JESUS
AND THE RISE OF **CHRISTIANITY**

EXAMINING IN CONTEXT THE NUMBER ONE
HISTORICAL FIGURE OF ALL-TIME

PHILIP
MCFARLAND

Creation Enterprise Books
Suffolk, Virginia

Creation Enterprise Books
Suffolk, Virginia
Copyright © 2010 by Philip McFarland

Requests for information should be emailed to:
Creation Enterprise Books
prmcfarland@liberty.edu

For orders or to obtain a catalog, please call 757.567.6979

ISBN-13: 978-0-615-37225-9
ISBN-10: 0615372252

All passages unless otherwise stated are taken from the New King James Version of the Bible; BibleGateway.com Copyright 1995-2006 Gospel Communications International; http://www.biblegateway.com/

All NIV passages are taken from BibleGateway.com; Copyright 1995-2006 Gospel Communications International; http://www.biblegateway.com/

BibleGateway.com is a free service for reading and researching Scripture online providing advanced tools to search keywords or verses, as well as other tools to enhance your study of the Bible.

Cover Design: Philip McFarland
Printed in the United States of America

This book is dedicated to
Stefani McFarland,
Allen and Doris McFarland,
family and friends

TABLE OF CONTENTS

PREFACE

Over 2,000 years ago, there was an individual who influenced the hearts and minds of thousands with his teachings and works of miracles. He was the catalyst in causing Christianity to become the dominant religion across Europe during the Roman Empire. He is none other than Jesus the Christ. He not only impacted the lives of people during ancient Palestine, but is still affecting the lives of people today with his absence. Although he was discarded and abandoned by many, there is no other person today who has impacted people's lives as he did.

Jesus lived during a period when Roman authority was strongly affective in shaping the viewpoints of those under its rule. The entire civilized world, with the exception of the little-known kingdoms of the far East, was under the domination to Rome. What was the political, social, economical, and religious world like before Jesus came on the scene? How were the common people treated during that era? What was life like living in the Roman Empire being either rich or poor? These and many other questions will be answered to show the environment of which Jesus came into and why such a hero was needed to change the hearts and minds of mankind.

Jesus' teachings were considered "strange" because they went against the entire social norm of his day. He spoke against the way the common people viewed their "neighbors" and he challenged the religiousness of the religious leaders. His miracles were not only unique but were life-changing. To reject Jesus' miracles is to disregard accurate inductive procedure where all essentials are investigated before a decision is made. On the same premise, to reject his resurrection is to disregard the same premises.

There has only been one single event throughout history which changed the entire world and that event is the resurrection of Jesus of Nazareth. Even the most scientifically minded people remain baffled concerning these events, and what they can't get over is the fact that it is real history. The events surrounding his life and death have been frequently read and spoken more than the stories surrounding any other person in history. Because of this fact, the resurrection established the truthfulness of Jesus and provides hope for millions around the world in several ways.

His resurrection, arguably the most important event in the history of Christianity, was not only responsible for the establishment of the Christian Church, but it spawned a movement toward moral perfection from Jesus' followers. Because of this phenomenal event, hundreds of millions of people have found comfort in the Christian Bible and they aspire to live their lives accordingly. Nations have proclaimed to be founded from Jesus' actual resurrection and people everywhere testify to the truth of God and his Son Jesus Christ.

But without investigating, there is no way to claim the occurrence of certain events, such as the resurrection of Jesus Christ. Just to state that there was a resurrection without stating any proof does not stand on solid group. Yet if there were numerous convincing proofs and solid unwavering evidence that he actually rose from the grave, than there is a strong case that he indeed was resurrected. In this book, I will discuss all such details.

I pray that you will not only enjoy this book but that this book will change how you live each and every day. For all those who are skeptics, atheists, or just non-believers, this book will certainly change your outlook in how you view God, life, and Christianity as a whole. I know that that this God-given information will be a blessing to everyone who reads this book because it has personally changed my life.

- Philip McFarland

CHAPTER 1
A HERO IN THE MAKING

The people in the Roman Empire looked to Caesar Augustus and many thought of him as the peace maker. Yet, Jesus was needed not only as Savior, Messiah, and Lord, but as the one who brings ultimate peace on earth. This was the peace of the Kingdom of God, a peace based upon justice.

The Political World

While the Hebrew Scriptures give a good amount of information about the life of Jesus and his teachings, they are of little historical value in relation to the problems that Judea faced during his life. Therefore, I will attempt to give much of this historical value beginning with the political world of the Roman Empire.

The events that took place before Jesus life occurred in Palestine, also known as the land of Israel. Israel was a tin piece of real estate positioned at the hinge of the European, Asian, and African continents. When empires clashed along a north-south axis between the Nile Delta and whoever controlled the Anatolian Plateau or the Mesopotamian Plain, tiny Israel was there in the middle.[1]

In spite of its small size, Palestine was a bridge between two continents, giving it a pivotal role in international politics, commerce, and culture of the ancient near east.[2] Located on the west bank of the Jordan River are Judea and Samaria, with Jerusalem approximately in the middle. Both are historical parts of the land of Israel. In 63 B.C., Rome organized Syria into a province and annexed Judea. Rome's

1

rapid territorial expansion brought great changes in the life of the Roman people. As each military leader increased power, Rome began to use armies not only for foreign conquest, but also for enforcing their supremacy at home. Thus, the people in the land of Israel greatly felt the Roman presence and domination.

THE ROMAN EMPIRE

Rome took its name from the capital city in Italy, the original settlement from which the Roman state grew. Founded in 753 B.C., it was at first a community comprising a union of small villages in its vicinity and ruled by a king.[3] Through five hundred years of almost uninterrupted war, Rome grew from an obscure village on the banks of the Tiber to become the ruling empire of the world.

If there was one thing that Roman was noted for, it was their exercise of power and authority over territory. Rome was a highly class determined society. At the head of their social order were kings, queens, diplomats, emperors, senator's ambassadors and governors. The government of the empire appointed a governor to oversee the collection of taxes and keep order and peace in the land. These leaders ruled through violence and they flourished on force and power. Those who were conquered were compelled by treaty to keep the peace and were absorbed gradually into the Roman province. The emperors of Rome were loved, worshipped, and held in high esteem because of their many successful conquests that aided in furthering their kingdom.

What Rome acquired, Rome kept. Rome was one of the most successful conquering states in all history, but it was the most successful retainer of conquests. Rome institutionalized the rule of its legions more stably and over a longer period than any other society before or since. Rome's empire of domination eventually became a true territorial empire.[4] For example, from 265 B.C. to about 56 B.C., Rome was engaged in a great struggle with Carthage, the chief maritime power of the western Mediterranean. As Rome expanded, it came into conflict with the Carthaginian Empire. Aside from the fact that the two civilizations were alien to each other in racial origin and in political theory, there was not enough room for both of them in the same territory, and thus, one had to succumb. The wars between them ended in 146 B.C. when the Roman general

Scipio Aemilianus captured the city of Carthage and razed it to the ground. Rome thus established dominion over Spain and over North Africa.[5]

The Roman Empire symbolizes the zenith of the best of the man-made empires. It could acclimatize any culture on earth into the Roman system. The Roman Empire utilized a social structure of exercising their power and placing people in hierarchal classes. Rome's social power is a combination of four types of power united together: military power, the monopoly or control of force and violence; economic power, the monopoly or control of labor and production; political power, the monopoly or control of organization ad institution; and ideological power, the monopoly or control of interpretation and meaning.[6]

Rome's military power was stationed along the Rhine, the Danube, the Euphrates, and the North African frontiers, and they built weather proofed roads and bridges. With this infrastructure, they could move with all their baggage and equipment at a guaranteed fifteen miles a day to crush any rebellion anywhere.[7] Rome's economic power came from their military infrastructure. After one of their conquests, the captured people were romanized by urbanization for the means of buying and selling. For those individuals who opposed this system, they came upon them violently. Their roads and bridges were now able to be used for business and trade, and as a result, there was quick and easy access for merchants to conduct and maintain good business relations. Rome's political power was instituted through the Roman elite and upper-class. These individuals not only had money but influence. They were able to allow some high local elites to be members of the Roman Senate. These elites saw very obviously what they received in return for their loyalty. And Rome's ideological power was a means of sustaining their internal relations.

THE MACCABEES

The Jewish nation was characterized as a people free to exercise their religious beliefs to God. Their freedom not only included individual worship but public worship and they were able to perform religious ceremonies in their religious temples. As part of the conquest of the ancient world by Alexander the Great (332 BC), the Jewish nation continued to be a theocracy under the Seleucid rulers. God was their civil ruler and only he instituted divine justice. At the same time, the Jews, like any group of people, did not like being controlled, conquered, and in subjection to other nations.

But after a successful invasion in Egypt, Antiochus IV, who reigned from 175-164 BC, moved on to bring strict domination over Israel and the Jewish people. Although he encouraged Greek culture that was brought about because of Alexander the Great, he attempted to suppress Judaism. Around 167 BC, he did not allow the Jews to perform their religious ceremonies and ransacked Jerusalem and its temple in order to restrain their religious and cultural observances. This was done for the purpose of enforcing Greek-oriented culture and customs on the entire population. In addition, the temple and priesthood were used for pagan worship and sacrifice. In fact, a statue of Antiochus as Zeus was built in the Jewish temple in Jerusalem and pigs were offered on the altar.

As a result, the Jews rose up and revolted. The Maccabees priestly family, lead by Judah Maccabee, started a rebellion and his four sons refused to accept the Greek gods which were introduced to them. His son Judah the Maccabee led an army of Jews and they entered Jerusalem in order purified the Temple in 164 BC. They ultimately gained victory and successfully revolted against Antiochus IV. Four years later in 160 BC, Judas Maccabee was killing in a battle and was succeeded by his brother Jonathan. In 142 BC, Jonathan died and his only living brother Simon followed him.

Despite of overwhelming odds against them, the Maccabees' family was successful in driving out the Greeks. The temple was cleansed and rededicated and this led to the independence of the Jewish society. The new generation of Jews and people living under this kingdom was proud of the Maccabean victories and hopeful of even greater successes at home and abroad.

Many years after Israel won their freedom Antiochus IV, Pompey came to Jerusalem with troops and ended the Jewish independence. He brought Palestine under the Roman sphere of control and in 63 B.C., Palestine was conquered by the Romans when Pompey captured Jerusalem. In 47 BC the Hasmonean high priest Hyrcanus II was made a ruler by Julius Caesar for his help in the Roman civil wars and was given authority over most of Palestine.[8]

The Hasmonian dynasty was so important to Jews of whom Jesus would soon come from because this kingdom was the only self-governing Jewish state to exist in the four centuries after the

Babylonians conquered Judah in 586 BC. The Jews were looking for peace and prosperity, and desired not only God but also a Messiah to free them from foreign control. They were tired of the wars and rumors of wars that had plagued them for centuries and were looking for a savior, a hero, a military leader to rescue them. The revolt that took place under the Maccabee's would be followed by a revolt that would take place in 66-72 AD. Both revolts would show how much the Jews desired freedom.

CAESAR AUGUSTUS

Caesar Augustus, of which he was first known as Octavian, is only mentioned once in the Bible when he ordered a census to all the people in the empire. This census brought about the birth of Jesus the Christ and allowed him to be born in Bethlehem, which was spoken of by the prophets. The Roman senate appointed the title Augustus to him on January 17, 27 BC. This title was given to him in acknowledgement of his renowned services to the state.

His Power for Life

In 23 B.C. when he came to power, he was given the power for life, which meant that he had control over the popular assemblies and was appointed the permanent representative of the people. During his reign, many reforms were put into effect. He organized or rather reorganized the government, including the police and fire departments. He brought in public assistance programs such as feeding the poor and public baths. He established the positions of public officials such as police for the safety of his people. The Senate was purged of unworthy members and sought also to improve the morale of the people. Augustus believed that a province should be governed locally, so he appointed a prefect to take charge of Judea, in the time of Christ that prefect was Pontius Pilate.[9] He revived the state religion and rebuilt many temples. He left Jewish religious matters to their highest level of law known as the Sanhedrin. However there was a great resentment among the Jews over Roman control that continued when Augustus was succeeded by Tiberius in 14 A.D.[10]

His Prestige

Caesar Augustus was also the human being in the First Century who was called "Divine," "Son of God," "God" and "God from God". He was considered to be "Lord", "Redeemer", "Liberator" and "Savior of the World". Those titles were fully appropriate for one who had saved "the world" from war and established peace on earth. To proclaim these titles to anyone else would be to deny them of Caesar Augustus.

The people of the Roman Empire were loyal citizens towards their emperor. He was adored and popular by many because of his strong leadership qualities and his ability to conquer nations and expand the empire. A grateful populace reverenced him greatly, and some, especially in the East, actually worshipped him. Thus, emperor worship was born.[11] In many places, Augustus himself was worshipped as lord and god, although he did not demand such worship.

To pay tribute to the one whom they held so dearly in their hearts, Augustus had various statues erected in his name. One of these statutes was the Shrine of Augustan Peace. Erected by Caesar Augustus himself, this shrine was located in the same place of his renowned tomb. This Augustan peace represented a world of peace and not just of Rome and Italy.

His Peace

The Roman Empire had a vast population at the time of his reign and having at first a war filled society, the Roman people were anxiously awaiting contentment and peace. They deemed to find some means of rest in their times of war, for they were tired of the wars and rumors of wars that were continual throughout his reign. Though both Julius Caesar and Caesar Augustus were both intended to be great leaders, the people thought that Julius Caesar was the better leader and that Caesar Augustus was the bearer of peace. Though some turned on him, Augustus still managed to bring tranquility.

Augustus' rule brought an unmatched forty years of peace in Italy. With minimal hindrances, Rome and its territories enjoy a steady increase in prosperity, trade and peace. During the period of Augustan peace, things in Rome were reported as calm and content for many people. After peace had been reinstated throughout the empire and the lawful political order reestablished, the people began to enjoy quiet and happy times. To remind themselves of this peace and tranquility, the Roman people built an altar of peace to remind them of this era that Augustus ushered in.

This peace that was offered however was not always beneficial. Although there was tranquility in Rome, it was brought about at a great cost. It was during this era that the impact of war, patron-client relationships, and slavery were viewed in a much more dangerous light. Outside its walls, Augustus brought war and despair to others in order to maintain his precious peace. Emperors like Augustus often went to any extent to build their empires, even if it meant waging war on innocent countries and forcing them to surrender in the name of so called "peace". Yet inside its walls under this peace laid the injustice of patron-client relationships, which was advantageous to the elite but cruel slavery for the poor. The individuals who were not as privileged as the elite were put under a lifetime of poverty and servitude. As a result, the elite received all the blessings in life.

Jesus' Power for Life, Prestige, and Peace

How do you find peace in the time of war? The people living in the Roman Empire, including the Jews, looked to Caesar Augustus. Many thought of him as the peace maker because he brought peace and unity to the people after much war. Yet, his title of being the ultimate peacemaker would be challenged by the birth of a baby boy born in Bethlehem who was stated by angels to be the Prince of Peace. A small few revered this baby as having this power for life and he was even adored by wise men from the East who considered him one of prestige.

Most people who knew the Western tradition would probably answer that Jesus of Nazareth was this Divine Son of God, who was God, who came from God, who was and is Lord, Redeemer, Liberator, and Savior of the World. And most Christians probably think that those titles were originally created and uniquely applied to Christ. But before Jesus ever existed, all those terms belonged to Caesar Augustus.[12] Yet Jesus was needed not only as Savior, Messiah, and Lord, but also as the one who brings peace on earth. This is the peace of the Kingdom of God, a peace based upon justice.

7

HEROD THE GREAT

In the New Testament, Herod was known for the killing of innocent babies in Matthew 2. Ultimately, he was trying to kill Jesus, but an angel of the Lord appeared to his father Joseph in dream and told him to take Jesus and his wife to Egypt and stay there until further notice, for Herod would soon seek him to kill him (Matthew 2:13). Knowing Herod's history, it was entirely natural for his way of thinking to seek to kill a potential rival to his kingdom. He would have exterminated anyone who would have had a claim to his kingdom, even if it were one of his family members. This is the very reason why it is important to discuss the nature and character of King Herod, for he and Jesus seemed to be rivals, along with their distinct kingdoms.

His Person

Herod was an exceedingly complex person. Racially, he was an Arab. His father was from an Arab tribe in the southern part of the Holy Land called Idumea. His mother was from Petra, which was the capital of the Nabatean Kingdom, an Arab Kingdom that inhabited the northern part of Arabia in the First Century.[13] Culturally, he was Greek. Greek culture had spread widely throughout Palestine by that time, and Greek was the lingua franca of the international community. Indeed, Greek was his first language.[14] Politically, he was Roman and religiously, he was Jewish. In 31 AD, Caesar Augustus, who had outlasted all other Roman supremacy, established Herod's status as a supporter and friend of Rome.

His Kingdom

Before beginning to build a kingdom, one must know what kind of kingdom he wants to build. If this does not take place, it can be taken for granted that there is only one type, one model, one scenario. Is a kingdom always about power and glory, force and violence? Is it about the very few controlling the very many?[15] Well, it was for Herod. The Herod dynasty began with a man named Antipater, the father of Herod the Great. After his rule, Herod inherited all of his father's ability in international relations and regime. The Senate bestowed upon him the title "King of the Jews" and gave him authority to rule the territories of Idumea, Judea, Samaria, and Galilee as a client of Rome.[16] He not only took over the rule of Judea, which was vacant for some time, but he ruled over Judea from 37 - 4 B.C.

After returning from Rome, Herod first freed his family besieged in the fortress atop Masada, and then began in Galilee a violent struggle to obtain his kingdom. According to Josephus, he captured the Hasmonean garrison town of Sepphoris in Lower Galilee during a snowstorm, and from there began to root out all opposition to his rule. He laid siege to the last remaining opponents in the Arbel cliffs overlooking the northwest shore of the Sea of Galilee. He set fire to their caves, swung his soldiers down on cradles from an overhang above, and pulled them to their death with grappling hooks.[17] After destroying the final resistance in Galilee in 40 BC, he established his new kingdom.

He needed a lot of wealth for his kingdom. Why, because he had many and expensive building projects. One of them was the entire city of Caesarea including its artificial port, and another was the city of Samaria. He also began a monumental restoration of the Jerusalem Temple although he didn't really seem to care who was going to be worshipping in them. This massively expanded temple project took ten thousand laborers and a thousand priests. He established new towns and harbors and brought neighboring regions into his own kingdom and in alliance to Rome. He built along the coast and sponsored projects in faraway Mediterranean cities. Yet, he ignored Galilee.

His Killings and Brutality

He is not only known for his expensive building projects and magnificent structures but also for his political ruthlessness and killings even among those closest to him. He was the smooth talking, jealous, and murderous type, and this all pointed to the fact that he had chronic insecurity. Although he was an Idumaenean, he took it personal that the Jews disliked him because of this very fact. Another reason the Jews disliked him was because although he practiced Judaism, he did not practice it with all his heart. As a matter of fact, he practiced numerous faiths and gave acceptance to other religious philosophies. Thus to the Jews, he was a compromiser and had a diluted faith.

Understanding his bad case of insecurity, he showed his true character in practicing political ruthlessness. Although the Roman Senate appointed him king of Judea, he was perhaps the vilest human being ever to serve as a Jewish king. He inaugurated his regime by murdering forty five members of the Jewish high court, the Sanhedrin. He soon became suspicious of the political loyalty of his favorite wife, Mariamene, and had her killed. After that he was known to wander through the palace calling her name and sending the servants to fetch her. When they failed to do so he would have them beaten.[18]

In addition, he murdered Mariamene's two sons, as well as his mother in law, brother-in-law, and the High Priest.[19] He killed many of the Hasmonean remnants who would have had a claim to rule. He also killed many Pharisees.[20] With intelligence given to him concerning the birth of another "king of the Jews" (Matthew 2:2), it was documented that he sent and killed all the male children in Bethlehem and in the surrounding reasons who were two years and under. This information backs up the character and brutality of Herod, king of the Jews.

Herod's last days were no better than the brutality he had shown during the prime of his life. Seemingly the only good thing that took place was the fact that he found a way to make peace with Caesar Augustus, the very one who established his status as a supporter and friend of Rome. Unfortunately, his last days were filled with violence, hatred, and revolts. He literally became "mad", and for that he was hated. Realizing that when he died there would be no grand funeral service for him and not even mourning, he sent letters to the principle heads of every family in Judaism demanding their company. After they arrived in Jerusalem, he locked them up and commanded them to all be killed. For Herod, this would assure him that people would mourn when he died, yet he knew they would not mourn for him. After being struck with cancer of the intestines and dropsy, he died on April 1, 4 B.C. Fortunately right after he died, his sister released the imprisoned Jews and allowed them to go back home. At that time, revolts broke out all over the Jewish homeland. It eventually took three of the four legions of the Syrian governor Varus to put down all the rebellions.[21]

Jesus' Kingdom

Herod was officially appointed King of the Jews by Roman authority and became even more famous for his numerous building projects and murders. The jealous and crooked character of this man explains the duplicity of his dealing with the Magi from the East and his brutality in ordering the massacre of the children in Bethlehem (Matt. 2:1-18). The silence of history concerning the massacre at Bethlehem can be explained easily, for the slaughter of a dozen infants in an obscure Judean village would not arouse much comment in comparison with the enormity of Herod's greater crimes.[22]

Yet the Hebrew Bible stated in Matthew 2 that a new and replacement King of the Jews had been appointed by God to take over completely. This little boy was whom Isaiah the prophet spoke of when he stated, "Of the increase of his government and peace there shall be no end, upon the throne of David, and upon his kingdom, to order it, and to establish it with judgment and with justice from henceforth even for ever. The zeal of the LORD of hosts will perform this" (Isaiah 9:7). It was to be his kingdom that was to be the "real" kingdom, one that would never end. This is in contrast to the "man made" kingdoms that comes and goes, and that becomes conquered and that conquer. It would be Jesus' Kingdom that would increase and become ever more powerful and not Herod's Kingdom. That is why Herod tried to kill all boys two years and under in Bethlehem and its neighborhood in an attempt to get rid of this possible king.

HEROD ANTIPAS

The Herod who was most prominent in the New Testament was Herod Antipas. When Herod the Great died in 4 BC, both Antipas and Archelaus his sons appeared before Caesar Augustus in Rome to plead their opposing cases. The Herodian family members preferred direct rule by a Roman governor, but unfortunately they supported Antipas over Archelaus. Augustus gave half of the Jewish homeland to Herod Archelaus, but entitled him "people-ruler" and not monarch. He divided the rest between two tetrarchs, with Herod Antipas getting Galilee and Perea on either side of the Jordan and Philip getting the far northern reaches of the country. Antipas began his rule sorely disappointed.[23]

After inheriting his territories, Antipas ruled them as a client state of the Roman Empire. Like his father, he was known for his building projects, specifically the cities that he erected. During his reign of 43 years, he erected a new capital on the shores of the Lake of Galilee named Tiberias. Tiberias, which was named after the reigning Roman emperor, was built in A.D. 18-20. Antipas also built the city of Sepphoris, which was the capital and heart of the Galilee province, and the city of Betharamphtha, which he fortified and named after Julias the emperor's wife.

Yet his morals and character was another subject. He divorced his first wife, the daughter of King Aretas IV of Nabatea, in favor of Herodias the daughter of Aristobulus, son of Herod the Great, who had formerly been married to his brother. Because of this, John the Baptist condemned this arrangement of union and as a result, Antipas had him arrested. Antipas did not want to put John to death, for he liked to hear him preach (Mark 6:20), and he probably also was afraid of a potential riot from the people. Yet it was Herodias who played a major role in John's death, for she used her daughter to dance seductively before Antipas and then to ask for John's head as a reward.

Antipas is most renowned by Christians for his role in the events that led to the executions of not only John the Baptist but Jesus of Nazareth. He is the one whom Jesus calls "that fox" (Luke 13:32), which was not given in any way to be complementary. Yet Jesus said this in order to characterize his slyness, craftiness and vindictiveness. In Mark 8, Jesus cautioned his followers to be aware of the "leaven" of the Pharisees and of Herod Antipas. Antipas is also the one before whom Jesus was tried (23:7-12). He presided over Jesus' trial with Pontius Pilate and both of them determined Jesus' death sentence, although most historians state that it was only Pilate who sentenced Jesus.

The Social World

Jewish people from the land of Israel were Mediterranean people. When Jesus was born, he came into a Mediterranean society. He spent most of his life in and around the farming village area of Nazareth, and he taught the people and worked miracles among them to show the power and authority of God. Shortly after he went back to heaven, his kingdom movement that he started rapidly spread throughout this society. His disciples, his brother James, and Saul of Tarsus were some of the most influential people who continued to spread the good news of Jesus' resurrection and the validity of God's Kingdom. The communities that were formed after his ascension consisted of Mediterranean people and many of the writings in the New Testament were written to these people.

Therefore, it is important to look at the social society that Jesus came into not only to show why he was needed but to ascertain to whom he came to minister to and save. It may seem easy to view these people from a western point of view but this must not be done, for one will unfortunately miss the entire social world that existed in the first century.

MEDITERRANEAN PEOPLE

The Mediterranean people were those who live in Palestine or modern day Israel and the Romans were obviously in control during the First Century. The hierarchy of accountability included the Jewish people reporting to the Jewish government, who reported to the Roman government who was King Herod, who reported to the Roman Emperor Caesar Augustus. The major city of Palestine was the infamous city of Jerusalem and it was more multi-ethnic than other cities in the region.

The universal language was Greek, but it was normal for Jews to speak Hebrew, Aramaic (the everyday language), and Latin. The synagogue was an assembly house used for prayer, worship and teaching, and was the essential meeting place for Jews.

The family structure was important among the Mediterranean people. Men were the spiritual head of the house. Women were not only second class citizens but were comparable to slaves. Yet Jesus allowed women to not only follow him during his ministry but to minister to him out of their own means. And children were to show honor and respect to their parents.

It was impossible for these Mediterranean people to ignore each other for several reasons. First, from a geographical perspective, they all shared the sea. Because of the close geographic proximity, many people of different areas were in contact with each other to sell goods to one another, to go to war together, and to be able to have interrelations. Because of their natural geography, they could not ignore each other and as a result, they were forced to have to deal with both the good and the bad.

Secondly, they could not ignore each other because of the similarities of their daily lives. In our world today, there not only is a strong middle class but there are endless professions that people can aim for to achieve greatness and higher status. Yet this was not the case in the First Century. The daily lives of the people were very similar, for many were farmers and fishermen and the majority were poor and perhaps illiterate. There were either rich or poor people and the vast majority of the land was peasants. At the same time, most all of the people understood the injustice that they daily experienced.

Thirdly, the people understood the fact that they were all vulnerable. Since they could not control their geography and the fact that they all had to work together, they understood that they were surrounded by a "hostile landscape". The Jew's history has been one of being conquered continuously and they lived their lives knowing that there was always uncertainly. They realized that without each other, they and their country would not survive. Ignorance of each other was certainly impossible because in order for them to conquer and grow, they had to face their customers who were mainly near, and their enemies who many were outside their land.

And last, it was impossible for Mediterranean people to ignore each other because of their inter-connections. First, they were not able to avoid each other in this way was because of the sea, weather, topography, and mode of production that made it possible for them to need each other and to effectively communicate. Second, since it was hard to produce in such rough environments and terrains, they had to help each other out in any way possible. They worked together to solve problems and by their efforts, they were able to obtain the necessary resources from different parts of their hostile land. And third, as a result of their communication and friendships, their relations over time caused for many of them to intermarry, which then made it possible for them to appreciate different cultures and customs. They married into other societies and some even took over another society introducing their beliefs and traditions. At the same time, they shared values such as not allowing their women to be used as a form of sexual hospitality. Because of these similarities, the Mediterranean people were united in a way which did not allow them to ignore each other.

THE GALILEANS

Israel under the Roman Empire was divided into three sections, Judea, Samaria, and Galilee. Galilee, which is the largest of the three, was located in the whole northern section of the country, roughly making up one-third of the geography. It was divided into Upper Galilee, Lower Galilee, and Western Galilee. A meager 100 kilometers separate its northern border from its southernmost boundary. The majority of Galilee had rocky terrain at heights between 500 and 700 meters. A couple of its highest mountains include Mount Tabor and Mount Meron. Lower Galilee ranged from 500 feet above sea level to around 700 feet below sea level at the Sea of Galilee.

The term "Galilean" was a simple geographical designation for all those who live within the territory of Galilee. Galileans were the people group of whom Jesus came from. His boyhood home of Nazareth was located in Lower Galilee, which is one of the region's most fruitful areas, and this region was his home during at least thirty years of his life. His public ministry took place in Galilean cities such as Nazareth and Capernaum. He told parables that evoked the fields, skies and humble dwellings of Galilee including the lilies of the field, the mustard seed, the vineyard and the fig tree. Galilee is also cited as the place where he cured a blind man. Although many villages were located in this area during Jesus' ministry, only a few were mentioned in the Hebrew Bible. Yet it is almost certain that Jesus performed many works and ministered to people in many of these cities. Herod Antipas, the son of Herod the Great, ruled Galilee during Jesus' day, and some estimate that approximately 350,000 people including slaves and Jews would have been present during his rule.

The Galileans were peasants who were of the countryside and villages and not of the cities and metropolitan centers. Their very attitudes as country people were different from the people in the towns. It seems that they felt that their way of life was, at times, threatened by the urban areas in the surrounding regions. They had no interest in war, and the men were trained and military disciplined. This caused them to ready for a social revolution of poor against rich and peasantry against gentry. The one thing they feared more than anything was the Roman legions, which in ancient times consisted of an army division of 3,000 to 6,000 soldiers including cavalry. Because of this fear, they were more than willing to blend into the peasantry population in order to evade being massacred for their aggressive behavior.

Josephus, a First Century Jewish historian, describes the nature of the Galileans who were his loyal supporters. There were Galileans under his leadership numbering around 5,000 who were able to blend in with the peasantry instantaneously. They felt a strong hatred towards the towns of Sepphoris, Tiberias, Gabara, Gischala, and Rome, and they could well imagine a world with certain administrative centers devastated. This hatred chiefly stemmed from the pro-Roman attitudes those cities had and the miseries these people had brought upon them even before the war. Sepphoris and Tiberias were the governmental capital of Galilee, and this was a big reason for the tension between the groups.

WOMEN

Ancient History

In every world religion, the history of women and their rights has been discussed. Although they have been uniquely considered as a creative source of human life and although wifehood and motherhood were regarded as their most significant professions in life, they have not always had the same rights as men.

For example, Greek legends believed that the women brought the plagues, diseases, and ultimately unhappiness to the world. Even early Christian writers believed some of the same similar views. Tertullian believed that women were the devil's gateway. St. Jerome stated, "Woman is the gate of the devil, the path of wickedness, the sting of the serpent, in a word a perilous object".[24] Ambrose, who was the bishop of Milan, believed that man was superior. Martin Luther believed that women only existed to bear children, and if they died during childbearing, then it did not matter because that was all they were here for in the first place. Thomas Aquinas believed that women were made to be man's helpmeet, but her sole responsibility is to bear children, for men would be better assisted by other men for all other purposes.

Women were believed to be both intellectually inferior to men as well as the prime source of temptation and evil. They have long been viewed as naturally weaker individuals than men and thus not capable of executing work that involves not only muscle but intellect. In most pre-industrial societies, the house chores were given to women. The men concern themselves with nothing but the more laborious hunting and the waging of war. Their wives are regarded and treated as slaves. Women perform the drudgery and bring home the food slain by their husbands, fetching wood and water, tanning the skins, and making them into clothing. The labor of erecting the tents and hauling the sleds when on their journey during the winter falls upon them. They were considered inferior to men, and in their social life they soon show the effects of the hardships they undergo.[25]

This same attitude permeated the social world in Jesus day. The New Testament not only mentions but describes detailed instances of Jesus' interactions with women. The book of Matthew include five women mentioned in Jesus genealogy including Mary his mother, Tamar, Rehab, Ruth, and (Bathsheba) the wife of Uriah. Although it would have been unheard of for this to take place, these women were held up as examples of how God uses the unexpected to triumph over human obstacles. We observe a woman kissing and anointing Jesus' feet, and drying them with her hair (Luke 7:36-50), which went against the cultural norm of their day. We even see Jesus having a detailed conversation with a woman during the middle of the day (John 4). Jesus truly went against culture as he conversed and interacted with women during his day.

Honor and Shame

The world that Jesus came into was an "honor and shame" society. The three main form of stratification during this time were the government, class, and honor. Honor was arguably the most important of the three. Honor was the value of a person in his own eyes and in the eyes of his society. It was not only his estimation of his own worth, his claim to pride, and his acknowledgement of that claim, but his excellence recognized by society.[26] Because of this, people would constantly reevaluate themselves because they were seen through the eyes of others. Thus, one was entirely dependent on society at large to uphold and maintain one's own self-worth, and if one had lost his honor he ceased to exist.

A women's dignity was not easily protected and honor was not considered an appropriate or relevant factor for them. Thus, their honor and shame were the responsibility of the men, including their fathers, brothers, and husbands. Therefore, if a woman were to do a heinous act like appearing naked as Bathsheba did in front of King David (2 Samuel 11) or committing adultery as Mary would have been suspected of (Matthew 1:18-20), their honor would have been completely taken away. More importantly, they would have had no reason to live. That is why stoning was commanded to be the form of death for a women who was getting married as though she was a virgin and she really was not (Deuteronomy 22:13-21).

Divorce

Marriage was first instituted by God in the Garden of Eden and was intended to be a monogamous, physical, and spiritual union between a man and a woman. Unfortunately, because of the fall of man, divorce was the method that breaks this God given covenant. Divorce was basically the dissolution of marriage and was an official process that leads to the extinction of a marriage.

In the Bible there was divorce. In the Old Testament, only men were able to divorce their wives (Deuteronomy 24:1-4) and the nature of divorce was seen as adultery against women. A man could steal a woman's honor by divorcing her and remarrying. The Jewish law gave rights only to the husband regarding adultery and divorce, and the crime of adultery was seen as something that went against male honor and male rights. Although a man could divorce his wife, it was unheard of or never mentioned of a woman divorcing her husband. This was simply not allowed and not practiced. It was also considered disloyal to a woman for her husband to remarry again. Thus, a woman could not initiate divorce and her self-respect was not easily guarded.

Although this was the law, Jesus would soon see how terribly unfair and plainly wrong this system of justice was. When he came, he would soon introduce a radical idea for that time period, which involved reversing the order of this Jewish mindset. He stated that "every one who divorces his wife and remarries another commits adultery, and he who marries a woman divorced from her husband commits adultery" (Luke 16:18; Matthew 5:21-32). On the same lines, he said that "whoever divorces his wife and marries another, commits adultery against her" (Mark 10:11). So in this way, it was seen that he recognized honor as not merely equated it to men, but to a women as well. He instituted the new idea that if a man committed adultery or if a woman committed adultery, they would be taking away each others honor, and not just the man taking the women's honor. Thus from Jesus' perspective, a woman's honor could be stolen by a man whenever he divorced her.

By teaching this new doctrine and strange message, Jesus certainly cause division within the family structure especially among the men, who was more dominate in the society. He introduced the concept of equal rights for men and women and the issue of honor for both. His stance helped the preservation of the dignity of men and women. Yet, for Jesus to describe this process was not an easy concept to accept.

Virginity

As was stated before, women were considered a creative source of human life, and both wifehood and motherhood were regarded as their most significant professions. Women helped defined and uphold the honor and shame of their social group. They were looked upon as a special and unique resource, much like land or cattle were resources at that time, when it came to the family's future. The obtaining of a wife was contingent upon the wife's relations and dealings with other groups of people and the future of the family depended on a new wife.

One of the most vital ways that typified the quality of a woman was her virginity. Virginity symbolized her purity and if she was not a virgin at the time of her marriage, she would bring shame to the family. It would appear as if the men of her house, specifically father and brothers, had not done their job in keeping the woman from being dishonored. On the same note, the virginity of their women unified their men because together they could bask in their most prized possession, their pure, holy, and virgin women.

When virginity was defiled, we see the anger of her brothers who were in the women's household. In Genesis 34, Jacob's daughter Dinah was sexually defiled and when Jacob's sons heard what had happened, they were filled with grief and anger because of the disgraceful act that should not have been done. Three days later, two of Jacob's sons took their swords and attacked the city where Dinah was defiled and killed every male. In addition, they detained their flocks and herds and donkeys and everything else in the city and out in the fields. They also carried off all their wealth and all their women and children. In this example, we recognize not only the quality and special resource of a woman's virginity but the unity of the male members in the family.

Mary the mother of Jesus was said to be a virgin before she and Joseph ever came together. She would be a clean vessel whom God would use to give birth to the Savior of the world. She would represent the competition for a pure and virgin resource that had not been defiled. Her virginity makes complete sense symbolically in that she represents what every man wants but can never have, and thus, she was considered an honorable and unreachable woman.

Religiously Impure

Women not only lived in an honor and shame society and in a world where men could steal their honor by divorcing them and remarrying, but they were also considered religiously impure. To understand this fact, we must look at one of Jesus' disturbing parables, at least for the people of his day, which compared the Kingdom of God to leaven and the actions of a woman.

In this parable, Jesus said, "The Kingdom of Heaven is like unto leaven, which a woman took, and hid in three measures of meal, till the whole was leavened" (Matthew 13:33). Leaven in the ancient world was a symbol of moral corruption. It was made by taking a piece of bread and storing it in a damp, dark place until mold forms. The bread thus rots and decays.[27] In Israel, the process of leavening was allowing a new, pure substance to rot and decay. It was considered unholy everyday. On the other hand, unleavened bread was holy and considered a sacred feast.

In light of the leavened bread, women as a symbolic structure were associated in Judaism, as in other Mediterranean cultures, with the unclean, the religiously impure. The male was the symbol for purity.[28] In this parable, a woman secretly using leaven to make her bread was a very negative implication.

For Jesus to compare his kingdom with both leaven and religiously impure women held not only a negative connotation but was very shocking. What he was doing was comparing the Kingdom of Heaven, a new religious movement, to a woman, who was considered religiously impure, and to leaven, which was unholy and a symbol of moral corruption. This was similar to him comparing his kingdom to the dangerous mustard seed (Matthew 13:31-32) that has a tendency to take over when it is not wanted. With Jesus using this parable to describe the kingdom implies that it consisted of that which was undesirable. Thus the people were confronted with an image of the kingdom that is immediately shocking and provocative.

LAND AND INJUSTICE

During the pinnacle of the Roman Empire, peasant Jews living in Israel depended on land for their security and livelihood. In order to "live to tell the tale", they needed to make a profit on the food they raised at least until the following harvest. In addition, they needed food for their animals, trade, and their ceremonies and parties.

The Romans who were in control demanded the peasants to generate an excess of harvest. Yet, it was stolen from the ruling elite by means of taxation and used for their benefit and profit. The people were not only given a general taxation, but were required an additional taxation in the form of tribute. Thus, they were taxed doubled, which sometimes amounted to as much as 40% of production. To make matters worse, they would also obtain additional resources from the people during times of war often demanding funds instantly. Not to mention natural disasters or droughts that could come and make it virtually impossible to even pay tribute. For these Jews, this typical injustice was not just robbery but impossible to meet. They had to pay the Romans, for non-payment was considered rebellion and the Romans usually responded with military force. Families who could not live off their profit after paying all these taxes were required to borrow, and if they could not make enough money to escape their debt, they would lose their land and would be considered as slaves to the Romans.

The Jews understood the Torah when it stated, "Whatever the land yields during the Sabbath year will be food for you, for yourself, your manservant and maidservant, and the hired worker and temporary resident who live among you, as well as for your livestock and the wild animals in your land. Whatever the land produces may be eaten" (Leviticus 25:6-7). Deuteronomy reiterates the covenantal stipulations of how Israel was to live in the land. It includes, among other things, a system of checks and balances to ensure a just distribution of the land and its produce since, of course, that land belonged to God, so that all its inhabitants were, as Leviticus put it, but tenant farmers and resident aliens.[29] The Jews understood that land, as the basis of life, was not just a commodity for normal entrepreneurial manipulation but rather belonged to God. God's people were all tenants on divine property.[30] Yet, many were frequently required to become farmers on the very land that had belonged to their ancestors for generations.

So, the thought of comprehending all these factors created a situation for Jews that was impossible to escape. With the high demands of taxes, the intimidation of military action for non-payment, and the natural disasters that added to the burden, Jews were left with essentially two options. They could either accept Roman oppression, injustice, and slavery, or reject oppression and taxes, and thus become an enemy of the empire.

BANDITRY - JEWISH RESISTANCE

Their Past History

Those specific Jews who resisted Roman oppression often did so by resorting to banditry. Banditry was one of the most universal social phenomena known to history and one of the most amazingly uniform wherever societies are based on agriculture.[31]

Banditry apparently began during the Maccabean era and peaked in the middle of the First Century. For the longest time, history was not recording much detail of this practice in antiquity. Yet shortly after the death of Herod Agrippa I in 44 A.D., Rome's greed was further extended into Galilee. As Rome became more and more oppressive, banditry became more and more commonplace. As a result, banditry increase and there was the mention of bandits during each of the prefects in power apart from Tiberius Alexander in 46 to 48 A.D. An unexpected famine that came after Tiberius Alexander's death did not help the bandits' situation, for it added to some of their debt and lack of hope. There were repeated accounts of revolts and upheavals throughout Judea and during Jesus' era, Judea was infested with bandits.

Their Practice

Banditry is the practice of stealing by a group or gang because individuals refused to submit to their lot in life as a poor person. Because of the injustice of being heavily taxed, no longer having their land, being in serious debt, and ultimately being oppressed, banditry was the means of life gained by plundering.

Who were bandits? Bandits were outlaws and robbers. Some of them may have been common thugs or general criminals, but imperial situations often make it difficult to distinguish between the systemic violence of the conqueror and the individual counter-violence of the conquered.[32] They attained their name when they left their families and friends and tried to change things that they did not like.

What did the bandits actually do? They basically operate primarily within human violence alone. But it must be remembered that any such violence represents response rather than initiative.[33] They were fighters for what they wanted or thought was right and were found in one of three forms: the noble robber; the resistance fighter; or the terror bringing avenger. All three types used violence in one form or another. They would steal from the rich and give to the poor, although it was hard to really decipher if they were actually doing this. Villages were looted and temples were defiled at their hands. As a result, the Roman government and their system of justice were flooded with corruption.

To their fellow Jewish people, bandits served as their leaders in revolutionary situations. Because they were out for power of which few people even had, many rose to great heights within their society and were admired by the people. The common people considered them as heroes, champions, avengers, leaders of liberation, and fighters for justice. Bandits encouraged the people to stress their liberty and not to submit to the Roman Empire. In return, the people supported them. The more successful bandits were, the more protection they needed, and it was given to them not only by the common people but by the politicians and elite.

Their Purpose

The Bible presents the radicality of a just and nonviolent God repeatedly and relentlessly confronting the normalcy of an unjust and violent civilization. Again and again throughout the biblical tradition, God's radical vision for nonviolent justice is offered.[34] Yet, for the bandit, if God was not going to act then and now, they in return would take it into their own hands.

It was their response to the Roman government treating them cruel and inhumane that they acted substandard to the laws and orders of their day. They acted different than normal criminals, for criminals disobeyed certain laws, but bandits live against those laws with a final goal to change them. They would encourage people to declare their independence with Rome and they urged them to use arms to fight for their liberty and to stop being treated like slaves.

Their Penalty

Although it was not clear how numerous the bandits were, it was clear that they were a common phenomenon in the Roman Empire. Because bandits were peasant outlaws whom the empire believed to be much worse and dangerous than everyday criminals, their penalty consisted of the most brutal of the death penalties. Despite their number, Roman reaction to this form of rebellion was extremely violent. Their punishment included crucifixion, being thrown to wild animals, or being burned alive. All this was done so that they could be used as an example for anyone else desiring to rebel against the empire.

Legally, if a person caught a bandit, they were expected to take them to the authorities by force or by killing them. The Roman Empire did its best trying to rid the bandits, but consequently due to shifts in attitude, impending growth of religion in the cities, and the growth of injustice, this form of rebellion only increased.

Banditry and Jesus

This subject of banditry is extremely important because it reflects the mindset and attitude of the world in which Jesus came into. In the

New Testament, the word for bandits is sometimes also translated revolutionaries, robbers, and murderers. A couple of these instances included the bandit named Barabbas who was freed in order that he might be crucified and the two men who were crucified alongside Jesus were not only thieves, but bandits. During Jesus' adult life, he was linked to banditry several times (Mark 14:48; 15:27; 15:6-16). Jesus was even portrayed as bandit-like because he was from the villages, he was connected with disreputable people, and he made rebel-like comments.

The very practices and beliefs that comprised Roman culture were completely challenged by Jesus. He showed how important it was to love one's enemies and to do good to those who despitefully misused them. Although the Zealots were the most passionate about eliminating Roman rule and who went as far as to exempt themselves from Roman taxes, believing that they only needed to pay the Jewish Temple,[35] Jesus told them to pay taxes to the Roman government as well as to God. He did not advocate treason in any way. He even came from a family, specifically his parents, who obeyed the law by registering themselves to be taxed by Caesar Augustus (Luke 2). He destroyed the idea that support and robbery was necessary for people to have their needs fulfilled, and he called for them to look to God as their activist and not the bandits. Although Jesus' ministry was rejected by so many, it challenged the way of thinking held by Jews living in the Roman Empire.

After his death and ascension, banditry did not decelerate but rather flourished. In the late 40s, disturbances in Judea led to severe retaliation against Zealots and Nazarenes by Roman forces. In 52 AD, the situation had grown acute enough for the official representative of the Roman government of Syria, the immediate superior of the prefect of Judaea, to intervene. But terrorism continued. Radical Zealots in the late 50s began assassinating Jews who collaborated with the Romans.[36] These were all key facts that led to the first Jewish Roman War (66-73), or the Great Revolt. This was the first of three major rebellions by the Jews of Judaea against the Roman Empire. Bandits actually made up a significant portion of the forces who fought against Rome in the first Revolt (66-70 A.D.).

It is interesting to know that within the first four hundred years of foreign control, specifically under the Persian Empire and Greek replacements, there was only a single revolt, which took place at the very end of that period. But within the first two hundred years of

Roman control there were three major revolts. All of this tension only shows that if you repress a group of people either socially, economically, or religiously for long enough, they will revolt and history has shown us this over and over again.

The Economic World

What was the nature of the economic world in Jesus' day? How did the Roman Empire and Jews living in Palestine make their money? How was the system broken down and who received the money? To answer these questions, we must discuss the nature of land and the agrarian society, of which the Roman Empire was made up.

The Land

The Supremacy of Rome

Owning land was the major source of wealth and whether the land was inherited or seized during war did not matter. The Roman Empire at the very least was an empire of domination and control. During the onset of their quest, their political, military, and economic domination took over countries and citizens alike. As their empire continued to grow, they urbanized their land of which they had much of. Roman imperialism sought land for commercial operation as well as territorial expansion and this physical growth of rural land into areas with high density was a means of control of the people.

Unfortunately, Jews clashed predictably with that Roman policy, and it clashed not only because peasants usually resist rural commercialization but also because Jewish peasants had a long and sacred tradition of such resistance.[37] On the one hand, there was the recognition that land was a unique resource that must receive special regulation in order to prevent the ruin of the people. On the other hand, there was a movement toward greater individual freedom in the use and disposal of the land, allowing for the possibility of agribusiness and the pauperization of masses of people. It appears that the ancient near East was pulled in the latter direction and it was in such a context in which Israel came into being.[38] Thus, the economy of First century Israel begins with the land upon which they lived and governed their lives.

The Society – Agrarian Society

How the Roman Empire received their money was characterized in an agrarian society. The word agrarian is defined as relating to or concerning itself with the land. It concerns itself with the ownership, nurturing, and possession of land for means of support, and the equitable distribution of land. An agrarian society bases itself on farming for its prime means of support and sustenance and it promotes agricultural interests. It was Rome who regularly invented better tools and improved processes that would make farming better. They were noted by the amount of land they owned and for being ingenious to improve their jobs and functions.

Agrarian societies were also marked by social inequality. Without exception, one would find pronounced differences in power, privilege, and honor associated with mature agrarian economies.[39] Because the Roman Empire was an agrarian society, many of the poor people immediately felt a divide, for they were living in a "rich get richer and the poor get poorer" society. In a traditional agrarian empire, land was a familial inheritance to be retained by the peasantry. Yet, in a commercializing agrarian empire, land was an entrepreneurial commodity to be exploited by the aristocracy.[40] Thus, one of the facts of urbanization was that it brought with it a measure of oppression. The gap between the wealthy and the poor was frequently widened and those who thrived in the city often did so at the expense of those in the dependent villages who do not.[41]

This is the world that Jesus came into and we see him frequently speaking of parables that pertain to the land, crops, and farmers alike. He was not oblivious to what was going on, for he saw and understood both the good and bad. He could not help the world in which he came into, yet, he would soon become the revolutionary that his Jewish counterparts needed to help change their mindsets and attitudes in light of what they were going through.

THE UPPER CLASS

In every society, it is a good feeling to sit among the rich and elite. With power, one can control how things are run. With money, one can buy that which seems appealing to the eyes. This was no different with the upper classes that existed during Jesus' era. During the reign of Caesar Augustus, separation according to class was the common practice. There were basically two classes, the free men and freed slaves (lower class) and the men in power (upper class), with an abysmal gulf separating the five upper from the four lower.

Their Classifications

The first class was the *Ruler Class*. They were a class of their own because they were the rulers who owned all of the land beneath them in their domains. They had the proprietary rights and were considered private owners. Much of the peasants and slaves were on their land and they had much control and influence.

The second class was the *Governing Class*. Like the Ruler Class, the Governing Class was a very small portion of the society (about 1 percent), but on the basis of available data it appeared that they probably received at least a quarter of the national income of most agrarian states.

The third class was the *Retainer Class*. Making up about 5 percent of the population, this class was made up the political "servants" such as scribes, bureaucrats, solders and generals. They were dedicated to serving the political heads, and were indispensable as groups, but expendable as individuals.

The fourth class was the *Merchant Class*. Probably advancing upward from the lower classes of society, this class managed to accumulate a large portion of wealth. Yet they were in disagreement with the Governing Class on their rank of advancement that they received rather than their level of authority. This class rarely had political power.

The *Priestly Class* was the last of the upper classes and they were located at the bottom of the privilege classes. This class covered all those who claim to be religious leaders, all those whose assertion of authority was not intrinsically dependent on Governing Class or rulers, and all those whose loyalty to aristocratic exploitation was always a little suspect.[42] This class was not only made up of privileged people who were able to maintain their status throughout history, but they were able to accumulated goods and own land. Their religious leadership included priests or prophets, visionaries or teachers, institutional or charismatic individuals, and officials or popular personage as long as their claimed authority was transcendental or divine.[43] On many occasions, especially in the Judaic-Christian tradition, the priestly class opposed tyranny and injustice and supported the needs and interests of the weaker elements of society. They did this understanding that God was above all a God of justice and that his awesome power would be used to punish the unjust.[44]

The longevity and stability of a culture is largely sustained by those who possess the wealth to eat what they visualize, rather than what they can afford. The upper class in the Roman Empire was of course no exception. Public displays of status were a very important feature of Roman society. It was not enough to belong to one of the upper classes, for status and rank had to be publicly recognized in order to be meaningful. Hence the clothing of upper class Roman males had distinctive features which made their rank immediately visible to all around them.[45] In addition to their clothing, they lived in gorgeous houses on the hills outside Rome. Many of the elite would host private dinner parties and serve their visitors the foreign dishware. They enjoyed an excessive lifestyle with comfortable furnishings, surrounded by servants and slaves to provide to their every desire.

Their Commodities and Privileges

For wealthy Romans, life was good. The wealthier a person was the more influential they were in Roman society, especially in politics.[46] Education in the empire was the prerogative of the wealthy. Unfortunately, the poor did not have the time, the money, or the need for an education that was designed to prepare the upper classes for positions of public service. In addition, the upper class felt that physical labor was beneath them but appropriate for the lower classes.

The extravagant living of the upper class was also taken out against those who were less fortunate. In a traditional agrarian empire, the aristocracy takes the surplus from the peasantry and in a commercializing agrarian empire, the aristocracy takes the land from the peasantry. The former devours the industry and productivity of the peasantry while the latter their very identity and dignity.[47]

The upper class had the privilege of covering up their operations and treatment of the people by claiming law, order, peace, and protection as returns for the poor's surplus. Yet, they knew that they could only raise taxes to a certain point and push peasants below survival levels only to a certain volume before rebellion occurs.[48] Thus, in the steady-state operation of a tradition agrarian empire, the peasants saw the aristocracy as something like a natural evil.[49]

Jesus' Significance

When Jesus would soon come on the scene, he would have a different philosophy concerning those who were rich. He would state that "it is easier for a camel to go through the eye of a needle than for a rich man to enter the Kingdom of God" (Mark 10:25). Here, Jesus would state that in order for the rich to enter into his kingdom, they must part with the burden of their worldly wealth and stoop to the duties of a humble religion. They must ultimately become disentangled from their riches,[50] and must sell everything they have and give to the poor (Matthew 19:21).

He would warn against the accumulation of wealth. Against the very mindset of the upper elite, Jesus would state, "Do not store up for yourselves treasures on earth, where moth and rust destroy, and where thieves break in and steal. But store up for yourselves treasures in heaven, where moth and rust do not destroy, and where thieves do not break in and steal" (Matthew 6:19). He would warn the multitudes of people who came to hear him that they cannot serve both God and money (Matthew 6:24). He was not against the rich because they had money but rather because it was wrong for some people to live in wasteful luxury while others starved.

His ministry would even showcase a number of wealthy individuals who came to understand the truth about riches. One truth being that money can be a useful means of helping the poor and less fortunate. The New Testament records wealthy women among the earliest followers of Jesus (Luke 8:3). Two of Jesus' followers, James and John, came from a family who owned their own fishing boat and could pay and provide work for servants (Mark 1:19-20). Zacchaeus was a wealthy but hated tax-collector, but when he came to know

Jesus, his attitude changed when it came to the usefulness of money (Luke 19:1-10). His concept of riches, his teachings, and his whole philosophical system of worshipping God and not money would be needed among the upper class of his day.

THE MIDDLE CLASS

The middle class did not make much of an impact during the Roman Era. For persons to be classified as a middle class, they had to have political power, wealth and some means of status. These attributes weren't based on what one had now, but what one could bring to the table in the future. They could have liquid assets, the ownership of property, or something that could put them in this financial class. The middle class could be considered as a group of people who may have had economic autonomy but not a great deal of social power. Unfortunately, few could accomplish or prove this status.

Thus, there was not a strong middle class since the persons with some wealth were not able to enter into or desired power. This made the people all somewhat unequal in an essence when referring to power. Although money could be gained, political power and ethical status only came though one's family. Unless you were born into a family with status, like those in government, you could not obtain status.

Their Skilled Jobs

For some who were in the Middle Class, they had skilled jobs such as merchants, stonecutters, masons, sculptors and craftsmen. Some of the religious leaders including the Pharisees, scribes, and teachers of the Law were also a part of this class. Other religious leaders like the temple priests and the Sadducees were a part of the Upper Class. Jesus and his family could have been among some of these people, since he and his father was a carpenter.

The Separation and Disparity

Outside of the few who were in the middle class, there were only those who were rich, those who were poor and not much in between.

For there to not be a real and definite class, there was certainly a wide gap in both income and power. During the reign of the first Roman emperor Caesar Augustus, separation according to class was the common practice but even before this, the Jewish prophets saw a huge discrepancy not only coming but already existing. These prophets were not radical liberals but, if anything, conservative traditionalists who spoke and wrote in light of what they saw.

Solomon stated "Do not exploit the poor because they are poor and do not crush the needy in court" (Proverbs 22:22). He was stating that it was not good to simply steal from those who were of a disadvantage just because it was easy to do so. He also stated, "Do not move an ancient boundary stone or encroach on the fields of the fatherless" (Proverbs 23:10). Solomon understood the inheritance of land that was intended to be passed down through generation and he saw the injustice that took place when land was taken from the very people of whom it was to be passed down to.

Around 760 BC, the prophet Amos was horrified by the widening discrepancy between rich and poor during the reign of King Jeroboam II. He stated that some of the people "sell the righteous for silver, and the needy for a pair of sandals. They trample on the heads of the poor as upon the dust of the ground and deny justice to the oppressed" (Amos 2:6-7). He states concerning Israel, "You trample on the poor and force him to give you grain. Therefore, though you have built stone mansions, you will not live in them; though you have planted lush vineyards, you will not drink their wine. For I know how many are your offenses and how great your sins. You oppress the righteous and take bribes and you deprive the poor of justice in the courts" (Amos 5:11-12). Notice the very specific details of the accusations of Israel. The prophet was not just giving a general condemnation but rather was getting down into commercial transactions in which "clever" landowners or merchants were swindling and taking advantage of the so called "unintelligent" peasants or workers with bogus weights and measures.

Jesus' Significance

A noteworthy individual was truly needed to challenge the Roman culture and their economic world that existed in the First Century. Someone was needed who was not afraid and who had a message worth hearing to challenge the issues of advocacy and patronage. Jesus was the one needed who would argue against this unfair reliance on those who held the upper hand and he needed to bring about another totally different way of thinking. People no longer had to be taken advantage of by the patron-client relationships that sought to entrap so many. All they had to do was to put their trust and reliance on him and his teachings. Yet, it was no wonder why such a teaching was so hard to accept for those who held power and money.

THE LOWER CLASS

In many societies today, the poor and enslaved are but a small minority. Unfortunately, during the Roman era the peasant class was the majority of the population. Numerically, the middle and lower peasant groups were the largest part of the rural population and the peasantry carried the greatest burden of taxation. That is why Jews hated tax collectors. Their place in the lower orders of the social hierarchy was virtually accepted although they did not believe it was right.

Some occupations the lower class people held ranged from working the land, farming, mining, well digging, road builders, camel drivers, and those who loaded and unloaded goods. They were given their earnings by means of gold, silver, goods and food. The people of higher status controlled the land, money, jobs, food and all resources that people needed to survive. Many of the lower class people were servants to the rich and were employed in the palace. I have already mentioned the five upper classes. Now I will talk about the nature of the four lower classes.

Their Classifications

The *Peasant Class* was made up of the bulk of the population. This class felt the overwhelming burden of the injustice of the Roman government, for they were the ones who were financially supporting the state. They were not only abused by the elite but their very existence was to sustain their wealth and power. Most peasants lived on a farm, produced agriculture, and worked in local markets. Because agriculture was the basis of most ancient empires, the peasants ultimately paid for wars, royal courts, bureaucracies, and religious establishments.[51]

The *Artisan Class*, representing about 5 percent of the population, was the homeless peasants or powerless class. They were not only below the peasants in class but also in income. Both peasants and artisans were considered to be illiterate.

The *Unclean and Degraded Classes* were so bad off that they were separated from both the Peasant Class and the Artisan Class. The reason was because they had profession like prostitutes, gatekeepers, shepherds, and miners that were considered unclean or degraded. They were forced to live exclusively by their intelligence or by donations. During the Roman society, they probably averaged between 5 and 10 percent of the population.

The last class was the *Expendable Class*. Like the Unclean Class and Degraded Class, they also made up about 5 to 10 percent of the population. This class was made up of about everyone else including criminals and the extremely poor. They lived entirely on people's donations. Despite the ravages of war, famine, plague, and other disasters, and despite the influences of infanticide, abortion, monasticism, and prostitution, those segments of the population which were at, or above, the subsistence level continued to produce more offspring than could be employed except by a steady reduction in privilege. Thus, barring an effective method of controlling fertility, which no agrarian society ever discovered, there seems to have been no alternative to the existence of a class of expendables, as harsh as such a statement may sound to modern ears.[52]

The Peasant World

All four of the lower classes were poor, while some were far worse than others. Peasants throughout history were near the bottom of the Agrarian social structure. A peasant was quite simply, an exploited farmer.[53] They were definitely rural and lived in relation to market towns. They formed a class segment of a larger population which usually contained urban centers, sometimes metropolitan capitals. They constituted part-societies with part-cultures. Peasants were not totally in isolation from civilized cultures due to their close proximity to market towns. By being mostly rural, they were often influenced by townspeople who passed through or lived nearby. They were a group of people who had self identity and who desired things in life such as land, money, good health, friendship and love, honor and respect, rank and authority, and influence. Unfortunately, all of these were in short supply. The peasant world consisted of several factors. First, they lacked many necessities for their everyday needs. They were not only poor but powerless. Whatever they acquired from their hard work, they were to keep very little for themselves and family. They had to use the rest to pay for supplies, rent, and their preparation for future tough times. It was a struggle to pay taxes, to find labor, food, and rent, and many lacked steady employment and were worse off than slaves who had a least assurance of food and of clothing. Food was just not enough to spread around to meet their health needs, and their food supply was severely reduced even though they worked for the crop production. Those who were unemployed were ready to follow any man who would give them anything to feed their stomachs. In seemingly every aspect of their lives, including respect, health, and housing, there was a "short supply."

Second, peasants lived under the conditions of being "nonexistent". They were mere "nobodies" from virtually those who were not peasants. They did not have any status in the community and were a group who would generally band together to protest in both non-violent and violent ways. They did not have a major voice concerning issues or political matters of their day. Many kept their inferior status due to land tenure, and were considered inferior to all other classes in every way. They were typically defined not only by where they lived but by their lack of social and political power. They had no opportunity to go up in status, but only down.

At the same time, they had not contributed to any of the making of history, since they were looked upon as being endlessly chasing their conservative daily routines. Since they were merely trying to survive, they had no time to change history or make it better. The peasants were look upon as not being able to trust, suspicious, aggressive, competitive, passive, stubborn, and even stupid. It is quite interesting that they were the largest of the social class, yet made the least impact in history. However, the only time they would be noted in history was when they made trouble for the elites. Jesus of Nazareth and the great Jewish revolt of 66-70 were just a couple of examples of Jews from possibly the Peasant Class that made history.

Third, understanding that peasants did not have control over their lives, they were always in confrontation with the authorities and the elite. Most subordinate classes throughout most of history were always being controlled by power, and for the Jews living in Palestine, their surpluses were given over to a dominant group of rulers who then distribute it to the rest of society. When the peasants did have the resources to make extra money, they could not because their resources were taken by those above them. They always owed someone for something and there was always a higher ranking person taking what little they had.

Knowing this, there was no real clever way for them to strike back. Even a drive to revolt against the higher powers was unheard of and thus, they generally avoided direct conflict with authority figures because of this. However, in defiance, some peasants would resist by hiding their true feelings and thoughts, running away, disobedience, robbery, ignorance, slander, and disruption. Collectively they had courage to protest which only demonstrated that many would have been successful in other areas if society would have given them a chance. Since there were so many dimensions in their life, peasants saw religion as one area in which they could control.

The Slave World

The lack of a strong middle class helped to bring with it the institution of slavery. Because of this institution, which was built upon the use of military captives, the middle class was almost crushed out of the empire. Slaves made up a large proportion within the Roman Empire and they were the lowest of the low while the patrons were the highest of the high. A slave was one who had to go without proper family life, money, and dignity, and they unfortunately had to live a life of their own.

The very existence of slavery during the First Century took place because of debt that families or individuals were brought into. It was of course, very easy, even in the absence of interest, to get more and more deeply in debt. As a result, debt could build up, slowly but surely, to an amount that could never be paid off. Individuals or families could sell themselves into slavery or be enslaved by their creditors when debt became too desperate.[54] People would become slaves because they were unable to afford food and shelter, and as a result, they viewed slavery as a better option. Indebtedness not only created a desperate situation but the loss of land, which was the very thing that God gave.

As a whole, all slaves were put to work. The degree of hardship experienced in a slave's life depended strongly upon what task they occupied within the agrarian society. The slaves were responsible for tending to the agriculture. They were use to working on farms, building public structures, and working as civil servants in the administration of emperors. Life's basic needs of shelter, food, and clothing were in no way abundant for slaves. Their whole lives were spent working in order to provide luxury for the upper class. The only rights or freedoms experienced by slaves were those granted by their masters. Provincials, though not considered citizens of Rome still had to pay taxes on their homes, land, and slaves that were owned in Rome. They were generally ruled by governors who had been appointed by the senate rather than directly by the emperor. Provincials usually lived as farmers and produced agriculture.[55]

The treatment of slaves is another topic. The effects of slavery as a whole were debasing. It carried a dark but apparent link to the same means of injustice that took place between patron-client relationships. The impact of patron-client relationships within the Roman Empire played an important function in determining how people behaved, which ultimately helped to fashion Roman culture. Even though patron-client relationships caused for special privileges and incalculable services for the elite, they also meant discrimination and dependence for the less fortunate.

As a whole, slaves weren't treated as human beings but rather as a useful product that was expected to deliver a service. The aristocrats and rich had the upper hand over another human being, and at any time, they could use their power to get what they wanted. The ownership of slaves made the masters dependent upon the labor and skill of those who served them to the extreme that they lost both originality and aspiration.

Jesus' Significance

Jesus was going to be born and would come to change the mindsets of the peasants toward those who controlled them. Other prophets, including Amos and Micah, came before Jesus and they rebuked the society for its injustice. They both had their condemnations collected into books in which they were read to the people in order to give them hope. Yet this was not good enough. Jesus had to come and he would be the hero that the peasants needed. Although he was not among the upper classes, he did not act in defiance and he would soon come with the ambition of spreading the words of God. He spoke of a kingdom that was under divine rule. This kingdom would judge all human rule, yet its focus would not be on kings, rulers, and power, but on the justice of God. Jesus understood that the Galilean peasants were considered nobodies, and yet he told them, "Blessed are the poor in spirit, for theirs is the Kingdom of Heaven" (Matthew 5:3). This was, however, in direct opposition to those who are rich.

The Religious World

The religious world of the Roman Empire was diverse, with its primitive religion in the early days being animism. Gods of the forest and field, gods of the sky and stream, gods of the sowing and of the harvest – all received his worship in their proper places and at their proper seasons.[56] Emperor worship was a growing consciousness in the empire seeing the great success of leaders like Caesar Augustus and Herod the Great. There were mystery religions, occult worship, and numerous philosophies and schools of thought.

Although there were many beliefs within the Roman Empire, I will specifically emphasis Judaism, the religion of the Jews, as the main focus within the religious world. The reason is because the New Testament specifically stated that Jesus came into his own, yet, his own did not receive him (John 1:12). "His own" specifically pertained to the Jews and although Jesus came to save all men, he came specifically during his ministry to confront and amend the Jewish though and religious way of life.

BELIEFS

We must begin with four of their key principles. The first is the belief in one God who is over all nations. Second, God chose Abraham and his descendants as his special people and promised they would be a great nation in the Promised Land. Third, God made a covenant with the Hebrews at Mount Sinai where he gave the law to the people through Moses as their prophet. And last, Abraham's people were chosen to be the model of behavior for all nations in the future age of Messiah, who will rule the world in justice and peace.

Several beliefs define the Jewish religion. First, the Jewish people were monotheistic. The captivity confronted the Jewish people with a stern alternative. Either they had to commit themselves utterly to the worship of Jehovah, the one true God, by which allegiance they would retain the genius and purpose of their national existence or they would be absorbed both religiously and politically by the nations among whom they were driven into exile.[57] They choose the former and to commit themselves wholly to God. On the same lines with their belief in one God, Jews believe that God, who revealed himself at Sinai, was the highest reality in history and to act in harmony with the will of this God was the highest goal of life.[58]

Second, failure to live in harmony with God is sin. They considered the two dimensions of sin as being idolatry and injustice. The Jewish attitude of sin is reflected in the New Testament stating, "For whoever keeps the whole law and yet stumbles at just one point is guilty of breaking all of it" (James 2:10). Even failure to obey one of God's proscribe commands were regarded as sin.

Third, Judaism considered belief in the divine revelation of God through the written and oral Torah as one of its fundamental core belief. The Torah taught individuals to maintain ethics and holiness and that the two, when separated, could cause serious damage. They were taught of not only how to think but how to behave and that righteous thinking resulted in right and appropriate behavior.[59] Because of righteousness, God would give rewards, but for evil doers, he would punish them. A day of judgment in which the wicked would be sent to a well-deserved doom and the righteous would be vindicated also appeared in their literature. Sheol was regarded as an intermediate state preceding the resurrection and the final rewards and punishments.

Fourth, the Messiah was one belief that Jewish people could agree on no matter what movement they followed. By definition, he would be someone who was regarded to be a savior or rescuer of their country. He would be represented as someone who would restrain all enemies, establish a universal kingdom, and make Jerusalem the capital on the earth. It was not written in Jewish writings of any specified year or century he would come, but what was only recorded was the fact that he would come. The Messianic expectation of the advent of a political deliverer for Israel was strong in the inter-testamental period. The Psalms of Solomon, written in the First Century before Christ, depict the coming of a righteous ruler for Israel who shall be sinless and who shall rule over the Gentiles. Unfortunately, the Messiah was nowhere represented as suffering for men or as redeeming them by his personal sacrifice.[60]

PLACES OF WORSHIP

Synagogue

The name synagogue refers primarily to a "gathering" or a "gathering place". It was a Jewish place of worship both in and outside of Palestine. Concerning its origin, some scholars believe that it was instituted by Moses (Exodus 18:20), while others believe that it went back to the time of Asaph (Psalm 74:8) where the name synagogue was actually mentioned. Still others believe that it originated during the Babylonian captivity and it was there where the system of worship was introduced and organized. But one thing is sure and that is the fact that the synagogues did bring a new center of worship to the Jewish people. The wide dispersion of the people in the captivity and their wanderings in the years that followed made some local form of gathering necessary.[61]

In the First Century, one of the areas in which the Roman Empire flourished was by allowing their people to maintain their own customs and beliefs. The synagogues during Jesus' day were one of the ways for the Jews to accomplish this. There was not just one synagogue but many were spread out all over Palestine and they were a great social outlet for many Jews. They were utilized for both worship and education. Young boys starting at age five began their formal education, five years later they would learn Jewish law, and by age 18, formal education was complete. They would learn from scribes or doctors of the law and the manual they used was the Torah. The Torah was the educational medium for keeping the law before the people and for providing instruction for their children in the ancestral faith.[62] The Jews main areas of learning included religion, law, history and ethics, and this was in contrast to the Greek education system which emphasized science, arts, linguistics and bodily training. It was also in these synagogues that the Jews were taught to keep their hope alive in the soon coming Messiah.

The synagogues held a much more central role in community life than just a meeting place. Regular worship, studies, the administration of punishment, the organization of sacred meals, the collection of charitable donations, and assembly for political and social purposes all took place at the synagogue.[63] We would see that Jesus and his disciples regularly taught in the synagogues (Matthew 13:54; Mark 6:2).

The Temple

Initially, the synagogue was central to First Century Judaism in a different sense then the temple. Whereas the temple was the dwelling place of the holy God and a place where sacrifices were made, the synagogue was socially central in Jewish life. The temple began as the central focus for First Century Jews, while the synagogue was a peripheral place of social activity.[64]

The first temple was not the temple standing that Jesus saw but was actually King Solomon's Temple that stood from 957 B.C. to 587 B.C. After coming back to Jerusalem from exile, the second temple was built by Zerubbabel and it stood from 520 B.C. to 19 B.C. The temple Jesus knew was the refurbished and enlarged temple by Herod the Great and it stood from 19 B.C. to 70 A.D. Herod's Temple was not the third temple, for he declared himself that his work was only to be considered as an enlarging and furthering of the magnificent work of Zerubbabel.

Herod undertook the task to rebuild the temple because the previous temple built by the exiles had been standing for about five hundred years and had experienced considerable natural decay and the physical attacks of war. To gain favor from the Jews, he refurbished it and carried out the expensive building project. The work needed 10,000 skilled laborers, 1,000 Levites, and 10 years to complete the main phase of the building. The entire project would not be complete until 65 A.D. Unfortunately five years later, his refurbished temple was destroyed by the Romans and has yet to be reconstructed.

Leading up to the time of the coming of Jesus, the temple was the main center of worship in Jerusalem. The temple was also a place of sacrifice. Jews from both inside Palestine and outside Palestine would come and bring their gifts to the temple. Although the synagogue was the everyday home for Jewish life and worship, the Jerusalem temple was the symbol of national Jewish life and worship. Its religious presence conveyed to all humanity of the one true and living God.

Jesus' Significance

Yet, both the religious and nonreligious Jews would soon hear and observe a disturbing message from Jesus about their religious centers of worship. Was the temple supposed to be a place for God or a place for commerce? Was it a place for all people to enter throughout or just the Jews? The money bankers and brokers would soon feel the heat of Jesus as he would make a whip of cords to drive them all out of the temple. He stated, "Do not make My Father's house a house of merchandise" (John 2:16). He seemingly chose to stop at the "Court of the Gentiles" in the temple to showcase his anger and more importantly his righteous zeal for his father. Instead of it being a house of prayer, it was used as a showcase for monetary exchange, something that greatly angered Jesus.

If this was not enough, Jesus would even promise the demise of the temple. Herod's temple had certainly become an icon for Jews all over the world not just because of its religious symbolism but also because of its magnificence and beauty. However in Matthew 21:1-2, Jesus said that "not one stone here will be left on another" and that "every one [stone] will be thrown down". In Luke 21:24, Jesus states that the Jews "will fall by the sword and will be taken as prisoners to all the nations." In addition, he states that "Jerusalem will be trampled on by the Gentiles until the times of the Gentiles are fulfilled." And that is precisely what happened many years later. The Romans destroyed Jerusalem in 70 A.D. and again in 132 A.D. During those two destructions, over a million Jews were killed and over 100,000 were forced into slavery and exile. Although the Jews had put much attention on their religious institutions, Jesus was trying to make a statement concerning where they need to put their trust. Man-made institutions were all temporary and Jesus came on the scene promoting a kingdom that would be permanent. He was needed to turn their direction, hope, and attention on him.

Festivals / Feasts

I will mention only seven festivals or feasts that were important to Judaism in the First Century. The seven were the Passover, the Feast of Unleavened Bread, the Day of Atonement, the Feast of Tabernacles, the Feast of Dedication, the Feast of Purim, and the Feast of Weeks. Five were prescribed by the Mosaic Law and two were post-exilic in origin. All of the biblical ceremonies and festivals contained significance. God never instituted the need for remembrance without a greater truth and anticipation. In addition to the mentioning of the festivals, I will state how each applied directly toward Jesus.

The Passover

The Passover began on the 15th day of the Jewish month of Nissan, particularly the full moon of that month. It was the most renowned of all the Jewish holidays, both historically and religiously. In Exodus, God inflicted a total of 10 plagues on the Egyptians so that Pharaoh would release the Israelites from slavery and the tenth plague was the killing of the firstborn of every Egyptian. So that the Jews were not killed, they were commanded to mark the doorposts of their homes with the blood of a lamb. When the death angel of the Lord saw this, he would "pass-over" and not kill those in that house. The Passover not only marked the anniversary of the liberation of the Jews from Egypt but their establishment as a self-governing people by God.

Yet, this ongoing tradition was to come to an end with the slaying of Jesus on the cross. The sacrifice for the Passover had to be a perfect lamb without spot and blemish, and Jesus was that perfect lamb that had been killed (Revelation 5:6). In addition, there was always much preparation before Passover began, for the house was to be completely cleaned and no leaven was to be left in the house. In looking at Jesus, there was much preparation when he took part in the Passover, and not only did he spend over three years training his disciples but he spent the last few hours before his arrest with those dearest to him. With Jesus' death, he brought the focus of the Passover to himself, and by his resurrection, he provided redemption for not only the Jews but for all humanity. For those who believed in him, the death angel would "pass over" and they would not spend eternity in the Lake of Fire.

43

Feast of Trumpets

The starting point of this feast comes from Numbers 10:1-2 and 10 which states, "And the LORD spoke unto Moses, saying, "Make thee two trumpets of silver; of a whole piece shalt thou make them: that thou mayest use them for the calling of the assembly, and for the journeying of the camps. Also in the day of your gladness, and in your solemn days, and in the beginnings of your months, ye shall blow with the trumpets over your burnt offerings, and over the sacrifices of your peace offerings; that they may be to you for a memorial before your God: I am the LORD your God." In addition, Leviticus 23:24-25, "Speak unto the children of Israel, saying, 'In the seventh month, in the first day of the month, shall ye have a Sabbath, a memorial of blowing of trumpets, a holy convocation. Ye shall do no servile work therein: but ye shall offer an offering made by fire unto the LORD.'"

This festival refers to the mandate to execute the ceremony of the blowing of horns and trumpets from morning to evening on the Jewish holiday of Rosh Hashanah. It is named "trumpets" because of the use of trumpets to sound the alarm to go to war. Unlike the Passover and Pentecost, this feast did not attract many pilgrims to Jerusalem, for it was celebrated in the synagogue as well as in the temple. Nehemiah states that those who returned from the exile observed the feast by the public reading of the law and by general rejoicing (8:2-12).[65]

The trumpets were used in giving signals of war and the Jews were looking for a Messiah who would lead them "to war" against their foreign opposition, the Romans. During Jesus' entire ministry, he was constantly making war against both physical and spiritual opposition. Yet when he rose from the grave, he defeated sin, which was actually the main struggle for Jews and for all mankind, and he defeated the governments of this world, specifically Satan and his spiritual enemies. It has also been prophesied that there will be a "blowing of the trumpet" at Christ's return and Christians will also triumph over the evil forces (Ephesians 6:11-13). The apostle Paul prophetically stated that in the near future, Jesus will descend from heaven with a "shout, with the archangel's voice, and with the trumpet of God, and the dead in Christ will rise first" (1 Thessalonians 4:16-17). Therefore, the greater fulfillment of this feast was in Jesus.

The Day of Atonement

More of a fast than a feast, the Day of Atonement, also known as Yom Kippur, was a marvelous ceremony that took place once a year. Leviticus 23:26-32 is where God gives Moses the instructions of holding a sacred assembly (the Day of Atonement) in which an offering was to be made to the Lord by fire. The people were not to work on that day when the atonement was made and this festival was to be a lasting ordinance for the generations to come. The special feature of the festival, apart from the ordinary daily sacrifices, was the presentation of the annual atonement by the High Priest. One of the key Old Testament passages that sets the tone for this ceremony was Leviticus 17:11 which says, "For the life of a creature is in the blood, and I have given it to you to make atonement for yourselves on the altar; it is the blood that makes atonement for one's life."

Described in Leviticus 16, the High Priest was obligated to follow a certain procedure or he would die. After washing his entire body, the priest put on a white garment and offered a bull for his sin and his family's sin. He would then fill a censer with burning coals and enter the Holy of Holies. This was the one time he could enter into the presence of God. He would exit and take some of the blood from the bull and sprinkle it on the mercy seat in order to pay for his sin. Next, after the goat was slaughtered, he would take the blood and perform the same ritual to pay for the sins of the people. After confessing the sins of the Israelites, the goat was taken away into the desert. After the ceremony had ended, the High Priest took off his clothes, washed up and the usual routine of sacrifices continued.

This once a year routine would showcase a one time act of Jesus' death that would eliminate the need of this festival. The lambs that were killed every morning and evening would only serve as a future platform of the one great atonement of Jesus for the sins of the world. Understanding the fact that the Holy of Holies was a sacred place that the High Priest could enter only one time a year on the Day of Atonement, Jesus was needed to separate this gap between man and God. This ceremony accomplished by the High Priest was costly if not performed correctly, and at the same time, Jesus was needed to show the people of his day how costly sin was. He was needed to allow the special privilege of allowing all those who believe in him to because priests themselves who can go directly to God (Revelation 1:6; Hebrews 4:16). He took away the covering of death that shadowed man, allowed all those who believed in him to "not perish but have everlasting life" (John 3:16), and he cleared the way by the blood of his sacrifice by acting as our priest before God. (Hebrew 10:19-20). He did not use the blood of bulls and goats, but rather his own blood, and his sacrifice was once and for all.

The Feast of Tabernacles

The name of the Feast of Tabernacles comes from God's mandate to the Israelites to build temporary "tabernacles" or booths to live in during the festival. As a result, the people left their houses and built temporary residences to live in while they rejoiced before God. The purpose was for them to reflect over their liberation from bondage in Egypt and when they actually lived in booths after God freed them. This was the last and most central holiday of the year. Also referred to booths, this holiday commemorated the Israelites 40 years of wandering in the dessert and it began five days after Yom Kippur on the fifteenth of Tishri (September or October). This feast was mentioned in the New Testament in John 7:1-13. During this occasion, Jesus went to the feast in private.

When Jesus went to celebrate this feast, he used it as an occasion to disclose his very person and duty. He came to make known to man that he was the tabernacle and dwelling place of God. Although Peter offered to put him in a "box" or booth-like structure during his transfiguration, God rebuked him to show that he was not contained. Paul emphasizes in his writings stating, "For we know that if our earthly house of this tabernacle were dissolved, we have a building of God, a house not made with hands, eternal in the heavens" (2 Corinthians 5:1-2). Prophecy states that people from the nations of the world will come up to celebrate the Feast of Tabernacles with the Jewish people in Jerusalem (Zechariah 14). This stage has already been set, for Jesus declared that he would come back and receive all those who believed in him. One day in heaven, all believers will finally leave their temporary homes and forever dwell with God in the New Heaven and New Earth. During that time, they will be able to reflect over their liberation from sin on earth. Therefore, although this festival has not completely been fulfilled, prophecy has already declared that it soon will be.

The Feast of Dedication

This was one of two feasts that were added later in post-exilic times. Also called Chanukah, the Feast of Lights, and Hannukah, the Feast of Dedication reminded the people of their liberation from totalitarianism. It was a Jewish holiday celebrating the rededication of the temple in Jerusalem during the Maccabean Revolt. It fell on the 25th of Kislev on the Jewish calendar. During the reign of the Antiochus Epiphanes, the temple and priesthood were used for pagan worship and sacrifice. A statue of Antiochus as Zeus was built in the temple in Jerusalem and pigs were offered on the altar. As a result, in 167 B.C., a priestly family, the Maccabees, lead by Judah Maccabee, started a rebellion. Despite of overwhelming odds against them, they were successful in driving out the Greeks. The temple was cleansed and rededicated which led to the independence of the Jewish society.

This festival commemorated a divine victory, which again gave to Israel their good land, after they had once more undergone sorrows like those of the wilderness.[66] The primary ritual of this festival was the stimulation of lights, one light on each night of the holiday gradually moving to eight lights on the final night. The purpose for lights was not for the illumination within the house but for the illumination of the outside of the house. This was so that spectators and casual observers would see it and be reminded of the miracle of liberation that took place. The only reference to this feast in the New Testament is in John 10:22-23 where Jesus went to Jerusalem to celebrate this festival.

Although the Feast of Dedication was to be a festival of lights, Jesus was stated as being that continual light that all men would see. Isaiah prophesied that the people of Galilee walking in darkness would soon be blessed because they would see a great light. The true light would come into the darkness and would be a light no one could extinguish (Isaiah 9:1-7.) Jesus preached three sermons stating that he was the "light of the world" (John 8:12; 9:5; 12:46) and perhaps all three could have taken place during the Feast of Dedication.

The Feast of Purim

The name Purim was derived from "the lots" which Haman, a Gentile, cast in order to wipe out the Jews, specifically those in Persia.

The story was found in the book of Esther when King Xerxes governed Persia during that particular period. Esther, a Jew, was selected to be queen and was told by her relative Mordecai to not tell anyone of her race. Sometime later, Xerxes elevated Haman over all the nobles. When all the people would bow down to Haman because of his high rank, Mordecai refused and his actions angered Haman. Once he found out that Mordeci was a Jew, he set about to get rid of all Jews in the kingdom. A declaration was issued that on the 13th day of the 12th month (Adar), all Jews were to be destroyed. When Queen Esther found out, Mordecai persuaded her to go to Xerxes and intervene. Knowing that she could be killed for coming into the king's presence without permission, she put on her robe and stood in the inner court. The king graciously found favor in her and Esther invited both the king and Haman to a special banquet. After a second banquet, Esther tells of the plot Haman had devised to destroy the Jews, including her. Xerxes was furious at Haman and immediately had him killed.

This festival was celebrated to remember the deliverance from the plot to exterminate the Jews from Haman. It reflects on the unforgettable story concerning an exiled people with no temple, no priests, no prophet, and no religious leader. Yet, they were liberated by a God who saw the need to come to their aid. Purim was celebrated annually according to the Hebrew calendar on the 14th day of the month Adar, and this was the day after the victory of the Jews over their enemies.

The theme for the Feast of Purim is deliverance. But God had an even greater purpose. This deliverance would only shadow the greater and permanent deliverance that he would bring by sending his son Jesus to die. The Jews were liberated on the seventeenth day of Nisan, which is the same day that liberation for the Israelites in Egypt began, which is the same day Jesus arose and freed man from the bondage of sin. God did not always bring about deliverance according to man's expectations. We see this from the fact that the Jews were looking for a Messiah who would lead and rule, yet they did not expect him to die. But Jesus was both the Jews and Gentile's Savior and he ultimately delivered them and from their sin. This was indeed the greater purpose for the Feast of Purim.

The Feast of Weeks

Last but not least, the Feast of Weeks, also known as Harvest, Shavuot, the Day of First fruits, or Pentecost, was considered the closing festival of the Passover season (Exodus 34:22; Leviticus 23:15). This festival was observed for only two days and was celebrated in the month Sivan, which was seven weeks after the offering of the wave sheaf after the Passover. The word "weeks" portrayed a time period from grain harvest to the barley harvest and ending with the wheat harvest. It was linked to the giving of the Ten Commandments and Jews believe that it was at that particular time that God gave the Torah to them through Moses on Mount Sinai.

Historically, the main happenings on the Feast of Weeks was the giving of a wave offering to the Lord, two loaves of bread with leaven. The bread was to be given with seven male lambs, a young bull, and two rams as a burnt offering. Although the feast was not mentioned in the Old Testament, it is of great importance in the New Testament as the time at which the Holy Spirit was poured out upon the disciples of Jesus, who, in obedience to His command, were waiting in Jerusalem.[67] It was a celebration to revive and reinforce personal relationships with God by the rite and study of the Torah.

There was not only a Feast of Weeks or Pentecost in the Old Testament but there was one in the New Testament as well. Jesus was the one exalted at Pentecost in the New Testament, for God sent his Spirit and he filled the room where Jesus' disciples were. During the first Pentecost, the Ten Commandments were given in stone to the people, which was 50 days from the crossing of the Red Sea, and three thousand were killed. In the New Testament, God's law was written on the hearts of men during Pentecost, which was 50 days from Jesus' resurrection, and three thousand lost Jews were saved. Historically, Jews represented the vast majority of the early church, but later Gentiles would represent the majority.

Religious Sects

In the centuries after Alexander the Great, there grew up considerable diversity within Judaism, leading to several First Century Jewish movements. These groups were the Pharisees, the Sadducees, the Essenes, the Zealots, the Hellenists, the Samaritans, and the Nazarenes – all of which were engaged in ongoing debate.[68] All of them were religious, yet they all believed that their way of practice and belief should represent the "true God" and the "true Israel". To understand their debates, it is important to remember that in the beginning of the First Century, there was no official Bible and no set practices and commitments accepted as normative by all Jews. It was only at the end of this century that the Tanak, or Bible of Judaism as we have it today, came into existence. [69] Therefore, each group desired to set the standard of practices by which all Jews were to live by.

The Pharisees

The Pharisees are the first religious group mentioned mainly because they were the leading and largest sect. Their origin went back to the reign of Hyrcanus I (134-104 B.C.) and from there, it is probable that they were one of numerous groups to grow out of the resurgence and resistance movement of the Maccabean period (ca. 166-160 B.C.). Around 100 B.C., the Pharisees and the temple nobles were in disagreement pertaining to who should control and govern Judaism. Later on under Queen Alexandra (76-67 BC), the Pharisees gained a strong voice,[70] and eventually, it was their religious practices that became the standard for Judaism.

Their name comes from the word "separate" or "separation" which typifies them as being separatists and puritans of that which should be considered "true Judaism". They looked on themselves as the godly core of the nation and Josephus typified them well by stating that they were a body of Jews with the reputation of excelling the rest of their nation in the observance of religion.[71] They were good and moral people who retreated from anything that was evil or that even appeared evil. Their ritualism was of such that their meals were consumed in a ritualistic manner and all aspects of their life were governed by the law and the constant strive for purity. In addition, they were organized into brotherhoods, binding themselves with an oath to observe faithfully the ordinances of the Levitical code. Yet, the prevailing mood in this organized group was not that of desire to learn but to establish grounds for criticism. Thus, they zealously accepted the function of watchdogs ready to investigate any spiritual leader who came on the horizon.[72]

The Pharisees' education allowed them to be scholars of the law. They were very powerful within the Jewish society holding much influence over the common people of their time. They were also popular and prominent in the communal gatherings. They prided themselves in their ability to interpret Mosaic Law with precision, which often times caused strife between them and the Sadducees. They held education in high regard and, in comparison with the Sadducees, were liberal in their desire to promote a religion centered on the written and unwritten Law.[73]

They were more likely of the middle class. They did not have the political power, wealth, and status that put them in the higher echelons of the upper class, yet they were not oppressed and violated like the peasants in the lower class. Some of them were scholar scribes, wealthy enough and situated in urban settings with enough support and leisure to read and write.[74]

Their beliefs were many. First and foremost, they believe God alone was their chief and master and would rather die than say that another man was their "master." They believed in the spirit world, specifically angels and spirits. They believed in the immortality of the soul and in the resurrection of the physical body. They looked forward to when God would reward the righteous and pure and would punish the wicked and impure. They, like many Jews, looked forward to the coming of a Messiah, who would escort in an era of universal peace.

About the time of Christ, two schools of Pharisaic interpretation were coming into being, the one taking its name from Hillel, the other from Shammai. Having come to Palestine from Babylonia, Hillel held to a looser construction of the law than most Palestinians, for the reason that some features of the code were unfitted for life in a foreign land.[75] Eventually the school of Hillel became dominant.

The Sadducees

This Jewish sect was the Pharisees' opponents. According to custom, they obtained their name from the sons of Zadok, who was high priest in the days of David and of Solomon. They were a priestly group, particularly Levites, connected with the leadership of the Jerusalem temple. During the Hasmonean Era, they characterized the noble group of their High Priests who were replaced by the previous high priestly lineage.

The Sadducees did not believe in fate and supposed that God was not concerned in one's actions. Rather, they believed that to act what was good or what was evil was at men's own choice. They also took away the belief of the immortal duration of the soul and the punishments and rewards in Hades.

The Pharisees and Sadducees differed greatly in aspects of their culture from education to the law. They had some orally transmitted traditions of their own explaining how to carry out the Torah's law. They rejected the oral law of the Pharisees and came close to being biblical literalists. For example, they interpreted literally "an eye for an eye." They rejected the notion of an after life because it did not appear in the Torah.[76] They believed that souls die with the body and that is why there is no afterlife and no resurrection of the dead. They denied the existence of angels and spirits and did not believe in personal immortality.

The Sadducees were of the upper class. They had the political power, ethical status, and the monetary earnings of being put among the higher echelons of society. Less numerous and powerful than the Pharisees, they did not have the education as the Pharisees did. They had little influence over the common people they dwelt with and their appeal was primarily to the rich and aristocracy. Unfortunately, they went out of existence after the destruction of the temple in the year 70 A.D. Their religious life was apparently so centered on the temple that its destruction robbed them.

The Essenes

The third religious sect was the Essenes. They thrived from Second Century B.C. to First Century A.D. According to history, the Essenes had settled not in one particular city but in large numbers in every town.[77] There was a reference to one of their places of habitation as having a "gate", which suggests a community living in a section of a city.[78]

Unlike the Pharisees and the Sadducees, this group was an ascetic brotherhood. They were separatists and their philosophy consisted of celibacy and in the observance of the Sabbath. Believing that city life was tainted and evil, they moved to meagerly populated areas of Palestine, particularly to the desert near the Dead Sea. Their survival depended on constantly winning new converts. After a three year trial period, recently joining members would take a vow that included the commitment to practice piety towards "the Deity", living virtuously towards all human beings, upholding a pure way of life, and refraining from criminal and immoral practices.[79] Members ate their meals together in strict silence, except for prayers at beginning and end. Members who violated the group's regulations were excommunicated. ·

Their beliefs included the immortality of the soul and that God would receive them back after death.[80] They were compared to the followers of Greek philosopher Pythagoras with their belief in immortality. Their customs consisted of observances such as collective ownership,[81] and the selection of a leader to make sure that everyone obeyed their orders.[82] They were prohibited from swearing oaths,[83] from sacrificing animals,[84] and they had to control their temper and be peacemakers.[85] They carried weapons only for protection against thieves.[86] They could not have slaves but rather had to serve each other,[87] and they did not engage in trading.[88] Unlike the Sadducees, the Essenes wanted nothing to do with the temple, for they apparently felt it had been corrupted by the Sadducean priests.

The Zealots

The Zealots emerged around the onset of the era mainly because of their opposition to the Roman regime. In 6 A.D., the Zealots, lead by Judas of Galilee and Zadok the Pharisee, rebelled against Judah because it was put under direct Roman rule. They believed that God was to be their only Ruler and Lord[89] and that Israel belonged only to a Jewish king who was a descendent from King David. Unfortunately, the rebellion was quickly obliterated.

What was typical of these sectarian movements was a strong distrust of the Sadducees, who were viewed as having sold out to the Romans. The Zealots, the most hostile of all, had nothing but contempt for the Sadducees and chose to directly oppose them. If the Sadducees urged "don't rock the boat," the Zealots were committed to rocking the boat as often as possible.[90]

Compared to a modern day terrorist group, the Zealots were renowned for frequently living in rebellion. Their existence was in the formation of a political party that had a designated leader.

Their very doctrine constituted a necessity of aggressive and hostile actions against the enemies of Judaism. They were openly hostile to the Gentile world, whereas the Nazarenes, like the Hellenists, were very positive toward Gentiles and sought their conversion.[91]

The Hellenists

The Hellenes were the early residents of Greece and from this people group came the term "Hellenism", which portrayed Greek language and culture. Those non-Greeks who spoke Greek and resided among Greek people were eventually called Hellenists. Specifically speaking, a Hellenist imitated the manners and customs or even the worship of the Greeks. Although they spoke Greek, they most likely were not born on Greek soil. They were in contrast to "Hebrews" who assume a more established Jewish lifestyle.

They were mentioned in Acts 6:1 which states, "And in those days, when the number of the disciples was multiplied, there arose a murmuring of the Grecians against the Hebrews, because their widows were neglected in the daily ministration." The Grecians were the same as the Hellenists. What was taking place in Jerusalem during this time was that those who were more loyal to a Jewish Christianity were finding dissimilarities with the Jews who were more Hellenistic in manner.

Although Palestine was the traditional homeland of the Jewish race, the largest number of Jews in the Roman Empire lived outside the borders of the Holy Land. Known as the Diaspora, or the Dispersion, they were found in almost all of the large cities from Babylon to Rome and in many of the smaller settlements also, wherever commerce or colonization had taken them. Within the Diaspora were two distinct groups, one of which were the Hellenists.[92] The Hellenists were the great missionaries of Judaism who used Greek philosophy to explain the meaning of the biblical stories. They were anxious to promote Judaism as a religion that had a place for Gentiles, and they adapted Judaism to Greek customs whenever feasible. They successfully encouraged large numbers of Gentiles to come and worship the one true God of Israel.[93] Leading up to the coming of Jesus, the Hellenists did not congregate with the Hebrew-speaking Jews of Jerusalem, but had their own synagogues.

The Samaritans

During the Roman era, the Samaritans lived in the district of Samaria, the hill country north and west of Jerusalem. Yet their history goes way back to the conquest of the Northern Kingdom of Israel in 722 BC by the Assyrians. Because of disobedience, God allowed an Assyrian monarch to siege the Northern Kingdom with Samaria being its capital and brought the rule of the ten tribes of Israel to a close. Many Jews were taken as captives along with foreign nations. This assimilation of nations was introduced in order to reduce the chances of rebellion among those taken captured. This mixing of Jews and foreign nations resulted in the formation of a crossbreed race who came to be the Samaritans.

Later on, the Southern Kingdom of Judah was taken captive to Babylon in 586 BC also because of disobedience. When the Judean exile ended in 538 BC and the Jews returned from the Babylonian exile and began to rebuild the temple, they quickly observed their former native soil occupied by people who claimed the land was theirs. Many, of whom were Samaritans, offered to assist with the building of the new temple, but their proposal was rejected. After being rejected, "the peoples around them set out to discourage the people of Judah and make them afraid to go on building. They hired counselors to work against them and frustrate their plans during the entire reign of Cyrus king of Persia and down to the reign of Darius king of Persia. At the beginning of the reign of Xerxes, they lodged an accusation against the people of Judah and Jerusalem" (Ezra 4:4-6). This rejection hastened a further hindrance not only with the rebuilding of the temple but with the rebuilding of Jerusalem.

From then on, the Samaritans and the Jews have been hostile against each other. The Samaritans were never accepted by the Jews of the south and there was never a feeling of connection knowing that at one point they did not worship the true God. The Jews even considered them as mongrels, which was an offensive name denoting the fact that they were of mixed racial ancestry. Their alienation increased causing the Samaritans to not desire to worship in the Jewish Temple. Rather they built their own temple on Mount Gerizim, near Shechem.

Leading up to the years before Jesus, the Samaritans were severely despised by the Jews. It was well understood that "Jews have no dealing with Samaritans" (John 4:9) and they were hated so bad that they were put on the same level as the despised tax collectors and sinners. But even more humiliating, the Jews believed that they could be infected by even passing through their territory. That is why those who journeyed from Judea to Galilee or vice versa would cross over the Jordan River to evade Samaria. They would then cross back over the river once they arrived at their destination. On the other hand, the Samaritans were sometimes aggressive to the Jews and they often mocked them. They even claimed to have an older copy of the Hebrew Scriptures than the Jews.

Religiously, they considered themselves true worshippers of Yahweh, like all the other Jewish sects. They placed ultimate importance on the Pentateuch as a detailed way of life. Like many Jews, they looked for the Messiah but specifically expected him to rule from the location of their temple on Mount Gerazim. They placed a worship-like emphasis on Moses and they believed in the final judgment, with rewards for the righteous.

The Nazarenes

The Nazarenes were a member of a Jewish sect who preserved and followed many of the prescribed Jewish observances. Their beliefs, like most Jews, started with a zeal for the Torah. But unlike the Ebionites, they believed in the virgin birth and the divine nature of Jesus. They did believe in a Messiah figure that was coming and they expected Jesus to specifically fulfill that duty. The origin of their name is uncertain but some believe that it came from the word that means "to separate" in Aramaic. However, this term Nazarene is more of a broad term for this Jewish movement, which may have included the Ebionites who considered themselves as the "Poor Ones".

Historically, the Nazarites in the Old Testament took special vows of dedication to Lord to refrain for a specific time period from alcohol and fruit from the vine. They could not cut their hair or touch any dead corpses (Judges 13:7). Leading up to the coming of Jesus, there was certainly an Ebionite/Nazarene movement that was made up of mostly Jews and followers of John the Baptist. Their locale was in Palestine. When we refer to the Nazarenes, we are not talking about someone from the small town of Nazareth. It is true that Jesus himself was referred one time as a Nazarene (Matthew 2:23), yet in all other cases, the word is rendered "of Nazareth" (Mark 1:24; 10:47).

Jesus' Significance

Understanding that this was the religious world before Jesus came, one may ask why would Jesus have been needed at all? All of these Jewish sects believed in the one true God, a Messiah who would soon come, and most were God-honoring and pious living individuals. Unfortunately, Jesus would be needed to confront them about their very "religion". Even more baffling, he came with his own "religion", to promote the Kingdom of God.

By Jesus coming into this era, he would bring about more controversy and conflict among the religious Jews than they had among each other. Pharisaic opposition to Jesus was a persistent theme in all four gospels. The arguments between Jesus and the Pharisees centered mainly on purity, tithing, and Sabbath laws. As a matter of fact, the Pharisees and the Sadducees, although they did not like each other, teamed up against Jesus numerous times during his ministry. For example, they both in Matthew 16 came together to tempt Jesus asking him to show them a sign from heaven. Jesus sharply rebuked them and left them. Though Jesus taught with the same methods as the Jewish leaders and teachers, his teachings often eluded them or spoke against them. In the end, the Pharisees could not understand him, his actions or his claims. Only the few religious leaders who eventually believed and followed him, namely Nicodemus and Joseph of Arimathea, were greatly affected by him and their lives were forever changed.

Regarding the hated Samaritans, Jesus went out of his way to show that they were among those whom God loved. Although they were despised, Jesus came to break the walls of division. He came to "seek and to save that which was lost" (Luke 19:10) and his teachings on love and acceptance would pierce far deeper than the Jews of his day would have ever expected. For example, his ministry included three noteworthy Samaritans, a leper, a woman, and a man mentioned in one of his parables. The Samaritan leper showed an attitude of gratitude to Jesus the Jew for healing him. After Jesus broke cultural barriers between him and a woman in Samaria, she not only listened to Jesus and believed him, but she went to the city and encouraged other Samaritan men to come and see Jesus the Jew. And the parable of the Good Samaritan portrayed a man who showed kindness beyond measure to seemingly a Jew.

Concerning those who were only pro-Jewish like the Zealots, Jesus showed them that he excluded no one and his kingdom is for all those who believed both Jew and Gentile. His teachings included paying of taxes to Rome and submitting to those who have the rule over you. He did not act in defiance but left an example of how to show love. Overall, he showed them that their religious beliefs had become a dead system of works that blinded men from the real truth.

CHAPTER 2
HIS COMING TO THE WORLD

...He comes to us as one unknown, without a name, as of old, by the lakeside, he came to those men who did not know who he was.[94]

The Genealogy of Jesus

The genealogy of Jesus is recorded in both Matthew and Luke. In order to appreciate and better understand this genealogy, one must first understand why Jews even regarded ancestral records in the first place. One reason why they kept precise records was because of property rights. In Israel, property rights were connected with family legacy and tradition, for Jews were given land as an inheritance by God when they settled in Israel. This was land that was promised to Abraham their father as an incentive for leaving his family and country. Even individual families were allotted parcels of land and one could do whatever he felt was right with the land they had. Thus, they desired to keep good records of that which was given to them.

A second reason concerned the prophecies that God had given them concerning the Messiah. Prophets of old had been assuring Israel for years of a leader who would come to save them and God specifically stated that this person would come from one of their descendents. Although the Jews did not know who he would be or when he would come, it was important to maintain accurate genealogical records to prove this descent.

MATTHEW'S ACCOUNT

In the order of New Testament books, Matthew's account comes first and he wrote to the Jews to present Jesus as their king. His genealogy charts the family line of Joseph, the legal father of Jesus, and his account opens by stating, "The book of the generation of Jesus Christ, the son of David, the son of Abraham" (1:1). These very words present Jesus was the legal heir to David's throne. He sets the tone and credibility for his book up front and establishes the facts of Jesus' relationship to David the king of Israel before that of Abraham, the father of the Jewish nation. As a whole, he placed more emphasis on Jesus' Davidic origins.

The structure of his genealogy was of such that he divides his account into three groups of fourteen generations. His somewhat condense account traces the lineage from Abraham to Jesus, totaling 41 generations. His divisions include the following: Abraham to the reign of David (the patriarchs), David's reign to the captivity in Babylon (the kings), and ending with the Jew's discharge from this captivity to the birth of Christ (private citizens). This account is more of a historical progression throughout history than just an ordinary lineage. It begins with the establishment of the Jewish family, then it escalates to the power of David and the kings, then it weakens from these royal families to the lowly beginnings of Jesus.

There are other genealogies in the Old Testament that looks similar to this one. Genesis 5 gives a list of the generations of Adam. Yet, there is a distinction between the genealogy of Jesus and the genealogy of Adam. The genealogy in Genesis 5 leads from Adam to Noah and is a genealogy of his descendants. However, the genealogy of Jesus is a genealogy of his ancestors.[95]

LUKE'S ACCOUNT

While Matthew gives a somewhat condense account totaling 41 generations, Luke records a more detailed account from Adam to Jesus totaling 76 generations. Matthew's account, similar to Genesis 5, follows the order of chronological succession beginning with the ancestors and moving forward. Yet Luke's account is unusual in that it starts with Jesus and moves backward through history.

Luke's earliest readers were Greek Christians which differs from Matthew who was writing to the Jews. In light of this, Luke was not necessarily trying to emphasize king David but rather the facts that Jesus' origins come from God. He starts off his genealogy stating the facts that "Jesus himself was about thirty years old when he began his ministry. He was the son...of Joseph, the son of Heli" (3:23). He then ends his genealogy by saying that he was "the son of Enosh, the son of Seth, the son of Adam, the son of God" (3:38).

Being a physician by trade, Luke was careful to look at the ends and outs of his account. He even stated at the beginning of his book that "many have undertaken to draw up an account of the things that have been fulfilled" concerning Jesus and they were "handed down to us by those who from the first were eyewitnesses and servants of the word" (1:1-2). He then states that he himself had "carefully investigated everything from the beginning" and because of this investigation that was undoubtedly true, it seemed only good for him to "write an orderly account" so that others may "know the certainty of the things you have been taught" (1:3-4). Thus, his genealogical records are certainly among the "carefully investigated" material that proved to be true and worth writing "an orderly account" of.

Skeptics are usually quick to attribute the differences of these accounts. In addition to the differences of 41 generations in Matthew and 76 in Luke, there are only four names that are the same in these genealogies. They are David, Jesus, Shealtiel and Zerubbabel. Why are the genealogies so different? Although some critics try to point to the inaccuracy of the Bible or that these genealogies were only made up, one must first understand that it is unimaginable that the two authors would just build two entirely contradictory genealogies of the same lineage. However, one of the reasons for their differences could be that Luke was taking into consideration of the "Levirate marriage" tradition. With this view, Joseph, the father of Jesus had both a legal (Heli) and biological (Jacob) father through this marriage. A second reason for their difference could be that Matthew was tracing the ancestry of Joseph while Luke was tracing that of Mary. With this view, Jacob was Joseph's biological father, while Heli, who was Mary's biological father, became Joseph's surrogate father. In addition, Jews referred to the word "son" as not only the biological son but also a grandson, great grandson, or son of a more distant generation. Thus, all of these considerations must be kept in focus as one looks at these genealogies.

JESUS' HISTORICITY

Jesus did not write an account of his life but available to us are four different accounts written some thirty to seventy years later after he left this earth. These accounts are found in detail in the gospel accounts of Mark, Matthew, Luke, and John. The book of Acts does give some information on his ascension. All of these records relied upon tradition that was handed down to them from eye witness accounts.

These genealogies of Jesus are part of an attempt to explain his biblical and ministry significance as well as his historical significance. Very few scholars hold the view that Jesus never lived. This conclusion is generally regarded as a blatant misuse of the available historical data. Christians are by no means at the mercy of those who doubt or deny that Jesus ever lived.[96] Although some people actually wonder if Jesus ever existed, both of these genealogies set the record strait that Jesus was indeed a human figure of actual history.

Since this same Jesus, who is a man of history, started Christianity, then Christianity must certainly be a religion of historical facts. Therefore, it is not based on legends concerning people who never lived but rather has its very foundation on people who lived at a particular time in a particular place among real people. He was born just before the death of Herod the Great in 4 B.C. and lived during the violent attempts to replace the injustice of Rome.In addition, Paul, who was not only a contemporary of Jesus but helped to further and strengthen the early Christians, shared his beliefs and message concerning the facts of the historical Jesus. He states that if the facts of Jesus' life, death, and resurrection are bogus, then there are absolutely no grounds for the Christian faith (1 Corinthians 15:12-19, 32).

THE UNLIKELY WOMEN

In addition to Mary, the mother of Jesus, Mathew includes four women in his genealogy: Tamar, Rehab, Ruth, and (Bathsheba) the wife of Uriah. Since it was not customary for Jews to include women in their records, why would a genealogy written in the First Century include women when virtually all of Middle Eastern genealogies only included males? Even more notable is the fact that most of the women had disgraceful past. Thus, it had to be a special purpose for these women to be mentioned and an even greater purpose as it related to Jesus, the soon to be Messiah.

Tamar

Tamar was seen in pre-Christian literature as an Aramean.[97] Found in Genesis 38:6-30, she was the daughter-in-law of Judah and was married to a man named Er, but because he was wicked, God killed him. Judah then asked his second son, Onan, to have sexual relations with Tamar so that children could be declared that of Er's. However, Onan did not do this knowing the child would not be his. Instead, he spilled his semen on the ground while having sex in order not to produce offspring. Because of this, God killed him. Judah then told Tamar to be a widow until his youngest son, Shelah, gets older, but unfortunately when he did get older, Judah still will not give Tamar to Shelah in marriage.

The custom at the time, as stated in Deuteronomy 25:5-6, was that when a woman's husband died without leaving an heir and the deceased had a brother, the family was expected to marry the widow to that brother.[98] Yet looking at what Judah had done to Tamar, it was not only unlawful but also negligence on his part in not giving Tamar his surviving son. As a result, he exposed Tamar to temptation.

Sometime later, Tamar took the opportunity, after it was communicated to her that Judah was on his way to Timnah to shave his sheep, to expose herself as a prostitute. After covering her face, which was customary of prostitutes, Judah, thinking that she was a prostitute, gave Tamar his seal and its cord, and his staff, and had sexual relations with her. Tamar eventually became pregnant and then exposed the wickedness of Judah by revealing the valuable he had left with her. Tamar later gives birth to twins named Perez and Zarah. Perez is in King David and Jesus' lineage.

Rahab

Rahab, most likely a Canaanite, was a prostitute by trade. Beginning in Joshua 2, she was supposedly so well known in her profession as a prostitute that when it was told to the king of Jericho that some spies came into their land, he sent his men to Rahab's house telling her to "bring out the men who came to you and entered your house, because they have come to spy out the whole land" (2:2-3). After hiding the men, she lied and said that they did come but had just left and she did not know which way they went.

After the king's men had gone, she talked with the men who were sent from Joshua that she knows that the Lord has given this land to them and that a great fear has come on all the people of Jericho. She asked them to promise to show kindness to her and her family for the kindness that she had shown to them. The men assured her that they would treat her kindly and faithfully when the Lord gives them that land, starting with the city of Jericho.

Ruth

Ruth was a foreigner from Moab and her story takes place in the book of Ruth. During the time when the Judges ruled, she unfortunately experienced the tragedy and unfortunate circumstances of loosing her father in law Elimelech, who was married to Naomi, and her husband Mahlon. During this tragedy, they were living in Moab and with nowhere else to turn, Naomi decides to return to Bethlehem. She encouraged her daughters-in-law to return to their own country and to remarry. Although one of Naomi's daughter returns, Ruth went with Naomi to her hometown of Bethlehem.

After returning to Bethlehem, Ruth went into the field to collect the leftover crops from the farmers' fields after being commercially harvested. It just so happened that the field she went to was owned by a man named Boaz, a close relative of Naomi's husband's family. Boaz was friendly to Ruth and his friendliness gets back to Naomi. Ruth was soon notified from Naomi that because Boaz was a near relative, he was therefore obligated by the Levirate law to marry her in order to carry on his family heritage.

Naomi tells Ruth to go to the threshing floor at night and when Boaz lied down, she must "uncover" his feet in order to show that he was the one who had the right to redeem her. Ruth figured out that if she uncovered the feet of the sleeping Boaz, he would wake up naturally when his feet got cold, and she could have an interview with him in total privacy – a brilliant plan.[99] After being startled and awakened during the night, Boaz comforted Ruth and stated that he was able and willing to redeem her. Yet, he must check with another closer male relative who had the first right of redemption. Because this other redeemer refused to endanger his heritage, Boaz married Ruth.

Bathsheba

In Matthew's genealogy, Bathsheba's name was not even mentioned because of an act that Jews take very seriously when it comes to their "honor and shame" society. Her story was recording in 2 Samuel 11:1-27 and began in the spring time when the kings went off to war. The Bible states that for some unknown reason, David decided to stay back at home in Jerusalem. During this time, he got up from his bed one evening and walked on the roof of his palace. It must be noted that in a traditional Middle Eastern village, only powerful men had second and third floors to their homes. Such people could look down and see into their neighbor's homes, walled courtyards and windows. The rest of the town would not observe their private spaces.[100]

To his surprise, David sees a woman who was bathing. Whether she was naked or not, the Bible does not specifically say. But certainly in any culture and in any society, it is hard to bathe with clothes still on the body. In light of exposing her bare flesh for others to see, no self-respecting woman in any culture would do such a thing.[101] The Bible also states that she was very beautiful and her name was Bathsheba. Bathsheba knew what she was doing and certainly was no fool. Her plan succeeded in getting noticed by the king and within a short time, David arranged to have her taken to his palace where he would have sexual relations with her. She ended up conceiving and this matter was immediately made know to him.

To try to cover up his sin, David tried to get Uriah the Hittite, the legal husband of Bathsheba, to go home and have sexual relations with his wife. Uriah did come home to Jerusalem, but refused to lay with Bathsheba because the armies of Israel were at war. After refusing on several occasions, David sent word to his army general telling him to put Uriah on the front line where he knew the strongest defenders were. As a resuult, Uriah was killed and David took Bathsheba as his own wife.

Mary

Mary was by far the most famous out of all these women and some think that because she was the Jesus' mother, she should be mentioned in this genealogy. But in Middle Eastern genealogies, women were never mentioned and that would also apply to Jesus' mother. Her story took place in Matthew 1:18-25 and in Luke 1:26-56 where she was legally engaged to Joseph.

An angel of the Lord came to her and drastically disrupted her life plans. He told her that she was pregnant and would give birth to a son who would be great and would be called the "Son of the Highest." Her son would be a king that would not only reign over Israel but would reign forever with a kingdom that would have no limits. Knowing that she had not had sexual relations, the angel assured her that this was the work of the Holy Spirit and not of man. And by way of confirmation, the angel told her something that no one would know and it was that her cousin Elizabeth, who was living "locked-up" in her house, was pregnant. When she received the message from the angel, she responded, "Let it be to me according to your word" (Luke 1:38).

Mary accepted her pregnancy as a miracle of God, but it is hard to imagine that many people in community believed her story. Most of them probably saw her as an immoral woman who should be stoned. Yet, she humbly accepted a discipleship that she knew would bring shame on her in the eyes of the community and could be the cause of her death.[102] When Joseph, her betrothed husband, found out that she was pregnant, he decided to put her away secretly. Yet, it took another divine act of God through an angel to affirm to him that what she was telling him was true and that he needed to continue with the engagement process.

THE SIGNIFICANCE OF THE WOMEN

Nothing ever happens by accident! The women should not have been mentioned; yet this very genealogy sets the stage for Jesus' coming into the world. So then, was there a better outcome of these stories that may not have been easily noticed? Is there a greater truth that can be sought even though some of the women acted "scandalous" and immoral? What about the women, like Mary, who seemingly were innocent persons but their lives were drastically changed? Did God have a better plan in store for them? The answer is emphatically, yes!

Tamar

The story of Tamar presents a bold Gentile woman who was determined to acquire her rights, even if she had to use an irregular method. When all hope of having children seemed gone, she stepped out of her comfort zone and acted. She may have certainly committed this act because of her faith in the Messianic promise coming from Judah's ancestry. Yet, despite her sin of prostitution and deception, God was making a powerful statement concerning the function and status of woman in his kingdom and those in the family of faith. Only God was notorious in bringing about the good in a situation in the midst of transgression and dishonesty, and he did just that in the story of Tamar.

Rahab

It was only the providence of God directing the men to the house of Rahab the prostitute. She had the courage to save the spies even when her life was threatened by her own people. Despite her profession, she believed in the God of Israel and put her faith into works by saving the very people of God who came to spy on the land. On the basis of her new faith, she acted against her own people, her former gods, and even the king of Jericho. She was looked on as a heroine and was commended as being a spiritual giant of faith in Hebrews 11. God was certainly making a statement that despite the immensity of the sin, he still looks for faith, boldness, and the act of audacity.

Ruth

Ruth conveyed faith, love, dedication, astuteness and determination. Despite the tragedy of loosing family members, she could have easily gone back to her hometown just like her sister. Yet she chose to cling with her mother-in-law. She demonstrated faith by stating to her, "Where you go I will go, and where you stay I will stay. Your people will be my people and your God my God" (Ruth 1:16). God blessed her not only with a man who could redeem and marry her but in allowing her to have a son named Obed, who was the descendant of Perez, the son of Judah, the grandfather of King David.

Bathsheba

Bathsheba waited to take a bath in front of an open window facing King David's palace until her militant husband went away to fight. Unlike Ruth and Tamar, she was unfaithful to her husband. On the positive side, she demonstrated intelligence, daring, initiative and courage in the advancement of her interests as she understood them.[103] Her name was not recorded because in the Middle East, men and women were exceptionally modest about exposing their bodies. Yet God was trying to make a statement against this very Middle Eastern standard of honor and shame. He allowed her and David to give birth to Solomon, who was most renowned for building the first Jewish temple. The fact of her being mentioned in Jesus' genealogy shows that God can use the most disgraceful act to bring about an unforgettable work.

Mary

Mary had the privilege of birthing the Messiah. But can you image her telling the surrounding and close community that she was pregnant and the baby's biological father was not Joseph, her soon to be husband, but actually the Holy Spirit. Certainly most if not all the people in her community would say her story was both far-fetched and absurd. Yet after telling God, "Let it be to me according to your word", she went down in history as playing one of the most vital roles in God's plan to save humanity.

In all these women's stories, there was something extraordinary or irregular in their unions with men, yet they all showed initiative and played an important role in God's plan.[104] These women were all esteemed as being role models of how God used the unforeseen to generate victory over human obstacles. Thus, Matthew's gospel was written to show that Jesus was to be a Savior for women and men who were both saints and sinners, as well as Jews and Gentiles.[105]

The Prediction of the Birth of John

John's prediction comes before Jesus not because he was better or his parent's revelation was greater but rather because chronologically his foretelling comes first. At the same time, his very existence was to be the forerunner of Jesus the Messiah, and thus, the stage must be set first for the forerunner who would soon set the scenery and backdrop for the Christ. In light of this, the Christmas story of Jesus must not start with Jesus but with John. God had a purpose for not only John to be his forerunner, but for the gospel writer to put his prediction narrative first. Thus, the correct teaching of this story should begin with how John laid the groundwork for Jesus to come on the scene.

This narrative begins in Luke 1 with Zechariah and Elizabeth, John's parents. To make sure they were not mixed up with anyone else, the author states that Zechariah belonged to the priestly order of Abijah and his wife Elizabeth was a descendant of Aaron. Both Zechariah and his wife were not only upright in their relationship with God but also in their walk with him. They were blameless in observing the laws of the land as well as the laws of God.

THE DISGRACE OF BARRENNESS

Because Zechariah was a priest, his character would have been known throughout the community. Yet his priestly order and he and his walk with God were not the central themes in Matthew's opening scene. It was rather the disgrace that they both experienced as a result of not having children. By this time, Elizabeth was barren and they both were both well advanced in age. Their hope of even having children had long gone been expired and the author illustrates a human impossibility. What seems even more ironic was that this couple truly pleased God, yet the one thing that their culture demanded during their era, especially among women, was that of having children.

They lived in an honor and shame society. In this society, people would constantly reevaluate themselves and their situations, for one's very self-worth were seen through the eyes of others. Although they pleased God, they were naturally observing themselves, for perhaps they may have believed that they were not totally meeting God's expectations. Certainly because of Zechariah's priestly order, the communities knew them or of them and since these people were well acquainted with each other, they would also have known them as being childless. So Luke opens up his first scene by not only telling his audience who Zechariah and Elizabeth were but of their unfortunate circumstance of not being able to have children.

THE DUTY AND PRIVILEGE OF OFFERING INCENSE

God intentionally waited for Zechariah and Elizabeth to be well advanced in age before setting the stage for an unforgettable and life-changing encounter. God used Zechariah's priestly division to create an opportunity for a special encounter. Luke 1:8-10 states that Zechariah "was chosen by lot, according to the custom of the priesthood, to go into the temple of the Lord and burn incense." It was the custom of the priests to partition the various functions of the priesthood office among themselves and it was a privilege for Zechariah to receive this allocation, for only a few priests would have even had this opportunity. After entering the sanctuary of the Lord, the priest would enter the Holy Place, to the inner Holy of Holies (Hebrews 9:1-7) and he would take the incense from a bowl, put it on the burning coals, and scatter it.[106]

It also would be an unforgettable experience not just of entering the Holy of Holies but of what awaited him outside. The people praying and the act of incense being offered to God were both symbolic, for incense itself was a symbol of the prayers and praises of God's people (Psalm 141:2). Therefore, the ceremony of the priest and the prayers of the people were virtually the same act as seen from God's point of view. It was not a coincidence either for God to have allowed a multitude of people to become spectators of this special event. Although it was customary for people to gather while waiting for the benediction to be given by the priest performing this religious act, God would set an even greater stage for them to see an even greater work.

THE DIVINE ENCOUNTER

Zechariah was most likely nervous, for one mistake against the specific guidelines given by God concerning how to execute this specific act could be life-threatening. All that was most likely on his mind was to do what he came to do and in getting out of there alive. Yet God interrupted his plans, for "an angel of the Lord appeared to him, standing at the right side of the altar of incense" (Luke 1:11). Luke states that the angel was in the standing position located "at the right side of the altar of incense". He did not approach or come through the walls and curtains, but rather appeared in an instant of time. In other words, Zechariah, after observing his surrounding, knew that he was the only person in the small room, then suddenly, another person appeared standing there right with him. How shocking! In addition, the angel was a way of describing God's visible presence among men and there had been neither prophecy nor divine intervention for about 400 years.

Knowing that he was the only person near the altar of incense, more less in the Holy of Holies, Zechariah was startled and gripped with fear. Literally, his calmness of mind was taken away from him and he was troubled and restless. After being shocked, the feeling of dread came upon him. Although this was the natural reaction of people in the Bible when they come into the company of a divine being, Zechariah could not believe what he was seeing. Yet he was about to be prepared for a special purpose concerning his part in the Kingdom of God.

The angel said, "Do not be afraid, Zechariah, your prayer has been heard. Your wife Elizabeth will bear you a son, and you are to give him the name John." The specific prayer that he and his wife had been apparently praying continually in their hearts was for a child. Yet because his wife was past due having children, his prayers had long been over. How was God planning to work this situation out? Certainly, this human impossibility had to be overcome by God.

The angel did not stop there. He told Zechariah that his child would be a "joy and delight to you" and that "many will rejoice because of his birth", with an emphasis on "many." How ironic was this saying, for in the First Century, women and babies were nowhere as significant as the dominant male. In many situations, if a girl was born, she would be quickly discarded as trash. So to have a community birthday celebration for baby John was almost unheard

71

of. The angel then said that he "will be great in the sight of the Lord." However, this was in direct contrast to Herod, ruler of Judea, who was renowned for his greatness.

The angel assured Zechariah that John was to be set apart for the Lord in three ways. First, he was "never to take wine or other fermented drink, and he will be filled with the Holy Spirit even from birth." This prohibition of wine and all intoxicants seems similar to Samuel, Samson, and to all Nazarites alike. Yet, for him to totally have been a Nazarite, some other facets were not specified included.

Secondly, "many of the people of Israel" will be brought back to the Lord their God because of him. The idea of turning or returning to the Lord God is standard Old Testament connotation for the repentance of a people. It has been a long cold 400 years of silence in hearing from God, and at the same time, because of so many Jewish sects competing to have the right Jewish philosophy and theology, many people needed to be turned to God. Not to forget the suppression of the Roman government and the injustice they brought on the Jewish people.

And third, John would "make ready a people prepared for the Lord." He would be like Elijah who would "turn the hearts of the fathers to their children and the disobedient to the wisdom of the righteous." Just like Jeremiah, God appointed him a prophet to the nations before he was formed. God was simply setting the stage. Little did Zechariah know but his son would not be the one to prepare for the advent of God, but rather for the arrival of Jesus.

DISBELIEF, DUMB, AND DEAF

What was Zechariah's reply in light of all this shocking information? He asked the angel "How can I be sure of this? I am an old man and my wife is well along in years" (Luke 1:18). It seems like a simple and relevant question in light of the new and unanticipated information that he had just received. Yet, his statement was an element of unbelief refuting the even possibility of what the angel had assured. This would be a sharp contrast to the submissive belief of Mary and her encounter with an angel.

What the angel then had to do was to assure Zechariah that all things are possible with God and that no natural obstruction can have any power when indeed God has affirmed that it would take place.

The angel first confirms to him who he was, as if Zechariah did not know who he was already. He states that he was Gabriel who stands in the presence of God and that he has been sent to speak and tell him this good news. Then second, the angel tells him that he will be silent and not able to speak until the day this happens because he did not believe the angel's words, which has been assured him that they will come true at their proper time (Luke 1:20). The punishment was appropriate since Zachariah had not believed God's word and God not only took away his speech but his hearing as well (Luke 1:62). Zechariah knew immediately that this was a work of God, for only God could immediately cause the absence of hearing and speech to happen immediately.

THE DISGRACE TAKEN AWAY

The people waiting outside were certainly going to be hit by a surprise. They knew how long it was needed for Zechariah to carry out this priestly duty, probably about half an hour, and they wondered why he took so long. When he did come out, the people were expecting him to come down the temple steps and lift his hands over the congregation of Israel and bless them. In return the people would be prostrate in worship and would be urged to praise the God of all who would grant them joy of heart.[107] But this did not take place because Zachariah came out making signs but was unable to speak. What a disgrace! This special opportunity for him to offering incense before the Lord with a community outside watching him ended in ignominy.

But what the people and the surrounding community would see would be an even greater work of God than that which took place in the temple. God would not only take away the disgrace that Zechariah experienced by being struck dumb and deaf in front of all the people, but also the disgrace of barrenness. God would do something new and definitive for his people, for Elizabeth would become pregnant. Yet she would remain in seclusion for five months. No one outside her husband would know about this seclusion, that is unless God intervened and would tell someone. A natural explanation for her seclusion would be the embarrassment that came to a person of her age undergoing such a life-changing encounter. Or maybe it could be that she waited until any doubt of her pregnancy had been removed.

If she experienced one or more miscarriages in the past, it may be just one reason why she would hide for five months. Graciously, God's miraculous encounter overshadowed all past experiences. This couple had lived a godly life and God never forgot their faithfulness, for "the eyes of the Lord are on those who fear him, on those whose hope is in his unfailing love" (Psalm 33:18).

The Prediction of the Birth of Jesus

After the prediction of John's birth, Luke moves to the prediction of Jesus' birth. Again, John's birth is predicted first because he comes first chronologically and he is the for-runner of Jesus. Yet, Luke is about to make it very clear that there are considerable differences not only between the two predictions but between the two persons. Although John is mentioned first, Luke will exalt Jesus above him in every way.

The opening scene found in Luke 1:26 begins in the sixth month of Elizabeth's conception with John. God sends Gabriel, the same angel who appeared to Zechariah, to a town in Galilee named Nazareth. Nazareth, a tiny village located off a trodden path and about four miles from Sepphoris, was a farming town that remained rural despite the urbanization. This more or less village on the outskirts of another town, had no signs of wealth, no special schools, or even notable people. It would appear that nothing good could come from this city or it would have been mentioned and this city was never mentioned as a town in many different texts which listed other Galilean towns. There was nothing noteworthy or remarkable about Nazareth that would make it a likely location for such a miraculous event.

THE DIVINE MESSAGE

Yet these facts do not stop a divine messenger from coming to visit Mary who was a virgin and who was pledged to be married to Joseph, a descendant of David. Mary is the same name as Miriam, the sister of Moses and Aaron, and it means exalted.[108] Mary's virginity was important, for a women's virginity was a living symbol. Men wanted their prospect wives to be assured of the purest form and women were looked upon as a special and unique source in the family's future. Even the way a woman acted was a major part in how a social group's honor was defined.

So Mary, being legally engaged to Joseph, had not yet come to live with him nor did she had sexual relations (Matt 1:18; Luke 1:27, 34). During this stage, things were looking promising and hopeful as they were about to complete their long awaited marriage process, for it was important for them to keep a good testimony in the eyes of others. Yet God surprised Mary and sent her an angel. The angel went to her and said, "Greetings, you who are highly favored! The Lord is with you" (Luke 1:28). This greeting was intended to raise her up by letting her know that she was not only dignified but that the presence of God was with her. Mary's favor was similar to that which God gave Moses (Genesis 6:8). She was about to receive the most convincing proofs of God's special favor on her and she would soon have to evaluate the proofs and decide for herself if she indeed would take God at his word. It would be natural for a young girl, maybe as early as 13 years of age, to wonder what kind of greeting this was. Yet, the very objective of angels was to remove all doubt, confusion, and questions.

He tells her to not be afraid for she has not only found favor or "grace" with God but will be with child and will soon bring forth a son. When he does come, she must give him the name Jesus, which is the New Testament form of the Old Testament "Joshua," meaning "Jehovah is salvation." Mary knew that she would soon complete her marriage process with Joseph and that they both would have children. Yet the angel was telling her that the birth process would come before they complete their marriage process. Thus, the meaning was clearly of a promise of an immediate conception. How shocking!

Although Mary herself lives in poverty and triviality, the angel discloses the admiration of the child stating that he "will be great and will be called the Son of the Most High. The Lord God will give him the throne of his father David, and he will reign over the house of Jacob forever; his kingdom will never end" (Luke 1:32-33). Not only will he perform great things but his very name will unveil his greatness. He will rule specifically over all who belong to Israel and although other kingdoms come and go, his kingdom will endure forever. Certainly, Mary knew about Herod's kingdom and rule and of his power and greatness, yet the angel was not only exalting Jesus much higher than that of Herod but was disclosing a kingdom and reign that Herod would not even come close to fulfilling.

THE METHOD OF CONCEPTION AND MIRACLE OF ELIZABETH

It was a reasonable enquiry for Mary to ask "How will this be since I am a virgin" (Luke 1:34). She has not yet had sexual relations and is currently on a marriage contract with Joseph that would soon be finalized. Yet she knew that she has not acted in any way to bring about this "so called" conception and she modestly inquires by what means will this promise occur.

The angel then tells her that the Holy Spirit will come upon her and the power of the Most High will overshadow her, so that the Holy One that would soon be born will be called the Son of God. Jesus would be conceived in the womb of a woman, not after the manner of men, but by the singular, powerful, invisible, immediate operation of the Holy Spirit, whereby a virgin, beyond the law of nature, was enabled to conceive and that which was conceived in her was originally and completely sanctified.[109] The word "overshadow" is always used of divine power. It recalled the cloud over the tabernacle during the wilderness wandering and was used in all the synoptic Gospels of the cloud that came at the transfiguration. The concept is reminiscent of the Spirit hovering over the waters in Genesis 1:2. Here, the Spirit would be active in a new "creation" of God.[110] Thus, Mary understands that the child would be totally a work of God and a new creation, yet mystery in nature. This pregnancy process would be a miracle like no other to accomplish the purpose of God.

To give further encouragement to her faith, the angel confirms to her this truth and tells her, "Even Elizabeth your relative is going to have a child in her old age, and she who was said to be barren is in her sixth month. For nothing is impossible with God" (Luke 1:36-37). Since Elizabeth was of the tribe of Levi and Mary was of the tribe of Judah, they were relatives by their mother's side. No one would have known of Elizabeth's pregnancy because she was in hiding. So for the Angel to reveal this secret to Mary was not only a miracle in itself but also a means of confirmation. The words the angel told Mary are similar to those that were spoken to Sarah, "Is anything too hard for the Lord? I will return to you at the appointed time next year and Sarah will have a son" (Genesis 18:14).

THE MODEL OF SERVANTHOOD

Although it may seem to be an easy decision to make, Mary understood the repercussions if she were to go along with God's divine plan. She knew that if a bride was caught in adultery during the betrothal period, it was considered a capital offense. Deuteronomy 22:23-24 states, "If a man happens to meet in a town a virgin pledged to be married and he sleeps with her, you shall take both of them to the gate of that town and stone them to death--the girl because she was in a town and did not scream for help, and the man because he violated another man's wife. You must purge the evil from among you." At the same time, there was a test for proof of a girl's virginity. If she was found a liar, she would be "brought to the door of her father's house and there the men of her town shall stone her to death." Why, because "she has done a disgraceful thing in Israel by being promiscuous while still in her father's house." The stoning would take place to "purge the evil" from among the people (Deuteronomy 22:20-21). These laws gave a powerful caution to young women to flee fornication.

So what was Mary's response? She said, "I am the Lord's servant, may it be to me as you have said" (Luke 1:38). She leaves the results with God and submits entirely to his will. As a believer of the divine favor, she is not only content that it should be so, but humbly desires that it may be so.[111] Zechariah previously doubted the words of the angel but now Mary has accepted it. Mary is the prototype of a handmaid or servant of God and replies as a true disciple who is obedient to the call of God. What was she going to say to Joseph and to the surrounding community? What would everyone perceive her as once she told them the truth?

After saying these words, "the angel left her." This is an ordinary characteristic of angelic manifestations, since such a heavenly announcement has to be momentary. Angels do not come to develop relations or to have unnecessary conversation. Rather, they come to accomplish the work of God and then they are gone.

THE MAGNITUDE OF JESUS

The parallelism is clear. The angel Gabriel says of John that "he will be great before the Lord," yet for Jesus, the angel states that "he will be great, and will be called the Son of the Most High." The prediction of Jesus' birth was intended to be greater than that of John. In addition, John's miracle of infertility and being born to aged parents does not compare to the miracle of Jesus being born without a human father. What God has done for Mary far outshines what God has done for Zechariah and Elizabeth.

The Visitation of Mary to Elizabeth

Mary's Salutation

In Luke 1:39-56, we have the narrative of Mary visiting Elizabeth. Despite the cultural norm of disgrace and frustration that Mary should have felt, she was stated to have made herself ready and she hurried to a town in the hill country of Judea. She left her business behind to travel the long journey, for many miles separated the two regions. After hiding for six months, certainly people in this society may have wondered why they have not seen Elizabeth for so long. Being such a close society were people knew about each others affairs, Elizabeth and possibly Zechariah were finding ways to exclude people from coming into their house.

Why did Mary rush off to see her cousin? She possibly could have left to escape the shame of people seeing her undergo the initial signs of pregnancy. But more than anything, she possibly desired to confirm the validity of what the Lord had said to her through the angel. If her cousin was pregnant, more or less six months pregnant, she would obviously be showing. If indeed she was showing, then the miracle of birthing a son will certainly come true, even though she knows that she has not had sex with Joseph or any man.

Despite how she was able to enter the house, the Bible states that when she did enter and Elizabeth heard Mary's greeting, "the baby leaped in her womb and Elizabeth was filled with the Holy Spirit" (Luke 1:41). This movement was more than any ordinary motion of the child. The babe leaped as it were to give a signal to his mother that he was now at hand whose forerunner he was to be.[112] This leaping also shows that not only was Elizabeth filled with the Spirit, but John.

ELIZABETH'S SALUTATION

Upon entering, Elizabeth stated to Mary in a loud voice, "Blessed are you among women, and blessed is the child you will bear! But why am I so favored, that the mother of my Lord should come to me? As soon as the sound of your greeting reached my ears, the baby in my womb leaped for joy. Blessed is she who has believed that what the Lord has said to her will be accomplished" (Luke 1:42-45). The Spirit inspired her words of blessings and she uttered them out of pure joy. She gave monumental words of encouragement to Mary beginning with the fact that she is blessed and the child inside her is also blessed. These are similar words of encouragement that the angel gave Mary when he told her that she has "found favor with God" (Luke 1:30). It was God's act of placing his son in her womb that has allowed her to be esteemed, favored, and blessed. Although her conception was not as miraculous as Mary's, Elizabeth rejoices and there is no rivalry between the two mothers since the same angel Gabriel has been sent to publicize both conceptions.

Elizabeth continued to state, "But why am I so favored, that the mother of my Lord should come to me." Here, she was stating why she was thankful for Mary coming to visit her. Yet even more specifically, she was proclaiming her son as God and the Messiah. Despite how she was notified of her pregnancy, Elizabeth's words were stated as factual and with great faith. She now has a clear knowledge of the mystery of the long awaited Messiah, and to prove her words of blessings and encouragement, she interprets the leaping of her child as proof of his identity.

MARY'S SONG OF PRAISE

After hearing the unanticipated blessing and encouragement of Elizabeth, Mary sings a song of praise. Recorded in Luke 1:46-56, Mary's song is comprised of three parts: her praise to God for what he has done for her (46-50); her praise to God for what he had done and would do against the proud, rich, and ultimately the oppressors (51-53); and her praise to God for his people Israel (54-55).

She begins her song by expressing to whom it is directed to. "My soul glorifies the Lord and my spirit rejoices in God my Savior" (Luke 1:46-47). These were the same words that Hannah sang who experienced a similar situation, for she stated, "My heart rejoices in the Lord, mine horn is exalted in the Lord" (1 Samuel 2:1). From Mary's point of view, the only way in which God could be lifted up was by his people taking action and doing so. Nothing can be added to him, for he is infinite and eternal. However, understanding her situation, it is unimaginable that Mary would say such words or more less would have thought any such thoughts. Yet she does what only few true worshippers ever do and that is extolling and glorifying her Lord despite her situation.

Understanding her poverty condition, Mary realizes that God "has been mindful of the humble state of his servant." Even from the humiliation that awaits her, she understands that God's divine presence also awaits her. She knows that "from now on, all generations will call" her "blessed" (Luke 1:48). In the Old Testament, it is often illustrative that God rescues his people from persecution or oppression (Deuteronomy 26:7; Psalm 136:23; 1 Samuel 1:11). In addition, she states "for the Mighty One has done great things for me - holy is his name" (Luke 1:49). These "great things" are set expressions for God's wonderful endeavors, especially during the Exodus. Knowing that she is not worthy to receive such blessings, she states "his mercy extends to those who fear him, from generation to generation" (Luke 1:50).

Mary even knows that God is against the proud, for she states, "He has performed mighty deeds with his arm, he has scattered those who are proud in their inmost thoughts. He has brought down rulers from their thrones but has lifted up the humble" (Luke 1:51-52). Pride caries the meaning of rising up and portrays arrogance and haughtiness. It characterizes one with an arrogant assumption of his own worth who looks down on others and even treats them with disrespect and scorn. The proud look down on others because they do not look up to God. Prideful individuals believe that they no longer have a need for God and they don't need to worship him. This is why the proud are constantly presented as God's enemies (Isaiah 13:11). In addition, God "has filled the hungry with good things but has sent the rich away empty" (Luke 1:53). God is not against the rich because they are simply rich, but rather is against those who exploit the poor. It is a common occurrence in the Bible that the fortunes of the wicked rich will be taken away (Job 15:29), and even given to the righteous.

Mary concludes her praise to God for his dealings with his people Israel. She states, "He has helped his servant Israel, remembering to be merciful to Abraham and his descendants forever, even as he said to our fathers" (Luke 1:54-55). She understood that with the birth of her son, Israel will be revived and restored. Certainly, she did not possess a complete understanding of all that her son would do, nor of every prophecy that was spoken of him. But certainly, God gave her the words of this song and what she did know, she proclaimed.

The Birth of John

Knowing that Mary stayed for three months after visiting Elizabeth, she had to have left before John was born, for she is no longer mentioned in the impending narrative with Elizabeth. Elizabeth's time had now come to give birth and "she gave birth to a son." After being in isolation for six months, God remembered her, and her shame and disgrace left her. What was fulfilled of the word of God through Gabriel to Zacharias came true and now she is a living witness of a miracle of God. God's promised mercies came when the full time for them had come and not before.

Unlike the cultural norm, many came to rejoice over her birth. The Bible states that "her neighbors and relatives heard that the Lord had shown her great mercy, and they shared her joy" (Luke 1:58). This rejoicing had a way of alleviating the many years of feeling rejected possibly by God and the reproach from the surrounding community. The people were able to rejoice because she had been barren for long time, she was currently old and should not have had a child, and her child would be extraordinary. No one even knew of her pregnancy the entire nine months, but after she gave birth, no one was resentful or displeased.

THE CIRCUMCISION AND NAMING

On the eighth day the people in the community came to circumcise the child. The biblical law specified that "every male among you who is eight days old must be circumcised, including those born in your household or bought with money from a foreigner..." (Genesis 17:12) and that circumcision could be performed by both men and by women (Exodus 4:25). The community was coming to name him after his father Zechariah and the eager but somewhat intrusive neighbors meant well, for it was traditional to name a male child on the day of circumcision. Yet to the crowd's astonishment, his mother Elizabeth stepped in and spoke up and said, "No! He is to be called John." She had somehow learned earlier that God appointed John to be his name. The name John describes the grace or mercy of God that would be displayed in allowing his son to come into the world and save mankind.

Unfortunately, the people rejected Elizabeth's name and said, "there is no one among your relatives who has that name" (Luke 1:61). Turning now to Zechariah who officially was responsible for the naming, the community "made signs" to him "to find out what he would like to name the child" (Luke 1:62). Their actions showed that Zechariah was certainly both dumb and deaf. In the annunciation, the angel had predicted that many would rejoice at John's birth and that has been fulfilled. Now the other prediction must be fulfilled that the child would be called John. The neighbors and relatives did not know of this prediction but they could sense the stirring of great things in the marvelous agreement between the two parents on the name.[113]

Responding back through these same signs, Zechariah "asked for a writing tablet, and to everyone's astonishment he wrote, 'His name is John'" (Luke 1:63). He thus verified the angel's word and that the name had already been established and therefore, there was no further need to discuss this issue. As a result of his faith, his mouth was immediately opened and "his tongue was loosed, and he began to speak, praising God" (Luke 1:64). His impediment was quickly removed. God's divine words were again true after all, for his handicap only lasted until his son was born as stated by the angel.

What did Zechariah say with his first words? The Bible states that he blessed the name of the Lord and extolled him with praise. He understood for a long nine months that he must believe the words of God despite the odds of the situation. In addition, he understood the use of his tongue and the true power of God.

THE CHILD'S FUTURE GREATNESS

As a result of seeing this, "the neighbors were all filled with awe and throughout the hill country of Judea, people were talking about all these things" (Luke 1:65). God has done something new and definitive for these people and the people's reaction was just a natural result of seeing a miracle of God. The people in this region are now well acquainted with the circumstances of Zacharias and Elizabeth, and now "everyone who heard this wondered about it, asking, 'What then is this child going to be?' For the Lord's hand was with him" (Luke 1:66). The angel only told Zechariah that the child would be great, now the entire region sees that this child is extraordinary. In addition, they see that he will do an extraordinary work. Now for many years to come, the community will remember the events that surrounded John's birth and the hand of God that will be upon his life.

In light of John's greatness, the angel prophesied concerning him that "he will go on before the Lord, in the spirit and power of Elijah, to turn the hearts of the fathers to their children and the disobedient to the wisdom of the righteous, to make ready a people prepared for the Lord" (Luke 1:17). What did Elijah do? He challenged the emperors of his day, specifically Ahab and Jezebel, and he would do the same by challenging Herod and Herodias. John was not the "light" but came to testify of that "light." He was not the Messiah and rather desired to decrease so that Jesus would increase. He was not only a prophet but was "much more than a prophet" (Luke 7:26) and he was the last of the prophets (Luke 16:16).

THE SONG OF PRAISE

Zechariah now praises God through song. His song was somewhat unusual, for it consisted of prophetic sayings. He did not say his words under his own will and power but rather was qualified to prophesy because of the filling of the Holy Spirit. His opening words stated, "Praise be to the Lord, the God of Israel, because he has come and has redeemed his people" (Luke 1:68). Speaking of Jesus and not of his newly born son, he uttered a prophetic word when he had not yet even been born. He trusted in the certainty of God's fulfillment and believed with confidence that what God had promised was as certain as if it had already happened. He would no long doubt God words but would believe in them with assurance. His wife Elizabeth believed in the same revelation when she told Mary, "But why am I so favored, that the mother of my Lord should come to me" (Luke 1:43). Both realized that this special person had been sent by God to this world to do a special and marvelous work.

He understood the history of David his "father" and the covenant of royalty that was made with him. God's promise to David was unconditional and gave numerous promises. Among these promises included that he would provide a place for Israel and would give them a home in their own land. He would give them rest from all their enemies and would establish a house for them. He would raise up their offspring and would establish his kingdom forever (2 Samuel 7:10-13). Understanding this promise, Zechariah prophesied with confidence that God "has raised up a horn of salvation for us in the house of his servant David (as he said through his holy prophets of long ago), salvation from our enemies and from the hand of all who hate us - to show mercy to our fathers and to remember his holy covenant, the oath he swore to our father Abraham: to rescue us from the hand of our enemies, and to enable us to serve him without fear in holiness and righteousness before him all our days" (Luke 1:69-75).

Then, Zechariah prophesied concerning his own son. First, concerning his dignity he states that his son will "be called a prophet of the Most High" (Luke 1:76). He will not only speak of future events that had not yet come to pass but will preach the very word of God to the people in his day. He will be honorable, respected, and noble.

Second, concerning his occupation he states that he will "go on before the Lord to prepare the way for him" (Luke 1:76). Before Jesus would even come on the scene, he will make ready his appearance and help mold the hearts of the community of Israel to believe in his Messianic manifestation.

Third, concerning his doctrine he states that he will "give his people the knowledge of salvation through the forgiveness of their sins because of the tender mercy of our God, by which the rising sun will come to us from heaven to shine on those living in darkness and in the shadow of death, to guide our feet into the path of peace" (Luke 1:77-79). Zechariah believed in the mercies of God to give man a second chance in life. But despite their wrongdoing, God offered mercy to those to those who believed and in return would guide them to the path of peace.

After his prophetic song, the Bible states that John "grew and became strong in spirit, and he lived in the desert until he appeared publicly to Israel" (Luke 1:80). Just like his mother hid for nine months John is hidden in the wilderness preparing himself for the soon coming Messiah.

The Birth of Jesus

Although the birth of John was great, Jesus' would be even better. The book of Matthew states, "This is how the birth of Jesus Christ came about: His mother Mary was pledged to be married to Joseph" (Matthew 1:18). They were betrothed or engaged and they had already taken the first step in the matrimonial procedure by exchanging consent.

THE CIRCUMSTANCE

Mary knew of the revelation of her pregnancy, yet Joseph her spouse was in for a surprise. Matthew 1:18 continues to say "but before they came together, she was found to be with child through the Holy Spirit." Somehow Joseph was informed or he observed some signs that indicated pregnancy. Although the passage states that "she was found to be with child through the Holy Spirit", we know that Joseph did not either believe or understand this concept, for he was still going to divorce her. Mary was going through trying circumstances where her character and nobility was at stake within the community. She knew that she was pregnant and that it was of God, for she had never had sex with a man. Yet, she did not know how she was going to get out of this situation, more less alive.

So after Joseph somehow found out that she was pregnant, he tried to do what he understood best. Because he "was a righteous man and did not want to expose her to public disgrace, he had in mind to divorce her quietly" (Matthew 1:19). It is not clear what "quietly" meant or how Joseph hoped to accomplish it, but according to the practice from later rabbinic writings, a totally secret divorce was not possible, since the writ of repudiation had to be delivered before two witnesses. Nor could Joseph have kept Mary's shame hidden indefinitely. Mary's pregnancy would eventually have become a matter of public knowledge. Probably, all that Matthew meant was that in the divorce, Joseph was not going to accuse Mary publicly of adultery and thus not going to subject her to trial. To avoid the accusation of adultery, Joseph could have offered less serious grounds.[114] Other men would have been quick to expose their wives, but Joseph exemplified the trustworthy man in Proverbs 11:13 stating, "A gossip betrays a confidence, but a trustworthy man keeps a secret."

THE REVELATION

What was needed was a divine revelation, yet it came only "after he had considered this" (Matthew 1:20). The Greek word here translated "he considered" has two meanings. One of them is "he considered or pondered." But a second meaning is "he became angry."[115] After hearing the news about Mary's pregnancy, he did not initially have any other news to base the decision he was about make. So how would he or anyone feel after hearing such shocking news? He would certainly have felt upset and emotionally disturbed. Perhaps long centuries of veneration for "Saint Joseph," have led to an assumption that he could not have become angry, particularly not with Mary! But this is to overlook the pure humanness of the man. On hearing that his fiancée was pregnant, is he expected to sit quietly and "consider" this matter? Or would he naturally feel deeply disappointed and indeed angry?[116]

The angel appeared to him in a dream and said, "Joseph son of David, do not be afraid to take Mary home as your wife" (Matthew 1:20). He was telling Joseph to take Mary home rather than divorcing her as he intended. He would have to take public responsibility for not only the child but for the pregnancy of his wife that came about before they were legally married. In addition, the angel was giving him a convincing reason for him to do so, for "what is conceived in her is from the Holy Spirit." The angel told him that this child was actually conceived through the Holy Spirit, just as she had said (1:18). He continued to tell him that "she will give birth to a son, and you are to give him the name Jesus, because he will save his people from their sins" (Matthew 1:21). By naming the child, Joseph would be acknowledging him as his own, for generally a man would not accept the responsibility of a child if it was not his. If he were to obey, he would be the legal father of Mary's son.

Joseph was also told to give him the name Jesus. The role that Jesus will have would be parallel to the role that Moses had in the Old Testament. Both of them would be deliverers of the Jews from bondage and enslavement. Jesus would not only be a type of Moses but of Joshua, who led the Jews into the promise land. Yet, he would be greater than them both, for he would save men from their sins and lead mankind to heaven.

THE FULFILLMENT OF PROPHECY

Matthew tells us that the preceding narrative had to take place because it was fulfilled "by the Lord through the prophet, saying, 'Behold the virgin shall be with child, and shall bring forth a son, and they shall call his name Immanuel; which is, being interpreted, God with us'" (Matthew 1:22-23). Spoken of by Isaiah, it is a fact that he and other prophets did not always know the true meaning of the words God gave them to preach. While sometimes they preached deliverance through someone anointed as God's agent, there is no proof that they anticipated with accuracy even a single detail in the ministry of Jesus. For example, in Isaiah 7:14 where this prophecy is given, the Hebrew word *alma* for virgin describes a woman, normally a young girl, who has reached the age of puberty and was marriageable. This word gives no emphasis on her virginity and there is another word that could normally indicate someone who has never had sex. Although prophecies often had dual meanings (one current and one in the future), Isaiah's prophecy was spoken to give comfort to the people of his day. The sign he prophesied about concerned the imminent birth of a child, probably Davidic, who would be naturally conceived. The child would help to safeguard the lineage of David, would signify that God was still with his people and that he still cared for them. There was nothing in the Jewish understanding of Isaiah's passage that would bring about the notion or idea of a son that would be born with the aid of the Spirit of God acting as the father.

But God would use this same prophetic passage given by Isaiah to apply to his soon coming son. Matthew read the prophecy of Isaiah as one of hope rather than despair and took its term virgin to apply not only to the prior state of the mother but to her continuing state even during and after conception.[117] Although Isaiah's prophecy would be miracle from God during his era, the young and virginal conception of Jesus would be an even greater miracle and a greater sign of God's involvement and providence. Jesus' virgin birth even brings credibility to the Christian faith. It is affirmed in the Apostles' Creed and in view of the brevity of the Creed, the inclusion of the virgin birth is a significant testimony to the importance the early church attached to this article of faith.[118]

The Belief, Faith, and Sanctity of Joseph

Joseph had a big decision to make, but it was the divine confirmation of God that gave him confidence to make the right decision. The Bible states, "When Joseph woke up, he did what the angel of the Lord had commanded him and took Mary home as his wife. But he had no union with her until she gave birth to a son. And he gave him the name Jesus" (Matthew 1:24-25). Joseph first submitted to God and he obediently did as he was told. He took Mary home and completed the marriage process. Matthew presents him as a human being of remarkable spiritual stature. He possessed the boldness, daring, courage and strength of character to stand up against his entire community and take Mary as his wife. In short, he was able to reprocess his anger into grace.[119]

Joseph was a believer! He showed a tremendous amount of faith. Soren Kierkegaard, the famous Danish theologian, wrote that authentic faith requires an absolute relationship to the absolute.[120] Joseph was God fearing and his faith portrayed his relationship to him who does not change. Although his world would change forever, he understood that he needed to trust God who does not change. His obedience and faith was shown when he gave his son the name Jesus just as the angel had commanded. By doing this, he gave a strong statement to his family and community that he would take responsibility for this child, which was only after him taking Mary home and claiming her as his wife.

Matthew also shows his discipline and sanctity, for "he had no union with her until she gave birth to a son." The author would not have mentioned this if it was not significant. As mentioned earlier, Jesus' parents were models of virtue. Joseph could have easily had sex with her before the marriage process was complete since she was already pregnant and most of all the entire community was aware of Mary's situation. Joseph did not have to maintain integrity but he did and now his name is recorded for the entire world to see.

In addition, his character shows the kind of person that God uses. Yes, God can allow every situation to work out for his honor and glory, but it is consistent throughout Scripture that he desires to use clean vessels. He could have used King Saul to do a great work for him, but Saul chose to disobey God on at least two occasions. Obedience, faith, and a righteous life is what God is looking for, and because he saw this in Joseph, he allow him to be the earthly father of his son, the Messiah.

THE BALLOT

Jesus was not only a real person, but his birth took place during a real time surrounded by real historical figures. How do we know this? Luke 2:1-7 is where we find the facts of his actual birth and it took place the days of Caesar Augustus. Luke 2:1-2 states that he "issued a decree that a census should be taken of the entire Roman world. (This was the first census that took place while Quirinius was governor of Syria)."

Archeology prepared the way for this investigation by the discovery of census papers in Egypt showing that under the Romans it was customary to take a count of the population every fourteen years.[121] This decree or edict involved the formal royal action taken with the consultation of the Roman Senate, and "the entire Roman world" was the civilized world of which the Roman Empire ruled. Although we cannot tell from history that there was no universal census at the time, it is argued that Luke is referring to the first stage in a census which was actually taken only a dozen years later. The presumed purpose of the census would have been taxation, rather than military service from which the Jews were exempt.[122]

Caesar Augustus' census caused for "everyone" to go "to his own town to register" (Luke 1:3). The phrase "his own town" means one's ancestral city. For Joseph, that would have been Bethlehem. For Mary, according to Luke 1:26 and 2:39, that would have been Nazareth. But it did not matter where Mary was from but rather where Joseph was from. Thus, the census was brought about to explain how the child was born in Bethlehem, which was the ancestral home of Joseph.

BETHLEHEM'S JOURNEY

Understanding the need of going to Bethlehem, "Joseph also went up from the town of Nazareth in Galilee to Judea, to Bethlehem the town of David, because he belonged to the house and line of David. He went there to register with Mary, who was pledged to be married to him and was expecting a child" (Luke 2:4-5). Bethlehem is a village south of Jerusalem in the Judean hills. It is 2,250 feet high, it is situation on a ridge, and it is significantly elevated more than Nazareth, which is 1,600 feet above sea level. Thus, Joseph's journey encountered a climb which could have been somewhat difficult.

The city he was going to was the town of David, who, like Jesus, was destined to be king. Both Luke and Matthew stated that Jesus was not only the new Moses who would "save his people from their sins" but also the new David who would rule on the throne. In a land of social prejudice, foreign supremacy, and colonial mistreatment, the Jewish people envisioned a future Davidic leader who would bring back the peace and splendor that they so desperately needed. Jesus would be the new Davidic Messiah, a new David, who would establish justice and peace for God's people.

THE BIRTH AND LOCATION

After staying in Bethlehem for some time, "the time came for the baby to be born, and she gave birth to her firstborn, a son" (Luke 2:6-7). Jesus' birth is dated two years before the death of Herod in 4 B.C. (Matt 2:16) and it was here that these circumstances needed to unfold for the Old Testament Scriptures to be fulfilled. God strategically brought about a census from Augustus so that what he spoke of through the prophets long ago would eventually come true.

Mary "wrapped him in cloths and placed him in a manger" (Luke 2:7). For the western mind, the word "manger" involves the words stable or barn. But in traditional Middle Eastern villages this is not the case. In the parable of the rich fool (Luke 12:13-21) there is mention of "storehouses" but not barns. People of great wealth would naturally have had separate quarters for animals.[123] This "wrapping" is an ancient custom that is referred to in Ezekiel 16:4 and is still practiced among village people in Syria and Palestine.[124]

Why was Jesus wrapped in "cloths" and "placed" in a manger? "Because there was no room for them in the inn" (Luke 2:7). The western mind interprets this scenario as being an "inn" that is similar to a hotel that had many rooms and unfortunately they were all occupied. Therefore, Jesus was put in a cave-like barn somewhat outside the city where numerous animals stayed. But the Greek word does not refer to "a room in an inn" but rather to "space". How do we know this? Well, simple village homes in Palestine often had but two rooms. One was exclusively for guests and the other room could be attached to the end of the house. The main room was a "family room" where the entire family cooked, ate, slept and lived. The end of the room next to the door was either a few feet lower than the rest of the floor or blocked off with heavy timbers. Each night into that designated area, the family cow, donkey and a few sheep would be driven. And every morning those same animals were taken out and tied up in the courtyard of the house. Such simple homes can be traced from the time of David.[125]

The Greek word that we have here in Luke 2 is *katalyma*, which means an eating room or dining room. Literally, it is "a place to stay" and can refer to many types of shelters. The three that are options for this story are inn, house and guest room.[126] This Greek word is different for a commercial inn (*pandocheion*). In Luke 10:25-37, the Samaritan takes the wounded man to a commercial inn and not to an eating or dining room. Thus, the child was born, wrapped and literally "put to bed" in the living room in the manger that was either built into the floor or made of wood and moved into the family living space. They were not invited into the family guest room because the guest room was already occupied by other guests. The host family graciously accepted Mary and Joseph into the family room of their house.[127]

The Visits to Jesus

THE SHEPHERDS

God had not spoken in nearly 400 years. He had not used angels, prophets, or any other divine means to communicate to man. But during this particular era of time, God would unleash his divine

91

presence to man and he seemingly choose to do this among some of the most unlikely people. After the birth of Jesus, God did not want to keep his son's birth a secret but rather choose to allow others to see the magnificence of his son.

Their Location

Luke 2:8-20 gives us the unanticipated narrative of the shepherds and the angels, and it starts off with "shepherds living out in the fields nearby, keeping watch over their flocks at night." The open country where the shepherds abode was known as "Shepherd's Fields" and they were located some two miles from Bethlehem toward the Dead Sea.[128] This low-lying shepherds' plain must have been a place located nearest to Bethlehem where scarcely any snow falls in winter, and where in the case of need flocks can remain at night in the open.[129]

Their Lowly Classification

Unfortunately, the shepherds would have been the last group mentioned in any First Century text, more less in the narrative of the Jew's Messiah. Their classification was of such that they were not only from the peasant class but were among the lowly and the socially and economically unimportant. They were the ones to experience oppression and exploitation by Rome, and like many classes of people living in the First Century, they dreamed of a different kingdom than the one that was currently ruling.

Secondly, far from being regarded as either Gentile or noble, they were often considered as dishonest, outside the law.[130] Herdsmen were added by the early rabbis to the list of those ineligible to be judges or witnesses since they frequently grazed their flocks on other people's lands. Thus, they were among the type of dishonest people who were excluded from court.[131]

Third, shepherds were poor and rabbinic traditions label them as unclean.[132] This classification was as such that they were label on the same terrain as those who had leprosy and other skin diseases. They were not a group of people who easily made friends with the people in the community or even those who passed through the towns.

The Angel's Appearance

Despite their lowly classification, God's divine presence would come to them. The Bible states, "An angel of the Lord appeared to them, and the glory of the Lord shone around them, and they were terrified" (Luke 2:9). What is significant with this angel is not only the fact that he appeared, but his appearance to the lowly shepherds. The shepherds were of low status, they were considered unimportant, unclean, despised, and were dwellers among sheep. In contrast, the angel was of high status, he was holy, clean, divine, and he dwelt among a holy God. The shepherds were surrounded by darkness, which is associated with being cold and remote, with the feeling of grief and morning, and with death and disparity. Darkness brings a sense of uncertainty, for people easily get lost and they stumble around. It also brings fear of danger that may be lurking. In contrast, the angel was surrounded by light and glory, which is associated with radiance, warmth, closeness, life, and festivity. It symbolizes the glory of God in a dark world, for darkness cannot overcome light. The light of the angel was only a foretaste of the light that Jesus would bring, for he would also bring light to the hearts of man.

The Angel's Message

The angel speaks and said to the shepherds, "Do not be afraid. I bring you good news of great joy that will be for all the people" (Luke 1:10). These first words almost seemed as if he accidentally appeared to the wrong group of people. These lowly shepherds are not use to having someone approach them to tell them that they have "good news of great joy." They have been exploited their entire lives and despised from even their closest neighbors. Yet, the angel seemingly came to tell them truth, but it seemed too good to be true.

The good news the angel was referring to concerned the fact that "today in the town of David a Savior has been born to you; he is Christ the Lord" (Luke 2:11). Probably being Jews themselves, the shepherds needed no explanation of where the town of David was located, for they knew it was Bethlehem. But what they did need clarification on concerned the fact of why the angel told them that a "Savior has been born" to them. "Savior" has the primary meaning of "rescuer" and "deliverer." The term "Christ" specifically meant Messiah. There was no unified Messianic expectation in First Century Judaism, but rather an array of expectations. But when the specific term "Messiah" was used, it was in the perspective of the one promised and anointed by God to be the Jew's deliverer. So, the shepherds were certainly in need of a "Savior" but they knew that they were among the most unlikely to received this deliverance.

At the same time, the shepherds knew who was the contemporary human being considered to be savior of the world, and he was Caesar Augustus. He was called divine, son of god, God, and God from God. His titles were lord, redeemer, and liberator. He had saved the world, specifically the Roman Empire, from war, and he established peace "on earth." If Augustus could be pictured by Luke as giving an edict affecting the whole world, it was precisely because he was remembered as the founder of the empire who had pacified the world. Yet, the angel was telling the shepherds that a baby boy who was just born in Bethlehem was the Savior and source of peace. How shocking!

The Angel's Confirmation

The angel anticipated the anxiety of the shepherds desiring some form of confirmation to this truth, so he continued to say, "This will be a sign to you: You will find a baby wrapped in cloths" (Luke 2:12). Luke seems more concerned with where Mary laid the newborn baby, for he is careful to report him swaddled and laid in a manger because of the lack of space in the main section of the house. What was unique was that this baby Messiah would be wrapped in strips of cloth. This is the same form of wrapping that the peasant shepherds did with their newly born children. Furthermore, they were told that he would be "lying in a manger"! That is, they would find the Christ child in an ordinary peasant home such as theirs. He was not in a governor's mansion or a wealthy merchant's guest room but in a simple two room home like theirs. This was really good news.[133]

Despite the fact of being labeled "unclean," this was truly a sign for them and a means of encouragement despite their "low degree". Since the Messiah child would be born in the normal surroundings of a peasant home, they would feel the common respect of a Middle Eastern society. There would be no heartless innkeeper with whom to deal and they would not feel rejected, but honored. What a sign!

The Host of Angels

As if the message of the angel was not enough confirmation, the Bible states that "Suddenly a great company of the heavenly host appeared with the angel, praising God and saying, Glory to God in the highest, and on earth peace to men on whom his favor rests" (Luke 2:13-14). The author confirms that the angels acknowledged at the beginning of Jesus' life what the disciples came to know only at the end, namely, the person of the Messiah King. There was a so called peace on earth, for Rome and its emperors saw themselves as having brought peace and one of their ways of handling bandits and violence was through crucifixion. But now millions of angels were proclaiming that this baby would be the source of real peace. This peace would not be based on oppression and violence but rather on justice and equality.

This breath-taking and unbelievable experience was certainly too good to be true. If the child was truly the Messiah, the parents would naturally reject the shepherds if they tried to visit! But is the angel's news of joy was indeed true, then they would feel welcomed. So what did thy do? The Bible states, "When the angels had left them and gone into heaven, the shepherds said to one another, 'Let's go to Bethlehem and see this thing that has happened, which the Lord has told us about'" (Luke 2:15).

Their Discovery

Searching for truth, they wasted no time and they immediately left their occupation behind. When seeking Jesus, all delays are dangerous, for Satan longs to create fear and doubt. But with these shepherds, this seemingly did not exist. "They hurried off and found Mary and Joseph, and the baby, who was lying in the manger" (Luke 2:16). The poverty and humbleness in which they found Christ was similar to their poor and humble circumstances.[134]

Their Propagation

After hearing the angels, searching for the Christ child, and actually seeing exactly what was foretold to them, the shepherds were convinced. As a result, "they spread the word concerning what had been told them about this child, and all who heard it were amazed at what the shepherds said to them" (Luke 2:17-18). Amazingly, the first people to hear the message of the birth of Jesus were a group of lowly shepherds who were near the bottom of the social class. Yet, they were the forerunners, not of the apostles, to all future believers who would believe in Jesus the Messiah without even seeing him for themselves. Their public proclamation would even be a foreshadowing of the teachings of Jesus who himself came to "preach good news to the poor", to "bind up the brokenhearted", to "proclaim freedom for the captives and release from darkness for the prisoners" (Isaiah 61:1).

Their Adoration

Not only did the shepherds publicly proclaim the good news of great joy, but they themselves worshipped and praised God. Luke 2:20 states that "the shepherds returned, glorifying and praising God for all the things they had heard and seen, which were just as they had been told." Praise means to boast, to shine, to make a show, and to celebrate. It may be given in many circumstances and is always directed to God. It is not just a sense of belonging in the community but rather is participation in the worship of God and is the expression of delight in knowing him and in learning more about the Savior.[135] What amazed the shepherds was the fact that everything that had been told them came true, and thus, only God could have been strategically involved in the entire situation. That is why the shepherds gave glory and praise to God.

In conclusion, being a shepherd may have been a despised trade, but David's occupation before he was king involved "keeping the sheep" of his father Jesse (I Samuel 16:11) and protecting them (I Samuel 17:15-36). In addition, this same David wrote the psalm stating, "The Lord is my shepherd" in Psalm 23. The ending of the story does not portray shepherds who are considered low, from the peasant class, unimportant, unclean, despised, and dwelling among sheep. Nor does it portray shepherds who are associated with being cold and remote, with grief, and morning, with death and disparity. Rather, we see shepherds who have been in the presence of the King of kings, the Lord of lords, and the Savior of the world.

THE MAGI

The shepherds were not the only ones who came to see the Christ child. Matthew 2:1-12 gives the narrative of Magi coming to Jerusalem from the East in search for the King of the Jews. In order to understand why they were coming to see him, it is important to find out who they were and where exactly were they from.

Their History

The Magi had a reputation for wisdom (I Kings 5:10; Proverbs 30:1; 31:1), which was a "secret wisdom," a kind not known by ordinary people. The term "magi" refers to those engaged in occult arts and covers a wide range of astronomers, fortune tellers, priestly auguries, and magicians of varying plausibility.

Historically, their commercial relations between Israel and South Arabia went back to Solomon's time.[136] They were descendants of the magicians, the enchanter, the Babylonians, and the diviners who were opponents of Daniel. They were thought to have the power of interpreting dreams and visionary messages (Dan 1:20; 2:2; 4:4; 5:7). They survived both the transfer of power from the Medes to the Persians and the rising religious governing powers of Zoroastrianism.

They specifically came from the East to Jerusalem (Matthew 2:1) and in the Old Testament, the "people of the East" were most often desert Arabs and were Gentiles or from "the nations". These people were known for their idolatrous practices of reverencing the stars and regarding the planets and the fixed stars as deities. This worship was perhaps the oldest form of idolatry observed by the ancients. Knowing this, Moses strictly cautioned Israel during their early establishments against worshiping the sun, moon, stars, and all the host of heaven.

Their Search for the King

After arriving in Jerusalem, they asked, "Where is the one who has been born King of the Jews? We saw his star in the east and have come to worship him" (Matthew 2:2). What caused these people to come so far from the East? In the First Century, there were remarkable astronomical occurrences surrounding the period around the birth of Jesus along with a general interest in astrology and celestial events surrounding human destiny. Magi were famous among both Jews and Gentiles as having special powers, both good and bad. In their country, they somehow had seen an extraordinary star, such as they had not seen before, which they took to be an indication of an extraordinary person born in the land of Judea, over which land this star was seen to hover. This differed so much from anything that was common that they concluded it to signify something uncommon.[137]

After discovering this unusual but striking radiant appearance, they most likely reflected on the prophecies relative to Israel's redemption. It probably was not hard for them to see this as being the possible fulfillment of Balaam's fourth oracle in Numbers 24. In this story, King Alak summoned a famous seer named Balaam to put a curse upon Israel. He was not a Jew, but rather was an occult visionary and a practitioner of enchantment. Balaam, a man with magical powers, came from the East and predicted that a star would rise from Jacob. In this prophecy, one of Balaam's oracles stated that "a star will come out of Jacob; a scepter will rise out of Israel. He will crush the foreheads of Moab, the skulls of all the sons of Sheth. Edom will be conquered; Seir, his enemy, will be conquered, but Israel will grow strong. A ruler will come out of Jacob and destroy the survivors of the city" (Numbers 24:17-19).

Surely this must have been a real star, else these astrologers would not have been awed by it. At the same time, the star appeared but apparently was no longer present, for they stated they "saw his star" or "have seen" the star. What they did not say was that the star was still in the sky or they could still see it but rather they "saw his star". This piece of information is important, for soon the star will "reappear" and lead them to the place of Jesus. Strangely, the same star that was misused and used for idolatry purposes was the same star that God used to lead men to his Son.

Their Encounter with Herod

These men came to Jerusalem because they believed that Herod and the people would have seen the star, would have known its purpose, and would have been worshipping the King of the Jews as well. But unfortunately, their question was received with worry and distress by all Jerusalem. Eventually King Herod heard this and "he was disturbed and all Jerusalem with him" (Matthew 2:3). They were "disturbed" because all Jerusalem and the entire Roman Empire knew that Herod was King of the Jews, for he had built a magnificent kingdom that was full of power and glory. He restored the Jerusalem Temple, established new towns and harbors, and sponsored projects in remote cities. Since Herod was known by this title, the suggestion that a new king was a challenge to him.

Seeing the tension rise in his blood, Herod immediately called the proper persons, specifically the chief priests and teachers of the law, to ask them "where the Messiah was to be born." Although he was Jewish by religion, Herod did not notice the countless prophecies concerning the coming of the Messiah and that is why he had to assemble the most religiously educated people of the day to ascertain the whereabouts of this coming king. Certainly none of these priests and teachers were fearful knowing that Herod was the only king. Yet they quickly but wisely took refuge in the Jewish Scriptures and told Herod, "In Bethlehem in Judea for this is what the prophet has written: 'But you, Bethlehem, in the land of Judah, are by no means least among the rulers of Judah; for out of you will come a ruler who will shepherd my people Israel'" (Matthew 2:5-6). The ignorance of Herod concerning the Jew's Messianic hope was in line with his secular monarchial character.

After finding out the prophetic location of the Jewish Messiah, he "called the Magi secretly and found out from them the exact time the star had appeared." As cunning as he could be along with his evil character, he called them secretly because he did not want to openly disclose his fears and jealousies. This particular action put him in the same arena with sinners who are frequently plagued with secret doubts and insecurities, of which they try to keep with themselves.

Then he sent them to Bethlehem and said, 'Go and make a careful search for the child. As soon as you find him, report to me, so that I too may go and worship him'" (Matthew 2:7-8). He knew the birthplace along with the child's age, now he needed to find the exact location. But Herod's crowned head could not endure to think of another successor, much less a rival. For him, nothing less than the blood of this infant would satisfy him.[138] His duplicity is shown to all of Matthew's readers, for they immediately knew that he did not wish to worship the child but to destroy him! History proves that he was politically ruthless, smooth talking, jealous, chronically insecure, and the murderous type, and we see how his actions fit right in line with this biblical narrative. He was now an old man and had reigned thirty-five years, but this "new" king was but newly born and not likely to enterprise anything considerable for a many years. Yet Herod is jealous of him.[139]

Their Continued Search for the King

After receiving their edict from Herod, they continued to set out on their expedition. The Bible states that as "they went on their way," the luminous star they had seen "went ahead of them until it stopped over the place where the child was" (Matthew 2:9). The star they were given to understand were they might enquire for this king eventually disappeared, which was why they inquired of Herod where he was to be born. Then the star reappeared and did not simply shine in the sky but amazingly moved and went ahead of them. While a star guiding persons to a location is known in ancient times, the accuracy of it guiding them to a particular house is certainly abnormal.

Upon seeing the star, the Bible states, "they were overjoyed" (Matthew 2:10). Now they realized they were not deceived by the star after all but that it would truly serve as their guide. They no longer had to feel that they traveled to Jerusalem in vain but now they could be assured that God was with them.

Their Worship and Gifts to the King

When they came to the house, they saw the child with his mother Mary, and they bowed down and worshiped him" (Matthew 2:11). Although the shepherds "came with haste and found Mary, and Joseph, and the babe lying in a manger," the first to pay homage to him were Gentiles from the East. Their act of worship was signified through prostration, which was usually offered to persons of dignity or authority and to deities. At the same time, we only see them worshipping the child and not Herod in Jerusalem.

Matthew's readers may have remembered that the Magi in the Old Testament failed to read God's revelation in the form of a handwritten message on the wall that told the king that his kingdom would be taken (Daniel 5:9). But now they have comprehended the message of the star and have clearly interpreted God's revelation of the coming Messiah. It is amazing to know that they learned from the Jewish Scriptures of God's plan of salvation before they even came to worship the Messiah.

After bowing down and worshipping him, "they opened their treasures and presented him with gifts of gold, frankincense and myrrh" (Matthew 2:11). Rich people usually possess gold, and gold was mined in Arabia. But more specifically, frankincense and myrrh were harvested from trees that only grow in southern Arabia. Wealthy dwellers of those desert regions would naturally have gold, frankincense and myrrh.[140] There are even early writings that confirm that fact that wise men from Arabia came to Bethlehem and worshipped the child.[141]

Yet Jesus was not the only king that was brought special gifts from the rich. When King Herod completed the building of Caesarea Maritima, envoys from many nations came to Palestine with gifts.[142] In A.D. 44, Queen Helen of Adiabene, a kingdom that paid tribute to the Parthians, converted to Judaism and came to Jerusalem with bounteous gifts for those affected by the famine which was devastating the land. Tiradates, king of Armenia, came to Italy with the sons of three neighboring Parthian rulers in his entourage. Their journey from the East was like a triumphal procession. The entire city of Rome was decorated with lights and garlands, and the rooftops filled with onlookers, as Tiradates came forward and paid homage to Nero.[143]

Yet, the divine circumstances that led these rich Gentiles to this exact location and the fact of them worshipping this child and not an established king signifies a uniqueness of worship and adoration than all previous examples. In addition, there can be no denying of the prophecies given over 400 years earlier including the fact that, "nations will come to your light, and kings to the brightness of your dawn" and "all from Sheba will come, bearing gold and incense and proclaiming the praise of the Lord" (Isaiah 60:1-6). Inhabitants from Sheba consisted of descendants of Ham and specifically pertained to a nation in southern Arabia. Thus, this was no ordinary migration of kings and wealthy people groups to Jerusalem and then to Bethlehem. Rather, it was a prophetic and divinely led expedition.

Their Warning by God

Because this was a prophetic and divinely led expedition, God divinely warned them "in a dream not to go back to Herod" and as a result, "they returned to their country by another route" (Matthew 2:12). Herod told them to report back to him and they certainly remembered his edict, for they would not have "returned to their country by another route." By giving heed to God's message, these men were not only earthly wise, but possessed God fearing wisdom, which is much superior. Their sensitivity to God not only saved Jesus' family but if they had not taken a different route home, their lives may have been in jeopardy as well. These men were not the same enchanters depicted in Daniel who could not interpret God's message but rather are men who have been in the presence of God himself.

Because of what they had seen and heard, they go back to their country where Matthew's readers never hear of them again. Most assuredly, they brought the good news of Jesus to their country that was infested with idolaters and those who claim to have a "secret wisdom". Now these people, including those who were thought to have the power of interpreting dreams and visionary messages, were now able to hear the truth of God's divine providence and the actuality of his Son. From the Jewish perspective, these men were not depicted as evil Gentiles but rather pro-Jesus. There is now no insinuation of false practice but rather men who should be admired.

The Escape and Return of Jesus

JOSEPH'S DIVINE WARNING

After the Magi left, an angel of the Lord appeared to Joseph in a dream and said, "Get up, take the child and his mother and escape to Egypt. Stay there until I tell you, for Herod is going to search for the child to kill him" (Matthew 2:13). Joseph has already been described as "an upright man" and one faithful to the law. Now after he has proven himself in being obedient, God is able to trust him in a much different way. He is the main protagonist during this entire episode, for Mary does not speak nor does she receive any divine revelation.

Although Herod is the Rome appointed king, God uses Joseph to save his Son who is the Davidic Messiah and is the God appointed king.

If the angel just told him go to Egypt, there would not be a sense of urgency. But for the angel to tell him to "escape" meant that he had to flee immediately and secretly. Since the angel came to him in a dream and most likely at night, Joseph did not wait till the morning to flee but rather he did so that night. Why, so that others in their small community would not have seen him leave and in return no one would tell Herod that a family left and traveled down south. Again, the Mediterranean society was a close society and everyone knew about everyone else's whereabouts. Thus, God used a strategic method in telling Joseph to immediately flee in order to protect his Son.

Joseph's specific instructions were for him to stay in Egypt till God communicated with him again because "Herod is going to search for the child to kill him." It had been God's plan from the beginning that Jesus should be both a revelation to the Gentiles and Jews, and he was not going to let Herod exterminate his plan. So what did Joseph do? The Bible says that "he got up, took the child and his mother during the night and left for Egypt, where he stayed until the death of Herod" (Matthew 2:14-15).

All this took place so that it could be "fulfilled what the Lord had said through the prophet: 'Out of Egypt I called my son'" (Matthew 2:14). This prophecy came from Hosea 11:1 stating, "When Israel was a child, I loved him, and out of Egypt I called my son." Hosea's text contained a meaning intended by God to be fulfilled shortly after his birth. Israel was first called "out of Egypt" in Exodus when God liberated them from Pharaoh, but it was fulfilled even greater when the Jesus returned from Egypt to Nazareth.

HEROD'S MASSACRE

Somehow "Herod realized that he had been outwitted by the Magi" and as a result, "he was furious." "Outwitted" signifies that he was outsmarted and ultimately defeated by them. He understood that they took another route, for they did not come through the streets of Jerusalem as they did before. Now his emotions signify the utmost fury of his cruel and crafty character, and knowing that it was useless to try to chase after the Magi, he takes his anger out on the inhabitants of Bethlehem. The Bible states that "he gave orders to kill all the boys in Bethlehem and its vicinity who were two years old and under, in accordance with the time he had learned from the Magi" (Matthew 2:16). Rome, which had political and ideological power, had established a very successful method for avoiding royal tyranny. They were renowned for the exercising of power and authority over their territories. So now Herod sees that there is another "kingdom" that has come up against his and he will go out of his way to have this king destroyed before his ministry could begin. The battle between the Kingdom of Rome and the Kingdom of God had now begun!

Because Rome and its leaders ruled through violence and they flourished on force and power, Herod portrayed this by this massacre. "All the boys" gives the intuition of large numbers, yet, those interested in establishing the historicity of this event have calculated how many children there would have been in a village like Bethlehem and its surroundings. Because of the high infant mortality rate, we are told that if the total population was one thousand, with an annual birthrate of thirty, the male children under two years of age would scarcely have numbered more than twenty.[144]

Herod and his malformed character typified just the kind of person he was. This killing occurred toward the end of his life and history confirms that some short time later he discerned that no one would morn at his funeral. As a result, he ordered his soldiers to kill notable political prisoners as soon as he died to ensure morning for him when he died. Josephus and other Jewish or Roman historians did not note this slaughter in their writings because it was well understood that Bethlehem and its vicinity was small and the list of those killed would be very few. In other words, this slaughter would not create much of a rouse.

For the Jews living in Bethlehem, this was a major happening. Matthew states that these events were fulfilled through the prophet Jeremiah saying, "A voice is heard in Ramah, weeping and great mourning, Rachel weeping for her children and refusing to be comforted, because they are no more" (Matthew 2:17-18). Although prophets like Jeremiah did not understand the full extent of their prophecies, God intended for this prophecy to be fulfilled in this narrative. At the same time, because this killing was a fulfillment, this occurrence reflects Matthew's reluctance to attribute to God an evil purpose. This same fulfillment took place with Judas and the thirty pieces of silver used to betray Christ. God is not the author evil but allows everything to happen according to his purpose and plan in history.

There are numerous similarities to the story of Herod seeking the life of Jesus and the wicked Pharaoh who sought after baby Moses. 1.) Innocent Moses was born in the midst of a slaughter; Jesus was born during the murderous attempt of Herod. 2.) Pharaoh seeks to do away with Moses and Moses flees (Exodus 2:15); Herod searched for Jesus to destroy him and Joseph took him and his mother and went away. 3.) Pharaoh commanded that every male born to the Hebrews be cast into the Nile (Exodus 1:22); Herod desired to kill all boys two years and younger. 4.) Moses escapes from Pharaoh's massacre and leads the Jews from Egypt to the Promised Land; Jesus escapes from Herod's plot, flees to Egypt and would lead all those who trust in him to Heaven. 5.) Moses escapes from Egypt, but for Jesus it is to Egypt. 6.) And the place of past doom and death for Moses has become the place of refuge and life for Jesus.[145] Thus, Jesus is now seen as the new and greater Moses.

JOSEPH'S RETURN

The death of Herod occurred not long after the massacre in Bethlehem. In Egypt where Joseph and his family were in hiding, an angel of the Lord appeared to Joseph in a dream and said, "Get up, take the child and his mother and go to the land of Israel, for those who were trying to take the child's life are dead" (Matthew 2:19-20). These words were similar to the Lord saying to Moses in Midian, "Return to Egypt, for all those who were seeking your life are dead" (Exodus 4:19).

Although the Bible specifically states that Herod wanted Jesus' death, there were more people desiring his demise, for the angel told Joseph that "those" who sought his life are now dead. Yet, we only see Herod trying to take the child's life in this narrative. This is where history comes into perspective concerning the death of Herod. Historically, Herod caused the death of many of his prominent and important people right before he died by shutting them up at Jericho and killing them with darts. This was all apart of God's provision in allowing Herod to take so many of his vicious nobles to the grave with him. Although the enemies of Jesus wanted God's plan to fail, God cause all of them to die close together.

So what did Joseph do? The Bible states that "he got up, took the child and his mother and went to the land of Israel" (Matthew 2:21). Again, we see the same similarity with Moses taking along his wife and his children and returned to Egypt (Exodus 4:20). We observe once more the obedience of Joseph and the providence of God. However, somewhere along his journey, Joseph heard that "Archelaus was reigning in Judea in place of his father Herod he was afraid to go there." Archelaus was a son of Herod by one of his ten wives. His kingdom in Judea was established by the will of his father. Unfortunately, just like his father, his was ruthless. Joseph might have thought that since Jesus was born in Bethlehem, he should be raised there as well. Yet because of Archelaus, he is wisely cautions but afraid to enter into his dominion.

Knowing his concern, God warned Joseph "in a dream" and as a result "he withdrew to the district of Galilee." (Matthew 2:22). Philip was the ruler of Galilee and unlike his father and half-brother Archelaus, he was of a different temperament. He was differentiated as one of the mildest and least vicious of the numerous rulers that came from Herod the Great's malevolence dynasty. This is Matthew's reasoning as to why Jesus was born in Bethlehem in Judaea but was reared in Nazareth of Galilee. Here, God allowed Joseph and his family to be in a mild environment, especially in light of all that they went through with Herod the Great. If the promise of God can thrive in a world that produces the slaughter of the innocents, it can certainly thrive anywhere.

"HE WILL BE CALLED A NAZARENE"

Matthew 2:23 states, "And he went and lived in a town called Nazareth. So was fulfilled what was said through the prophets: "He will be called a Nazarene." By him settling down in Nazareth, Jesus fulfilled two Jewish expectations. One was that he being the Messiah would be born in Bethlehem and the second was that he would be a Nazorean, which Matthew interprets to mean "from Nazareth." Jesus' residence there resulted in his being called a "Nazarene" and although he was "called" this, he did not display the strict disciplinary life attributed to "Nazarites" such as Samuel, Samson, and John the Baptist.

The town of Nazareth was named after the Nazarites and was a city on a hill located in the middle of Zebulon. It was a small Jewish settlement with no more than two to four hundred inhabitants. Like the rest of Galilee, which lay relatively uninhabited until the Late Hellenistic Period, Jews settled in this town under Hasmonean expansion. The people of Nazareth were very likely the descendants of Hasmonean colonizers or Jewish settlers who migrated there over a century earlier.[146] All archaeological evidence from this period points to a Jewish, yet simple peasant existence.

During the First Century, if someone would have stated that their Messiah and Savior would come from Nazareth, it would have created a stumbling block. We know that this was true because Nathaniel the Jew later asked, "Can any good thing come out of Nazareth". There were at least five major reasons why Nazareth would have been the most unlikely city for the Messiah, King, and Savior of Israel to dwell. First, it was virtually unknown to almost everyone outside of it. Prior to Rome's conversion, the literate elites and politically powerful in the empire knew nothing about Nazareth. It was only locally known.[147] There were many towns spread apart around Nazareth, but Nazareth itself was simply a shadow of a major administrative city. Because of this, the idea of anything good coming from it seemed less probable.

Second, the physical location of Nazareth did not help its fame through the region. At an elevation of approximately 4,000 feet with only a single well-spring, it was clearly isolated and so far off the beaten path that its chances of gaining any notoriety were virtually non-existence before Jesus came.

Third, it was seemingly unknown in the Old Testament. We know this was true because when Zebulon's tribal allotment lists about fifteen Lower Galilean sites in the surrounding areas of Nazareth's vicinity, Nazareth was not mentioned (Joshua 19:10-15). It almost seemed unreal that the city where the future Savior of the world would dwell was insignificant in Jewish writing preceding his existence.

Fourth, Nazareth was a place of agriculture, which meant that the less educated and poorest people would settle in its town. No person of prominence or anyone with ambitions in life would not have settled in this town. Therefore, it was seem almost as a "forgotten city".

And last, during the Roman-Jewish wars, the temples in Nazareth were constantly destroyed and the defeated Jews moved on to other locations. Although some did resettle back in Nazareth, it was a very "unlikely city", since it was continuously being demolished during the wars.

In light of these five facts, it was no accident that Jesus came from Nazareth and was known as a Nazorean. To say that Jesus "put Nazareth on the map", would be by no means an understatement.

The Presentation of Jesus in the Temple

This narrative, located in Luke 2:21-40, must be examined because it is that tradition which leads to the encounter with Simeon and Anna. There are no accidents in Scripture nor is there information or narratives that are less important than others. This narrative is vital to Jesus' physical arrival to earth because it prepares the readers of Luke to understand that although Jesus is being presented in the temple, he will soon come to provide the same services that the temple offered, and yet, he would be an even greater temple.

JOSEPH AND MARY THE JUST

Our narrative begins by portraying the righteousness of Jesus' parents as we see them obeying the Jewish laws. Luke states, "On the eighth day, when it was time to circumcise him, he was named Jesus, the name the angel had given him before he had been conceived" (2:21). With regard to the birth of her child and not to her conception or pregnancy, a Jewish woman was considered unclean for a week. Leviticus 12:2-3 states, "A woman who becomes pregnant and gives birth to a son will be ceremonially unclean for seven days, just as she is unclean during her monthly period. On the eighth day the boy is to be circumcised" (Leviticus 12:2-3).

After circumcision, Luke states, "When the time of their purification according to the Law of Moses had been completed, Joseph and Mary took him to Jerusalem to present him to the Lord" (Luke 2:22). Mary's time of uncleanness had just ended and now was her time for purification. Here, Jesus' parents were taking him to the Jewish Temple in Jerusalem because it was written in the Law of the Lord that "every firstborn male is to be consecrated to the Lord" (Luke 2:23). Yet the law did not require for them to take their child and migrate up to the mountain of Jerusalem.

In addition to taking Jesus to the temple, the Bible states that they came "to offer a sacrifice in keeping with what is said in the Law of the Lord: 'a pair of doves or two young pigeons'" (Luke 2:24). The background for their observance of the law also takes place in Leviticus which states, "When the days of her purification for a son or daughter are over, she is to bring to the priest at the entrance to the Tent of Meeting a year-old lamb for a burnt offering and a young pigeon or a dove for a sin offering....If she cannot afford a lamb, she is to bring two doves or two young pigeons, one for a burnt offering and the other for a sin offering. In this way the priest will make atonement for her, and she will be clean" (Leviticus 12:6-8). Their only two choices were a lamb and a pigeon/dove or if they could not afford these, they had to bring a pair of doves. Joseph and Mary's offering of a pair of doves or young pigeons showed that they offered the offering of the poor and not of someone who could afford a lamb and pigeon.

This same story is modeled after the Samuel story in the Old Testament when he was presented in the sanctuary at Shiloh. After the miraculous conception and birth of her child Samuel, Hannah brought him to the sanctuary at Shiloh and offered him to the service of the Lord (1 Sam 1:24:28). Here, Joseph and Mary took Jesus to Jerusalem to present him to the Lord (Luke 2:22).

By Joseph and Mary carefully observing these ceremonies, they were making the statement that all legal requirements under the law were carefully observed. Luke 2:39 even states that both Joseph and Mary "had done everything required by the Law of the Lord". Although we will find out that Jesus was sinless from birth and that his mother conceived him through the Holy Spirit, this purification process shows that Jesus was not exempt from identifying himself with mankind. He as well as his parents had to submit to the laws of their day and they did just that.

SIMON THE RIGHTEOUS

Now that Joseph and Mary have come to Jerusalem to present their son before the Lord, Luke introduces his audience to a man named Simon. He is described as both "righteous and devout". His walk and actions were not only virtuous and blameless but were caution and wise. He was not a man making hasty judgments but one who was led by the Lord.

In addition to his lifestyle, Luke states that he "was waiting for the consolation of Israel, and the Holy Spirit was upon him" (2:26). He was one of the many who longed for the coming of the Messiah and he was one of the ones who continued to believe and anticipate when others had lost hope. He lived his life directly under the influence of the Holy Spirit and would not act unless he knew that the Spirit was guiding him to do so. But more importantly, "it had been revealed to him by the Holy Spirit that he would not die before he had seen the Lord's Christ" (Luke 2:26).

Understanding his Spirit led life, he, being moved by the Spirit, entered into the temple courts at a particular day and time. When Jesus' parents brought him inside the courts so that they could perform "what the custom of the law required," Simon saw Jesus and was told by the Spirit that he was the Christ child whom he had waited for. It was this same Spirit that gave him his promise and upon seeing him, he took the child "in his arms and praise God" saying, "Sovereign Lord, as you have promised, you now dismiss your servant in peace. For my eyes have seen your salvation, which you have prepared in the sight of all people, a light for revelation to the Gentiles and for glory to your people Israel" (2:29-32). At the end of his life, the aged Simeon embraced this child who was only beginning his life. He knew that he could now die in peace no longer worrying if God was still going to be true to his word that was spoken of from the prophets and also to him. Then he prophetically spoke to this child because he had looked into the future and had seen God's long-awaited salvation to both Jews and non-Jews. His prophetic song would now be sung for generations to come.

To Simon's unexpected actions and words, "the child's father and mother marveled at what was said about him." Simeon was not telling his parents anything they had not previously heard, yet for them to see a stranger verify the very words of God under abnormal circumstances could have served a means of confirmation to them. What Simeon stated was a double proclamation of Jesus' greatness and future destiny which could not have taken place except it be God-given. Now Joseph and Mary would certainly have been assured that what God said about their son was going to happen as if it had already taken place.

Seeing their reaction of astonishment, "Simeon blessed them and said to Mary his mother, 'This child is destined to cause the falling and rising of many in Israel, and to be a sign that will be spoken against, so that the thoughts of many hearts will be revealed'" (Luke 2:34-35). He addressed his words directly to Mary and not to Joseph, but he continued to prophecy and to give them both words of assurance and encouragement. Concerning this "falling and rising of many", Simeon is assuring his mother that Jesus is destined to convert many to the Father who are spiritually dead in their sins and who are sunk in hopelessness. Some of those who would "rise" would soon include some unlikely fishermen who would be world changers, a hated and sinful tax collector who would give back to those whom he cheated, and a persecutor of the believers who would soon rise and be the greatest evangelists of his era. Some of those who would "fall" would soon include one of Jesus' own disciples who would be more in love with money than in him, religious leaders who simply made up in their minds that they would not believe in him, and a married couple who would lie to the Holy Spirit.

The last prophetic message from Simeon would not only be personal to Mary but depressing. He looked at Mary and told her that "a sword will pierce your own soul too" (Luke 2:35). We know that Jesus went through agonizing pain at the cross and that literally a sword/spear went through him (John 19:34), but now Simeon is telling Mary that "a sword will pierce" her soul as well. In other words, although this child was destined to be a great blessing, Mary needed to be prepared for the agony and pain that not only her son would undergo but also what she would undergo as well. Jesus would soon have to suffer and Mary would have the unfortunate experience of seeing it and feeling the same pain. In addition, this prophecy may have also referred to the fact that Mary would also die a martyr's death just like her son. This is the reason why Simeon looked directly at her because God revealed to him this important truth. Since Joseph was not looked upon or given reference to concerning this specific prophecy, it is possible that he was not around to see the unfortunate circumstances that his son would experience.

ANNA THE PROPHETESS

No less significant than the prophetic message of Simeon is words of Anna the Prophetess. Understanding the fact that women usually would not be mentioned in Jewish writing, the author shows no reservation in mentioning her. Luke 2:36-37 states, "There was also a prophetess, Anna, the daughter of Phanuel, of the tribe of Asher. She was very old; she had lived with her husband seven years after her marriage, and then was a widow until she was eighty-four..." Although she being a prophetess was noteworthy, she had the unfortunate circumstance of being a widow for 84 years. She would have been a maiden of about 12 when she married, and we can calculate 12 years approximate of her virginity and the seven years of her marriage. Together, this would have been a lifespan of about 103 years making her age to be over a century. Thus, the author was precisely trying to call consideration to the great length of her widowhood and current age.

But what was more noteworthy is the fact that "...she never left the temple but worshipped night and day, fasting and praying" (Luke 2:37). Although some people feel incomplete and unsatisfied when single, Anna proved them all wrong, for her devotion and worship to God took precedence over everything. The fact that she never left the temple but worshipped night and day probably does not mean that she literally "set-up shop" and lived there. Rather, she never forsook her religious duties and was a faithful worshipper. Even when others her age would have stayed at home, she did not become weary of well-doing. It would be her life of devotion, prayer, and fasting that would virtually open the door to her recognition of Jesus and to her prophetic message concerning him.

She came up to Mary and Joseph "at that very moment" and "she gave thanks to God and spoke about the child to all who were looking forward to the redemption of Jerusalem" (Luke 2:38). Her intimacy with God allowed her to recognize his true significance. Nowhere do we see that she received a vision or revelation like Simeon but rather being led by the Spirit of God, she was able to speak a prophetic word because God spoke through her at that very moment. The basis of her prophecy centered on thanksgiving and she was grateful that God had looked upon his people to redeem them. Now Anna would be seen as a forerunner to the soon-to-be Christian community in Jerusalem who would be seen in Acts as devoting themselves to prayer and daily continuing to meet together in the temple courts (2:42;46).

The expectations of both Simeon and Anna are fulfilled in the temple courts, yet the law did not require Joseph to take his son to Jerusalem. Thus, it was no accident that Jesus came to the temple to be offered back to God, for he would soon replace the temple and all that it stood for.

The Boy Jesus among the Teachers

Because the attendance at the Feast of the Passover in Jerusalem was commanded by God in Exodus 23:17 and Deuteronomy 16:16, Jesus' parents would take the migration every year in observance of the law. Luke 2:42 states, "When he was twelve years old, they went up to the Feast, according to the custom." Specifically, the Jewish males were obligated to attend the feast but the entire family would make these trips to Jerusalem together. Since many people took this journey, the roads would be full of people. Jesus' traveling party consisted of at least relatives and friends from Nazareth and their journey would cover a distance of about twenty miles.[148]

HIS STAY IN JERUSALEM

After celebrating this feast, "while his parents were returning home, the young Jesus stayed behind in Jerusalem, but they were unaware of it" (Luke 2:43). The first day crowd leaving Jerusalem would have been great and the roads would have been filled with people. It would have been easy for Joseph and Mary to lose track of him. Probably when the night approached and the roads started to thin out a bit, Mary and Joseph caught up with each other thinking that he was in their company. "Thinking he was in their company, they traveled on for a day. Then they began looking for him among their relatives and friends" (Luke 2:43-44). After searching among their neighbors, they searched for him among their family members and acquaintances. The overwhelming answer that they received from everyone was that they had not seen Jesus since they left Jerusalem.

Since Joseph and Mary were not careful in watching their son in Jerusalem, they lost his presence and thus had to search for him grief-stricken. They took no rest until they had found their son, for the absence of his presence only brought worrying and confusion. As soon as they could, they "went back to Jerusalem to look for him" (Luke 2:45). I'm sure there were many disturbing thoughts that went through their mind. They may have remembered that Herod and his men had searched for the child and never found him, and just perhaps one of these men had finally found the soon-to-be king and killed him. They may have even remembered the terrifying news that Jacob received when his sons showed him Joseph's coat of many colors that looked like "some ferocious animal has devoured him" (Genesis 37:32-33).

HIS SITTING AMONG THE TEACHERS

Fortunately after three days of sorrow, they gladly "found him in the temple courts, sitting among the teachers, listening to them and asking them questions" (Luke 2:46). Although during his ministry, he would be often described as a teacher, he is not presented as one here. He is seen as an avid learner and as one listening to the teachers and doctors of the law. We observe the wisdom that he had at this early age, for he desired to increase his understanding and readiness to communicate truth. His presence among these teachers would also forecast his interests, for he would soon be constantly engrossed in debates with them over the law. Unfortunately, these same religious teachers and doctors of law would be hostile toward him and would try to ask trick questions on numerous occasions. But here, only piety and respect permeates the temple courts.

Joseph and Mary also observed that everyone in the courts who heard their son "was amazed at his understanding and his answers" (Luke 2:47). What is amazing is the fact that for three days, this twelve year old dumbfounded his listeners because of his understanding and answers. We see his development of understanding already attained at such an early age, for if Jewish Rabbis who were expects of the law were amazed at his understanding and answers, Jesus must have been an extraordinary young man. Yet they did not know that he had a unique relationship with God and all he was simply doing was portraying his love to him through his answers.

After finding their son after three days and then seeing the reaction of the doctors of law respond to his questions, Luke states, "When his parents saw him, they were astonished" (2:48). This astonishment literally meant that they were stuck with shock and amazement. Was it that they were surprised to see him in the temple or just surprised to even see him alive? Was it shocking to see the teachers and doctors amazed at Jesus' answers or were they shocked that he was still in Jerusalem when they all left to go back to Nazareth?

HIS STATEMENT – "FATHER'S HOUSE"

With Mary probably being more grief-stricken than Joseph, she spoke quickly and said, "Son, why have you treated us like this? Your father and I have been anxiously searching for you" (Luke 2:48). She immediately cross-examines him and the basis of her trouble stemmed from her view that Jesus put her and Joseph through this stress. To his mother's question, Jesus responds in a much less stressful tone of voice, "Why were you searching for me? Didn't you know I had to be in my Father's house?" (Luke 2:49). These first recorded words of Jesus emphasize at least two important truths. First, he based his relationship on the God of Israel and not on the people of Israel. The focal point was not his aptitude but his reference to God as his Father. He was stating that his presence in the temple and his listening to the teachers was indicative of where his vocation lied, namely, in the service of God who was his Father, not at the call of his natural family.[149]

The second truth conveyed the purpose of his existence, that is being in his "Father's house." In the Jewish society, boys at age 12 had to learn a trade. By him stating that he must be about his Father's house, he was letting his parents know his ambition and purpose. Although his earthly father was a carpenter, Jesus would ultimately follow in his spiritual father's footsteps in helping to provide salvation to all mankind. During his earthly ministry, he would "received from God the Father honor and glory when there came such a voice to him from the excellent glory, 'This is my beloved Son, in whom I am well pleased'" (2 Peter 1:17). But this did not make him who he was, for he had already established this fact at this young age. Therefore, he did not leave them, but rather they left him.

After hearing these profound but unexpected words from their son, both Mary and Joseph "did not understand what he was saying to them" (Luke 2:50). Joseph heard the divine messenger tell him that his son would save people from their sins (Matthew 1:21) and it was revealed to Mary that her son would be reign over the house of Jacob forever and that his kingdom will never end (Luke 1:33). Yet they both had not until this moment understood his full significance and mission. They were too busy looking in other areas and they seemingly forgot his purpose and what he came to earth for.

HIS SUBMISSION AND MATURATION

Luke states that after Jesus responded back to his mother, "he went down to Nazareth with them and was obedient to them. But his mother treasured all these things in her heart" (Luke 2:51). By him staying behind in the temple, he was not showing defiance. He is esteemed not just because he knew his purpose and existence in life but because he was obedience as a youth. Although he had just stated his divine purpose, he was still a child and had to show submission to his parents just as any Jewish boy had to do. Although the hour awaited him to show his heroism, he would not show incompetence in not submitting himself to his parents.

In addition to his submission, he "grew in wisdom and stature, and in favor with God and men" (Luke 2:52). The author mentions the mental, physical, social, and spiritual development of Jesus and although some would soon deny his humanity, the author sets the tone early that Jesus fulfilled all the attributes of humanity.

CHAPTER 3
STRANGE TEACHINGS

"He comes to us as one unknown, without a name, as of old, by the lakeside, He came to those men who knew him not. He speaks to us the same word: 'Follow thou me!' and sets us to the tasks which he has to fulfill for our time. He commands. And to those who obey him, whether they be wise or simple, he will reveal himself in the toils, the conflicts, the sufferings which they shall pass through in his fellowship, and, as an ineffable mystery, they shall learn in their own experience who he is.[150]

Introduction to Teachings

Early in his ministry, the Gospel writer Mark states that Jesus went to Capernaum and when the Sabbath came, he "went into the synagogue and began to teach. The people were amazed at his teaching, because he taught them as one who had authority, not as the teachers of the law" (Mark 1:21-22). Mark was trying to set the tone early for Jesus' teachings in view of all those under the sound of his voice.

Jesus' teachings were not just original, but were atypical. Just imagine a normal way of life, whatever that may be, and then a teacher out of nowhere comes and teaches a message that goes against the entire social norm. This would typify Jesus' teachings like no other. In addition, by understanding the culture that permeated the Mediterranean society and then to compare that with Jesus' teachings, you will see that virtually every message he spoke went against some cultural norm of the day. That is why Jesus' teachings to the people of his day were "strange".

The traditions and values that embraced Roman culture were completely challenged by Jesus' life and teachings. Although the Roman culture put people in hierarchical structures which virtually segregated the society, Jesus showed them that this was not how God viewed people. Instead of people looking to bandits as their saviors, Jesus told them to look to him as their advocate. Although Caesar Augustus was renowned during this era, Jesus wanted the multitudes to understand that he was greater, for he would conquer death, which was something Augustus was unable to do. Consequently, Jesus' teachings were rejected by many, yet it challenged the philosophical norm held by the society.

HE COMES UNKNOWN

When he came into a village of Lower Galilee, he would come unknown and although many would soon worship him, his presence among the people would appear normal. Between the ages of twelve and thirty, he would live in Nazareth and the call of Jeremiah included God appointing him "to build and to plant" (1:10). His social trade would be that of a carpenter (Mark 6:3), which made sense in view of the world where sons usually followed into their father's professions. One's social degree would easily be known in a Greco-Roman world and Jesus' trade of being a "carpenter" would indicate a lower-class status.[151]

In any given village, serious-minded Jews would gather and devote themselves to studying the Torah and applying its laws to their day. Everybody "kept their jobs" but spent their spare time discussing the law. Growing up in Lower Galilee, Jesus most likely joined nightly in discussion of the law with the local people. We can be confident that he was a part of this group because in the Gospels he demonstrates skills in the rabbinic style of debate such as were nurtured in these fellowships. After those eighteen years of "theological education" he would be ready to begin his public ministry.[152]

Before his ministry began, he did not come working miracles or promoting his new kingdom but rather came learning and sitting under the teachers and doctors, of whom he would some day be. He would fit right in with the everyday crowd and seemingly all the people who heard about the wonders surrounding his birth quickly forgot the true person he was. But yet, that was intended.

HE COMES AS A TEACHER

The New Testament writers make it clear that Jesus' public ministry began by preaching (Matthew 4:12-17; Mark 1:14-15) and this is how he presented himself to the Mediterranean people of his day. In Israel's history, the office of a teacher was respected in the community ever since the giving of the law on Mount Sinai. Jesus was commonly acknowledged as a teacher because of the titles given to him and it was an expected title for him to have, particularly in light of the fact that he assembled disciples around him. His teachings always centered on God and he enabled his followers and disciples to understand the God of the Scriptures.

The object of Jesus' teachings was to give direction rather than directions and to point to the goal rather than to give goals. His aim was to point men to the Father and to inform them about the Kingdom of God. At the same time, he informed his followers that their goal in reaching the Father was only through him. Therefore, the important aspect from Jesus' standpoint was not whether the goal was near or far away, but whether the direction was correct. If the object of Jesus was so to guide his followers that their lives should fit into the great purpose of God, the question whether that purpose would be realized in ten years or ten thousand became a minor consideration.[153]

The purpose behind the object of his teaching was to save men. His kingdom message in the form of parables were not merely wise sayings to better one's life but were permeated with destiny. Thus, to ignore his teachings was to bring destruction to one's own life.

His main form of teaching was the parable. The word "parable" denotes a comparison or similitude, which is the putting of one thing alongside another. It is an observation about nature or human life constituting a spiritual lesson relating more or less closely to the natural counterpart.[154] It is used for warning as well as for an example and its application may be hidden from the hearers.[155] Along with parables, Jesus used proverbs (Matthew 16:1-4), hyperbole (Matthew 7:3-4), metaphor (Matthew 11:7), epigram (Matthew 22:21), and paradox (Matthew 16:25).

The characteristics of Jesus' teachings were many. First, his teachings brought wisdom. Although Solomon was a wise man and taught wise sayings, Jesus' teachings were much greater, for Solomon's teachings were mostly beneficial for one's life on earth while Jesus' teachings were mostly beneficial to one's life and destiny once an individual died.

Second, his teachings were radical. His use of extravagant language was a device to stimulate interest and impress the point being made.[156] He had no shame calling out the Pharisees' on major issues and in using them as examples in his parables for the entire multitude to hear. He cut no corners but exclaimed the truth with boldness.

Third, his teachings were simple. People could understand him because he spoke their everyday language not just in dialect but in relation to their day after day struggles. He would relate the Kingdom of God to their everyday professions and would inform the multitude that God knows and cares about their situation. Hence, his words were simple and yet reflective.

And fourth, his teachings were original. All writers, Jewish and Christian alike, grant a difference between Jesus' teaching and the rabbinic in that his words are free of the wearisome casuistry that clutters the Talmud.[157] At the same time, a spirit and atmosphere pervades his teachings that are not found elsewhere.[158] One of the key examples of his originality comes from the fact that virtually his entire messages centered on aspects that were totally uncommon to the people and yet it is his teachings that elevates him to hero status and that sets him apart from all other admirable persons.

HE COMES FULFILLING PROPHECY

During the onset of his ministry, Jesus not only set the stage as a teacher but as one who fulfilled Jewish prophecy. In Luke 4, "He went to Nazareth, where he had been brought up and on the Sabbath day he went into the synagogue, as was his custom. And he stood up to read" (14-16). He came to this village as a nomadic rabbi and was given a chance to talk to the people who came to the synagogue. The Jews allowed the law to be read only with the reader standing up.

The scroll of the prophet Isaiah was given to him and after unrolling it, Jesus found a specific passage that the Jews knew about and he read, "The Spirit of the Lord is on me, because he has anointed me to preach good news to the poor. He has sent me to proclaim freedom for the prisoners and recovery of sight for the blind, to release the oppressed, to proclaim the year of the Lord's favor" (Luke 4:18-19). His audience of settlers understood this text and with everyone listening intently, he chose this familiar and deeply beloved passage.

But to their shock and amazement, he stopped reading at the point at which judgment and servitude was pronounced on the Gentiles, whom they, as a settler community, were there to displace.[159] This prophecy from Isaiah foretold the coming of the Messiah's Kingdom and ministry. Jesus, knowing that he was the Messiah, understood that there would be two "comings", with the Second Coming occurring after the rapture. Therefore, he did not read the rest of Isaiah which only pertained to the Messiah's role in the Second Coming.

After reading, he "rolled up the scroll, gave it back to the attendant and sat down" making an even greater statement that he intentionally stopped at that specific passage. Knowing that there was more to the Isaiah text, "the eyes of everyone in the synagogue were fastened on him" (Luke 4:20). It was probably just as intriguing to the Jewish audience that Jesus picked such a bizarre prophetic passage to read in the synagogue. After seeing the looks on their faces, Jesus said to all those listening, "Today this Scripture is fulfilled in your hearing" (Luke 4:21). This was his way of boldly stating that he was the Messiah and was the Spirit-led anointed Savior sent to rescue the Jewish people. Jesus' statement declared that these Scriptures were a present reality fulfilled through him and he left the crowd with two alternatives, either to believe that he was the Messiah or that he was not.

After stating these bold words, everyone "spoke well of him and were amazed at the gracious words that came from his lips." Then they ask each other, "Isn't this Joseph's son" (Luke 4:22). These people recognized Jesus as Joseph's son, but more importantly, because he grew up in their Jewish village, they were amazed that Jesus would say such words, for they certainly understood how the Jews felt regarding that Jewish text.

But then Jesus stated, "I tell you the truth, no prophet is accepted in his hometown" (Luke 4:24). Then he purposefully gave examples of two of the most renowned prophets in the Old Testament, Elijah and Elisha, and stated how they chose to bestow their favor among outsiders rather than those among their own people as if they were not accepted. Concerning this, he said, "I assure you that there were many widows in Israel in Elijah's time, when the sky was shut for three and a half years and there was a severe famine throughout the land. Yet Elijah was not sent to any of them, but to a widow in Zarephath in the region of Sidon" (Luke 4:25-26). In 1 Kings 17:9, God indeed told Elijah to "go at once to Zarephath of Sidon and stay there", for he would command a widow in that place to supply him with food. But Zarephath was a "heathen" village located between Tyre and Sidon, and Sidon was an ancient Phoenician city. Yet, God purposefully told him to go to this region and would ultimately use this narrative to show that the ministry of the Gospel would soon be open to outsiders. Concerning Elisha, Jesus said, "And there were many in Israel with leprosy in the time of Elisha the prophet, yet not one of them was cleansed-only Naaman the Syrian" (Luke 4:27). Syrians or Armenians were not only foreigners but enemies of the Jews.

Upon hearing these words, "all the people in the synagogue were furious when they heard this" (Luke 4:28). They were furious because Jesus, who from their eyes was only Joseph's son and a carpenter, was comparing himself to the ministry of these great prophets, who worked miracles and challenged the great kings and queens. But just as damaging to their ears was the fact that Jesus dared to say that God had reserved the truth of the gospel for the Gentiles to hear and grasp hold of. Yet Jesus was trying to let them know that their religious ancestors willingly obeyed God as they foresaw the hopes of adding the Gentiles to family of God. He desired to inform them that God indeed loved Israel, but he also loved Gentiles as well.

Detesting Jesus' assessment and ideology, "they got up, drove him out of the town, and took him to the brow of the hill on which the town was built, in order to throw him down the cliff. But he walked right through the crowd and went on his way" (Luke 4:29-30). Many of the messages of Old Testament prophets almost cost them their lives, and this seemingly almost happened to Jesus. His teachings were rejected in Nazareth, yet his prophecy would soon reveal to be true.

He Comes Promoting a New Kingdom

The Jews knew all to well about kings and the political term of kingdoms. Their history consisted of constant struggles between empires and they as a people were conquered by the Assyrians, Babylonians, Medes and Persians, and the Greeks. Currently, they were under the rule of the Romans and they knew all about the rule of Caesar August and the ordering of his census that brought the entire empire under his rule. They understood his "power for life" title that meant that he had control over the popular assemblies and the people. They understood Herod's Kingdom and the many and expensive building projects that he erected. Unfortunately, the downside of their understanding of kingdom consisted of the oppression and segregation that they constantly experienced. Herod would not only try to kill anyone who threatened his kingship, but he saw urbanization and oppression as a means of control and stifling even the very hint of revolt. Therefore, kingdom and rule was not foreign to the Jews of the fist century.

Yet when Jesus would come on the scene, he would not just promote a kingdom but from the standpoint of the people living in the Roman Empire, he would promote a new and different kingdom. Luke 4:14-15 states that after Jesus' baptism and a period of temptation in the wilderness, he returned to Galilee to begin a popular public preaching ministry. The Gospel writer Matthew states that early in Jesus' ministry, he began to preach, "Repent, for the Kingdom of Heaven is near" (Matthew 4:17). Matthew stated that Jesus' daily activity consisted of going "throughout Galilee, teaching in their synagogues, preaching the good news of the kingdom, and healing every disease and sickness among the people" (Matthew 4:23). Kingdoms and rulers had sovereignty, majesty, dominion, power, and domain. Yet Jesus' Kingdom would consist of all of this, but from the perspective that it would not be under man's rule. Almost every instance in which he spoke about his kingdom, he would introduce it with the Kingdom of God or the Kingdom of Heaven. He would teach that the Kingdom of God consists of people under divine rule and it is God that transcends and judges all human rule. The Kingdom of God is what the world would be if God were directly and immediately in charge.[160] To advance toward his kingdom, Jesus would state that it is through the knowledge of loving God (Mark 12:32-34). To enter his kingdom, one must do so like a child (Mark 10:15), one must be born again (John 3:5), and one must be a doer of God's will (Matthew 7:21).

Jesus would soon pick 12 disciples to follow him, and they like most Jews had imaged a kingdom. Yet their kingdom would only pertain to the future of Israel. Unfortunately, this was not what Jesus came promoting, for he would soon die for not only the Jews but for Gentiles alike. In addition, the disciples and all the people who imagined a kingdom had a problem in not recognizing its actual presence among them. Many were only waiting its advent, but Jesus was going to let them know that the kingdom is actually among them, right now! Thus, this kingdom was a much greater thing than the disciples and people had imagined.

Jesus' Kingdom would thus be a "code word" for community and would encompass all those who sought for it and would exclude none. Jesus actually took it to the extreme that his kingdom consisted of the "nobodies" of the First Century. Although their world was governed by a male dominate society and the rich were often seen as noteworthy, Jesus would boldly proclaim that his kingdom was open to the children and women, poor and destitute, and to the non-Jews alike. Children were considered nobodies and there was nothing exceptional that would define their stage of life. The only possibility of them becoming important depended on their parent's status in the community. Yet Jesus would embrace children and proclaim, "Let the little children come to me, and do not hinder them, for the kingdom of heaven belongs to such as these" (Matthew 19:14). Concerning women, he would not look down on them because of their sex but would allow them to be his followers and financial supporters. In a society, where women did not have rights and were considered immorally impure, Jesus did not condemn them but encouraged them to remain pure.

Jesus community would also encompass the poor. Jesus would preach that being rich does not save a person from death, and death shows no favoritism among the poor and the rich. He would tell the poor that earthly physical riches will not gain admission into the Kingdom of Heaven and that those who possess these riches generally have a difficult time in parting with them. Yet, he would give hope to the poor of his day. From Jesus' point of view, the poor and the meek are the ones who will inherit the earth. Soon, his followers would understand this fact and say as Jesus lived, "Has not God chosen those who are poor in the eyes of the world to be rich in faith and to inherit the kingdom he promised those who love him" (James 2:5).

Yet to these "nobodies" of the First Century, they were not really concerned about the comparisons and contrasts of Jesus' Kingdom to the Roman Kingdom. Rather, what they really want to know was what this new kingdom could do for their current needs. In a society filled with physical infirmities, the oppressions of tax and dept, and spiritual blindness and demonic possession, the people were not concerned that Jesus looked like them but rather could his teachings help them. They soon would find out that he could and did.

Teachings of the Baptism Movement

For the Jews living in Palestine, hope became more of a rarity. Many individuals and groups turned apocalyptic and desired God to act in light of the violence that constantly surrounded them. Thankfully, God did show up and brought his servant John into the wilderness to proclaim a special message in the midst of the silence all around. He appears, and cries, "Repent, for the Kingdom of Heaven is at hand." Soon after, Jesus came in the knowledge that he was the coming Son of Man and he took control of the world to set it moving on that last revolution, which was to bring all ordinary history to a close.

The stern warning of judgment upon sin that characterized John's preaching were accompanied by the command to repent and to manifest works in keeping with a true repentance. Various groups who came to him sought instruction as to the type of conduct expected of them, and John replied in terms appropriate to their special situations.[161] John's urgency pertained to the fact that the Kingdom of Heaven was at hand and his teachings also set the stage for the Messiah and his teachings. Seemingly, all Jerusalem and Judea and the territory around the Jordan would eagerly come out to not only catch a glimpse of this desert figure and to see his act of baptism, but to listen to his teachings on the advent of God and the coming of the long awaited Messiah. Thus, the teachings of the Baptism Movement would serve as the foundation to the entire New Testament message and would bring together all of what the former prophets had preached.

JOHN'S PROPHETIC FULFILLMENT OF ISAIAH

The angel told John's parents that he would be "great", but they did not know or even comprehend how great he would be. John would be so great that the law and prophets would stop with him. Luke 16:16 states this fact in saying, "The law and the prophets were proclaimed until John. Since that time, the good news of the Kingdom of God is being preached, and everyone is forcing his way into it." No more prophets were need with his coming, and Jesus even stated, "Among those that are born of women there is not a greater prophet than John the Baptist..." (Luke 7:28). The prophets would not only end with John being the last of the prophets, but he would be greater than any of the prophets before him. His greatness would not be because of his ascetic practices or religious conduct but because of the task that was set before him.

It was John and not Jesus who was the initiator of the Gospel and of the Kingdom Movement, specifically speaking in the New Testament. One of the Gospel writers states that "the beginning of the gospel about Jesus Christ, the Son of God" began with John (Mark 3:1-3). John's coming would not be a mishap, for it would be foretold hundreds of years earlier of his special purpose of being the forerunner of the Christ. All three of the Gospel writers who mentioned his message of repentance also mentioned that his very coming was a fulfillment of Old Testament prophecy.

After stating that he went into all the country around the Jordan preaching a baptism of repentance for the forgiveness of sins (Luke 3:3), Luke the author desires to make it clear that his coming was purposeful. He states, "As is written in the book of the words of Isaiah the prophet: "A voice of one calling in the desert, prepare the way for the Lord, make straight paths for him. Every valley shall be filled in, every mountain and hill made low. The crooked roads shall become straight, the rough ways smooth. And all mankind will see God's salvation'" (Luke 3:4-6). John's self-identification as the voice of one crying in the wilderness implies that he leaned heavily upon Isaiah's prophecy for the knowledge of his mission. Isaiah, the most evangelical of all the prophets, preached this message to the people of his day (40:3-5) and he began this message by comforting his people Israel. He desired to let them know that their "hard service has been completed", that their "sin has been paid for", and that they have "received from the Lord's hand double" for all their sins (40:2). In the same way, John's message in the New Testament would provide comfort to the people of their day in view of all the oppression they have been experiencing. He would let them know that the Messiah would be coming and that he would "baptize" them "with the Holy Spirit and with fire" (Matthew 3:11).

Isaiah would state the prophetic words of "a voice" calling to "prepare the way for the Lord." John would prepare the way for the

Messiah by using his voice. Mark 1:2 states that Isaiah the prophet stated, "I will send my messenger ahead of you, who will prepare your way." The Roman Empire used force to "prepare the way" within the empire, yet John would use a totally different method. John's specific purpose would be that of preparing "the way" for the Messiah. His voice would be used to simply inform people of his coming.

Although the prophets as a whole did not understand the full extent of a future individual coming to be the forerunner of Jesus of Nazareth, the New Testament authors recognized this prophetic message to be fulfilled through John. It would be John who would "make straight paths" for Jesus the Messiah and because of his message of preparation, "every valley" would be "filled in", "every mountain and hill" would be made "low", "the crooked roads" would become "straight", "the rough ways" would be made "smooth" and "all mankind" would be able to "see God's salvation." With the current oppression, injustice, and spiritual void in society, Jesus would be the only one who would be able to rectify this epidemic. Although the Roman Empire believed to be powers that would fix the current world, Isaiah the prophet stated hundreds of years earlier that it would be another. Therefore, John's message would provide a smooth transition for the coming of Jesus and when Jesus' ministry would end, he would have brought all things together.

JOHN'S LOCATION

John is depicted in being located in two general locations. The first location is in the "wilderness of Judea" (Mark 3:1). Judea (or Judah) was the southern portion of Palestine positioned on the side of the Jordan and the Dead Sea and although there were people who lived in that region, it was mostly unpopulated because of the desert. The wilderness of Judea is located west of the Dead Sea and extends from these waters to the very edge of the central plateau. The wilderness stretches as far as the eye can see and is virtually mountainous. Because this area receives less than two inches of rainfall a year, it is almost completely devoid of any vegetation. In Joshua's days, this wilderness included Betharabah, Middin, and Secacah (Joshua 15:61) and Betharabah actually means "house of the desert valley" or "place of the depression".

The second location is in "all the country about Jordan" (Luke 3:3). Jordan is located on the eastern side of the Jordan River and is in both the northern and eastern hemispheres in Israel. Bordered by Israel, Syria, Iraq and Saudi Arabia, the Jordan region is generally a flat desert plateau. This location is not just a commonplace segment of Israel but rather carries great significance within God's historical timeline. Jordan is the part of the country which Israel took possession first when entering into the land that God promised. Numerous men including Abraham, Job, Moses, Ruth, and Elijah accomplished essential tasks that aided God's evangelist plan within this region. Moses delivered God's Law to Israel in this region and it would be here where Jesus would be baptized by John.

When did John settle in the desert? We must remember that after Elizabeth gave birth to John and the surrounding community was amazing at the wonders surrounding his birth, Luke states that John "grew and waxed strong in Spirit, and was in the deserts till the day of his showing unto Israel" (1:80). Although his father was a priest, John did not go up to minister before God like Samuel but rather, he knew his calling and at a young age, probably at age 13, he went into the desert to prepare for his long-awaited calling. He did not sit under rabbis nor did he receive formal training but rather, he would be prepared to introduce the Messiah because he "waxed strong in Spirit", which was the primary agent to help him effectively fulfill his calling.

The Dead Sea Scrolls discovery has attached new importance to the question of John's possible relation to the Esssenes. Historically, Essenes moved to meagerly populated areas of Palestine, particularly to the desert near the Dead Sea because they believed that the city life was tainted and evil. They were separatists and their philosophy consisted of celibacy. Since John spent his sheltered years in the Judean desert, the possibility of contact with this group must be admitted. His location in a remote and almost desolate area demonstrates the powerful working of God, for God lets it be known that no place is so secluded that man is unable to hear from him. Although David was located in this same wilderness, he was still about to seek God early (Psalm 63:1).

JOHN'S APPEARANCE AND DIET

His appearance, diet, and demeanor mirrored that of the land from which he came. Only Luke and Mark give reference to John's location and only Matthew and Mark give reference to his appearance and diet. Matthew states, "John's clothes were made of camel's hair, and he had a leather belt around his waist" (3:4). Mark's details are similar stating, "John wore clothing made of camel's hair with a leather belt around his waist" (1:6).

His appearance was similar to that of Elijah, for it was stated of him that "he was a man with a garment of hair and with a leather belt around his waist" (2 Kings 1:8). He and Elijah both wore clothes made out of hair cloth and it was stated that John specifically wore camel's hair. In contrast with soft raiment, both of their garments of hair were girdled with a leather belt. Contrasted with today's society, the New Testament writers rarely stated anything concerning the attire of an individual and this thought would have been irrelevant in light of the everyday appearance of people. Yet for Luke and Mark to mention details of his attire show that it was not only significant but striking.

In addition to his dress, both authors state that his diet consisted of locusts and wild honey. This was not John's casual meal but rather was his everyday food. Although both he and Elijah had a similar semblance, only John went to the extreme. Locusts, the swarming of short-horned grasshoppers, may reach lengths of six inches and because of their ability to breed quickly, John would have no shortage of "meat." Locusts eat many types of plants but they prefer to eat plants grown by people. This fact supports the notation that John's residence in the wilderness was not in a totally uninhabited area but that there had to have been some residences in the area. In addition to eating swarming grasshoppers, John's diet also consisted of wild honey. The term wild in the New Testament gives the connotation of living or growing in the fields or woods, which was precisely where John was located.

His diet was a means of buffeting his body from the pleasures of this world as he lived in a world where some would only indulge themselves (Luke 16:19-21). His ascetic practice allowed him to be better prepared to become the forerunner of the Messiah. Like Elijah who called men to repentance, he would fearlessly call Israel to repentance.

JOHN'S MESSAGE OF REPENTANCE AND URGENCY

John's message centered on the need for the people to "repent, for the Kingdom of Heaven has come near" (Matthew 3:2). Repentance is literally the stopping of habitual practices of sin and it is an individual's changed mindset regarding how God views sin. Although the Jews were currently experiencing oppression and injustice, John dealt with their greater issue and need, that is their personal relationship with God.

As a result of his preaching, "people went out to him from Jerusalem and all Judea and the whole region of the Jordan" (Matthew 3:5) and they came "confessing their sins" (Matthew 3:6). His fame spread throughout the region to the extent that great crowds came out to him. Then he gave his message of repentance with urgency. He told the crowds, "You brood of vipers! Who warned you to flee from the coming wrath? Produce fruit in keeping with repentance" (Luke 3:7-8). After asking the question, he gave them no time to answer but rather gave them the remedy of producing fruits of repentance. The people could identify with "fruits", for they lived in an agrarian society. At the same time, they could identify with producing fruits versus not producing fruits. Their livelihood was dependent on the weather, which was essential for their livelihood. Yet, John's message of producing "fruit in keeping with repentance" was relative to the people and they could all understand his teachings.

Then John told them, "And do not think you can say to yourselves, 'We have Abraham as our father'" (Matthew 3:9). Jews even to this day pride themselves because of their history and they live their lives based on past customs. Abraham was a historical figure and a great man of faith. He was even the biological father of the Jews. But here, John was trying to tell them that Abraham will not help them in God's coming wrath and that each individual is going to have to give an account of their "fruits". If they don't repent, they will consequently suffer the judgment of God.

In addition, John honestly told them how insignificant it really was to pride themselves as being one of Abraham's descendents, for he told them not to use Abraham as a crutch because "out of these stones God can raise up children for Abraham" (Matthew 3:9). There were innumerable amount of stones in southern Israel and for John to make this statement, he was telling them that by priding themselves as being one of Abraham's descendents was certainly a lame excuse.

If God wanted to, he could destroy all the Jews and then could replace them with those million of stones who would repent and produce fruit. Therefore, the urgency of his preaching was enforced even greater.

John's urgency continued by him informing the people that "the ax is already at the root of the trees, and every tree that does not produce good fruit will be cut down and thrown into the fire" (Matthew 3:10). He had been in the "Spirit" long enough to recognize the heartbeat and temperature of God. His life of solitude allowed him to recognize that the time is very short for those who have been living bogus lives before God.

JOHN'S APPLICATION TO REPENTANCE

Yet for those who still seemed confused on the whole "bearing fruit" message, John told them how to put repentance into action. Someone in the crowd freely spoke forth and asked him, "What should we do then? John answered, 'The man with two tunics should share with him who has none, and the one who has food should do the same'" (Luke 3:10-11). Since "fruit" consists of that which is seen or displayed, John told the people to share with the one who does not have anything. It was hard enough living in a world where people constantly struggled and John knew this. Yet his answer coincided with his producing "fruit in keeping with repentance" message and informed them that their mindset on giving to others needed to change.

Some tax collectors came to John and asked him, "Teacher, what should we do?" They probably saw some of the other people ask John about their situation and they then proceeded to ask him how they needed to evaluate their own lives. John replied to them, "Don't collect any more than you are required to" (Luke 3:12-13). Tax collectors were hated by the Jews because they would demand above and beyond the amount due for taxes. Because they would pocket the excess money, tax collectors were among the rich and wealthy in the land. Yet he gave them the simple message of only collecting what is required. They would unfortunately have to go against the grain and act differently than the rest of the tax collectors of the land. John's message only dealt with the particular issue in which the tax collectors needed to change, for repentance is the ceasing of habitually practicing sin and not a mistake.

After the tax collectors, some soldiers came to him and asked what should they do. He replied, "Don't extort money and don't accuse people falsely - be content with your pay" (Luke 3:14). John gave them three areas of repentance. First, he told them not to extort money. Because of their legal authority, soldiers would obtain money through coercion and oftentimes through force. Yet, John told them to not do this.

Secondly, he told them not to accuse people falsely. The people of whom they would threaten for money and accuse falsely (that is if they did not give them the money) would most likely be the common peasants of the land. These were the same people who were constantly being oppressed, especially from Roman government. Yet John told them not to use their legal position to present false information concerning the poor to the chief priests.

And third, he told them to be content with their pay. We know that after the resurrection, the soldiers, who went to the chief priests after undergoing the earthquake and seeing the angels, were given money in order to keep quiet about the truth and were told to spread false information about what took place at the tomb site. John's rebuke of the soldiers made sense, for if they were well paid men, the bribe from the chief priests would not have been as enticing. Yet, he told them that their constant negative attitudes regarding their pay needed to be brought under the submission of God.

JOHN'S MESSAGE OF THE MESSIAH

Because of his liberal spirit and the divine presence upon his life, the multitudes began to believe that now was the time for the Messiah to emerge and they "were all wondering in their hearts if John might possibly be the Christ" (Luke 3:15). Isaiah's prophetic words of "a voice" calling to "prepare the way for the Lord" came true in light of the very thoughts of the people. Their language demonstrated that their hearts were already prepared for God's advent and it was up to John to clarify to them of God's purpose for the Messiah.

John had certainly fulfilled his prophetic duty, yet he would have to tell the people one more important truth. He said, "I baptize you with water. But one more powerful than I will come..." (Luke 3:16). John quickly renounced all pretensions to being the long-awaited Messiah, but verified to them that their expectations will soon be fulfilled. He let them know that if they thought that he was great, the Messiah would be even greater. To prove his greatness, he told them that he was "not worthy to untie" his sandals and that he will baptize them with the Holy Spirit and with fire (Luke 3:16). In Matthew 3:11, John states that he was "not fit to carry" his sandals and in Mark 1:7, he states that was "not worthy to stoop down and untie" his sandals. The feet were among the most insignificant and dirtiest parts of the body within the Mediterranean world, yet these references give attention to the feet of the Messiah and how John believed that he was unworthy to even become associated with them.

He then gave an important message concerning the authority and work of the Messiah during the apocalyptic era of God. He told them, "His winnowing fork is in his hand to clear his threshing floor and to gather the wheat into his barn, but he will burn up the chaff with unquenchable fire" (Luke 3:17). The act of winnowing in the Old Testament meant to scatter, fan, cast away, disperse, and spread. The threshing floor was a place in the field made hard after the harvest by a roller and was a place where grain was threshed out. The people here understood the negative act of winnowing from Jeremiah the prophet when the Lord spoke through him to tell the rebellious Jews, "I will winnow them with a winnowing fork at the city gates of the land. I will bring bereavement and destruction on my people, for they have not changed their ways" (15:7). John's message to the people was clear in that God was ready to clear out and separate those who were not willing to repent and they will burn forever.

Yet John did not know that this would be the same message that Jesus would speak in one of his parables. He would soon preach, "The field is the world; the good seed are the children of the kingdom; but the tares are the children of the wicked one; The enemy that sowed them is the devil; the harvest is the end of the world; and the reapers are the angels. As therefore the tares are gathered and burned in the fire, so shall it be in the end of this world. The Son of man shall send forth his angels, and they shall gather out of his kingdom all things that offend, and them which do iniquity. And shall cast them into a furnace of fire: there shall be wailing and gnashing of teeth" (Matthew 13:38-42).

John's message of the Messiah may have seen harsh but to the people, they were seen as encouraging words. We know this because Luke 3:18 states, "And with many other words John exhorted the people and preached the good news to them." His encouragement to the people was that they could prepare themselves for the coming of the kingdom. He spoke as if he already knew the outcome and he gave reassurance to them who were never given a second change in life. His hope could even be attained by the poorest of the poor.

JOHN'S PRACTICE OF BAPTISM

There were many great inventions in the First Century, but none were as unique as John's practice of baptism. Matthew states that "people went out to him from Jerusalem and all Judea and the whole region of the Jordan. Confessing their sins, they were baptized by him in the Jordan River" (Matthew 3:5-6). Mark gives a similar depiction by saying, "And there went out unto him all the land of Judea, and they of Jerusalem, and were all baptized of him in the river of Jordan, confessing their sins" (Mark 1:5). Before this practice, the only place in the country where Jews could legally offer sacrifices was Jerusalem. Jews, who could afford the services, migrated there to offer sacrifices for their sins. But the expense of the trip and the long travel prohibited many from taking this trip regularly. So the Jews not around Jerusalem were seldom atoned for. Yet John allowed people to repent and be baptized for their sins, and when this news spread around the region, people immediately saw an inexpensive, accessible, and suitable substitute for the long pilgrimage to Jerusalem.

John saw baptism as a way to obtain forgiveness for one's sins (Luke 3:3) and it represented a physical symbol of a spiritual reality. He preached that if one became baptized, he would be introduced to God when he came back for his apocalyptic intervention. John's desire was to prepare man for the coming of God's Kingdom, and baptism would demonstrate one's dedication to him which would prepare for his advent.

Josephus, a notable First Century historian, associates John's baptism with righteousness. He states that he was a pious man and that he offered the Jews who practiced virtue and exercised righteousness toward each other and piety toward God to come together for baptism. He stated that his baptism was not a convenient means of clearing sins formerly committed but rather a symbolic act demonstrating the achievement of righteousness by good deeds.[162] His desire was to arrange a distinct and unified community of the baptized across the Jewish native soil that was repentant and waiting for God's advent.

THE POLITICAL INJUSTICE OF HEROD

Unfortunately, John's boldness in his preaching and teaching came at a cost. He had no problem speaking about repentance, the advent of God, and people's behaviors. He gave no thought to speak the words of God in front of tax collectors, soldiers, or even Herod the King. Yet his popularity and public preaching would soon come to an end.

Around the year 30 B.C., Herod Antipas rejected his first wife in order to marry Herodias, who was the wife of his half-brother Herod. John spoke up and told him that it was not "lawful" for him to have her (Matthew 14:4) and he rebuked him for "all the other evil things he had done" as well (Luke 3:19). Herod then became concerned that his teachings would gain him too much power and influence over the people, for John was teaching the multitudes to become ethical individuals. So to prevent him from becoming too powerful, Herod wanted to kill him but "was afraid of the people because they considered him a prophet" (Matthew 14:5). Instead, he had him arrested and bound and put him in prison.

Herod's wife Herodias even "nursed a grudge against John and wanted to kill him. But she was not able to because Herod feared John and protected him, knowing him to be a righteous and holy man" (Mark 6:19-20). She then sought an opportunity to show revenge on the prophet and one day her opportunity had come. On Herod's birthday, Herodias' daughter danced before Herod and his guests, and she pleased Herod so much that he promised with an oath to give her whatever she asked. She then went out and said to her mother, "What shall I ask for?" Her mother responded, "The head of John the Baptist." "At once the girl hurried in to the king with the request, 'I want you to give me right now the head of John the Baptist on a platter'" (Mark 6:24-25). Herod was "distressed" when he heard this, but because of his oath and his dinner guests, "he did not want to refuse her. So he immediately sent an executioner with orders to bring John's head. The man went, beheaded John in the prison and brought back his head on a platter. He presented it to the girl and she gave it to her mother" (Mark 6:27-28).

John would be remembered as a just and righteous man. It was written of him that he was a good man and had exhorted the Jews to lead righteous lives, to practice justice towards their neighbors and to live faithfully to God.[163] God's advent did not come during John's imprisonment but rather Herod's cavalry and the sword. Yet he was remembered by Jesus during his ministry as being more than a prophet and a man of righteousness.

Teachings to the Twelve

INTRODUCTION

Early in Jesus' ministry, he focused on raising future leaders who would carry on his work when he would no longer be present. He identified the kind of successors he wanted and among his prospective leaders were not those of the upper classes of society like the Pharisees and Sadducees. To avoid individuals who had a chip on their shoulder, he wanted everyday blue-color workers with lowly circumstances. He even sought his followers from the detested and demoralized district known as Galilee.

The twelve he appointed were as following: Simon Peter, mentioned first in Mark, also had the names Cephas, and Bar-Jona (son of Jona) and was the younger brother of Andrew. Simon was married during Jesus' ministry (Matthew 8:14) and continued to be married after his death (1 Corinthians 9:5). Andrew, along with Simon Peter, were from Bethsaida in Galilee and both were fisherman and followers of John the Baptist. James, son of Zebedee, was one of the Sons of Thunder and was a fisherman from Galilee. His younger brother John was commonly believed to be the "beloved disciple" of Jesus. Philip, who was also from Bethsaida in Galilee, was the first to be asked by Jesus to follow him (John 1:45) and his responsibility may have been in charge of the disciples' food supply. Bartholomew, a Galilean, was seemingly one of Philip's friend (John 1:45). Matthew was a hated tax collector in Capernaum of Galilee. He was possibly the brother of James, son of Alphaeus. Thomas the Galilean was a twin and most of the information we have concerning him comes from John's gospel that seemingly always portrayed him as one who could not understand the message and truth of Jesus. Thaddaeus, whose name means "gift of God", is only mentioned twice in the New Testament and nothing personally is mentioned about him at all in the Gospels. Simon, also known as the Zealot, was a revolutionary Galilean and was anti-Roman. And Judas Iscariot was the only disciple from Judea and was the treasurer of the group (John 12:5-6). After his betrayal and death, he was replaced in the twelve apostles by Matthias (Acts 1:20-26).

These chosen followers were all men and they would all be put to use. Although they represented all different kinds of people, they were all able to be taught and molded by the master. They were ordinary individuals whom Jesus would use to do an extraordinary work. Among the twelve were fishermen, a tax collector, and an anti-Roman zealot. They were men who were slow learners, who had power struggles and disbeliefs, and who spoke often times without thinking. Yet at the same time, they would be men who would witness stunning miracles that only the Old Testament prophets could only dream about. They would be men who would "turn the world upside down" (Acts 17:6) and who would see thousands come to the knowledge of Jesus Christ.

What was the purpose of their calling? Jesus appointed the twelve and designated them apostles "that they might be with him and that he might send them out to preach and to have authority to drive out demons" (Mark 3:14-15). They were chosen first "that they might be with him" and secondly that "he might send them out to preach and to have authority to drive out demons". Their first commission would be in a limited way, but after Jesus' departure, they would be trained to lead the church.

It would be established that the 12 apostles represented the 12 tribes of Israel. The number 12 suggests the new Israel and their selection and training constitute evidence that the Lord envisioned a church that he would build.[164] At the end of his public ministry, Jesus had nothing tangible to leave as a monument of his life work. There was no literature, nor was there an institution to memorialize him. He had chosen instead to invest himself in a small group of men.[165] It was these men whom he devoted himself almost exclusively to, especially before his death and after his resurrection. Their activities with Jesus prepared them for their future purpose when they would go into society, sometimes alone, carrying the gospel message to the ends of the earth. Jesus visualized them covering the whole human race and by starting the church, all of them would be used to carry out its work. They would "go" into many sectors of the Roman Empire and would proclaim the gospel with boldness and assurance.

ON EVANGELISM

The Samaritan Woman

All of Jesus' teachings to his followers would pertain directly or indirectly to the Kingdom of God. In light of his kingdom, he would prepare his followers and disciples to look at the harvests of people and at the same time, he would send them out to the harvest and teach them valuable lessons on evangelism. To teach his disciples about the importance of evangelizing the lost, Jesus first allowed them to observe him talking to a Samaritan woman (John 4). Despite the odds of even Jesus the Jew talking to an anti-Jewish Samaritan women, they were able to see the women leave her water pot and proclaim to the people of a nearby city that Jesus was truly the Messiah. Then almost immediately, the disciples observed lost and needy people coming out to see him.

Right after this incident, he told them to not say that there are yet four months till harvest time, but rather to look at the harvest and observe that they are already white. Jesus was not talking about the fields of crops and produce but rather of people. He was explaining to them that they did not have to wait to reap, for it was ready and waiting for them. He was trying to get them to see not only the scarcity of laborers and a gigantic field, but a world of people who are spiritually ready to receive his gospel. John the Baptist was instrumental in making ready a people prepared for the Lord and in the same way, Jesus, with all his sovereignty and wisdom, chose his disciples to be the means of sharing his good news to the lost as well.

The Seventy

In addition to his teachings on evangelism, he would send men and women into cities and towns and would use this to teach a valuable lesson to his disciples. In Luke 10, we see Jesus appointing "seventy-two others" and he sent them two by two ahead of him to every town and place where he was about to go. Who were these seventy? They would have been witnesses of his wonders, hearers of his teachings, and believers in him being the Messiah. Unlike his disciples, they were not close with Jesus during most facets of his ministry but they were glad to find out that he was interested in them enough to send them into the "harvest". Many of these individuals would have been the same followers who were companions with the apostles after Jesus' resurrection. They were sent out "two by two" not only for protection but for the strengthening and encouragement of one another. Even the wisest man aside from Jesus stated the benefits of two over one saying, "Two are better than one, because they have a good return for their work. If one falls down, his friend can help him up. But pity the man who falls and has no one to help him up" (Ecclesiastes 4:9-10).

These men and women were set out with an expectation of trouble and persecution awaiting them, for Jesus told them that he was going to send them out like lambs among wolves. Metaphorically, wolves were portraits of cruel, greedy, ravenous, and destructive men. Yet his followers were to act as lambs or sheep, portraying peaceable and non-threatening men and women of God who were easy targets as prey.

Jesus instructed them to not take a purse, bag, or sandals on their journey. In other words, they literally carried their homes with them. All they needed could be carried in a simple knapsack slung over their shoulders. Their command not to burden themselves with masses of provisions was to show reliance upon God, and the people whom God would use to provide for their needs. Jesus' instructions were similar to Elisha' instructions to his servant Gehazi stating, "Tuck your cloak into your belt, take my staff in your hand and run. If you meet anyone, do not greet him, and if anyone greets you, do not answer. Lay my staff on the boy's face" (2 Kings 4:29). Yet how strange and anti-cultural was this message, for if Jews were going in unfamiliar territory, especially from Jerusalem to Jericho, they would carry the necessary provisions to keep them safe (Luke 10:30).

When they entered a town and were welcomed, Jesus told them to eat what was set before them. They were not to be concerned about their diet or that which would be fulfilling to the stomach, but were to eat and drink only such as they were served. They were to be thankful and grateful, which would portray them as being true marks of Jesus' disciples. This way of thinking would be in direct contrast to the religious leaders, for they would fast to receive attention of men. They were to heal the sick that are there and were to tell them that the kingdom of God was near to them. This message of the kingdom would not only be Jesus' message but John's message who came before him. John spoke of the urgency of the kingdom and the seventy would have to do the same.

However, if they entered a town and were not welcomed, they were to go into its streets and say, "Even the dust of your town that sticks to our feet we wipe off against you. Yet be sure of this: The kingdom of God is near" (Luke 10:11). These men and women were to be bold as John in rejecting those who did not obey the words of God or his messenger. For those individuals who rejected them, they were to denounce the judgments of God against them. Since the gospel was brought to their very neighborhoods and they rejected it, they might just very well forfeit the grace of God. Jesus then told them that it would be more bearable on that day for Sodom than for that town. Although the people of Sodom and the surrounding cities rejected the warning given to them by Lot, Jesus was letting them know that the rejection of the gospel of his kingdom is a more dreadful crime and they will be chastised during the day of wrath.

After doing what they were commanded, these men and women returned with joy and told Jesus the good news, including the demons submitting to his name. Then Jesus would use this teaching as a valuable lesson for his disciples and would say to them, "Blessed are the eyes that see what you see. For I tell you that many prophets and kings wanted to see what you see but did not see it, and to hear what you hear but did not hear it" (Luke 10:23-24). He wanted to let them know of the unique blessing they had and that they must not take it for granted, for many former worshippers of God desired to have seen and experienced what they have.

The Twelve

On a different occasion, Jesus sent out his 12 disciples as recorded in Mark 6 and gave them virtually the same commissions as he gave the seventy other men and women. In the coming days, these men could look back upon this preaching mission and reflect that although the Lord was not with them in person, his power had accompanied them to accomplished great things.

ON PRAYER

In addition to teaching his disciples about being laborers in the harvest, he sought the opportunity to teach them about prayer. Luke states that "one day Jesus was praying in a certain place. When he finished, one of his disciples said to him, 'Lord, teach us to pray, just as John taught his disciples'" (Luke 11:1). Jesus would then proceed to speak to all of "them" and to teach them about prayer. In Matthew 6, we see Jesus actually talking to the multitudes and not specifically just to his disciples. Yet both passages would serve as teaching opportunities for Jesus to instruct them on how to pray.

Before giving them an example of a model prayer, he cautioned them to not be like the hypocrites who love to "pray standing in the synagogues and on the street corners to be seen by men" (Matthew 6:5). But rather praying in the open, he instructs them to "go into your room, close the door, and pray to your Father, who is unseen. Then your Father, who sees what is done in secret, will reward you" (Matthew 6:6). In addition, they were not to keep "babbling" like the pagans but rather to recognize that God their Father knows what they need before they ask.

The Model Prayer

Then Jesus proceeded to give his disciples and followers a model prayer. He states, "This, then, is how you should pray: 'Our Father in heaven, hallowed be your name'". By this opening address, Jesus criticized the Gentiles for long prayers, for they would open by addressing their deities with long greetings. Why? Because they desired to make sure that they used all the correct titles for their god. Addressing God with one title was in direct contrast to Caesar who understood himself as being "the emperor Caesar, Galerius, Valerius, Maximanus, Invictus, Augustus, Pontifex Maximus, Germanicus Maximus, Egypticus Maximus..."[166] Jesus invited his followers to see a new reality where words were petite but powerful.

Jesus lived in a world where the public reading of the Bible was only in Hebrew, and prayers had to be offered in that language. When he took the giant step of endorsing Aramaic as an acceptable language for prayer and worship, he opened the door for the New Testament to be written in Greek (not Hebrew) and then translated into other languages.[167] He taught his disciples to pray "abba" (meaning Fathers), yet it appeared that when he addressed his prayers to abba, he was to some extent differentiating himself from the common practice, and perhaps many if not most Jews would have found it awkward to address God simply as 'abba.'[168] Yet, Jesus' strange teachings of how to address God would serve as a model for his future followers despite how uncomfortable it may seem. He was telling all of the Jews that this address was not sacra-religious or heresy but rather the proper way of addressing God.

The location of God from Jesus' standpoint was "in heaven" and Jesus was letting his followers know that God was far but at the same time was still near. Despite the physical distance, his children were still able to call him "our" Father. "Hallowed be thy name" is an expression of giving glory to God. Mankind was created to praise and worship God, and even if everything else is unclean, God's name was holy.

Jesus' prayer gave reference to his kingdom, for he states, "Thy kingdom come." The Lord's Prayer contained no reference to Jerusalem or the temple, and the disciples were taught to pray for the Kingdom of God to come "on earth," which reflects a global concern for all people.[169] What God has promised should be prayed for by his people and Jesus preached that his Father's kingdom could arrive at any moment. Therefore, it should be sought for at all times.

Bread symbolized all that we eat and Jesus desired his followers to ask God to "give us today our daily bread" and to "forgive us our debts as we also have forgiven our debtors" (Matthew 6:11-12). Debts were unfulfilled obligations toward either God or fellow human beings and consisted of those things one has left undone. This prayer was relevant to the Galilean peasants of that day because food and debts were their most troubling issues. It brought them relief and comfort to be able to pray for help with these issues. At the same time, the disciples were able to understand that there was no need to worry about tomorrow. Those who trust in him must continually depend on him for provision and providence, and must not worry. In addition, they must recognize that their relationships with God and with their neighbors were closely tied.

Jesus knew that the multitudes and his followers needed protection and he included in his prayer that they ask God to lead them "not into temptation, but deliver" them "from the evil one" (Matthew 6:13). The word "temptation" can also mean trial and his disciples would understand this reality sooner or later, for Peter stated, "Be self-controlled and alert. Your enemy the devil prowls around like a roaring lion looking for someone to devour" (1 Peter 5:8).

In conclusion, Jesus wanted his followers to acknowledge God's supremacy and position as the almighty ruler. He states, "For yours is the kingdom and the power and the glory forever. Amen" (Matthew 6:13). This concluding phrase elevates God and puts him on display. "Amen" confirms and grants their prayer as already taken place and sealed with God's approval.

The Example of Prayer

Jesus even taught the importance of prayer by being a model. Luke 3:21 states that "when all the people were baptized, it came to pass, that Jesus also being baptized, and praying, the heaven was opened." Luke 5:16 says, "And he withdrew himself into the wilderness, and prayed." Luke 6:12 says, "And it came to pass in those days, that he went out into a mountain to pray, and continued all night in prayer to God." The example of Jesus often withdrawing himself to lonely places shows that private time with God must take place. He prayed because he desired to maintain communion with his Father and to know his will. By his example, the disciples certainly took notice and they were able to see it as a delight and not an obligation.

ON SERVANT-HOOD

Faithfulness to God

Jesus desired his disciples to be seen as individuals who were servants. One of his teachings to his disciples on servant-hood came right after a parable of the shrewd manager (Luke 16:1-13) who was esteemed by his master at the end of the story. Then looking at his disciples, Jesus said, "Whoever can be trusted with very little can also be trusted with much, and whoever is dishonest with very little will also be dishonest with much. So if you have not been trustworthy in handling worldly wealth, who will trust you with true riches? And if you have not been trustworthy with someone else's property, who will give you property of your own" (Luke 16:10-12). Portraying the insignificance of money, Jesus was telling them that if an individual was not faithful in managing the little he has, he would never be faithful in managing that which is great.

These words then led up to Jesus telling them that "no servant can serve two masters. Either he will hate the one and love the other, or he will be devoted to the one and despise the other. You cannot serve both God and money" (Luke 16:13). One of the meanings of service is to minister and Jesus was not only stating the impossibility of serving both God and money, but the deceptiveness of the one who thinks he can. He then gave an incentive that if any man will serve him, he will be honored by the Father (John 12:26).

Humility before God

Jesus gives another story in Luke 18 about a Pharisee and a tax collector who went up to the temple to pray. The Pharisee's was full of pride and self-centeredness, and his character consisted of arrogant assumptions of his own worth as he looked upon others with disrespect and ridicule. But the tax collector was more honest in his appraisal of himself when he looked to God alone for mercy. Instead of declaring to God his personal acts of righteousness, he was willing to humbly give his whole life to him. His humble prayer only consisted of asking God for mercy because of his many transgressions.

After the story, Jesus explained to his disciples that the tax collector went home forgiven and justified rather than the Pharisee. He then uttered these powerful words, "Everyone who exalts himself will be humbled, and he who humbles himself will be exalted" (Luke 18:14).

Jesus' Teachings and Example

Throughout his ministry, Jesus taught servant-hood in many settings and surroundings to both the multitudes and to his disciples. He stated, "If someone strikes you on the right cheek, turn to him the other also" (Matthew 5:39) and "if someone forces you to go one mile, go with him two miles" (Matthew 5:41). He gave them these commandments so that they would be obedient to him and that others would recognize that they were his followers and disciples (John 13:35).

Although Jesus was essentially a leader, he did not "come to be served, but to serve." In John 13:5, he took a basin and towel and washed his disciple's feet, which showed meekness. As he washed his disciples' feet, he told them, "I have set you an example that you should do as I have done for you. I tell you the truth, no servant is greater than his master, nor is a messenger greater than the one who sent him. Now that you know these things, you will be blessed if you do them" (John 13:15-17). He reminded his followers that the motivation of his mission was to minister rather than to be served (Mark 10:45). When the Jews tried to make him king, he avoided their actions (John 6:15). Instead of riding upon a strong horse, he fulfilled prophecy by riding into Jerusalem upon a weak and unattractive donkey.

The multitudes and his disciples were able to hear and see his teachings of servant-hood that totally went against society. In a world where the poor and destitute only looked out for themselves and the religious leaders only desired to be seen of others, Jesus taught just the opposite. He encouraged his disciples to think differently and to act atypical regardless of what the culture demanded.

ON DISCIPLESHIP

Throughout his entire ministry, Jesus taught his followers the nature and character of discipleship. A disciple, which is simply the Greek word for student, means a learner or a pupil. One of his teachings spoke of a disciple as not being "above his master, nor the servant above his lord" (Matthew 10:24). This teaching was totally in direct contrast to the life of the religious leaders, specifically the Pharisees, for they believed that they were above the law. They not only lived a self-righteous life but they would pride themselves in their ability to interpret Mosaic Law with precision, which often times caused strife. Unfortunately, they could not constitute as a disciple of Jesus.

On one occasion, he told large crowds, "If anyone comes to me and does not hate his father and mother, his wife and children, his brothers and sisters, yes, even his own life, he cannot be my disciple. And anyone who does not carry his cross and follow me cannot be my disciple." (Luke 14:26-27). He was not just telling them of what discipleship is all about, but rather the conditions of what it would take to be one of his disciples, which grants a special privilege and eternal reward. An individual must consider his family and even his own life as being second, and must elevate Jesus as number one. To sum this teaching up, Jesus stated that if "any of you who does not give up everything he has cannot be my disciple" (Luke 14:33).

Jesus elevates the facts of knowing truth to discipleship and states, "If you hold to my teaching, you are really my disciples. Then you will know the truth, and the truth will set you free" (John 8:31-32). The word "hold" means to remain, abide, and to not depart. Speaking specifically to the believing Jews, he was telling them that holding on to his teachings qualifies one to being his disciple. At the same time, he was letting them know that truth was not relative and could not be reasoned with, and therefore, it was of necessity to know the unchanging truth. We know that his disciples were around and eventually grasped on to this truth, for John later stated in his epistle, "Dear children, this is the last hour; and as you have heard that the antichrist is coming, even now many antichrists have come. This is how we know it is the last hour. They went out from us, but they did not really belong to us. For if they had belonged to us, they would have remained with us; but their going showed that none of them belonged to us" (1 John 2:18-19).

ON FAITH

Jesus' disciples learned the essentials of faith during their early encounters with him, for having left their various occupations, they were without a means of livelihood. But so was their Master. Jesus had left the carpenter shop behind even as they had left their nets behind. His example taught that being grateful and content with what they had and for their daily provisions was the true essence of faith.

The Power of Faith

The disciples would visibly see a man's faith who was not even a follower of Jesus. Matthew 8 states that a centurion, an officer in the Roman Army, came to Jesus telling him that his servant lies at home paralyzed and is suffering terribly. Jesus told him that he would go and heal him but the centurion replied, "Lord, I do not deserve to have you come under my roof. But just say the word, and my servant will be healed. For I myself am a man under authority, with soldiers under me. I tell this one, 'Go,' and he goes; and that one, 'Come,' and he comes. I say to my servant, 'Do this,' and he does it" (Matthew 8:8-9). After hearing this, Jesus was astonished and responded to those around him, "I tell you the truth, I have not found anyone in Israel with such great faith" (Matthew 8:10). He then assured the centurion that his servant would be healed.

The centurion did not have a pre-planned speech but his words came from his heart. More importantly, he knew something about Jesus that the disciples did not yet comprehend. He understood the power of God and the fact that his very words were able to heal and not just his actual presence in his home. His measure of faith would be the foundation of the faith that all future "disciples" of Jesus would need to have once he would leave earth. All of his future followers would not physically have the luxury of having Jesus come to their house but would need to have faith like the centurion in believing and trusting that he could heal by his very words.

The Lack of Faith

Later on in his ministry, there were specific occasions where Jesus taught his disciples on the disposition of faith. One of these occasions occurred when a man approached Jesus and knelt before him saying, "Lord, have mercy on my son. He has seizures and is suffering greatly. He often falls into the fire or into the water. I brought him to your disciples, but they could not heal him" (Matthew 17:15-16). The disciples' faltering faith caused themselves to be ineffective and powerless in ministry. Because of this, they were embarrassed and their lack of faith was put out in the forefront in view of both Jesus and a crowd of people.

After hearing these embarrassing words, Jesus replied, "O unbelieving and perverse generation, how long shall I stay with you? How long shall I put up with you? Bring the boy here to me" (Matthew 17:18). After being with his disciples for a long time, his frustration was made evident and he even wondered how long was this wavering faith going to continue. Yet, he did not loose faith in his followers but prepared to show his love to both them and to the distressed boy. Immediately, he rebuked the demon inside the boy and after the demon came out, the boy was healed.

After seeing Jesus succeed in healing the boy after his disciples had disastrously failed, they came to him in private and asked, "Why couldn't we drive it out?" He replied, "Because you have so little faith. I tell you the truth, if you have faith as small as a mustard seed, you can say to this mountain, 'Move from here to there' and it will move. Nothing will be impossible for you" (Matthew 17:20-21). The disciples desired to avoid embarrassment that might have resulted publicly and asked their question in private. Yet, Jesus boldly tells them that it was their lack of faith that caused them to be ineffective. They knew that they had some faith, for they tried to help the child. But Jesus was trying to tell them about having the faith that can move mountains and the faith that they can live life knowing that nothing would be impossible to them. His lesson encompassed the fact that all things were possible through faith despite the situation.

<u>Teachings Promoting Blessings</u>

INTRODUCTION

The peoples of whom Jesus primarily ministered to were the lower classes of society. This class was made up of peasants, artisans, those who were unclean, and those who were criminals and extremely poor. Peasants were not only poor but they were relatively powerless. Comprising of the largest of the classes in the Roman society, these people constantly carried the greatest burden of taxation, military mobilization, and of being controlled. Because of this, they were always in confrontation with the authorities and the elite. They certainly desired to have self identity, the ownership of land, money, good health, honor and respect, rank and authority, and influence, but these were all hard to obtain. They lacked many necessities for their everyday needs and they lived under the conditions of being nonexistent, for they were mere "nobodies" from virtually those who were not peasants. Their land, money, jobs, food and resources were mostly controlled by the upper class and they constantly lived their lives searching for happiness.

Yet, these very people would soon understand that Jesus the Messiah came to earth for this very reason, that is to meet their particular needs. He came to promote blessings and happiness in a world that only oppressed them. He came to give them hope and a future in a world that constantly suppressed them and took away their hard earned living. To both the lower classes and the upper classes of society, Jesus' teachings were considered "strange" and atypical, for he truly went against the norm of his day. However, Jesus was not concerned about how he was perceived, for he knew his vision, mission, and objective.

Matthew 5 states that upon seeing a great multitude, "he went up on a mountainside and sat down. His disciples came to him, and he began to teach them saying..." (Matthew 5:1-2). It was typical for Jesus to be moved with compassion upon seeing crowds and he probably was heart-felt when he saw such these people coming to him to hear him. The traditional site of this mountain is seven miles southwest of Capernaum known as the Horns of Hattin.

In the first twelve verses of Matthew 5, Jesus gives declarations of happiness to the multitudes. (The word "blessed" actually means "happy" in the Greek). These nine simple sayings to the multitudes are known as the "beatitudes", a declaration of both mundane happiness but God-inspired happiness. A beatitude is a declaration that someone or something is blessed by God, and it often has a dual configuration involving, in the first part, a statement of who or what is blessed and, in the part, the explanation of why someone or it is blessed. The first statement affirms a happy state that already exists and the second statement affirms a future that allows one even now to live a happy life.[170]

TO THE DESTITUTE

Jesus' first declaration stated, "Blessed are the poor in spirit, for theirs is the Kingdom of Heaven" (Matthew 5:3). The Greek word here for poor is *ptōchos*. Yet, Jesus could have used the more general word *penēs*, a less severe word for poor, and not the word *ptōchos*. If "the poor" are understood only spiritually, it makes no difference whether the text is phrased as "the poor" or "the destitute," for humans standing spiritually before God, both terms mean the same thing. But it makes a world of difference which term you use when you are speaking both economically and socially as well as spiritually and religiously.[171]

So, from an economical standpoint, what really was the difference between the Greek words for poor and the destitute? Well, those who were poor (*penēs*) were family farmers who made a bare subsistence living from year to year. Although these people needed to work, they had enough to survive. However, the destitute (*ptōchos*) were sharecroppers and/or day-laborer whose status were pushed, by disease or debt, draught or death, off the land into destitution and begging.[172] They suffered from the more severe forms of poverty and were not only helpless but had nothing at all. They would have lost many if not all of their family and social connections, and they lived life wandering. They were virtually outsiders to all those around them, they would be unable to pay taxes, and they possessed little or no resources.

In addition, the distinction between poverty and destitution was much more absolute in rural areas than in urban situations. The great divide between the poor and the destitute coincided generally with that between the landed peasant and the landless peasant, and especially between the landed peasant and the dispossessed peasant.[173] Thus, Jesus was not speaking to the well off peasants (*penēs*) but to the dispossessed peasants (*ptōchos*) seeking to reinstate their dignity and security.

But he did not stop with just the "poor" but stated blessed are the "poor in spirit". The word spirit generally coincided with the third person of the triune God, the Holy Spirit, who is coequal and coeternal with the Father and the Son. But more specifically, Jesus was referring to the attitude and character of individuals who emphasized and portrayed his personality and character. One thing the destitute understood in Jesus' day was that unless they persistently wandered and yearned for food, water, and the basic necessities in life, they would physically die. Thus from the spiritual perspective, they had to apply this same desire with the acquisition of the attitude and character of the Spirit of God in order to enter the Kingdom of God.

And yes, it was this very Kingdom of God that Jesus stated that these destitute Jews were able to enter. This Kingdom of God or Heaven had to do with the rule of God in the lives of individuals and societies. Yet for Jesus to say "for theirs is the Kingdom of Heaven", he was letting those who were destitute, wanderers, and had nothing at all to know that they could have the privilege of becoming members of God's Kingdom. But why? Did he really think that bums and beggars, who were haters of Roman authorities and aristocrats, were actually blessed by God? The answer is emphatically yes! From Jesus' perspective, his kingdom was precisely focused on the destitute and the dispossessed and not the rich. He was teaching especially to those dispossessed peasants with an intense desire to reinstate their dignity and disposition.

To the Mourners

Jesus' second declaration stated, "Blessed are those who mourn, for they will be comforted" (Matthew 5:4). Suffering is an extraordinary teacher and one knows little about the great depths of the human spirit until he has endured suffering. In addition, pain has a way of rearranging one's priorities.[174] This is exactly what has rearranged the poor Jews in their Mediterranean society, for they had many reasons to mourn.

Despite the unpredictable weather that could destroy their toiled vegetation, the Jews sorrowed over their constant oppression from the Roman authorities. When the soldiers demanded John to tell them what they needed to repent from, John told them to not "extort money and don't accuse people falsely - be content with your pay" (Luke 3:14). Who were these soldiers accusing "falsely" and acting violently against because their "wages" were low? It was these very people that were sitting and listening to Jesus. Apparently, Roman soldiers would demand money from the poor Jews and if they resisted, they would falsely accuse them of a misdemeanor before the chief priests. Why would they act in this manner? Because their wages were low. They were trying to get ahead in society and with the money they were receiving from the government, they were not able to do so. This was just one of the many examples why these poor people were "mourning".

At the same time, it is one thing to mourn, yet it is another thing to know that one's mourning will never cease. This was the case for the people sitting and listening to Jesus. The words "comfort" would have been a word that would not even be in their vocabulary. Their economic situation was an ongoing phenomenon and there was no way of getting out of it. Even though many of the farmers would produce enough harvest to get ahead in society, their surplus was taken away from the Roman elite so that they would never arise above their current situation.

Nonetheless, Jesus told them some strange teachings regarding their current situation. His teachings pertained to mourning, yet from a kingdom's perspective. He would equate this same mourning that the Jews would have full knowledge about to a mourning that would soon be "comforted". From the people's perspective, this comforting would be impossible in light of their current world in which they lived. But from Jesus' perspective, he would be able to comfort them and his presence would reassure them and conciliate their situation. They would not have to repeatedly endure their hardships because comfort would soon arise.

As these people would continually listen to Jesus' teaching, they would soon find out that this comfort could only be found through him. But for the moment, although this was strange teachings, it was truly teachings that promoted blessings and happiness for them. It truly gave them hope to know that their current situation did not have to stay the same.

To the Meek

Jesus' third declaration stated, "Blessed are the meek, for they will inherit the earth" (Matthew 3:5). Meekness means mildness of disposition and gentleness of spirit, and is the opposite of self-assertiveness and self-interest. One who is meek is not engaged with their own identity at all, and from Jesus' perspective, it was these people who would inherit the land. The Jews understood inheritance to mean receiving a lot, becoming an heir, receiving their assigned portion, receiving as one's own, and ultimately becoming partakers of. Yet this was strange teachings to them in light of knowing who usually would inherit the land. In the First Century, the area that encompassed Galilee, Samaria and Judea was torn with wars and rumors of wars, and such an affirmation would have resonated deeply with the powerless in Jesus' audience. Here, Jesus is promising that the meek will inherit the land rather than the powerful. Rome and the Zealots would soon be engaged in all-out war to win political and military control over that same land. Yet Jesus had a different idea about who had rights to it.[175]

Jesus' teachings about the meek inheriting the earth was also strange because it seemed as if he was ignoring Jewish history and the Jew's current state of affairs regarding the land that was supposed to have been theirs. Their unfortunate circumstance consisted of the fact that they were frequently required to become farmers on the very land that had belonged to their ancestors for generations. Yet for many of them, their land was taken from them and was controlled by foreigners. In return, they wanted divine justice! Those specific Jews who resisted Roman oppression often did so by resorting to banditry. Bandits encouraged the people to stress their liberty and not to submit to the Roman Empire. However, Jesus teachings were against the common thought patterns of the day. He stated that it would be those who had a mild disposition, a gentle spirit, and one who was self-less who would actually possess the land and not the bandits.

The Jews would soon come to the realization that Jesus' terminology of "inherit" would portray a meaning that they were not accustomed to. They only understood inheritance to mean the acquiring of a physical portion of land that they would currently dwell. In the Old Testament, we see examples of this in Numbers 32:32, 1 Chronicles 16:18, and in Zechariah 2:12. Yet, Jesus came on the scene speaking of inheritance from a kingdom perspective and he spoke of the opportunity for people to "inherit" eternal life (Matthew 19:29; Mark 10:17; Luke 10:25). His disciples and followers caught on to this and they only spoke of "inherit" as pertaining to "the Kingdom of God" (1 Corinthians 6:9), salvation (Hebrews 1:14), this blessing (Hebrews 12:17), and the kingdom he promised those who love him (James 2:5). John the apostle sums up this New Testament thought by telling the churches that "he who overcomes will inherit all this" (Revelation 21:7), specifically speaking of "the Holy City, the New Jerusalem, coming down out of heaven from God, prepared as a bride beautifully dressed for her husband" (Revelation 21:2). This was certainly the theological perspective of what Jesus was talking about concerning the meek inheriting the earth, for he was not talking about the physical land that was taken from them but rather a lot and portion of the Holy City, the New Jerusalem.

To the Hungry and Thirsty

Jesus' fourth declaration stated, "Blessed are those who hunger and thirst for righteousness, for they will be filled" (Matthew 5:6). There were an innumerable amount of people living day to day looking for food. Lazarus the beggar desiring to receive food from the rich man's table in Luke 16 was certainly not a rare occurrence in Israel. Those who were destitute of food were so common that Jesus even alluded to this fact saying to his disciples, "The poor you will always have with you, but you will not always have me" (Matthew 26:11). This was not an understatement for Jesus to say this and these very people were the ones who lived lives hungry and thirsty.

Yet Jesus gave these very people a hope and a future, and he would compare this same hunger and thirst that would daily consume their minds to a hunger and thirst after "righteousness." This word righteousness encompassed several similar meanings of which the Jews would have certainly understood. Righteousness incorporated the keeping of God's laws, but more profoundly it denoted a way of living that was acceptable to God and a lifestyle which one could attain his approval. It characterized one who portrayed honesty, virtue, decency, rightness, and correctness of thinking and feeling. In a narrower sense, it meant the bestowal of justice. Thus, for Jesus to talk about people hungering and thirsting after righteousness was a way for him to use words embedded in physical needs but actually illustrating spiritual realities.

Concerning this righteousness, Jesus does not say, "Blessed are those who live righteously and maintain a righteous lifestyle" but rather, "Blessed are those who hunger and thirst after righteousness". The statement presupposes that righteousness is something the faithful continuously strive after. The blessed are not those who arrive but those who continue, at whatever cost, in their pilgrimage toward a more perfect righteousness. The constant, relentless drive toward righteousness characterizes the blessed.[176] Righteousness does not mean the ethical quality of a person nor does not mean any quality at all, but rather a relationship. That is, righteousness is not something a person has on his own, rather it is something he has in the verdict of the "forum" to which he is accountable.[177]

The affirmative promise that Jesus gave to these physically hungry and thirsty people was that "they will be filled". The people certainly remembered Moses and the Israelites and how God "filled" them with manna from heaven. Yet they were assured that just as God provided for them, he would be able to provide and fill them. However, this filling from Jesus' perspective was not physical satisfaction of hunger and thirst, but rather the satisfaction that God's Kingdom would bring them if they "hunger and thirst for righteousness."

It was evident that Jesus was concerned about their spiritual satisfaction that could never cause them to be hungry again. Physical hunger could only be satisfied for the moment and this was the same message that Jesus was trying to tell the woman at the women (John 4:14). Regardless of how full these people may become in their earthly state, death always resulted. This is why Jesus' "filled" concerned a spiritual state and not a physically one. From his perspective, the desire for righteousness was the only desire of man that could be truly and finally satisfied, and he would be the only one who could give them what they physically lack.

To the Merciful

Jesus' fifth declaration stated, "Blessed are the merciful, for they will be shown mercy" (Matthew 5:7). The word "mercy" was almost unheard of during Jesus' epoch on earth. In light of what all the Jews had experienced since Rome took over their land, the only thing that was on their mind was vengeance.

The people were not only given a general taxation, but the Romans required an additional taxation as well. Not only were they taxed doubled but their taxing occasionally amounted to as much as 40% of production. The Romans would also obtain additional resources during times of war. If the people didn't pay, the Romans usually responded with military force. In addition, the Jews and all the people felt the urbanization of Rome's conquest. As the empire continued to grow, Rome sought land for commercial operation and territorial expansion. As a result, this prompted social inequality and the need for the people to be totally dependent on others.

However, from Jesus' perspective, to respond to human need with compassion and action was at the core of what being merciful was all about. To be merciful and to obtain mercy were profoundly related to forgiving and being forgiven.[178] It would be unheard of for these people to show mercy to the Romans who were so undeserving. But Jesus states that all types of unmerciful conduct are condemned. Here, the very meaning of the word merciful not only meant "compassion", "kind", and "lenient" but also "forgiving" and "gracious". Thus, Jesus was trying to let these people know that they must not only show love and kindness to those who are undeserving, but they must also forgive. To him, this was the very essence of what showing mercy was all about.

Although this would not be easy, Jesus assured them that if they are "merciful", they "will be shown mercy". The Jews would soon come to realize that this showing of mercy would only come from God, yet it would not be like the mercy they have seen in the past. This showing would be guaranteed and unconditional. The New Testament writers soon understood the extent of God's mercy shown to them, for Paul stated, "...I was shown mercy so that in me, the worst of sinners, Christ Jesus might display his unlimited patience as an example for those who would believe on him and receive eternal life" (1 Timothy 1:16). After Paul believed on Jesus, he was shown this mercy from him and was able to received eternal life. This same eternal life obtained through God's Kingdom would be the same focus of Jesus' teachings on earth.

TO THE PURE

Jesus' sixth declaration stated, "Blessed are the pure in heart, for they will see God" (Matthew 5:8). The meaning of pure applies to those who are physically clean like in a levitical sense as well as to those who are ethically blameless. These people understood the disposition of being pure before God. Their very history testified of the fact that God strikes people dead for seemingly simple acts of disobedience (1 Chronicles 13:9-10) and that he had to deal with acts of impurity (Exodus 32).

But Jesus did not just say, "Blessed are the pure" but rather "Blessed are the pure in heart". According to the Scriptures, it is the heart that understands, that reasons and thinks, and that believes and loves. The feelings, the mind and the will were all part of "the heart."[179] The New Testament describes the heart in terms such as soul, spirit, heart, mind, and conscience. These terms showcase the heart as being used to describe the immaterial part of man. It is the nucleus of the real person and is the main catalyst by which man is able to serve and obey God. The physical heart was fully responsible for man's life, but in the spiritual sense, there was just as much value. The Jews would have remembered how Moses understood the importance of the heart when he warned the Israelites to not let their hearts "be not deceived" so that they would "turn aside" and worship other gods (Deuteronomy 11:16).

As a result, the blessings for those who are pure in heart was the assurance that "they will see God". The Jews would have certainly remembered when God told Moses, "When my glory passes by, I will put you in a cleft in the rock and cover you with my hand until I have passed by. Then I will remove my hand and you will see my back; but my face must not be seen" (Exodus 33:22-23). But Moses never saw God's "face" but rather his "back". So here, Jesus was telling the Jews that they would be able to experience something that Moses was unable to experience.

This "seeing" him would not be from a spiritual or mystical perspective, for this word actually means to physically look at, to behold, and even to allow ones self to be seen. There was certainly an Old Testament expectation of seeing God, for Job stated, "And after my skin has been destroyed, yet in my flesh I will see God" (Job 19:26). When Jesus came on the scene, he would introduce the Kingdom of God and would tell the Jews, "I tell you the truth, no one can see the Kingdom of God unless he is born again" (John 3:3). Later, he would assure the Jews, "Did I not tell you that if you believed, you would see the glory of God" (John 11:40). Therefore, Jesus assures them that if they are "pure in heart", they shall "see God" face to face (Revelation 22:4; 1 John 3:2).

TO THE PEACEMAKERS

Jesus' seventh declaration stated, "Blessed are the peacemakers, for they will be called sons of God" (Matthew 5:9). The Jews primarily saw peace as the absence of war or the cessation of violence. They saw wars as solving problems and were use to living in a world where nations would conquer other nations as not only a means of maintaining control but in establishing peace. They remembered their ancestors having long periods of rest for 40 years (Judges 3:11) after being subdued by foreign nations. They remembered having their own democratic rule beginning with King Saul only to have it taken away from them by the Assyrians and Babylonians. They remembered their times of peace in the midst of war, for this was their world and how they saw life.

Yet Jesus came teaching strange messages concerning a different kind of peace then what the multitudes were used to seeing. The actual word for peacemaker means one who loves peace. The opposite of this kind of person would be one who was hostile and aggressive. Jesus' interpretation of a peacemaker was one who did not see war as its first or even last option. He saw a world where men would not try to overthrow the Roman government because of injustice but rather would promote tranquility. He proclaimed blessings for those who could bring peace to their fellow men who are at strife between or among themselves.

It was apparent that the surroundings and temperament of Jesus' world did not consist of the way of peace. One of the ways we know this was true was through the angels' proclamation of good news to the shepherds stating, "Glory to God in the highest, and on earth peace, good will toward men" (Luke 2:14). From the lowly shepherd's standpoint, this peace would be one of the enticing facets that would convince them of the coming Messiah and the change he would bring to the world. During Jesus' ministry, he encouraged the people stating, "Have salt in yourselves, and be at peace with each other" (Mark 9:50). Because of an apparent deficiency of peace, Jesus had to encourage the multitudes to "be at peace with each other." He would even inform his followers that his peace would be different. He stated, "Peace I leave with you; my peace I give you. I do not give to you as the world gives" (John 14:27).

Yet Jesus assured them that if they "are the peacemakers," they will be called "sons of God". The word "son" means sonship through physical descent or from a legal transaction. The Jews may have remembered the past references of "sons of God" being applied to divine angelic beings (Job 1:6; 38:7), but they would soon come to realize the unique privilege of being a member of God's family just like the angels, but with a greater privilege. From the kingdom's standpoint, men are not by nature a child of God but are considered "children" of wrath (Ephesians 2:3) and are typified as being disobedient (Ephesians 2:2-4). However, those who are "sons of God" are adopted in a legal sense into the family of God (John 1:12). This adoption is based on faith (Galatians 3:26) and the benefits are numerous. Although the multitudes listening to Jesus would not understand the full extent of son-ship, they would soon find out that this special privilege would include God's unconditional love, his comfort and care, his inheritance and special access to God himself. Such shall be called the "sons of God" because they are most like God when they promote peace and not hostility and aggravation.

To the Persecuted

Jesus' eighth declaration stated, "Blessed are those who are persecuted because of righteousness, for theirs is the Kingdom of Heaven" (Matthew 5:10). In essence, persecution meant harassment, maltreatment, and the suffering on an account of something. Along with Jesus' other declarations, the multitudes understood persecution quite well. The Jew's history displayed numerous encounters of persecution from foreign nations. The Assyrians were known to have put hooks through their captive's nose and would carry them away with shackles. This is exactly what the Jews experienced when they were conquered by this nation some hundreds of years earlier. At the same time, they were currently experiencing persecution from the Roman authorities and the elite. Certainly, they would have been able to identity with those who were persecuted.

Yet Jesus equated what the multitudes understood as persecution in their current state to being persecuted for living righteous. Righteousness was a state and not simply an act, and it was a position of an individual of where he ought to be and not where he thinks or desire he should be. It is the condition acceptable to God, the way in which man may attain his state of approval, and includes the attributes of integrity, virtue, purity, and rightness. So from Jesus' perspective, no blessing would occur for those who were simply persecuted. If there was, virtually all of those in the lower classes of society would receive it. But here Jesus is showcasing the blessings for those who are persecuted "because of righteousness". He is elevating the persecuted moral above the persecuted masses.

To the people, this was certainly strange and unfamiliar teachings. Yet Jesus would declare that those who are persecuted because of righteousness sake would receive the blessing of his kingdom.

TO THE INSULTED, PERSECUTED AND FALSELY ACCUSED

Jesus' ninth and final declaration stated, "Blessed are you when people insult you, persecute you and falsely say all kinds of evil against you because of me. Rejoice and be glad, because great is your reward in heaven, for in the same way they persecuted the prophets who were before you" (Matthew 5:11-12). It was no accident or a random excess of words that Jesus targeted three groups of people. The first group included those who were reproached and reviled. These were the ones who had been criticized, reprimanded, blamed, and even scolded for whatever reasons. The second group were those who were persecuted. These people could have been harassed, molested, and/or even mistreated. And the third group included those who were falsely accused of all kinds of evil. These were people who were lied against, deceived by a lie, and/or those who were deliberately spoken against falsely. Jesus seemingly would attempt to cover all of the people's personal and economical hardships and maltreatments with no one left out of needing a blessing.

But it was not the maltreatment alone that constituted a blessing but rather those who suffered because of his name sake. Out of all the prior eight beatitudes given, Jesus put himself on a pedestal for the multitudes to consider. He basically told them that unless they were insulted, persecuted and falsely accused because of his name sake, no blessing would be granted. It was obvious that no one currently was being mistreated because of his sake, for these teachings were spoken more towards the onset of his ministry. But very soon, his followers would have to make a choice whether they would take a stand for his name or deny him. For those who would suffering for his name, Jesus tells them to "rejoice and be glad," a more a unusual response. It was unheard of for anyone to rejoice because of being criticized and blamed, for being harassed and molested, and for being lied against and deceived. Yet he went against the cultural norms of the day to tell the multitudes how they should react in light of the blessedness of the Kingdom of God.

But why did they need to rejoice? Because Jesus said their "reward" would be "great" in "heaven." The Jews recognized heaven as being a place where God "thundered" from (2 Samuel 22:14), where he was ruler over (Ezra 5:11), and where the entire expanse was located in the sky. Yet Jesus was not talking about all this but rather about an eternal and perfect place where God and other heavenly beings reside; the place where he was going "to prepare" for those who believe in him (John 14:2), where one's "citizenship" dwells (Philemon 3:20), and where "names are written" (Hebrews 12:23).

In addition, Jesus gave them further comfort in knowing that they would not be the only ones who would have to suffer for his name, for he states that even "the prophets" were persecuted who were before them. Some of the examples the Jews would have remembered of those persecuted included Isaiah, Elisha, and Daniel. From his perspective, the prophets would serve as examples of suffering and affliction, for they were also reproached and reviled, molested and mistreated, and falsely accused of all kinds of evil. Thus, the multitudes would not be alone if they suffered for his name sake and Jesus was trying to assure them of this fact.

Teachings of Parables

INTRODUCTION

Jesus' teachings were "strange", for they would go against the entire social norm of his day. Yet at the same time, they were original. He came proclaiming a kingdom, which all people were familiar with, but his kingdom was different than all others. It was not based on violence but on love and forgiveness, and it was open to the children and women, poor and destitute, and to the non-Jews alike.

The Nature of Parables

Unlike the other teachers of his day, Jesus used simple word-pictures, called parables, to help people recognize the nature of God and what his kingdom was all about. We know that this was his preferred way of teaching to the multitudes and to his disciples because Matthew 13:34 states, "Jesus spoke all these things to the crowd in parable. He did not say anything to them without using a parable."

Parables were everyday, simple, memorable stories, often including imagery, which give a single message in which people can relate to. They are quite difference than fables, myths (imaginary or unverifiable existence) allegories, and proverbs. A myth is something that you can't prove or disprove and today's meaning is typified as a parable or allegory. Although myths can be seen as "lies", Jesus' teaching of parables carried with it a disposition of truth, actuality, and credibility.

Jesus' stories were relative and appealed to the adolescent and to the aged, to the poor and to the prosperous, and to the scholar and to the simple. They had a dual meaning with the first incorporating a literal meaning and the second incorporating a deeper meaning of spiritual truth about his kingdom. What would really keep his audience on their toes was the often element of surprise or unexpected twist at the end.

The Understanding of Parables

It is not enough to just understand the parables of Jesus but rather to understand that which led up to the parable. It was what Jesus stated before the actual parable that actually constituted the basis and starting point for the rationale of why the parable was mentioned in the first place. In addition, the application and/or conclusion of the parable was important to understand the reason why the parable was given in the first place. His parables were interrelated because the common ground of them all focuses on the Kingdom of God. In looking at all the parables, the people were able to grasp bits and pieces from them all and were able to create a detailed profile of what will occur in the future. Yet without the background surrounding Jesus giving telling the parable and the application or conclusion at the end, the parable itself would have no significance.

THE BARREN FIG TREE

The Background

What led up to this parable was the allegation that Pilate had sent soldiers into the temple to perform bloody wrath on some of the Galileans while they were worshipping. This news was brought to Jesus of the death of these people "whose blood Pilate had mixed with their sacrifices" (Luke 13:1). Their blood unfortunately intermingled with that of the blood from the sacrifices that they were offering. This matter could have been brought to Jesus for several reasons. Maybe, they simply wanted to inform him of what had just taken place or perhaps anger him because he himself was from Nazareth of Galilee. Or maybe they simply wanted Jesus to take revenge on the Galileans who had died.

Regardless, Jesus responded to them and asked if they thought that they "were worse sinners than all the other Galileans because they suffered this way" (Luke 13:2). The Jews asked this question because they were self-righteous and they thought that they were not wicked sinners like those Galileans, and Jesus knew this. Although they had ancient prejudices reaching as far back as Job, Jesus had a different message, for he demanded repentance from these self-righteous Jews and stated, "But unless you repent, you too will all perish" (Luke 13:3).

The Parable

Then he spoke a parable intended to enforce his words of repentance. He said, "A man had a fig tree, planted in his vineyard..." (Luke 13:6). A fig tree with leaves would ripen in late May or early June, and if it didn't, it would be barren for the entire season. The common place for these trees to be raised would have been the way-side. Yet the advantage of this tree was that it was planted in a vineyard where it had better soil and care from the owner.

The owner of the tree, expecting fruit to have been grown on the tree, came and "went to look for fruit on it, but did not find any." He then vents and grumbles "to the man who took care of the vineyard" and tells him that for three years, he's been coming to look for fruit and has not found any. The tree was certainly not three years old because the owner had "planted" it and he was patient and not hasty, for he had waited a long time to see the results of his hard labor. Yet because of three years of frustrating encounters with no fruit on the tree, the owner proclaims its fate and tells the man to "cut it down." His reasoning behind his thought was "why should it use up the soil?" In other words, the tree was only taking up needed space in the vineyard and from the owner's perspective, there was no use of having a vineyard raised tree with no intention of bearing fruit.

But the man who took care of the vineyard had a different perspective. Instead of telling the owner to immediately cut the tree down, he tells him "leave it alone for one more year" and during that tenure, he would "dig around it and fertilize it" so that it would be given a better chance to produce. The keeper desired to give the barren tree a second change to produce, and thus, the owner would have the discomforts of maintaining more patience while the keeper of the vineyard would have the discomforts of toiling the ground. Yet the patience and labor of the men would not last forever, for the keeper stated that "if it bears fruit next year, fine! If not, then cut it down." To see the barren tree bring forth fruit would cause for rejoicing but to see yet another year of barrenness would cause for the demise of the tree. If the tree had to be cut down, it would certainly take work, but it would be the only hope for the future of the vineyard.

The Application

We can compare the potential cutting down of this tree to the unwatchful servant in Matthew 24:50-51. Jesus says, "The master of that servant will come on a day when he does not expect him and at an hour he is not aware of. He will cut him to pieces and assign him a place with the hypocrites, where there will be weeping and gnashing of teeth." In addition, the potential results of the tree is similar to the results of bad weeds that would be tied in bundles to be burned (Matthew 13:30) and bad fish, typifying the wicked, who would be thrown "into the fiery furnace, where there will be weeping and gnashing of teeth" (Matthew 13:50).

It is evident that Jesus compared repentance to that of bearing fruit. In the narrow and physical sense, his unusual teaching referred to the Jews, but in the spiritual sense it would refer to all persons alike. He would not only call them to repent and bear fruit but also all those who desire to enter into his kingdom. God did choose the Jews as a people and he led them through history for his special purpose. However, they deliberately chose to disobey and many chose not to repent. Therefore from his and John the Baptist's perspective, repentance was the way to escape perishing. Jesus was trying to let them know that his patience has been shown and would continue to be shown in hopes that repentance on their part would take place.

THE BUDDING FIG TREE

In the Gospels of Matthew, Mark, and Luke, we see the parable of the budding fig tree. Since most of Jesus' parables were only mentioned in either one or two Gospels, there must have been a noteworthy motivation for these Gospel writers to have all mentioned this parable.

The Background

What led up to this parable was Jesus' prediction of his Second Coming that would occur after the Rapture and the Great Tribulation. He states that "the sign of the Son of Man will appear in the sky...They will see the Son of Man coming on the clouds of the sky, with power and great glory" (Matthew 24:30). Yet instead of all the people on the earth rejoicing at his return, he states that they will all "mourn". After they observe the "signs in the sun, moon and stars" all the "nations will be in anguish and perplexity at the roaring and tossing of the sea. Men will faint from terror, apprehensive of what is coming on the world, for the heavenly bodies will be shaken" (Luke 21:25-26). This mourning will only take place from those who are destined to destruction, for he states that "he will send his angels with a loud trumpet call, and they will gather his elect from the four winds, from one end of the heavens to the other" (Matthew 24:31) and will obviously cast them into the fire.

The Parable

In light of these chilling words, Jesus demonstrated his great love, mercy, and forgiveness, and uses these future facts to give his disciples a parable that would give them warning and encouragement. He tells them, "Now learn this lesson from the fig tree: As soon as its twigs get tender and its leaves come out, you know that summer is near. Even so, when you see all these things, you know that it is near, right at the door." (Matthew 24:32-33). Jesus gave an obvious fact that all the Mediterranean people would understand. Because their very livelihood depended on produce harvested, they all would recognize the signs of a fig tree that would let them know that summer is near, for the budding and blossoming of the leaves are the pre-stages to this change.

The Gospel of Mark states Jesus saying that "when you see these things happening, you know that it is near, right at the door" (13:29). In light of what he was telling them before this parable, his disciples would be able to use this same judgment in their agrarian society to know that the advent of Jesus and the signs of his return are "right at the door". Luke also states that when they see "these things happening", they will "know that the Kingdom of God is near" (Luke 21:31). Again, this parable and every parable had "the Kingdom of God" at its main focus, and Jesus desired his followers to understand this foundational theme.

The Application

What a joy it was to know that Jesus did not want his followers or any individual to undergo the fear, anguish, and grief that would accompany his return. This parable would serve not only as a relief for those who would believed his words but also as a warning for those who chose to reject his teachings, despite how strange they may have been.

THE FRIEND AT MIDNIGHT

The Background

The rationale of this parable focuses on prayer. We know this because Luke 11:1-4 starts off with Jesus teaching his disciples how to pray, and it was this basis that led him to tell this parable. But what specifically about prayer was Jesus desiring to highlight? It would be one's boldness and shamelessness regarding one's prayers to God that he would soon portray in a story.

Leading up the parable, one of his disciples asked Jesus, "teach us to pray, just as John taught his disciples." He graciously answered his request and told them, "When you pray, say: 'Father, hallowed be your name, your kingdom come. Give us each day our daily bread. Forgive us our sins, for we also forgive everyone who sins against us. And lead us not into temptation" (Luke 11:2-4). His teachings on prayer emphasized not only its privilege and greatness but its detail and precision. He taught them how to address God, how to expect his future kingdom, how to ask for forgiveness, and how to ask God for protection against temptation. Throughout his ministry, the disciples were able to observe his habitual practices of going away and praying. From Jesus' perspective, people should not only expect great things from God when they pray but should make bold requests and not concern themselves with the shame that may accompany their praying endeavors.

The Parable

Then he stated a parable saying, "Suppose one of you has a friend, and he goes to him at midnight and says, 'Friend, lend me three loaves of bread, because a friend of mine on a journey has come to me, and I have nothing to set before him'" (Luke 11:5-6). Palestinian peasants bake on a daily basis and people in the village generally know who has some left over bread in the late evening. Because this Mediterranean society was a close-nit society, guests must leave villages with a good feeling about the warmth and generosity. The host must set something before him before he leaves, whether the wayfarer is really hungry or not.[180] He must offer the guest a complete unbroken loaf and to feed a guest with a partial loaf left from another meal would be an insult.[181] But from this friend's perspective, it was not easy in making the journey to the neighbor's house. As a matter of fact, it was quite embarrassing. Yes, the neighbor would desire to show hospitality to the borrower but it would be a rare occurrence for someone to ask this request at such an odd hour of the night when everyone in the house would certainly be asleep.

Yet to the borrower's surprise, "the one inside answers, 'Don't bother me. The door is already locked, and my children are with me in bed. I can't get up and give you anything'" (Luke 11:7). To even mention these words as the door remained shut during the midnight hour was to emphasize the hesitancy of the neighbor inside. Traditionally, we assume that the borrower persists in his knocking. Yet, he does not knock at all but rather calls. To knock on a neighbor's door in the night would frighten the neighbor. A stranger knocks in the night but a friend calls. When he calls, his voice will be recognized and the neighbor will not be frightened.[182] From Jesus' perspective, he is asking, "Can you imagine going to a neighbor asking for help and then he receives this unwelcoming response?" From his perspective, the arrival of the friend at midnight would be certainly unusual.

However, the friend outside continues to call out and tells him he will not stop till he receives what he came for. We know this because Jesus states, "Then I tell you, though he [the man inside] will not get up and give him the bread because he is his friend, yet because of the man's *boldness* he will get up and give him as much as he needs" (Luke 11:8). The neighbor inside eventually gets up and gives the borrower what he needs despite the shame and embarrassment the man outside experienced. It was his "boldness" that eventually allowed his neighbor to "get up" and give him his request.

The Application

The important lesson that Jesus desired to communicate to his disciples involved "boldness" in praying to God. Although shame was an extremely important quality in this Eastern culture, Jesus simply told them, "Ask and it will be given to you; seek and you will find; knock and the door will be opened to you. For everyone who asks receives; he who seeks finds; and to him who knocks, the door will be opened" (Luke 11:9-10). This parable teaches that God is a God of honor and that man can have complete assurance that his prayers will be heard.[183] It would be this same boldness that the New Testament authors state that believers in Jesus are able to obtain, for Paul states, "Let us therefore come boldly unto the throne of grace, that we may obtain mercy, and find grace to help in time of need" (Hebrews 4:12). Thus, man can come boldly before God, and because of their faith he has a greater reason to rest assured that his requests will be granted.

THE GOOD SAMARITAN

The Background

A lawyer, desiring to discuss matters of eternal life and the Kingdom of God with Jesus, preceded the giving of this parable. Luke 10:25 states, "On one occasion an expert in the law stood up to test Jesus. 'Teacher,' he asked, 'what must I do to inherit eternal life?'" Jesus could have exposed him in front of all the people, but rather he used this question as way to teach him how one needed to view God's Kingdom and those who have the right to enter into it. So he answered him with a question and asked, "What is written in the Law? How do you read it?" (Luke 10:26). Jesus first tells him that the answer to his question must be found in the Hebrew Scriptures, specifically the Pentateuch, and second, that he must invest in the task of reading them for himself in finding his answers.

The lawyer then replied back and said, "Love the Lord your God with all your heart and with all your soul and with all your strength and with all your mind and love your neighbor as yourself'" (Luke 10:27). Jesus replied to him, "You have answered correctly. Do this and you will live (Luke 10:28).

But from his perspective, he was trying to achieve acceptance before God on his own, and he needed more of an answer. Therefore desired to "justify himself" to Jesus, he asked him, "And who is my neighbor?" (Luke 10:28-29). After asking this question, he probably expected Jesus to respond with a list that he hoped he could handle including loving his fellow Jew. He may have remembered the command of God to Moses saying, "Do not seek revenge or bear a grudge against one of your people, but love your neighbor as yourself. I am the Lord" (Leviticus 19:18). He could certainly go back to this passage to understand that his "people" would constitute as one of his "neighbors". However, he asked a bad question. Although lawyers are portrayed as one who never backs down from a challenge and who desires to prevail over the "testimony" of others, he unfortunately would be overpowered by the wisdom of Jesus.

The Parable

Jesus then intended to give a parable to explain to the lawyer who exactly was his neighbor, how he was to treat him, and whom by the second great commandment was he indebted to love. He said, "A man was going down from Jerusalem to Jericho, when he fell into the hands of robbers" (Luke 10:30). The road from Jerusalem to Jericho was approximately eighteen to twenty miles long. The way was rocky and the descent could be very rapid. About halfway in between these two cities, there was a huge rock which could present a convenient place for robbers to lie in wait. This place and many other hiding places gave this highway the unfortunate reputation as the "Way of Blood."

These robbers unfortunately took advantage over the man, for they "stripped him of his clothes, beat him and went away, leaving him half dead." Robbers in the Middle East were known to beat their victims only if they resist. It can be assumed, therefore, that this poor fellow made this mistake and consequently suffered a sever beating and was left naked and unconscious on the road. The wounded man would naturally be assumed to be a Jew.[184] Unfortunately, he had little to offer, for all the robbers took were his clothing.

Then Jesus said, "A priest happened to be going down the same road, and when he saw the man, he passed by on the other side" (Luke 10:31). Many of the priests during this time lived in Jericho. They would go up to Jerusalem for a two week assignment and then return to their homes in Jericho.[185] They were known to be wealthy and would have not traveled down steep and rocky roads without a ride. Therefore, this man could have easily transported the man to a hospital. In addition, they were men of public character and rank, and they professed holiness. They would have taught others to perform respected obligations in society including helping those who were drawn unto death. However, this priest would not take any action to aid this poor and dying man. If he did, he would have become ceremonially defiled. If defiled, he would then have had to return to Jerusalem and go through the long process of ceremonial purification. But certainly he did not want to go through all of this.

After the priest, "a Levite, when he came to the place and saw him, passed by on the other side" (Luke 10:32). The Levite not only saw him, but came and looked on him. Yet one thing that must be noted was that the Levite's functioned in the temple was to be assistants to the priests. This particular Levite probably knew that a priest was ahead of him on the road and may had been an assistant to that same priest. Since the priest had set a precedent, the Levite could pass by with an easy conscience.[186] And that was exactly what he did. Although he was another man of public character and rank, and one who professed holiness, he did not want anything to do of this defiled Jewish man.

But the hero of the story was not a Jewish aristocrat or religious elite but a hated outsider. Jesus stated the uncharacteristic words, "But a Samaritan, as he traveled, came where the man was; and when he saw him, he took pity on him" (Luke 10:33). Although Samaritans were despised from their Jewish neighbors in the First Century, this man saw that there was some life still left in the dying Jew and unlike the religious priest and Levite, "he took pity on him." The priest and Levite did not open up to one of their own, but the Samaritan had compassion on a "hate" foreigner and seemingly never considered his past history with their people.

What actions did the Samaritan take? First, "he went to him and bandaged his wounds, pouring on oil and wine" (Luke 10:34). He first had to find out how this man came to his condition before he could take therapeutic action. Then he used all his available resources including his own linen, oil and wine which he may have kept with him, and did what was necessary to ease the pain and blood flow.

Secondly, "he put the man on his own donkey, took him to an inn and took care of him." The Samaritan risks his life by transporting the wounded man to an inn within Jewish territory. Such inns were found in villages, not in the wilderness, and there were no archaeological remains to indicate that there was an inn in the midst of the wilderness between Jerusalem and Jericho at the time of Jesus.[187] Therefore, it was a sacrifice on his part, and he did the right thing regardless of the convenience or shame he may have experienced in a Jewish setting.

And last, "the next day he took out two silver coins and gave them to the innkeeper. 'Look after him,' he said, 'and when I return, I will reimburse you for any extra expense you may have'" (Luke 10:35). As if he was a member of his immediate family, the Samaritan left money with the landlord. It must be noted that two silver coins or two denarii would have covered the bill for food and lodging for at least a week and perhaps two.[188] From today's perspective, this money would have gone a great way. This huge sacrifice was the kind and generous treatment from a very close relative or maybe friend, but certainly not from a hated foreigner.

The Application

Then Jesus' skills as a teacher emerge as he asked the tough and even degrading question to the lawyer. "Which of these three do you think was a neighbor to the man who fell into the hands of robbers?" (Luke 10:36). The lawyer knew immediately who was neighbor to the poor Jew but because of his prejudices and hatred of Samaritans, he simply stated, "The one who had mercy on him." Then Jesus said to him, "Go and do likewise" (Luke 10:37).

The application of the parable is clear. To "go and do likewise" is to put these same teachings into action, something that would be hard for this racially prejudiced lawyer to do. Why, because this lawyer valued himself much upon his learning and his knowledge of the laws, and in that he thought to have puzzled Christ. But Christ told him to learn from a Samaritan and to learn his way of life. That is why he told him to "go and do like him."

It would have been more acceptable to the audience if Jesus had told a story about a good Jew who helped a wounded Samaritan on the way to Shechem. The Jewish audience might have managed to praise a "good Jew" even though he helped a hated Samaritan. It was, however, a different matter to tell a story about a good Samaritan who helped a wounded Jew, especially after the Jewish priest and Levite failed to turn aside to assist the unconscious stranger![189]

THE GREAT SUPPER

The Background

The setting of this parable begins with Jesus eating "in the house of a prominent Pharisee" and him being carefully watched by those around him (Luke 14:1). Sometime during the meal, he noticed how the guests picked their places of honor at the table and he immediately sought opportunity to reprove what he saw wrong. He told them, "When someone invites you to a wedding feast, do not take the place of honor, for a person more distinguished than you may have been invited. If so, the host who invited both of you will come and say to you, 'Give this man your seat.' Then, humiliated, you will have to take the least important place" (Luke 14:8-9). But as a means of encouragement, he told them when they are invited to not look for the "highest seat" but to take the "lowest place." Desiring to teach them about authentic humility, he told them that if they do this, they "will be honored in the presence of all your fellow guests" and not humiliated.

Then he took the opportunity to rebuke the master for inviting so many of the upper classes of society and those close to him because they were not the only ones in the society. Jesus wanted him to desperately broaden his horizons and thus, he explains to him those whom he should invite to his meal. He said when you give a banquet, "invite the poor, the crippled, the lame, the blind, and you will be blessed. Although they cannot repay you, you will be repaid at the resurrection of the righteous" (Luke 14:13-14).

Then someone at the table with him heard this and he said to him, "Blessed is the man who will eat at the feast in the Kingdom of God" (Luke 14:15). Seemingly, this man desired to invoke Jesus' views on the topic of the coming kingdom that he had been talking about through his ministry as well as the Messiah who would launch that kingdom. But even more surprising, this man heard and understood the connection of Jesus' rebuke of whom to invite and he associated it with God's Kingdom. But who were those who would be able to enjoy the meal? Speaking to a Jewish majority, Jesus would respond to this man's statement in a strange and atypical way.

The Parable

He replied, "A certain man was preparing a great banquet and invited many guests" (Luke 14:16). The man probably understood a couple of facts regarding the food he was preparing. First, in all societies, eating would be the primary way of initiating and maintaining human relationships, and to know what, where, how, when, and with whom people eat was to know the character of the society.[190] And second, eating was a behavior which symbolized feelings and relationships, mediates social status and power, and expressed the boundaries of group identity.[191] For whatever reason he was inviting these people over for, he put much preparation into his work. For the Jews listening, they may have remembered Isaiah dreaming of a great banquet at the end of history that would be held in Jerusalem and guests will include peoples from all nations (Isaiah 25:6-9).

When the banquet was ready, the man sent his servant to tell those who had been invited saying, "Come, for everything is now ready" (Luke 14:17). In a traditional Middle Eastern village, the host of a banquet invites a group of his friends. On the basis of the number of people who accept the invitation, he decides how much and what kind of meat he will serve.[192] It was certainly the friends who were invited just as the master prior to this parable invited his friends to his meal.

But to the man's surprise, "they all alike began to make excuses. The first said, 'I have just bought a field, and I must go and see it. Please excuse me'" (Luke 14:18). This man's reasoning, though it was an excuse, could have been postponed till after the banquet. Another person stated, "I have just bought five yoke of oxen, and I'm on my way to try them out. Please excuse me" (Luke 14:19). Although this was an excuse, his worries and concerns pertaining to his mundane affairs should have not kept him from coming to the banquet at all. And the third person stated, "I just got married, so I can't come" (Luke 14:20). He could have certainly brought along his bride to the great feast and he had no excuse either. But more noteworthy, his excuse was offensive because he did not even ask to be excused especially in a culture saturated with chivalry. Sadly, all of their excuses were unjustifiable, for they all had something that pertains to self and the gratification of selfish desires above duty and obligation.[193]

After hearing these excuses, the servant came back and reported these very words to his master. "Then the owner of the house became angry and ordered his servant, 'Go out quickly into the streets and alleys of the town and bring in the poor, the crippled, the blind and the lame'" (Luke 14:21). The owner now moved to a wider circle than before and would replace the absent guests with anyone off the streets. These people would be the outcasts of Israel, the "people of the land", and they would now be welcomed into the banquet even though they were not praiseworthy to be placed next to such a dignified host.

However, if people are brought in off the streets, one could, in such a situation, have classes, sexes, and ranks all mixed up together. Anyone could be reclining next to anyone else, female next to male, free next to slave, socially high next to socially low, and ritually pure next to ritually impure. And a short detour through the cross-cultural anthropology of food and eating underlines what a social nightmare that would be.[194] But that does not concern the master, especially when so many of his close friends and neighbors have rejected his invitation.

"'Sir,' the servant said, 'what you ordered has been done, but there is still room'" (Luke 14:22). So the master states to "go out to the roads and country lanes and make them come in, so that my house will be full" (Luke 14:23). This request, like the last one, seems easier said than done, for when an outsider, with no social status, is invited to a banquet in the home of a nobleman, the outsider has a very hard time believing that he is really wanted. The recipient of the invitation will at once feel they don't really want me.[195] Therefore the messenger would need a unique way of persuading them that they are liked and desired. That is why the master uses the word "make" or compel.

Jesus then concludes by saying, "I tell you, not one of those men who were invited will get a taste of my banquet" (Luke 14:24). The speaker was no longer the master addressing the servants in the parable but Jesus addressing the guests with whom he was eating. More notably, he identified himself as the servant and the Father as the master giving the supper, for he would reach out to the poor and Gentiles because most of his own people would reject and not believing in him.

The Application

Therefore in light of the opening response saying, "Blessed is the man who will eat at the feast in the Kingdom of God", Jesus lets it be known that God's Kingdom is open to all, shows no discrimination, and clashes with the current honor and shame society. What must be noted by the last request of the master was that it has long been affirmed that the third round of guests symbolized the Gentiles. Of course these people would certainly be considered as rejects, but Jesus included them along with the poor and destitute in the land as those who would be welcomed into his kingdom. Although his teachings were strange, he would make it be known that it would not be the proud who enter into his kingdom but the humble.

THE GROWING SEED

The Background

Just before this parable, Jesus had just stated a parable of a farmer who went out to sow his seed. Some of his seed fell along the path, some fell on rocky places, other seed fell among thorns, and still other seed fell on good soil. When Jesus was alone, his disciples and other people in the crowd asked him the meaning of the parable. He stated to them that the seed was the word and some people were like seed along the path where the word was sown. To this seed, Satan takes it away. The seed that was sowed on rocky places would receive the word with joy but would only last a short while because trouble or persecution would cause it to fall. The seed that was sown among thorns would be choked by the worries of this life, the deceitfulness of wealth, and the desires for other things. But the seed that was sowed on good soil would be the only seed that would produce a crop.

Immediately after this parable, Jesus gave another parable and Mark the author stated, "With many similar parables Jesus spoke the word to them, as much as they could understand" (Mark 4:33). This saying by Mark brings a small connection with each of these parables.

The Parable

In Mark 4:26-27, Jesus states, "This is what the Kingdom of God is like. A man scatters seed on the ground. Night and day, whether he sleeps or gets up, the seed sprouts and grows, though he does not know how." The farmer contributed nothing towards its growth and almost forgot that he even sowed this seed. Yet he cannot explain its growth, for the seed not only grows but produces.

In giving a more specific detail concerning its growth, Jesus says that "all by itself the soil produces grain - first the stalk, then the head, then the full kernel in the head" (Mark 4:28). He gave the progression of its growth starting with the grass-like core, then the "ear" of the produce, and then concluding with the full extent of the harvest.

Then he states, "As soon as the grain is ripe, he puts the sickle to it, because the harvest has come" (Mark 4:29). Although many of the Jews pulled much of their grain by hand, we know that they also used sickles. A sickle was the reaping hook or pruning hook and was what reapers and vinedressers used when the harvest was ripe. When the fruit was brought forth and was fully ready, the farmer would put his sickle in the harvest and carry it away.

The Application

We know that the parable teaches truth regarding the Kingdom of God. But what does the closing stanza of the parable mean in light of the parable as a whole? The reference of sickle was only mentioned 11 times in both the Old Testament and New Testament. Apart from its references as being simply a tool used by farmers, every reference (apart from Mark 4) speaks clearly of judgment and the wrath of God being poured out because of man's wickedness. For example, Joel speaks of the future prophecy of a "sickle" needing to be swung for the harvest is ripe. Then he states, "Come, trample the grapes, for the winepress is full and the vats overflow - so great is their wickedness" (3:13). It will be the wickedness that was grown and would be fully ripe in the harvest, and it was now in need of a sickle. Similarly, Jeremiah 50:16 states, "Cut off from Babylon the sower, and the reaper with his sickle at harvest." And lastly, the most detailed and vivid example of its use was in Revelation 14. In his vision, John saw one like a Son of Man with a crown of gold and a sharp sickle in his hand. An angel loudly proclaimed to him to take his sickle and reap, "because the time to reap has come, for the harvest of the earth is ripe." Then he "swung his sickle over the earth and the earth was harvested" (verse 15-16). Then another angel said to take his sharp sickle and "gather the clusters of grapes from the earth's vine, because its grapes are ripe." Then the "angel swung his sickle on the earth, gathered its grapes and threw them into the great winepress of God's wrath" (verse 18-19).

The sickle represented the sword of God's justice, the field represented the world, and the reaping represented the cutting of the residents of the earth down and carrying them away. The harvest time was when the grain was ripe and when the measure of the sin of men was filled up. Then he will spare them no longer and will thrust in his sickle, and the earth shall be reaped.[196]

Although it may seem that this parable represented good" seed and "good" produce, we understand from these prior examples that this was not always the case. Because "sickle" only has one interpretation throughout Scripture, we must use this same interpretation to clarify the full meaning of this parable. Although most references to bringing forth fruit in the New Testament carried a good connotation (Romans 7:4), there were also references to bringing forth "fruit for death" (Romans 7:5), and this was exactly the end result of what will take place to this seed that "sprouts and grows" and that "produces grain". Its end result would be to experience the full wrath of God.

THE HIDDEN TREASURE

The Background

Money was commonly lost among the peasants of the land, for they depended on monetary gains to allow them to live each day. Money was a focus for the rich in the land because they would constantly take from the poor in order to build up their wealth. Yet Jesus used a different perspective in demonstrating an unorthodox way a particular man would use the money he found. He did this to show where man's ultimate focus should be centered on, that is the Kingdom of God.

The Parable

Jesus said in Matthew 13:44, "The Kingdom of Heaven is like treasure hidden in a field." To the poor peasants of his day, this story would have certainly grasped their attention, for they would have all understood the value of the treasure. But what Jesus did not say but rather implied was that no one knew how long the treasure had been passed and how many people may have crossed over it. There could have been hundreds or thousands of people who may had passed its way, but failed to find it.

Eventually, whether it had been three decades or three generations, the treasure was eventually found. What a great joy and a shock it must have been for an ordinary man to find this great treasure. And for all of Jesus' listeners, they would have immediately thought that he would celebrate his great discovery with his friends. But he did not, for when he found it, "he hid it again, and then in his joy went and sold all he had and bought that field." He would profit off of the field by his knowledge of the treasure of which the previous owner had no idea about.

The Application

Many if not most of Jesus' parables were shocking to his listeners and this one fit right in to this common theme. First, it was atypical for Jesus to even compare God's Kingdom to buried treasure in a field. Second, in order to obtain it, he had to what was socially unacceptable for his time to obtain it. And last, it was shocking to think that the man would not share his story but rather would rather hide it. But despite this, his great deliberation for those listening was that the kingdom was indeed a treasure, a treasure surpassing all others in riches and desirability.

From his standpoint, it would be a great thing to discover the treasure of the kingdom hidden in the field of the world. Yet it was even greater to comprehend its value and advantage, and to do whatever it was necessary to personally obtain it regardless of the cost involved. Although the treasure of God's Kingdom would be hidden to most, indeed only a few would find it.

THE JUDGE AND THE PERSISTENT WIDOW

The Background

In Luke 18, Jesus tells a parable of an unrelenting widow desperately making her plea to an unjust judge. The audience was assumed by the text to be the disciples (Luke 17:22; 18:1) and the parable was addressed to those who were self-righteous like many of the religious leaders. Luke states the nature of this parable in the first verse saying, "Then Jesus told his disciples a parable to show them that they should always pray and not give up." Neither Luke nor Jesus was intending to promote that the disciples should never stop bowing in prayer but rather to continually be in an attitude of prayer and to never stop asking until a request is actually granted. In addition, he knew how easy it was for people to give up and that is why he gave a parable to show them to never stop asking God until he granted their request.

The Parable

The parable begins, "In a certain town there was a judge who neither feared God nor cared about men" (Luke 18:2). This judge's position would have been given to him by either Herod or the Romans. Unless a plaintiff had money and influence to bribe his way to a verdict, he had no hope of ever getting his case settled.[197] But this was not God's preferred manner of how one was to rule. Hundreds of years earlier, judges were told by King Jehoshaphat to "consider carefully what you do, because you are not judging for man but for the Lord" and to "judge carefully, for with the Lord our God there is no injustice or partiality or bribery" (2 Chronicles 19:6-7). Contrary to Jehoshaphat's instructions, Jesus began by establishing the character of this particular judge who had neither godly respect for God nor the terror and dread that only God could bring. These two aspects go together, for one who has no regard for God can not be expected to have none for man.[198]

But in contrast to this high and lofty judge was "a widow in that town who kept coming to him with the plea, 'Grant me justice against my adversary'" (Luke 18:3). In this culture, poor widows would have numerous opponents, enemies, or just people who wanted to manipulate and misuse them. These people would take advantage of the poor and needy even in legal situations. Unfortunately, this was not a new phenomenon, for injustice took place hundreds of years earlier in King Solomon's time. That was why this king stated, "Do not exploit the poor because they are poor and do not crush the needy in court" (Proverbs 22:22). In this parable, it was this same injustice that the poor widow experienced that necessitated her to make a petition. Her legal rights were somehow being violated and her plea was for him to act and to give her the justice that was due her.

What the disciples would recognize as customary would come from Jesus' next words. He said, "For some time, he [the judge] refused." According to his usual practice and the injustices of society, this judge would not even give her request thought. The poor widow had no money or bribes to give him, no influence in society, and no lawyer who would give her a lending ear. The judge's neglect would fit right in to his everyday injustices of the lower class and he was not doing anything out of the norm.

However, his neglect was only "for some time" because he finally said to himself, "Even though I don't fear God or care about men, yet because this widow keeps bothering me, I will see that she gets justice, so that she won't eventually wear me out with her coming'" (Luke 18:4-5). Before he acted publicly, he inwardly spoke to himself, which from Jesus' perspective gives the truth and power of the human conscious. More importantly, it was what he said about his own character that was striking. He knew his disposition was corrupt and his reverence and dread of God was non-existing. He ultimately knew that there was a God but daringly chose to neglect him.

Yet because he did not continually want his conscience to bother him because of his lack of spiritually and humanitarian interests, he would see that she received justice. He would only acted because he foresaw her wearing him out and he did not want to continually be bothered by her demands.

The Application

From Jesus' perspective, if this woman's needs were eventually met, how much more the needs of the pious who pray not to a harsh judge but to a loving Father. However discouraged and hopeless one's situation may seem to be, it would not be as bad as that of this widow, and thus, one could rest assured that his petition would be heard and acted upon.[199]

Then the parable reallocates from general prayer to a brief conversation pertaining to the vindication of God's people. Jesus said, "And will not God bring about justice for his chosen ones, who cry out to him day and night? Will he keep putting them off" (Luke 18:7). The "justice" of God was future tense while those who "cry out to him day and night" were present tense. What was evident about God in this verse was that he does not immediately put an end, either to the wrongs of the wicked or the sufferings of good men.[200] Although the phrase "will he keep putting them off" pertains to the longsuffering of God relating to his elect, his supremacy and fury were always against those who harassed his people.

But Jesus does not stop with his vindication that he would soon pour out on his saints, but also states, "I tell you, he will see that they get justice, and quickly. However, when the Son of Man comes, will he find faith on the earth" (Luke 18:8). While assurance was given that God will punish or avenge his own, he wondered if he would find faith on the earth. Although this is scary feeling, the answer to this question is even scarier, for it is implied that he will not. There seems to be a definite prophetic implication of the deteriorating of faith before the end of time and one can consider from Jesus' perspective that it would be this faith that he will be looking for.

THE LABORERS IN THE VINEYARD

The Background

In Matthew 20:1–16, we have the parable of the laborers in the vineyard. Like all of the parables, this one represents a unique characteristic of the Kingdom of God and those who have the right to enter into it. Its main focus comes from Jesus' last words stating, "So the last will be first, and the first will be last" (Matthew 20:16). This central theme was important to those self-righteous Jews and religious leaders and this teaching went against the cultural norm of his day.

The Parable

Jesus began by saying, "For the Kingdom of Heaven is like a landowner who went out early in the morning to hire men to work in his vineyard" (Matthew 20:1). The destitute peasants in the First Century were virtually homeless and were always in need of either food or work in which they could buy food. When there was no work, it was a humiliating experience, for they would have nothing to bring home to their families at the end of the day.

This landowner finds some peasants interested in work and he "agreed to pay them a denarius for the day and sent them into his vineyard" (Matthew 20:2). A denarius or penny was the wages sufficient for a day's work during this time. Jesus' listeners would observe very early the character of the landowner, for he was not into exploiting the poor but was one who gave the allotted amount of money for the allotted amount of work. The term that he gave these desperate workers would only be for a day, which was the common timeframe one would be contracted for. Upon hearing these terms, they all simultaneously agreed.

"About the third hour he went out and saw others standing in the marketplace doing nothing. He told them, 'You also go and work in my vineyard, and I will pay you whatever is right.' So they went" (Matthew 20:3-5). The landowner makes a second selection, however he does not tell them what they will get paid. Rather he says, "I will pay you whatever is right." The desperate men are convinced and they all agreed to the terms as well.

The landowner then "went out again about the sixth hour and the ninth hour and did the same thing" (Matthew 20:5). There must have been much work for the landowner and therefore he needed many workers. Then about the eleventh hour, "he went out and found still others standing around. He asked them, 'Why have you been standing here all day long doing nothing?' 'Because no one has hired us,' they answered" (Matthew 20:6-7). It was truly shameful for these men not to have any work. How would they explain to their families back home that they were not able to bring back any food? But to their delight, the landowner said to them, "You also go and work in my vineyard."

When the evening had arrived, "the owner of the vineyard said to his foreman, 'Call the workers and pay them their wages, beginning with the last ones hired and going on to the first'" (Matthew 20:8). The workers who were hired first knew what they were going to make because the landowner specifically told them. Yet the other workers, some of whom were hired much later, were presumptuously told that their wages would be fair. So as each of the workers came to receive their money, the workers who were hired about the eleventh received a denarius. Then when those who were hired first came, "they expected to receive more. But each one of them also received a denarius" (Matthew 20:10).

What a shock it was for the first group of workers to receive the same amount of money that the last group of workers received. From the first worker's perspective, how dare the landowner compare them to the workers who were hired the eleventh hour. Thus, to vent their frustration, they "began to grumble against the landowner" and said, "These men who were hired last worked only one hour and you have made them equal to us who have borne the burden of the work and the heat of the day" (Matthew 20:12). From their eyes, they had a perfectly justifiable case that the landowner could not deny.

But the landowner answered one of them and said, "Friend, I am not being unfair to you. Didn't you agree to work for a denarius?" (Matthew 20:13). The word here for friend is a kind address meaning comrade or partner. It was a general form of address to someone whose name one does not know and is a polite title for a stranger.[201] In the midst of the tension, the landowner calls him friend and Jesus' listeners would quickly observe his meek and composed spirit. His words were used carefully not to cause further tension, for he used a "gentle answer" which can turn "away wrath", rather than "a harsh word" which only "stirs up anger" (Proverbs 15:1).

Now the truth would really hit home to not only this worker but to all of them, for the landowner continued to say, "Take your pay and go. I want to give the man who was hired last the same as I gave you. Don't I have the right to do what I want with my own money? Or are you envious because I am generous?" (Matthew 20:14-15). These workers who were hired first were basically told to be content with that which they received, for they could not deny that they agreed personally to the landowner that they would work for this wage. Therefore, they had no reason to vent their frustration and grumble.

The Application

Then Jesus concludes his parable stating, "So the last will be first, and the first will be last" (Matthew 20:16). This phase is seemingly not a part of the parable but rather he was speaking to those listening to him to give them the summation of the parable. Thus, from Jesus' perspective, what is the interpretation of the parable? The message is again atypical for it represented the overpaid and not the underpaid. For the first workers to receive the same pay as the latter workers almost seem to be an injustice on the part of the landowner. But Jesus went against culture to tell them an important truth regarding those who are able to enter his kingdom.

The Jews during his day prided themselves as being heirs of God's Kingdom. They were all aware of God's future promises to Abraham and to his descendants, but he was trying to explain that the mystery of his kingdom includes both Jews and Gentiles and that his good news should also reach the Gentile's ears. He was promoting equal privileges and advantages for all people alike, not just Jews, and that God his Father distributes his rewards by grace and not by race. But because he knows all men's hearts, he used the complaints of the first group of workers to show how the Jews were just like them. They would be jealous of Gentiles just like the oldest brother in the parable of the prodigal son would be at the grace shown to his sinful younger brother. His strange message through this parable would let the world know that the Gentiles had as much of the privileges of the God's Kingdom as the Jews would have and that is why he said, "the last will be first, and the first will be last." Therefore, don't pride yourself in being first (Jews) because the last (Gentiles) will also be first.

THE LEAVEN

The Background

In just one verse (Matthew 13:33), the author records the parable of the leaven. But this parable must be looked at from the scope and understanding of the previous parable. Just two verses earlier, Jesus stated, "The Kingdom of Heaven is like a mustard seed, which a man took and planted in his field. Though it is the smallest of all your seeds, yet when it grows, it is the largest of garden plants and becomes a tree, so that the birds of the air come and perch in its branches" (Matthew 13:31-32). The overall interpretation of that parable emphasizes the fact that Jesus' gospel message was like the small seed. Yet it was so powerful in nature that it had a tendency to takeover all of its adjacent territory, invading even those locations where it was not wanted. In a comparable way, we will see how the parable of the leaven had a similar effect.

The Parable

Jesus states, "The Kingdom of Heaven is like yeast [leaven] that a woman took and mixed into a large amount of flour until it worked all through the dough" (Matthew 13:33). He first began by comparing the kingdom to leaven, yet this was a negative association. The Israelites were instructed earlier in their history to purge out the old leaven during Passover. In ancient times, leaven represented both mental and moral corruption because it involved hiding and storing bread until it molded and then yeast was formed from the mold. In addition, leaven was perceived in its tendency to contaminate others. Although the act of leavening was an everyday occurrence and necessary in order to make the bread for consumption, the process was not discussed but taken for granted.

Not only was the kingdom-leaven comparison strange, but comparing the kingdom to a woman was strange as well. This woman took the leaven, which was her own work, and hid it in dough to create large loaves of bread. But culturally, she symbolized the religiously impure. In contrast to the man who was a symbol of spiritual or religious purity, this woman would have been inappropriate to perform this duty. Therefore, for Jesus to compare his kingdom with these images that normally held a negative connotation was very shocking and provocative at the time.

The specific actions of this woman must be noted as well. What were her results? Jesus stated that she mixed the leaven into a large amount of flour until it worked all through the dough, thus she accomplished her task.

The Application

With Jesus using this parable to describe his kingdom implied that it consisted of that which was undesirable. The leaven had a negative social connotation because it was thought of as unholy, unclean, and religiously impure. The woman was also unclean and religiously impure, yet it would be both of these images that Jesus would compare his kingdom to. This woman's action of hiding leaven was compared to the kingdom in the same way as the dangerous mustard seed and the poisonous darnel. For Jesus, it was a natural comparison, yet the people would have a problem with it.

In addition, Jesus' gospel message of the kingdom would be "mixed into a large amount of flour until it worked all through the dough." It would accomplish its purpose regardless of the individual who took upon himself the responsibility of the task. For the people of his day, the gospel message of the kingdom was like the leaven in that it would not be easily accepted nor discussed. It would certainly be compared to a woman whom people believed was religiously impure. His gospel messages would be strange teachings to the multitudes and heresy from the religious leader's viewpoint, yet Jesus was prophetically stating that his "leaven" will accomplish his intended purpose despite the opposition and cultural norm.

THE LOST COIN

The Background

There is a similarity with this parable to the parable of the lost sheep (Luke 15:1–7), which Luke records just before this parable. The parable of the lost coin in Luke 15:8-10 is one out of a few parables emphasizing the joy of finding something that was lost. Everyone sometime in their life would loose something valuable and those who found what they lost would certainly find a sense of joy and relief. Although Jesus would use something that everyone could relate to, he would compare the delight of finding what was valuable to his priceless kingdom.

The Parable

He begins by stating, "Or suppose a woman has ten silver coins and loses one. Does she not light a lamp, sweep the house and search carefully until she finds it?" (Luke 15:8). To begin a parable emphasizing the actions of a woman was culturally unacceptable. But Jesus, going against the cultural norm, uses her to show a key feature of the Kingdom of God. What must be first understood is the woman's coin was probably a part of her necklace, for Bedouin women wear their dowry in the form of coins hanging on their veils. Village women do not.[202] Secondly, the movement of peasant women in the village was extremely limited. Therefore this woman clearly knew that the coin was in the house. Her diligence was prompted by the knowledge that it could be found.[203]

The woman took several actions to find the lost coin, for she not only treasured her coin but it would have been an embarrassment for those who knew her. She would light a lamp, sweep the house, and use every available means she had to find it. And to her amazement and joy, her actions paid off in finding her coin. Instead of keeping her joy to herself, she "calls her friends and neighbors together and says, 'Rejoice with me; I have found my lost coin'" (Luke 15:9). Because of the close connection of the Mediterranean world, the community, especially those who were close to her, would have known of her missing coin. Now that she has found it, they all share in her joy, for before it was a community loss and now it was a community discovery.

The Application

Now Jesus brought the earthly story to life with a spiritual application. He states, "In the same way, I tell you, there is rejoicing in the presence of the angels of God over one sinner who repents" (Luke 15:10). From his perspective, the greatest of sinners may be brought to repentance and until a person was deceased, there was still hope and mercy available.

This parable, like the preceding one, stressed the joy of the angels of heaven over the salvation of the lost. There was a connection with the angels rejoicing over a sinner and that which the writer of Hebrews states, "Are not all angels ministering spirits sent to serve those who will inherit salvation" (1:14). Although their name actually means "one who is sent", we observe that they were not only sent by God to give special announcements and revelations but were sent to "those who will inherit salvation". Therefore, when a sinner gets saved, the angels greatly rejoice, thus showing the fruits of their labor.

In addition to this application, Jesus was crossing over cultural lines. We know that he was again rejecting both Jewish and Pharisaic attitudes toward groups of people in society. He was indirectly letting the Jews know that even a Gentile who repents will have this same rejoicing from the angels. Even the Pharisees who had self-righteous attitudes believing that they were not "like other men-robbers, evildoers, adulterers" or even sinful tax collectors (Luke 18:11), were not exempt from this parable. Indirectly, Jesus was also letting them know that his kingdom was made up of the repentant and not of those who believed that they were righteous from their good works.

THE LOST SHEEP

The Background

In Matthew 18:12–14 and in Luke 15:1–7, we have the parable of the lost sheep. Both Gospels record the same parable but a different account leading up to the parable. It was possible that Jesus told this parable twice and under two totally different circumstances, and this could be justifiable in light of other teachings and statements that he gave on more than one occasion. Matthew's gospel centers on Jesus telling his disciples that unless they "change and become like little children", they "will never enter the Kingdom of Heaven" (18:2). Luke's gospel centers on Jesus being criticized because of eating with tax collectors and sinners.

The setting surrounding Luke's gospel begins by stating, "Now the tax collectors and sinners were all gathering around to hear him" (Luke 15:1). Tax collectors or publicans gathered the taxes from the people of the land and transferred it to the Roman government. But they were detested not only by Jews but by other nations because they would take more than required and keep the surplus for themselves. The peasant Jews were prejudiced against them, for their actions totally contradicted the nature of God and all that was written in the Torah. In one instance, they were put on the same status as the harlots (Matthew 21:32), thus showing how sinful they were. As a result, they were regarded as "sinners". In this parable, these publicans and sinners were surrounded by Jesus and from their outlook, Jesus, a teacher of the law and one who claimed to be a righteous person, was keeping company with tax collectors and sinners, who were known as offenders and reprobates.

This is the very reason why "the Pharisees and the teachers of the law muttered" against Jesus saying, "This man welcomes sinners and eats with them" (Luke 15:2). The terminology used here portrayed him as hosting the meal. If this took place, it would have been a much more serious offense to these religious leaders than just for him to eat with them casually, for Jews and most nations throughout the world consider "table fellowship" as being a relatively serious affair. To understand what Jesus was doing in eating with "sinners", it would be important to realize that in the East, even today, to invite a man to a meal was an honor. It was an offer of peace, trust, brotherhood and forgiveness, and sharing a table meant sharing life.[204] In addition, when guests were received, the one receiving the guests would eat with them, and the meal was a special sign of acceptance. Thus, Jesus was seen as engaging in social relationship with publicans and sinners. No wonder the Pharisees were upset![205]

The Parable

Seeing their frustration and anger, he told them a parable stating, "Suppose one of you has a hundred sheep and loses one of them..." (Luke 18:4). The decision to address Pharisees as shepherds carried cultural and theological significance. In the East, the social status identified with particular professions was a very serious matter. A camel driver was very careful not to be known as a fisherman, and if caught fishing, he would point out to the visitor that he was a camel driver, not a fisherman.[206] So for Jesus to say "suppose one of you has a hundred sheep" would have caused offense to them because shepherds in the First Century were considered unclean and immoral. Therefore, the very beginning of this parable could be understood as an indirect and yet very powerful attack on the Pharisaic attitudes toward proscribed professions.[207]

Jesus continued to state that after loosing one of his sheep, "Does he not leave the ninety-nine in the open country and go after the lost sheep until he finds it?" Sheep were not only defenseless but were animals known for having no sense of direction. If and when one of them would get lost, one would not even recognize that danger was prevalent. At the same time, anyone wealthy enough to own a hundred sheep will hire a shepherd, or let some less affluent member of the extended family take care of them. The average family may have had five to fifteen animals and a number of families would get together and hire a shepherd.[208] Thus, having a hundred sheep could mean to be accountable or in charge of a hundred sheep. The shepherd most likely counted the flock while they were still in the wilderness (not after they got back to the village), and after discovering that one was missing, he naturally departed from them in the wilderness, leaving a second shepherd to guide the flock back to the village.[209] So in loosing just one of the sheep would be a serious matter to not only the wealthy owner but to the family and community.

After searching over hills throughout the open country, Jesus states that he eventually "finds it" and "joyfully puts it on his shoulders and goes home. Then he calls his friends and neighbors together and says, 'Rejoice with me; I have found my lost sheep'" (Luke 18:5-6). The endless trouble that the hireling goes through to find the lost sheep was a deep satisfaction once it was found. But Jesus did not stop with the finding but with the restoration. Since the lost sheep was a community loss, it must be brought back into the village and to the fold, and this caused for the occasion of joy from all the neighbors.

The Application

Then Jesus states the spiritual application of the parable saying, "I tell you that in the same way there will be more rejoicing in heaven over one sinner who repents than over ninety nine righteous persons who do not need to repent" (Luke 18:7). Jesus' theme was repentance and the joy over one who repents is the core message of his teaching. From his perspective, everyone should have the opportunity to repent because all people were lost and in need of a shepherd to guide them. The one hundred sheep could certainly stand for millions of people and God and his heavenly angels would take pleasure in just one of the worst of sinner's repentance.

Jesus was also giving an application of which was certainly out of the ordinary. First, his meals with the publicans and sinners were an expression of his mission and message (Mark 2:17) and an anticipatory celebration of the feast in the end-time (Matt. 8:11). Second, the inclusion of sinners in the community of salvation, achieved in table fellowship, was the most meaningful expression of his message of the redeeming love of God.[210] And third, although many Jews believed that no one but them had the opportunity to repent and be forgiven, Jesus gave them a different approach. He believed that "outsiders" could repent and his message was no different than that of Jonah, Daniel and other Old Testament prophets who encouraged foreign and despised nations to turn from sin. From Jesus' perspective, grace could abound to all people and not just the Jews.

THE MERCHANT LOOKING FOR FINE PEARLS

The Background

In Matthew 13:45–46, Jesus states, "Again, the Kingdom of Heaven is like a merchant looking for fine pearls. When he found one of great value, he went away and sold everything he had and bought it." In looking at this parable, there was a striking and yet important similarity in the parable that immediately preceded this one. In just one verse earlier, Jesus stated, "The Kingdom of Heaven is like treasure hidden in a field. When a man found it, he hid it again, and then in his joy went and sold all he had and bought that field" (Matthew 13:44). Both parables show the value of a precious thing that was worth great value, especially in light of him who found it, and the extreme measures the individual went through to obtain it.

The Parable

Jesus begins by comparing the kingdom to "a merchant looking for fine pearls." A merchant was a business profession whose journey, whether by land or sea, dealt in some way with trade. Yet this man was portrayed a little different than the man in Matthew 13:44 who seemingly just stumbled upon the treasure. Here he has his heart set out on finding pearls and Jesus did not coincidentally mention this fact, but rather used it for a purpose. To the First Century Jew, pearls were not considered a valuable ornament but rather were valued and highly sought after by Gentiles. The individual looking for the pearl may certainly have been a Gentile and not a Jew, and those listening to him would have caught this parallel rather quickly. Nonetheless, Jesus intentionally used this ornament to paint a specific picture about his kingdom.

What made pearls an ideal ornament to search for? First, they were very rare. The ideal ones were perfectly round and smooth, and the most priceless ones were found in the wild. In addition, pearls from the sea were more expensive and sought after more than those in freshwater. Secondly, the way a pearl was formed carried significance. Its very existence was a representation of difficulties overcome, for its formation was caused by an aggravation and irritation to an oyster. And thirdly, in biblical times the pearl was associated with many other costly things. For examples, in 1 Timothy 2:9, Paul wanted the women "to dress modestly, with decency and propriety" and not "with braided hair or gold or pearls or expensive clothes." John describes a woman in Revelation who was "dressed in purple and scarlet, and was glittering with gold, precious stones and pearls" (17:4). Therefore, what this merchant was looking for carried high levels of significance.

This merchant here was out on business seeking many pearls and not just one. However, Jesus stated that "he found one of great value." Because of his finding, he did not need to search anymore, for "he went away and sold everything he had and bought it." Those listening would have known that he would have brought money with him since he was on a business trip looking for a rare gem. But Jesus was letting them know that this particular pearl was of such "great value" that he needed to "literally" sell all he had to obtain it. His actions here were similar to the man in the previous parable that found hidden treasure, then hid it again, "and then in his joy went and sold all he had and bought that field."

The Application

It was not a coincidence that three Gospels record Jesus telling a rich man to "sell everything" he had, to "give to the poor", and then to "come" and "follow" him (Luke 18:22; Mark 10:21; Matthew 19:21). It would be clearly evident by many who had followed him during his ministry to see that he was referring to himself as being that pearl of great value and of fathomless worth. Therefore, the merchant would apply to any man on earth who would be searching for a priceless gem. For one who desired to follow him, Jesus was letting them know that he must not have second thought in their life but rather priority. The one who desired to follow him must leave all behind, deny himself, take up his cross, and follow him (Luke 9:23).

THE MUSTARD SEED

The Background

Before looking at the parable of the mustard seed in Matthew 13:31-32, we must first look at that parable of the seed and the weeds mentioned previously. In Matthew 13:24-30, Jesus stated that the Kingdom of Heaven was compared to a man who sowed good seed in his field. To his dismay, his enemy came and sowed weeds among the wheat and escaped. The owner's servants came and asked him if he knew where the weeds came from that was sown among his good seeds. After the owner recognized that an enemy did this wicked act, the servants asked him if he wanted them to go and pull them up. The owner said no because they may accidentally pull up the wheat with the weeds. Instead, he said to let both the wheat and the weeds grow up together until the harvest, and then he will tell the harvesters to first collect the weeds and burn them and then gather the wheat and bring them into his barn.

The application of this parable carried with it a particular prophetic message. The weeds that were burned and the wheat that was brought into the owner's barn portrayed both the sinners who would be thrown into the Lake of Fire (Revelation 20) and the church who would reign with Jesus during the Millennium and in the New Jerusalem (Revelation 21). In light of this parable, Jesus spoke another parable that portrayed a similar but significant disposition of his church in the future.

The Parable

He said, "The Kingdom of Heaven is like a mustard seed, which a man took and planted in his field" (Matthew 13:31). One must first understand some facts about a mustard seed. Mustard, with its pungent taste and fiery effect, was extremely beneficial for the health, and it grew entirely wild. As for the seed, when it falls, it germinated at once.[211] Once the seed was sown, it becomes a mustard plant. The mustard plant was dangerous even when domesticated in the garden, and was deadly when growing wild in the grain fields. It started as a proverbially small seed and grew into a shrub of three, four, or even more feet in height. It had a tendency to take over where it was not wanted, to get out of control, and to attract birds within cultivated areas where they were not particularly desired.[212]

The man who took the mustard seed to plant it in his field knew the general outcome of the size plant that it would become. But here, Jesus states an abnormal outcome of the planted seed. He says, "yet when it grows, it is the largest of garden plants and becomes a tree." The seed is said to be small, but once it fell on the ground and grew, it not only became a plant but an extremely large tree. In addition, he continues to state the abnormality of the plant in saying that it was large enough to allow the "birds of the air to come and perch in its branches." This feature was added, no doubt, to express the magnitude of the tree, for it could now provide protection and a home to house birds and other creatures.

The Application

Jesus' progression from smallness to greatness and the allegorical value of the seed and the plant it produces was symbolic. Since the mustard seed grew so tall that it protected birds and other creatures of life, the Kingdom of God was explained in the same manner. It was a fact that the fully grown mustard plant or shrub had a powerful nature and tendency to takeover all of its surrounding territory, invading even those places where it is not wanted. And yet Jesus was stating that his kingdom had these same takeover properties and it too could grow and become extremely large. Yet, what specifically was Jesus talking about within his kingdom that would produce this effect?

We know that he stated during his ministry, "I will build my church, and the gates of Hades will not overcome it" (Matthew 16:18) and two verses later he "warned his disciples not to tell anyone that he was the Christ" (Matthew 16:20). Here, he prophetically stated the inauguration of the church and the unstoppable force it would continue to be. At the same time, the parable that preceded this one had a prophetic message of the separation of the wicked from the church. Yet before both groups of people become separated, church history records the fact that the Christian faith did begin small but grew despite persecution. Historical documents show that in the first three centuries of the Common Era, the Christian church endured regular persecution from Roman authorities (from Nero in 64 A.D. to the Edict of Milan in 313 A.D., Christians experienced 129 years of persecution). Christianity's most severe persecution occurred under Diocletian, for he ordered the burning of Christian books and churches which caused the faith of the martyrs to blaze. Yet Jesus' church grew and the "gates of Hades" did not "overcome it", for after Diocletian and Galerius' reign (303-324), Christianity became the "world" religion under Emperor Constantine.

Therefore, we know that he was referring to his church in this parable for several reasons. His church would be "extremely beneficial" for those who were apart of it, it would immediately grow once it "falls into the ground", it would grow "wildly" and to unforeseen "heights", and it would "take over" in areas where it would not be wanted. Still today, Jesus' church is continuing to stay strong and useful. Today, Christianity is the largest religion in the world and the church is like the great tree in which the fowls of the air lodge.

THE NET CAST INTO THE SEA

The Background

The parable of the net cast into the sea is one of several parables in Matthew 13 that prophetically expresses what will take place with the church and the wicked once God's dragnet is full. In looking at the ending of the parable of the seed and weeds, there is a strikingly similarity to that of the parable of the net cast into the sea. Therefore, the same conclusion from both parables can be sought out and explained similarly in light of the Kingdom of God.

The Parable

Jesus begins by saying, "the Kingdom of Heaven is like a net that was let down into the lake and caught all kinds of fish" (Matthew 13:47). Because fishing was a well known trade among the Mediterranean world, those listening could personally relate to this parable. This net was a large fishing net or dragnet which drew everything and allowed nothing to escape. This is a different word used for a casting net as seen in Mark 1:16. Because the dragnet was so large, it was often practiced using two boats. The word here for "kinds" in view of "kinds of fish" is an expression that seemingly is used to describe people. Those listening to him could not only see the diversity of the fish brought in and the all-encompassing nature of the catch.

Then Jesus stated, "When it was full, the fishermen pulled it up on the shore." (Matthew 13:48). Because the dragnet was so large, there were all types of fish caught, and there were no more fish able to be taken into the net because it was filled to the brim. Now that their catch was completely full, the fisherman then "sat down and collected the good fish in baskets, but threw the bad away." The word for "good" meant useful, excellent in its nature, such as one ought to be, and morally good and noble. In contrast, the word "bad" meant rotten, corrupted and no longer fit for use.

Then Jesus summed up the parable and stated, "This is how it will be at the end of the age. The angels will come and separate the wicked from the righteous and throw them into the fiery furnace, where there will be weeping and gnashing of teeth" (Matthew 13:49-50). Those listening just heard that the fisherman would separate the good and the bad. Now, Jesus was letting them know that "at the end of the age", the separation will take place by angels and not by men. Yet gratefully, it would be understood that the righteous' future would not consist of this misery and weeping.

The Application

Now after hearing these spiritual yet factual applications, the crowds would be able to understand the true disposition of the parable. The lake or sea would represent the world and the dragnet which caught all kinds of fish would represent every person in the world both small and great from every kindred and nation. No people would be taken in unless it had first been captured in God's "dragnet", thus showing that there was no other way to escape his capture. The fact of the dragnet being full represented the completion of the "catch" being filled to the brim.

After pulling it to the shore, the fisherman sitting down would express the intentional and planned judicial separation that will occur. Thus, the world would remain divided right up until the end with the church being mixed in with the sinners (Matthew 13:24-

30). But when the time came, the angels would come and separate the wicked (the rotten and corrupted) from the righteous (the good, useful, and morally noble), and consequently, the wicked would be thrown into the fiery furnace where there would be weeping and gnashing of teeth.

THE PHARISEE AND THE TAX COLLECTOR

The Background

In Luke 18:9-14, we have a parable that was not only strange to the Jewish people but to the religious leaders as well. Virtually all the people living in this era had a favorable impression of the Pharisees, yet from Jesus' perspective, they were unfavorably represented and were scolded as being hypocrites. To show their true disposition among the Jews, Jesus shared a simple story of a Pharisee and a tax collector's prayer.

At the onset of the parable, Luke explains the direction in which the story was heading stating, "To some who were confident of their own righteousness and looked down on everybody else, Jesus told this parable" (Luke 18:9). Here, the author was targeting not just people in general who fit this description but the specific sect of the Pharisees. Their name came from the word "separation" and they looked on themselves as the godly core of the Jewish nation. They were organized into brotherhoods and they bounded themselves to observe the ordinances of the law. They were people who were self-righteous and believed that they needed no help from God. Yet at the same time, they would look down on others believing that no one was as righteous as they were.

The Parable

So Jesus told a story saying, "Two men went up to the temple to pray, one a Pharisee and the other a tax collector" (Luke 18:10). The temple in Jerusalem stood up on a hill and everyone who went to this place of worship literally went "up" in elevation. It was a place of public worship and religious ceremonies where people would come from far and near to worship God and celebrate religious festivals. With the temple being a renowned public place to offer up personal devotions, both men felt the need to go and pray to God. Yet knowing the mindset of the religious leaders, this Pharisee possibly went to be seen by all those who were not as righteous as he was so that he could receive attention and praise. On the opposite scale of the "righteous" Pharisee was a tax collector whom all the Jews knew were dishonest people. They were hated and despised for they promoted Roman oppression by their deceitful gain in taking more money than needed for taxes.

Although both men went to pray, both came to God in different ways. "The Pharisee stood up and prayed about himself" (Luke 18:11). His non-verbal action of standing up, probably looking up as well, was done to be seen of others, and he most likely prayed in a loud voice. If it was ever possible to have the intentions of speaking to God but for one's prayer to never leave one's lips because of selfish motives, this entreaty from this Pharisee would have been the epitome of such a prayer.

He egoistically stated, "God, I thank you that I am not like other men - robbers, evildoers, adulterers - or even like this tax collector" (Luke 18:11). He began on the right note by stating, "God, I thank you", yet the words that continued to come out showed his true character and motives. The scandalous and depraved people that he thanked God he was not like included robbers, evildoers, adulterers, and tax collectors. Most likely, he was not practicing these gross sins, he was not oppressing the people of the land like tax collectors, he was not living in infidelity, nor was he taking what was not his. Yet he was comparing himself to this tax collector" whom he had left behind, probably in the court of the Gentiles.

He continued to state how good he was saying, "I fast twice a week and give a tenth of all I get" (Luke 18:12). Although God had commanded only one day of fasting each year on the Day of Atonement, the Pharisee impressed those around him by stating that he fasts twice a week. In addition, he proclaimed he was not "robbing" God by not bringing his "tithes to the storehouse" as many Jews had failed to do in the past (Malachi 3:8). Certainly those listening to his "so-called" prayer would be amazed by such a high degree of righteousness. Yet according to First Century Judaism, prayer was of three types: confession of sin, thanksgiving for gifts received, and petitions for oneself and for others. Unfortunately, his prayer did not fall into any of these categories. He was neither confessing his sins nor thanking God for gifts, and he did not make any requests for help. His public remarks were an attack on others clothed in self-advertisement. Rather than comparing himself to God's expectations of him, he compared himself to others.[213]

Conflicting to the Pharisee's prayer, the tax collector "stood at a distance. He would not even look up to heaven, but beat his breast and said, 'God, have mercy on me, a sinner'" (Luke 18:13). Before even mentioning his prayer, his non-verbal actions were revealed. First, he "stood at a distance" or the more accurate translation was that he was standing by himself and apart from others. He knew he was a social outcast and ashamed to be counted among the religious Jews, he knew he did not consider himself worthy to stand near the "righteous" Pharisee who was in front of him praying aloud, and most importantly, he knew he was unworthy to draw near to God. He may have remembered when the psalmist stated that "God is good to Israel, to those who are pure in heart" (Psalm 73:1). Yet he understood his sinful heart and actions, and that his heart was far from purity.

Second, "he would not even look up to heaven". He did not even lift up his hands which was the common gesture at that time, for he was ashamed to look where God dwelt. He knew that his sinful trade of ripping people off was wrong, and his shame and disgrace gave him neither assurance nor audacity to reverence the God of heaven.

And third, he "beat" or smote his breast where his heart was located. This was a common action for one who was smitten with anguish and self-reproach. This same action is mentioned in Luke 23:48 where people beat their breasts after seeing the earth become darkened, the veil of the temple torn, and Jesus dying after crying aloud. These actions show not only remorse but indignation for grievous actions.

Then Jesus records the surprising words from the tax collector, "God, have mercy on me, a sinner" (Luke 18:13). The more accurate translation presents the great theological term meaning to "make an atonement". Thus, his cry was different than that of a beggar.[214] In other words, he was asking God to be merciful to him through his atoning sacrifice for sins because if there ever was a sinner, he would model that individual perfectly. His prayer was short and because of fear and disgrace, he felt reluctant to say many words.

Then Jesus gave his deliberation on the results of the two men's prayer saying, "I tell you that this man [the tax collector], rather than the other [Pharisee], went home justified before God" (Luke 18:14). He would now show the Pharisee's folly and disfavor before God, for he went before him with self-assurance knowing that he did not practice gross sins. His prayer, simply being a monologue, recognized no need of God, confessed no sins, asked God for no pardon, but only recognized his achievements. Because he only looked at himself, his prayer not only failed to receive anything from God but was rejected. He came to the temple a sinner and left the same way he came, and from Jesus' standpoint, it would have been better for him to have stayed home.

But the prayer of the publican resulted in his justification which took place immediately. In essence, justification is the rendering or pronouncing of righteousness and from God's standpoint, it is the way one ought to be. By Jesus stating that he was justified meant that God had received him and confirmed him to be righteous. Why did God receive the tax collector? Because he humbly approach him knowing how wretched and corrupt he was, and he prayed to him on the basis of his atoning sacrifice.

Then Jesus stated, "For everyone who exalts himself will be humbled, and he who humbles himself will be exalted." What a blow this was to the religious leaders! The people of the land had looked up to them favorably, but from his standpoint, they would not be "exalted" unless they first humbled themselves. Jesus concluded this parable making it clear that those who would enter into heaven would consist of the humble.

The Application

In looking at this parable, Jesus was targeting the religious Pharisees, as he had done in so many other parables. From his standpoint, self-glorification seriously tarnished their image and he saw a serious imbalance in their actions. For example, they would tithe more than the law required, yet they neglected the weightier matters of the law such as justice, mercy and faith (Matthew 23:23-24). In another instance, he accused them of being like "whitewashed tombs, which look beautiful on the outside" and appeared "to people as righteous but on the inside" they were "full of hypocrisy and wickedness" (Matthew 23:27-28). When he called them "hypocrites" he did not mean that they were merely "play-acting" or "pretending," but rather that they sincerely thought that they were good men while all the time they failed to see that their goodness was largely counterfeit. As Jesus pointed out they were "blind guides", for moral and spiritual blindness was their chief defect, though all the time they fondly supposed that nobody could see as clearly as they did.[215]

It was these kinds of dialogue with the Pharisees and other religious authorities that led them to seek Jesus' death. They wanted to put out this light, for their "goodness" and "righteousness" were being exposed to his true light. At the same time, compared to their formal training, Jesus was only a man from Nazareth. He was one who had received no special training, yet his words had a divine, convicting power about them that was unique.[216] He taught the people with authority and not as they did (Mark 1:22; Matthew 7:29) and this created amazement from all the people but hatred from their point of view.

THE PRODIGAL SON

The Background

Almost all of Jesus' parables were short; hence, the very meaning of a parable is a short story. Yet, the parable of the prodigal son found in Luke 15:11-32 was one of the few longer parables given by Jesus. The scope of this story is the same of the two that preceded it, for they demonstrate how gratifying it was to God to see just one sinner converted and how ready he was to show forgiveness. Yet this parable expressed a greater scope of the riches of God's grace to one who had wasted his life on riotous living and the restoration that would be given to him despite his sin. In addition, this parable, along with many others, showed that God was not just the God of the Jews but allowed all people to experience his grace and restoration.

The Parable

Jesus begins by setting the scene. He states, "There was a man who had two sons. The younger one said to his father, 'Father, give me my share of the estate...'" (Luke 15:11-12). During this time, a father

202

would usually divide his living between his children before his death. Yet, there was no law or custom which permitted a son to share in his father's wealth while he was still alive. So the younger son asked an unheard of request by demanding his father to give him his share immediately, that is while he was still alive. Although this was an insult and a dishonor to the family, it would have been even more of a shock for the father to grant his son's outrageous request. But the father demonstrates unbelievable love by granting his request and he "divided his property between them." Although the younger son asked for the request, the father divided his "property" among both of his sons. He more than likely knew what would happen to the younger son and perhaps the older son as well, yet he generously gave into the request.

Not long after the younger son received his money, he "got together all he had, set off for a distant country and there squandered his wealth in wild living" (Luke 15:13). He had his hopes set from the onset of his request to experience life away from home. Although he desired to become independent from his father, he quickly found himself in a worse situation that he had never dreamed of. His unruly life resulted in squandering his money, profligacy, and immoral living, and it would soon cost him his well-being. His result is similar to what happened to Dinah the daughter of Jacob who "went out to visit the women of the land" and eventually was taken and sexually violated (Genesis 34:1-2). In both situations, they desired to explore the "land" away from their home, they both had ulterior motives in their adventure, and both fell into misfortune.

But Jesus went the extra step to show the seriousness of his adversity and ruin in saying, "After he had spent everything, there was a severe famine in that whole country, and he began to be in need" (Luke 15:14). He literally spent his money so fast that he made himself into a beggar aimlessly wandering from place to place looking for aid. But it was not necessarily because he "squandered his wealth in wild living" that caused him "to be in need" but more prevalently, it was the "severe famine in that whole country" that caused him to be among the lowest of the classes of people in his day. Although famines were rare, they would come more than desired and would cause the farmers and virtually all the people in the land to suffer, for the Mediterranean world was an agrarian society. Therefore, all the people listening to Jesus would understand the effects of such a famine and the reality of this young man's adversity.

Because of his destitute state, he "went and hired himself out to a citizen of that country, who sent him to his fields to feed pigs" (Luke 15:15). From today's point of view, it seems harmless for this young man to work for a "citizen of that country". Yet every Jew listening would know that he, being a Jew, went to feed pigs for Gentiles. This was a great sin and a serious matter to the Jewish culture, for he lost his family inheritance to Gentiles and now he is working for them. If his community back home ever found out about this, it would not only be a disgrace, but he would be excommunicated from them. In addition, pigs were considered unclean by Jews as stated in Leviticus 11:7.

One would think his life would gradually improve, but Jesus proved otherwise. He stated that while he fed the pigs, "he longed to fill his stomach with the pods that the pigs were eating" (Luke 15:16). Still used today, pods were rough, locust-like bean with small sugar content. Only the shell of the bean was suitable for eating, for the seed itself was hard and valueless as food. Jesus said that "he longed to fill his stomach "with what was given to pigs implying that someone else was feeding the pigs and at the same time was making sure that the young man did not eat the pig's food. He most likely was receiving something but whatever he received was not keeping him healthy and alive. In addition, "no one gave him anything" which implied that he miserably failed in asking for assistance. He was totally in a destitute and was dying slowly.

But the turning point of the parable was when he "came to his senses" and said, "How many of my father's hired men have food to spare, and here I am starving to death" (Luke 15:17). It actually came to the point of no one giving to him because of the severe famine as well as him slowly dying because of starvation that he realized how much better it would be if he were at his home. He realized that his father's hired servants had not just food but "food to spare". In other words, if there was food to spare for the hired servants, he, being his father's begotten son, would never have to wonder if there was any food.

He not only contemplated going back home but also the response he would give to his father once he arrived. Jesus states his initial response saying, "Father, I have sinned against heaven and against you. I am no longer worthy to be called your son; make me like one of your hired men" (Luke 15:18-19). This young man quickly realized that there would be no way of covering up the fact that he "squandered his wealth in wild living" and lived the life of a fool. Thus, he decided to repent and to tell the truth.

But in looking at his initial response more closely, we must notice a couple of details. First, he desired to say that he had sinned against "heaven" or simply against God. By him saying this, he understood the source of who he had sinned against and he desired to make this point of truth known at once. Secondly, because of his shame, he desired his father to make him one of his hired servants because he felt he was no longer worthy to be called his son. During this time period, a hired servant was an outsider who did not live in the house. Although he was a free man and was employed when required, he did not have any personal interests in the issues of the master's house. Therefore, the son was really feeling worthless when he said these words and he desired to even command his father to show no grace to him but to treat him like a hired servant. He knew that shame would overshadow him once he returned to the village, yet, this was his most thought out plan that he felt would possibly come into fruition.

With this plan, "he got up and went to his father. But while he was still a long way off, his father saw him and was filled with compassion for him" (Luke 15:20). Up until now, everyone back in the village understood the severity of the famine and the reality of the prodigal's survival in a foreign land. Therefore, the thought of him still being alive would only be weakened each day he was away, especially as the famine continues to linger. But there was at least one person who never lost hope and that was his father. Not only did he wait but he never forgot his son although he would be fully aware of how he would be treated from the community once he returned.

Upon seeing his son "a long way off", the father showed a sequence of theatrical actions that restored his son back into the fold. First, "he ran to his son", which men of his dignity never did in public. The community watching him would only see his disregard of cultural tradition. Second, he "threw his arms around him" which showed a demonstration of possession and ownership. And third, he "kissed him." His actions of hugging and kissing him would show the unexpected visible demonstration of love in humiliation.

After seeing this portrayal of love, the son at once states his rehearsed speech, "Father, I have sinned against heaven and against you. I am no longer worthy to be called your son" (Luke 15:21). Yet there was an important element that he left out from what he had earlier rehearsed. He did not say to "make me like one of your hired men", for he saw the unexpected visible demonstration of love in humiliation from his father.

As if he had simply ignored his son's stressful and preplanned speech, the father said to his servants, "Quick! Bring the best robe and put it on him. Put a ring on his finger and sandals on his feet. Bring the fattened calf and kill it. Let's have a feast and celebrate" (Luke 15:22-23). The father took several actions to restore his lost son to the family and community, and to show him that he was loved. First, the best robe would have been the fathers, and it was needed not only to clothe and adorn the son but to show the community that he was accepted and not condemned. Second, the ring or possibly the signet ring would indicate that his son's debts would be paid and his trust would be restored. Third, the shoes would portray his ownership and status of freedom in the house, which would be opposite of that of a hired servant. And fourth, the significance of the father bringing the "fattened calf" versus a goat showed that the community would be invited to the celebration.

Why did the father go to the extreme and take such actions to restore and show love on his wayward son? Because his son "was dead" and is "alive again"; "he was lost and is found" (Luke 15:24). The purpose of this celebration was to bring reconciliation to him and to show the community that he was accepted, despite his sin. Yet soon, the father would realize that he did not have one lost son, but actually two.

Jesus then states, "Meanwhile, the older son was in the field. When he came near the house, he heard music and dancing. So he called one of the servants and asked him what was going on. 'Your brother has come,' he replied, 'and your father has killed the fattened calf because he has him back safe and sound'" (Luke 15:25-27). Suspicious at the music he hears and the dancing he sees, he rightfully inquires from one of the servants about what is going on. After hearing the news of what his father had done, he "became angry and refused to go in. So his father went out and pleaded with him" (Luke 15:28). The brother was not angry simply because of hearing the music and seeing the joyous celebration but because his father restored his brother back to the family and community. From his perspective, his unruly actions should not have been erased and because of this, he refused to attend the celebration for his brother.

After the father pleaded with him to attend his brother's "homecoming" celebration, the older son states, "Look! All these years I've been slaving for you and never disobeyed your orders. Yet you never gave me even a young goat so I could celebrate with my friends.

But when this son of yours who has squandered your property with prostitutes comes home, you kill the fattened calf for him" (Luke 15:29-30). There was an obvious break in fellowship between the two and the selfish views of the older brother seemed to have now come to surface. By him telling his father that he never gave him "a young goat so I could celebrate" showed he was accusing him of favoritism. At the same time, he was boasting of his own high merits and submission to his father. We also see him not acknowledging his brother as being "his" brother but rather says the words "this son of yours" as a means of telling his father that he was not a part of the family.

But the father tells him, "My son, you are always with me, and everything I have is yours. But we had to celebrate and be glad, because this brother of yours was dead and is alive again. He was lost and is found" (Luke 15:31-32). He does not offer an apology for his wayward son's actions nor did he criticize his oldest son's actions and words because there was much truth in what he said. But the father simply centered his speech on the celebration of the lost. In a calm and collective manner, he reminded his oldest son that this was your brother and that there were some very important reasons why he needed to rejoice in his restoration. The two reasons he gave were that he was "dead and is alive again" and that he was "lost and is found". By this simple and well calculated speech, the father was not only trying to bring him back to the oneness of his brother but to inform him that since he was his brother, he needed to rejoice as well.

The Application

The themes of this parable include sin, repentance, grace, joy, and son-ship. The application must first be understood by discussing the two sons. The first was a lawless prodigal who was open to his father about his sin. He was similar to the sinner who expressed to God his true heart in the parable of the Pharisee and the tax collector. The second son was lawless but within the law, he unfortunately was hypocritical, for he was hiding his true feelings while hating his father and brother. He even denied kinship with his brother while at the same time stated how moral and righteous he was.

Yet Jesus, in a clever and skillful manner, was depicting the immoral Gentiles as representing the younger son and the religious leaders as representing the elder son. These pro-Jewish leaders did not want Gentiles and sinners to be included in the family of God and they would pride themselves in their good works and moral behavior. Yet, he was trying to convey the message of how gratifying it was to God to see a sinner restored and shown forgiveness despite how immoral they may have been. From Jesus' perspective, the same unexpected love could be demonstrated to anyone despite who they were or what they may had done.

THE RICH FOOL

The Background

In Luke 12:13-21, we have a parable where Jesus discussed money with the application that those who store up treasure on earth will not be rich toward God. This parable speaks of a man who failed to understand that he was accountable to God for all his possessions and that ultimately, all things belong to him.

To understand the scope of this parable, we must observe a couple of earlier messages spoken of by Jesus. We see him giving warnings concerning worrying when he stated, "I tell you, my friends, do not be afraid of those who kill the body and after that can do no more" (Luke 12:4). We see him giving warning about those who do not acknowledge him on earth when he stated, "I tell you, whoever acknowledges me before men, the Son of Man will also acknowledge him before the angels of God" (Luke 12:8).

Just before the parable was given, a man said, "Teacher, tell my brother to divide the inheritance with me" (Luke 12:13). Despite what Jesus had just stated earlier about worrying, this man interrupts him to ask that he take his side in a domestic financial dispute. The demand meant that the split between the brothers had already taken place, and the assumption behind such a request is clear. The father had died without an oral or written will, there was an estate that was held by the two brothers, and according to the law of the times, the inheritance could not be divided until the older brother agreed. The petitioner therefore must be the younger brother, who was ordering Jesus to press his older brother into making the division. Apparently, the older brother did not want this to happen. The issue was important because justice was a critical part of life.[217] The law additionally stated that the elder brother would receive two-thirds and the younger would receive one-third. Yet this man did not want Jesus to listen to both sides but only to his side and that is why he asked him to speak as a prophet or as one with authority to his brother.

Jesus then replied, "Man, who appointed me a judge or an arbiter between you" (Luke 12:14). Although the man may have had an honorable motive, Jesus refused to act as a mediator. Although he hoped Jesus would take his case, he did not come as a divider of the two brother's estates nor did he take upon himself legislative or judicial authority.

Instead of answering the man, Jesus stated, "Watch out! Be on your guard against all kinds of greed; a man's life does not consist in the abundance of his possessions" (Luke 12:15). He said this not just because he knew all men's heart but because he knew this man's heart. It was not that he was not concerned about justice but rather he was concerned about the deeper problem of "greed". From Jesus' perspective, greed would damage this man more than him not receiving his allotted inheritance. In addition, his teachings against greed and the abundance of possession were atypical, for it contradicted the way of the common life. It was upon this premise that he stated a parable that demonstrated the follies of worldly living and the miseries that riches could bring in this life.

The Parable

He began his parable stating, "The ground of a certain rich man produced a good crop. He thought to himself, 'What shall I do? I have no place to store my crops'" (Luke 12:16-17). This man Jesus introduced seemingly had a whole countryside to himself and he desired to expand his storage facilities in order to preserve all his surpluses for himself. But his possessions were attached to a deep fear of having no place to store his surplus of crops. Regardless of how much he put away, he wanted to acquire more. His question of "What shall I do" sadly resembled the poorest of beggars living in the land wondering the same question.

After reasoning within himself, the rich man states, "This is what I'll do. I will tear down my barns and build bigger ones, and there I will store all my grain and my goods" (Luke 12:18-19). His project would entail him tearing down what he currently had and building newer and bigger barns to store his surplus. Yet what was interesting was that he stated the words "my barns", "my grains", and "my goods" which seemed to lay an emphasis of what he had done. In addition, there was no mention of other workers but simply only himself as being the one who accomplished all the work.

Even more staggering, this rich man seemed to have no one else to talk to for he continues to say, "And I'll say to myself, 'You have plenty of good things laid up for many years. Take life easy. Eat, drink and be merry'" (Luke 12:19). He "dialoged with himself" which was a very sad scene. In the Middle East, village people made decisions about important topics after long discussions with their friends. Families, communities and villages were tightly knit together, and everybody's business was everybody else's business.[218] Unfortunately for this man, there was no one else to get wisdom from and seemingly, he was all alone. After he dreamed about what he would do, his satisfaction and comfort in his bigger barns would allow him to relax and celebrate, for he would have plenty of "good things" stored up for many years to come.

The rich man's way of thinking would have been the common mindset of those listening to Jesus. From the elites' perspective, the more they could obtain for their increase, the more prosperous they would become. However from Jesus' perspective, they had it all wrong, for he continues to say, "But God said to him, 'You fool! This very night your life will be demanded from you. Then who will get what you have prepared for yourself'" (Luke 12:20). The neighbors and friends of the rich man would have commended him for his thoughts, but God would only commend him for his foolishness. Everyone but God highly praised him and although he was rich, he was a fool. God told him that his life would cease to exist that very night and that someone else would obtain all that he had left for himself. Solomon, the wisest man who ever lived, was also a rich man, and he stated similar words saying, "I hated all the things I had toiled for under the sun, because I must leave them to the one who comes after me. And who knows whether he will be a wise man or a fool? Yet he will have control over all the work into which I have poured my effort and skill under the sun" (Ecclesiastes 2:18-19).

The Application

By way of application, Jesus states, "This is how it will be with anyone who stores up things for himself but is not rich toward God" (Luke 12:21). The rich man in this parable never shared with those who were in need. He coveted his possessions and his human anxieties about his possessions were only futile. Yet, Jesus let it be known that all material possessions belong to God who in return gave them to mankind. Thus, man is accountable to God for all his actions and his life does not consist of the abundance of things he possesses as most men are accustomed to thinking. From Jesus' perspective, the one who continues to labor for himself alone will fall short to obtain riches for God.

THE SEED AND THE WEEDS

The Background

In Matthew 13:24–30, we have the parable of the seed and the weeds and in verses 36-43 of the same chapter, we have Jesus' interpretation of this parable. This parable is one out of several that sheds light on a profession that all of the people in the Mediterranean world would be able to identify with. Farming was a way of life for almost all peasants in some way or another and Jesus skillfully used this way of life to discuss truths regarding the apocalypse of his kingdom.

The Parable

He begins by stating, "The Kingdom of Heaven is like a man who sowed good seed in his field" (Matthew 13:24). It seemed a little strange that Jesus would begin stating that the farmer sowed "good" seed because since the peasants were so dependent on the land, no one in their right mind would plant any other type of seed but that which would produce a crop.

But he continued to say, "But while everyone was sleeping, his enemy came and sowed weeds among the wheat, and went away.

When the wheat sprouted and formed heads, then the weeds also appeared" (Matthew 13:25-26). By definition, weeds are plants out of place which grow aggressively and unrelentingly where they are not desired. They are problematic in numerous ways. First, they contend with the good crops for water, light, soil, nutrients and space, and thus, they overall reduce harvest quality. Second, they serve as hosts for crop disease and third, they produce chemical substances that are lethal to other harvest plants. Despite some of their good qualities, their negative qualities far outweigh that which is good. Although they could spread to outrageous number, weeds only made up about 3% of all the plant species, yet they were the biggest headache to farmers. In Jesus' day, weeds (sometimes stated as tares) were a kind of darnel which resembled wheat except the grains were black. At the same time, it was a fact the experts could only differentiate some species of this darnel from true wheat, for weeds were hard to distinguish.

Jesus continued to say, "The owner's servants came to him and said, 'Sir, didn't you sow good seed in your field? Where then did the weeds come from'" (Matthew 13:27). Once the weeds started to grow among the good crop, the servants of the owner recognized the crime that was done and they brought the concern to the owner. The owner quickly was aware of who had done this for he stated, "An enemy did this" (Matthew 13:28). He did not blame the servants or the neighbors but rather the enemy. From the owner's perspective, the enemy was the one who was his adversary and opponent and who desired to bring him harm by way of his vineyard. He did not try to do physical harm to the master or the servants but rather desired to contaminate his crop and work.

Foreseeing the harm that the weeds would do to the good crop, the servants quickly asked him, "Do you want us to go and pull them up?" Because of the difficulty to differentiate between the weed and the wheat, the master answered back, "No, because while you are pulling the weeds, you may root up the wheat with them." Then the master devised a plan regarding how he would rid the bad and keep the good. He stated, "Let both grow together until the harvest. At that time I will tell the harvesters: First collect the weeds and tie them in bundles to be burned; then gather the wheat and bring it into my barn" (Matthew 13:29-30). The order that the master would take seemingly out of frustration would be in taking the weeds out first, which had cause much turmoil in his garden, and then he would gather the good and useful wheat.

The Application

Soon after the parable when Jesus left the crowd and went into the house, his disciples came to him and asked him, "Explain to us the parable of the weeds in the field" (Matthew 13:36). Knowing that Jesus' teachings had some unique and spiritual application, these men were inquisitive to know what the parable truly meant.

Jesus then replied, "The one who sowed the good seed is the Son of Man. The field is the world, and the good seed stands for the sons of the kingdom. The weeds are the sons of the evil one" (Matthew 13:37-38). Jesus was the Son of Man and he frequently used this title during his ministry to refer to himself (Matthew 12:32; Luke 6:5). He would be the one to sow good seed, which represented the sons of the kingdom, into the world of people. We know that he would start his church (Matthew 16:18) and after its initiation, those whom would follow him and his teachings would be considered "sons of the kingdom".

Yet the weeds that grew right next to the sons of the kingdom would be the "sons of the evil one". The evil one was Satan or the devil of whom Jesus stated, "My prayer is not that you take them out of the world but that you protect them from the evil one" (John 17:15). The "sons" of the evil one were not demons put rather people who were of their father the devil. These would be those who were not apart of the church but would be "planted" right next to those who were apart of the church. These sons of the evil one would be those who would grow aggressively and unrelentingly where they were not desired. They would be problematic and would contend with the sons of the kingdom for water, light, soil, nutrients and space, and at the same time, they would serve as hosts for spiritual disease.

Jesus continued to say that the one who planted the seed was the devil, and that "the harvest is the end of the age, and the harvesters are angels" (Matthew 16:39). After the devil had planted the seed, there would be some time lapse between that time and the end of the age of which the weeds would be pulled and "burned in the fire".

Then Jesus gave a chilling description of what would actually take place with those "sons of the evil one" saying, "the Son of Man will send out his angels, and they will weed out of his kingdom everything that causes sin and all who do evil. They will throw them into the fiery furnace, where there will be weeping and gnashing of teeth" (Matthew 13:41-42). The furnace that the people used during this era was used either for baking bread, burning earthen ware, or for smelting. Here Jesus was describing a similar furnace, yet it would be used for burning people and not bread or earthen ware. In this furnace, people would not die but rather would intensely suffer through weeping and the gnashing of teeth. Gnashing would have been known by the people as depicting extreme anguish and utter despair, and from Jesus perspective, this would be the feeling of what the "sons of the evil one" would experience.

But graciously, Jesus did not end his interpretation of the parable on a negative note but rather states, "Then the righteous will shine like the sun in the kingdom of their Father. He who has ears, let him hear" (Matthew 13:43). In contrast to the utter destruction of the "sons of the evil one", he used the word for "righteous" to describe the "sons of the kingdom". Although the typical interpretation of righteousness during his time constituted one who obeyed divine laws and one who was virtuous and faultless, he took this term to another level. We know that the Pharisees were "righteous", for they fulfilled the general criteria for righteousness. Yet in John 8, he boldly told them that although they considered themselves to being children of Abraham, they belonged to their father the devil (8:44). So if Jesus told them that they were simply "sons of the evil one" who were not "holding to the truth" (8:44), then he had a different and strange view of righteousness that contradicted the common viewpoint of the day.

THE SOWER

The Background

In Matthew 13:3–23, Mark 4:1–20, and Luke 8:5–15, we have the infamous parable of the sower, which is often called "the sower and the seed". Why such an infamous parable? First, this parable began a new method of teaching (Matthew 13:10-17) and would serve as a catalyst for all other parables because Jesus would explain in this parable why he speaks to the multitudes in this manner.

Second, up until this time, neither the former prophets nor angels totally understood the total mystery of redemption. Although many prophecies were foretold, the prophets did not see nor totally understood their entire prophecy. But now the disciples and even the world had the opportunity to hear Jesus state the overall meaning of his mission through this parable. Third, Jesus himself named this parable as "the sower" (Matthew 13:18), for there were few parables, if any, in which he actually stated the actual name. And fourth, it was one of the few that was mentioned in all the synoptic Gospels (Matthew, Mark, and Luke), and this fact shows the magnitude of its significance and interpretation.

The Parable

Jesus begins by stating, "A farmer went out to sow his seed" (Matthew 13:3). The beginning of this parable fit right into the agricultural society and into the minds of all those listening. As the farmer would sow wheat by scattering seed from a bag, he would hurl the seed in the air in front of him in an arc form as he walked through the field. After the seed was scattered first, it was plowed into the ground.

As he scattered the seed, "some fell along the path, and the birds came and ate it up" (Matthew 13:4). The path would have been the wayside and a frequently traveled road. The seed would have fell along a place where people commonly would walk and trample the seed, and where the ground would not have been fertile. The purpose of the seed would have no chance to take root but would only serve as an open invitation for the birds to easily see them and eat them up.

In addition, some seed "fell on rocky places, where it did not have much soil. It sprang up quickly, because the soil was shallow. But when the sun came up, the plants were scorched, and they withered because they had no root" (Matthew 13:5). The rocks would have been on top of potentially good but thin soil and the seed would be able to grow quickly because of the warmth of the soil. Yet, it would be unable to take root because of the rocky shelf. Therefore, when the sun came to give nourishment, it would only kill the plant because there was no root, and as a result, the plant quickly perishes.

Other seed fell between "thorns, which grew up and choked the plants" (Matthew 13:6). Thorns could portray thorny places as well

215

as bushes and thorny plants. This soil was fertile, perhaps too fertile, and both thorns and grain could grow in the same earth. However, as the good seed grew, the thorns would only suffocate the plant and cause it to drown.

Lastly, other seed fell on "good soil, where it produced a crop - a hundred, sixty or thirty times what was sown" (Matthew 13:8). Good ground describes soil that was both fertile and weed free. Only good and useful crops grew and produced the intended results in good quality soil. Despite the previous two soils having potentially good soil, it would only be last that would be interference free. Then Jesus encouraged the crowds to understand this parable stating, "He who has ears, let him hear" (Matthew 13:9).

After the conclusion of the parable, Jesus' disciples came to him and asked, "Why do you speak to the people in parables" (Matthew 13:10). This was the beginning of a new method of teaching and it was not the fact that parables were a bad form of teachings from the disciple's perspective but rather it was a strange way to showcase the Kingdom of God. They had heard many messages regarding his new kingdom, but not in this manner. So from their point of view, they had a reasonable question.

In response to why he spoke in parable, Jesus first gave them the basis of his teachings in light of the people he was ministering before. He stated, "The knowledge of the secrets of the Kingdom of Heaven has been given to you, but not to them. Whoever has will be given more, and he will have an abundance. Whoever does not have, even what he has will be taken from him" (Matthew 13:11-12). This word for secrets or "hidden things" was another word for "mysteries". This word typified that which was not obvious to the understanding of the majority, and specifically, it was those things of purely divine revelation.

Jesus' first answer was to plainly let his disciples understand that they would obtain knowledge of the truth and the secrets of his kingdom from simply being with him. Yet the crowds of people would not. From his perspective, these people were "harassed and helpless, like sheep without a shepherd" (Matthew 9:36) and they could be instructed regarding the mysteries of God's Kingdom. And second, he also understood that what little the people spiritually had would continually be taken away unless he imparted in them the truths of God's Kingdom, something far beyond religiousness and obeying the law. Therefore, parables would serve as an effective way for the multitudes to understand these secrets. It would be an illustrative way for them to gain understanding that would not be taken away from the enemy. Thus, Jesus would use something familiar and ordinary to the people like farming as a means of illustrating truth. He would not use any philosophical notions or speculations but rather illustrations in their own language.

After giving the basis of his teachings and the nature of the people, Jesus continued to say, "This is why I speak to them in parables: 'Though seeing, they do not see; though hearing, they do not hear or understand.' In them is fulfilled the prophecy of Isaiah: 'You will be ever hearing but never understanding; you will be ever seeing but never perceiving. For this people's heart has become calloused; they hardly hear with their ears, and they have closed their eyes. Otherwise they might see with their eyes, hear with their ears, understand with their hearts and turn, and I would heal them'" (Matthew 13:13-15). He further explained the condition of the people of whom he was speaking to and he states his point by quoting the words of the Old Testament prophet Isaiah. Isaiah, the evangelical prophet, spoke of the state of the Jewish people (6:9-10), and it was foretold to him that these people whom he would be sent to would be so "calloused" in their heart that they would actually become worse because of his message. They would not hear nor see the truth of what God desired to tell them and that was why Jesus said that if they did hear with their ears and understand with their heart, he would heal them.

Then he encourages them by saying, "But blessed are your eyes because they see, and your ears because they hear. For I tell you the truth, many prophets and righteous men longed to see what you see but did not see it, and to hear what you hear but did not hear it" (Matthew 13:16-17). He desired to let them know how fortunate his disciples were for understanding the truths of his kingdom message and in not having such a hard and calloused heart. And to even further encourage them, he stated that the prophets of old, including Moses and Elijah, desired to look into those things which they could not fully understand (1 Peter 1:10-12). Although many prophecies were foretold, the prophets did not see the entire picture nor did they truly know the extent of their prophecy. But the disciples had the privilege to not only see Jesus and his miracles but to understand the total mystery of redemption.

The Application

Then Jesus proceeds to interpret the parable by saying, "When anyone hears the message about the kingdom and does not understand it, the evil one comes and snatches away what was sown in his heart. This is the seed sown along the path" (Matthew 13:19). It would be now obvious that the assorted classes of soil represented the various conditions of the human heart. Although man's heart would be capable of bearing fruit, the seed that fell along the soil of the path had no change to even germinate. Since this man's heart did not understand the word that was given to him, his soul became an easy target for Satan to come and snatch it away like birds.

"The one who received the seed that fell on rocky places is the man who hears the word and at once receives it with joy. But since he has no root, he lasts only a short time. When trouble or persecution comes because of the word, he quickly falls away" (Matthew 13:20-21). Although soil exists under the rocks, this seed only produced quick but transient results. Jesus let his disciples know that this person would show tremendous emotions at the onset of their religious experience but would unfortunately have no depth. And because of this, when "trouble or persecution" arise because of the word, he would have no stability because of the shallowness of ground he stood on and the lack of spiritual depth he possessed in their hearts.

"The one who received the seed that fell among the thorns is the man who hears the word, but the worries of this life and the deceitfulness of wealth choke it, making it unfruitful" (Matthew 13:23). This ground was much more fertile than the one before and was even too fertile, for much more than wheat was able to grow in the soil. This person desired to grow but unfortunately did not understand what surrounded him once he made his commitment to the word. He had good motives but eventually was chocked and drowned in the process and thus, was "robbed" of eternal life.

However, the "one who received the seed that fell on good soil is the man who hears the word and understands it. He produces a crop, yielding a hundred, sixty or thirty times what was sown" (Matthew 13:24). It was Jesus' intention that his followers bear fruit, for anything less than bearing fruit would not allow one to enter into his kingdom.

THE TEN SERVANTS AND THE TEN MINAS

The Background

One of the few parables given within the scope of a geographical location was the parable of the ten servants and the ten pounds. Found in Matthew 25:14–30 and Luke 19:11–27, Jesus taught a parable on stewardship in relation to the Kingdom of God. Just before the parable, he had gone to be the guest of Zacchaeus the sinner and had told him that salvation had come to him. Then he stated that "the Son of Man came to seek and to save what was lost" (Luke 19:10).

Luke makes the point that "while they were listening to this, he went on to tell them a parable, because he was near Jerusalem and the people thought that the Kingdom of God was going to appear at once" (Luke 19:11). Being "near Jerusalem" meant that Jesus and the people were going up a steep incline and this would be the same place where he would suffer and die. From Luke's perspective, it was right after Jesus' words of him coming to save the lost that he speaks this parable.

The Parable

Jesus began the parable stating, "A man of noble birth went to a distant country to have himself appointed king and then to return" (Luke 19:12). Jesus used a political scene familiar to his audience as the background for this parable. The people would have remembered Herod the Great making a voyage to Rome in 40 B.C. desiring that Rome appoint him as king. In addition, Archilles, who had built a palace in Jericho, had gone to Rome in order that he might be elevated to the title of king, for only the Roman senate could bestow this title. So as the story opens, Jesus uses some familiarity to portray his character who was one of high birth and him going into a far country to receive for himself kingship.

Yet before the nobleman left, he "called ten of his servants and gave them ten minas. 'Put this money to work,' he said, 'until I come back.'" Out of his many servants, the nobleman only called ten and gave them ten minas or pounds. The weight and sum of one mina was equal to 100 drachmae. He desired that these men literally "do business" with the resources that they were entrusted with. They were expected to invest and to generate interest.

After giving the money to his servants and arriving in the distant country, the nobleman was given a surprise response. The "subjects hated him and sent a delegation after him to say, 'We don't want this man to be our king'" (Luke 19:14). These subjects were the inhabitants and citizens of the distant country of whom the nobleman came to and they showed hatred and disdain in his arrival for an unspecified reason. To let this nobleman know how they really felt, they even sent an ambassador to tell him that he was not welcome. Yet despite the hatred of the citizens, "He was made king" and then he "returned home."

After being made king, he "sent for the servants to whom he had given the money, in order to find out what they had gained with it" (Luke 19:15). The first servant came and said, "Sir, your mina has earned ten more." The master replied, "Well done, my good servant! Because you have been trustworthy in a very small matter, take charge of ten cities" (Luke 19:17). Although the increase was great, the reward was even greater, for seemingly each one mina that was increased equaled one entire city he would rule.

The second servant came and said, "Sir, your mina has earned five more. His master answered, 'You take charge of five cities'" (Luke 19:18-19). This servant like the first one used the little money given to him and he increased it. For his increase, the master puts him in charge of cities as well. For both of these servants, the master commends them for being faithful and not successful, and their reward does not consist of privileges but rather greater responsibilities.

Then Jesus states that a third servant came and said, "Sir, here is your mina; I have kept it laid away in a piece of cloth. I was afraid of you, because you are a hard man. You take out what you did not put in and reap what you did not sow" (Luke 19:20-21). This servant claimed to be afraid of his master and because of his fear, he was unfaithful and careless. He never really positioned himself to do good with the monies that was given to him in the first place. He not only critically misjudged his master but he developed a wrong and twisted view of his true character.

Then his master replied, "I will judge you by your own words, you wicked servant! You knew, did you, that I am a hard man, taking out what I did not put in, and reaping what I did not sow? Why then didn't you put my money on deposit, so that when I came back, I could have collected it with interest?" (Luke 19:22-23). What the third servant actually stated of the master was true and because of this truthful statement, the master asks why he did not invest the monies that were given to him. It was to this question that this servant never responded to.

Then the master stated to those standing by, "Take his mina away from him and give it to the one who has ten minas" (Luke 19:24). No longer would this servant be able to keep what the master gave him for he was no longer worthy nor competent. Although the master was informed that "he already has ten", he was not concerned for he stated, "I tell you that to everyone who has, more will be given, but as for the one who has nothing, even what he has will be taken away" (Luke 19:26). From Jesus' perspective, it only will benefit those who actually increase that which was given to him, for he would only receive more in addition to what he already had. In addition, seemingly to vent his frustration to those who resisted him earlier, the master stated that "those enemies of mine who did not want me to be king over them - bring them here and kill them in front of me" (Luke 19:27).

The Application

This is one of the parables of Jesus that not only opposes the religious leaders but actually broadcasts their doom. The Pharisees and others religious leaders certainly opposed Jesus throughout his ministry when he came proclaiming his kingdom ministry. They not only hated him but wanted to kill him, which they eventually did. But in this parable, Jesus actual stated that they would be brought forth and killed in front of him, as well as all those who do not trust and believe in him.

In addition, Jesus professed that the one who responds with faithfulness to his gifts will be the one who receives the greater gifts. Yet the one who proves to be unproductive will lose that which they have. Thus, all of Jesus' followers must be mindful of their stewardship and of him promises.

THE TEN VIRGINS

The Background

This parable mentioned in Matthew 25:1-13 is actually a continuation of Jesus' discourse which began in the previous chapters regarding his Second Coming. He earlier told the religious leaders that they would not see him again until they said, "Blessed is he who comes in the name of the Lord" (Matthew 23:39). In light of this saying as well as others statements made by him, his disciples were inquisitive in knowing what the signs would be of his coming at the end of the age. Jesus proceeded to tell them these numerous signs and he now spoke this parable of the ten virgins to quicken them in being diligent and ready for his return.

The Parable

He begins by stating that the "Kingdom of Heaven will be like ten virgins who took their lamps and went out to meet the bridegroom" (Matthew 25:1). By way of background, the three stages to a Jewish weddings was first the engagement, which was the formal agreement made by the fathers, then the betrothal, which was the ceremony where the vows are made, and then the marriage, which occurred about one year later when the bridegroom came at an unanticipated time for his bride.

This opening scene focused on preparations for the third phase of the wedding which was to take place in the home of the groom. A great crowd of family and friends would fill the house and into the streets, and as the crowd was gathering, the groom and several close friends would make their way to the home of the bride, which was assumed to be across town or in a nearby village. From there, the groom would collect his bride and escort her back to his family home, where the crowd awaited and the marriage feast would be held.[219] The virgins were obligated to meet the bridegroom, which was a great means of happiness for them, and the wedding party would consist of the ten virgins. The fact that Jesus mentioned virgin women here would be atypical from one standpoint because of how insignificant women were during this era. Yet it was a common occurrence for Jewish women to be virgins before they were married which portrayed their purity.

In describing the disposition of the virgins, Jesus states, "Five of them were foolish and five were wise. The foolish ones took their lamps but did not take any oil with them" (Matthew 25:2-3). As these virgins come to wait for the bridegroom, their main duty was to have lights in their hands, which symbolized honor and service. Yet the five foolish virgins only had enough oil to make their lamps burn for the current moment as if the bridegroom would have no delays. They had no bottle of oil with them and they were only prepared for the moment but not for the long-haul. But the next five virgins were in direct contrast to these first five because they "took oil in jars along with their lamps" (Matthew 25:4). They understood their need to not only be prepared for the now but also for the later. And their understanding proved them right and fit because "the bridegroom was a long time in coming, and they all became drowsy and fell asleep" (Matthew 25:5).

The parade, which was currently winding through the streets, took much longer than anticipated and the hour was getting very late. All ten of the women's enthusiasm wore out and as a result, they all fell asleep. There was nothing wrong with this fact because both the wise and foolish virgins fell asleep. Yet the concern was not in them all falling asleep but rather those who were not prepared when the bridegroom would finally came.

And that time eventually came, for "at midnight the cry rang out: 'Here's the bridegroom! Come out to meet him!'" That fact of him coming at midnight was the time when the people least expected it. Then all the virgins "woke up and trimmed their lamps." They were all getting ready to show their respect and honor to the bridegroom, and although the bridegroom and the party were not currently outside the house, they would be there within moments. So as they all trimmed their lamps, the foolish ones realized that their oil was gone and because of this, they "said to the wise, 'Give us some of your oil; our lamps are going out'" (Matthew 25:8). The five foolish lamps were lit, for oil would not light an extinguished lamp. But their lamps were quickly disintegrating and they had no oil left to continue to keep their lamps lit. It was certainly an honorable request seeing the current need of the five foolish virgins.

But to their dismay, the five wise virgins replied, "No, there may not be enough for both us and you. Instead, go to those who sell oil and buy some for yourselves'" (Matthew 25:9). It was at this moment that these foolish virgins realized their folly and the wisdom of the others. They had no choice but to leave the house where the bridegroom was coming to and to go to find some oil from someone else.

But while they were going to buy oil, "the bridegroom arrived" and the "virgins who were ready went in with him to the wedding banquet. And the door was shut" (Matthew 25:10). It was customary for the door to be shut when all the guests came in to secure those who were inside and to keep anyone from coming in. Now only those inside were able to experience the joy and excitement of seeing the bridegroom.

Sometime later, the foolish virgins came and said, "Sir! Sir! Open the door for us!" They would have been speaking to the bridegroom and would have been begging him to let them in. But he replied, "I tell you the truth, I don't know you" (Matthew 25:11-12). What an utter dismay and shock it was for those women who came to the door, for they were not allowed to come and experience the joy of celebration. Even more demoralizing to them was the reply in which the bridegroom stated that he did not even know them. Certainly others in the house would have known them, but it was the answer from the man at the door who gave them these disheartening words. Consequently, it did not matter what others thought but rather what the bridegroom thought and how foolish these virgins must have felt knowing that they were not prepared.

The Application

Jesus ends the parable by saying, "Therefore keep watch, because you do not know the day or the hour" (Matthew 25: 13). As was often the case, those listening to Jesus' parables were left hanging with the outcome of the story. Yet from his perspective, it was the spiritual message that he desired his listeners to walk away from. For those who desire to be his followers, they would have to make up in their minds to watch and be prepared.

There are many applications to this parable of which I will explain a few. First, every individual must participate in God's Kingdom with his own resources. Too many parables illustrate the fact that man must use wisely that which God has given him and one will be judged according to how he use what has been given him.

Second, participating in God's Kingdom required a long commitment. Therefore, advance planning was necessary. Third, although the depiction of virgins symbolized that which was good within Jewish standards, Jesus made his point clear by letting his audience know that some people will be lost. They would appear respectable, clean and moral, but because of negligence and a lack of preparation, they would not be able to enter into the door.

THE TWO SONS

The Background

In Matthew 21:28–32, we have the parable of the two sons. Just before this parable, Jesus entered into the temple courts and while he was teaching, the chief priests and the elders came and asked him by what authority had he been doing these things and who gave him this authority. Jesus told them that he would ask a question and they must answer his question in order for him to answer their question. Jesus then asked the question of where John's baptism came from. After discussing it among themselves, they realized that it was best for them to not answer the question, and they did not. Then Jesus told them that he would not tell them by what authority he was doing these things.

The Parable

Then in their very presence, he told this parable stating, "What do you think? There was a man who had two sons. He went to the first and said, 'Son, go and work today in the vineyard'" (Matthew 21:28). He began by asking a question which would set the tone for the entire parable. This question would cause for the people listening in the temple courts to begin comparing these two sons and to make an analysis at the end. Both sons would have the same father and would be given the same instructions, beginning with the first son. The simple statement that the father gave this son was not a question or a proposal but rather a command, for he told him to "go and work."

The first son replied, "I will not" but sometime later, "he changed his mind and went." This son was certainly rude to tell his father initially that he would not go and work. Yet although his initial response was careless and reckless, he somehow "changed his mind." This word for change would actually be the word for repentance. As a result, the master not only forgave him but gave him a second chance to work in his vineyard.

Then the father went and told the second son to go and work in his vineyard as well. He answered, "I will, sir, but he did not go" (Matthew 21:30). Different from the first son, he gave the right answer but his actions showed a different response. He gave a profession but he did not validate it with obedience. After this response, Jesus asks the question, "Which of the two did what his father wanted? 'The first', they answered" (Matthew 21:31). Both sons had their blunders but it was evident that only one obeyed.

The Application

Then Jesus puts real life application to this parable by analyzing both sons starting with the first. He states, "I tell you the truth, the tax collectors and the prostitutes are entering the kingdom of God ahead of you." The tax collectors and prostitutes were mostly despised by the religious leaders. These sinners had at first rejected the message of John and Jesus, but they eventually came to believe. Here, Jesus told these leaders that these sinners would enter into God's Kingdom ahead of them, which was a definitive insult. Jesus did not encourage or promote their sin but rather simply emphasized their obedience to his message.

Then speaking directly to these religious leaders, he analyzed the second son by stating, "For John came to you to show you the way of righteousness, and you did not believe him, but the tax collectors and the prostitutes did. And even after you saw this, you did not repent and believe him" (Matthew 21:32). John was the one who initiated the kingdom movement and he showed the true way of righteousness, repentance, and submission, which was something far different than what the religious leaders practiced. Jesus was plainly letting these religious leaders know that they rejected this message but the "sinners" obeyed. Then he showed how callous and hypocritical they were in not believing even though they saw these sinners believe.

The overall premise of this parable was for Jesus to portray how ignorant and callous of heart the religious leaders were in not receiving his kingdom message even though they saw the worst of sinners receive it. The first brother, representing the worse of sinners, initially disobeyed. Yet when the truth was preached to him, he submitted to God and his messengers John and Jesus. Because he obeyed, his hope of entering the kingdom would not be taken away. On the other hand, his brother, representing the scribes and Pharisees, claimed to believe in God all along but his actions did not line up with his beliefs. He professed obedience but never submitted to God or his messengers. Another premise of this parable represents the Jews and Gentiles. The first son would represent the Gentiles who would obey and come to salvation while the later would represent the Jews who would reject Jesus.

Although it was strange teachings from the religious leader's mindset, Jesus made his point clear. What ultimately matters to God most was not what one said but rather what one does. The scribes and Pharisees talked the talk but were coldhearted and unable to come to the truth. Just before this parable, they were so concerned with what authority Jesus was doing these things. Yet Jesus was trying to let them know that they needed to be concerned about their own unrepentant hearts and not about what he was doing. Unless they changed, he assured them that they would not enter into his kingdom.

THE UNJUST STEWARD

The Background

In Luke 16:1-9, we have Jesus' most notorious parable, for he actually commends an unjust steward for acting wisely once he had his "stewardship" taken away. Following the parable, we have Jesus' application in which he reminded his disciples that they are but stewards of God in his kingdom. Although this parable was spoken to his disciples, Jesus was actually talking about the Pharisees, of which he often did in most of his teachings, for they "heard all of this" (Luke 16:14). Thus, he would not only be cautioning his disciples about the nature of his kingdom but he had a second intention in rebuking the religious leaders.

The Parable

The parable begins with Jesus telling his disciples, "There was a rich man whose manager was accused of wasting his possessions" (Luke 16:1). The same word for manager is steward or superintendent and it would have been known for him to manage money or property. Since everything the manager handled belonged to the rich man who owned everything, somehow he heard that his manager was cheating or wasting his goods. We don't know who brought these charges on the manager, but clearly the intelligence came from sources that were reliable to the rich man. What was disheartening to him was that his manager was not only wasting goods but was actually wasting *his* goods.

Now the manager was being called on to give an account of what he had done. The rich man called him in and asked him, "What is this I hear about you? Give an account of your management" (Luke 16:2). The manager was not asked to balance his account but rather to turn them in so that they could be inspected. And on top of this, he was given the disheartening news that he was no longer needed because he was told, "you cannot be manager any longer."

Now that his world has come crashing down, he said to himself, "What shall I do now? My master is taking away my job. I'm not strong enough to dig, and I'm ashamed to beg. I know what I'll do so that, when I lose my job here, people will welcome me into their houses" (Luke 16:3-4). Although he had not taken his life seriously in the past, his priorities concerning what he would now do was taken seriously. He quickly understood the unattractive options that were available for him. He was probably a feeble man for he initially understood that he was too weak to dig. At the same time, he understood the shame that accompanied begging for food and money. Now at the bottom of his life, he forced upon himself to come up with a workable plan that would take away his shame.

So "he called in each one of his master's debtors. He asked the first, 'How much do you owe my master?' 'Eight hundred gallons of olive oil,' he replied. The manager told him, 'Take your bill, sit down quickly, and make it four hundred.' Then he asked the second, 'And how much do you owe?' 'A thousand bushels of wheat,' he replied. He told him, 'Take your bill and make it eight hundred'" (Luke 16:5-7). Knowing that he was losing his job and was guilty of wasting the rich man's goods, his objective was to make social contacts with his master's debtors who were tenants behind on their payments. He quickly began to reduce their debts to his master so that he would at least receive half of what they owed instead of receiving none. In addition, the manager was making those debtors obligated to show kindness to him.

What was the reaction of the rich man? Surprisingly, he "commended the dishonest manager because he had acted shrewdly" (Luke 16:8). While not endorsing his conduct of dishonesty, the rich man did approve of his shrewdness, perceptiveness, and clever thinking.

But how could Jesus use an example out of a dishonest man and why would he commend this steward? First, he did not commend him for his actions but rather for his sharp thinking and assessment on his current situation once he realized that he had done wrong. From the owner's perspective, the manager's honest assessment of his life portrayed true wisdom and was worth commending. Second, the manager took advantage of his present position to set up a secure establishment for many years to come. And third, the very nature of Jesus' parables constituted strange concepts regarding his kingdom and he sometimes uses malevolence to make a respectable and noteworthy point regarding his kingdom.

The Application

After commending the manager, Jesus made the point that "the people of this world are more shrewd in dealing with their own kind than are the people of the light." From his perspective, if his followers would pursue the Kingdom of God with the same vigor and zeal that the world pursued mundane affairs, the entire world would be different, and his kingdom would be filled with authentic and strong Christians.

Then he proceeds to make application of the parable as it concerned man's place in the kingdom. He states, "I tell you, use worldly wealth to gain friends for yourselves, so that when it is gone, you will be welcomed into eternal dwellings" (Luke 16:9).

Jesus transferred the principle illustrated by the story of the unjust steward to a contemporary application. From his perspective, one needed to use their present resources to plan ahead for eternal life. For him to say "use worldly wealth to gain friends" meant to "turn to one's advantage", and this steward did just that. He began showing mercy to those who were bound by debt and he turned them to his advantage. His mindset and actions were changed and it became evident among everyone including his boss. Seemingly, this manager, although he was accused of wasting his master's possessions, still had a chance to enter into the Kingdom of God despite his previous failures.

Then Jesus continued to make application by telling his disciples that "whoever can be trusted with very little can also be trusted with much" and if "you have not been trustworthy in handling worldly wealth, who will trust you with true riches" (Luke 16:10-11). He basically let them know that everything "belongs to God" and "no servant can serve two masters" for "either he will hate the one and love the other, or he will be devoted to the one and despise the other" (Luke 16:13). His message was uncharacteristic from the Pharisees' standpoint because they loved money. Yet because of their covetous ways, Jesus cautioned his disciples to watch out for them and their hypocritical behaviors. He also desired to let everyone know that one day they will stand before him to give an account of the things that they have done, for this was the very reason why he spoke this parable.

THE UNMERCIFUL SERVANT

The Background

In Matthew 18:23-35, Jesus gave a heavy duty lesson on forgiveness. Leading up to this parable was Peter's question to Jesus asking him how many times he should forgive his brother when he sins against him. In asking this question, Peter may have used the Old Testament background to justify his answer, for Amos 1:3 states, "This is what the LORD says: 'For three sins of Damascus, even for four, I will not turn back my wrath.'" Therefore from his perspective, to forgive someone seven times would have not only been a great matter but would have gone far and beyond the Old Testament mandate. To him, this would have shown extreme love and repentance.

Yet Jesus answered him saying, "I tell you, not seven times, but seventy-seven times" (Matthew 18:22). He gave an unexpected answer to Peter not saying that he was to forgive 490 times but rather that he needed to forgive as many times as it was needed and sought. He was stating that he needed not to keep records of one's trespasses, and therefore, he should never come to the point of refusing forgiveness when someone asked. Soon, Peter would understand that this same unconditional repentance was a pre-condition to not only man's forgiveness by God but also for one's entrance into the kingdom.

The Parable

Then Jesus begins his parable stating, "Therefore, the Kingdom of Heaven is like a king who wanted to settle accounts with his servants. As he began the settlement, a man who owed him 10,000 talents was brought to him" (Matthew 18:23-24). The word "therefore" was mentioned because it showed that this parable was given in reference to the matter that just preceded it. This parable begins with a king who decided to inspect and settle the accounts of those who owed him money. As he looked throughout his record books, he could not help but notice an unbelievably high debt that was needed to be paid. The size of this debt was significant! The English Revised Version shows that one talent would be about $1,000. Therefore from this margin, this servant owed 10 million dollars. However, other figures factored this amount to be between 12 million and 1 billion dollars. Clearly, this figure represented an unpayable debt for even the average wealthy person living in this time period. To this man's disfavor, he was brought to the king.

"Since he was not able to pay, the master ordered that he and his wife and his children and all that he had be sold to repay the debt" (Matthew 18:25). It was common during this time period for a man's entire immediate family to be sold into slavery and for their land and possessions to be taken for not being able to pay a debt. The sale of the man's family rested upon the general supposition that they were the king's property in the first place. But unfortunately, this selling would not pay off the debt because slaves at their highest price were only sold for one talent.

Seeing the misfortune that would befall him, "The servant fell on his knees before him. 'Be patient with me,' he begged, 'and I will pay back everything'" (Matthew 18:26). His actions of falling on his knees before the master demonstrated the Old Testament's act of worship. This was the servant's last plea for help and hope from the king who was in total control of his life, his family's life, and his well-being. After seeing his actions and hearing his desperate cry for mercy, the "master took pity on him, canceled the debt and let him go" (Matthew 18:27). The master showed an unbelievable and uncharacteristic act by not only nullifying all that he owed but also by letting him and his family go free. Although the servant told the master that he would "pay back everything", the master understood that his debt could never be repaid, no matter what pleas and promises he made.

Those listening to this parable may have believed that this would be an appropriate end of the story. Yet Jesus does not stop but continues to say, "But when that servant went out, he found one of his fellow servants who owed him a hundred denarii. He grabbed him and began to choke him. 'Pay back what you owe me!' he demanded" (Matthew 18:28). This servant seemed to have immediately forgotten the debt that he owed the king and he actually went out to search for one of his fellow servants who owed him a significantly smaller amount of money. A hundred denarii, which was less than one to a million of what he owed the king, equaled 100 day's wages for the average peasant. The Jews listening would have quickly understood that this was an insignificant amount of money in light of the 10,000 talents.

This fellow servant demonstrated the exact same actions and words as the servant did in front of the king, for he "fell to his knees and begged him, 'Be patient with me, and I will pay you back'" (Matthew 18:29). Unlike the king, the servant refused to forgive and more shocking, he threw his fellow servant "into prison until he could pay the debt." How could one repay a debt sitting in the walls of a prison? Yet, the king never threw the servant in prison for his unpaid debt! But here, the servant took action and actually locked up his fellow servant.

His sin would come to the ears of the mighty king because "when the other servants saw what had happened, they were greatly distressed and went and told their master everything that had happened" (Matthew 18:31). From the other servant's perspective, how could this man not forgive his fellow servant of a payable debt when the king forgave him of an unpayable debt?

After finding out all that this servant had done, the "master called the servant in. 'You wicked servant,' he said, 'I canceled all that debt of yours because you begged me to. Shouldn't you have had mercy on your fellow servant just as I had on you?'" (Matthew 18:32-33). The master called him wicked not because he was a murderer or thief, nor because he was associated with sins that the culture would have labeled as repulsive and abominable. Rather, he called him wicked because of his unforgiving and merciless heart.

Because he did not show mercy and forgive his fellow servant, the master not only put him in jail but delivered him "to be tortured". This expression also meant "delivered him to the tormentors". During this era, jailers would have been assigned the task to being instrumental in torturing those in prison. This action showed the severity of the treatment that the master thought such a case would require in light of the servant's wickedness. In addition, although the master appointed these actions to this servant until he "should pay back all he owed", everyone listening would have understood that he would never actually pay back this debt, especially sitting in a jail cell.

The Application

Then Jesus gave the application of the parable saying, "This is how my heavenly Father will treat each of you unless you forgive your brother from your heart" (Matthew 18:35). What a tough message to swallow and what strange teachings this was in light of the kingdom. His message was plain and simple. If God has forgiven you, you must forgive your brother. Even more, one must forgive the "payable" grievances against one's brother because there would be no way for him to pay back in full the debt he owed to God. In addition, Jesus made it clear that forgiveness is a matter of the heart and one must always be willing to forgive.

The overall analogies in the parable begin with God as the king and all people on earth as the servants of the king. Unfortunately, all servants have an unpayable debt, yet through God's grace and clemency, he not only forgives but cancelled all debts with no strings attached. The servant who was forgiven and refused to forgive his fellow servants could represent any human being. Therefore, if any man refuses to show mercy and forgiveness, he will be put in prison and turned over to the tormenters.

"Tormenters" is mentioned several times in Scripture. First, when the rich man died in Luke 16:28, he opened his eyes in a place of torment because of his wicked actions on earth. Here, the place of torment represents a place apart from God when one dies. Second, torment was associated with The Great Tribulation (Revelation 9:5; 14:11; 18:7), for God will send locust with scorpion tales that sting to "torment" people on earth for five months (Revelation 9). Here, we see God turning one over to the tormentors. And last, the Lake of Fire is represented as a place of torment for not only man but for Satan and his angels. We know this is true because there were three references in the Gospels where demons literally begged Jesus not to "torment" them before it was time (Matthew 8:29; Mark 5:7; Luke 8:28). These evil spirits understood that they would be tormented in the future and this time of torment would occur when they get thrown into the Lake of Fire with Satan their leader. We know that Satan would be thrown in the Lake of Fire in Revelation 20:10 and since demons are little "devils" and are only associated with their leader the devil, they will be thrown with him in the Lake of Fire.

In conclusion, it was evident in relation to the Kingdom of God that man must forgive or he would be eternally condemned to not only a place of torment but to God's "tormentors". Peter was able to see the importance of forgiveness and he would be able to understand how quickly God could humble the most arrogant and pitiless human being. Therefore, it was important to forgive the payable trespasses of man while on earth to experience the joys of God's Kingdom.

THE VINEYARD OWNER AND WICKED TENANTS

The Background

In Matthew 21:33–46, Mark 12:1–12, and Luke 20:9–19, we have the parable of the vineyard owner and the wicked tenants. This parable was an autobiography of Jesus himself and it not only proclaimed what took place in the past with the killing of the prophets but prophetically stated what would occur in the future with the killing of Jesus and the destruction of Jerusalem.

There were a couple of major occurrences leading up to this parable. In the previous chapter, we see Jesus "driving out those who were selling" in the temple area and because of this, the "chief priests, the teachers of the law and the leaders among the people were trying to kill him" (Luke 19:47). Then right before this parable, the chief priests, the teachers of the law, and the elders came up to Jesus asking him by whose authority he was doing "these things". Consequently, Jesus never answered their question. But what must be understood as a background to this parable is the fact that Middle Easterners have always taken their sacred sites, including the temple, very seriously. Thus, it was not a surprise that they wanted to kill him not just before this parable but right after it as well.

The Parable

Jesus begins the parable by stating, "A man planted a vineyard, rented it to some farmers and went away for a long time" (Luke 20:9). This parable seemingly was taken literally from Isaiah's parable of "The Song of the Vineyard" in chapter 5. His parable portrayed one who "had a vineyard on a fertile hillside" and he "planted it with the choicest vines" and eventually desired a crop of good grapes. However, "it yielded only bad fruit". The owner wondered what more could have been done and after reasoning with himself, he eventually decided to "take away its hedge" and to destroy it so that nothing would grow there. He then concluded the parable by stating that the vineyard is Israel.

Jesus continued to say, "At harvest time he sent a servant to the tenants so they would give him some of the fruit of the vineyard. But the tenants beat him and sent him away empty-handed" (Luke 20:10). In the Herodian period, the wealthy often lived some distance from their estates[220] and the tenants did not own the vineyard but rather they were only keepers and tillers of the soil. The owner would have sent his servants across the land so that the tenants would give him some fruit. But they beat the servant and sent him away with no fruit. In this society, actions of this nature were very rare understanding the facts of the owner's prestige and power over the tenants and the shame that would have accompanied such actions.

Yet graciously, the man "sent another servant, but that one also they beat and treated shamefully and sent away empty-handed" (Luke 20:11). Seeing the actions that were done to his first servant, it was certainly atypical for the owner to send yet another one. Still even more surprising, the same result occurred but in addition, the servant was also treated shamefully. In the Mediterranean world, shame and honor were a huge factor, for people would often try to avoid shame as much as possible. At the same time, personal honor was held in extremely high esteem.

But to the amazement of everyone listening, the owner "sent still a third, and they wounded him and threw him out" (Luke 20:12). There was a progression with the way each servant was treated. The first one was beaten, the second was beaten and "treated shamefully" and the third was wounded and cast out.

Then the owner asked himself the question, "What shall I do?" He knew that he could not afford to allow his servants to experience more shame and disgrace. And because of this, he said, "I will send my son, whom I love; perhaps they will respect him" (Luke 20:13). The owner was acting out of unspeakable nobility and he profoundly hoped that his choice of total vulnerability would awaken a long-forgotten sense of honor in the hearts of the violent men who were waiting in the vineyard. He was willing to take this risk.[221] His servants had already been beaten and wounded and no longer was he willing to allow his enemies to dictate the nature of his response. He believed that by sending his son, the tenants would not only feel shame but that they would reverence him.

But when the tenants saw the owner's son coming from afar, "they talked the matter over. 'This is the heir,' they said. 'Let's kill him, and the inheritance will be ours.' So they threw him out of the vineyard and killed him" (Luke 20:14-15). Unfortunately, the renters forgot that they were merely renters and tillers of the vineyard and they now assumed that they were owners. They desired to take for themselves all that the master worked hard for and their actions showed this by them dragging his son out of the vineyard to avoid defiling the good grapes and killing him. This progression of violence, displayed from the actions of the tenants, escalated to its pinnacle by their act of murder.

Then Jesus asks, "What then will the owner of the vineyard do to them?" Those listening to this story would unanimously agree that these tenants should be destroyed. And that is what Jesus said stating, "He will come and kill those tenants and give the vineyard to others" (Luke 20:16). The vineyard owner was clearly the hero of the story. From Jesus' perspective, the tenants had opportunities to do right even after they had done wrong. Yet they did not learn from their actions but only increased their violence.

The Application

Although Jesus never gave a formal application of the parable, at least of yet, the people listening to him understood some real life application, for when they "heard this, they said, 'May this never be!'" They probably did not say these words in hopes that the owner would not kill the tenants but rather that the tenants would never betray the owner of the vineyard in this way. But he indirectly answered the people's question by letting them know that this action would take place and that the fate of the owner's son would apply to him.

After looking directly at the people, Jesus asked them, "Then what is the meaning of that which is written: 'The stone the builders rejected has become the capstone.' Everyone who falls on that stone will be broken to pieces, but he on whom it falls will be crushed" (Luke 20:17-18). The stone was a symbol of God and the Jews listening would have remembered the Old Testament passages of the Lord being "the Rock" (Deuteronomy 32:4). Jesus was trying to let the people know that he was that stone that was rejected by his own people (John 1:10-11).

But Jesus continued to talk about that stone for he referred to Daniel's prophecy by stating that "a rock was cut out, but not by human hands. It struck the statue on its feet of iron and clay and smashed them. Then the iron, the clay, the bronze, the silver and the gold were broken to pieces at the same time and became like chaff on a threshing floor in the summer. The wind swept them away without leaving a trace. But the rock that struck the statue became a huge mountain and filled the whole earth" (2:34-35). This passage in Daniel reflected well what Jesus stated about the impact of the stone. Jesus was letting the people know that those that acknowledged him as being insignificant and those who were offended in him would be the ones who "will be broken to pieces" and "will be crushed". Because of that stone, the builders would fall and become broken.

These were fighting words not from the crowd's perspective but from the religious leader's perspective, for "they looked for a way to arrest him immediately, because they knew he had spoken this parable against them. But they were afraid of the people" (Luke 20:19). These leaders not only perceived that Jesus spoke against them but they clearly knew it. Jesus was interested in the heritage of Israel and he knew that the religious leaders were against this and that was why they killed God's past servants. Now they had a guilty conscience and instead of submitting themselves to the words of Jesus, they were now trying to kill him. But only because they feared the people was the reason why they did not take him right then.

There were many analogies and applications to this parable that must be revealed. God was the one who let out his vineyard, representing Israel, to the leaders of Israel, representing the farmers or tenants. The actions he took to plant and hedge the winepress represented the establishment of Israel to receive the message from his servants the prophets. Yet it was the leaders of Israel who abused and shamefully mistreated the prophets. The son of the master represented Jesus and although he would be killed outside the city of Jerusalem, he would be "appointed heir of all things" (Hebrews 1:1-2).

This parable clearly shows that the leaders of Israel recognized Jesus as the true heir and the Messiah, yet they willingly chose not to believe that he was God. Although Jesus would be rejected, he would be the head cornerstone and exalted to his Father's right hand. He would eventually cause all others to be "broken" and "crushed" and all his enemies could expect no other punishment but to be destroyed.

CHAPTER 4
MIRACLES OF WONDER

Unfortunately, some claim that man has now "come of age," that we now have a scientific and empirical worldview that is obviously linked up with reality and which cannot take miracles seriously.[222] Yet this perspective is not only offensive to the biblical emphasis on miracles but it undeniably wipes out the world religions of Christianity and Judaism. From Christianity's standpoint, the absence of miracles would have not allowed the early church to come into being, yet the belief in miracles lies at the heart of authentic Christian faith.

The Introduction to Miracles

It is important psychologically for human beings to believe that a supernatural power directs their affairs in life. In a world that is unpredictable, human beings need to believe in a divine spiritual presence and they need not only to believe in the God of heaven but in his ability to work miracles. This belief helps man to cope with his own fears and gives him security and hope throughout their life.

Miracles are unique occurrences that appear in distinct periods of crisis situations involving revelation and redemption. Although the miracles of Jesus were incredible and sometimes hard to believe, Christians accept them as actual events. In the New Testament, Jesus constantly equated his miracles with faith and the faithful. Those who were willing to heed him and follow his teachings were the people who benefited from the miracles. According to the Bible, miracles were witness by vast numbers of people, both those who supported Jesus and those who did not. Jesus' critics never denied the accuracy of the miracles, only the power behind them.

AN HISTORICAL INSTITUTION

Some people today do not believe in miracles because they do not see any "miraculous" happenings right in front of them. Because of this, many even refuse to believe in Jesus of God. Unlike the present world, the ancient world was not suspicious of miracles, for they were regarded as a normal, if somewhat extraordinary, part of life. They typically believed not only that supernatural powers existed, but that they intervened in human affairs.[223]

Moses and Joshua's Era

We first see an example with they drying "up the water of the Red Sea" that has been considered the most significant miracle of the Old Testament. Known as the centerpiece of Israel's history and of Old Testament religion, it was this miracle that the Jews were able to understand God's mighty hand as well as his power and might. It was also this very miracle that the Jews forgot which caused them to not trust in God and to forsake him and his commandments.

A second example is in the book of Joshua concerning the secular nation Jericho. After hearing what God had previously done, Rahab of Jericho told two men of Israel, "I know that the Lord has given this land to you and that a great fear of you has fallen on us, so that all who live in this country are melting in fear because of you. We have heard how the Lord dried up the water of the Red Sea for you when you came out of Egypt..." (Joshua 2:9-10). This nation did not deny or question the miracles of God but rather became scared at its extent. If these people did not believe that a miracle could take place, they would not have been "melting in fear." But since they were not suspicious of miracles, they regarded them as not only extraordinary but certainly able to occur.

Elijah and Elisha's Era

Signs and wonders were not restricted to the time of the exodus, though in some sense they may be seen as a continuation of it. There were mighty miraculous works that were done from the life and ministry of Elijah and Elisha. These two men were not only prophets but were instrumental in working miracles that promoted God and his future work for Israel.

Elijah's greatness was portrayed in the New Testament stating that John the Baptist would come in his spirit (Luke 1:17). Both Jesus and John during their ministries were sometimes thought as being Elijah. In the Old Testament, Elijah was introduced in 1 Kings 17:1 as Elijah the Tishbite. Some of his miracles included causing the rain the cease for three and a half years (1 Kings 17:1), resurrecting the widow's son (1 Kings 17:22), causing fire from heaven on the altar (1 Kings 18:38), causing it to rain (1 Kings 18:45), calling fire from heaven upon 100 soldiers (2 Kings 2:10; 12), and parting the Jordan River (2 Kings 2:8).

The transfer of leadership from Elijah to Elisha was breathtaking. Elisha was being coached by Elijah for 10 years and he had seen God's deliverance of the Jewish people and many of his works. But it was time for him to depart and for Elisha to emerge. After he was taken up in a fiery chariot, Elisha accepted the leadership of the sons of the prophets and became a renowned man of God throughout Palestine. He requested and received "a double portion" of Elijah's spirit (2 Kings 2:9) and his ministry as prophet lasted for sixty years (2 Kings 5:8). Some of his miracles included parting the Jordan (2 Kings 2:14), cursing the she bears (2 Kings 2:24), filling the valley with water (2 Kings 3:17), resurrecting the Shunammite's son from the dead (2 Kings 4:34), healing a man named Naaman (2 Kings 5:14), and restoring the sight of the Syrian army (2 Kings 6:20).

Concerning the miracle of Elijah controlling the rain, one must understand the problem of rain in Palestine. Rain falls only in the rainy season, which is from October to April. Its timing was everything and its quantity and quality had to work together from the people's perspective to provide them the quality of life they needed. If the rain fall was not kept in equilibrium, then all the people in the land would be affected. Too much rain would demolish the soil, as would too little. Since whoever could control rain could control life itself, the miracle of causing rain not to fall on the earth for three and a half years made one of the greatest impacts of all time for the people in that entire county. This miracle would have become well known throughout the region because of the extent of people that would have been affected by it.

The New Testament Era

In looking at the New Testament, the phrase signs and wonders appear some sixteen times. There was a shift in the focus of miracles from the exodus to now concentrating on the birth, life, death, and resurrection of Jesus. Just like miracles did not present a problem to those in the Old Testament, the people in the New Testament did not have a problem accepting them either. As a matter of fact, the early Christians used miracles as a means of giving credibility to their faith in light of their surrounding culture.

The central miracle of the New Testament was the resurrection of Jesus. Its credibility was given in each New Testament book with either a direct mention of the event or either a proclamation or assumption that it actually took place. This miraculously event was discussed meticulously in each Gospel and was affirmed by the Apostle Paul in 1 Corinthians 15 to be the foundation of Christian faith.

JESUS' IMPACT

The Jewish people waited over 400 years for a leader who would deliver them from their oppressors and set up a kingdom that would never end. The prophets of old had prophesied that he would come from the lineage of David. The Jews knew that God's promise of this future Messiah would be unconditional. Thus the Jews understood the surety of his coming just as sure as God existed. Yet no one knew the exact time or century when he would come.

Then during the reign of the Herod dynasty, God sent his son in the midst of a depressed and suppressed Jewish nation, and he came and informed the people that he was the fulfiller of the Old Testament prophets. On one specific occasion, he stated to the Jews who did not believe in him saying, "If you believed Moses, you would believe me, for he wrote about me. But since you do not believe what he wrote, how are you going to believe what I say?" (John 5:46-47). Jesus came as teacher and he eventually gathered 12 devoted disciples to help him promote the kingdom movement. Despite some opposition from the Jewish leader, he continued to promote the teachings of God which would eventually lead to his demise.

He first made an impact through his teachings in the synagogues and because of this, "The people were amazed at his teaching, because he taught them as one who had authority, not as the teachers of the law" (1:22). Teaching was Jesus' first way of not only impressing the crowds but in differentiating himself from the religious leaders.

But teachings were not all that he did to promote his kingdom. He also was a miracle worker. Yet this was a bit surprising to the Jewish people who understood Old Testament prophecy. Although some of the previous prophets like Elijah and Elisha performed miracles, they did not initially expect that their Messiah would also perform miracle. We see this on one occasion when the Pharisees desired to justify Jesus' miracle of casting out demons by saying that he only casts them out by Beelzebub who is the prince of devils (9:34; 12:24). Yet despite their justification and excuses, Jesus used miracles not to promote himself but God's work.

But by far, his greatest impact came from his miracles. We observe this when he had finished teaching in the synagogues, a man who was demon possessed cried out to Jesus saying, "What do you want with us, Jesus of Nazareth? Have you come to destroy us? I know who you are - the Holy One of God!" (1:24). How shocking this must have been for the crowds listening to him teach. Even more shocking were the words of the man telling him that he knew who he was and desired that he not destroy them. But Jesus sternly rebuked the demon possessed man saying, "Be quiet!" and "Come out of him!" Then "the evil spirit shook the man violently and came out of him with a shriek" (1:25-26). The people who saw this was amazed and asked each other, "What is this? A new teaching - and with authority! He even gives orders to evil spirits and they obey him" (1:27). But what was interesting was the fact that after he performed this miracle, "news about him spread quickly over the whole region of Galilee" (Mark 1:28) and that very evening after sunset, "people brought to Jesus all the sick and demon-possessed. The whole town gathered at the door, and Jesus healed many who had various diseases. He also drove out many demons, but he would not let the demons speak because they knew who he was" (Mark 1:32-34). It was his miracles and not his teachings that gave him the greatest impact. Yet after this incident, he let it be known to his disciples that despite the fact that everyone was looking for him, he came to preach (Mark 1:37-38).

JESUS' INDIVIDUALITY

Jesus was more than just a physician, for he was the Great Physician. His miracles of healing separated him from all other past doctors, magicians, and miracle workers. As his miracles were recorded one by one in the Gospels, he was unique as a miracle worker in several ways. First, he did not require an appointment for his special touch like many doctors and men of prestige did. We see in Mark 1:28-31 that after the news quickly spread over the whole region of Galilee that he had the authority to cast out demons, he left the synagogue and went with a couple of his disciples to the home of Simon and Andrew. Although he was not expecting to perform another miracle, some of the people surrounding him told him that Simon's mother-in-law was in bed with a fever. Despite any reservations or excuses, he "went to her, took her hand and helped her up" and the "fever left her". Throughout his entire ministry, he was never bothered or inconvenienced by someone's request for healing. We never see where he made prior arrangements to heal someone but rather at man's convenience, he was ready and available to meet their physical and spiritual need.

Second, he volunteered to be on call. In Mark 1:32-34, when the evening had come after sunset, "the people brought to Jesus all the sick and demon possessed. The whole town gathered at the door, and Jesus healed many who had various diseases. He also drove out many demons, but he would not let the demons speak because they knew who he was." He made himself available to heal as many who desired to be healed. And what was particularly strange was the fact that he healed numerous people "that evening after sunset". In other words, when the sun had gone down, he was still making himself available for the needs of the people. What the Gospel writers did not say was how long he was healing people that night, but since "the whole town gathered" at his door, we know that it probably took him a considerable amount of time. From his perspective, this was one of the reasons why he came and he did not see it as a task or obligation but rather as a part of his ministry.

Third, he practiced compassion. This seems easier said than done, for we must remember that he was 100% fully human just like you and I. He not only wept (Luke 19:41) and became angry (Matthew 21:12), but he would have become tired and weary, especially after a long day of working miracles. Yet he consistently practiced compassion and portrayed a genuine love for people despite his feelings. We see an example of this in Mark 1:39-42 when he traveled throughout Galilee preaching in the synagogues and driving out demons that unexpectedly, "a man with leprosy came to him and begged him on his knees, 'If you are willing, you can make me clean.' Filled with compassion, Jesus reached out his hand and touched the man. 'I am willing,' he said. 'Be clean!' Immediately the leprosy left him and he was cured." Jesus was probably teaching the people in the synagogues when he was interrupted with this man's plea. Even though the average person may have easily become frustrated, Jesus was moved with compassion. This example was just one of many that demonstrated his emotions as he sought to minister to people.

Fourth, he specialized in impossible cases. When even the best doctors and magicians would have past up an unachievable task, Jesus let it be known that nothing was too hard for God. We see an example of this in Mark 5 when a demon possessed man came out from the tomb to meet Jesus after he came across the lake to the region of the Gerasenes. This was no ordinary man, for Mark makes the point clear that no one could bind him with chains because previously he had broken even the strongest of chain. At the same time, no one was "strong enough to subdue him." But Jesus took upon himself to handle this hopeless case and would not only relieve this man from the demons but would carry on a personal conversation with him afterwards. People throughout the region were now able to see this man, who had been previously possessed, now sitting there with Jesus and in his right mind. Thus, the cases that were without a solution and not viable were easily solved and made possible by only Jesus.

The Definition of a Miracle

I suggest that a miracle is an irregular event that violates the laws of nature which shows an indication of power with the final intent of showing a specific purpose. Gary Habermas states that a miracle as an event in which God temporarily makes an exception to the natural order of things, to show that God is acting.[224] He specifically notes that miracles are only "temporarily", thus they are not revolving occurrences.

In my definition of miracle, I did not incorporate the workings of the true God in heaven, for there is biblical evidence that Satan and his demons work signs, wonders, and miracles. It has been said that only God can do miracles and that Satan only performs signs or wonders. I would agree that "true and authentic" miracles are workings of God alone but Satan has the capabilities of working miracles which are irregular, which violate the laws of nature, which demonstrate power, and that show purpose. Thus, all thoughtful persons should pay attention to the structure of their own worldview, for that worldview inevitably influences what they believe and how they live.[225] It is my purpose to promote the truth of what a miracle is and how it can change the average person's worldview. I will show this by explaining how a miracle is an irregularity of an event, how it is an infringement of nature's laws, how it is an indication of power, and how it intends to show a specific purpose.

AN IRREGULAR EVENT

A miracle is by definition at least a highly unusual and irregular event. If persons were to say that a miracle took place, they would be promoting a rare occurrence and not something that happens every day. Because miracles are irregular, greater claims must be supported by greater evidence. In other words, the adequate eyewitnesses and strong evidence can make it reasonable to trust that an implausible event has actually occurred.

An example of this comes from the narrative of Lazarus in John 11. The unfortunate situation for this man was that his sickness slowly led to his death. After he died, he had been given a common Jewish burial in one of the tombs and it had been four days before Jesus came and found him already in the tomb. The best possible scenario that his sister Martha could give Jesus would be that he would rise again during the resurrection at the last day. Yet Jesus told her that he was the resurrection and the life and even if someone was currently lifeless, he would raise them up immediately. Yet,

Martha and everyone around understood the impossible situation at hand. Even both sisters told Jesus that if he had been there, Lazarus would not have died. But Jesus simply asked the Jews where they had laid him so that he could change their natural way of thinking. Despite one of the sisters telling Jesus that he had been dead for four days, Jesus told the Jews to take away the stone. After weeping and groaning in himself, he cried in a loud voice and told Lazarus to come forth. To everyone's surprise and amazement, he came out.

Lazarus was not resuscitated but resurrected, the same way in which Jesus would be some time later. If he was resuscitated, this narrative would not have been an irregular event but rather would have been like many other past cases. But only Jesus could use an unusual situation and bring about a miraculous result even when virtually everyone around him could not see how it would take place. At the same time, this irregular event was able to be witnessed by many of the Jews. They would be able to serve as eyewitnesses in promoting this miraculous rare occurrence to people throughout the land. Consequently, it would be no surprise that many of the religious leaders wanted to kill Jesus.

AN INFRINGEMENT OF NATURE'S LAWS

Natural law or the Law of Nature is a theory that posits the existence of a law whose content was set by nature and therefore has validity everywhere. Laws have their foundation in scientific practice and that which is stated to be a law can not happen accidentally. There are at least three conditions necessary for the existence of a law within nature. First, it is a truth based on fact and not logic like the boiling point of water or sulfur. Second, it is true regardless of time and place. And third, it is universal. Therefore, all laws of nature must work the same way everywhere and it doesn't matter who does the experiment or where it occurs, the same results should appear.

In light of this, a miracle is not only an irregular event but is a violation of nature's laws. Specifically, a miracle runs contradictory to the observed processes of nature. Our knowledge of nature is a limited knowledge, yet from God's perspective, it is not contradictory. That is why a miracle is a violation of what man knows to be contradictory to nature's law and nothing is considered a miracle if it ever happens in the ordinary course of life. For example, it is no miracle that a man, seemingly in good health, should die all of the sudden because such a kind of death, though more unusual than any other, has been frequently observed to happen. But it is a miracle that a dead man should come to life.[226]

In looking at Lazarus' narrative, the fact that he was dead for four days assured his sisters, Mary and Martha, and all the Jews present that his chances of rising again were non-existent. They all understood one of nature's laws concerning the fact that dead people do not come back alive. To make sure that Lazarus was dead, Jesus purposefully waited till he died to come to his aid, and when he had come to the town of Bethany, he found out that he had been dead for four days (John 11:17-18). Then he caused an infringement of natural law by resurrecting Lazarus from the dead. This act was certainly an exception to the ordinary course of nature. As one author writes, "since it was Lazarus's nature to die in the circumstances of his illness, his resurrection was, in the strict sense, supernatural, going beyond what was natural for him. It was, therefore, a miracle."[227]

AN INDICATION OF POWER

Every human being who has ever lived knows that man himself cannot cause an irregular event or an infringement of nature's laws. Yet history points that irregular events causing an infringement of nature's laws has indeed taken place. Therefore, miracles point to the existence of God.

A well rounded Christian worldview will rule out opinions signifying that man cannot attain knowledge about God. At the same time, it has been implanted in the heart of every human being that God exists. Romans 1:19-20 states this in saying, "Since what may be known about God is plain to them, because God has made it plain to them. For since the creation of the world God's invisible qualities - his eternal power and divine nature - have been clearly seen, being understood from what has been made, so that men are without excuse." Even such early Christian thinkers as Augustine wanted the world to know that the Christian God and the Christian view of creation differed totally from the Platonic picture. Plato's god was not the infinite, all-powerful, and sovereign God of the Christian Scriptures. Plato's god was finite and limited.[228]

Given that there is factual confirmation that God exists, there is reason to expect that he would give a revelation. One of the central claims of Christian thought is that God acts in history. At least some of the events that occur in history – particularly miraculous events – occur because God brings them about. God is an agent in human history and in human lives, and he is a God who acts.[229] Only he is powerful enough to produce irregular events in time and space and to cause an infringement of nature's laws. When he came on the scene, he did not come promoting God as one who exists, for everyone knew this fact, but rather as God who acts and reveals. And because he exists, he was capable of producing miracles.

After understanding that God exists and that he acts and gives revelation, miracles exist and indicate the power of God. One of the words for miracle used in the New Testament is *dynamis* and this is where we get our English word for dynamite. This word not only means strength, power and ability but even more specifically, it means inherent power or power existing in a person by virtue of nature. Miracles worked by men of God throughout the Old and New Testament demonstrated the intervention of power not limited by natural laws. When Jesus walked on water (Matthew 14:25) or when Elisha caused an ax-head made of iron to float on the water (2 Kings 6:1-7), it showed the world that their miraculous work demonstrated such great power that was superior to the control of physical forces and gravity. At the same time, miracles are not acts of power displayed by man but by God using man as a simple tool.

AN INTENT TO SHOW PURPOSE

If a "God-ordained" miracle consisted only of an irregular event that caused an infringement of nature's laws and showed only an indication of God's power, it would not serve its true purpose. Why? Because miracles not only point to God and his revelation but they also demonstrate purpose.

The signs and wonders in the Old Testament served mainly as indicators of the continuing redemptive work of God in the history of his people. The Gospels teach that Jesus' miracles were prophesied works of the Messiah and were signs rather than merely wonderful works. However, they were only signs to those who had the spiritual discernment to recognize them as such.[230]

When Jesus came on the scene, he came promoting the Kingdom of God. He began his ministry by preaching and teaching in the synagogues. Yet he used miracles as a means of promoting his kingdom and from his perspective, the work of God consisted of believing in him (John 6:29). We see an example of this in Luke 8 when a man named Jairus begged Jesus to come to his house because his daughter was dying. While on his way to his house, someone told Jairus that his daughter was dead and there was no more use to bother Jesus anymore. But Jesus' message to him was for him to not "be afraid" and to "just believe and she will be healed" (8:50). After arriving at the man's home, Jesus took the girl by the hand and she stood up. By this miracle, Jairus was able to understand Jesus' true scope of God's divine power and that was for him to believe despite the bad news and loss of hope.

We see another example of Jesus' purpose of desiring faith in John 11. After Lazarus was dead, he states to Martha concerning him that he was "the resurrection and the life" and "he who believes in me will live, even though he dies" (John 11:25). In addition, he stated that "whoever lives and believes in me will never die. Do you believe this?" (John 11:26). Then Jesus showed his power by raising Lazarus from the grave after he had been buried for four days.

Biblical miracles have a clear objective: they are intended to bring the glory and love of God into bold relief. They are intended, among other things, to draw man's attention away from the mundane events of everyday life and direct it toward the might acts of God.[231] And this was exactly what Jesus desired to do as he worked his miracles and wonders. Other stated purposes of New Testament miracles include Jesus' endorsement by God (Acts 2:22), the verification of the message of God's grace (Acts 15:12) and the salvation he offers (Hebrews 2:4), to lead unbelievers to faith (Romans 15:19), to strengthen the belief of those of the house of faith (Acts 2:43), and to mark out those who were apostles (2 Corinthians 12:12).

Deceptive Miracles

Not only does God perform miracles but Satan performs them as well. Yet it is God's workings that are "authentic" and it is Satan's workings that are deceptive. Certainly, Satan has the capabilities of working miracles which are irregular, which violate the laws of nature, which demonstrate power, and that show purpose. Yet since all of his works are against God, he gives miracles a negative and misleading connotation.

IN THE OLD TESTAMENT

For those who do not believe that Satan and his kingdom have the capabilities of working miracles, we will look at Scripture to ascertain this truth. In the Old Testament, we see the miracles of not only God but of Pharaoh's magicians. In Exodus 7:10-12, "Moses and Aaron went to Pharaoh and did just as the LORD commanded. Aaron threw his staff down in front of Pharaoh and his officials, and it became a snake. Pharaoh then summoned wise men and sorcerers, and the Egyptian magicians also did the same things by their secret arts: Each one threw down his staff and it became a snake. But Aaron's staff swallowed up their staffs." Since miracles go against the laws of nature, the very fact that a staff was able to turn into a snake certainly endorses this miraculous work. Yet Satan's Kingdom was of no match for God's Kingdom, for Aaron's staff literally swallowed up all of theirs.

Later on in the book of Deuteronomy, Moses notes that the signs and wonders in and of themselves are not definitive proof of God's approval. Lest the people focus in the wrong direction, Moses let them know that false prophets may perform miracles and then call the house of faith to serve other gods (Deuteronomy 13:1-2). We see in this passage that the purpose of these false and deceptive miracles was to point the people away from God and to cause them not to ultimately worship, serve, and obey him.

IN THE NEW TESTAMENT

In the New Testament, all three Greek words for miracles including power (*dynamis*), sign (*sēmeion*), and wonder (*teras*) have also been attributed to Satan and his kingdom. Concerning the "man of lawlessness" who would come in the future, the apostle Paul warns the believers not to be deceived, for this man "will oppose and will exalt himself over everything that is called God or is worshipped, so that he sets himself up in God's temple, proclaiming himself to be God" (2 Thessalonians 2:4). Then Paul states that his coming "will be in accordance with the work of Satan displayed in all kinds of counterfeit miracles, signs and wonders" (2 Thessalonians 2:9). The words here in this verse for miracles, sings, and wonders are the same three Greek words that are also attributed to the workings of Jesus. Thus, Satan will be instrumental in working miracles in order to deceive men on earth.

The most common of these Greek words that is used to portray the deceptiveness of Satan is the word for sign (*sēmeion*). In describing his future workings, John states in Revelation 16:13-14, "Then I saw three evil spirits that looked like frogs. They came out of the mouth of the dragon, out of the mouth of the beast and out of the mouth of the false prophet. They are spirits of demons performing miraculous *signs*, and they go out to the kings of the whole world, to gather them for the battle on the great day of God Almighty." Yet despite these miraculous signs, John also predicts this false prophet's demise saying, "But the beast was captured, and with him the false prophet who had performed the miraculous signs on his behalf. With these signs he had deluded those who had received the mark of the beast and worshipped his image. The two of them were thrown alive into the fiery lake of burning sulfur" (Revelation 19:20).

Miracles or Magic

In the New Testament, at least three words were used to designate miracles. First, power (*dynamis*) meant inherent power residing in someone or something by virtue of its nature. This was power that a person or thing would exercise. These powerful works were done through superhuman power as seen in Acts 2:22 and Romans 15:19 and this word was where we get our English word for dynamite. The majority of the times this word was used did not pertain to miracles but rather referred to power 77 times, mighty works 11 times, and strength 7 times.

Second, a sign (*sēmeion*) was a certain mark or token which distinguished someone or something from another. It was an unusual occurrence and it exceeded the common course of nature. This word was viewed a little differently than an outward display of power, for signs pointed to a spiritual truth and was the testimony of a divine message (Matthew 12:38-39). There were about 50 times this word was used to refer to a sign and 23 times it was referred to a wonder.

And third, a wonder (*teras*) simply meant a miracle that was performed by someone, and was a marvel that made its appeal to the senses. In Acts 2:19, wonders produced astonishment to those who watched. There were 16 times in which this word refer to a wonder in the Bible.

THE DEFINITION OF MAGIC

I suggest that a miracle is an irregular event that violates the laws of nature which shows an indication of power with the final intent of showing a specific purpose. However, there are many groups of people both of the past and of the present that believe that Jesus was a magician rather than a miracle worker. Thus, we come to the section of discussing the nature and disposition of magic so that we can ascertain whether or not it was associated with Jesus' works.

In the ancient world, the word magic obtained a negative association because some magicians were renowned to be cheats and frauds. Yet today, there are many who have come up with various definitions, many of which are favorable, as to what they consider to be magic. Harold Remus believes that unlike tricks or natural events, some marvelous events might be caused by spiritual forces and from his perspective, these are sometimes called magic. As understood traditionally, he believes magic involves harnessing spiritual beings or powers through incantations and other arts. For example, in the ancient Mediterranean world, magicians used recipes or performed rituals to help their clients and to damage their clients' enemies.[232] Some believe that magic is the art that makes people who practice it feel better rather than worse. For some, it provides the delusion of refuge to one who is insecure, the feeling of help to the helpless, and the comfort of hope to the hopeless. Howard Clark Kee believes that magic is a technique, through word or act, by which a desired end is achieved, whether that end lies in the solution to the seeker's problem or in damage to the enemy who has caused the problem.[233] Thus, magic may be seen as an art through word or action that produces a desired effect through various means which gives man a level of hope and certainty and is brought about through supernatural forces of nature.

From a secular point of view, magic may not be seen as an evil or dreadful technique. Yet in considering the biblical standpoint, magic was only seen as negative and damaging. Biblically, magic was described as the art of bringing about results beyond man's capabilities through superhuman intervention. Early in the Pentateuch, the works of God were in hostility with the works of Pharaoh's magicians. Although they had real power to perform superhuman achievements and although they were able to duplicate some of Moses' miracles, their magic was limited, for they could not duplicate all of the miracles. Acts 8:9-13 states that a man named Simon practiced sorcery in the city and he amazed all the people of Samaria. "He boasted that he was someone great, and all the people, both high and low, gave him their attention and exclaimed, 'This man is the divine power known as the Great Power'" (8:9-10). Yet although many followed him because of his wonders, he soon no longer believed in himself but rather in the message of the apostles. After he was baptized, he started to follow Philip everywhere and was astonished by his great signs and miracles which were accomplished by God.

There were numerous magical terms mentioned in the Bible of which all were against the nature of God. First, divination consisted of a means of securing secret knowledge especially concerning the future. Second, sorcery was the use of administering drugs and those who were distressed used sorcery as a suppliant to seek release by magical means. Third, witchcraft had reference to drugs used in exercising the magical rite and was associated with divination. Fourth, repeated utterances referred to the false notion that the repeated expression of a word would secure one's desire. And fifth, magic was associated with imposters of which were given the name "seducers".

THE DEBATES CONCERNING JESUS' MIRACLES

The Gospels portray the act of healing through touch as one of Jesus' ways of performing miracles. During the First Century, the injustice of taxation caused many people in Palestine to become malnourished, which opened the way for disease. Curing could only be done in the temple but the travel expenses and the nature of the trip would cause most to not be able to afford the trip. Thankfully, Jesus came and used his act of healing as a means to not only show the people the Kingdom of God but to cure people who were not able to travel to Jerusalem.

However, not everyone during his day believed that his miracles were justifiable. The Pharisees' believed that he was only able to accomplish this work because he was merely an exorcist. They believed he simply used prayers or religious rituals to drive out these evil spirits who were only believed to possess a person. During one occasion when Jesus healed a demon-possessed man who was blind and mute, the Pharisees tried to explain it by saying, "It is only by Beelzebub, the prince of demons, that this fellow drives out demons" (Matthew 12:24). They could in no way refute the reality of these cures, but they simply sought ways to work around them in order to liquidate the power of God and the violation of the laws of nature.

In addition to the Pharisees' debates regarding how they could best explain Jesus' miracles, there are several contemporary controversies concerning his works. Concerning this same miracle mentioned in Matthew 12, Ioan Lewis tries to give his reasons on what took place. He believes that Jesus possibly did in fact use demonic powers to cast out a demon possessed man because shamans, who are "spiritual" leaders having special powers to heal, have been accused of witchcraft because they were caught curing something that they caused.[234] Therefore, since healers of the past happened to create a problems, such as disease, and they cured it, Jesus must have done the same thing.

John Crossan argues that a symbolic story could have been the true intended purpose of what took place in Mark 5:1-17 than a miracle itself. In this narrative, a man named Legion who lived in tombs was demon possessed with many demons. Jesus cast out the demons into a herd of pigs and the man instantly received his sanity and eventually his life back. Concerning the nature of the story, Crossan believes that although a man was cured, the symbolism is hard to miss or ignore.[235] When the demon is cast out of the man and into the pigs, which run off the cliff to die by drowning, he believes that it was symbolic of the revolution the Jews hoped for, which was the death of the power of Rome. His overall view concerning his miracles was not about the facts but about their attestation.[236]

David Aune believes that Jesus actually used a technique rather than a miracle to heal an individual. In Mark 8:22-26, there was a narrative of a blind man who begged Jesus to touch him. Jesus took the man by the hand and led him outside the village and after spitting on the man's eyes, the man eventually was able to see everything clearly. He then sent the blind man on his way but asked him not to go in the village, for he didn't want the people to know what he did. Yet Aune claims that the use of Jesus' saliva to heal was a technique known to both Jewish and Greco-Roman magical practitioners. Therefore, no miracle was performed but rather a merely medicinal practice of that time.[237]

And last, Karl Venturini overall debates Jesus' God-given miracles as authentic and supernatural. He believes his healings, for example, were affected by medicines and Christianity's most notorious miracle of him rising from the dead is discredited as well. He states that Joseph of Arimathea and Nicodemus noticed signs that he might still be alive while they were preparing his body for burial, and they signaled the Essenes, who later removed his body. After having recovered somewhat, Jesus was periodically seen by his disciples.[238]

THE DEBATES CONCERNING JESUS' CHARACTER

In addition to trying to find a reasonable explanation without denying the validity of the miracle, there are several contemporary controversies concerning Jesus' character and person. It was clear that the Gospel writers state that he was and is the Son of God and that he was a worker of miracles. Yet many have tried to find some other explanation to portray who he was.

A. A. Barb states that Jesus, although he was a religious man offering his adorations in humble submission to "the deity", was also a magician who attempted to force the supernatural powers to accomplish what he desired and avert what he feared.[239] He believes that since a miracle is what the god's will and magic is the will of man by the use of a deity, magic is in fact derived from religion. Thus, he equates Jesus to merely a religious man who characterized himself as a humble servant to the deity, yet he equates him to a magician and not a worker of miracles. Because he believes that magic and miracle are similar and that magic comes from religion, he uses the word magic to characterize the person and works of Jesus.

Morton Smith states that the difference between the terms such as Son of God, divine man, or magician in the early Roman Empire was one of social status and success. He believes that once the requirements of social status and decorum were met, the same man would customarily be called a divine man, son of a god by his admirers, or a magician by his enemies.[240] Thus, Jesus was able to receive his title from man because he worked his way up in the higher echelons of society and that was how he was able to be given the title as the Son of God.

The Distinctions of Jesus' Miracles

Although many during Jesus' day as well as today believe that his works were only magic or surreal and although many have questioned his character and person, it must be noted that his works were indeed miraculous and nothing short of it. There are several distinctions of his works that I will give to the alleged controversies.

His Works Were Unlike Magic

First, his works were unlike magic. To liquidate the distinction between the miracles of Jesus, some try very hard to argue that there is no difference between miracles and magic. Yet this belief, regardless of how accurate it sounds, is absolutely absurd in a theological context.

Although the Pharisees believed that he only "drives out demons" by "Beelzebub, the prince of demons" (Matthew 12:24), Jesus distinguished his works as truly miraculous by his response. After knowing their thoughts, he stated, "Every kingdom divided against itself will be ruined, and every city or household divided against itself will not stand. If Satan drives out Satan, he is divided against himself. How then can his kingdom stand? And if I drive out demons by Beelzebub, by whom do your people drive them out? So then, they will be your judges (Matthew 12:25-27). He quickly shut down their ill-advised logic by simply telling them that Satan cannot cast out Satan and that no organized society can prevail when turned against itself. From his perspective, it makes no sense and is inconsistent for him to place demons inside of a man to then to cast it out.

Then he distinguishes himself from Satan and his kingdom by stating, "But if I drive out demons by the Spirit of God, then the

Kingdom of God has come upon you...He who is not with me is against me, and he who does not gather with me scatters" (Matthew 12:28, 30). As a means of representing the power of God, Jesus states that his works not only destroys Satan's but his very nature and person is not in his league. In addition, he removed any neutral ground by telling them that they must either be totally for him or they are totally against him.

Jesus' works (including his encounters with demonic spirits) were unlike magic in that he performed miracles by his own power and authority.[241] Since magic is caused by spiritual forces and involves harnessing spiritual beings or powers through incantations and other arts, Jesus did not use outside forces but rather his own power and authority. He gave reference to his own power and authority when he stated in Matthew 9:6 "'So that you may know that the Son of Man has authority on earth to forgive sins" he said to a paralytic man "Get up, take your mat and go home.'" Therefore, Jesus did not need to use outside forces to cause his works to take place.

His Works Were Not of a Magician

Many claim that Jesus was simply a magician. Yet, the writings within the New Testament show a disdain for witchcraft. We see at least one example of this in Acts 8:4-24 when Peter and John encounter a man named Simon who practiced sorcery. Sorcery in essence is the use of supernatural or natural power, and is the same as witchcraft. However, Simon was eventually swayed to believe in the preaching and miracles of the apostles. After he believed, he saw Peter and John laying hands on the newly baptized and when they saw the results of the people receiving the Holy Spirit, he propositioned them saying, "Give me this power too, so that anyone I lay hands upon may receive the Holy Spirit" (Acts 8:19). Peter immediately rebuked him for this saying and said, "May your money perish with you, because you thought you could buy the gift of God with money! You have no part or share in this ministry, because your heart is not right before God" (Acts 8:20-21).

The core of the problem with Jesus being a magician was that if indeed he was one, then so too were his apostles, for they performed some of the same works as Jesus even after he had ascended. Then if the apostles were magicians, what makes them different from Simon?

But we do see a distinct difference with the works of the apostles and the works of Simon, for Simon saw a distinction and was interested in receiving the same powers of the apostles. What he lacked was the ability to lay his hands on someone who believed and had been baptized so that they could receive the Holy Spirit. Therefore in this narrative alone, we see a distinction with Jesus' apostle's works and that of Simon. Simon was certainly a magician, yet his works were less significant than that of the apostles.

It is a fact that magicians usually use objects or materials (like spittle) to perform their miracle. We see Josephus' in his writings telling about one who exorcised demons by putting something up to a person's nose and drawing the demon out through the nostrils.[242] Yet this is much different from Jesus' miracles. Although he occasionally used spittle, he typically healed simply by speaking. Mark 3:15 states that he simply cast out the demons without the need to draw them out through the nostrils. Matthew 8:16 states that "many who were demon possessed were brought to him and he drove out the spirits with a word." He simply commanded the demons by his own authority to come out, and they came.

His Works Were Truly Miraculous

There is both biblical and historical proof that proves that Jesus' works are truly miraculous and we see this when he conquered death by raising himself from the dead. Romans worshipped Caesar because he conquered many nations, but the followers of Jesus worship Jesus because he conquered death. Death is a natural law that cannot be done away with nor overlooked, for it is a fact that when people are truly dead, they cannot be brought back. No magic trick, no forms of sorcery or witchcraft, and no works of supernatural forces of nature can bring back a dead person. Many magic spells can heal a sick person, but to raise a dead person would be a violation of the laws of nature.

However, it was a miracle for Jesus when he raised his friend Lazarus and several others from the dead, for he demonstrated power over death and the laws of nature. Yet what is significant is that when he stated that he was the "resurrection and the life", he could also allow this statement to refer to himself. In other word, he was not only the resurrection and life over someone else deceased but also for his own deceased body. Caesar's mere act of conquering other nations meant nothing when placed next to Jesus' act of conquering death. Simon's acts of sorcery does not come close with Jesus' supernatural miracles either.

Although the New Testament states that the Spirit of God and God the Father raised up Jesus from the dead, Jesus himself stated in John 2:19 that if they destroy this temple, speaking of his body, he would raise it back again. Jesus was speaking to those disbelieving Jews and eventually, the disbelieving religious leaders destroyed him by taking his life. But Jesus defied all the powers of magic by raising himself up from the grave. He stated later in Revelation that he is the one who lives and was dead and more importantly that he holds the keys of hell and death (1:18). Since he holds the keys to death, he was able to not only raise those who were dead, but also to raise himself. When he died, he proved that his death was only temporary and in no way had him bound.

His Works Prove He is the Son of God

Previously we observed those who suggested that Jesus was not the son of God, but only a medicinal, magic-performing social reformer. They said that he only used old healing technique to work his miracles which caused him to hold authority. They also said that he was a good man and that he was able to receive this title as the Son of God because he worked his way up in the higher echelons of society. Yet, his works have actually been proven that he indeed was the Son of God.

In the book of John, a Pharisee, of whom most would have been hostile towards Jesus' teachings and miracles, actually told him that he was a teacher come from God and that no man could do these miracles except God be with him (3:2). What was interesting was that out of all the individuals who could have given this statement, a Pharisee clearly explained that God had to have been with Jesus for him to have done these miracles. There would have been no reason why this gospel writer would have lied or twisted this statement especially since so many Pharisees had been unreceptive of Jesus' teachings and miracles during his entire ministry.

To give validity to his miracles, there were numerous times when Jesus desperately tried to tell the Jews that God was his Father and that he was God himself. He told the Jews in John 10 that the works that he does in his Father's name bear witness of him (10:25) and that he and his Father were one (10:30). For virtually every Jew, this statement would have not only been hard to believe but it would have been heresy. They all during this era believed in God but they would need much persuasion to believe that Jesus was not only his Son but God himself. That was one of the major reasons why Jesus used miracles and not magic as a means of giving this undeniable proof. And even more surprisingly, a Pharisee believed in him because he was convinced that his works were miraculous. Thus, if there was any reason why a Jew during the First Century or even a skeptic today would not believe that Jesus was the Son of God, his miracles would undeniably prove that he was.

The Purpose for Jesus' Miracles

INTRODUCTION

One of the best examples that demonstrate the overall purpose of Jesus' miracles comes from Satan's temptations in the wilderness. After he was baptized of John the Baptist in the Jordan region, he was "led by the Spirit into the desert to be tempted by the devil" (Matthew 4:1). God had just given him divine approval through a heavenly voice and this approval would remain with him for what lied ahead. This next step for him was not in the area of public affairs, but rather in a state of solitude. His temporarily home became the wilderness and his companions would not be people but rather the wild beasts.

After fasting for forty days and nights, Satan came to him to tempt him when he was most vulnerable. The story of the failure of Adam under Satanic pressure stands in the background. Now Jesus comes on the scene and redemption history revolves around him. If he fails as the first man failed, all hope for the race would be gone.[243] If Jesus had no way of sinning, he could not have been compared with Adam who made the choice to sin and thus brought sin into the human race. In addition, all of the New Testament writers would be wrong in their assessments of all of his righteous volitional acts especially in the light of temptation.

Satan then gave his first temptation to Jesus saying, "If you are the Son of God, tell these stones to become bread" (Matthew 4:2). It is a fact that Satan knew that he was God's Son, for even the prophets of old prophesied this fact. Yet he had motives for asking this question. It would be his effort to persuade Jesus to such action as would be contrary to complete dependence on God, by asserting a measure of independence based on self-interest. But Jesus was committed to living man's life and sharing his lot, despite his supernatural origin, and he knew that if he failed in principle now, he would not succeed in practice later.[244]

Then Jesus responded to his temptation by stating a purpose of his use of miracles. He stated, "It is written: 'Man does not live on bread alone, but on every word that comes from the mouth of God'" (Matthew 4:4). To satisfy his hunger was not a sin, for eating was a part of man's life. Although he had a need which bread would supply, since no bread was given to him when he went into the wilderness and no direction was given to him about meeting his need, it would be wrong for him to use any special power such as his status to produce bread apart from divine direction. Rather, he had to wait upon divine provision.[245] From his point of view, miracles were not to be used for selfish interests but for direction and purpose in someone else's behalf. He certainly had the power to make stones turn into bread but that was not why came to perform miracles. In addition, he established a pattern that would be reproduced in those who came after him. If he had yielded to this temptation by providing himself with bread through means at his command, discipleship would have been out of the question for those who must earn their daily bread by the sweat of their brow.[246]

Afterwards, Satan took him to "the holy city" and had him stand on the highest point of the temple. He stated to Jesus, "If you are the Son of God, throw yourself down. For it is written: 'He will command his angels concerning you, and they will lift you up in their hands, so that you will not strike your foot against a stone" (Matthew 4:6). Since Jesus had the capabilities of walking on water (Matthew 14:25), he certainly could have thrown himself down to only find himself protected from harm. But he responded and told him, "It is also written: 'Do not put the Lord your God to the test'" (Matthew 4:7). Jesus again responded by citing Scripture and that his miracles were not to be used for selfish interests or even for protection. He would have had the capabilities of preventing himself from dying on the cross, yet he came to earth to die and his death was needed for the redemption of the world.

Again Satan tried to give him one more temptation. This time he "took him to a very high mountain and showed him all the kingdoms of the world and their splendor. 'All this I will give you,' he said, 'if you will bow down and worship me'" (Matthew 4:8-9). Satan, already having the title of being the "prince and power over the air", sought to astonish Jesus by riches and power that could be his. Yet this "kingdom" that Satan was showing him was not same kingdom that Jesus came to promote. What Satan was offering was only temporary, for he could not offer a kingdom that endured like God's righteousness, joy and peace. He could only offer outward grandeur. In addition, Satan's character is shown to being in direct contrast to that of the angels in heaven, for heavenly angelic beings abhors the very thought of being worshipped (Revelation 22:8-9).

Then Jesus responded to him and said, "Away from me, Satan! For it is written: 'Worship the Lord your God, and serve him only'" (Matthew 4:10). Jesus demonstrated to all his future followers that he would be obedient unto death and afterwards, he would be in position, just like all his future followers, to receive from God himself the reward of faithfulness. By this rejection, he not only indicated his messianic role but the ultimate purpose of why he chose to perform miracles. From his perspective, he wanted man to "worship the Lord" and to "serve him only". That is why he asked so many individuals if they "believed" even before he worked a miracle for them. Although he was sent out into the desert and was hungry, thirsty, and weak in a physical, emotional, and spiritually vulnerable state, he resisted each of the devils temptation, for he was focused on the spiritual and not the physical.

To Inaugurate the Kingdom of God

After establishing the fact that Jesus' works were miraculous and not magical, we must attempt to understand the purpose of his miracles. One of these purposes was to inaugurate the Kingdom of God. All of the people living in the Roman Empire understand what a kingdom was and how it was supposed to operate. They understood that it was to be led by a king and all the people within were to be his subjects. Yet Jesus came promoting a new kingdom while still operating under the laws of the Roman Kingdom. His kingdom did not entail promoting an earthly king like Caesar Augustus but rather God as King. Virtually everything he said and did was encompassed within his kingdom movement and he gave a picture of God's Kingdom as a way of life that was lived in the present. This kingdom would be a permanent society established and made up of redeemed men and women, and Gentiles as well as Jews.[247] Nothing would ever happened by accident but everything would serve as a vital purpose within the kingdom.

His miracles caused many people to see that the Kingdom of God had indeed arrived and his workings of miracles actually had the effect of bringing together multitudes of people who were likely to listen to his spoken word. It was because of his miracles that allowed him to gather record number crowds of which he was able to teach and to heal their many infirmities. Matthew 4:23-25 states this in saying, "Jesus went throughout Galilee, teaching in their synagogues, preaching the good news of the kingdom, and healing every disease and sickness among the people. News about him spread all over Syria, and people brought to him all who were ill with various diseases, those suffering severe pain, the demon-possessed, those having seizures, and the paralyzed, and he healed them. Large crowds from Galilee, the Decapolis, Jerusalem, Judea and the region across the Jordan followed him." In addition, great multitudes were in position to hear his "Sermon on the Mount" because the people had brought their sick from far and near and he healed them.

We see an example of the purpose of Jesus' miracles from Nicodemus and Jesus' dialogue in John 3. Since his miracles were not intended to promote himself, as magic is accustomed to doing, but rather his kingdom, Nicodemus the Pharisee understood this when he stated to Jesus at night, "Rabbi, we know you are a teacher who has come from God. For no one could perform the miraculous signs you are doing if God were not with him" (John 3:2). This religious man not only understood that Jesus was doing miracles that no one else could do but that his works were accompanied by God.

Yet Jesus desired to tell him the true purpose of both his teachings and miracles. He replied to him saying, "I tell you the truth, no one can see the Kingdom of God unless he is born again" (John 3:3). In giving a more specific reply, he continued to say, "I tell you the truth, no one can enter the Kingdom of God unless he is born of water and the Spirit. Flesh gives birth to flesh, but the Spirit gives birth to spirit.

You should not be surprised at my saying, 'You must be born again'" (John 3:5-7).

TO INDUCE FAITH

If the miracles were designed simply to authenticate the claim of Jesus to be sent of God, the execution of a few signs here and there would have been sufficient.[248] But Jesus did not do just a few signs here and there. Although he healed in his own right, so to speak, not calling upon God in prayer in order to gain the needed power from on high, it was doubtless his intention that the miracles should serve as a revelation of his divine nature and purpose.[249] Certainly, his miracles did serve as a means of revelation, but there must have been a greater purpose in addition to authenticating the claim that he had came from God. This greater purpose was to induce the faith of people.

The Multitudes of People

Unquestionably, there were many who were compelled to put their faith in God because of his miracles and by believing in his message and miracles, they too could enter into his kingdom. Since a miracle was to serve as genuine evidence for faith, it had to be identifiable as a miracle by people not already faithful to Jesus. The people coming to him with various needs and conditions were just as lost, helpless, and curious as the next person and they all desired to know the truth of what they had seen. Thus, Jesus' miracles demonstrated validity in front of all the people and since they were not already committed to him, they were able to see his works and believe in him because of what they had seen.

Early on in his ministry, we see him encouraging the people to have faith concerning the basic necessities in life. In Matthew 6, he told the multitude that if God "clothes the grass of the field", he will certainly clothe you, "O you of little faith" (6:30). In order to challenge them in light of their "little faith", he told them to not worry about what they would eat, drink, or wear but rather to seek his kingdom and his righteousness.

In Matthew 8, we see not only an example of faith, but of a miracle that accompanied this faith. After entering into Capernaum, a centurion came to Jesus telling him that his servant was home paralyzed and in terrible suffering. After Jesus stated that he would come and heal him, the centurion told him that he did not deserve him coming into his house but rather he could "just say the word" and his servant would be healed. After hearing this, Jesus was astonished and he encouraged the crowds by telling them, "I tell you the truth, I have not found anyone in Israel with such great faith" (8:10).

Yet there were instances when Jesus was troubled because of the lack of faith. In Mark 6, he came to his hometown with his disciples and he began to teach in the synagogue. But the people asked many questions in disbelief stating, "Where did this man get these things", "what's this wisdom that has been given him that he even does miracles", "isn't this the carpenter", "isn't this Mary's son and the brother of James, Joseph, Judas and Simon", and "aren't his sisters here with us" (6:2-3). Following their questions, all the people "took offense at him." After hearing their questions and experience their "offense", Jesus "could not do any miracles there, except lay his hands on a few sick people and heal them. And he was amazed at their lack of faith" (6:5-6). Why? Because these people were not able to get past the fact that he grew up in their hometown and that his family currently resided in the area. Because of this, they were not able to truly see who he was and the true purpose of his miracles. From his perspective, if they were not willing to believe in him, it would be no use to conduct many miracles.

In John 10, we see another example of the unbelief of the multitudes. During one occasion when Jesus was in the temple, the Jews gathered around him asking him if he was the Messiah. Jesus replied in saying, "I did tell you, but you do not believe. The miracles I do in my Father's name speak for me, but you do not believe because you are not my sheep" (10:25-26). After stating that God was his father and that he "and the Father are one", the disbelieving Jews picked up stones to stone him. But Jesus said to them, "I have shown you many great miracles from the Father" (10:32) and "do not believe me unless I do what my Father does. But if I do it, even though you do not believe me, believe the miracles, that you may know and understand that the Father is in me, and I in the Father" (10:37-38). These words stated were very important in light of his miracles. Jesus told them that he did tell them that he was the Messiah but it was not through what he said but rather through his works. From his perspective, his miracles proved that he was God, yet, they did not want to believe. Thus, since they did not believe in his miracles, they would not be able to believe that he was God because his miracles speak of his oneness with God.

The Disciples

Concerning Jesus' disciples, we see that they spent numerous intimate occasions with him. Yet, very few miracles were performed with only them present (fig tree). The impression persists for the reader of the Gospels that the miracles were designed to induce faith and not simply to stimulate or confirm it.[250] His works were intended to serve as faith-based miracles not specifically for those who knew him closely like his disciples, but rather for the people who did not spend intimate time with him. Miracles were intended to endorse his person and mission (Luke 4:16-21) and he did not have to do many miracles in front of his disciples, for they even testified with assurance who he was (Matthew 16:16).

In John 14, we not only see Jesus' last moments with his disciples but also a powerful message concerning faith and miracle. Thomas and the disciples wondered where Jesus was going and how they could know the way. He told them that he was the way, truth, and life and that no one comes to God the Father except through him. Another disciple named Philip asked for Jesus to show them all the Father and that would be enough for us. Troubled by this question, Jesus told them all that anyone who has seen him has seen the Father and that he was in the Father and that the Father was in him. Then he states, "Believe me when I say that I am in the Father and the Father is in me; or at least believe on the evidence of the miracles themselves. I tell you the truth, anyone who has faith in me will do what I have been doing. He will do even greater things than these, because I am going to the Father. And I will do whatever you ask in my name, so that the Son may bring glory to the Father. You may ask me for anything in my name, and I will do it" (14:11-14). Faith in his miracles was the least that Jesus was asking for from his disciples and he was encouraging them that if they truly believe, they would do even greater works than he did.

TO IMPROVE MAN'S NEEDS

Last but not least, Jesus worked miracles to improve the needs of mankind and he basically gave countless people their lives back. Through his miracles, people began to see that in the Kingdom of God, sickness and suffering, and death and evil could be conquered. They no longer had a barrier to overcome but rather they were freed to listen and accept the message of the kingdom. He improved the needs of the people by bringing healing, peace, life, and joy, and by him meeting these needs, they would be able to understand the future life of having no more tears and sorrow in heaven.

There are various needs of man. In naming just a few, man has a physical need, which is basically the same as his biological need. This encompasses the need for not only food, water, and air but also the need for homeostasis. This need is mentioned first because it is the strongest of all the needs. Second, man has an emotional need to belong especially in the areas of family and friends. This need consists of both giving and receiving love and affection. And third, man has a social need which includes the need for esteem. This shows the need for high levels of self-respect from others. When this need is filled, one feels valuable, but when it is discouraged, one feels substandard, weak, powerless and insignificant.

Physical Need

In looking more closely at the three needs, we see that when Jesus healed individuals, he was improving their physical needs. In order to really understand the physical needs of the people, we must look at the nature of diseases. A disease is an abnormality in the structure and function of bodily organs and system.[251] A disease refers to a malfunctioning of biological and/or psychological processes, while the term illness refers to the psychosocial experience and meaning of perceived disease.[252] During the First Century, there were countless people in the land with various illnesses and diseases. Numerous passages in the Gospels, including the parables of Jesus, shed light on the widespread ailments that affected the society.

One of these physical diseases was called leprosy. There is a distinction between what we call leprosy today and the leprosy that existed during Jesus' day. Leprosy is caused by Mycobacterium leprae, a bacillus discovered in 1868 by the Norwegian physician. That disease was, in fact, known in New Testament times but was then called elephas or elephantiasis. Ancient lepra or leprosy, on the other hand, covered several diseases, all of which involved a rather repulsive scaly or flaking skin condition – for example any fungus infection of the skin.[253]

We see an example in Luke 5 when a man with leprosy came to Jesus begging him to make him clean. He reached out and touched him and healed him immediately. From this, we observe this man desiring Jesus to heal him of his most basic need, the physical need, and because he healed him, "the news about him spread all the more, so that crowds of people came to hear him and to be healed of their sicknesses" (5:15).

Thankfully, Jesus' works freed people from their most basic need. His works were useful in meeting pressing human needs such as the relieving of hunger, the cleansing of leprosy, the restoration of bodily powers atrophied through crippling illness, and many other conditions. One good reason for refusing to perform a miracle in the presence of Herod and his men was the inappropriateness of the situation, since it presented no genuine human need.[254]

Emotional Need

It is a fact that humans desire to be freed from the things they fear including grief and the fear of death itself. At the same time, they are searching for love and affection from those that know them best. Jesus' miracles improved man's need to belong especially in the areas of family and friends and he understood man's desire to be alienated from society because of their illness and disease.

We see an example of this restoration process in Jesus' miracle of healing a demon-possessed man in Mark 5. The author carefully and clearly describes this demon-possessed man by stating that he "lived in the tombs", "no one could bind him any more, not even with a chain", "no one was strong enough to subdue him", and "night and day among the tombs and in the hills he would cry out and cut himself with stones" (5:3-5). It is clear that the demons that entered him drove him away from his family and friends and caused him to be psychologically impaired.

But Jesus saw his needs and told the demons to come out of him. After they left, the man would now have the privilege in being in his "right mind". Then as Jesus was getting into the boat, the man begged to go with him. But Jesus did not let him, but said, "Go home to your family and tell them how much the Lord has done for you, and how he has had mercy on you. So the man went away and began to tell in the Decapolis how much Jesus had done for him" (5:19-20). This man was not only able to be socially restored but also emotionally restored with his family. He would no long have to live in fear and bondage, and he would now be able to belong and receive the love and affection that he much desparetly needed.

Social Need

We must first remember that this era that Jesus live in was an honor and shame society. People not only valued themselves from their own eyes but also through the eyes of others. They would constantly reevaluate themselves because of the society in which they lived in. In light of this, those who had diseases were suffering not only physically and emotionally but also socially. Those suffers were in mourning for their lost lives, because in their honor and shame society where, as we have seen earlier, their existence was dead.[255] After working a miracle in someone's life, Jesus truly demonstrated the triumph of hope. Persons who were once socially unacceptable were now socially acceptable. They now had hope again and this hope caused them to go and tell "the whole world" what Jesus had done, even when he told them not to say anything.

In looking at an example, we look at John 9 when Jesus healed a man who was blind. In Jesus' parable of the unjust steward in Luke 16, we get a glimpse of how shameful it was to be a beggar (16:3) and to make matters worse, this man had never been able to see. Beggars who were physically impaired were often carried everyday to certain places around the city where they could ask for money or food. After seeing this blind man, Jesus had pity on him and "spit on the ground, made some mud with the saliva, and put it on the man's eyes. 'Go,' he told him, 'wash in the Pool of Siloam'. So the man went and washed, and came home seeing" (16:6-7). As the man was returning home, "his neighbors and those who had formerly seen him begging asked, 'Isn't this the same man who used to sit and beg'" (16:8). What was evident was the fact that after he washed, he started to return home "seeing". It was his home where he was socially accepted and no longer did he have to spend endless hours begging. Even the neighbors of the man saw that he was changed and different, and they now could restore him to the community.

In addition to this example, the demon-possessed man who had been healed by Jesus would also serve as an example of a man who was socially accepted by his family and friends (Mark 5). Thus, Jesus is to be esteemed by using his miracles to help improve man's social needs. Only he could rightfully restore man to his community and family with no strings attached.

The Historical Validity of Jesus' Miracles

Although we have looked at the facts of the nature of miracles and how Jesus' miracles were distinguished from magic, I propose the question of whether Jesus' miracles were historically valid and credible. There are a number of questions that must be analyzed regarding this validity and some of them include whether his miracles in the biblical accounts were consistent and reliable, and whether other Jewish men who also worked wonders and signs could compare with him.

On the same lines, we must understand the importance of witnesses and reports. If the witnesses of miracles contradict each other at anytime, if there are but few witnesses, if the witnesses are of unreliable character, and if they give their evidence with indecision or with too violent asseverations, there is skepticism in the validity of the miracle. While it is certainly true that when something altogether extraordinary is reported, the wise man will require more evidence than usual and will check and re-check the evidence very carefully.[256] Yet, this is because miracles are extraordinary and would go against the laws of nature. In addition, when reports of miracles arise in religions where the early history devalues miracles, this raises doubts about the historicity of those stories. In light of this, we will look at the historical validity of Jesus' miracles and will evaluate and investigate the accounts. After this evaluation, we will come up with a well supported conclusion.

COMPARING THE BIBLICAL ACCOUNTS

The Prediction in the Old Testament

Jesus' coming was predicted far in advance by prophets sent to Israel. God stated through Isaiah the prophet saying, "Here is my servant, whom I uphold, my chosen one in whom I delight; I will put my Spirit on him and he will bring justice to the nations" (42:1). While the servant here is called "Israel," this figure is also distinguished from Israel as the one who will bring the nation Israel back to God. The servant is a mysterious but glorious figure, abhorred by the nation and seemingly unsuccessful, but ultimately vindicated and honored even by rulers. This figure is to become a "light to the Gentiles" and bring God's "salvation to the ends of the earth." The New Testament recognizes their fulfillment in Jesus.[257]

God speaks of the ministry of his servant Jesus in saying that he would come "to open eyes that are blind, to free captives from prison, and to release from the dungeon those who sit in darkness" (42:7). He would not only spiritually fulfill these prophecies but he would even physically open the eyes that were blind and would perform many miracles that would give authenticy that he came from God. It was also prophesied that he would be a light to the Gentile nations. Isaiah 42:6 states, "I, the Lord, have called you in righteousness; I will take hold of your hand. I will keep you and will make you to be a covenant for the people and a light for the Gentiles." Isaiah 49:6 states, "It is too small a thing for you to be my servant to restore the tribes of Jacob and bring back those of Israel I have kept. I will also make you a light for the Gentiles, that you may bring my salvation to the ends of the earth."

The Fulfillment in the New Testament

The complete text of Isaiah was available during Jesus' times and was available in both Hebrew and Greek and probably paraphrased in Aramaic. Furthermore, when the New Testament writers applied these passages to Jesus, they were making this claim long before Christianity had become very successful. This was not a safe gambit on their part if we assume that they were merely guessing.[258] It was certainly not popular to make these claims in the midst of a hostile Jewish culture, yet many of them understood the Scriptures and saw a complete and valid fulfillment in only one person, namely Jesus of Nazareth.

The question must be asked as to what is the evidence that Jesus was the literal fulfillment of Isaiah's prophecy concerning the servant? Initially, he is the founder of the largest religion in the world and although he only reach a small number of Gentiles and Jews while he was still alive, his followers carried his message to the ends of the earth. Interestingly, he was the only person claiming to be the Jewish Messiah who had founded a world religion among Gentiles. This accomplishment would have been very difficult to stage.[259]

The Eyewitnesses of the New Testament

His miracles were set in a framework of the truly historical and were represented as having really happened. One of the major factors to this truth comes from the validity of the eyewitness accounts. After he raised up Lazarus from the dead in John 11, many of the Jews had seen what he had done and they put their faith in him. Some of them went to the Pharisees and told them what Jesus had done. Understanding the fact that they could not deny the eyewitness reports, "the chief priests and the Pharisees called a meeting of the Sanhedrin. 'What are we accomplishing?' they asked. 'Here is this man performing many miraculous signs. If we let him go on like this, everyone will believe in him, and then the Romans will come and take away both our place and our nation'" (11:47-48).

From the chief priests and Pharisees' perspective, the eyewitness reports would have caused everyone to believe in Jesus, and they did not want this to happen. In addition to this example, we see that after Jesus rose from the dead, he "appeared to more than five hundred of the brothers at the same time", most of whom were still living during Paul's day (1 Corinthians 15:6).

The Reliability of the New Testament

In addition to the eyewitness reports, the historical reliability of the New Testament documents enjoys powerful support in several ways. First, several key miracle accounts surrounding his ministry were well supported. When Jesus came on the scene to begin his ministry, he began to speak of God not as imminent apocalypse but as present healer. His miracle of feeding about five thousand men was document in all four gospel accounts and the miracle of him walking on the sea was documented in three out of the four gospel accounts.

Second, the gospels possessed solid confirmation based on both internal and external considerations. Internally, they are consistent without being identical and they have many characteristics of eyewitness accounts. Externally, they enjoy confirmation from other ancient documents and archaeological finds. They faithfully reflect the cultural conditions of First Century Palestine and correctly identify many people and places of that era.[260]

Third, his miracles did not involve retaliation and in no record did he use his authority to impose chastisement on those who hated and disputed against him. He maintained honest motives even though there was pressure on him by his disciples on at least one occasion to do this very thing (Luke 9:52-56).

Fourth, he maintained pure motives throughout his ministry of working miracles. He did not intentionally perform miracles in order to gather large crowds and most of his miracles were performed openly and not in secret. On more than one occasion, he intentionally did not want people in the cities to know that he worked a miracle because he did not want all the attention, nor did he want them to make him their "king". He did not perform any "show off" miracles and he even warn against false prophets who would perform signs and wonders so great as to deceive even the elect (Matthew 24:24-26).

Fifth, in contrast to many of the other wondrous signs that took place during his era, his miracles were completed instantly in nearly every case. He did not have to call upon anyone or work with any charms but rather he acted or spoke and the person was healed.

And sixth, concerning the quality and general reliability of any documents reporting miracle events, one must consider the issue of dating. Virtually all ancient miracle stores outside the Bible are described in texts written long after the events they reports. But we read the stories of Jesus' works in documents composed within a generation of his life by people who claimed to see the events, and in a context where friends and foes alike could either confirm or dispute the stories (see Acts 2:22; 26:26).[261]

COMPARING THE ACCOUNTS OF OTHER MEN

It is a fact that the faith-healing "business" attracts many impostors who look for anyway to gain credibility and fame through religious and spiritual works. Charlatans often feed off the prestige of a respected religion. The first century Mediterranean world produced many accounts of miracles allegedly performed by Jewish holy men, various magicians, and Hellenistic "divine men." Some scholars, especially of the history of religions school, portray Jesus as a representative of one of these groups.[262] Yet was Jesus a charlatan and was there any difference between his miraculous accounts and the accounts of other men who were somewhat contemporaries of him?

In looking at some of the First Century accounts, the Babylonian Talmud mentions a Jewish holy man named Honi who ended a drought when he drew a circle on the ground, stepped inside the circle, and told God he would not leave until rain came. According to the Talmud, God relented and sent the rain.[263] The Talmud is the records of rabbinic conversations regarding Jewish ethics, customs, law, and history. The Babylonian Talmud, which mentions this story of this man naned Honi, was historically compiled about the year 500 A.D. and continued to be edited later.

Although this miracle may have taken place, the historical validity of Jesus' miracles gain much more credibility, for the four gospels and the book of Acts was written less than 60 years after his ascension. At the same time, the accounts in the New Testament were not continuing to be edited over and over again. Although rabbis continue to add to the Talmud, the Old and New Testament has remained the same for these past 2,000 years. In addition, the countless witnesses give even more validity to Jesus' miracles as absolute fact than Honi's alleged miracle.

There was another man named Apollonius who allegedly exorcised demons and raised a girl from the dead.[264] Yet, Philostratus, the biographer of "Life of Apollonius of Tyana", raises serious doubts about whether the girl was really dead. This book tells the story of Apollonius who was a philosopher and teacher and who lived most of his life in the First Century (40-120 AD). It speaks of his voyages to numerous countries including Africa and India. Yet the credibility of the book from a scholastic standpoint is more of invention and fabrication, for many believe that he may have never traveled to any of these countries but rather spent his whole life within the Roman Empire.

His miracle of driving out demons and raising a girl from the dead does not come close to comparing to Jesus' miracles of driving out demons, for the gospel writers are seen as credible and their narratives do not contradict each other. In addition, the eyewitness of Jesus' miracles of driving out demons and healing the dead were numerous and even those who hated him could not deny validity of his works.

Some classify Jesus as one of these Jewish holy men and others place him in a loosely defined group of Hellenistic holy men.[265] Despite superficial similarities, however, Jesus is quite distinct from all these. As a Jew, he obviously shared much with Jewish holy men but the stories of his life do not borrow directly from accounts of Jewish holy men. For one thing, he corrected the teachings of his contemporaries (Matthew 5-7) and he connected with the Old Testament but resisted the official Judaism of his day.[266]

Additionally, the New Testament reports concerning Jesus' miracles are far more reliable than accounts of the Jewish holy men. During his public ministry, he worked Moses-like miracles, walking on the water and feeding the crowds of 4,000 and 5,000 miraculously with bread in a desert place. There was also a pattern of Elijah/Elisha-like signs that causes him to be hailed as a prophet. Yet he was never remembered as gathering crowds or leading them to symbolic places with promises that he was going to perform miraculous signs, for there were prophets and miracle workers who did this very thing. Although many stories are fabricated in order to achieve credibility and although magicians achieve wondrous works in order to draw attention to them, Jesus' works were unlike these. Even Josephus himself gives credibility to Jesus in not referring to him as a charlatan prophet.

Narratives of Miracles

INTRODUCTION

All of the "miracles" recording in the Gospels were indeed miracles, for they were irregular, they violated the laws of nature, they demonstrated power, and they showed a specific purpose. In light of miracles violating the observed laws of nature, it is not a miracle for someone who was sick to eventually get well. It is the body's natural prerogative to gradually maintain homeostasis and to fight illnesses and disease. However, it is a miracle for a healing to take place instantaneously and for a man's withered hand to be instantly restored just like his other one. An instantaneously healing totally goes against man's observed views of how the law of nature works.

Jesus' miracles are simply divided up into four sections: his nature miracles, his general healings, his resurrections, and his casting out of demons. His nature miracles are examples of his most extraordinary claims over the earth and the elements. Some of them include him feeding 5,000 men, feeding 4,000 men, stilling the turbulent storm, walking on water, and turning water into wine. Some of his general healings include him cleansing a leper, healing the sick, healing a paralytic, opening the eyes of blind men and restoring a servant's ear. By far, these healings are more numerous then his nature miracles, his resurrections, and his casting out of demons. The three resurrections of Jesus include him raising a ruler's daughter, raising a widow's son, and raising Lazarus. And last, there were about four miracles of Jesus casting out demons and they include him casting out a demon-possessed blind and mute man, an unclean spirit, him curing a demon-possessed mute individual, and him allowing demons to enter into a herd of swine.

Additionally, it must be noted that the miracles recorded in the Gospels are not the only miracles that Jesus performed. Mark 1:32-34 states that during one evening "after sunset, the people brought to Jesus all the sick and demon possessed. The whole town gathered at the door, and Jesus healed many who had various diseases. He also drove out many demons, but he would not let the demons speak because they knew who he was." We don't know specifically all the manners of diseases and sicknesses that he performed but all we know is that he performed many miracles late that evening. At the end of his ministry, John the apostle makes it clear that "Jesus did many other miraculous signs in the presence of his disciples, which are not recorded in this book. But these are written that you may believe that Jesus is the Christ, the Son of God, and that by believing you may have life in his name" (John 20:30-31). So therefore, even though we do not have all the miracles, signs, and wonders that Jesus did, what we do have is sufficient for faith in Jesus in order to obtain eternal life.

STILLING THE STORM

The Background

In Matthew 8:23-27, Mark 4:35-41, and Luke 8:22-25, we have the miracle of Jesus stilling a violent storm. The same day that he had spoken many parables to the people, Jesus said to his disciples, "Let us go over to the other side." Leaving the crowds of people behind, the disciples and Jesus went over to the other side of the lake.

As they sailed, he fell asleep and soon thereafter, a furious storm came up on the lake so that the waves swept over the boat, and everyone on the boat was in great danger. Immediately, the disciples awoke him saying, "Master, Master, we're going to drown" and "Teacher, don't you care if we drown". Jesus obviously knew what was going on despite being asleep and in spite of where he was located on the boat, it would be very hard for him to maintain any good sleep. Maybe it was not a coincidence that he was asleep and perhaps he desired to see the faith of his disciples who were struggling to stay alive on the boat. But consequently, they did not have any faith.

The Miracle

After being awaken, Jesus replied to them, "You of little faith, why are you so afraid" (Matthew 8:26). Then he got up and rebuked the winds and the waves and immediately it was completely calm. Storms on the water certainly come and go but once the winds and the waves are raging, they never instantaneously calm down. There is always a progression to its peak of violence and a progression to its former state of quietness. But what makes this narrative unique is that Jesus not only spoke to the storm and it immediately departed but he rebuked the wind and the waves. This Greek word for rebuke means to chide, reprove, and sharply admonish. He rebuked the weather as a father would rebuke and admonish his child to "behave", and he spoke with authority and claimed absolute control over the weather and virtually all forces of nature.

Wind, which is air molecules in motion on earth, is the flow of air and other gases that create an atmosphere. For Jesus to rebuke the wind, which actually causes the waves to act violently, he was exercising control over the entire atmosphere including the sun, the air molecules in motion on the earth, and all the other gases that make up the atmosphere. He was directly going against all forces of nature in order to instantaneously stop the wind from causing the waves to violently sweep over the boat.

After the miracle, all of his disciples in fear and amazement asked one another, "What kind of man is this? Even the winds and the waves obey him." The disciples quickly recognized Jesus as being extraordinary or superhuman. They had seen him perform miracles but not one like this in which the forces of nature obeyed his very command.

The Application

Matthew's gospel records that after being awaken, Jesus stated to these men, "You of little faith, why are you so afraid" and then got up and rebuked the winds and the waves. Mark's gospel states that after Jesus performed the miracle, he asked them, "Why are you so afraid? Do you still have no faith?" In Luke's gospel he asked, "Where is your faith?" It is evident that Jesus desired faith of his followers. Yet it was not faith that they would actually perform the miracle of calming a storm that he desired but rather the faith in believing that he could protect them from the physical and spiritual storms of life.

Although Satan and his kingdom have influence over the weather (Job 1:19), he has never been described as having authority and absolute control over nature. His works are actually under the authority of God, for he even had to ask God for permission before he could muster up a tornado to destroy Job's house and kill all those inside. But Jesus, who was God himself, exercised direct control over nature and he did not have to get permission from anyone.

The Feeding of the 5,000

Probably one of the most well known miracles of Jesus and certainly one of the most unbelievable and indescribable miracles that could have even been done was when he miraculously fed large multitudes with only a lunch portion of fish and bread. The only miracle recorded in all for Gospels is the feeding of the 5,000 (Matthew 14:13-21; Mark 6:30-44; Luke 9:10-17; John 6:1-15). The feeding of the 4,000 was recorded in Matthew 15:29-39 and Mark 8:1-13.

The Background

The background of Jesus feeding the 5,000 began with him telling his disciples to come with him by themselves to a quiet place so that they could eat and get some rest. He took them and they departed by boat crossing over the far shore of the Sea of Galilee to the solitary place of Bethsaida. But somehow the crowds of people heard where he and his disciples went and they followed him by running from their various towns and they arrived ahead of them. Surprisingly when Jesus and the disciples landed, there were large multitudes waiting for him. After seeing them, he had compassion on them and he taught and healed their various sicknesses and diseases.

The Miracle

After finding a boy with five small barley loaves and two small fish, the disciples told Jesus what they had found from this young boy. Then Jesus said to bring them here to me. It started to get late in the day and everyone was hungry. The disciples came to Jesus telling him, "This is a remote place, and it's already getting late. Send the crowds away, so they can go to the villages and buy themselves some food." Jesus replied, "They do not need to go away. You give them something to eat" (Matthew 14:15-16). John's gospel records Jesus seeing the great crowds coming to him and him telling Philip, "'Where shall we buy bread for these people to eat?'" (John 6:5-6).

Luke 9:14 makes it clear that "about five thousand men were there". It was common to only include the men in a counting, for children and women were not as significant or noteworthy to be included in the count. If most of the men had wives and each couple had about 3-4 children, there would have been over 20,000 people present who made somewhat time-consuming journeys to that remote solitary place. Certainly, Jesus and his disciples did not have food to feed all the people, yet Jesus was going to demonstrate to everyone present that nothing would be too hard for God.

Then he directed his disciples to seat all the people in groups on the green grass and they sat down in groups of hundreds and fifties. After taking the five loaves and two fish and thanking God, he gave them to the disciples, and they gave the food to the people. Even more specifically, the people were able to receive "as much as they wanted" (John 6:11). After everyone was satisfied, Jesus told his disciples to gather all the pieces that were left and to let nothing be wasted. After gathering all the broken pieces of bread and fish, the disciples picked up twelve basketfuls. Then after the people saw this miraculous sign, they began to say, "Surely this is the Prophet who is to come into the world" (John 6:14).

It is not a miracle for approximately 20,000 people to be fed and filled with fish and bread. Yet, it is indeed a miracle for 20,000 people to be fed and filled with only five loaves and two fish. From man's world, this was impossible. Yet somehow Jesus was able to actually duplicate and miraculously create new barley loaves and fish before he actually handed them to his disciples in order for them to feed the people. How did he do that? No one would ever know. But this act of his allowed all the people to recognize this miracle and to hail him as Prophet.

The Application

Concerning the 5,000, John's gospel records Jesus seeing the great crowds coming to him and him telling Philip, "Where shall we buy bread for these people to eat?" Then John makes it clear that Jesus asked this only to test him, for he already had in mind what he was going to do" (John 6:5-6). Again we see the desired outcome of faith that he initially wanted out of his disciples. Of course, they failed again, but they would never forget the miracle that Jesus performed that day.

THE FEEDING OF THE 4,000

The Background

Jesus, his disciples, and the multitudes of people were also in a desert and another large crowd began to gather around him after he healed the lame, blind, crippled, and mute. Jesus told his disciples that he did not want to send them home, for those that came long distances would collapse on the way. In addition, they had been with him for three days and they have nothing to eat.

The Miracle

His disciples asked him where in this remote place anyone could get enough bread to feed all these people. Jesus asked them how many loaves they had and they replied that they had seven and a few small fish. After telling the crowd to sit, he took the food, gave thanks and had his disciples to distribute it to the people. Just like the feeding of the 5,000, all the people at and were satisfied. Afterward the disciples picked up seven basketfuls of broken pieces that were left over.

WALKING ON WATER

The Background

Mentioned in Matthew 14:22-36, Mark 6:45-56, and John 6:16-24, the events of this miracle begin right after he fed about 5,000 men in an isolated area. Immediately after he fed this multitude, he compelled and forced his disciples to get into a boat and to go on ahead of him to the other side, while he dismissed the crowd. Afterwards, he went up on a mountainside by himself to pray.

The Miracle

When the evening had come and it had become dark, a violent storm came as his disciples were on the lake. Jesus saw them in trauma because the wind was against them and he set out to go toward them. Yet he went to them walking on the water. After rowing three or three and a half miles away from the land, the men saw him walking toward the boat on the water and they were horrified. As if he didn't even see them, Jesus was about to pass them, but they all cried out in fear saying, "It's a ghost." Then Jesus immediately spoke, "Take courage! It is I. Don't be afraid."

But Peter replied, "Lord, if it's you, tell me to come to you on the water." Jesus replied and said, "Come." Peter got out of the boat and amazingly he began to walk on the water. Yet when he saw the waves, be became afraid and thus began to sink. After crying, "Lord, save me", Jesus caught him and told him, "You of little faith, why did you doubt?"

Then when Jesus climbed into the boat, the wind immediately stopped. Recognizing that Jesus did not speak to the wind but rather his presence entering the boat caused it to cease, his disciples worshipped him saying, "Truly you are the Son of God." Yet, Mark makes it clear that they had completely forgot the previous miracle that Jesus performed of feeding 5,000 men and it was because "their hearts were hardened" (Mark 6:52).

This miracle was not just about Jesus walking on water, but also of him calming a raging storm by just his presence. No where did any of the writer's state that he told the storm to cease as he did on a previous occasion. Yet when he entered the boat, the raging storm instantaneously ceased. What a miracle!

The Application

It seems that Jesus purposefully compelled his disciples to go across the lake right after miraculously feeding thousands of people and hearing them hail him as prophet. It seemed that he was just trying to set them up for their next test of faith. Yet there were many instances in other miracles that the writers of the Gospels recorded the fact that Jesus either purposefully did something or said something to test someone's faith. He did this very thing in the previous miracle by asking his disciples where they would get food to feed the multitude.

It was also clear from Mark that Jesus saw them in distress and fear but it seemed that he purposefully was about to pass them and not come to their aid. Yet, he did desire to help them but was waiting for them to acknowledge him and their need for help. This acknowledgment fits right in line within his ministry, for he purposefully desired those who needed help from him to acknowledge their need. Numerous times he would ask those who came to him for healing what was it that they would like for him to do. He obviously knew what they wanted but from his perspective, it must be man's initiative to acknowledge the specific help that they were in need of.

Turning Water into Wine

The Background

Recorded in John 2:1-11, we see Jesus' first miracle. The setting was at Cana in Galilee and Jesus, his disciples, and his mother were invited to wedding. The unfortunate situation that arose was when the wine ran out. Immediately, Jesus' mother came to him and said, "They have no more wine." She did not tell him this to inform him of the situation at hand but rather so that he could "miraculously" fix the unfavorable situation. She knew what he was capable of doing and that is why she came to him. Appearing to be reluctant, Jesus asked her why she desired to involve him in this situation for his time had not yet come. As if she paid him no mind, she told the servants of the house to "do whatever he tells you."

The Miracle

Nearby, there were six stone water jars and each held twenty to thirty gallons of water. Jesus told the servants to fill the jars with water and they filled them to the brim. Then he told them to draw some of the water out and take it to the master of the banquet. The master tasted the water that had been turned to wine and he did not know where it had come from, yet the servants knew.

After calling the bridegroom aside, he stated, "Everyone brings out the choice wine first and then the cheaper wine after the guests have had too much to drink; but you have saved the best till now" (John 2:10). This water that Jesus changed to wine was not cheap but rather was the best of wine which should have came out first. Thus, Jesus' wine was much better than the wine that the people previously had.

The Application

At the conclusion of the miracle, John the author makes it clear that this was Jesus' first miraculous sign and this miracle revealed his glory to his disciples. As a result of this miracle, his disciples put their faith in him. Jesus had to start somewhere in order to show his close followers that he was indeed the Messiah and ultimately God himself. Graciously, his disciples put their faith in him, yet, they would be tested as we have seen earlier.

In addition, Mary knew what Jesus was capable of doing and we see this from their brief conversation. If this was Jesus' first miracle, how did she know that he was capable of performing miracles? In understanding the purpose of Jesus' miracles from a biblical perspective, he would not have performed miracles before his ministry. He intended miracles to serve as a means of faith, as a means of inaugurating the Kingdom of God, and for other purposes. Thus, this was the first miracle that Jesus ever performed while on earth. At the same time, we must not forget that Mary was informed by the angel that Jesus would be no ordinary child. Certainly, she recognized from the Scriptures who he really was, what he was capable of doing, and what he would do for the Jewish people. Even more interesting is the fact that this miracle may not have even occurred unless his mother requested and even demand that it would take place.

WITHERING THE FIG TREE

The Background

In Matthew 21:18-22 and Mark 11:12-25, we have the miracle of Jesus causing a tree to immediately wither. The setting begins with him and his disciples leaving Bethany and heading back to Jerusalem. As they were nearing the city, Jesus was hungry and in the distance, he saw a fig tree with leaves by the road and he went to it to find some fruit.

The Miracle

Unfortunately, there was no fruit on the tree because the season had not yet come for figs. But because he saw leaves with no fruit, Jesus said to the tree, "May no one ever eat fruit from you again" and immediately the tree withered. A fig tree with no leaves would show no signs of fruit but a fig tree with leaves must at least show some young fruit in the process of growing or it would be barren for the entire season. Since Jesus saw leaves, he was expecting to the very least see some young fruit which would have been located underneath the leaves. Because he saw none, he condemned the tree because of its lack of any sign of fruit. After seeing this sight, the disciples were amazed at how the tree withered so quickly. That very next morning as they went along that same path where the tree was, the disciples saw that it had withered all the way from the roots.

There seems to be two miracles in this narrative and not just one. The first miracle was the immediate and visible withering of the tree, specifically the leaves. Yet the second miracle was him causing the tree to wither all the way down to the root in less than a day. The reason why the second miracle may have been distinct from the first seems to come from the disciples seeing a difference in the tree that next morning. The withering of the leaves is miraculous because trees do not instantaneously shrivel. The second miracle is even more shocking because all in less than a day, the entire tree had been dried up and dead all the way down to its roots.

The Application

After seeing the tree wither all the way from the roots, Peter remembered what Jesus had previously said to the tree. Then he said to him, "Rabbi, look! The fig tree you cursed has withered!" In order to teach Peter and the disciples about faith, Jesus replied and stated, "I tell you the truth, if you have faith and do not doubt, not only can you do what was done to the fig tree, but also you can say to this mountain, 'Go, throw yourself into the sea,' and it will be done" (Matthew 21:21). Jesus' first application to the situation at hand centered on faith. His encouragement to them pertained to believing and never doubting.

Then he continued to say, "Therefore I tell you, whatever you ask for in prayer, believe that you have received it, and it will be yours. And when you stand praying, if you hold anything against anyone, forgive him, so that your Father in heaven may forgive you your sins" (Mark 11:24-25). His second teaching concerned both prayer and faith. Jesus wanted his followers to believe that what they prayed for would be accomplished. At the same time, he did not want their prayers hindered because of unconfessed sin in their life. He used this same tree that he miraculously caused to wither to teach his followers about faith and prayer. As a result, his disciples were given confidence that they could believe and exercise this similar means of power that he did.

THE DROUGHT AND CATCH OF FISH

The Background

In Luke 5:1-11, we have Jesus astonishing numerous fishermen with a miraculous catch of fish. During a particular day when Jesus was standing by the lake, he saw two boats that were left there by fishermen who were washing their nets. With intent, he got into Simon's boat and asked him to pull the boat a little from the shore so that he could continue teaching the people. After he had finished speaking to the people, he told Simon to take his boat out into the deep water and to let his net down for a catch. Simon told him that he and others had been working all night and have not caught anything. But because Jesus told him to do so, he complied.

The Miracle

It was a preposterous suggestion that Jesus made in telling Simon to take his boat out into the deep water for a catch. First, Peter was exhausted. He and his partners had fished all night and caught nothing. They worked at night for one simple reason - the fish in the Sea of Galilee feed at night. In the daytime they hide under rocks.[267] All fishermen during this time knew that the most thriving fishing took place at night, for during the day they could see and avoid the nets. Second, the Sea of Galilee drops off into deep water close to the shore, and in most areas, it was too dangerous for swimming.[268] All fishermen primarily fished near the shore where fresh water feeds into the lake and Simon and the others knew this. And third, the very idea that Jesus of Nazareth, who has never wet a line, should presume to tell a seasoned fishing captain what to do would be preposterous.[269] Thus, to launch into the deep in broad daylight would have been ridiculous!

Yet after letting down their nets, Simon and his fishermen caught so many fish that their nets began to break. They quickly signaled to other fishermen in the other boats to come and help them. Even more shocking, both boats were filled with fish so that they began to sink. After seeing the miraculous catch of fish, Simon fell at Jesus' knees saying, "Go away from me, Lord; I am a sinful man!"

The Application

Jesus did not ignore Peter's request but rather sought an opportunity to teach him an important lesson about "fishing". Jesus replied and said to him, "Don't be afraid. From now on you will catch men." Jesus approached Peter at his greatest strength and told him that he would be "fishers" of men. Dismissing his fears, Jesus assured him that his fishing skills would still be needed but for a different kind of catch, for he would now be catching people. The word catching in this scene means "to catch alive."[270] Jesus intentionally began with a preposterous suggestion in order to work a miracle with the purpose of moving Simon and his friends into the world of "fishing for people."

Then after pulling their boats up on the shore, Simon and some of the other fisherman left everything and followed Jesus. Once man's weaknesses and inabilities are exposed in front of Jesus, it only makes sense to leave everything behind and follow him. These men made the best decision of their lives in making this first step toward the Savior.

HEALING BLIND BARTIMAEUS

The Background

On several occasion, Jesus was instrumental in healing the blind. The most famous of these narratives was when he healed a blind man named Bartimaeus, for three out of the four Gospels records this miracle (Matthew 20:29-34, Mark 10:46-52, and Luke 18:35-43). The setting begins with Jesus walking the streets of Jericho with large crowds following him and he was on his way out of the city. While many were walking with him, two blind men were sitting by the roadside. One of the men's names was specifically mentioned as being Bartimaeus the son of Timaeus.

The Miracle

When Jesus drew near where these two men lay, someone told them that Jesus was coming by. As a result, they shouted, "Lord, Son of David, have mercy on us!" Many rebuked them including those who led the way and they all told them to be quiet. But these men shouted even louder saying, "Lord, Son of David, have mercy on us!"

It was obvious that the crowds of people around Jesus were talking and making noise and certainly everyone was not quiet. So why did the beggars have to keep quiet? Because they were outcasts! That was why they were told to literally, "shut your mouth" even by "those who led the way" (Luke 18:39). Even when these blind men had a glimmer of hope, they were despised and given no hope.

289

Could some of these people who rebuked this man have been Jesus' own disciples? Certainly, for they may have been leading the way and serving as Jesus' "right hand" helpers. They even helped lead the way in many other instances in the Gospels.

Yet, Jesus stopped and ordered the men to be brought to him. So they called to the men and told them to "cheer up" and to get "on your feet" for "he's calling you." Mark specifically states of Bartimaeus that after "throwing his cloak aside, he jumped to his feet and came to Jesus." Jesus then asked, "What do you want me to do for you?" They answered, "Lord, we want our sight." After having compassion on them, Jesus touched their eyes and immediately they received their sight.

The Application

The purpose of his miracle was obvious, for after performing the miracle, Jesus told them, "Go, your faith has healed you." Instead of literally going, these men stayed and followed Jesus along the road praised God along their way. When all the people saw it, they also praised God. It was faith all along that Jesus desired to see from those who wanted healing. It would also be their faith which caused them to receive a miracle in their lives.

In addition, we see Jesus siding with the oppressed as he had always done. His teachings and his miracles show him giving special attention to the poor, the widow, and the outcasts, which would have included the blind. By him extending grace to these men, he was rejecting the views of the crowd and their cultural ways. He gave them all, possibly even his disciples, a verbal slap on the wrist by calling the blind men to him and healing them in the presence of everyone.

HEALING TWO BLIND MEN

The Background

A second narrative of Jesus healing the blind comes from Matthew 9:27-31. The setting begins with two blind men following him crying out for him to have mercy on them. They also use the term "Son of

David" as Bartimaeus used in the previous narrative. The blind men continued to follow him despite Jesus going "inside" a building, and here we see the desperation of these men.

The Miracle

Jesus saw what was going on and eventually asked them if they believed that he was able to heal them. They replied, "Yes Lord." Then Jesus touched their eyes and told them, "According to your faith will it be done to you" and their sight was restored. Although we don't see the specific word for "immediately" in light of this miracle, we do see the author stating that he touched their eyes and that they were open. We know that this miracle happened instantaneously because there was no gap between what Jesus had said and what actually took place. In addition, the result of this miracle fits right in to the holistic disposition of Jesus' miraculous works happening instantly.

After the miracle, Jesus strictly warned the two men to tell no one about this miracle. However, they went out and spread the news about him all over that region. If there was any group of people that Jesus did not want to know about this miracle, it would have been the religious leaders, for they were against him and desired to kill him. He was not afraid of them but he knew that it was not his time to die and that he needed to continue ministering to the people of the land. Certainly he wanted the entire region to know about God's goodness and grace, for he told many individuals including a man who had been demon possessed to "go home to your family and tell them how much the Lord has done for you, and how he has had mercy on you" (Mark 5:19). But sometimes we see him telling people to not say anything about what was done except to their loved ones.

The Application

It was the faith of the two men that Jesus actually saw than anything else. These men had the boldness to follow him literally wherever he went to receive their miracle. In addition, they were crying out to him for mercy and they told Jesus that they did believe that he could heal them. It was this faith in action that eventually allowed these men to receive their miracle.

HEALING A MAN BORN BLIND

The Background

The third narrative of Jesus healing the blind takes place in John 9. What makes this narrative different from the previous narratives was that this man was specifically stated as being born blind. Perhaps the previous men were born blind, but from John's perspective, he gives a greater emphasis on him being blind from his birth and the faith that needed to have been accompanied as a result of this miracle.

John begins this narrative by stating that Jesus saw a man who was blind from his birth. Assuming that this man or someone in his family must have done wrong, the disciples asked him, "Rabbi, who sinned, this man or his parents, that he was born blind?" Jesus told them that neither of them sinned but rather he had this blindness so that God's work might be displayed in his life. In addition, he told his disciples that we all must do work while it was still day and while he, who is the light of the world, was still in the world.

The Miracle

After saying this, he "spit on the ground, made some mud with the saliva, and put it on the man's eyes." Then he told the man to go and wash in the Pool of Siloam. After the man wash, the man was stated as coming home "seeing". As he came home, his neighbors and those who saw him begging wondered if he was the same man who used to sit and beg. Some claimed it was him and others claimed that he looks like him. Yet this man insisted that he was the man who used to sit and beg. After being asked how he was now able to see, the man told them all what Jesus did.

After a thorough investigation from the Pharisee, they themselves became divided. Some of them questioned Jesus as not being a man of God and one who does not keep the law while others stated that sinners can not do miraculous signs. Even many of the Jews did not believe that this man was born blind and because of their disbelief, they sought out his parents. The parents confirmed to everyone that the man born blind was indeed their son. Yet they told the Jews and Pharisees that he was of age to talk concerning how he was now able to see. His parents said this because they were afraid of the Jews, for the Jews had already decided that anyone who gave credit that Jesus was the Messiah would be put out of the synagogue.

The Application

One common denominator that we see in all three narratives consisted around faith. During the first two narratives we see Jesus asking the men questions in order to see their faith. The third narrative shows the man's confidence in letting the Jews know that he was blind and that Jesus indeed healed him. This man gave credit to whom credit was due. He not only went against the culture norm of his day but he believed in the miraculous workings of Jesus. Unfortunately, he was thrown out of the synagogue for his belief.

HEALING AND CLEANSING A MAN WITH LEPROSY

The Background

The most famous narrative of Jesus healing the intractable disease of leprosy was mentioned in three of the four Gospels (Matthew 8:1-4; Mark 1:40-45; and Luke 5:12-16). Leprosy is characterized by scabs and shining spots appearing to be deeper than the skin. Other signs included the affected hairs turning white and the escalation of quick raw flesh. Those who contracted leprosy were considered unclean and those who even touched a leper would have been considered unclean. From the general accounts of these Gospels, this miracle happened early in his ministry.

The Miracle

This account began with Jesus coming down a mountainside into one of the towns and him being approached by a man with leprosy. This man came on his knees begging Jesus saying, "Lord, if you are willing, you can make me clean." Filled with compassion, Jesus reached out and simply touched the man and said, "I am willing, be clean!" Immediately the leprosy left him and he was cured.

Then Jesus ordered him to not tell anyone but to go and show yourself to the priest and offer the sacrifices that Moses commanded for your cleansing. Instead of going to the priest however, the man went out and began sharing freely and spreading the news of what he had done so that crowds of people came to hear him and to be healed of their sicknesses.

As a result of this miracle, Jesus could no longer enter a town openly, but stayed outside in lonely places where he prayed. Yet still, people came to him from everywhere.

The Application

What makes this miracle famous was not necessarily the actual healing of the leper but the after affects of the healing. First, Jesus told the healed man to go to the priest because lepers needed to be confirmed as being healed before they could return to their homes. This comment shows Jesus' commitment to the law, for he said earlier in his ministry that he did not "come to abolish the law or the prophets" but "to fulfill them" (Matthew 5:17).Yet after the man realized that he was clean, he did not go to the priest and did not obey the custom of the land. Why? Because from his perspective, he did not believe it was needed especially since he was immediately healed.

Secondly, instead of going to the priest, this cleansed leper went and began freely spreading the news of what Jesus had done to the effect that large crowds of people came from everywhere to be healed of him. Ironically, although Jesus ordered him to not tell anyone, the exact opposite effect happened and now he would still be surrounded by large crowds.

And third, Jesus realized that he was not welcomed in these large towns most likely from the religious leaders and not from the people. So he made the choice to stay outside of the city and in the countryside regions where he could spend time with God. But the authors state that the crowds of people found out where he was and they came to him from everywhere in rural regions. From these three perspectives, we are now able to see the true impact of this miracle and why it was mentioned in three of the four Gospels.

HEALING 10 MEN WITH LEPROSY

The Background

Another miracle of Jesus healing leprosy took place in Luke 17:11-19. This narrative began with him traveling on his way to Jerusalem along the border between Samaria and Galilee. The fact that he traveled near Samaria shows that his actions were different than most Jews during his era. It was well understood that "Jews have no dealing with Samaritans" (John 4:9), and those who journeyed from Judea to Galilee or vice versa would cross over the Jordan River to evade Samaria. They would then cross back over the river once they arrived at their destination. On the other hand, the Samaritans were sometimes aggressive to the Jews and they often mocked them.

The Miracle

As Jesus was passing through a village, ten men with this disease came to him and at a distance they cried to him in a loud voice saying, "Jesus, Master, have pity on us!" Without any hesitation, he instructed them to go and show themselves to the priest. Miraculously, as they were traveling, they were cleansed.

After being cleansed, one of the ten came back to him and was praising God in a loud voice. He bowed down at Jesus' feet and thanked him. Ironically, he was a Samaritan. After seeing what was done, Jesus asked, "Were not all ten cleansed? Where are the other nine? Was no one found to return and give praise to God except this foreigner?" Then Jesus said to this cleansed leper, "Rise and go, your faith has made you well." Although it was not specifically stated, all ten of these lepers were immediately healed just like the man in the previous narrative. We know it happened quickly because as Jesus was still traveling to Jerusalem, this leper quickly found his way back to him in order to thank him.

The Application

Certainly, it was the unexpected thanksgiving coming from an unexpected foreigner that Luke the author desired to bring out in this narrative. We don't know if all of the cleansed lepers were Jews but what was unexpected was that this Samaritan would come to Jesus who was a Jew and would offer up praise and thanksgiving to him. Seeing this man's attitude of thanksgiving, even Jesus wondered about the other nine knowing that they were healed as well. Although the faith of the man is significant in his healing, his thanksgiving was the centerpiece and main objective of the miracle.

HEALING THE WITHERED HAND

The Background

In Matthew 12:1-14, Mark 3:1-6, and Luke 6:1-11, Jesus openly healed a man with a withered hand. Two of the three authors were careful in mentioning the background for this miracle. They began with him and his disciples going through the grain fields on the Sabbath and because his disciples were hungry, they began to eat some of the heads of grain.

The Pharisees, presumably looking at them in order to find fault, saw this and told Jesus that his disciples were doing what was unlawful on the Sabbath. Jesus replied saying, "Haven't you read what David did when he and his companions were hungry? He entered the house of God, and he and his companions ate the consecrated bread which was not lawful for them to do, but only for the priests. Or haven't you read in the law that on the Sabbath the priests in the temple desecrate the day and yet are innocent?" (Matthew 12:3-5). Then Jesus, speaking of himself, stated the piercing words that one greater than the temple is here, that he desires mercy and not sacrifice, and that "the Son of Man is Lord of the Sabbath."

The Miracle

On another Sabbath while teaching in the synagogue, a man whose right hand was shriveled was present. The Pharisees and teachers of the law were also present and were looking for a motive to charge Jesus, so they observed him closely to see if he would heal on the Sabbath. Knowing what they were thinking, Jesus told the man with the shriveled hand to get up and stand in front of everyone. After the man did this, he said, "If any of you has a sheep and it falls into a pit on the Sabbath, will you not take hold of it and lift it out? How much more valuable is a man than a sheep" (Matthew 12:11-12). Then he asked, "Which is lawful on the Sabbath: to do good or to do evil, to save life or to kill?" But they all remained silent. After looking around at the people in anger and after being deeply distressed at their stubborn hearts, he told the man to stretch out his hand. Once he stretched it out, it was completely restored as the other hand. Then the Pharisees left the synagogue in anger and began to plot with the Herodians how they might destroy Jesus.

The Application

It is interesting to note that it was not recorded that this man ever asked Jesus to heal him. Maybe he was simply in the synagogue to hear him teach, and depending on the extent of his withered hand, it may have still been able to have been used in some form or fashion. Did Jesus purposefully use this man's weakness to show the people and religious leaders the importance of saving a life rather than not taking any action at all? Did he resolutely have this man stand up in order to heal him for the purpose of demonstrating that he was greater than the temple and synagogue? Certainly this cannot be overlooked, for the Gospel writers were careful to mention individuals asking and begging Jesus to heal them. But we don't see this man asking for anything.

Therefore, this miracle possibly encompasses an even greater purpose seeing that Jesus came to his need in order to show the purpose of him being greater than the Sabbath and that it was more beneficial to do good than not do anything at all. Although the religious leaders and teachers of the law were more interested in custom, Jesus was more interested in reaching out to a man with a need.

HEALING A PARALYTIC

The Background

In Matthew 9:1-8, Mark 2:1-12, and Luke 5:17-26, we see the miracle of Jesus healing a man who was paralyzed. A paralytic was one who had loss his voluntary movement and it was an offensive term for a physically challenged person. In the Greek, this word represented one who was weaken and enfeeble, and one who was suffering from the "relaxing" of the nerves.

The background of this parable began with him crossing over the lake and coming to Capernaum. Upon seeing him, people gathered around him, for they heard that he had come home. The Pharisees and teachers of the law had also come from every village of Galilee and from Judea and Jerusalem. After entering into a house, he began teaching the people and healing the sick. So many people gathered in that house that there was no room left in the house and not even outside the door.

The Miracle

While he was teaching, four men came bringing to him a paralyzed man on a mat and they tried to take him into the house to lay him in front of Jesus. But since they could not find a way in because of the crowd, they went to the roof, made an opening right above him and after digging through it, they lowered the paralyzed man on the mat into the middle of the crowd, right in front of him. When Jesus saw their faith, he told the paralyzed man to cheer up for his sins were forgiven.

But when the Pharisees and teachers of the law heard this, they said to themselves, "Why does this fellow talk like that? He's blaspheming! Who can forgive sins but God alone?" (Mark 2:7). Immediately, Jesus knew what they were thinking in their hearts and he asked them why they entertained evil thoughts in their hearts. He asked them which is easier to say to the paralytic, "Your sins are forgiven," or to say, "Get up and walk." To prove the power of God, he then told them "so that you may know that the Son of Man has authority on earth to forgive sins", he said to the paralyzed man, "Get up, take your mat and go home". Immediately the once paralyzed man stood up in front of them all, took his mat, walked out in full view of everyone, and went home praising God. When the crowd saw this, they were amazed and gave praise to God saying, "We have never seen anything like this" and "we have seen remarkable things today".

It seemed that Jesus set up the Pharisees and religious leaders by not immediately healing the man but first stating that his sins were forgiven. He knew that many of them came from every village of Galilee and from Judea and Jerusalem. In addition, it is true that there were no other miracles that Jesus performed where he told someone that their sins were forgiven. He did tell a women who anointed his feet that here sins were forgiven (Luke 7:36-50) but no miracle was present. So did he purposefully delay in healing the man so that he could show all the people that he had authority and power to forgive sins? Possibly so!

The Application

What is most meaningful is the faith of these four men bringing the paralyzed man to Jesus. There was no way for them to get into the house and they went through extreme measures to get to him. Going to the roof would not have been so difficult, for there were stairs that led to the roof in many if not most of the typical homes of that day. But it was the extreme measures of careful precision that these men took in making a hole through the roof. If they weren't careful, all four of them could have fallen through and could have possibly injured themselves. But yet they took the risk and were successful in not only lowering the man in front of Jesus but in seeing the paralyzed man healed.

What is not coincidental is the fact that these men made an opening in the roof right above him and they lowered the man into the middle of the crowd. This was purposefully arrayed so that the power of God could be seen by all including the Pharisees and teachers of law. This act shows that God makes no mistakes but rather strategically organizes and arranges the things in life for a particular purpose. And what was this purpose? He wanted to show the religious leaders that he had power and authority on earth to forgive sins. They knew that no one but God could forgive sins but it was Jesus' strategic purpose in letting them know that his miraculous power proved that he was God and that he was able to forgive sins.

HEALING THE INFIRM WOMAN

The Background

In Luke 13:10-17, we see Jesus healing a woman with an infirmity. This narrative begins with him teaching on a Sabbath day in one of the synagogues. There was a woman present who had an infirmity and her infirmity was caused from a demonic spirit. The Greek word used for infirmity (*astheneia*) meant one who was devoid of strength, weakness of body, and feebleness of health. It also referred to a disease. Her particular condition caused her to be "permanently" bent over and she had lived with it for eighteen years.

The Miracle

Although she did not come to Jesus for help, Jesus saw her need and came to her. He gave her the good news that she was now set free from her infirmity. Then he put his hands on her and immediately she straightened up and praised God. Offended and angry because he healed on the Sabbath, the ruler of the synagogue told the people that since there were six days for work, he ought to heal people on those days and not on the Sabbath.

But Jesus replied to him saying, "You hypocrites! Doesn't each of you on the Sabbath untie his ox or donkey from the stall and lead it out to give it water? Then should not this woman, a daughter of Abraham, whom Satan has kept bound for eighteen long years, be set free on the Sabbath day from what bound her?" (Luke 13:15-16). After saying this, all his opponents were put to shame but the people were overjoyed with what Jesus was doing.

The Application

Although it was both the demon and the infirmity that Jesus immediately overcame, he had to also overcome the brainless beliefs of the ruler of the synagogue and all his opponents. Because he was surrounded by so many people who were looking for a way to catch him in sin, he performed this miracle to show them all how commonly they overlook the simple things in life. He appealed to the common practice among the Jews of untying their cattle from within the stable and leading them out to water. It would be barbarous not to do this, for letting the cattle rest on the Sabbath would be worse than working them.[271] Yet Jesus applied this fact to a daughter of Abraham who needed to be let loose of an infirmity, and from his perspective, since it was unthinkable not to untie cattle in order to lead them to war, it would be unthinkable for him not to loose a woman from the hands of Satan.

HEALING THE INFIRM MAN

The Background

In John 5:1-15, we have a second narrative of Jesus healing one with an infirmity. What differentiated the first narrative from this one comes from Luke 13:11 which explain that the woman's physical infirmity was ascribed to the influence of an evil spirit. After going to Jerusalem to celebrate a Jewish feast, Jesus saw a man who had an infirmity for thirty eight years at a pool where other disabled people were. Far from any ordinary pool, it was known that an angel came down at certain seasons into the pool and troubled the water. Whoever stepped in first after the water was troubled was made whole of whatever disease he or she had.

The Miracle

When Jesus saw this infirm man lying there and after understanding how long he had lived with this infirmity, he asked him if he wanted to get well. Only thinking about the miracle that accompanied the pool, the man told him that he had no one to help him into the pool when the water is stirred, for while he tries to get in, someone else always gets in ahead of him.

Then Jesus said to him, "Get up! Pick up your mat and walk." At once the man was cured of his infirmity and he picked up his mat and walked. Because that day was a Sabbath day, some of the Jews saw this man carrying his mat home and told him that the law forbids one to carry their mat on that day. But the man told the Jews that the one who cured him commanded him to pick up his mat and walk. The Jews asked him if he knew who it was that told him to do this. Unfortunately, the man did not know who it was because Jesus had slipped away in the crowd of people.

Sometime later, Jesus found the cured man at the temple and said to him, "See, you are well again. Stop sinning or something worse may happen to you." The man obviously recognized that this was the man who healed him and after inquiring who he was, he went away and told the Jews that it was Jesus who had miraculously healed him.

The Application

Again, we see another miracle that took place on the Sabbath. But it was specifically what one of the laws of the Sabbath prohibited that was particularly interesting. The Jews told the man that the law prohibited him from carrying a mat on the Sabbath. How strange of a law, for we had just previously seen that the Jews would untie their ox or donkey from the stall on the Sabbath and lead it out to give it water. Yet, one was not allowed to carry their mat home. It was these dimwitted practices that Jesus was against.

In addition, the way this man had incurred this infirmity most also be noted. The fact that Jesus told him to stop sinning or something worse may happen to you suggest that he was infirmed because of his sin. Amazing, we see a major effect of sin and the consequences of continually sinning. The lesson to be learned from Jesus for the Christian life is that sin can cause physical problems for the human body while the cessation of sin can avoid the harmful consequences of sin.

HEALING THE NOBLEMAN'S SON

The Background

In John 4:46-53, we see Jesus healing the son of a nobleman. A nobleman was an officer of the state in the service of Herod Antipas and his very office belonged to the king. He most likely was born into an upper class or royal family. This narrative begins with Jesus visiting Cana in Galilee where he had previously turned water into wine.

The Miracle

When this nobleman at Capernaum found out that Jesus was coming, he immediately when to him begging him to come and heal his son who was dying from a fever. As a means of reproof and in order to show him his sin and weakness, Jesus replied, "Unless you people see miraculous signs and wonders, you will never believe." Yet the nobleman begged him again saying, "Sir, come down before my child dies." Then Jesus said, "You may go. Your son will live."

Taking Jesus at his word, the man left to go home. While he was on his way, his servants met him with the good news that his son was living and well. Then the nobleman asked as to the time when his son started to get better. After finding out that the fever left him yesterday at the seventh hour, he realized that it was the exact time at which Jesus had said to him that his "son will live." Then he and all that was in his house believed.

What is noteworthy from this narrative is when the nobleman realized that Jesus instantaneously healed his son. We know that this healing took place immediately because the servants of the nobleman did not know when he had talked to Jesus nor when Jesus said that his son would live. They were only reporting the facts of when the fever left and surprising, it was the exact time that Jesus spoke his words. Therefore, this miracle just proves again of Jesus' instantaneous healings and the power of God.

The Application

For Jesus to say, "Unless you people see miraculous signs and wonders, you will never believe" just after the man asked him to come and heal his son seems to be a very incongruous way of answering a request. But for him to say the words "you will never believe" shows again that he was looking for faith. This man could have been offended at Jesus' harsh words and could have quickly walked away or tried to justify himself. As a result, his son may not have ever been healed. However, this man continued to demonstrate faith and as a result, his son was healed.

RAISING THE RULER'S DAUGHTER TO LIFE

There were three resurrections recorded in the Gospels (aside from Jesus' resurrection) and they include Jesus raising a ruler's daughter, raising a widow's son, and raising a man named Lazarus. Since I have previously mentioned the miracle of Lazarus' resurrection, I will concentrate on the other two resurrections. The most famous of the three is Jesus' miracle of raising the ruler's daughter, for it is mentioned in three of the four Gospels (Matthew 9:18-26; Mark 5:21-43; Luke 8:40-56). What is interesting in this particular miracle is the fact that Jesus not only raises a dead girl but he heals a sick women as well.

The Background

This narrative begins with Jesus crossing over the lake and being welcomed by a large crowd while by the lake, for they were expecting him. While he was talking to the people, a synagogue ruler named Jairus came and fell at his feet begging him to come to his house because his only daughter, about twelve years old, was dying. He desired him to put his hands on her so that she would be healed. Jesus got up and went with him and his disciples followed.

As Jesus was going to his house, a large crowd followed and pressed around him almost to the point of crushing him. There was a woman nearby who unfortunately suffered from bleeding and anguish for twelve years. She spent all her money on doctors for healing but instead of getting better, her condition intensified. When she heard that Jesus was coming, she believed that if she could only touch his clothes, she would be healed. So she found a way to come up behind him and touched the edge of his cloak. Immediately, her bleeding stopped and she was delivered from her suffering.

Right away Jesus realized that power left him and he stopped and turned around in the crowd and asked, "Who touched me." Trying to be realistic as possible, Peter and the disciples told him, "You see the people crowding against you and yet you ask, 'Who touched me?'" But Jesus kept looking around to see who had touched him because he knew that healing power had gone out from him. Knowing that she could not continue to go unobserved, the women who touched him came and fell at his feet trembling with fear. She told him the truth about her bleeding and condition and why she touched him. Then Jesus said to her, "Take heart, daughter, your faith has healed you" and "go in peace and be freed from your suffering."

While Jesus was still talking to the woman, some men came from Jairus' house and told him that his daughter was dead and that he should not bother Jesus anymore. But Jesus ignored what they said and told Jairus to not be afraid but believe and she will be healed.

The Miracle

When Jesus had arrived at Jairus' house, he saw a commotion of people crying and sobbing loudly. He kept the crowd outside and only allowed Peter, James, and John to enter along with the child's mother and father. When he entered the house, he also saw a noisy crowd and asked why there was so much commotion and crying. He then told them all that the child was not dead but asleep, but they all laugh at him for they knew that she was dead.

Then he took the girl by the hand and said, "Little girl, I say to you, get up!" Immediately her spirit returned and she stood up and walked around in front of all the people. Then Jesus told them to give her something to eat. Seeing what was done, everyone was completely astonished but Jesus gave strict orders not to let anyone know about this. Yet, the news of what he had done spread through that entire region.

The Application

It was not a haphazard statement for Jesus to have told all the people in the house that the girl was only sleep. He had stated many other similar statements to various people before he performed miracles in order to test their faith. The people knew that the girl was dead and Jesus and writer of this Gospel knew as well. But Jesus desired to see who would believe that what he was saying was realistic and that she would live. If Jairus knew that Jesus was a healer, certainly other people in the house knew as well. Consequently, they all laughed at him which showed Jesus had faithless they all were.

Yet it was the faith of the dead girl's father that Jesus went on ahead and raised her to life. It is evident this man's faith was tested, for some men came from his house and told him that his daughter was dead and that he should not bother Jesus any more. Even more importantly, we see Jesus' willingness to go to the house despite the bad news and to raise a dead girl despite the lack of faith present.

RAISING THE WIDOW'S SON TO LIFE

The Background

We see another miracle of Jesus raising someone from the dead in Luke 7:11-17. When he and his disciples were entering a town called Nain, a large crowd followed him. As he approached the town gate, a funeral procession was taking place. A dead boy, being the only son of his mother, was being carried out to be buried, and there was a large crowd from the town supporting the funeral procession.

The Miracle

After Jesus saw the woman crying, his heart went out to her and he told her to not cry. Then he went up and touched the coffin, and those carrying it stopped walking. He said, "Young man, I say to you, get up!" Immediately, the dead man sat up and began to talk. After seeing this, everyone was filled with amazement and they praise God saying, "A great prophet has appeared among us" and "God has come to help his people." This miracle spread throughout Judea and the surrounding country.

The Application

What is interesting is that Luke makes it clear that there were two different crowds of people. One large crowd was following Jesus and a second was following the widow whose son died. Yet from God's point of view, it was a strategic occasion for all these people to see his power displayed.

In addition, it was important to recognize what the people stated following the miracle. They stated, "A great prophet has appeared among us" and "God has come to help his people." Yet, these were similar words which the angel spoke to Joseph, the father of Jesus. In reference to his son, the angel told him that "he will save his people from their sins" (Matthew 1:21). In other words, the people recognized that Jesus was someone who not only appeared to them but had come to help them, especially in light of their oppression and suppression. And yet Jesus' very name meant that he would come to save his people.

CASTING OUT A DEMON IN THE SYNAGOGUE

The Background

There were more than a half a dozen instances where Jesus encountered demons and miraculously cast them out of people. Mark 1:21-28 and Luke 4:31-37 gives us probably the earliest example of him performing this type of miracle. The narrative begins with him going to a town in Galilee named Capernaum and him teaching the people in the synagogue on the Sabbath. All the people were amazed at him because he taught with authority and not like the teachers of the law.

The Miracle

Suddenly, a man in the synagogue who was possessed by a demon yelled out saying, "What do you want with us, Jesus of Nazareth? Have

307

you come to destroy us? I know who you are - the Holy One of God" (Mark 1:24). Jesus immediately told the demon possessed man to be quiet and to come out of him. After shaking the man and throwing him down on the ground in front of everyone, the demon came out without harming him. Everyone who saw this was amazed and asked each other, "What is this? A new teaching - and with authority! He even gives orders to evil spirits and they obey him" (Mark 1:27). As a result of this miracle, news spread quickly about what Jesus did around the whole region of Galilee.

There are a couple interesting facets about this miracle. First, when Luke states that the demon came out of the man without harming him, he mentions this because there was at least one other instance when a demon almost killed a young boy before coming out (Mark 9:26). And second, this miracle was one of the first miracles relating to demonic possessions that aided Jesus' fame all across Galilee. He was already becoming famous, but this miracle added to his prestige.

The Application

The demon possessed man was initially seen as a listener sitting in the synagogue. Since it was common for Jews to consistently come into the synagogue to listen and learn from the Torah, he possibly was one of those consistent attendees. But when Jesus came that particular day, we see the demon speaking through the man acknowledging who he was and his future mission. Although the people listening to him did not know specific details of the final judgment that the demonic world would undergo, the demon certainly knew, for he stated, "Have you come to destroy us." Yet this would not be the only time in which a demon would ask Jesus about this future judgment.

CASTING OUT A DEMON FROM A MUTE MAN

The Background

On a second occasion after healing two blind men, Jesus was met by a man who was demon possessed. Matthew 9:32-33 specifically states that this man could not talk and because of this, he was brought to Jesus. There was no indication that the demon was violently attacking the man or even hurting him. But rather, the demon caused the man to be mute.

The Miracle

Jesus did not let the demon continually affect this man but rather he drove the demon out of him. As a result, the man immediately was able to freely speak. Upon seeing this, the multitudes were astonished and they said, "Nothing like this has ever been seen in Israel."

It is interesting to know that some demons cause physical deficiencies as in this narrative while other demons violently hurt people intending to kill them (Mark 9:26). Both were dreadful circumstances and both could only be overcome by the power of God.

The Application

What the crowds of people stated following the miracle was important. Although Israel had seen its shares of magic workers, the people stated that Jesus' works separated him from everyone else. They saw a distinction between him and the religious leaders and even the other "so-called" workers of magic. That is why they said, "Nothing like this has ever been seen in Israel."

CASTING OUT A DEMON FROM A GENTILE

The Background

On a third occasion, Jesus was instrumental in healing a Gentile woman's daughter. In Matthew 15:21-28 and Mark 7:24-30, Jesus went to the region of Tyre and Sidon. Sidon was located less than 20 miles of Tyre and both cities were large ancient Phoenician cities with power and wealth. After coming in this region, he entered into a house but he did not want anyone to know he was there. Yet, crowds of people were still able to find him.

The Miracle

A Canaanite woman born in Syrian Phoenicia found out that Jesus was there and she came and fell at his feet. She asked him to have mercy on her, for her daughter was suffering terribly from a demon. Jesus did not immediately say anything and that troubled his disciples to the point that they insisted that he send her away because she kept begging them all. Then Jesus stated, "I was sent only to the lost sheep of Israel," but the woman came again and worshipped him saying, "Lord, help me!"

Then Jesus said, "First let the children eat all they want, for it is not right to take the children's bread and toss it to their dogs" (Mark 7:27). In a discouraging manner, he was implying that the Jews have all the miracles shown to them because they are God's chosen people and thus, his works were not intended to be given to the Gentiles who were considered as dogs from the Jews.

But what was shocking to Jesus was the woman's reply stating, "Yes, Lord, but even the dogs eat the crumbs that fall from their masters' table." Her answer showed that she was not trying to eat loaves but only crumbs. She wanted to receive the crumbs of God's power and grace and if she could receive that, she would be content. Although she understood that Jesus the Master came to the Jews, she showed faith by letting him know that even Gentile should have the opportunity to be able to eat from his table.

Her response was all Jesus needed to know, for she was a woman of faith. Then he told her, "Woman, you have great faith" and "for such a reply, you may go; the demon has left your daughter." At the very hour, the girl was healed. The woman went home and found her child lying on the bed with the demon gone.

Both Gospels state in their own way that the demon came out immediately. Mark states that after seeing the woman's faith, Jesus told her that she may go because "the demon has left her daughter." In other words, that very instance of demonstrating faith, the demon left. Matthew states that "her daughter was healed from that very hour" after Jesus saw her faith.

The Application

In analyzing this parable, Jesus was not advocating the prejudiced mindset of the Jews and certainly he was open to healing anyone and everyone. At the same time, he was stating the facts of him coming specifically to the Jewish people (John 1:11). But yet again, we see Jesus' purposeful actions with not initially answering the women and we see his purposeful words in light of what he said to the woman. Certainly all Gentiles would have recognized that they were hated by the Jews and Jesus stated these words to see what she would say. To his surprise, the Gentile woman gave a true statement of dogs eating crumbs from the master's table and applied it to her lowly state. She demonstrated unbelievable faith and as a result, her daughter was healed.

CASTING OUT A DEMON FROM AN EPILEPTIC BOY

The Background

A fourth narrative of Jesus encountering demons comes when he heals an epileptic boy. In Matthew 17:14-21, Mark 9:14-29, and Luke 9:37-43, the narrative begins with him coming down from a mountain where he was transfigured and he was approached by a large crowd. Among the crowd, Jesus saw his other disciples arguing with the teachers of the law and he asked what they were arguing with them about.

The Miracle

Just as he was talking, a man in the crowd came to him and pleaded with him to have mercy on his only son who was possessed by a demon. The man stated that the demon not only took away his speech but seized the child which caused him to suddenly scream and foam at the mouth. The father claimed that the demon scarcely ever left him and would throw him to the ground and would cause him to gnash his teeth and become rigid. Seeing that the demon was literally destroying the child, the man claimed that he begged his disciples to drive it out, but they could not.

Frustrated at their lack of faith, Jesus replied, "O unbelieving and perverse generation, how long shall I stay with you and put up with you? Bring your son here" (Luke 9:41). Some of the people brought the boy to Jesus and while they were bringing him, the demon through him into a convulsion. He fell to the ground, rolled around, and foamed at the mouth. Jesus asked the boy's father how long this had been going on and the father answered, "From childhood. It has often thrown him into fire or water to kill him. But if you can do anything, take pity on us and help us" (Mark 9:21-22). Jesus told him that "everything is possible for him who believes and the father immediately stated, "I do believe; help me overcome my unbelief!"

By this time, a large crowd started running to the scene and when Jesus saw this, he scolded the demon stating, "You deaf and mute spirit, I command you, come out of him and never enter him again." After the demon yelled and convulsed the boy aggressive, he came out and the boy was healed from that moment. The boy was left on the ground believing by many to have been dead, but Jesus simply took his hand and lifted him up to his feet. The boy stood up and Jesus gave him back to his father. After seeing this, all the people were astonished at the power of God.

The Application

After seeing the embarrassment, the disciples asked him why they could not drive out the evil spirit. Jesus replied, "Because you have so little faith. I tell you the truth, if you have faith as small as a mustard seed, you can say to this mountain, 'Move from here to there' and it will move. Nothing will be impossible for you" (Matthew 17:20). By giving this reply, Jesus proves once again his purpose in performing a miracle. He wanted not only the boy's father to believe but he wanted his disciples to believe that they could accomplish anything by faith.

If there was any narrative from Scripture where we could truly understood the power and effect of what one demon could do, we find it in this miraculous encounter. Yet Jesus proves once again his power and authority over the spirit world. We see some encounters in which Jesus does not say anything when a person comes to ask him for help. Yet in this encounter, Jesus quickly casts out the demon in order to avoid a public show.

CHAPTER 5
THE TURNING POINT

Although many tried to take his life on previous encounters, we see that God strategically handed him over to the Romans for a particular purpose. Because he was strategically handed over, it was meant for him to be betrayed, unjustly tried, unjustly condemned, brutally beaten, and executed.

Introduction

If there had to be one narrative or sequence of events centering in on the life of Jesus that has captured the awareness and thoughts of people worldwide, it would undoubtedly be his betrayal and trial. We see this portrayal in passion plays, Christian art, and in Christian music. This sequence of events touches the hearts of Christians all over the world and has created a lasting impact in their personal and public lives.

This section deals with Jesus' last moments with his disciples both in the Upper Room and in the Garden of Gethsemane, and it covers both the Roman Trial and the Jewish Trial. I have entitled this section of the book "The Turning Point" because although Jesus' life was threatened numerous times during his ministry, there was no actual arrest. He was seized on one occasion when people in the synagogue drove him out of the town in order to throw him down the cliff, but Jesus miraculously escaped (Luke 4:28-30). From the disciple's perspective, they never felt fear around him although his teachings and actions went against the religious norm of the day. We don't see these men living discouraged or hopeless lives. Even during one occasion, Jesus told him that "he will be handed over to the Gentiles" and "they will mock him, insult him, spit on him, flog him and kill him" but "on the third day he will rise again" (Luke 18:32-33). Yet this did not seem to discourage them at all.

However, it is at this point of his ministry, that we see his disciples as we had never seen them before, for their hearts were described as "troubled" (John 14:1). Although they had shown the emotions of agitation on the ship in the midst of a storm, we now see a troubled spirit during Jesus' last hours with them. Even more discouraging, right after his was arrest, we see all them fleeing for their lives as if they too would be taken. Although many tried to take his life on previous encounters, we see that God strategically handed him over to the Romans for a particular purpose. Because he was strategically handed over, it was meant for him to be betrayed, unjustly tried, unjustly condemned, brutally beaten, and executed.

Beginning with his last meal with his disciples followed by their journey to the Garden of Gethsemane, we shall see how this was certainly the turning point to Jesus ministry and life. The four Gospel writers may not have all been eyewitnesses of each event surrounding Jesus' betrayal and trial, but their information came down from trustworthy eyewitnesses. When the Gospel writers set out to write their narratives, they understood that their readers and listeners would want to know details that would have been less obvious and most significant and unique. Thus, the accounts of Jesus' life including his betrayal, arrest, and trail would consist of countless unique details that would separate these sequences of events from all others.

The Last Supper

It does not due justice to "The Turning Point" of Jesus' ministry without first beginning with the events that transpired around his last meal. It was during this encounter with Jesus' disciples that changed their disposition, way of thinking, and way of behaving. It was during this meal where it actually hit these twelve men that Jesus was really about to leave their presence...for good. Therefore, it only does justice to begin with the sequence of events and words that transpired during this meal.

THE BACKGROUND

The Last Supper, also referred to as the Lord's Supper, was the last meal Jesus partook with his disciples. This meal took place only hours before he was taken into the hands of the Romans. Not many of his teachings and miracles were mentioned in all four Gospels, but the Last Supper was described in all four Gospels (Matthew 26:17-29; Mark 14:12-25; Luke 22:7-30; John 13:1-30).

This narrative begins on the first day of the Feast of Unleavened Bread when it was expected out of Jewish tradition to sacrifice a lamb. During this time of celebration, Jesus' disciples asked him where he wanted them to go and make preparations to eat for the Passover. Jesus told Peter and John to go into the city and a man carrying a jar of water will meet them and they were instructed to follow him to the house that he enters. They were then to tell him that the teacher asks where is the guest room where he is to eat the Passover with his disciples. He will show them a large upper room already furnished and ready and they were to make preparations for him and the other disciples. Peter and John did as Jesus had told them.

THE PASSOVER MEAL

Jesus desired to eat with these men during this meal in order that he and they might have a little time together for private conversation. Although the Passover celebration was to be a reminder that a lamb had suffered, Jesus brought the entire focus to himself. John 13:1 sets the tone for the Passover meal because "Jesus knew that the time had come for him to leave this world and go to the Father." Because he knew this, he told his disciples as they all were reclining at the table, "I have eagerly desired to eat this Passover with you before I suffer. For I tell you, I will not eat it again until it finds fulfillment in the Kingdom of God" (Luke 22:15-16). These were very important words for him because he set the tone for the occasion. Although he let them know that he was eager to eat with them, it was the next words that he stated that brought about discomfort to the disciple's spirit. He stated that he was going to suffer and even more distressing, he told them that this undeniably would be the last time that he would eat with them "until it finds fulfillment in the Kingdom of God."

His Betrayal Prophesied

As if the news he just stated was not bad enough, he told them that one of them would betray him. He stated that although he must "go" as it was prophesied by the prophets, it would be better for the one who betrays him to have never been born. Knowing that everything he had said in the past took place, the disciples were saddened by the news, for they did not know which one he was talking about. Then one by one they asked him, "Surely not I, Lord?" To all of their responses, he replied telling them, "It is the one to whom I will give this piece of bread when I have dipped it in the dish." Then, dipping the piece of bread, he gave it to Judas Iscariot, son of Simon" (John 13:26). As soon as Judas took the bread, Satan entered into him and Jesus told him, "What you are about to do, do quickly!" After taking the bread, he went out into the night.

Satan did not just sporadically enter into him for no reason but rather Judas opened himself to his influence and devices much earlier. The Gospel writers carefully depicted his character during Jesus' ministry. For example, after a woman named Mary anointed Jesus' feet with expensive ointment, Judas objected stating, "Why wasn't this perfume sold and the money given to the poor? It was worth a year's wages" (John 12:5). Because he kept the money for Jesus' ministry, he was implying that some of this money be given to him so that he could put it in the bag that he kept and to use it for the poor. Yet John the disciple plainly noted that he "did not say this because he cared about the poor but because he was a thief" and unfortunately "as keeper of the money bag, he used to help himself to what was put into it" (John 12:6).

Just before Jesus met with his disciples in the Upper Room, Luke makes it clear that "the chief priests and the teachers of the law were looking for some way to get rid of Jesus, for they were afraid of the people" (Luke 22:2). Then Luke makes the striking statement that "Satan entered Judas" and because of this, Judas "went to the chief priests and the officers of the temple guard and discussed with them how he might betray Jesus" (Luke 22:4). Somehow, Judas made it clear that with some sum of money, he would watch "for an opportunity to hand Jesus over to them when no crowd was present" (Luke 22:6). Through it all, Judas allowed himself to be used by the Devil and Jesus was fully aware of it. Although Jesus talked about his betrayal several time, he never mentioned Judas by name, yet he did identify him circuitously.

His Acts of Servanthood

After Judas left, Jesus demonstrated the marks of servanthood. Jesus arranged the dinner intentionally to demonstrate this intimate time of fellowship especially since it would be his last. It was known that sharing a meal and eating with someone symbolized fellowship and helped to develop and maintain a close relationship. While the disciples were eating their meal, Jesus took the bread and after giving thanks, he broke it and gave it to his disciples. Afterwards he took the cup of grape juice, gave thanks and told them to drink. He explained to his disciples that the bread was a symbolism of his body and the cup of juice was a symbolism of his blood of the covenant which would be poured out for the forgiveness of man's sins.

His disciples would have understood that females were known to being preparers and servers of the family food. At the same time, a host during this era would occasionally serve guests a lower quality meal to differentiate between ranks. Yet Jesus took on himself the role not only of servant but of female. He also shared the same food amongst his followers which illustrates that all his followers were equal. In addition, the Gospel writers states the verbs he used in the telling of what took place in the Upper Room. They state that Jesus *took, blessed, broke*, and *gave*. Yet these are not ordinary words but rather are symbolic, for the first two verbs, *took* and *blessed* are actions that a master would take but the later two actions, *broke* and *gave*, are that of a slave.

Not only did he demonstrated servanthood during the meal, he demonstrated servanthood after the meal by taking "off his outer clothing", wrapping "a towel around his waist", pouring "water into a basin", washing "wash his disciples' feet", and "drying them with the towel that was wrapped around him" (John 13:4-5). If these actions that he took during the meal were not lowly enough, Jesus certainly demonstrated the actions of a house slave by washing and drying eleven men's feet.

THE WORDS OF COMFORT

In order to encourage Simon Peter, Jesus told him that Satan has asked to sift him as wheat. But he had prayed for him that his faith would not fail. Yet what struck Peter was Jesus' next words which he said, "And when you have turned back, strengthen your brothers" (Luke 22:32). By this expression, Peter understood that Jesus was prophesying that he would somehow turn away and loose strength. But he was not trying to hear this because for over three years, he was one of the three who spent intimate time with Jesus and he was comfortable with being by his side. Thus, Peter told Jesus, "Lord, I am ready to go with you to prison and to death" (Luke 22:33). But Jesus told him, "I tell you, Peter, before the rooster crows today, you will deny three times that you know me" (Luke 22:34).

Seeing his disciple's troubled spirit, Jesus sought to give them words of comfort and hope. He began by telling them to put their trust in God and to hope in God's provisions in heaven. He stated, "In my Father's house are many rooms; if it were not so, I would have told you. I am going there to prepare a place for you. And if I go and prepare a place for you, I will come back and take you to be with me that you also may be where I am. You know the way to the place where I am going" (John 14:2-4). It was after Judas left the scene that Jesus intentionally told them about their place in heaven and the glories that would await them. Consequently, Judas would have no part in these future glories. Jesus told them that he was the only way to the Father in heaven and he would not leave them empty handed but would "ask the Father" and he would "give you another Counselor to be with you forever" (John 14:16). This person would be the Spirit of Truth and he would "teach you all things" and "remind you of everything I have said to you" (John 14:26).

The Mount of Olives

THE BACKGROUND

In Matthew 26:30-35, Mark 14:26-31, Luke 22:39, and John 18:1, Jesus and the eleven disciples left to go to the Mount of Olives, which is literally the mount that is called Olivet. Located just east of Jerusalem, this place was special to Jesus because he regularly lodged there. Luke 21:37 states that "each day Jesus was teaching at the temple and each evening he went out to spend the night on the hill called the Mount of Olives." The prophet Zechariah mentioned this name in the apocalyptic context of the great battle on the day of the Lord. He stated, "On that day his feet will stand on the Mount of Olives, east of Jerusalem, and the Mount of Olives will be split in two from east to west, forming a great valley, with half of the mountain moving north and half moving south (14:4). This mount is the same place where Jesus would soon ascend to heaven with the assurance that he would come back in the same manner (Acts 1:9, 12).

It was specifically noted that after singing a hymn and praying that Jesus and the disciples left the Upper Room to head to the Mount of Olives. The singing of the hymn and the prayer not only served the purpose of focusing on God as they departed but also to set the framework for what was about to take place, hence the betrayal, arrest, and trial of Jesus. Now they should have been in the proper mood and mind frame that Jesus envisioned them to have. Although it was not a long distance from where they eat the Passover meal, it must have seemed extremely long distance for the disciples.

THE PREDICTION TO HIS DISCIPLES

The first thing that Jesus does upon leaving the supper is to utter a threatening prediction of the fate of his disciples. He tells them along the way that all of them would soon fall away because of him. Their scandal would be focused on him and would take place that very night. He even stated that the former prophet Zechariah verified this same claim stating, "Strike the shepherd, and the sheep will be scattered" (13:7). It is interesting to note that earlier in the book of Zechariah, God sought for someone to become a shepherd and to care for the sheep because they were being slaughtered by those who purchased them (11:4-5). Consequently, a foolish shepherd came to lead the flock. Because of the disappointment, God stated that he was "going to raise up a shepherd over the land who will not care for the lost, or seek the young, or heal the injured, or feed the healthy, but will eat the meat of the choice sheep, tearing off their hoofs" (11:16).

After giving the disappointing prediction, he predicts that after he has risen, he will go ahead of them into Galilee. Although Satan had already previously entered into Judas and now desired to destroy all of his disciples, it was Jesus who would be the model shepherd. He would be the one who would not abandon the sheep but would "go ahead of them". He was even pictured in John 18 as the one who interceded for his disciples despite their failures.

Then Peter spoke up and boldly proclaimed, "Even if all fall away on account of you, I never will" (Matthew 26:33). Peter insisted that he was willing to die with Jesus and that he was the exception to Jesus' prophetic words. Yet Jesus tells him a second time that most certainly tonight, before the rooster crows, he would disown him three times. But Peter insisted emphatically, "Even if I have to die with you, I will never disown you" (Mark 14:30) and all the other disciples joined in saying the same words.

Despite Peter and the other disciple's words, Jesus insisted that although they would be ashamed because of him, the ultimate outcome would not be negative. He would rise again and meet up with them again into Galilee. However, only in the case of Judas was the ultimate outcome negative and damning. Mark 14:28 and 16:7 gives no hope that he would be among those whom Jesus would rebuild as his followers in Galilee after he rose from the grave.

THE PRAYER IN GETHSEMANE

The Background

In Matthew 26:36-46, Mark 14:32-42, and Luke 22:40-46, we have a narrative centering on the location of a particular place called Gethsemane. Gethsemane is located somewhere in Jerusalem and is east of the walled city. Concerning its location on the Mount of Olives, it is impossible to be sure exactly where on the Mount of Olives Gethsemane was located. Since the Fourth Century, a site at the bottom of the Mount (where olive trees grow more abundantly than on the upper slopes) has been venerated and, in particular, a rock formation or cave has been discovered that might have housed an oil press.[272] This is the most likely spot of Gethsemane and its name actually means oil-press. It is the name of an olive yard and that is why it is often referred to as a garden.

His Prayer and State of Anguish

Upon reaching Gethsemane, Jesus told his disciples to not only "sit here" while he prays but for them to pray as well so that they would "not fall into temptation." Then he took his three closest disciples (Peter, James, and John) along with him and he began to be deeply distressed and troubled. Then he said to them, "My soul is overwhelmed with sorrow to the point of death. Stay here and keep watch with me" (Matthew 26:38). The disciples saw Jesus in a state that they had never seen before. He was greatly disturbed and distraught to the point of anguish for the simple fact that he was about to face his impending fate that had been planned by his adversaries for years. Jesus knew what they had been trying to do but in the next few moments, he would literally face this great trial. We see him facing a close and similar situation that David felt in Psalm 55:4-5. He stated, "My heart is in anguish within me; the terrors of death assail me. Fear and trembling have beset me; horror has overwhelmed me." This psalm lets us know that Jesus was not the only one to feel the anguish and terrors of death that awaited him.

Then Jesus want a little farther about a stone's throw beyond the three disciples and he knelt down and prayed to his Father. He asked him if he was willing and if it was possible that "this cup" be taken from him, yet not his own will but his will be done. Regardless of how far he was from the three disciples, at least one of them heard his distressing yet submissive prayer. Although his prayer was directed to God his Father, his disciples and future followers would be able to see his prayer as a model even in the most distressful times of life.

Why did Jesus asked his Father to take away the "cup" of suffering when he himself indicated that he would have to be rejected and crucified by God's divine plan on at least three different occasions (Mark 8:31; 9:31; 10:33-34)? The answer is this! What Jesus feared was that the suffering in Gethsemane might be too much for him and that he might die before he reached the cross.[273] Although he was 100% God, he was also 100% human. Not only did he show emotions of crying and anguish, he also knew that he would have to endure a gruesome beating and crucifixion. Even more distressing, many of the crucified victims did not make it all the way to the cross, for the beating and punishment they faced before the cross was often times lethal. Although no human in their right mind would have wanted to go through the crucifixion process, Jesus wanted to make sure that he carried out God's plan to the end.

At the same time, he knew that Moses interceded to change the Lord's determination concerning the Israelites after their idol worship of the golden calf (Exodus 32:10-14) and Hezekiah's prayer to change God's will about his death (II Kings 20:1-6). Certainly his request was reasonable, justifiable, and historical. Yet, hundreds of prophecies had already been stated by prophets of old declaring his fate. Thus, it would seem that Jesus would have no choice but to carry out God's plan.

Despite what actions God his Father would take, Jesus ended his prayer with his Father's will taking priority over his own. When he asked God to take the cup away from him, he was placing his concern over his own. Thus, he placed himself at the mercy of his Father despite his anguish and distress.

His Comfort from an Angel

After Jesus asked his Father to take the cup away from him, his Father answered. Luke 22:43 states, "An angel from heaven appeared to him and strengthened him." Jesus was pleased to allow his human nature to be so prostrate, so abandoned to its own weakness, as to need a creature's sympathy and a creature's aid.[274] God kept silent in response to his Son's request but he sent him an angel to indirectly let him know that the "cup" would not be taken away and that he would have to "drink it". Knowing that he would be a hero for generations to come, the angel served as a means of comfort, hope, and support for the spiritual and physical battle that approached him.

In light of the angel coming so quickly, it must be remembered that during another low point of his life when he was in the desert after fasting for 40 days, Satan came to him in order to tempt him. Now we see another low point of his life when he is in anguish, distress, and troubled, and God knew that this would be a prime opportunity for Satan and his forces to attack. So God providentially sent an angel before the enemy could come.

After the angel came to comfort him, Luke 22:44 tells of him "being in anguish" and praying "more earnestly" so that "his sweat was like drops of blood falling to the ground." His anguish was the same as agony which means "extreme pain". It is the kind of agony that a runner in an athletic contest experiences just before the start. An athletic parallel offers an explanation of the profuse sweat that follows: the runner is tensed up to begin the trial and sweat breaks out all over his body. In such an interpretation, the great trial, which Jesus now knowingly will enter, resembles an athletic contest.[275] It is understood that he quickly knew why the angel came to his aid and most importantly that he would have to endure the trial that lied ahead. Understanding the answer given back to him from his Father constituted his emotions of anguish.

In light of physical anguish and distress that Jesus went through, his future followers are told in Hebrews 4:14-16 to gain self-assurance in their time of need because they have a high priest (Jesus) who is able to sympathize with their weaknesses. He is "one who has been tempted in every way, just as we are - yet was without sin." Because of this, all of his future followers are able to "approach the throne of grace with confidence" so they can "receive mercy and find grace to help" in time of need.

His Reproof to his Disciples

After arising from his prayer, Jesus went back to his disciples and he found them sleeping and not praying, for they were "exhausted from sorrow." Specifically looking at Simon Peter, he asked, "Could you not keep watch for one hour? Watch and pray so that you will not fall into temptation. The spirit is willing, but the body is weak" (Mark 14:37-38). Jesus prophetically knew that he would not be ready when the trial came, for he would be the first to draw his sword in hopes of killing a Roman guard. Yet, it was this same Simon Peter who told him that he would be an exception to his prophecy concerning them all being scandalized. Therefore, it was intentional for Jesus to look directly at him and to ask him why he could not even pray one hour.

Fortunately, Jesus knew the weakness of the flesh and the power of the Devil. He knew that human weakness is the devil's weapon to defeat man. In addition, Jesus knew that his enemies were right around the corner and more importantly what it would take for not only himself but for his disciples to stand their ground against their adversaries. Jesus had done exactly what he warned in that parable the master would do (Mark 13:36), for he came suddenly and found his disciples sleeping. Matthew does not have the parable in the book of Mark but his readers too could catch the eschatological meaning of this Gethsemane dialogue by recalling the words, "Keep on watching for you do not know on what day your Lord is coming (Mark 24:42)"[276] We will even find out that the disciples were not strong at all but spiritually weak from this time forward, that is until Jesus' resurrection.

His Continued Prayer and Words to His Disciples

Jesus went away a second time and he prayer the same thing stating, "My Father, if it is not possible for this cup to be taken away unless I drink it, may your will be done." There are two famous Gardens in the Bible. Eden, where the first Adam failed, and Gethsemane, where the Last Adam wrestled in prayer and attained the victory and poise that carried him through the remaining hours of his earthly course. Here, where the olives were pressed, the Son of God endured his great soul travail.[277]

When he came back to them, he found them sleeping because they were tired and weary. After going back a third time, he came a third time and said to them, "Are you still sleeping and resting? Enough! The hour has come. Look, the Son of Man is betrayed into the hands of sinners. Rise! Let us go! Here comes my betrayer!" (Mark 14:41-42). At the last moment he has aligned his disciples with him to face Judas and the forces of evil, but Jesus does this with the sad experience of their threefold sleeping and the realization that they cannot come with him into this trial.[278] His disciples would have the unfortunate feeling of hearing these last words of their master before he was executed and their last moments together were humiliating and embarrassing. It was embarrassing for him to have come to them three times to tell them to pray just one hour. At the same time, it was embarrassing for the disciples to have their master come to them and to expose the weakness of their flesh.

THE ARREST

The Betrayer, the Soldiers, and the Kiss

It was ironic for Jesus to see his betrayer coming to him just as he was exposing his disciple's weaknesses and lack of spirituality. Yet he knew that the money had already been paid to Judas and the bargain was already completed. Thus, his betrayal had to continue as planned. While Jesus was saying to his disciples, "Rise, let us go, here comes my betrayer", Judas was leading a crowd of soldiers and officials from the chief priests and Pharisees to him. The soldiers were carrying torches and lanterns and they were armed with swords and clubs. They came for him alone because only he was a threat to the Sanhedrin. Yet, it seemed strange that there should be such a large number of men, armed and ready, sent out to apprehend a man who was not known for his belligerence and was only surrounded by a small band of disciples.[279] Yet, both Roman and Jewish troops came in such a fashion and their intended purpose was to take him away.

Before this encounter, the chief priests and scribes were seeking to seize and kill Jesus without a crowd of people present, for they wanted to avoid a riot. Judas knew where Jesus would be without a crowd because he had often met in this garden with his disciples. In the Upper Room, none of the other disciples knew what Jesus and Judas were talking about especially when he told him to do what he was going to do quickly. But now they understood Judas' intentions all along. They were now made aware that Jesus was fully conscious of his own betrayal and all the details that accompanied it. In addition, when Jesus told them that one of them was a Devil early on in his ministry (John 6:70-71), they now understood that he knew years before that he was talking about Judas.

Now Judas had arranged a signal with the soldiers that whomever he kissed, they should arrest him. After identifying him, he came to Jesus saying, "Greetings, Rabbi" and he kissed him. A kiss was an actual greeting as seen in 2 Samuel 20:9 and was a sign of forgiveness as seen in Genesis 33:4. Even the early church Christians developed a sacred kiss. Therefore this kiss was not strange at all but fit in line with the cultural salutation.

But Jesus asked him, "Judas, are you betraying the Son of Man with a kiss?" Jesus knew exactly what he was doing but he asked this

325

question as if Judas thought that he did not know what was going on. From Judas' standpoint, he agreed to a sum of money to hand him over to the authorities and his primary actions were not that of betrayal. He just wanted to complete the transaction and not let Jesus get away. But Jesus made it clear that it was certainly a betrayal and nothing less. Although Judas did not betray secrets but only made it possible to arrest Jesus, he was taking advantage of the Son of God and his intimate relations with him, and thus, he betrayed him.

But this question that Jesus asks Judas goes beyond him knowing his heart and actions. Although Satan had already entered into him, Jesus understood the human capability to make decisions and to be given at least one last chance to repent. Jesus was not only trying to reach out to him as a sinner but to allow him to really think about what he was doing. Judas was being given an opportunity to evaluate his horrific actions and to return to the Savior. Although his fate would soon be revealed (Acts 1:15-19), everyone would know that Jesus tried one final time to reach out to him and persuade him to repent. Unfortunately, Judas does nor says nothing, and now he will not be able to turn back what takes place from now on.

The Miraculous Drawback

After the kiss, Jesus went out to challenge the arresting party and he asked them who they wanted. They said, "Jesus of Nazareth." Jesus replied saying, "I am he." After he said this, the crowd of soldiers and officials all drew back and fell as if they were paralyzed. Despite the mob's apparent power, Jesus' words forced them all to the ground. After they got back up, Jesus again asked, "Who is it you want?" They replied again, "Jesus of Nazareth." Then Jesus told them, "I am he" and that if they were looking for him, then they were to let these men go.

Although it was obvious that these men had never seen Jesus, for Judas had to identify him, it was even more obvious that they had never heard of him and his miraculous power. Interestingly, Jesus would soon say to Pilate during his trial that he has "no power" over him except what has been given by God. Ironically, Jesus proved much more powerful than every since man present in the mob.

The Seize and the Careless Attack

Now after he has spoken, the arrest proceeded and the mob seized Jesus and arrested him. Although no hand had been laid on him during his public teaching in the temple, things were now different. When his disciples saw the drama that was going to happen, they asked him if they should strike with their swords. Jews could put on weapons for self-defense[280] and in some areas, carrying a sword was necessary and almost the equivalent as being clothed. There was also evidence that the Essenes carried weapons when traveling because of highway robbers.[281]

But before Jesus could even answer the disciple's request, Simon Peter drew his sword and cut off the right ear of a man named Malchus. Since Jesus had never been touched before in this way, Peter was trying to defend him. His attack showed defiance from that fact that he was determined to be faithful to his promise that he made to Jesus concerning him laying down his life for him. Unfortunately, he had not yet grasped the truth that the weapons of his warfare were not carnal but spiritual in nature. Although Jesus told them all to pray, it was not for him but for themselves. Thus, Peter in particular miscalculates the test that faced him and the consequence of his failure was exposed in his careless use of his sword.

To Peter's careless actions, Jesus states, "Put your sword back in its place, for all who draw the sword will die by the sword. Do you think I cannot call on my Father, and he will at once put at my disposal more than twelve legions of angels? But how then would the Scriptures be fulfilled that say it must happen in this way? (Matthew 26:52-54). In addition, he told him, "Shall I not drink the cup the Father has given me?" (John 18:11). Here we see three major components of his message to Peter and the disciples. First, without Jesus' displeasure, the rest of the disciples might think they too could use the sword to solve problems. So he quickly told Peter of his displeasure in him using his sword in the first place. Second, he lets his disciples know of his power in calling down legions of angels. Since one legion was equivalent to six thousand, Jesus was letting all of his disciples know just how much power he had. And third, he was telling them how essential it was for him to go to Jerusalem and die from these very men. His disciples had to understand that it was fulfilled that these events would occur this way and therefore it must not be stopped.

Then Jesus touched the man's ear and healed him. Unless the servant had been healed, this act of violent resistance would have been brought up against Jesus before Pilate. Because Jesus healed him, the servant eventually became a Christian, and that is how his name "Malchus" was known and preserved.[282]

The Rebuke to the Crowd

After Jesus chastised one of his disciples, he turns to chastise the crowds. He asks them, "Am I leading a rebellion that you have come out with swords and clubs to capture me? Every day I sat in the temple courts teaching, and you did not arrest me. But this has all taken place that the writings of the prophets might be fulfilled" (Matthew 26:55-56). Although one of his disciples acted out of ignorance and rashness, Jesus maintained control during his arrest. He had already shown the arresting party that he had the power to throw them back to the ground and now that he has grabbed their attention, he states a second time that all of what took place was simply a result of prophecy. Even though the mob could have come much earlier during his ministry, it was ordained for them to come at this particular time and place. His rebuke of Peter and then the crowd shows that everything comes under God's already designate plan.

How depressing it was for Judas to hear Jesus say, "But how then would the Scriptures be fulfilled that say it must happen in this way" and then to hear him say, "But this has all taken place that the writings of the prophets might be fulfilled." At first, he simply thought that he was just handing him over to the authorities for money. But now, life came at him faster than he expected and he soon realized that the actions he took were more serious than expected. How must he had felt knowing that Satan used him as a fulfillment of prophecy to hand Jesus over?

The Flight of his Followers

After hearing Jesus say on two occasions that prophecy must be fulfilled this way, the disciples "deserted him and fled". Ironically, just hours before this occasion, Peter stated that he would not deny Jesus and all the rest of the disciples said the same. Yet after the arrest, they all fled like chickens.

But Mark states that a "young man, wearing nothing but a linen garment, was following Jesus" even after all the disciples fled. It seems that the author is offering a glimmer of hope to his readers even though the most faithful followers of Jesus fled under pressure. The identity of this individual seems to be someone who was attracted to the scene from the lights of the torches and lanterns and from the commotion that accompanied Peter *trying* to cut someone's head off. This individual probably recognized Jesus and desired to follow him out of curiosity or out of sympathetic interests. Since his name was unknown, he probably was of no importance. Yet his apparel was of importance for he was described as one wearing a "linen garment" or more specifically a linen cloth. This material was fine and costly and was a light and loose garment worn at night over a naked body.

But when the soldiers found him and "seized him", he "fled naked" and left "his garment behind". Although he made an attempt to follow Jesus, the instant in which an official grabbed hold of him, he immediately became afraid. Nakedness was not something good and was something to be avoided. Mark's readers would have understood that if he left his expensive linen cloth behind, he had even more force in depicting the young man's desperate flight.[283]

The escape of this young man is comparable to the flight of the disciples. Both fled out of fear of their lives and none of them were willing to forsake all in order to follow Jesus (Luke 14:26). However, this last disciple has literally "left all" in not only following him but in fleeing from him. He left with a more desperate flight than the other eleven disciples. His attempt to follow Jesus showed that he wanted to be a "true disciple", but his attempt failed miserably, for he became afraid under pressure. Sadly, he would forever be known as a "would-be-disciple."

The Effects of Satan

In conclusion, we see the effects of the power of darkness and Satan. First, we see its effects on Judas. Satan entered into him, he put into his heart to betray Jesus, and he took him away from Jesus (Luke 22:3-4). After the betrayal, we see that he has found his proper position, for he is seen neither with the disciples nor with the Jews.

Now he is alone and unable to bear himself, he would eventually take his own life. The devolution of his soul would eventually become complete.[284] Looking back over his life, John the disciple refers to him as "the son of perdition" or the son of utter destruction (17:12) and this is the same phrase used in to describe the future antichrist who exalts himself to God's status (2 Thessalonians 2:3-4).

Second, we see the effects of Satan on Jesus. After trying to tempt him at the onset of his ministry, he left him until "an opportune time". Now when Jesus was in the garden, Satan sought his opportunity during Jesus' most vulnerable point in ministry. It was now Satan's "hour" that "has come" in order for Jesus to be "betrayed into the hands of sinners (Mark 14:41). With the mob arresting Jesus, Jesus was companied with sinners and was to be counted as one. Satan ultimately led him out with the stigma upon him as being one worthy of death.

Third, we see the effects of Satan on Jesus' disciples. He has now resumed his frontal attack and it was not just against Jesus and Judas but against his followers. Jesus told his followers earlier about the cost that comes with following him (Mark 8). Yet his eleven were found sleeping on more than one occasion when they should have been praying in Gethsemane. Instead of gaining strength, they were opening themselves up to the frontal attacks of the enemy. On one specific encounter, Jesus told Peter in the presence of all the disciples that Satan sought to sift him like wheat. Yet he and all the disciples fled away from him after he was arrested. Graciously after his resurrection, they all were given a second chance.

The Jewish Trial

THE BACKGROUND

There have been many famous trials in world history. Some of the famous individuals involved included: Adolf Eichmann, Adolf Hitler, Alfred Dreyfus, Charles I, Galileo, Gandhi, Jesus of Nazareth, Joan of Arc, Martin Luther, Mary Queen of Scotts, Nelson Mandela, Sir Thomas More, and Socrates. In addition to world's trial, there have been some famous American trials including individuals such as: Bill

Clinton, Charles Manson, Falwell vs. Flynt, John Hinckley, Moussaoui, O. J. Simpson, The McMartins, and Timothy McVeigh. After looking at these famous trail, there is only one trial that has affected our world today more than any trial in history and that trial is none other than the trial of Jesus of Nazareth.

Before looking at the Jewish trial of Jesus that took place about 2,000 years ago, it is beneficial to look at today's criminal justice system because there are numerous comparisons between the two legal systems. Although the United States judicial and legal system is well known to many, some don't take the time to look at the particulars of it. For example, individuals have several rights that they are afforded. The have the right to be free from unreasonable searches, to not talk or to provide a link in a chain that might lead to their prosecution, to have a fair and public trial, to confront their accusers and know what the nature and cause of the accusation that is against them, to bring witnesses and to present a defense, and to have a lawyer as an effective assistance of counsel. We have rules that state that a government official can not use ones confession unless the crime has already been proven first. In addition, we have rules on corroboration that state that lawyers can't just present one witness against you but have to verify it and back it up with two or three. These rights are afforded to everyone regardless of wealth, status, and wealth.

Now going back 2,000 years to the legal system during Jesus' day, the laws were not as detailed or impressive but were about the same. They had laws that were memorized, of which they relied on oral tradition, and they had written laws that came from the Torah. Their memorized laws were not codified until 175 years later after Jesus died and was arranged in the Mishnah. In looking at the laws that were stated in the Mishnah, we are not only able to see and understand the legal system during Jesus' day but we see that the Jews had a great system of law. Although they called their laws by different names, they were similar to the laws that we have today. For example, one of their laws stated that they could not condemn a person unless two people explicitly acquiesce on the misdemeanor from beginning to end. This is strikingly comparable to our corroboration law today. They had another law that stated that unless a crime was proven, you could not make the accused confessed. Concerning their written laws, we see an example in the Torah that there was a tendency to adjourn verdicts against the violators until the answer corresponded to God's will (Numbers 9:8; 15:34). Therefore, if one can comprehend the criminal justice and legal system today, one can understand the legal system during Jesus' day.

PETER'S FIRST DENIAL

After Jesus' arrest and his disciples fleeing in fear, Simon Peter and another disciple followed him out of love, but at a distance because of fear. Perhaps Peter saw the guard seize the young disciple wearing the linen cloth and perhaps that cause him to secretly follow Jesus to his first interrogation. He even had more of a reason to fear the soldiers because it was he who tried to cut one of their heads off, but only managed to cut off his ear.

Upon arriving at the high priest's house, John 18:15-16 states that "because this disciple was known to the high priest, he went with Jesus into the high priest's courtyard, but Peter had to wait outside at the door. The other disciple, who was known to the high priest, came back, spoke to the girl on duty there and brought Peter in." Their location was in the house of Annas and Caiaphas, for both their houses looked over a common courtyard. Because Peter remembered his promise of never forsaking his Lord, it was very exciting for him to have been privileged enough to enter into this hall. Jesus was above the courtyard about to be interrogated while Peter was below.

After the guards "kindled a fire in the middle of the courtyard and had sat down together, Peter sat down with them" (Luke 22:55). Nights in March and early April in Jerusalem could be very chilly[285] and the custom of soldiers to keep fires burning through the night was noted from history.[286] It has already been mentioned that "police" attendants, specifically soldiers and officials carrying torches, lanterns, and weapons, were apart of the arresting party and now they appear to be surrounded by Peter. Thus, it is not surprising that when Peter stands around the fire, there are attendants present warming themselves. There are also attendants guarding Jesus as he stands before Annas.[287] In putting together a vivid picture of where Jesus is interrogated and where Peter stands, the Gospels give the impression of a palace with a gateway, courtyard, and large room. This is a compound where servants and police attendants are within reach.

After having entering the courtyard, Peter was immediately asked by a servant girl at the door who, after looking closely at him, asked him if he was one of Jesus' disciples and if he was with him. Peter quickly denied and said, "I don't know or understand what you're talking about" and "Woman, I don't know him" (Luke 22:57). Then he went out into the entryway. Although this woman's status was of no importance to the aristocracy of the day, Peter did not have enough courage to stand up for Jesus. Unfortunately, he did not witness Jesus' example of how to carry himself when it should come his turn to suffer. Unfortunately, it was a much worse affair that he joined himself with those who were Jesus' enemies.[288]

BEFORE ANNAS

The Background

John 18:12-13 makes it clear that they bound Jesus and first brought him to Annas, the father-in-law of Caiaphas, who was still given the title of high priest. In 6 AD, Quirinius, legate in Syria, appointed him high priest but in 15 AD, Valerius Gratus, prefect in Judea, deposed him. Yet despite his deposition, he remained such a powerful force that in the fifty years after his deposition, five of his sons became high priests.[289] Yet the house of Annas made a much noticeable impact after his encounter with Jesus. As far as Christians are concerned, was it accidental that Jesus, Stephen (the first martyr), and James the brother of the Lord were all put to death during the tenure of priests of the house of Annas? Indeed, since Matthias, son of Annas, was high priest in 42/43 under Herod Agrippa I,[290] possibly James the brother of John (the first of the Twelve to be martyred) also perished under the house of Annas (Acts 12:1-3). That would mean that every famous Christian who died violently in Judea before the Jewish Revolt suffered in the tenure of a priest related to Annas.[291]

Jesus is led away from the place of arrest to the court or courtyard of the high priest. He was bound when he was taken to Annas alone for his "trial" and we see that he was still bound afterwards when he was taken to Caiaphas. Although we state that this was a "trial" of Jesus, it would be more appropriate to say that it was an "interrogation", "hearing", or "legal proceeding" of Jesus.

Of course, this is a late night session when the regular meeting hall should have been closed, for Jesus was arrested at night and was about to be interrogated by Annas alone and Caiaphas late that same night. But it was no accident that he was tried during this time. Although there is little or no solid evidence that mishnaic rules governed Sanhedrin proceedings in this period,[292] the Mishna, the written form of Jewish oral traditions, states that capital cases must be tried in the daytime.[293] Mark 14:1-2 reports that the Jewish authorities wanted Jesus arrested and put to death by stealth and with as little public attention as possible. Nighttime proceedings fit that desire very well.

The Interrogation and Response

During Peter's first denial, Annas "questioned Jesus about his disciples and his teaching" (John 18:19). Concerning his disciples, we see right after Jesus raised Lazarus from the dead that some of the Jews went to the Pharisees and told them what Jesus had done. "Then the chief priests and the Pharisees called a meeting of the Sanhedrin" saying, "Here is this man performing many miraculous signs. If we let him go on like this, everyone will believe in him, and then the Romans will come and take away both our place and our nation" (John 11:47-48). The religious Jews believed that if Jesus continued to do what he was doing, those who believed in him would become so numerous as to constitute a threat. Concerning his teaching, they were trying to prove him a teacher of false doctrine.

To his questions, Jesus responds by saying, "I have spoken openly to the world. I always taught in synagogues or at the temple, where all the Jews come together. I said nothing in secret" (John 18:20). He first let it be recognized that his motives were pure and he was not leading a revolt or teaching secret doctrines. During his ministry, he even asked the question, "Can any of you prove me guilty of sin" (John 8:46). At the same time, Annas certainly did not need to be informed where the Jews worship and he knew what Jesus was saying was true.

After stating the pure and innocent motives that he had, he then exposed the character of the High Priest saying, "Why question me? Ask those who heard me. Surely they know what I said." When he asked, "Why question me", he was objecting to what was currently happening, specifically the injustice of having no witnesses. This objection was similar to the protestation he gave to the mob who came at him with swords and clubs as if he was some rebel armed bandit. When he said to "ask those who heard me" "surely they know what I said," he was demanding that there be witnesses before he is condemned. From his standpoint, witnesses would be able to testify that he spoke openly and not secretly. Thus, if there was no one to defend him, he should not be questioned at this "trial".

The Physical Abuse

While Annas was unjustly questioning him, one of the nearby officials physically abused him by striking him in the face. After striking him, the official said, "Is this the way you answer the high priest? As Jesus was still bound, we see one of the officials taking advantage of the opportunity although Jesus neither said nor acted wrongly. However, these actions were meant to take place because Isaiah prophetically wrote that he gave his cheeks to them that plucked off the hair. In addition, Isaiah stated that he did not hide his face from shame and spitting (50:6). All this Jesus underwent for a strategic purpose and he knew what awaited him during this trail.

Then Jesus spoke up immediately and asked him, "If I said something wrong, testify as to what is wrong. But if I spoke the truth, why did you strike me" (John 18:23). Jesus was neither cursing the high priest nor talking bad about him. He was just exposing the facts of there being no witnesses. From his standpoint, the slap in his face was a decisive rejection of truth and he lets the official know again of his innocence and clean hands.

PETER'S SECOND DENIAL

To set the scene for his second denial, Peter now takes himself away from the courtyard and goes out to the gateway. He wants to avoid any further altercation and does not want to be known as one who was a follower of Jesus. Yet he is still not wanting to give up his oath of not being like the other disciples who would run away from him. There were no records historically that mentioned the guards ever attempting to arrest Jesus' disciples and the Gospel writers specifically mentioned that they were only after Jesus. But after seeing his first denial, Peter is not only afraid but ashamed to be recognized with Jesus.

Then a little later as he was warming himself by the fire, another servant girl saw him and told the people standing around, "This fellow was with Jesus of Nazareth" and that he was "one of them." This girl was also seen asking Peter, "You also are one of them."

To this accusation, Peter denied his affiliations with Jesus again and he even accompanied his denial with an oath saying, "I don't know the man!" His stance had become more reprehensible, for he was no longer claiming that he did not understand what the woman was talking about. Out of Jesus' twelve disciples, he quickly forgot that he was chosen first and that Jesus assigned him the name Peter (Mark 3:14-16). Unfortunately, he was now denying all of that and he backed up his claim with an oath.

PETER'S THIRD DENIAL

The setting of the third denial does not change, yet only the time has changed. Both Matthew and Mark states, "After a little while" while Luke gives a more specific time lapse stating, "About an hour latter". This was certainly enough time for Peter to have felt that he had gotten away from the servant girls and soldiers who believed that he was with Jesus.

Then we get the description of several individuals challenging Peter including a high priest's servant who was a relative of the man whose ear Peter had cut off. Matthew's gospel specifically states that those standing there actually "went up to Peter" as if they were going to confront him. As if each individual had their own questions to ask him, we see them stating several questions including, "Surely you are one of them, for your accent gives you away", "Surely you are one of them, for you are a Galilean", "Certainly this fellow was with him, for he is a Galilean", and "Didn't I see you with him in the olive grove?" Although Peter had previously told a servant girl that he did not understand what the woman was talking about, now we see that he was easily detected as being a Galilean, the same region where Jesus ministered.

To these accusations, Peter replied saying, "Man, I don't know what you're talking about" and "he began to call down curses on himself and he swore to them" that he did not know the man. He was now more serious in his responses and was boldly denying the truth. His disclaimer had reached a stage of passion that he agreed to take an oath that he did not know Jesus, yet he forgot that taking oaths under any circumstance was condemned by Jesus himself (Matthew 5:34).

Then immediately the rooster crowed and Luke states that "the Lord turned and looked straight at Peter." It was this encounter that he "remembered the word the Lord had spoken to him" saying "before the rooster crows today, you will disown me three times." With Jesus looking at Peter, we have to assume that he was present through all of these denials. In observing the setting of this scene, according to Mark 14:66, Jesus has been upstairs in the high priest's house while Peer was below. And so to harmonize Mark with Luke, we must imagine that Jesus turned and looked out of the window of the upper room and he caught Peter's eye in the courtyard.[294]

There was now no possibility of fulfilling his promise, "Lord, I am read to go with you both to prison and to death" (Luke 22:33) or "even if it be necessary for me to die with you, I will not deny you" (Matthew 26:35). Now that reality hit him and he realized that it was Jesus' words that came true and not his own, he understood that he had gravely failed his Lord. He then broke down and went outside where he wept bitterly. The word here used to describe his weeping is the same word that depicts someone wailing over the deceased. Jesus told his disciples to keep on praying lest they enter into trial, for he knew that they were not strong. Yet his remorse showed a glimpse of repentance which would give the entire narrative a positive thrust.

BEFORE CAIAPHAS AND THE SANHEDRIN

The Background of Caiaphas

After Jesus was interrogated by Annas, he was sent bounded to Caiaphas his son-in-law (John 18:24) and the houses of Annas and Caiaphas were not far apart. John lets his readers know that this was the same man who "advised the Jews that it would be good if one man died for the people" (John 18:14). After Jesus exposed the injustices of Annas' interrogation by stating, "Why question me, ask those who heard me, surely they know what I said", this examination consisted of witnesses. This trial or interrogation took place sometime before 5 a.m. Friday morning while it was still dark.

Caiaphas was considered high priest that year (John 11:49). Josephus tells us that after the prefect Valerius Gratus removed Annas from office in rapid succession, no more than a year apart, he appointed four different high priests, the last of whom was Joseph surnamed Caiaphas.[295] Out of the nineteen high priests in Jerusalem in the First Century, Caiaphas ruled by far the longest and was rivaled only by the nine year tenure of Annas.

His existence as mentioned from the Bible proved to be factual when archaeology discovered his remains about 18 mile outside of Jerusalem. In November 1990 near Abu Tor, there was an inscription on an ossuary were the words "Yehosef bar Kayafa," translated as "Joseph, son of Caiaphas". Not only was his ossuary found but also his family members as well. His status and title proved to be accurate when his burial gave validity to a Jewish former high priest.

Caiaphas' was a shrewd strategist who did not care about right or wrong. He was always ready to do whatever pleased the Jewish leaders while not wanting to upset the Roman leaders. While in office, Josephus the historian provides no information, but it is obvious that he was good at what he did in order for him to stay in office for as long as he did.

The Background of the Sanhedrin

In addition to Caiaphas being there, the Gospel writers state that the teachers of the law and the elders were present as well. Many if not all of these "teachers" and "elders" were apart of a greater group called the Sanhedrin. All four Gospels cite the Sanhedrin by name as having a contributory role in the death of Jesus. The root meaning of the Greek word *synedrion* (Sanhedrin) involves the idea of sitting together and this term can cover the place of doing this, the assembly of those involved, and even their functioning as council, court, or governing body. During the First Century, the Sanhedrin exerted authority under the watchful eye of the Romans. Generally, the Roman governor allowed them to have considerable autonomy and authority, yet during Jesus' trial, however, they did not have the authority to condemn people to death (John 18:31).[296]

"Judaism" Sanhedrin was a technical designation for a specific Jewish assembly and judicial body. It was the name for the Jewish high courts of ancient Judea. It has been customary to think of the Sanhedrin as a court acting like a judge and jury. By the time of the Mishna the Sanhedrin had become a body of experts in the law. In literature written before A.D. 100, when the Sanhedrin does sentence to death, there is little evidence of court-like procedures to protect the defendant.[297]

The highest court was known as the Great Sanhedrin and it consisted of seventy one scholars who were experts in the written Law of Moses and in the oral law that was developed through rabbinic debates. This number came about in Numbers 11:16 when Moses was joined by the seventy elders of Israel and it was reorganized by Ezra after the exile.

The functions of this assembly were more legal or judicial than political but there were legislative and executive elements as well. Although secular matters were treated, the overall tone was strongly religious.[298] Their most important mission was to interpret biblical laws, as the Supreme Court's mandate is to interpret the Constitution. Unlike the Supreme Court, however, they were also empowered to enact new laws when necessary.[299] The Jerusalem Sanhedrin was managed and organized by the chief priests, wealthy nobles or elders, Pharisees, and scribes. Overall, the Pharisees were very influential and they had gained much favor with the Romans. They were so influential that even after the Jerusalem temple was destroyed in 70 A.D., they were the only religious group that survived.

The False Testimony

Although the Sanhedrin had convened before, they were gathered during this occasion to carry out their long awaited plan – that is to look "for false evidence against Jesus so that they could put him to death" (Matthew 26:59). Yet, what they were seeking to do would totally violate the already established written law against false testimony (Exodus 20:16). Because Jesus had consistently handled himself above reproach during his three years of ministry, these leaders had no choice but to find false methods of putting him to death and that is why they were seeking testifiers probably during the middle of the night who would speak against him! However to their dismay, "they did not find any, though many false witnesses came forward". When many testified falsely against him, their statements did not agree, therefore their statements could not stand in their court of law.

Then two individuals stood up to give false testimony against Jesus saying, "We heard him say, 'I will destroy this man-made temple and in three days will build another, not made by man'" (Mark 14:58). The main institution of both public and religious life in Judea was the temple and any verbal threats or actions against it went beyond just theological concerns, for it would reach socioeconomic and political realms as well. Helpfully, the Gospel writer explains that although the Jews thought he was speaking of the Jerusalem Temple, he was actually speaking of the sanctuary of his body (John 2:21). So these false witnesses remembered Jesus' direct actions of clearing out the Jerusalem Temple (Mark 11:15-17) and the authority that he used to accompany these actions. They said that he claimed that there was something greater than the temple and they tried to make a case against him concerning this Jewish center of religious activity. However, a second blow came upon Caiaphas' interrogation, for even the two men's testimony did not agree. Thus, the whole case against Jesus was false and his opponents made a conscious use of prevarication we would never know.

Amazingly, the witnesses did not know that they were unconsciously fulfilling prophecy. The Old Testament gave many prophecies concerning Jesus including Psalm 27:12 which states that "false witnesses rise up against me, breathing out violence" and Psalm 35:11 which states that "ruthless witnesses come forward; they question me on things I know nothing about." Yet little did these witnesses know that their future would be prophesied, for Isaiah stated, "Once more the humble will rejoice in the LORD... The ruthless will vanish, the mockers will disappear, and all who have an eye for evil will be cut down those who with a word make a man out to be guilty, who ensnare the defender in court and with false testimony deprive the innocent of justice" (29:19-21).

The Interrogation of Caiaphas

Then Caiaphas the high priest stood up. Previously, the witnesses stood up and came forward but unfortunately they were unsuccessful. Now the high priest stands up and comes forward and he is determined to be more successful. His standing marks a definitive turn to the interrogation and the notion has now been given that the trial is now about to move in another direction. Interestingly at this interrogation, there were no judges, Jesus had no counsel, and there were no witnesses on his behalf.

So he asked Jesus, "Are you not going to answer? What is this testimony that these men are bringing against you?" But to his dismay, Jesus "remained silent and gave no answer." But did Jesus have to say anything since the witnesses against him could not agree? He refused to confirm anything or say any incriminating evidence against himself during this particular section of the trial. It was obvious that injustice was taking place and thus, he wisely handled himself above everyone else. His submission to the inconsistent statements that were brought against him was a matter of his choice. In order to make sure that prophecy would be fulfilled, he opted not to speak even though he was innocent, for Isaiah stated, "He was oppressed and afflicted, yet he did not open his mouth; he was led like a lamb to the slaughter, and as a sheep before her shearers is silent, so he did not open his mouth" (53:7). Even though the legitimacy of the temple authorities was a burning issue during this time, Jesus wisely chose to remain quiet. He knew that he had to die and since his Father did not take away his "cup", he chose to go down the road of death.

After seeing that all the Sanhedrin's years of planning for his death had just been crushed, Caiaphas decided to take matters into his own hands. Since he could not move his interrogation further with the sham testimony, he tries another scheme to see if he can get Jesus to open his mouth. He spoke up and said, "I charge you under oath by the living God. Tell us if you are the Christ, the Son of God." He basically wanted to know if Jesus was an imposture or really the Messiah who was the God's Son. This was a serious proposal that he asked and not just a mere question. He intentionally put him under oath and history records the fact that if one was put under oath by the divine name or a recognized divine attribute, one was bound.[300]

The English word "Messiah" is from the Greek translation *Christos* or "Christ" and the Greek terms means "anointed." The Messiah designation of Jesus comes indirectly through John the Baptist in Matthew 11:2-6 and on a different occasion, the Son of God designation comes directly from a divine voice in Matthew 3:17. But here, we see the specific demand that Jesus was to tell if he was the Messiah or Christ who was the Son of God, which narrows the focus.

During his ministry, Jesus himself responded to the Messiah question ambivalently, neither confirming nor refuting, somewhat because he had his own model of ministry and because he left the final expression to the responsibility of his Father. During his era, there were various types of Messiahs anticipated by Jews of Jesus' time. Their overall expectation consisted of this person being a special manifestation of the power of Yahweh who would deliver their people. In his writings, Josephus depicts numerous historical figures in the First Century including prophets, kings, and priests, yet he never calls any of them a Messiah. But he does state that Jesus was the Messiah.

The Response from Jesus

To this question, Jesus responded saying, "I am". Without a shadow of doubt, he was affirmative in his answer. Then he stated, "But I say to all of you. In the future you will see the Son of Man sitting at the right hand of the Mighty One and coming on the clouds of heaven." When he stated these words, "But I say to all of you", he was invoking judgment on all of them. By him speaking of himself as the Son of Man, he was certainly giving reference to himself without applauding himself. He specifically states that they would see him in two positions. First, he would be "sitting at the right hand of the Mighty One." He knowingly adapted Psalm 110:1 which states, "The LORD says to my Lord, 'Sit at my right hand until I make your enemies a footstool for your feet.'" Although he was currently bound, he knew that one day he would be in a position of not only resting on his throne but ruling with dignity and dominion. Thus, he indirectly was letting these wicked religious leaders know that he would subdue and triumph easily over them and all his enemies in the future.

His second position would consist of him being seen "coming on the clouds of heaven." Daniel 7:13-14 reports a future prophecy of "one like a Son of Man coming with the clouds of heaven" who was "given authority, glory and sovereign power" and all "peoples, nations and men of every language worshiped him." This same person as Daniel mentioned will come in the clouds and will "send his angels and gather his elect from the four winds, from the ends of the earth to the ends of the heavens" (Mark 13:26-27). These words that Jesus stated would prove to be true and before everyone's ears, he was stating their doom. Although Caiaphas and the Sanhedrin had power, Jesus was indirectly letting them all know that "true" power was associated with the Son of Man.

The Condemnation from Caiaphas

This was all Caiaphas needed, for he believed that Jesus had now condemned himself by his own declaration. Then Caiaphas tore his clothes and said, "'He has spoken blasphemy! Why do we need any more witnesses? Look, now you have heard the blasphemy" (Matthew 26:65-66). We see three actions of the Caiaphas. First, he tears his clothes. The historical actions of the tearing signified grief as Jacob tore his clothes after hearing of the death of his son (Genesis 37:34). Second, he tells the Sanhedrin that Jesus has blasphemed and third, he specifies through a question that witnesses are no longer needed.

But historically, what was considered blasphemy. Leviticus 24:16 states, "Anyone who blasphemes the name of the LORD must be put to death. The entire assembly must stone him. Whether an alien or native born, when he blasphemes the Name, he must be put to death." Blasphemy was specifically when one cursed the name of God or Yahweh. Numbers 15:30 states in a different way that "anyone who sins defiantly, whether native born or alien, blasphemes the LORD and that person must be cut off from his people." In the Greek, the basic meaning of blasphemy was to abuse, slander, or insult the name of God. Yet Jesus did not do any of this but rather he simply declared that he was God's Son and that the Son of Man would take future action against them all.

Although there was no charge of blasphemy and no death sentence, Caiaphas simply believed that there was no need for witnesses even though Jesus had no witnesses for him, for the witnesses against him had to be thrown out because of discrepancy. Seeing the obvious injustice that was taking place, it was of no surprise to Jesus because he had predicted years earlier that it was necessary for himself to be rejected by the elders, chief priests, and scribes and for him to die (Luke 9:22).

The Condemnation from the Sanhedrin

Then Caiaphas appealed to the bench and asked the Sanhedrin, "What do you think?" They replied, "He is worthy of death." The one who urged the others to decide Jesus' death was Caiaphas and when he had already prejudged the cause and pronounced him a blasphemer, then, as if he was willing to be advised, he asks the judgment of his brothers. He knew that by his authority he could sway the rest, and therefore declares his judgment, and presumes they are all of his mind.[301] Did every single person on the bench consent? Joseph of Arimathea, who was a member of the Council, was specifically noted as being one who "had not consented to their decision and action" (Luke 23:50-51) of condemning Jesus. Perhaps he was apart of that early morning meeting but he did not agree with their decision. However, the majority certainly agreed and now Jesus has been officially condemned.

The Maltreatment

The indignation that followed the sentence included the guards spitting on his face, slapping him, and striking him with their fists. Then they blindfolded him, punched him and said, "Prophesy to us, Christ. Who hit you?" Then the guards took him and beat him even more. After all this took place, we see Caiaphas fulfilling the words of his own prophecy. He purposefully did what he did to please the Jews and his actions showed even more how he was a shrewd strategist and a pleaser of the Jewish people.

DELIBERATELY BREAKING THE LAW

In looking back at this Jewish trial/interrogation, was Jesus' court case handled in a legal and humanitarian way? The answer was undoubtedly no! His trial was not a legal interrogation but rather a miscarriage of justice. It was judicial murder! There were about a dozen of Jewish laws that were broken by the high priests and the Sanhedrin. First, there were laws that forbad the trying of capital cases on the eve of the Sabbath or the eve of a Jewish feast day. All four Gospels specifically mention that Jesus was arrested and tried during the Passover weekend (Matthew 26:2; Mark 14:1; Luke 22:1-2; John 19:14-16). John's gospel mentions that Annas and Caiaphas' actions against Jesus occurred on the day before the Passover meal. The other three Gospels stated that his trial occurred on the day that began with the eating of the Passover meal. However, both the high priest and the Sanhedrin knew that they were breaking their oral laws of the day.[302]

Second, there were several laws broken during his arrest. He was arrested at night and on the identity of a paid informant or traitor which were both against their laws. When he was arrested, he was arrested by both the Roman guard and the temple guard which was against their law. Astoundingly, the Jewish people and the Roman soldiers' corroborated in arresting him. When they came to arrest him, they had no probable cause and even more interestingly, they did not know who they were arresting. These soldiers had Judas to identify him and without Judas, they would not have known who to take into custody.

Third, Jesus was taken for his interrogation to the homes of Annas and Caiaphas, the prosecuting attorneys. Today, trials or hearings would never take place at the homes of judges and certainly this was not supposed to take place during Jesus' trial. In addition, it was against the law for Annas to interrogate Jesus alone, for the Gospels do not record any other judges present. Certainly there were other people there including those who recorded the interrogation but there were no other arbitrators present with Annas. Yet this was against the laws of their day because the Mishna specifically states that judges were not to judge alone.

Fourth, the trials before Annas and Caiaphas took place at night and very early in the morning while it was still dark. We know this was true because Matthew 26:31 and 34 states Jesus' prophetic words that at night the disciples would become offended because of him and that Peter would deny him. At the same time, Peter denied Jesus at the same time when Jesus was before both Annas and then Caiaphas. Yet, the Mishna stresses that capital cases must occur during the daytime and not during the night. In addition, the decision to either condemn or free someone must take place during the daytime.

Fifth, in any court of law both past and present, false testimony is prohibited. Yet, the interrogation before Caiaphas begins with false witnesses testifying against Jesus. More interestingly, these false witnesses were sought out from those present including Caiaphas. These witnesses may have been paid or coerced to speak as imposters. Yet, the law during their day stated that capital cases must begin with reasons for acquittal.[303]

Sixth, their laws required special cares to be given to make sure that the witnesses speak the truth and that the defense had witnesses as well. Unfortunately, Jesus had no one to represent him and he even brought out this fact out in front of Annas. Isn't it amazing to know that a "jury" (Caiaphas, Sanhedrin, false witnesses) was put together for the very purpose of condemning the accused (Jesus)? Certainly, it does not sound like a fair trial.

Seventh, if the witnesses during the trial do not agree, the evidence must be thrown out. This should have taken place during Jesus trial. But since the Sanhedrin and Caiaphas were both in on the false witnesses, they proceeded to let the case continue. In addition, if false witnesses intentionally testified and it was found out that their testimony was indeed false, they were to suffer the penalty that the accused would suffer. Thus, the two false witnesses should have been crucified along with Jesus. But of course, this did not happen.

Eighth, Caiaphas and the Sanhedrin condemned Jesus of blasphemy, yet Jesus did not technically commit this offense against God. Since blasphemy consisted of pronouncing the divine name, it was not recorded that Jesus ever did this. However, Caiaphas and the Sanhedrin broke the law and condemned him for a crime that he never committed. In addition, there were 70 members of the Sanhedrin and it is difficult to believe that all of them were propelled out of their beds for a late night or early morning trial. Perhaps just the ones who wanted him dead were presence to condemn Jesus.

Ninth, when Caiaphas appealed to the bench and asked the Sanhedrin, "What do you think" and they replied, "He is worthy of death", he was ultimately breaking the law. The Mishna states that one judge should not tell the others to accept his view or beliefs. In addition, the law states that unanimity of judges voting for condemnation nullifies the conviction in capital cases. However, it seemed that Caiaphas intentionally acted against the law in order to condemn Jesus. Why? Because after seeing Jesus stand silent and the witnesses not able to agree, he knew that there was no case against him. That was why he took the initiative to speak up.

And tenth, the timing in which they were to have Jesus executed was illegal. Jesus was arrested at about 11:00 p.m. and a murder trail was to last over two Jewish days. This was so that the members of the Sanhedrin could walk home at night in pairs to talk about the proof, to look for ambiguity, and test the facts. However during Jesus' trial, he was arrested at night given several trials or interrogations the next day and executed before the sun went down. Therefore, all in one Jewish day, Jesus was judged and killed which was totally illegal during their day under their laws.

This is the first time in history when a person is condemned to death because of being who he was and proclaiming the truth. Although there were deliberate actions taken against him during this Jewish interrogation, Jesus proved to be better than the Jewish leaders. He truly humbled himself and would even asked his father on the cross to "forgive them" for they do not know what they are doing.

The Fate of Judas

Matthew's gospel puts the fate of Judas Iscariot between the Jewish and Roman trial (27:1-10). Although the Gospels tell us relatively little about him, what is written is not only vivid and striking but highly dramatic.

THE BACKGROUND

His name is the Greek version of the Hebrew name Judah, the same name of one of the sons of Jacob. Most likely he was Jewish and it was not uncommon among the Jews during Jesus' era to be given this particular name. In addition, the name "Iscariot" was given most likely from the town he was from. Iscariot is the Aramaic word for "man of Kerioth", which is a town near Hebron.

I have already talked about Judas' character as being one who "loved money". He acted as the treasurer for Jesus' ministry but was eventually portrayed as a thief by his disciples (John 12:4-6). Jesus predicted his betrayal in the Upper Room with his disciples and it was eventually found out from the other disciples that he betrayed him for money. Thus, it was not a coincidence that all of the Gospel writers place him at the end of the list of Jesus' called disciples.

HIS REMORSE

Matthew states that after he "saw that Jesus was condemned, he was seized with remorse" (Matthew 27:3). Somehow Judas did not just hear but rather "he" saw that Jesus was intentionally condemned by the Sanhedrin, the same people who asked him to turn him over. This verse gives the impression that he was actually present for the Sanhedrin decision and that it totally opened his eyes to what really was happening to his teacher and "leader". For the first time, he actually saw that he was set up so that his "enemies" could condemn Jesus to death. He knew all along that Jesus was innocent, but he especially saw his blamelessness in the courtroom with the Sanhedrin when they convicted him.

Although he was remorseful, he did not take full responsibility but rather tried to throw off much of it on the same people who set him up. He then "returned the thirty silver coins to the chief priests and the elders. 'I have sinned,' he said, 'for I have betrayed innocent blood'" (Matthew 27:3-4). Although he indirectly testified that Jesus was innocent, Judas was letting the religious leaders know that he was guilty with the sin of judicial murder. Yet nothing could be brought back and it was his actions of betrayal that ultimately sentenced Jesus.

Yet little did he know but he was unconsciously fulfilling Scripture, for Zechariah the Old Testament prophet stated hundreds of years earlier, "So they paid me thirty pieces of silver. And the LORD said to me, 'Throw it to the potter', the handsome price at which they priced me! So I took the thirty pieces of silver and threw them into the house of the LORD to the potter (11:12-13). It was foretold in obscurity that the Shepherd would be paid off and discharged and Judas unconsciously fulfilled this very prophecy.

After Judas returned the money, the chief priests replied, "What is that to us? That's your responsibility" (Matthew 27:4). This response shows how careless and insignificant they viewed Jesus and they indirectly tell Judas that they don't care about his wrong actions. They were glad at first to know that he was willing to turn him over, yet they did not care what happened to him after he was betrayed. Sadly, these were supposed to be religious leaders, yet they care nothing about sin or in the fact that they were about to shed innocent blood.

After seeing the response of the chief priests, "Judas threw the money into the temple and left" (Matthew 27:5). After he threw the money, "The chief priests picked up the coins and said, 'It is against the law to put this into the treasury, since it is blood money'" (27:6). Presumably, the money to pay him came from the temple treasury and that is why he threw it back there. Although the money was sacred and was supposed to be use for God's use, it was used to condemn his Son. At the same time, these religious leaders wanted to abide by the law in this case but not during the actual trial of Jesus. How sad!

In an attempt to avoid polluting the temple treasury by blood money, the chief priests "decided to use the money to buy the potter's field as a burial place for foreigners" (Matthew 27:7). Peter states, "With the reward he got for his wickedness, Judas bought a field" (Acts 1:18) and it was actually Judas' money that he returned to the chief priests that bought the field and not Judas himself buying it (Matthew 27:6-10). That particular field was called the Field of Blood and it was not named by the chief priests but by the people who used it to bury their dead.

Unfortunately, the chief priests were unconsciously fulfilling prophecy when they bought this field, for a prophet spoke of their actions hundreds of years earlier (Zechariah 11:12-13). The combined prophetic passage with the words of Zechariah and the career of Jeremiah serves to show the readers that even the most difficult aspects of Jesus' passion (his betrayal by Judah, his refusal of the chief priests and elders to be swayed by innocent blood) lay within God's plan. All of it was according to what the Lord directed (Matthew 27:10), even as was the hostile refusal of Pharaoh in dealing with Moses (Exodus 9:12).[304]

HIS DEATH

Judas now fully sees his betrayal and wickedness in light of Jesus' innocence and purity, and he can hardly live with himself knowing that fact. Matthew states that he died from hanging himself. If we look to his Gospel alone, we get the impression the he immediately went and hanged himself, but Matthew does not state immediately but rather that he hung himself after he threw the money.

There is only one other biblical passage that states how Judas died in addition to Matthew's account. Acts 1:18 states that after he bought a field, "there he fell headlong, his body burst open and all his intestines spilled out." Although this is one of the Greek translations, another translation states "and arriving in the midst of it (the acreage he had bought), he fell headlong." I believe this translation is more accurate in light of the four Greek words that are used. The first word "*ginomai*" means "to come into existence", the second word "*prēnēs*" means "headlong", the third word "*lakaō*" means "to burst open" or "to crack open", and the fourth word "*mesos*" means "in the middle of". Therefore, I believe the more accurate Greek interpretation states that after he bought the field, he literally "fell" headlong and came into existence in the middle of his field and as a result, his insides burst open.

From Peter the Apostle

Peter states specifically that "everyone in Jerusalem" heard about what happened to him and this shows that his death was not commonplace. A simple ordinary death would not have attracted the attention of all of the Jews. Peter, continuing to let a group of Christians know that his actions of betrayal were all apart of Scripture, stated, "Brothers, the Scripture had to be fulfilled which the Holy Spirit spoke long ago through the mouth of David concerning Judas, who served as guide for those who arrested Jesus. He was one of our number and shared in this ministry" (Acts 1:16-17).

In addition, Peter states that the aftermath of his death actually affected the land that was bought. He stated that the purchase of the land was written in the book of Psalms stating, "May his place be deserted; let there be no one to dwell in it" (Psalm 69:25), and "may another take his place of leadership" (Psalm 109:8). Now that he quotes a couple of passage from the psalms to coincide prophetically with Judas' "place" and "leadership", it may be possible to look at these passage to examine other possible prophetic passages in the same chapter that may also shed light on Judas.

From Historical Documents

In addition to these biblical accounts, it is not a coincidence that a reliable historical document mentions the death of Judas and could possibly give greater light to both the New Testament accounts and to Old Testament prophecy. Papias, one of the early leaders of the Christian church, wrote in the Second Century about the death of Judas. Although his writings no longer exist, this passage was quoted by Apollinariris of Laodicea in the Fourth Century. There is recorded a long version and a short version of Judas' death by Papias. The long version account states:

> Judas lived his career in this world as an enormous example of impiety. He was so swollen in the flesh that he could not pass where a wagon could easily pass. Indeed not even his oversized head alone could do so. His eyelids were so puffed, they say, that he could no longer see the light at all nor could his eyes be detected even by an optician's instrument, so far had they sunk below the outer surface. His private organ was gross and loathsome to behold in a degree beyond same. Carried through it from every part of his body, there poured forth together pus and worms, to his shame even as he relieved himself. After so many tortures and punishments, his life, they say, came to a close in his own acreage; and this acreage because of the smell has been until now a desert and uninhabited. Indeed, even until this day none can pass by that place without holding the nose with one's hands – so massive was the flow from his flesh and so widespread over the earth.

The short version of his death states:

> Judas lived his career in this world as an enormous example of impiety. He was so swollen in the flesh that he could not pass where a wagon could easily pass. Having been crushed by a wagon, his entrails poured out.

351

There are numerous details that I desire to bring out in light of these two accounts. First, there is a system of law that states that historical accounts like this can be considered credible and usable data. At the same time, it is evident that Papias' account was written apart from the New Testament writings or the prophecies in the Old Testament and there is no indication that he borrowed their information to make it fit his description of how Judas died.

Second, Papias does not state how he died but rather, he gives more of a description of the horrors that he experienced during the last days and hours of his life. He begins his long version by setting the tone of his sinfulness and wickedness. As Papias describes the horrors of his health, it is apparent that his condition took place after Satan entered into him and after he threw the money in the temple. We know this is true because none of the Gospel writers mention this physical condition and before he betrayed Jesus, his physical condition seemed normal.

Third, I wanted to bring out possible prophecies that back up Papias' account. Speaking of his physical condition, Judas is described as being not only "swollen" but "so swollen" "that he could not pass where a wagon could easily pass." Because of being "so swollen", he had an oversized head and his "eyelids were so puffed" that he could not see the sun's light. We know that Psalm 69:25 coincides with Judas fate because Peter prophetically mentions this writings. But could more of that psalm also apply to Judas? I believe that it does. Psalm 69:23 states, "May their eyes be darkened so they cannot see, and their backs be bent forever." Again, Papias did not right his description of Judas after he examined the Old Testament. However, it is not a coincidence that two verses earlier of Peter's prophecy, there is a description of dimmed "eyes". Certainly, I believe that because of Judas' oversized weight, it was prophesied hundreds of years earlier that his eyes and even back would be greatly affected.

Fourth, Papias talked about the "shame" that Judas encountered because of his condition. I believe that Psalm 69:24 speaks of Judas in saying, "Pour out your wrath on them; let your fierce anger overtake them." Certainly, Judas' physical condition was possibly a direct result of God's wrath and his suffering could have been an added element to God's anger. In addition to Psalm 69, other verses in Psalm 109 could possibly have prophetically declared judgments on Judas, especially since we know that Psalm 109:8 speaks of him. Verse 12 states, "May no one extend kindness to him or take pity on his fatherless children." This verse in addition to others may have directly been spoken to apply to his emotional suffering of tortures and punishments.

Fifth, in support of Peter's indirect words of Judas perishing in his own field, Papias states that his life "came to a close in his own acreage" because of "so many tortures and punishments." In light of both Peter and the psalmist's words, Papias actually describes in detail why his field remained deserted. He stated that his body, possibly already lifeless because of the hanging, was "crushed by a wagon" and his "entrails poured out" "so massive" that it was "widespread over the earth". Because of this widespread of entrails, it caused a smell that would cause people to hold their nose and not want to inhabit that particular place. Luke 22:3 states that Satan entered Judas and his death may have reflected Satan's influence, for evil spirits do cause physical defects and deficiencies. Therefore when Acts 1:18 speaks of Judas "bursting open" and his insides came out, Papias' account could very well support Peter's biblical account.

Sixth, a simple hanging would not have attracted "everyone in Jerusalem", specifically speaking of the Jews. Certainly hanging was out of the ordinary, but hanging alone would not have attracted everyone's attention. However, a unique and rare painful physical condition and the spilling of one's insides that was so severe that people would not even want to come into contact with a piece of land would have certainly attracted "everyone's" attention.

Thus, although it seems from Matthew's account that Judas immediately killed himself after throwing the money in the temple, it seems more reliable to say it did not happen right away. It would have taken time for his physical condition to be so extreme and for people to persistently say words of torture that would cause him to commit suicide. In addion to these words, the Bible states that it was the fact that Judas knew that Jesus was innocent and his guilt caused him to commit suicide. Certainly all these circumstances could have caused him to literally 'lose his mind'.

THE APPLICATION

So then, what was the difference between Peter's sin of denial and Judas' sin of betrayal? Jesus predicted both and both were against him and his character. Yet there were major differences between their sins.

First, Peter regained courage and was reaffirm and restored while Judas was not, for he committed suicide not long after his betrayal. Second, during Jesus' ministry, Judas consistently partook of sin by living the lifestyle of a thief but Peter consistently lacked wisdom and judgment as it was portrayed in numerous instances. Yet, Peter tried to do the "right" thing. Third, Judas consistently was consumed with sin (greed) and he left himself open and vulnerable to Satan. Although this same enemy desired to "sift" Peter, Peter did not open himself to his influences. And fourth, Judas played the major role in the shedding of "innocent blood" while Peter's sin did not. Because of Judas' sin, he was removed from his position and would forever be known as the one who gave Jesus over.

During Jesus' ministry, Judas had power and authority by just being apart of his great ministry. He even had a position of leadership in keeping the money for the use of the ministry. Yet towards the end, instead of focusing in on the leadership ministry of Jesus, he focused in on the leadership ministry in leading those who arrested him. Thus, just because many were numbered with Jesus, Jesus let it be known that only God truly knows those who are his.

The Roman Trial

BEFORE PONTIUS PILATE

Mark 15:1 states that "very early in the morning, the chief priests, with the elders, the teachers of the law and the whole Sanhedrin, reached a decision" and afterwards, "they bound Jesus, led him away and handed him over to Pilate." John 18:28 specifically states that the Jews led Jesus from Caiaphas to the palace of the Roman governor. John 18:28 states that the place was called the praetorium. The term "praetorium" was associated with "praetor" which means "one who goes before." This term signifies a Roman official who would serve as a general leading an army. The spot where he had his judgment seat set up was an area paved with stones (John 19:13) and modern excavations at the Castle of Antonia adjacent to the temple have disclosed a section paved with large stones, which seems to answer well to the situation pictured by the author.[305] This place was outdoors, for "Pilate came out to them", specifically the Jews (John 18:29) and the religious leaders seemed to be nearby, for they were able to talk with him and react to what he said. One of the important facts about this place was that the public might have had access to the governor at the praetorium since it served as an administrative headquarters.

The Background

Pontius Pilate was the sixth procurator of Judea and he ruled from 26-36 AD. Pontius was of Samnite origin and Pilate (specifically Pilatus) was a family name or cognomen which took its origin from "cap", "helmet" or "spear." He is best known in Christian and secular history as being one of the judges or prosecuting attorneys for Jesus' trial and he was the judge who condemned him to death, for the Jewish authorities could not do so at that time.

In Christian history, although the Gospels speak more favorably of him in trying to let Jesus go, I Peter 2:23 states that Jesus was "handed himself over to an unjust judge". In secular history, Pilate stood out as a notoriously vicious man, one who was stern and uncaring. According to Philo, Pilate was inflexible, stubborn, one of cruel disposition, and one who executed troublemakers without a trial. He stated that his actions consisted of violence, thefts, assaults, abusive behavior, endless executions, and endless savage ferocity.[306] According to Josephus, he frequently nearly caused rebellion and uprising among the Jews due to his uncaring attitude toward Jewish customs.[307] There was an incident when he deliberately spent money from the Jewish Temple to build Roman aqueducts and when the Jews protested, he hid soldiers in the crowd while he was talking to them. After he made a sign to them, they randomly assaulted, beat, and even kill numerous Jews to quiet their objection.[308]

Although many scholars at one point were skeptical of the Bible because of his historical existence, physical evidence was found of him in 1961. There was a block of limestone discovered by a group led by Antonio Frova in the ruins of a Roman theatre at Caesarea Maritima and inscribed on a rock was the name Pilate, the prefect or governor of Judea. It has been dated to 26-37 A.D. and is currently housed in the Israel Museum in Jerusalem. His title was customarily thought to have been procurator but this inscription states that his title was "prefect". Some commentators stress that this archeological evidence proves the veracity of the Gospels on his existence while others cite the inscriptions' significance in clarifying his title. Since I have already stated the historical findings of Caiaphas the high priest in 1990, it is interesting that history gives credibility to both a Jewish and Gentile prosecuting attorney of Jesus.

The Charge from the Jews

This trial began early in the mourning when most people would have still been in bed and the Jews who did come to Pilate's place did not enter because they wanted to avoid ceremonial uncleanness. This is why Pilate came outside to them. The trial seems to officially begin when Pilate came outside where the Jews were and he asked them, "What charges are you bringing against this man." He wanted to know the crime Jesus had committed and the proof that he committed the crime. Luke states that they began to accuse him of "subverting our nation", opposing "payment of taxes to Caesar" and claiming "to be Christ, a king" (23:2).

Concerning these three charges, the first was vague and did not specifically state what he did in "subverting" the nation. The second was untrue because after the Pharisees sent their disciples to Jesus to ask him if it was "right to pay taxes to Caesar or not", Jesus took a coin and told them all to "give to Caesar what is Caesar's, and to God what is God's" (Matthew 22:15-22). And concerning the third question, although the Romans considered a "king" as a political rival, Jesus was a king but he was not a political rival in the sense Pilate thought. He even tried to avoid making himself king by the people on a particular occasion.

Although Caiaphas and the Sanhedrin accused him of blaspheming the Jewish God, these Jews knew that Pilate, the Roman governor, would care nothing about a religious matter. So that is why these Jews brought up crimes that would be considered an infringement against the Roman government. Yet the Jews in their own minds did not see these civil matters they were bringing to Pilate as a threat to their laws and customs.

In addition to bringing up these civil crimes, the Jews told Pilate that "if he were not a criminal, we would not have handed him over to you." These religious leaders were demanding justice as if Jesus was already a criminal. Pilate replied saying, "Take him yourselves and judge him by your own law" (John 28:31). But the Jews knew that they would not get a death sentence by judging him according to their own laws. In addition, they had already judged him and found him guilty. So the Jews objected saying, "But we have no right to execute anyone" which signified their intentions all along. They wanted Jesus to die and from their perspective, this was the reason why they were bringing him to Pilate all along.

Yet, John makes it clear that all "this happened so that the words Jesus had spoken indicating the kind of death he was going to die would be fulfilled" (18:32). Even those who intended to defeat Christ's sayings were made serviceable to the fulfilling of them by an overruling hand of God. Those sayings of Christ in particular were fulfilled which he had spoken concerning his own death.[309] When Jesus prophesied that he would be turned over to the Gentiles and that they would put him to death (Matthew 20:19), the Jews fulfilled that very prophecy by declining Pilate's offer to "take him" and "judge him" by their laws. In addition, when Jesus said that he would be "crucified" (Matthew 20:19), this form of death would not have happened if the Jews did not turn him over, for he would have been stoned by them rather than crucified.

The Interrogation

Then Pilate, after going back inside the palace, called for Jesus and asked him, "Are you the King of the Jews?" Pilate asked this question to possibly find something on which to ground an allegation. But for him to even ask this question was out of the ordinary since there was no evidence that this title was every applied to him during his ministry. In addition, Jesus was never accused by the Romans of this title before this trial.

Yet these Jews had remembered several occasions in his life that may have constituted him being a king. They may have remembered the magi coming to look for the newborn child who was "The King of the Jews" (Matthew 2:1-2) and how Jesus' entry into Jerusalem was associated with the prophecy in Zechariah 9:9 (Matthew 21:5). They may have interpreted Jesus speaking of himself when he stated, "Then the king will say to those on his right, 'Come, you who are blessed by my Father; take your inheritance, the kingdom prepared for you since the creation of the world'" (Matthew 25:34). Therefore, we can see how the Jews may have twisted both sayings and occurrences to try to force Pilate to want to inquire about Jesus' kingship.

To his reply, Jesus stated, "Yes, it is as you say". John states a more specific answer saying, "Is that your own idea or did others talk to you about me" (John 18:34). Jesus wanted to know if this question was something that he wanted to know or simply was it just something that he had heard? From his perspective, it was clear that Pilate did not say those words from his own initiate but rather because the Jews told him that he was the King of the Jews. Again, we see Jesus not only telling the truth but exposing the lousy interrogation from the "interrogator". In addition, since Jesus was inside of Pilate's place and Pilate literally went outside his place to hear the charges of the Jews, it seems possible that Jesus did not hear his accusations. Yet because he was God, he knew the charges as they were being brought forth. It could be possible that Pilate was not expecting Jesus to know the details of what had just transpired and because of this, Jesus' answer amazingly caught him off guard. Certainly, this could be one of the reasons as to why Pilate would soon declare his innocence.

Then Pilate stated, "Am I a Jew? It was your people and your chief priests who handed you over to me. What is it you have done" (John 18:35). In a sarcastic way, Pilate was letting Jesus know that he does not meddle with Jewish questions and that he has nothing to do but to proceed on the information that was given by Jews. Since Jesus was being accused of many things, Pilate was simply trying to find out if Jesus could be charged on any rebellious matters.

In order to give a more detailed answer to Pilate's response, Jesus replied back saying, "My kingdom is not of this world. If it were, my servants would fight to prevent my arrest by the Jews. But now my kingdom is from another place" (John 18:36). It becomes clear that by Jesus stating that his kingdom "is not of this world", it did not threaten Caesar's or any Roman ruling authority. After contrasting his spiritual kingdom with Pilate's worldly kingdom, Pilate sought the opportunity to simply ask him, "You are a king, then!" It made sense from Pilate's perspective that if Jesus talked about having a kingdom then he certainly was a king.

Jesus answered him and said, "You are right in saying I am a king. In fact, for this reason I was born, and for this I came into the world, to testify to the truth. Everyone on the side of truth listens to me" (John 18:37). His reply consisted of three things. First, he told Pilate that he was a king. Yet by him stating this, Pilate knew that he was neither a rival king nor a king that would concern any of his political matters. Second, he stated his purpose for coming into the world and his reason was to give evidence to the truth. From his perspective, he came to reveal God's veracity and all those who listened and obeyed him would understand this very truth. And third, he was indirectly trying to witness to Pilate. Although he did not state specifically what truth was, he responded back to Pilate in a way that would spark his mind in wanting to know this truth. Jesus' answer did not only apply to Pilate but to everyone who desired to follow him and know the truth. In addition, Paul stated in 1 Timothy that this was a good response by Jesus, for "while testifying before Pontius Pilate" he "made the good confession" (6:12-14).

Then Pilate asked Jesus, "What is truth?" It does not seem that Pilate took the religious leaders accusations any more seriously than Jesus did. At the end of their dialog, we don't see either of them talking about the allegations but rather on truth. Yet it is sad that Pilate did not recognize the truth standing right in front of him.

The Declaration of Jesus' Innocence

Pilate did not stick around to find out the answer but rather he went out to the chief priests and the crowd of Jews and told them that he did not find a basis for a charge against him." From Pilate's point of view, Jesus was not setting himself up to be a rival king and therefore he was innocent.

In light of his actions after asking Jesus "what is truth", we see some comparisons and contrasts between him and Nicodemus in John 30. Just like Nicodemus asked Jesus spiritual questions, so did Pilate. Yet Nicodemus stayed around to hear Jesus talk about the Kingdom of God and how to be born again but Pilate seemingly did not want to. Pilate may have had his life changed forever just like Nicodemus, yet he was more concerned about political matters and in declaring Jesus' innocence before a hostile Jewish crowd.

But the Jews replied back to Pilate insisting that he was guilty. They said, "He stirs up the people all over Judea by his teaching. He started in Galilee and has come all the way here" (Luke 23:1-5). It seemed like the former three allegations were not strong enough for Pilate and these people decided to attempt one more allegation on him. Galilee was where all the rebellions started against Rome and by the Jews placing Jesus in this territory, they were placing him at the center of upheaval against the empire. They were promoting the fact that he was a leader of insurrection and was detrimental to Rome and its government. Certainly Rome was not going to take any rebellion from anyone and we see this many years later when they destroyed the Jewish Temple in 70 A.D. because of a Jewish revolt.

After Pilate asks him if he was the King of the Jews, Pilate states many accusations by the chief priests and the elders (Mark 15:3). Surprisingly, Jesus "gave no answer". He was able to answer Pilate's questions about kingship and truth, but he gave no answer to the numerous Jewish accusations. Then Pilate asked him if he was going to answer these charges, but Jesus made no reply, not even to a single charge. He never asserted or denied any of their basic charges for he knew that their allegations were false. This non-response amazed Pilate.

The Transfer to Herod

When the Jews insisted that Jesus stirred up the people all over Judea by his teaching beginning with Galilee, "Pilate asked if the man was a Galilean. When he learned that Jesus was under Herod's jurisdiction, he sent him to Herod, who was also in Jerusalem at that time" (Luke 23:6-7). Why did Pilate hand Jesus off to Herod when he did not have to? Certainly, he was hoping to flee from the difficulties of condemning an unjust man. But from his standpoint, Jesus was not just an ordinary man because from his history, he certainly did not care about acting notoriously. But there was something about Jesus that made him feel uneasy to condemn and instead of acting as a judge in making a difficult decision, he felt better by doing absolutely nothing and sending him off to someone else.

But little did he know that he was unconsciously fulfilling Scripture, for Peter and John stated in Acts 4 that Psalm 2:1-2 was a prophecy concerning Jesus. This psalmist stated, "Why do the nations conspire and the peoples plot in vain? The kings of the earth take their stand and the rulers gather together against the LORD and against his Anointed One." After stating this psalm, Peter and John stated that "both Herod and Pontius Pilate met together with the Gentiles and the people of Israel" in Jerusalem "to conspire against... Jesus" (Acts 4:27). This psalm was expressly said to be fulfilled in

Herod and Pontius Pilate and it is interesting to see that not only did they both conspire but that they conspired with both the Romans and the Jews in order to condemn Jesus.

BEFORE HEROD ANTIPAS

Herod Antipas, son of Herod the Great, was the one who earlier beheaded John the Baptist, the cousin of Jesus. For Jesus to have been from Galilee would constitute him being under Herod's sphere of power and this location is consistent with him being raised in Nazareth, which was a small town location in Lower Galilee.

The Interrogation

When Jesus came to Herod, Herod "was greatly pleased, because for a long time he had been wanting to see him. From what he had heard about him, he hoped to see him perform some miracle" (Luke 23:8). Sadly, he never took Jesus' works of miracles seriously but only saw him as some magic worker. He only wanted to be entertained! Luke states that he asked and demanded him to speak, "but Jesus gave him no answer". Certainly, these questions must have also consisted of his interrogations and perhaps he was also trying to find some means of fault or reason for condemnation.

The Response from Jesus

Yet Jesus gave him no answer, for he was able to see his heart and know that he was also filled with falsehood and deception. His silence here was also a prophecy stated in Isaiah 53:7, "He was oppressed and afflicted, yet he did not open his mouth." But how could Jesus not say anything to the very man who beheaded his cousin John and to the one who did not take him seriously? Knowing his evil heart and that he conspired against him with Pilate, how could he not open his mouth but rather be "led like a lamb to the slaughter"? The reason is because he knew what he had to do and that prophecy must be fulfilled. He understood that he had to drink of the cup of wrath and become "oppressed and afflicted." At the same time, he did not want to interfere with anything that would cause him not to die the horrible death of crucifixion.

The Accusation and Mocking

After seeing Jesus not say anything to Herod, the chief priests and the teachers of the law who were standing right there decided to do everything in their power to get Herod to condemn him. So they "vehemently" began "accusing him" and after doing so, "Herod and his soldiers ridiculed and mocked him." Specifically, these solders were Herod's bodyguards, men of war, and they unfortunately sought the opportunity to make Jesus look bad especially since he refused to amuse Herod with miracles or answer any of his questions. Apparently, Jesus continued not to speak but only stood and allowed all these people to oppress him and afflict him.

The Transfer back to Pilate

Herod knew he had no case! Jesus did not convict himself and Herod had nothing to judge him upon. With all the chief priests and bodyguards trying to get him to do or say something that was worthy of condemnation, Jesus remained irreproachable. Therefore Herod "sent him back to Pilate" and instead of releasing him, he showed no honor or boldness but rather sent him back. Like Pilate, it seemed that he too did not want to condemn a just man but at the same time, he did not want to stand up for what was right. He was a person who followed the crowd as we had just seen him follow the ridicule of the chief priests and teachers of the law. He ultimately was a lousy leader.

But he did not send Jesus back to Pilate without the feeling of maltreatment, for he purposefully dressed "him in an elegant robe" representing a king-like figure. Certainly, he was not trying to respectfully honor or exalt him, for he never took his miracles seriously and had just finished openly ridiculing and mocking him. Therefore, this splendid garment was meant to show mockery of Jesus.

If Herod really thought Jesus was even somewhat of a threat, he would have condemned him. We see him cutting off the head of Jesus' cousin John and this action shows that we are not dealing with a man who is not willing to take action. But there was something about

Jesus, something that would not allow him to take action but rather to send him to someone else. Even with all the scorn and rebuke, he had a conscious. Yet, he used it in the wrong way.

His actions showed that both he and Pilate had something in common. With him sending Jesus back to Pilate shows their common ground in their opposition to Jesus and this could have been one of the reasons why "that day Herod and Pilate became friends" for "before this they had been enemies" (Luke 23:12). With both of these weak leaders becoming friends shows something about both of their character.

BEFORE PONTIUS PILATE A SECOND TIME

Although we have seen Pilate's spineless character, now he is surprisingly stunned to see innocent Jesus before him again. He was nervous at him before Herod interrogated him but he will soon find out that he will be even more scared to condemn an innocent man. So right after Jesus has been sent back to him, he immediately "called together the chief priests, the rulers and the people, and said to them, 'You brought me this man as one who was inciting the people to rebellion. I have examined him in your presence and have found no basis for your charges against him. Neither has Herod, for he sent him back to us; as you can see, he has done nothing to deserve death'" (Luke 23:13-15). He seemingly wanted to make it clear that Jesus was innocent after a full investigation and that he wanted nothing more to do with him. He even points out that Herod also investigated him and came up with the exact same result.

Then he came up with an idea of how to make the Jews happy and he told them that he will punish him and then release him (Luke 23:16). He said this because he knew the "custom at the feast to release a prisoner chosen by the crowd" and he hopefully believed that the Jews would pick Jesus as the one to release. Or better yet, he hoped to release Jesus on his own initiative. But why would he chastise him if both he and Herod found him innocent especially since there was just as much injustice in scourging as in crucifying an individual? Certainly, he wanted to satisfy the people but he did not want to kill Jesus and that is why he offered him to be "punished".

The Notorious Prisoner named Barabbas

Then the New Testament authors set the stage for a man by the name Barabbas. Matthew states that he was a notorious prisoner (27:16) and that he had been put in prison for an "insurrection in the city and for murder" (23:19). Mark states that he was in "prison with the insurrectionists who had committed murder in the uprising" (15:7). John 18:40 states that he had "taken park in a rebellion." Thus, we see him as a violent revolutionary who was locked up with other revolutionaries who had committed murder during a particular rebellion. We are not told whether he was tried or convicted, but one thing for sure is that he would have been certainly condemned and sentenced to death because of his actions.

Now a large crowd had just gathered to add its presence to the whole Sanhedrin before Pilate and they began to ask him to do just as he had always done for them (Mark 15:8), that is to release one of their prisoners. Then Pilate asked them, "Which one do you want me to release to you; Barabbas or Jesus who is called Christ?" Pilate said this desiring to have Jesus released and Barabbas sentenced.

Yet to his dismay, the crowd yelled in one voice saying "away with this man! Release Barabbas to us!" From Jesus' ministry, we see no attempt of him acting in a violent way, for he was a nonviolent revolutionary. That is why Pilate and the Jews made no attempt to capture his disciples or followers. However, Barabbas and some of his followers were captured and he demonstrated his frustration to the Roman government through violence. Both Barabbas and Jesus opposed Roman injustice but Jesus handled his opposition in a nonviolent way. But ironically, we see the crowd desiring his demise.

Yet Pilate knew at least two reasons why the Jews gave this answer. First, he knew all along that "it was out of envy that they had handed Jesus over to him" (Mark 27:18). However he found out this information, he knew that the Jews knew that Jesus was innocent, for they did not hand him over because of him committing an offense but because of jealousy. Second, he had to have noticed the chief priests and the elders stirring up the crowd to have Barabbas released instead of Jesus, for the gospels confirm that these religious leaders did just that (Mark 15:11; Matthew 27:20). That is why Pilate most likely was not surprised at all to hear them say that they wanted Barabbas released.

The Message from his Wife

Certainly Pilate was nervous, but now his wife would add to his conscious and nervousness in knowing that he must not condemn this innocent man. Matthew states that "while Pilate was sitting on the judge's seat, his wife sent him this message, 'Don't have anything to do with that innocent man, for I have suffered a great deal today in a dream because of him" (27:19). Although her name is not mentioned in the Bible, alternate Christian traditions name her (Saint) Procla, and her message seemingly only intensifies the current miscarriage of justice.

In looking at this dream, there seems to be some immediate questions. First, how was she able to dream about Jesus at the very moment that he was on trial before her husband? Second, how did she know that Jesus was just? And third, why did she rather than her husband receive the dream? In answering these questions, we see the dream of Jesus' father Joseph and how God had given him revelation the very night that he was to take his family to Egypt (Matthew 2:13). In addition, we see how God warned the magi in a dream to return home a different route in order that they would avoid opposition (Matthew 2:12). God used extraordinary means to reveal Jesus to the Magi who were Gentiles since they did not have the Scriptures. Their promptness to accept the revelation is contrasted with the hostile rejection of Jesus by those who did have the Scriptures.[310] Therefore in looking at the revelation given to his wife, we are able to see precisely how this fits into God's plan. Even church writers such as Origen, Augustine, and Calvin considered her dream to be of divine origin. Certainly God could have told her that Jesus was just and she could have recognized that no dream or divine revelation would get through to her husband and that is why she received the dream instead of him.

The Freeing of Barabbas

After receiving this advice, Pilate wanted to let Jesus go and he asked the crowd, "Do you want me to release the King of the Jews? Matthew has Pilate asking the people which of the two do they want him to release and they all said "Barabbas" (27:21). He did not want to become tainted by Jesus' blood and he made the extra effort to ask the crowd on a second occasion who they wanted to release. Yet because the people shouted back, 'No, not him! Give us Barabbas'" (John 18:39-40), Pilate succumbed to their request of releasing Barabbas.

Although he knew that Jesus was innocent and Barabbas was guilty, he had no choice but to let Barabbas go, for he was a pleaser of the people. Despite causing turmoil and death, Barabbas was now a free man while the decision was still up in the air as to what would become of Jesus. Ironically, the protagonist is condemned while the antagonist is set free. Unfortunately, the Jerusalem crowd had picked the wrong savior.

The Scourging and Mocking of Jesus

Now that Barabbas has been "freed" from his crime, the complete focus of the interrogation turns to Jesus. Pilate thought that he would best please the Jews by taking him and having him flogged (John 19:1) and he would do just that. Flogged is the same as "scourged" and a scourge was a whip made up of small cords. Rods were used on freeman; sticks on military personnel; and scourges on others. These scourges were generally leather thongs fitted with pieces of bone or lead or with spikes.[311] We see Jesus making a scourge of small cords earlier in his ministry and he used it to drive out people who were in the temple (John 2:14-16).

Under Rome's method of scourging, an individual would be stripped of all clothes and would be tied in a bending posture to a pillar. The Roman guards would make their scourge out of leather thongs and would incorporate sharp pieces of bone or lead. When they would hit their victims, they would rip it around him and yank it, causing one's flesh including back and breast would tear. Many people unfortunately were eviscerated because of this. Christian historian Eusebius records not long after Jesus' era that he saw Christians suffered and died under this Roman treatment.

This scourging fits right in with David's prophecy concerning Jesus stating, "I can count all my bones; people stare and gloat over me" (Psalm 22:17). Interestingly, Jesus specifically prophesied to his disciples that he would be delivered to the Gentiles to be mocked, "scourged" and crucified (Matthew 20:19). Precisely, this took place just as he had stated.

After Pilate had him scourged, the soldiers mocked him by twisting together a crown of thorns and putting it on his head. After this, they "clothed him in a purple robe and went up to him again and again saying, 'Hail, king of the Jews!' And they struck him in the face" (John 19:2-3). Jesus had already experienced mocking from Herod, Pilate, Roman and Jewish guards, and he had already been hit in the face. But now this mocking and abuse has just escalated. Putting a crown of thorns on Jesus' head not only showed mockery but was extremely painful.

The Declaration of Jesus' Innocence Again

After this, Pilate once more came out to the Jews and told them, "'Look, I am bringing him out to you to let you know that I find no basis for a charge against him.' Then Jesus came out wearing the crown of thorns and the purple robe and Pilate said to them, 'Here is the man'" (John 19:4-5). Pilate hoped that the Jews would take their "man" and he continued to asked them, "What shall I do, then, with the one you call the king of the Jews" (Mark 15:12) and we see him making an appeal in a desire to release him (Luke 23:20). Although he had the final authority to do with Jesus as he pleased, he still sought the Jews because he was a people pleaser. He has now boldly shown that he will be persuaded by them and therefore, he is ultimately not only losing control of the situation at hand but he is not in control.

But as soon as the chief priests and their officials saw Jesus come out with Pilate, they shouted, "Crucify! Crucify!" We can still see the chief priests and the elders convincing the people to say these words and certainly this crowd did not know who Jesus was. From their eyes, they may have believed that he was truly guilty and worthy of crucifixion. But Pilate replied back and said, "You take him and crucify him. As for me, I find no basis for a charge against him." This is the second time we see him telling the Jews to judge him according to their law (John 18:31). Yet the Jews really wanted Jesus to die the ultimate death of crucifixion and from their standpoint, they needed something else that would possibly scare Pilate in condemning Jesus.

So they insisted to tell Pilate, "We have a law and according to that law he must die because he claimed to be the Son of God" (John 19:7). It was this statement that scarred Pilate because although he had already heard Jesus say that he had a kingdom that was not of this world and from another place (John 18:36), he did not see him as the "Son of God." He knew that the Jews had turned him over because of envy but now he truly sees why they were envious. Now that Pilate had just put together Jesus' statement about his kingdom and the Jews statement about him being the Son of God, he goes back inside of his palace to have one more talk with this Jesus.

The Interrogation

He tells Jesus in a stern and forceful manner, "Where do you come from?" This was a question about identity since people were known by where they were from. He knew physically that he was from the Galilean region but Pilate asks this question as if there was more to his origin and person. In his first interrogation, he only asked Jesus about his identity from the testimony of those who were envious of him. But now he saw the real reason why the Jews hated him and he knew that it was one thing for the King of the Jews to die but another for the Son of God to die.

To his dismay, "Jesus gave him no answer." Knowing that the pressure was on him, Pilate asks him, "Do you refuse to speak to me? Don't you realize I have power either to free you or to crucify you" (John 19:10). This statement shows that the final outcome did indeed come down to him and he had the power to free or crucify anyone in his empire.

But amazingly, Jesus puts Pilate on trial and gives him an interrogation concerning power, saying, "You would have no power over me if it were not given to you from above. Therefore the one who handed me over to you is guilty of a greater sin" (John 19:11). Jesus was telling him that he may have the power (given from above) to crucify and release but he has the power to discern sin. And more importantly, even though Pilate has been placed by God in the judicial position in this trial, he does not escape sin, for he does not choose the truth.[312]

The Declaration of Jesus' Innocence

This was all he needed in his conscious to know for sure that Jesus was innocent and "from then on, Pilate tried to set Jesus free."

There was nothing in him worthy of condemnation and crucifixion and that was why he wanted to let Jesus go. Certainly this was a huge blow to the chief priests and elders who had desired Jesus to suffer the horrible death of crucifixion and they needed something even more that could convince him to crucify Jesus.

So they came up with the tactic to scare him saying, "If you let this man go, you are no friend of Caesar. Anyone who claims to be a king opposes Caesar" (John 19:12). The Jews saw that they had an advantage over Pilate and that he would be swayed by their decision, so they made this statement to invade his dignity and sovereignty. This statement was particularly threatening to him, for it frightened him believing that he may be displaced or impeached. In addition, he thought that he would be no friend of Caesar's friend if he did not crucify Jesus. Yet this was a statement the Jews did not mean themselves knowing that it was Caesar's government that was severely oppressing them and not Pilate's.

The Jews never had a case against Jesus but all they could do in the end was to politically challenge Pilate's authority and friendship with Caesar. And their plan worked, for when Pilate heard this statement, it touched him in a sensible way and he realized that he could not be loyal to Caesar if he did not condemn Jesus. So "he brought Jesus out and sat down on the judge's seat at a place known as the Stone Pavement (which in Aramaic is Gabbatha)." Either he sat down on the judge's seat or he sat Jesus down on the judge's seat so that judgment could take place. This place was probably the place where Pilate would sit and hear cases and/or condemn criminals. Historically, this place seemed to either portray an enclosed place where he could have complete control or an elevated place so that other people would see what was taking place.

Then Pilate told the Jews, "Here is your king." Again, he wanted to not have to condemn him but the crowds of people shouted, "Take him away! Take him away! Crucify him!" Pilate replied back saying, "Shall I crucify your king?" The chief priests answered saying, "We have no king but Caesar." Why did the chief priests say this? We know that the Jews wanted a political Messiah to deliver them for Roman's foreign control. Yet Jesus, in their eyes, failed to do this. So now they were denying his kingship and messianic rule and were embracing Caesar's kingship. In addition, these same people who desired to embrace Caesar rule would soon die under Roman's foreign control because of an insurgence. So they were only concerned about their present objective to get Jesus crucified.

Knowing that he did not commit any offense, Pilate replied back saying, "Why? What crime has he committed?" Knowing that they never had a case against Jesus, the Jews never responded back to his question but they only continued to say "crucify him".

But for the third time Pilate responded to the Jews saying, "Why? What crime has this man committed? I have found in him no grounds for the death penalty. Therefore I will have him punished and then release him" (Luke 23:22). By Pilate referring to Jesus as "this man" he was portraying him as not only feeble and useless but as one who was of no competition to Rome. Yet the Jews never understood his tone but only continued to cry louder saying, "Crucify him! Crucify him!" And sadly, Luke states that "their shouts prevailed."

The Washing of the Hands

"When Pilate saw that he was getting nowhere, but that instead an uproar was starting, he took water and washed his hands in front of the crowd. 'I am innocent of this man's blood,' he said. 'It is your responsibility'" (Matthew 27:24). He was convinced that nothing could persuade the Jews and yet, he saw that a disturbance was already taking place and he wanted to avoid a riot as much as possible. It is ironic that not long before this trial, the chief priest and the elders wanted to avoid a riot and that is why they arrest Jesus at night. Now it seems that the tables have turned and they are the main ones stirring up the people to the point of causing a riot in front of Pilate. And it is this disturbance that now convinces Pilate to give the Jews what they want even though Jesus had done nothing wrong.

But before he hands him over, he tries to free himself from the sham of executing a blameless man. So he washes his hand so everyone can see to signify that he is innocent of his blood. Yet this act could not remove his responsibility for his blood no more than Judas could by him returning the 30 pieces of silver. Interestingly, if it were not for Pilate, Jesus would not have been crucified, for Pilate told him by his own mouth that he had the power to free or crucify anyone in his empire. In addition, if it were not for Judas betraying Jesus, Pilate and the Jewish Sanhedrin would have never seen Jesus and thus, he would not have been crucified. Therefore, Pilate's act of washing his hands only shows how much more of a coward he was in not wanting to take responsibility for his own actions.

The Hand-Over to the Jews

After Pilate said "it is your responsibility", the people answered him saying, "Let his blood be on us and on our children" (Matthew 27:25). These Jews boldly proclaim that they were willing to take the blame for his death and they didn't care about the future consequences of their actions but rather, they only want him to be condemned at the moment. After desiring to please the crowd, Pilate granted their demand and now Jesus, who was their only hope, would no longer be in their company.

But what was Pilate's sentence for Jesus? The answer is that he gave none! He was smart enough not to condemn him but rather all four Gospels state that he was "handed him over to be crucified" or that he "surrendered Jesus to their will" (Luke 23:25). He never passed sentence stating that he was guilty of charged as they do in all court cases. Yet he would still go down in history as the one who gave Jesus over to be crucified. He completely knew what was appropriate and fair, but he chose amiss so that he might keep his occupation, reputation, and manner of life. Yet his actions were orchestrated by God, for whenever "handed" "over" is in the passive voice with no agent mentioned, it means "handed over by God."

John specifically states that this judgment took place on "the day of Preparation of Passover Week" and that it was "about the sixth hour". The Day of Preparation was the day before the Passover and the sixth hour would have been about noon. Yet from his perspective, there seemed to be more significance than just the fact that Jesus was condemned the day before the Passover, specifically at noon. Scholars point to noon as the hour when the priests in the temple began slaughtering the lambs for the Passover meal to be eaten that night. Jesus the Lamb of God was sentenced to death at the very hour when lambs for the Jewish Passover began to be killed, and this concept would constitute a replacement theme.[313] From John's perspective, at the very moment in which Jesus was about to be condemned, the lambs for the Passover began to be slaughtered. Ironically, at that very moment, Jesus replaced the sacrificial system.

CHAPTER 6
EXECUTION AND BURIAL

It was obvious to those surrounding Jesus' cross and those who interacted with him during that day that his death was of no coincidence seeing the obvious events that took place immediately after his demise. Those who were mocking and laughing at him during his trial and on the wooden cross were certainly not laughing immediately after he died. Why? Because the God of heaven revealed himself in a way that demonstrated his anger and contempt to those in opposition to his only begotten Son.

Jesus Led out to Crucifixion

SOLDIERS MOCK JESUS

Now that Jesus has been handed over by Pilate to the Jews, John made it clear that the "soldiers took charge of Jesus." His fate would now exclusively be in their hands and seemingly, they were able to do whatever they wanted with him. So they who were in charge sought the opportunity to publicly humiliate him first by calling together the whole company of soldiers to join in. After doing so, they all took several actions in mocking and debasing.

First, they "stripped him" (Matthew 27:28). Ever since nakedness because associated with sin and shame, it continued to keep that same association during the era of the Romans. This act of stripping him was an act to prepare him for crucifixion, since all victims were crucified naked. Crucifying victims naked only added to their dishonor.

Second, they "put a scarlet robe on him" (Matthew 27:28). The soldiers knew that one of royalty, particularly a king, would often wear scarlet because the dyes in the fabric were expensive. Thus, this act was a cruel and shameful act by these men and they wanted everyone looking at him to see him being mocked as a "king".

Third, they "twisted together a crown of thorns and set it on his head" (Matthew 27:29). One of royalty would often wear a gilded wreath of leaves. Yet mockingly, they literally weaved together a crown of thorns that tortured him. The thorn bushes in this area were long, hard, and sharp thorns. Thus, it would have penetrated into Jesus' head. Certainly, this was humorous to the soldiers in portraying Jesus as a "mock-king".

Fourth, "they put a staff in his right hand" (Matthew 27:29), most likely made of reeds. The soldiers knew that kings hold a scepter and sometimes ornate scepters, of which symbolized power. Thus this was another way for them to mock his kingly authority. Yet little did they know that his throne "will last forever and ever" and "a scepter of justice will be the scepter of" his kingdom (Psalm 45:6). One day, he would judge these very people that were here mocking him as king.

Fifth, they "knelt in front of him and mocked him. 'Hail, King of the Jews!' they said" (Matthew 27:29). Kings were respected and bowing in front of them was a standard act. Yet, the soldiers were making fun of him and were giving him "mocking worship". In addition, kings were given royal names and it was customary to greet Roman emperors with the cry, "Hail, Caesar!" So their words to Jesus were intended to put down his "title" as being the King of the Jews. But little did they know that one day "every tongue" will "confess that Jesus Christ is Lord to the glory of God the Father" (Philippians 2:11).

Sixth, then "they spit on him" (Matthew 27:30). Kings would be given normal greetings of kisses that demonstrated respect and honor. Prophetically speaking about Jesus, Psalm 2:10 states to "kiss the Son, lest he be angry and you be destroyed in your way, for his wrath can flare up in a moment. Blessed are all who take refuge in him." Yet instead of doing this, these soldiers spat on him and the better translation states that they kept on spitting on him. Truly, this showed ignominy.

Seventh, they "took the staff and struck him on the head again and again" (Matthew 27:30). We just saw earlier that the soldiers gave him the staff to mock him. Now one of them took that same staff and repeatedly hit him in the head which added both discomfiture and extreme pain. It is probable that they took the staff and hit the crown of thorns that was on his head so that the thorns went deeper and deeper into his head. To the soldiers this was fun but to Jesus this was almost unbearable pain. Yet this was prophesied hundreds of years earlier. Not even knowing specifically what would happen to Jesus, Isaiah prophesied concerning him stating, "He was despised and rejected by men, a man of sorrows, and familiar with suffering. Like one from whom men hide their faces he was despised, and we esteemed him not" (53:3).

After doing this, the soldiers "took off the purple robe and put his own clothes on him" (Matthew 15:20). No one knows how long the cruel actions of the soldiers lasted, but this act was done seemingly to end the mocking and to begin preparing Jesus for the long road to crucifixion. Soon Jesus' clothes would be in the hands of one of the soldiers, but for now, it would serve as a meager covering for his long walk to his death.

Then the soldiers "led him away to crucify him." John specifically states that after Pilate handed him over, Jesus was "carrying his own cross" (19:17). Although Jesus and his disciples took long walks throughout Palestine, this certainly was his longest walk. Now it is even more evident to see him being "led like a lamb to the slaughter and as a sheep before her shearers" (Isaiah 53:7).

SIMON OF CYRENE

Jesus had been scourged by Pilate toward the end of his second hearing and we have just seen the soldiers physically beat him with his rod and push long thorns deep into his skull. Thus, the soldiers would have quickly realized that Jesus was not physically able to make it the entire way to the crucifixion cite. Why? Most likely because of the loss of blood from the scourging and beating. So they needed another option so that they could get the heavy cross and Jesus to their intended place. It is at this point were the New Testament writers introduced on the scene a man named Simon.

The Background

Mark 15:21 states, "A certain man from Cyrene, Simon, the father of Alexander and Rufus, was passing by on his way in from the country." Who actually was Simon? We don't know much but there is some information given in the gospels that is helpful. We see in Mark that his sons were Alexander and Rufus (15:21) and knowing that this gospel was written to the Romans, Simon's sons may have perhaps been familiar to those in the church at Rome, for Rufus apparently was known in the early church and may have been converted as a Christian.

He was specifically known as being from Cyrene. Cyrene was the capital city of the province of Cyrenaica and was located in northern Africa, the eastern part of present-day Libya. Cyrene was a Jewish community where about 100,000 Jews had occupied during Ptolemy Soter's reign (323-285 BC). During Jesus' era, there was a Cyrenian synagogue in Jerusalem (Acts 9:6). After Jesus' resurrection, we see that "men from...Cyrene went to Antioch and began to speak to Greeks also, telling them the good news about the Lord Jesus" (Acts 11:20). Thus there was somewhat a presence of Christian men from Cyrene.

Why was Simon of Cyrene going to Jerusalem anyway? There is no doubt that he came as a passover pilgrim for the Feast of the Passover. Adult males came all over to participate in this feast and he came some 800 miles away. Matthew states specifically where Jesus was when the soldiers saw Simon. He states, "As they were going out, they met a man from Cyrene, named Simon" (27:32). So Jesus and the soldiers had already exited out of the city when Simon was approaching the city.

His Force to Carry the Cross

Matthew 5:21 continues to say that once the soldiers saw him, "they forced him to carry the cross." No one in their right mind would carry a heavy wooden cross for any reason, for it was a reproach. In addition, he knew little if anything of who Jesus was and he certainly did not want to have any connection with one who was on his way to the crucifixion cite. But legally, everyone was obligated to do as they were told from a Roman officer. We know that soldiers were able to compel one to carry a load for one mile. After that one mile, one could dump the load and leave if they wished. We even see a hint of this when Jesus told the multitude, "If someone forces you to go one mile, go with him two miles" (Matthew 5:41). All the people he was talking to understand that he was referring to the Roman officials. So the soldiers told Simon to carry the cross flat side down and he had no choice but to do so.

Understanding the fact that there were Jewish writers of the Gospels, it is unusual that they would lie about Simon's role in helping Jesus, for he was a Gentile. It was certainly unexpected for Simon to realize that day that although he was going to Jerusalem to celebrate, he would play an active role in Christian history. He just happened to be there and the one the Romans saw to compel to help this innocent man. Although the Romans considered him and his ethnicity as one who was of no importance, Simon was graciously able to be used by the Lord. That is why, although he never knew Jesus, he may have become a Christian for what he did for Jesus and may have became a very important part of the early church.

From history, the Romans would not have usually asked a foreigner or better yet anyone to help out one of their convicted villains. But a more plausible suggestion as to why they allowed this to take place was because Jesus had become so physically weak from the flogging that the soldiers were afraid that he would die before he got to the place of execution. At the same time, they wanted the sentence of the governor to be carried out. This explanation gains some support from the swiftness of Jesus' death once he was crucified (Mark 15:44; John 19:33).[314]

THE DAUGHTERS OF JERUSALEM

It was Luke who helped to introduce Simon in order to transition to a group of women. Since Simon did not oppose Jesus, perhaps the women would not either. After the soldiers "put the cross" on Simon "and made him carry it behind Jesus", we now get a picture of Jesus walking in front of Simon.

The Background

As they were walking to the crucifixion cite, "A large number of people followed him, including women who mourned and wailed for him" (Luke 23:27). At the crucifixion cite, the gospel writers give a list of some of the women who made up this crowd. When the author stated that "a large number of people followed him" it gives the impression that there was a highly unexpected amount of people following this convicted man than usual. It was expected that the relatives and friends of the loved one about to be crucified would accompany the criminal. It would also be expected that there would be much crying and an array of emotions.

These people who followed Jesus would have not only been his friends but also everyday people who were not against him in any way. Yet, it is not safe to say that they were disciples of Jesus. Certainly many of them were not aware of the unexpected trial and condemnation from both the Sanhedrin and Pilate, and once they heard of his condemnation, many may have been moved with compassion and sorrow for him. At the same time, the crowd could have been curious of him as well.

Jesus Addresses the Women

Seeing the multitude, Jesus sought the opportunity to address them, particularly the women in order to tell them where they should channel their weeping. He stated, "Daughters of Jerusalem, do not weep for me; weep for yourselves and for your children" (Luke 23:28). We had already seen him weep for Jerusalem just before he cleansed the temple (Luke 19:41-44) saying, "The days will come upon you when your enemies will build an embankment against you and encircle you and hem you in on every side. They will dash you to the ground, you and the children within your walls. They will not leave one stone on another, because you did not recognize the time of God's coming to you" (Luke 19:43-44). But now he is indirectly telling the women that he foresees Jerusalem's destruction, which would actually take place in 70 A.D., and he bids them to cry over Jerusalem and not him. From Jesus' perspective, their tragedy will not save them from the fate of Jerusalem.

As if this was not enough, he continued to say, "For the time will come when you will say, 'Blessed are the barren women, the wombs that never bore and the breasts that never nursed'" (Luke 23:29). He could have continued to talk about the upcoming destruction of Jerusalem which would take place about 50 years later. We know earlier that he told the Jews, specifically the Pharisees, that because they have killed and persecuted God's prophets, "this generation will be held responsible for the blood of all the prophets that has been shed since the beginning of the world" (Luke 11:49-50). And we know that the destruction of Jerusalem was the prophetic utterance that Jesus was implying. At the same time, he could have been also talking about the upcoming tribulation. Just as prophets of old unconsciously prophesied about a future event, Jesus could have also referred to both the destruction of Jerusalem and the tribulation.

Despite which future event he was referring two, Jesus was telling them that it would be better to be childless when this harsh retribution would come, for children will not be able to protect themselves in such times, and parents would have the anguish of seeing those whom they brought in the world destroyed. If the parents would try to save the children, they both would unfortunately perish.[315]

In addition, Jesus also tells them that one future day, "they will say to the mountains, 'Fall on us!' and to the hills, 'Cover us'" (Luke 23:30), for they would wish to be buried alive. Pertaining to the tribulation period, John the apostle states that one day, every man alive from the kings and princes to the slaves would hide in caves and mountains, and would tell the mountains and the rocks, "Fall on us and hide us from the face of him who sits on the throne and from the wrath of the Lamb! For the great day of their wrath has come, and who can stand" (Revelation 6:15-17). Certainly there are some similarities to Jesus' words and the prophecies of John in Revelation specifically pertaining to the tribulation period.

Jesus' last words to these women state that "if men do these things when the tree is green, what will happen when it is dry" (Luke 23:31). It is evident that these women understood the injustice that the Jews and Romans were inflicting on him. Therefore, they could understand that if this injustice could be done to a blameless man, what would come on Jerusalem and even the world during the time of dearth.

GOLGOTHA

Then Mark 15:22 states that "they brought Jesus to the place called Golgotha." We see Jesus standing for all of his hearings but now the soldiers had to bring him to the crucifixion cite. Jesus apparently had no strength especially from scourging and the loss of blood that accompanied it. Interestingly, when he left the Praetorium where he was tried by Pilate, the soldiers were leading him. Now when Jesus arrived at Golgotha, the soldiers seemingly were carrying him.

The Name

We can narrow the exact place where Jesus was crucified to this general area "which means the Place of the Skull" (Mark 15:22) and it was at this place "where they crucified him" (Luke 23:33). Golgotha is an Aramaic word and was translated into the Greek. The English meaning of Golgotha is "skull" and the Latin equivalent called "Calvaria" means "bare head" or skull.

Why was this place called the Place of the Skull? First, since the Romans crucified most of their prisoners at this location, the site was covered with the "skulls of men" who were executed. It is a fact that most of the victims were left at the site to die and it sometimes took up to six days for a victim to die. In addition, animals would eat the flesh of dead victims. Second, some think that the place actually looked like a skull, for there seemed to be a shadow of a skull's face on the hillside.

The Place

Where was Jesus crucified? The writer of Hebrews states that he "suffered outside the city gate to make the people holy through his own blood" (13:12). This passage fits in with Old Testament teachings that states in Leviticus 24:14 to "take the blasphemer outside the camp" and stoned by everyone in the community. This site is depicted near a road or path where people could react to what was going on and it seemed that the road lead into the city from the countryside, for Simon was seen as one coming into the city from the field (Luke 23:26).

John's gospel states that he was entombed nearby the same place where he was crucified, for it was needed for him to have a hasty burial. He states that "the place where Jesus was crucified, there was a garden, and in the garden a new tomb, in which no one had ever been laid" (19:41). We know that history shows Herod Agrippa I (10 B.C. - 44 A.D.) building a "third wall" which expanded Jerusalem significantly to the north. After this expansion, Jesus' crucifixion cite would have probably been incorporated within the city.

So as far as excavations today of where we believe he was crucified, there are two main locations. One place was known as Gordon's Calvary. This site, which sits at the top of a hill, looks remarkably like a skull, and is near ancient garden tombs. The second is the traditional site which is located outside the city to the west of the temple area, and is where the Church of the Holy Sepulcher now stands.[316] This site has garden tombs almost beneath this site. While some believe that the Holy Sepulcher is a more precise location, what is now Calvary rose 35-40 feet above the original location. Evidence of tombs has been found cut into the rock of the knoll and this extensive excavation has strengthened the case for this traditional site.[317]

THE FIRST OFFERING OF WINE

Once Jesus arrived at Golgotha, the soldiers "offered him wine mixed with myrrh" (Mark 15:23). This is the first time that soldiers gave Jesus wine and we will see them offering it to him again right before he dies. One of the purposes and effect of wine can be traced back to the Old Testament. Proverbs 31:6-7 states, "Give beer to those who are perishing, wine to those who are in anguish; let them drink and forget their poverty and remember their misery no more." Wine had the effect of an anesthesia so that the prisoners would not experience the true horrors of crucifixion.

Mark states that they mixed myrrh in the wine. Myrrh was used as flavor for the wine and the ancients used it to give it not only flavor but fragrance. Matthew 27 states that they mixed gall in his wine. Gall was known as being a bitter herb and Matthew seems to be reflecting on the Old Testament passage that states, "They put gall in my food and gave me vinegar for my thirst" (Psalm 69:21). By parallelism, this psalm was stating the similar occurrence in Matthew and this passage has been noted by many as being a prophecy fulfilled in

Jesus. So it seems that right before the criminals would be crucified, soldiers would come out and give them this wine to subside the pain that would soon lie ahead.

But instead of taking in the wine to help with the pain, "he did not take it" (Mark 15:23). Matthew states more specifically that "after tasting it, he refused to drink it" 27:34). From this description, it seems that Jesus allowed the soldier to put some of the wine in his mouth but instead of taking it down, he spit it out. Perhaps he was not fully conscious when the soldiers were coming with the wine to the criminals for he would have told them no before they could give it to him. The reason why he may have refused to drink this wine may come from Hebrews 2:9 stating, "But we see Jesus, who was made a little lower than the angels, now crowned with glory and honor because he suffered death, so that by the grace of God he might taste death for everyone." The author of Hebrews states that he "suffered death" so that he "might taste death for everyone" and this seems to answer why he refused it.

Jesus' Crucifixion

THE BACKGROUND

Luke states that when "they came to the place called the Skull, there they crucified him" (23:33). What a devastating moment for the followers of Jesus to see him go through the agonizing pain of crucifixion. This moment is the centerpiece of Jesus' passion and this portrayal of him on the cross has been portrayed in art more than any other scene in not only Christian history but world history. The first followers of Jesus would have known almost everything there was about crucifixion, for it was a normal threat given to them from within the Roman Empire. This was certainly one reason why the Gospel writers did not go into much detail pertaining to the horrors of the gruesome death, for their readers would have assumed numerous details.

It's History

There were three supreme penalties that the Romans inflicted on its people for punishment and they included crucifixion, being devoured alive by animals, or being burned alive. Crucifixion appeared in various forms among various peoples of the ancient world, even among the Greeks, and it had and continued to be a political and military punishment. We can trace its practice back to Alexander the Great and his desire to Hellenize the empire. With his spread of Greek power in the East during the Fourth Century, crucifixion then became a widespread custom. Regarding the Jewish practice of crucifixion, one of the earliest references is the execution of 800 prisoners in the early First Century by Alexander Jannaeus.[318] Then Roman armies began to hinder their practice in Judea and as a result, crucifixion of Jews became a subject of policy and procedures.

There have been little references in literature given by the Romans regarding crucifixion mainly because the educated Romans considered it as a heinous punishment and thus, they did not want to talk much about it. As a whole, history shows that those who practiced this type of punishment did not excessively converse about its details.

It's Practice

Rome reserved this practice for foreigners, runaway slaves and for those in the lower classes who challenged or threatened the Roman order. Crucifixion was seen in itself as a slave-type punishment and Rome would not dare in crucifying one of its own people. Thus, the Romans safeguarded the upper class, the nobility, and even their own people from this cruel punishment.

Rome would crucify their victims on a cross, yet the English term for cross is different than the Greek or Latin meaning. The English term gives the image of two lines crossing each other like we typically see in most photos. But the Greek and Latin refer to a stake to which people could be attached in various ways including: impaling, hanging, nailing, and tying. Using a stake to impale would normally kill the victim instantly or quickly but using a stake or pole would normally affect a slow death since no vital organ would be pierced.[319]

How were individuals crucified on a cross? In first looking at history, we can go back to June of 1968 when building contractors were working just north of Jerusalem and west of the road to Nablus. There they made an exciting discovery. Led by team leader Archaeologist Vassilios Tzaferis, the group accidentally unearthed several cave-tombs dating to the First Century A.D. These tombs belonged to a Jewish cemetery and housed ossuaries which contained the bones of between 20 and 35 people. There were four tombs in all, carved like small rooms into the soft limestone, each with an anteroom and then a burial chamber with niches deep enough to accommodate a human body lengthwise at burial. Such tombs were used over and over again for generations, for the bones, after decomposition of their flesh within the niches, were buried together in pits dug in the floor or, as a much more costly alternative, were gathered together into ossuaries – limestone bone boxes.[320]

There were numerous forms of deaths discovered within the tombs and about nine of them had apparently suffered violent deaths. Some of the babies and children died of starvation and a child of about four died after suffering an arrow wound in the skull. A young man and a slightly older woman were both burned to death while the young man was found to being bound while he died. An elderly woman died because her occipital bone had been shattered and another woman apparently died during childbirth, for her body preserved a fetus in her pelvis.

Then there was one death that anthropologist Nicu Haas examined and this individual suffered the violent death of crucifixion. His body was placed in a stone ossuary that bore the Hebrew inscription "Yehohanan the son of Hagaqol". Yehohanan was in his late 20s and the date of his crucifixion was between 7 A.D. and 70 A.D. Nicu Haas states specifically what happened to his body in an article in *Israel Exploration Journal*. He reported: "Both the heel bones were found transfixed by a large iron nail. The shins were found intentionally broken. Death caused by crucifixion."[321] Yehohanan's right heel bone was pierced by an iron nail about 11.5 centimeters and this size makes it anatomically impossible to affix two feet with one nail. In addition, the tip of the nail had become bent, which suggested that after the nail penetrated the tree, it may have struck a knot in the wood which would cause it to become difficult to remove from one's heel. Thus, the wood most likely used was either olive wood or an olive tree.

As stated in Nicu's report, Yehohanan's legs were found broken. His claims show that John's gospel account was not fabricated, for John states concerning this practice, "Now it was the day of Preparation, and the next day was to be a special Sabbath. Because the Jews did not want the bodies left on the crosses during the Sabbath, they asked Pilate to have the legs broken and the bodies taken down. The soldiers therefore came and broke the legs of the first man who had been crucified with Jesus, and then those of the other. But when they came to Jesus and found that he was already dead, they did not break his legs. (19:31-33). When the legs were broken, the criminals could no longer release the tension on their pectoral muscles. More importantly, however, they could no longer push themselves "upward to exhale [carbon dioxide] and bring in the life-giving oxygen.

Concerning their arms, criminals were affixed to the crossbeam by being tied or nailed. The crossbeam was lifted up by forked poles and, with the body attached, inserted into the slot in the upright.[322] History does record that at times, criminals were tied to a tree and beaten while there. The gospels clearly allude that both Jesus' feet and hands had nails to go through them (Luke 24:39; John 20:25, 27).

Pertaining to the position of the cross in relation to the ground, we know that the feet of crucified victim would have been low enough for animals like dogs to ravage their feet. In addition, because the olive trees are not tall, the crucified victim would have been at eye level. Therefore, a victim's foot would have only been about a foot off the ground. So that the condemned would not be able to free his foot by sliding it over the nail, a piece of acacia wood was positioned between the bones and the head of the nail.

Its Horrors and Humiliation

The chief reason for its use was its allegedly supreme efficacy as a deterrent. And thus, it was, of course, carried out publicly. It was usually associated with other forms of torture, including at least flogging. By the public display of a naked victim at a prominent place – at a crossroads, in the theatre, on high ground, at the place of his crime – crucifixion also represented his uttermost humiliation, which had a numinous dimension to it.[323]

It is a fact that the Roman Governor Varus crucified about two thousand people in 4 BC,[324] that the Roman procurator Florus crucified about three thousand six hundred in 66 AD[325], and the Roman general Titus crucified five hundred or sometimes more in 70 AD.[326] Thus we can estimate that some 50,000 - 100,000 Jews were themselves crucified by the Romans in the First Century. With all those thousands of people crucified around Jerusalem in the First Century alone, we have so far found only a single crucified skeleton - and that, of course, preserved in an ossuary. This supports the view that a burial for one who was crucified was the exception rather than the rule and the extraordinary rather than the ordinary case.[327]

Understanding this fact leads one to see the true horrors and humiliation of this cruel practice. First, we see that crucifixion was an aggravated death and one of the most aggravated forms of the death penalty. If one was burned by fire or eaten alive, the aggravation would not last longer than three to five minutes. Yet crucified victims would suffer for several days. This form of execution was one of the cruelest and disgusting penalties that have ever existed in history. An example of this aggravated death is portrayed by the fact that the body of the crucified could be given physical support in several ways, not as an act of mercy but so that the suffering would last longer.[328] Biblically, we see that support was given through wine so that the pain could be deadened.

Second, we see the horrors of how crucifixion was essentially death by asphyxiation. While the body hangs in the "down" position, the intercostals and pectoral muscles around the lungs halt normal breathing. Therefore, faking a death on the cross still would not permit one to breathe, for one cannot fake the inability to breathe for any length of time.[329] If the condemned could lift himself up to get breath, he would survive longer than if the unsupported body were dead weight hanging from the nailed or tied arms.[330] Breaking the victim's ankles insured death even quicker, since the person could not push up in order to free the lungs for breathing. The Romans were knowledgeable in these matters, as indicated by the broken leg bones of a First Century crucifixion victim whose skeleton was recently discovered.[331]

Third, we see that crucifixion was a dishonor in every way. The normal Roman pattern would have been to crucify a criminal naked which was humiliating in and of itself. Then while they were on the cross, dice would have been thrown by the soldiers as prophesied in

Jesus' case (Psalm 22:18). In addition, victims were quite often not even buried. What it meant for a man in antiquity to be refused burial, and the dishonor which went with it, can hardly be appreciated by modern man.[332] The reason is because virtually everyone today receives some type of home going service or memorial. But for the Jews living during this era, crucifixion was aggravated further by the fact that many were never buried. Rome's intention was for them to rot on the cross and to serve as food for wild beasts and birds or be cast aside for carrion. From Rome's perspective, their process of humiliation was made complete in order for them to deter violators.

And fourth, there was no way of getting out of this humiliating death. Because of the ignominy and dishonor of this type of execution, it involved guarded crosses or at least severe sanctions against removal of the body before death and burial of the body after death.[333] Soldiers were assigned to watch over crucified robbers so that their bodies would not be taken down. Certainly, there was Roman supervision to make sure that the victims received their due punishment and we even see while Jesus was on the cross that the soldiers "kept watch over him there (Matthew 27:36).

THE TWO BANDITS

All four Gospels make it clear that when they came to Golgotha, they crucified two robbers with him, one on his right, one on his left. These two were included in the Gospels because their presence illustrates the indignity to which innocent Jesus was subjected.[334] The writers indirectly were making a distinction between Jesus and those who were truly sinners and wrongdoers. At the same time, it was probably set up for him to have two wrongdoers crucified next to him so that it would not look like he was crucified alone out of envy and injustice. He was intentionally crucified with the mortification of everyone seeing him as being a criminal like those next to him.

Yet it was no accident that he was crucified by two wrongdoers because the psalmist prophesied this hundreds of years earlier. Psalm 22:16 states, "Dogs have surrounded me, a band of evil men has encircled me" (Psalm 22:16). Figuratively, dogs meant those who were contempt or disrespected, and in the East, evildoers were given this description and were objects of hatred. Yet these same evildoers were surrounded by Jesus on the cross.

THE INFAMOUS WORDS - "FATHER FORGIVE THEM"

Just after the soldiers crucified him and before they gambled for his clothes, Jesus stated the infamous words, "Father, forgive them, for they do not know what they are doing" (Luke 23:34). He had just undergone the first wounds and misery of crucifixion by having the nails driven in both his hands and feet. Even more disheartening, he was earlier mocked and beaten by these same soldiers and he hardly slept the night before. The average human would have most likely prayed for his enemies to be devoured and destroyed, but Jesus did not pray this. Rather, he asked God to forgive them and even more interestingly, these words were just one of the many remarkable words that he spoke after being crucified and before he died.

Jesus asked his Father to forgive them because "they do not know what they are doing." It is obvious from his standpoint that if they did know what they were doing, they would not have crucified him. Paul states we "speak of God's secret wisdom, a wisdom that has been hidden and that God destined for our glory before time began. None of the rulers of this age understood it, for if they had, they would not have crucified the Lord of glory" (1 Corinthians 2:7-8). These rulers were certainly human rulers but they were led by "the rulers of the darkness of this world" (Ephesians 6:12), specifically Satan and his demons. These human rulers were blind and evidently did not know "God's secret wisdom" that had "been hidden...before time began." His enemies were not exempt from guilt but Jesus desired to put them in the best possible standing before God his father.

What was his purpose in stating the words? It is first evident that he wanted to act as mediator for these sinners and his desire was for them to receive clemency. We see him teaching his disciples in Matthew saying, "For if you forgive men when they sin against you, your heavenly Father will also forgive you. But if you do not forgive men their sins, your Father will not forgive your sins" (Matthew 6:14-5). He was certainly forgiving others who had sinned against him, yet he never sinned.

He also desired to show an example of love toward his enemies. He told his disciples and the multitudes earlier in his ministry, "You have heard that it was said, 'Love your neighbor and hate your enemy.' But I tell you: Love your enemies and pray for those who persecute you, that you may be sons of your Father in heaven. He causes his sun to rise on the evil and the good, and sends rain on the righteous and the unrighteous. If you love those who love you, what reward will you get?" (Matthew 5:43-46). While on that cross, he demonstrated to the entire world that he was a man whose actions backed up his words. Although he did not speak before the Jewish and Roman leaders while they were interrogating him, he certainly spoke to God when it came to forgiving those who wronged him.

THE DIVISION OF CLOTHES

All four Gospels mention that after crucifying him, the soldiers divided "up his clothes" and "they cast lots to see what each would get" (Mark 15:24). As mentioned previously, the condemned would normally have been led naked to the place of execution, so a soldier would have already had his clothes in his possessions. Sadly, while Jesus was in his dying distress, soldiers were merrily dividing his valuables.

It is John's gospel that gives a more detailed description of the division of Jesus' clothes stating, "When the soldiers crucified Jesus, they took his clothes, dividing them into four shares, one for each of them, with the undergarment remaining. This garment was seamless, woven in one piece from top to bottom." (19:23). It may be correct to assume that it was four soldiers who crucified him and these same men took his clothes and divided them among themselves. Each soldier claimed an equal share as close as to the same value.

The fact that his garment was "seamless" is significant because he would soon be seen as the great High Priest (Hebrews 3:1; 4:14) for mankind. The Old Testament sheds light on this same clothing that the High Priest would wear, for God states that his apparel was to be a "robe of the ephod entirely of blue cloth, with an opening for the head in its center. There shall be a woven edge like a collar around this opening, so that it will not tear" (Exodus 28:31-32). This robe was a basic covering of the priest and it was seamless and not torn from the head. Thus, Jesus' seamless tunic was not only a reminder but a fulfillment of his role as mankind's High Priest.

But the soldiers said to one another concerning his outer robe, "Let's not tear it, let's decide by lot who will get it" (19:24). Jesus' garment was seamless and woven in one piece from top to bottom and it denoted considerable skill and work. This garment could have been made from some of the women who "were helping to support them [Jesus and the twelve disciples] out of their own means" (Luke 8:3). Tradition states that his mother wove it for him probably when he was a child. But regardless, these soldiers certainly saw the skill that went into making this garment and because it was a piece of curiosity to them, they agreed to cast lots for it. Perhaps they heard of the woman who touched his garment and was healed from her disease or maybe they believed that they would be able to profit from it. To them, this was their wages for their work and they were willing to cast lots for his old clothes.

But John recognized that all "this happened that the Scripture might be fulfilled which said, 'They divided my garments among them and cast lots for my clothing'" (19:24). David foretold this state of affairs that he would undergo in Psalm 22:18 stating, "They divide my garments among them and cast lots for my clothing." The soldiers were actually gambling for his garment and dice would have been thrown. Yet God had control over Jesus' circumstance and he allowed all things to come to pass for a purpose.

THE THIRD HOUR AND THE SOLDIERS KEEPING GUARD

Concerning the time when Jesus was crucified, Mark 15:25 specifically states that "it was the third hour." During this time, the day began at 6:00 a.m. and the night watch began at 6:00 p.m. So approximate at 9:00 a.m., which was three hours after the morning watch, the soldiers crucified him. However, John calculated his time, the sixth hour or at noon (John 19:14), according to the Roman way of calculation.

Matthew 27:36 states that "and sitting down, they kept watch over him there." We don't see just one of the guards there but probably the four that crucified him and gambled over his clothing. We will soon see that after Jesus was buried, the chief priests and Pharisees told Pilate to make sure that he keeps Jesus' tomb extra secure so that Jesus' disciples don't come and steal his body. Certainly while he was on the cross, the chief priests most likely made sure that no one would come and rescue him. But God would soon use one of these same Roman guards to testify that he was indeed the Son of God.

THE INSCRIPTION AND CHARGE

All four Gospels make it clear that Pilate prepared a notice and "fastened" to Jesus' cross. The notice read "JESUS OF NAZARETH, THE KING OF THE JEWS" (John 19:19), for this was the charge by which he was condemned. Matthew calls it his accusation, Mark and Luke call it an inscription, and John calls it the title. This accusation of him being king was what the Jews brought before Pilate so that they could make him guilty of crime punishable by death. It would make sense that there was probably a charge over all the other criminals to denote what crime they had committed. What the writers portray here is not an official notification related to Roman records but a technique of informing the general public. If crucifixion was meant to deter crime, it would be useful to have the specificity of the crime publicized.[335]

It is also relatively certain, from Jesus' death, that Roman power considered him a lower-class subversive, since crucifixion was a warning against such criminal activity. Before Jesus, Herod the Great was officially appointed "King of the Jews" by Rome and after him, Herod Agrippa I was officially appointed "King of the Jews" by Rome. In between, Jesus of Nazareth died under a mocking accusation that was also a serious indictment, for he was accused as trying to be an illegal "King of the Jews" by Rome. Rome and Rome alone decided who was and who was not King of the Jews. But that title and that fate, in their full religio-political meaning, indicated that Jesus was executed for resisting to Roman law, order, and authority.[336]

Pilate did not intend to put this sign above him to show the seriousness of his crime but rather for a reproach. Remember that he more than once tried to set him free and he publicly declared his innocence in front of all the Jews. So, as a means of reproach, he states that Jesus who is from the small town of Nazareth has claimed to be the King of the Jews. What Pilate was doing was again promoting his blamelessness for the entire world at that time to see. Everyone reading would see that he had committed no crime worthy of crucifixion.

John then mentioned that "many of the Jews read this sign, for the place where Jesus was crucified was near the city, and the sign was written in Aramaic, Latin and Greek" (19:20). By John mentioning this fact, he was most likely referring to both Jews in Jerusalem and Jews out in the country side. And certainly the occasion of the feast brought many Jews around the area to observe the inscription that Pilate had written on the sign. Another reason why so many Jews were able to see the sign was that Pilate had it written in Hebrew, Greek, and Latin. Hebrew was the language of the country and of Old Testament prophecy and Scripture. Greek, the language Alexander the Great used to Hellenize the empire, was the everyday language. And Latin was the chief official language. Pilate knew that if his inscription was published in all three languages, more people would be curious to see who this person was and the reason why he was being executed. At the same time, no one would walk away and not know what the inscription said.

Yet Pilate unconsciously fulfilled the words of Jesus when he spoke earlier saying, "But I, when I am lifted up from the earth, will draw all men to myself" (John 12:32). Jesus said this to refer to the death of crucifixion of which he would die (John 12:33) and Pilate was used to make a sign in three languages to so that people would begin to draw towards him. It was at this time when these words that Jesus spoke had now begun to come to pass.

Seeing what he wrote above Jesus' head, "The chief priests of the Jews protested to Pilate, 'Do not write 'The King of the Jews,' but that this man claimed to be King of the Jews'" (19:21). Not long earlier, the chief priests told Pilate, "We have no king but Caesar." But now they see that Pilate has put for everyone to see that Jesus was their king and thus greater than Caesar. Yet they objected to this title and in their opinion, it was a false title. Certainly, it was obvious that their words portrayed jealously and ill-treatment toward Jesus but Pilate had seen this before.

Then Pilate answered and said, "What I have written, I have written" (John 19:22). He sticks with the fact that Jesus was the King of the Jews and he was publicly professing this fact to everyone. But unfortunately only minutes before, he did not have the backbone to stand up when he knew Jesus was innocent. Yet regarding an inscription, he decides to stand up to the Jewish leaders. The Jewish leaders quickly saw that Pilate was upset within himself for yielding to them when it came to Jesus' life and therefore, he was not going to give in to them again. Sadly, this issue was rather insignificant, for Jesus had already been condemned as a criminal and would soon be executed.

THE FIRST MOCKERY AND INSULT

Now that many people have been drawn toward Jesus, seeing that his inscription was written in three languages, the stage has now been set for them to either sympathize with him or to mock and insult him. Sadly, many choose the latter. The Gospels give three sets of mockery and the first begins with the common people. Matthew and Mark states, "Those who passed by hurled insults at him, shaking their heads and saying, 'You who are going to destroy the temple and build it in three days, save yourself! Come down from the cross, if you are the Son of God'" (Matthew 27:39-40). Luke states that "the people stood watching, and the rulers even sneered at him. They said, 'He saved others; let him save himself if he is the Christ of God, the Chosen One'" (23:35). We first see that the everyday people mixed in with the rulers who may have been apparently attracted by his signs had nothing good to say. Instead of sympathizing with him in his misery, they added to it by insulting him.

What was interesting was the gestures that the people used as they "hurled insults at him." They were wagging and shaking their heads at him. This Near Eastern gesture portrayed scorn and signified the people's triumph over him as was seen in the Isaiah 37:22 and Jeremiah 18:16. In addition, this very action was prophecied in the Old Testament saying, "But I am a worm and not a man, scorned by men and despised by the people. All who see me mock me; they hurl insults, shaking their heads" (Psalm 22:6-7). Psalm 109:25 also states, "I am an object of scorn to my accusers; when they see me, they shake their heads." It was no coincidence that God allowed the psalmists to experience the same insults that Jesus experienced and it is a fact that the psalmists also wrote of Jesus, perhaps unknowingly.

The reason why they shook their head was because in their eyes, he could not save himself. The people may have seen him saving others and now they believed that he was not able to save himself. Even the rulers were among these everyday people and joined in among their insults. The subject matter that gave rise to this first mockery was the change that Jesus would or could destroy the temple sanctuary and rebuild it in three days. These words come from his testimony at the trial by the Jewish Sanhedrin and although these Jews were only thinking about the great temple that took forty six years to build, the temple Jesus was speaking of was of his body.

THE SECOND MOCKERY AND INSULT

Probably moments later, a second mockery and insult came from the chief priests and teachers of the law. Matthew states, "In the same way the chief priests, the teachers of the law and the elders mocked him. 'He saved others,' they said, 'but he can't save himself! He's the King of Israel! Let him come down now from the cross, and we will believe in him. He trusts in God. Let God rescue him now if he wants him, for he said, 'I am the Son of God'" (27:41-42). In addition, "The soldiers also came up and mocked him. They offered him wine vinegar and said, 'If you are the King of the Jews, save yourself'" (Luke 23:36-37). Their words toward him were similar to the first group of people who insulted him, for if he was to be king and savior, he should have been able to save himself. They even told him that they would believe in him if he did come off the cross. The soldiers added to the mockery of the chief priests and sadly followed in their terrible example.

Yet if there was any group of people that should have been looked up to, it should have been these priests. These chief priests, sometimes interchangeably referred to as high priests or chief of the priests, went up by turns to minister in the temple at Jerusalem. They represented the people before God and offered the various sacrifices prescribed in the law. They were to be "selected from among men", to be "appointed to represent them in matters related to God", and were "to offer gifts and sacrifices for sins". They were to be "able to deal gently with those who are ignorant and are going astray" and were to "offer sacrifices for his own sins, as well as for the sins of the people" (Hebrews 5:1-3). But here, they were only leading people astray by their hatred for a Jewish man. They were not only mocking him instead of dealing gently with him, but were pouring vinegar on his wounds. There were other work for these chief priests to do during this time, but these men found nothing to do but to insult Jesus.

THE THIRD MOCKERY AND INSULT

The third and last mockery came from the "robbers who were crucified with him" (Matthew 27:44). To make sure that it was specifically one of the robbers, Luke states that only "one of the criminals who hung there hurled insults at him" (23:39). We don't know which robber on which side decided to insult him, but we do know that he said, "Aren't you the Christ? Save yourself and us!"

This criminal joins in with the other people who have passed Jesus by and his mockery is just an accumulation of all the hostility that was shown to him. From his perspective, if this man on the cross was what all these people said, truly he should be able to save himself and me. Certainly, we can see his motives in wanting Jesus to save him from the pain of crucifixion.

THE FAITH OF THE CRIMINAL

Hearing what he said, "the other criminal rebuked him. 'Don't you fear God,' he said, 'since you are under the same sentence? We are punished justly, for we are getting what our deeds deserve. But this man has done nothing wrong'" (Luke 23:40-41). We don't see Jesus answering those who mocked and insulted him but we do see a criminal who has spoken against one of Jesus' critics. Although everyone surrounding the crucifixion scene seemed to be negative, there was one individual who was positive and out of a bad situation, we see something good.

His rebuke to the other criminal demonstrated several things. First, he respected and feared God, and he understood God's power and authority. He was emphatically telling the other criminal to let others jeer but you must fear and respect God as the righteous judge. He understood that death could come on them in any moment and that he must respect God's coming judgment. Second, he recognized his own sin, for he knew that he was currently being punished justly for his actions. He understood that sin brings consequences of which he was experiencing at that very moment. But third, he recognized Jesus as being a man who has done nothing amiss or literally nothing out of place. Overall, his response to the other criminal was forthright and legitimate. He was horrified that the other criminal decided to follow in the same footsteps of the common people and the religious leaders. And last, his response was a means of bringing the other criminal to the hope that Jesus offered.

Then this criminal who spoke well of Jesus said to him, "Jesus, remember me when you come into your kingdom" (Luke 23:42). Instead of addressing Jesus with a title as virtually everyone else did during his ministry, this criminal instead addresses him by his first name. This is most likely his first encounter with Jesus, and with all the mockery that he hears and the sign he sees above his head, this man knows that there is something special about him. So he not only calls out to Jesus but with faith believes that he is king and that he has a kingdom. So by him asking to be remembered, he has expected an invitation already been given by Jesus. His request is more on the lines of being with Jesus and Jesus remembering him when he goes to his kingdom.

Seeing his faith, "Jesus answered him, 'I tell you the truth, today you will be with me in paradise'" (Luke 23:43). Jesus has once again shown mercy to the lost and has shown another example of healing and forgiving those who ask despite how sinful they were. His promise that the wrongdoer would be with him involves more than being in his company in paradise, for it involves sharing his victory.[337] With his words, Jesus wanted to give this man assurance that he would be with him despite the many unanswered questions he may have still had.

THE SUPPORTERS NEAR THE CROSS

Despite the groups who insulted Jesus at the cross, there were a small group who were supporters of him and his ministry. John states, "Near the cross of Jesus stood his mother, his mother's sister, Mary the wife of Clopas, and Mary Magdalene. (19:25). The "virgin" Mary was Jesus' mother and there was never a mention of Mary's sister in the Gospels. Clopas was the father of James the less, the husband of Mary the sister of the mother of Jesus. Mary Magdalene was the woman "who had been cured of evil spirits and diseases", for Jesus caused "seven demons" to come out of her (Luke 8:2). Jesus finds a mixture of disciples, friends, and relatives standing near him and from his viewpoint, these were his true family of believers.

If there was ever a moment when he could have cared for himself and his needs, it was at this moment. Yet he continued to put others first and their needs before his own. After seeing his supporters, Jesus determined to address his mother and when he saw her there "and the disciple whom he loved standing nearby, he said to his mother, 'Dear woman, here is your son,' and to the disciple, 'Here is your mother.' (19:26-27). His mom was his first concern and that is why he spoke to her first. The "disciple whom he loved standing nearby" was most likely John, for after Peter had denied Jesus, John was the only other faithful male to continue to follow him up till his death. Jesus knew his mother's cares and concerns and he desired to bring about a new relation between her and his beloved disciple. Most likely, Joseph her husband had been dead for some time and it was Jesus who had taken care of her and her needs. But no longer would this have to take place, for now Jesus was putting her mother in the hands of John.

It was at this moment when Simeon's words came true saying, "And a sword will pierce your own soul too" (Luke 2:35b). He said these words when Jesus was only a small child. Mary could have been so focused on her son's misery and torment that she may have wondered how she would have been taken care of. She saw Jesus' anguish on the cross and her heart longed for him. All the mocking and beatings that was said and done to Jesus fell on her as well and that is why Simeon stated that she too would feel the "sword" that Jesus felt. But now Jesus has provided for her at his death.

To John, Jesus was asking him to be a son who would stand by his mother. He gave him much responsibility to look after her and more than anything, it was a testimony for him to have been put in this position to care for the mother of the Savior of the world. And "from that time on, this disciple took her into his home" (John 19:27b). John was an obedient disciple and took care of Jesus' mom. Although Jesus would rise from the grave three days later, John would still have to take care of her after Jesus ascended into heaven.

Jesus' Death

THE DARKNESS AT THE SIXTH HOUR

The first sign that was given to show that the Son of Man was about to die came through nature. Matthew, Mark, and Luke state that at the sixth hour (noon), darkness came over the whole land until the ninth hour (3 p.m.), "for the sun stopped shining." This was seen as a sign by God, for nature itself refused the fact that the Son of Man was about to die.

It is interesting that this time of darkness coincides with the three hours of darkness that occurred in the book of Exodus. During this time, "the LORD said to Moses, 'Stretch out your hand toward the sky so that darkness will spread over Egypt - darkness that can be felt.' So Moses stretched out his hand toward the sky, and total darkness covered all Egypt for three days. No one could see anyone else or leave his place for three days. Yet all the Israelites had light in the places where they lived." (10:21-23). In Exodus, it was a thick darkness and perhaps, it was this same type of darkness here. In the Gospel of Peter, we are told that people went around with lamps because they thought night had come, yet they continued to fall on the ground because they could not see (5:18).

There are some prophetic references in the Old Testament that may have prepared the Jews for this moment. The prophet Zephaniah predicted that "the great day of the LORD is near - near and coming quickly...That day will be a day of wrath, a day of distress and anguish, a day of trouble and ruin, a day of darkness and gloom, a day of clouds and blackness" (1:14-15). The prophet Joel told everyone to, "blow the trumpet in Zion; sound the alarm on my holy hill. Let all who live in the land tremble, for the day of the LORD is coming. It is close at hand - a day of darkness and gloom, a day of clouds and blackness" (2:2). The most vivid prophetic warning came from Amos when he prophesied saying, "'In that day,' declares the Sovereign LORD, 'I will make the sun go down at noon and darken the earth in broad daylight. I will turn your religious feasts into mourning and all your singing into weeping. I will make all of you wear sackcloth and shave your heads. I will make that time like mourning for an only son and the end of it like a bitter day" (8:9-10).

Some reliable historical documents states that this was not just some extraordinary sign but it was an extraordinary eclipse of the sun. There was numerous Greco-Roman evidence that extraordinary signs were commonly thought to accompany the death of great or semi-divine men, and certainly there could have been one with Jesus. Origen and Eusebius quote words from a Roman historian named Phlegon in which he talks of an extraordinary solar eclipse and an earthquake about the moment of Jesus' crucifixion. Phlegon specifically states that it took place at the sixth hour of the day and it was so dark outside that the stars could be seen. He also states that there was an earthquake.

THE FIRST CRY TO GOD

About three hours after the darkness came upon the land, "Jesus cried out in a loud voice, 'Eloi, Eloi, lama sabachthani' - which means, 'My God, my God, why have you forsaken me'" (Mark 15:34). "Eloi, Eloi, lama sabachthani" are words in the Syriac tongue and were not recognized by the Roman soldiers. We don't see anywhere beforehand where Jesus ever prayed to God and addressed him as "God", but because he felt forsaken, he chose not to use an intimate word like "Father".

Many Jews including the one who had been crucified with him had mocked him and it seemed that Jesus' own Father was in no way coming to his aid. This cry was not an accusation against God, but we do see that he had to learn "obedience from the things he suffered" and at the same time, he was fully human.

Yet Jesus said these very words to fulfill prophecy spoken in Psalm 22 as he felt alone and deprived on the cross. In this passage, the psalmist said, "My God, my God, why have you forsaken me? Why are you so far from saving me, so far from the words of my groaning? O my God, I cry out by day, but you do not answer, by night, and am not silent" (22:1-2). Since Jesus' words are prophetic words from the psalmist, we can also get a glimpse as to why he spoke his words. He stated them because he felt that God was "far from saving" him, far from his groaning, and even when he cried out to God, he did not answer.

THE SECOND OFFERING OF WINE

After he said these words, some of the bystanders heard him and said, "He's calling Elijah" (Matthew 27:47), for they did not recognize the Syriac tongue. Elijah was a great historical figure as well as one who had popular expectations in the future. Yet the soldiers saw an opportunity for mockery during this last moment of his life.

So "immediately one of them ran and got a sponge. He filled it with wine vinegar, put it on a stick, and offered it to Jesus to drink. The rest said, 'Now leave him alone. Let's see if Elijah comes to save him'" (Matthew 27:48-49). For a casual encounter, vinegar wine was an enjoyable and social drink as seen from Ruth 2:14. In a second usage, vinegar with wine was meant to revive Jesus and keep him alive a few more moments so that he would not die so soon, for the soldiers wanted to see whether Elijah would come or not to his aid. Vinegary wine could certainly revive an individual, for when this bitter odor was put under someone's nose, it would have the effect of revitalization.

Yet, the soldiers as a whole and the one particular soldier who ran to get the vinegar wine were prophetically fulfilling Scripture, for the psalmist stated, "Scorn has broken my heart and has left me helpless; I looked for sympathy, but there was none, for comforters, but I found none. They put gall in my food and gave me vinegar for my thirst. May the table set before them become a snare; may it become retribution and a trap. (69:20-22). We see that it was out of scorn that they gave him this vinegar wine and yet God allowed this to happen as a sign to show the validity of the Old Testament Scriptures.

THE THIRD OFFERING OF WINE

The book of John states Jesus' last thoughts and actions saying, "Later, knowing that all was now completed, and so that the Scripture would be fulfilled, Jesus said, 'I am thirsty'" (19:28). Different from the second offering of wine, this third offering was purposely, for he intentionally asked for water and nothing that would slow down the process of crucifixion. But specifically he just wanted something to wet his parched lips and dry throat so he could fulfill Scripture one more time. In Psalm 69, Jesus was most likely trying to deliberately fulfill the situation he visualized and if this was the case, he would also be responsible for the immediate actions he took after the wine was offered to him.

John states that "a jar of wine vinegar was there" probably the same wine one of the soldiers tried to give him before, and "they soaked a sponge in it, put the sponge on a stalk of the hyssop plant, and lifted it to Jesus' lips" (John 19:29). A hyssop was a plant used by the Hebrews in their ritual sprinklings and was used early in connection with the institution of the Jewish Passover. It was capable of producing a stem three or four feet in length. Biblical descriptions of hyssop may not have always referred to the same plant. It could be portrayed as a small bushy plant that could grow out of cracks in the walls, a plant that I Kings 4:33 implies as being the humblest of shrubs. But in our case, a much better solution is to accept the fact that John meant the biblical hyssop despite the physical implausibility caused by the fragility of that plant.[338] Soldiers would have had both the wine and a lance to put the sponge filled with it up to Jesus' lips, for his head was about eye level to them.

THE DEATH CRY

"It is Finished"

But Jesus never drank the wine, for "when he had received the drink, Jesus said, 'It is finished'" (John 19:30). In the Greek, *tetelestai* (It is finished) is a one word which means "paid in full." In Mark's gospel, "Jesus cried with a loud voice, and gave up the ghost" (15:37) and we know that this loud voice stated these very words. Jesus said these words in a loud voice to show an earnestness and passion. concerning what he said and so that everyone around him might take notice of it.

Isaiah states, "Surely he took up our infirmities and carried our sorrows, yet we considered him stricken by God, smitten by him, and afflicted. But he was pierced for our transgressions, he was crushed for our iniquities; the punishment that brought us peace was upon him, and by his wounds we are healed" (53:4-5). This cry here was not the cry of a looser but of a winner. He had totally completed the work that his Father sent him to do and he had purposefully fulfilled prophecy in so many ways. At the same time, redemption was complete for mankind, for he had completed his act of reconciliation and had brought everlasting salvation to all those who trust in him.

After he stated those words, "he bowed his head and gave up his spirit" (John 19:30). Although we see a picture of physical exhaustion, we don't see a picture of anyone gaining victory over him. John 10:17-18 states, "The reason my Father loves me is that I lay down my life, only to take it up again. No one takes it from me, but I lay it down of my own accord. I have authority to lay it down and authority to take it up again. This command I received from my Father." We see him dying peacefully and of his own act, and he gave his life so that a greater purpose could unfold.

"Father, into your hands I commit my spirit"

Luke 23:46 states that "Jesus called out with a loud voice, 'Father, into your hands I commit my spirit.' When he had said this, he breathed his last." When Jesus cried out with a loud voice, John 19:30 states that he said the words, "It is finished!" therefore, the words, "Father, into your hands I commit my spirit" were not said in a loud voice but rather in one's everyday voice. It is interesting to know that this word "spirit" is not simply a partial component of the human being as in "soul" and body, but it is the living self or life power that goes beyond death.[339] Now his work was finished and there was no reason any longer for him to stay around.

Yet it was the psalmist in the Old Testament that said these exact words saying, "Into your hands I commit my spirit; redeem me, O Lord, the God of truth" (Psalm 31:5). Jesus borrowed these words from David, for he wanted to show the world that he came to fulfill Scripture. By stating these words, he was offering himself to be used by God the Father not only through his death but also through his resurrection.

Daniel the prophet prophetically stated that this drastic episode in Jesus' life would occur saying, "Know and understand this: From the issuing of the decree to restore and rebuild Jerusalem until the Anointed One, the ruler, comes, there will be seven 'sevens,' and sixty-two 'sevens.' It will be rebuilt with streets and a trench, but in times of trouble. After the sixty-two 'sevens,' the Anointed One will be cut off and will have nothing" (9:25-26). "Seven sevens" means 70 times 7 or 490 years. Within these years, the prophet stated that dark and hard times would occur. Although the Jewish city and temple would be destroyed within this time frame, the primary concern for the prophet would be that of the cutting off of the Messiah. Concerning the Messiah, the carnal Jews looked for one who should deliver them from the Roman yoke and give them temporal power and wealth. However, they were here told that the Messiah should come on another errand, purely spiritual. Christ came to take away sin.[340] Sadly, although Daniel prophesied this fact hundreds of years earlier, the Jews paid no attention to it.

THE FACTS OF JESUS' DEATH

Did Jesus really die or was there a chance that he was still alive? The apostle John sheds light on this matter. He states that right after he died which was on the day of Preparation, "the Jews did not want the bodies left on the crosses during the Sabbath." So "they asked Pilate to have the legs broken and the bodies taken down" (19:31) of those who were on the cross. All we know was that there was at least three people crucified and there could have been more. It was a reproach if dead bodies were left hanging on the crosses, for they were not to be left at any time (Deuteronomy 21:22-23). Many strangers from all over came to Jerusalem and it would have been an offence to them.[341] If the criminal's legs were broken, which was often done with clubs, their death would be hastened.

So "the soldiers therefore came and broke the legs of the first man who had been crucified with Jesus, and then those of the other. But when they came to Jesus and found that he was already dead, they did not break his legs" (John 19:32-33). Jesus never took a pain numbing substance and even more, he suffered greatly before he even came to Golgotha. So now in full view of all the Romans, they physically saw that he was dead.

But this did not suffice them, for they wanted to make sure that all of their criminals were in fact dead. This test was made whether Jesus was deceased or not and thus "one of the soldiers pierced Jesus' side with a spear, bringing a sudden flow of blood and water" (John 19:34). Tradition says that this soldier's name was Longinus.[342] This wound in him would have been both deep and wide. The Gospel writer probably never understood the medial significance of what he recorded, for which eyewitness testimony is claimed. Medical doctors who have studied this issue usually agree that this is a very accurate medical description. The water probably proceeded from the pericardium, the sac that surrounds the heart, while the blood came from the right side of the heart. Even if Jesus was alive before he was stabbed, the lance would almost certainly have killed him.[343] God had a further purpose in this, for he wanted to give evidence of the truth of his death, in order to prove his resurrection.

We know that this author (John) was present at the crucifixion cite, for Jesus acknowledged him and told him, "Here is your mother" (John 19:27). After stating the facts of his death, he states, "The man who saw it has given testimony, and his testimony is true. He knows that he tells the truth, and he testifies so that you also may believe" (John 19:35). John wrote faithfully not because of what he heard because of what he saw.

THE PHYSIOLOGICAL CAUSES OF JESUS' DEATH

There are organs that are vital to the body's existence, hence vital organs, and they include the brain, liver, heart, intestines, kidney, pancreas, stomach, and lungs. Yet, the process of crucifixion pierces no vital organ. So then what were the physical and organic factors that could have caused Jesus to die during crucifixion's heinous process?

The Respiratory Muscles Theory

One theory is called the Respiratory Muscles Theory. During normal breathing, the predominant muscle used is the diaphragm. During exercise, many muscles of respiration are used including the scalene muscles and there are other important respiration muscles include those of the abdominal wall (including the rectus abdominus, and the internal and external obliques.). Perhaps because of the effects of all his preceding suffering, his respiratory muscles were tantalized and it may have been that the scourging caused a hemorrhage in the pleural cavity between the ribs and the lungs producing fluid that ultimately separated into light serous and dark red parts.

The Hypovolemic Shock Theory

A second theory is called the Hypovolemic Shock Theory. In the areas of medicine and physiology, hypovolemic is the condition of decreased blood or specifically plasma in the body. The loss of about one-fifth or more of the normal blood volume, which could cause the heart not to be able to supply enough blood to the body, produces this shock. Even more, larger and more rapid blood volume loss results in severe shock. The rapid loss of blood contributes to one experiencing extreme thirst and the kidneys could shut down to preserve body fluids.

Dr. W. D. Edwards combines asphyxia and shock to his death and indeed insufficiency of blood to the various parts of the body[344] could have also produced this shock. Another author, Wilkinson, stated that both psychological and physical reasons would have produced this shock, as well as the spiritual agony in Gethsemane, exposure for three to six hours on the cross, and the loss of blood in the scourging. He believes that shock brought on by dehydration and the loss of blood is the only plausible medical explanation for his death.

Looking at these details and at Jesus' trial and execution, the Gospels may have provided evidence that he may have experienced this shock.   In addition to his spiritual agony in Gethsemane and his rare sleep the night before, he was flogged during Pilate's second trial. Then as he carried his cross out of the city leading to the hills of Golgotha, something happened so that soldiers realized he was unable to carry it any longer. Most likely he passed out or collapsed because of a lack of blood and even fluids. Knowing that he was unable to carry his cross, the soldiers saw Simon and "compelled" him to carry the cross. A second indicator comes from the words Jesus said on cross, "I thirst!" This showed that his body desired to replenish his fluids. He had six interrogations beginning the night before and he may not have received any fluids during that time either.

One of the symptoms of this shock would have been a sustained rapid heartbeat and this would cause fluids to gather around the lungs and heart. These fluids around the heart are called the pericardial effusion and around the lungs they are called the pleural effusion. This physiological fact explains why both blood and water came out when the soldier pierced his right side.

Happenings after Jesus' death

There were several happenings, most from nature itself, which occurred after Jesus gave up the ghost that the gospel writers recorded, and they were not only significant but predetermined. They were all apocalyptic signs that illustrate the partial fulfillment of the divine judgment implied by the Old Testament prophets.

It was obvious to those surrounding Jesus' cross and those who interacted with him during that day that his death was of no coincidence seeing the obvious events that took place immediately after his death. Those who were mocking and laughing at him during his trial and on the wooden cross were certainly not laughing immediately after he died. Why? Because the God of heaven revealed himself in a way that demonstrated his anger and contempt to those in opposition to his only begotten Son.

THE RENDING OF THE SANCTUARY VEIL

Matthew makes it clear that when Jesus died, "the curtain of the temple was torn in two from top to bottom" "at that moment" (Matthew 27:50-51). Luke states that it happened at about the sixth hour (23:44-45). In the order of events, Luke does put the rending of the sanctuary veil just before Jesus death, but most likely it happened immediately after he died.

Hebrews 9 gives a description of the veils or curtains that were located in the Israelite Tabernacle. The author states that there was in the first room a lamp stand, the table and the consecrated bread and apparently they were behind the first curtain. "Behind the second curtain was a room called the Most Holy Place, which had the golden altar of incense and the gold-covered Ark of the Covenant". "When everything had been arranged like this, the priests entered regularly into the outer room to carry on their ministry. But only the high priest entered the inner room, and that only once a year, and never without blood, which he offered for himself and for the sins the people had committed in ignorance" (9:2-7). To the Jews, the tabernacle was an important part of their religious life and daily experience.

In addition, there have been some portrayals of the veils from history. The outer veil was a huge linen draw curtain in the entrance porch that was ninety feet high. According to Josephus it had four different colors symbolizing the elements of the universe (fire, earth, air, water) and portrayed the panorama of the heavens.[345]

But who rented the veil rent? Certainly and without doubt, God was the agent. At the beginning of creation, he "rent" the heavens so that he could begin his impressive work of creation. Now he was renting the veil of the sanctuary and in the next verse, a Gentile would see his work, confess his existence, and understand that Jesus was his Son. This action by God is seen as negative, for Jesus had earlier chastised Jerusalem in stating, "O Jerusalem, Jerusalem, you who kill the prophets and stone those sent to you, how often I have longed to gather your children together, as a hen gathers her chicks under her wings, but you were not willing. Look, your house is left to you desolate" (Matthew 23:37-38). He actually predicted that something bad would happen not only within the temple, but to the temple itself, and this was certainly not a good thing for the Jews.

What was significant about God renting the veil? Well, the veil was what separated a holy God from sinful man and yet Mark 15:38 states that it was torn "from top to bottom" and "into two" and thus, it was not reparable. As a result, the building that continued to stand there was no longer a holy place anymore. God could not be approached any type of way and if any man entered beyond that veil except the high priest, he would die. But after the death of Christ, God ripped the veil to allow easy access between himself and man, and he would no longer dwell in temples made by hand. No longer would ceremonial law have to be enforced and no longer would Jews and Gentiles have to be separated, for, according to Hebrews, Jesus passed through the veil, which was his flesh, to the Holy of Holies in order to consummate there the sacrifice begun on the cross. By doing this, he opened the way for believers to enter the heavenly sanctum. Thus, God knew what he was doing so that man could have free access to him.

THE SHAKING OF THE EARTH

Matthew 27:51 states that at around this time, "the earth shook". We will see later that this earthquake was local for we see that the rocks were rent and the graves were open for the saints to enter into Jerusalem. The Jews would have recognized these signs as familiar apocalyptic signals of the last times stated in the Old Testament.

Yet this happening was predicted from Isaiah the prophet. There are several passages that may have spoken of this phenomena and one of them comes from Isaiah 13 where the prophet declared that God "will make the heavens tremble, and the earth will shake from its place at the wrath of the LORD Almighty, in the day of his burning anger" (13:10;13).

A more specific prophecy is given in Isaiah 24. Although this passage could certainly pertain to the apocalyptic writings in Revelations, it could also pertain to the happenings that occurred after Jesus' death. The first verse states, "See, the LORD is going to lay waste the earth and devastate it. He will ruin its face and scatter its inhabitants." This verse sets the tone for the verses that lie ahead, including verse 17-19, stating, "Terror and pit and snare await you, O people of the earth. Whoever flees at the sound of terror will fall into a pit. Whoever climbs out of the pit will be caught in a snare. The floodgates of the heavens are opened and the foundations of the earth shake. The earth is broken up, the earth is split asunder, and the earth is thoroughly shaken."

Perhaps the most detailed passage in the Old Testament comes from Joel's prophecy which states, "The LORD will roar from Zion and thunder from Jerusalem; the earth and the sky will tremble. But the LORD will be a refuge for his people, a stronghold for the people of Israel" (3:16). This prophecy specifically states that this "thunder" and "tremble" will take place "from Zion" or Jerusalem.

THE RENDING OF THE ROCKS

The rending of the rocks is a direct result of the earthquake that had just occurred. Earlier during Jesus' ministry when he made his triumphal entry into Jerusalem, "some of the Pharisees in the crowd said to Jesus, 'Teacher, rebuke your disciples!'" But Jesus replied saying, "I tell you, if they keep quiet, the stones will cry out" (Luke 19:39-40). Evidently, most all of the religious leaders did not bless him, the stones or rocks evidently cried out.

Certainly it was of no coincidence that creation itself acted in this way. This earthquake, which caused the rocks to "rent", was certainly visible to many people, for Jerusalem was a large city and this phenomenon took place during a busy weekend when many people from all over the empire came to celebrate the feast.

Yet the prophets in the Old Testament predicted that this would specifically take place. In general, Jeremiah 4:24 states that the shaking the earth was a sign of divine judgment of the last times. Stated specifically to Jerusalem, this prophet stated, "I looked at the mountains, and they were quaking. All the hills were swaying". The prophet Nahum prophesied and spoke of the jealous and avenging God stating, "The mountains quake before him and the hills melt away. The earth trembles at his presence, the world and all who live in it. Who can withstand his indignation? Who can endure his fierce anger? His wrath is poured out like fire; the rocks are shattered before him" (1:5-6).

In themselves these first three occurrences could have been natural since Palestine is prone to earthquakes. Yet, as with the darkness over all the earth, the timing shows that God was active in all this. In addition, these phenomena soon after Jesus died were a type of response given by God. Moments ago, Jesus stated to his Father, "My God, my God, why have you forsaken me" (Mark 15:34), but now that the temple sanctuary veil was torn and a centurion would soon confess him as God's Son, it shows that God had not forsaken him at all.

THE RAISING OF THE SAINT'S

In addition to the quakes, "the tombs broke open and the bodies of many holy people who had died were raised to life" (Matthew 27:52). Certainly if an earthquake was violent enough, it would open the tombs but no earthquake in itself could raise a dead body to life. Yet this is one of the most perplexing passages in the book of Matthew, for no other Gospel source mentions this fact nor does history confirm this occurrence. In addition, Matthew himself does not give us more details.

Yet this certainly did occur because this specific phenomenon was prophesied long ago. Isaiah 26:19 states, "But your dead will live; their bodies will rise. You who dwell in the dust, wake up and shout for joy. Your dew is like the dew of the morning; the earth will give birth to her dead." Ezekiel 37 may have been partially fulfilled during this phenomenon stating, "O my people, I am going to open your graves and bring you up from them; I will bring you back to the land of Israel. Then you, my people, will know that I am the LORD, when I open your graves and bring you up from them'" (37:12-13). This prophecy could have been fulfilled in several ways but it seems that it certainly had some specific applications during this occurrence. The saints of God are assured that they will come to know the Lord because of him opening up their tombs and leading them to Jerusalem.

Who were these saints? Some think that they were the ancient patriarchs who were much concerned in being buried in the land of Canaan. Others think these who were modern saints, such as had seen Christ in the flesh, but died before him. They may even have been the martyrs who in the Old Testament times had sealed the truths of God with their blood.[346]

Regardless, they were miraculously raised to serve as a testimony to the power of God. This occurrences was a glorious symbolic proclamation that Jesus had just overcome death in victory and the saints were "risen" so that they could accompany him when he would soon rise from the grave.

THE SAINTS ENTERING JERUSALEM

After the tombs were opened and their bodies came to life, these saints "came out of the tombs, and after Jesus' resurrection they went into the holy city and appeared to many people" (Matthew 27:53). The "holy city" is just another reference to Jerusalem as seen in Nehemiah 11:1. But this term is even given a greater symbolism, for John stated in Revelation that he "saw the Holy City, the new Jerusalem, coming down out of heaven from God, prepared as a bride beautifully dressed for her husband" (21:2).

The first few apocalyptic signs have been negative (darkness, rent sanctuary veil, earthquake), but this sign along with the opening of the tombs show the positive side of the divine judgment centered around the death of God's Son. The good are rewarded and the evil punished.[347] Thus it seems that Matthew is showing that the divine judgment has begun with both the negative and the positive.

Because Matthew's gospels state that the tombs were open and that the saints entered into Jerusalem, he gives us a more vivid picture of where the tombs were located. His context (27:53-54), in which the opening of the tombs is part of the phenomena visible to the centurion and other guards on Golgotha and in which those raised become visible in the holy city, indicates that the tombs were of the saints in the Jerusalem area close to where Jesus died.[348]

THE REACTION OF THE CENTURION AND GUARDS

Now we are about to see how God turned an "outsider" to recognize what the Jewish leaders of Israel could not. Matthew 27:54 states that "when the centurion and those with him who were guarding Jesus saw the earthquake and all that had happened, they were terrified, and exclaimed, 'Surely he was the Son of God!'" Mark states specifically that the centurion was the one who "stood there in front of Jesus" and when he heard his cry and saw how he died, he said those same words (15:39). Luke states that after he saw "what had happened" (earthquake, rocks rent, and darkness) he "praised God and said, 'Surely this was a righteous man'" (23:47).

The centurion was not only a military officer of the Roman Government but was the main superintendent over Jesus' execution. There were other soldiers present as well beneath him but he was the main one in charge. Not only did this lead centurion see what was going on but all of the other guards witnessed these events and although they were men of high rank, these events terrified them. They quickly understood that these occurrences were not natural but rather supernatural.

Previously, they had just mocked Jesus in the Praetorium and they continued to mock him while he was on the cross. They even divided up his clothes to see who would take them. They heard one of the criminals tell the other that he has done nothing amiss and they heard the "teachers of the law mocked him among themselves" saying, "Let this Christ, this King of Israel, come down now from the cross, that we may see and believe" (Mark 15:31-32). But now after they had seen these happenings and after putting together all that the criminal, the chief priests, and Pilate had stated about him, they believed. Because of all of their fears, they voiced their awe by stating Jesus' character and identity. They not only stated that he was "the Son of God" and "a righteous man" but they also "praised God." Ironically, this outsider was the first one to see Jesus in Jerusalem after his death and he glorifies God because of it.

It is interesting to see that out of all the words this centurion could have used to describe Jesus, he used the term "Son of God." The religious leaders had earlier accused him of blaspheming by claiming to do things that God alone could do. Yet, this military officer recognized that Jesus was no charlatan but actually was what he claimed to be. These words were remarkable because it shows that even the hardened Roman centurion was able to realize who Jesus was among all the injustice, mockery, and cruelty. Although he had been in charge of countless criminals, he understood the uniqueness of Jesus.

It is of no coincidence that the psalmist had already prophesied of people from other nations coming to the Lord. Psalm 22:28 states, "All the ends of the earth will remember and turn to the LORD, and all the families of the nations will bow down before him." The centurion and the guards who were Romans actually worshipped and reverenced Jesus the Jew as being God's Son, and by confessing Jesus, he becomes an example of the salvation brought to the Gentiles. Psalm 86:9 similarly states, "All the nations you have made will come and worship before you, O Lord; they will bring glory to your name." After Jesus' ascension, Acts 10 recounts how another Roman centurion named Cornelius came spontaneously to faith in Jesus. In addition, Acts 16:25-34 tells of a Roman guard in Philippi was convert by the apostle Paul.

THE REACTION OF THE PEOPLE IN THE CROWD

Not only did the Roman guards and centurion observe what was happening but Luke 23:48 states that there were "people who had gathered to witness this sight" and they "saw what took place." Luke does not specifically state what sex these people were. Yet, we can generally believe that they were a mixture of men and women. Certainly, they were among those who were mocking him after seeing the sign above his head.

Yet after seeing what happened, they "beat their breasts and went away" (Luke 23:48). This striking of the breasts not only represents their extreme sorrow but their repentance. Their mourning was not simply for the passing of a human life but for his unjust execution. The repentance of the crowd was not on the level of that of the centurion, for they neither gave glory to God nor did they confessed Jesus. But they beat their breasts implicitly signifying, "Be merciful to us sinner."[349] It was obvious that these people knew they were wrong, yet they could not do anything about their past actions and behaviors. They were sadly led astray by the religious leaders and they now saw how easily deceived they were.

THE REACTION OF HIS SUPPORTERS

Gratefully, Jesus did have supporters there watching what took place. Matthew states that "many women were there, watching from a distance" (Matthew 27:55). To specify who they were, he continues to state that they were the ones who "had followed Jesus from Galilee to care for his needs." Mark specifically states their names, "Mary Magdalene, Mary the mother of James the younger and of Joses, and Salome" (15:40), who apparently was the "mother of Zebedee's sons" (Matthew 27:56). Mary "Magdalene" was from Magdala on the North West shore of the Sea of Galilee.

By Matthew stating "among them" signifies that there were other women in addition to these who took care of Jesus' needs and thus, there were other women there at the cross. Mark confirms this by stating that "many other women who had come up with him to Jerusalem were also there" (Mark 15:41). Although they came up from Jerusalem, their location was in the same vicinity as the centurion and the guards. These women were truly followers of Jesus, for when all of his disciples fled and deserted him, they stayed with him. The fact that they are described as "standing" there, not having "returned" or gone away as did the crowds of the previous verse, prepares readers for what was still to come. In Luke, women will not only see where Jesus is buried but will immediately go and prepare spices and ointments, so that as soon as the prescribed Sabbath rest is over, they can set out for the tomb with the spices.[350]

These women were also apart of the psalmists prophecy, for Psalm 38:11 states, "My friends and companions avoid me because of my wounds; my neighbors stay far away." This fits rights in with Matthew 27:55 which stated that "many women were there, watching from a distance." Certainly they were his friends for they had followed him from Galilee to care for his needs. Yet because of the repugnance of the cross, they were located a good distance away.

THE UNIQUENESS OF JESUS' DEATH

In looking at these occurrences, it was widely understood in antiquity that the gods frequently gave extraordinary signs at the death of noble or important figures. For example, there was an eclipse of the moon on the night when Herod the Great put to death Mathias who had stirred up youth to purify the temple by removing an eagle Herod had placed there.[351] There were some reported occurrences that took place when Julius Caesar died, for history records that eclipses were "thought" to have marked his death along with Romulus and Virgil. Cassius Dio, a Roman historian, reported signs at the death of Claudius, including a comet seen for a long time, a shower of blood, a thunderbolt striking the soldier's standards, and the opening by itself of the temple of Jupiter Victor.[352] Josephus, a Jewish historian and apologist, tells of some eight wonders that occurred between 60-70 A.D. and served as ominous, God-given signs of the coming desolation of the Jerusalem Temple by the Romans. He said that in the heavens were a sword-shaped star and a comet that continued for a year.[353]

Perhaps, these were supernatural occurrences. But the occurrences centered around Jesus' death were far greater and supernatural than all those from history. Some could justify that the earthquakes that occurred happened because Palestine actually had occasional earthquakes. Even the eclipse that took place could have been justified as well. However, the fact that the graves were opened of only the saints and no one else could only have been caused by God. For these saints to have all migrated to the same city and for them to have all arrived there only after Jesus' resurrection was certainly unique and humanly impossible.

The Burial of Jesus

The burial of Jesus took place on the "day of Preparation" along with his crucifixion (John 19:14, 31, 42). Preparation day included the preparation of food, completing work and spiritual purification. The Hebrew day began at 6:00 a.m. and ended at 6:00 p.m., so the day of preparation extended from 6:00 p.m. on Thursday until the beginning of the Sabbath at 6:00 p.m. Friday.[354] So Friday was the day before the Sabbath and because the "evening approached" (Matthew 27:57), there was an urgency in getting Jesus buried.

JOSEPH OF ARIMATHEA

His Person and Character

Understanding that the day of Preparation was at hand, the Gospel writers set the tone for a man named Joseph. Matthew 27 states that "as evening approached, there came a rich man from Arimathea, named Joseph." Understanding the fact that he was rich, how could he serve as a model example to future Christians when Jesus stated that "it is hard for a rich man to enter the Kingdom of Heaven" and that "it is easier for a camel to go through the eye of a needle than for a rich man to enter the Kingdom of God" (Matthew 19:23-24)? Seemingly, the author wanted to portray to his audience that it was possible to be rich and to be a "disciple" of Jesus even though another rich man turned away from Jesus (Matthew 19:21-22).

He was from Arimathea, a location that is unknown. Yet Luke does describe it as a Jewish city, for he states that "he came from the Judean town of Arimathea" (23:51). Thus, it seems that this town was of no importance, for it had no other Scriptural symbolisms within history, and yet God would use a man from an unknown town to do a significant work for his Son.

His civil position consisted of him being "a prominent member of the Council" (Mark 15:43) and perhaps his riches allowed him to have been chosen to this prominent position. The word "council" means a company of individuals and the "Council" was spoken of as "counselors" who sat in public trials with the governor of a province as seen in Acts 25:12. In general, the Sanhedrin were the Jewish Council during Jesus day and they were the highest council of the land. Although Joseph sat on the "Council", the Gospels stated that he did not "consent to their decision and action" (Luke 23:51) in condemning Jesus to death. Either he was there for the trial and silently did not agree with the other Sanhedrin members or he may have not even been present during the trail because the other members may have known that he would not vote against him. Regardless, not all of the members of the Sanhedrin agreed with condemning Jesus and certainly Joseph was one of these persons.

In addition, he was converted by Jesus, for he eventually "had himself become a disciple of Jesus" (Matthew 27:57). But he was a disciple in secrete "because he feared the Jews" (John 19:38). Luke

23:50 states that he was a "good and upright man and he was waiting for the Kingdom of God.

His Request to Pilate

Although he feared the Jews, he did make a bold move and went to Pilate and "asked for Jesus' body" (Mark 15:43). We now see him with confidence and assurance to act against his fellow Sanhedrin "friends". Although he was either absence or silent when the council sentenced Jesus to death, he came back to defend him and to show his support.

By him going to Pilate, Joseph knew at least three aspects of Jewish culture. First, he knew the law concerning dead bodies left on crosses. The apostle John had already made it clear that it was the day of Preparation and "the Jews did not want the bodies left on the crosses during the Sabbath." The law behind this was the Old Testament command stating that if a man guilty of a capital offense was put to death and his body was hung on a tree, one must not leave his body on the tree overnight. They had to be sure to bury him that same day because anyone who was hung on a tree was under God's curse" (Deuteronomy 21:22-23). Joseph being a Jew seemingly knew of this law and felt obligated to bury him before sunset.

Second, he knew that it was common that those who hung on the cross fed the crows with their bodies. Not only did the crows feed on the body but after the soldiers guarded the body until death, it was left for the scavenger dog or other wild beasts to finish the brutal job.[355] In addition, he knew as Tacitus reported that people sentenced to death forfeited their property and were forbidden burial.

And third, he understood the Jewish mindset which included their desire to get Jewish bodies, including Jesus, off the cross before sunset. He knew that it was a dishonor to display a body on the cross during the Passover season and that the Romans were renowned to grant the bodies of deceased criminals to friends or relatives for proper burial.

Why was Joseph able to go to Pilate the procurator with confidence to ask for Jesus' body? First, political authority had crucified Jesus and it also took authority or at least authority's permission to bury him.[356] Second, Joseph was rich and among the few who were in the upper echelon of society and thus he would have been able to have access to Pilate. And third, he had influence, for he was not only a council member but was respected. In general, if one had influence, one was not crucified, and if one was crucified, one would not have influence enough to obtain burial. It would have been impossible, without influence or bribery, to obtain a crucified corpse. And it might also be very dangerous to request it.[357] Yet he had a special position and ranking with the Romans and his status as a Sanhedrin would undoubtedly have helped.

His Granted Request

After he asked for the body, "Pilate was surprised to hear that he was already dead. Summoning the centurion, he asked him if Jesus had already died. When he learned from the centurion that it was so, he gave the body to Joseph" (Mark 15:44-45). As already stated, crucified victims usually stayed alive for several days, but after Pilate found out from the lead centurion that Jesus was indeed dead, he granted Joseph's request. Pilate would not have given Jesus over to one of his disciples if they had political objectives and because he knew this, he gave him over to Joseph. At the same time, it seems that neither he nor the Sanhedrin had made any plans to give Jesus anything that would resemble an honorable burial and that is why Joseph took the initiative to give him one.

The fact that Pilate granted his request perhaps confirms the gospels conviction that Pilate really believed Jesus to be innocent.[358] We had seen earlier that he was the one who did not really exert himself on Jesus' behalf, for he could have freed him. But now he shows his certainty that Jesus was indeed innocent and was treated unjustly. Although we have seen Jesus given over by one antagonist to another (Judas, the Jews, Pilate, Herod, etc.), he is now given over, but to someone who loves him.

His Preparation of Jesus' Body

After receiving permission, Joseph "took it [Jesus' body] down" from the cross (Luke 23:53) and "took the body away" (John 19:38). Yet he did not do all this by himself, for "he was accompanied by Nicodemus, the man who earlier had visited Jesus at night" (John

19:39). When Jesus said, "But I, when I am lifted up from the earth, will draw all men to myself" (John 12:32), Joseph and Nicodemus were the first two drawn from those who had not publicly remained with him.

Nicodemus' name means "innocent of blood" and he is identified as a Pharisee, "a member of the Jewish ruling council" (John 3:1). Like Joseph, he was a member of the Sanhedrin, he was "a teacher of Israel" (John 3:10), and he was interested in the kingdom. Jesus had told him earlier that he would never see the Kingdom of God without being "born again" and/or "born of water and the Spirit." True to his name, he defended Christ before his peers as seen in John 7:51. Despite the appeal he felt for Jesus as a teacher from God, he was not eager at first to disclose openly his interests for him. But now he had come publicly before sunset to meet his needs. At this moment, we see these two men are now just becoming public disciples of Jesus.

After taking the body down, Joseph "brought a mixture of myrrh and aloes, about seventy-five pounds" (John 19:39) and he "brought some linen clothe" (Mark 15:46). Then both he and Nicodemus wrapped Jesus' body "in a clean linen cloth" (Matthew 27:59). Although the King James Version states "about a hundred pounds", we must understand that the roman *litra* or pound was about twelve ounces, and so the amount would be about seventy-five of our pounds.[359] Yet, seventy-five pounds of spices would have been an extremely amount of spices (myrrh and aloes). If powdered or fragmented spices are meant, such a weight would fill a considerable space in the tomb and smother the corpse under a mound.[360]

From Joseph and Nicodemus' point of view, they desired to give Jesus a burial fit for a king. This view corresponds well with the sign above Jesus' head stating "the King of the Jews." History has even shown that royal burials were given a large amount of spices, for the Jewish historian Josephus records that five hundred servants were required to carry the spices at the burial of Herod the Great.[361] Although Martha's sister Mary was chastised by Judas for using one "litra" of fragrance to anoint Jesus' feet, Joseph and Nicodemus use a hundred "litra" or seventy-five pound of fragrance for his burial.

The fact that both men brought some linen clothe to wrap him in shows that they followed the burial customs of that day the best they could (John 19:40), especially since they had little time. We know that their law mentions burial customs such as washing and anointing the corpse, laying it out and binding up the chin, and closing the eyes.[362] Since Joseph would not have touched the body by himself, for he would have become impure, he would have had others to accomplish this task.

Yet it seems by them bringing so much fragrance that they failed to understand that Jesus would live beyond his death and unfortunately, they disregarded his teachings concerning the fact that he would rise again. Their actions seemed as if they had come to a dead end, for they considered his burial as ultimate and final.

His Placement of Jesus' Body

After the preparation, they placed his body in Joseph's "new tomb that he had cut out of the rock" (Matthew 27:60). Not only was it a "new" tomb but it was one "in which no one had yet been laid" (Luke 23:53). The fact that the tomb was cut out of rock would not only help to identify the tomb near the garden but would signify that only a rich man would probably have this type of tomb.

John specifically gives the location of where they placed Jesus' body stating that "there was a garden, and in the garden a new tomb. Because it was the Jewish day of Preparation and since the tomb was nearby, they laid Jesus there" (19:41-42). Very likely, Jesus was crucified and buried north of Jerusalem, and each of the two suggested places for Jesus' death and resurrection bear this fact that it was close to the crucifixion cite.

John 20:12 may give the impression that Jesus' body was placed on a bench or on the shelf (acrosolia), for after his resurrection, there were two angels, one seated at the head and the other at the foot of the place where Jesus had lain. The tomb would have a small opening and possibly more than one partition where bodies were laid after spices, ointments, and linen strips were placed on them. The only types of tombs in the Greco-Roman world the entailed bending over in order to go through were acrosolia (bend tombs). These types of tombs were not only rare but were reserved for the wealthy and higher class of society. Even more authoritative, archaeologists have unearthed more than a few other acrosolia near Jesus' traditional burial. The incidental details that the tomb was unused and belonged to Joseph are quite probable, since Joseph could not lay the body of a criminal in just any tomb, especially since this would defile the bodies of any family members also reposing there.[363]

After placing his body in a tomb, Jesus had most likely several men to roll "a big stone in front of the entrance to the tomb" (Matthew 27:60). This wheel-shaped stone would have been the "door" of the tomb and would have been extremely heavy. The stone would have typically been put into a groove and it would have been settled down into channel. This would have prevented one or two men from moving the stone and disturbing the body. This was the customary way to seal an expensive tomb. But little did they all know that Jesus would only borrow that space for a few days.

His Accompany by Women

Matthew, Mark, and Luke make it clear that "the women who had come with Jesus from Galilee followed Joseph" (Luke 23:55). Joseph was clearly the leader and the women are seen now as coming and following him. It makes since that they knew of him going to Pilate to request Jesus' body and as soon as Pilate allowed him to take the body off the cross, the women were notified. John, who was there at the cross, seems to now have disappeared and now the women are following Joseph to the burial site.

These are the same ladies who have served Jesus in his public ministry out of their own means. Now they seem to be "serving" him till his death. How ironic and embarrassing it was for the writers to boldly proclaim that it was the women who followed Jesus all the way to his burial site and not his disciples. In a culture that considered women impure, God used them to be heroes and faithful followers of his Son.

The Gospels make it clear not only who these women were but also what they saw. The women were Mary Magdalene and Mary the mother of Joses (Mark 15:47) and the three things they saw were "the tomb", "how his body was laid in it" (Luke 23:55), and "where he was laid" (Mark 15:47). At the tomb site, the women did not have an active role, for they were "sitting there opposite the tomb" (Matthew 27:61).

After the completion of the burial, these women "went home and prepared spices and perfumes. But they rested on the Sabbath in obedience to the commandment" (Luke 23:56). It would make sense that since Joseph did not have much time to bury him, by the time the women arrived at their house, the Sabbath had already began.

Therefore, they only had time to prepare the spices and perfumes for Jesus sometime after 6:00 p.m. on Saturday.

THE CONCERN OF THE CHIEF PRIESTS AND PHARISEES

Sometime "after Preparation Day, the chief priests and the Pharisees went to Pilate. 'Sir' they said, 'we remember that while he was still alive that deceiver said, 'After three days I will rise again'" (Matthew 27:62-63). Instead of calling him by his "real" name, they called him a "deceiver" in front of Pilate, for they knew that Pilate saw his innocence and tried to set him free. They sarcastically implied that his entire ministry was a deception and ultimately misleading, along with the possibility of rising from the dead. They called Jesus a deceiver because they remembered the words he stated saying, "after three days I will rise again."

However, nowhere in the Gospels has Jesus actually said those words. For example, early in his ministry, the Jews demanded a sign and Jesus told them, "Destroy this temple, and I will raise it again in three days" (John 2:19). But John specifically states that they thought that he was speaking of the Jerusalem Temple. Later in Matthew 12, some of the Pharisees and teachers asked him for a sign and he replied, "For as Jonah was three days and three nights in the belly of a huge fish, so the Son of Man will be three days and three nights in the heart of the earth" (12:40). In addition, he told them that "one greater than Jonah is here" and that "now one greater than Solomon is here" (12:41-42). It didn't take a religious leader long to realize that Jesus was speaking of himself and perhaps they put together what he said earlier saying, "Destroy this temple, and I will raise it again in three days." Now we see a sense of uneasiness in their minds and hearts.

So they asked Pilate to "give the order for the tomb to be made secure until the third day" (Matthew 27:64). They want Pilate to make the tomb secure by guards only till the third day, for if Jesus' words would come true, it would only happen on the third day and not before or after. From the religious leaders' perspective, if he still was in the grave after the third day, then everyone would know that he truly was a deceiver. The reason why they wanted Pilate to do this was because they did not want his disciples to "come and steal the body and tell the people that he has been raised from the dead" so that "this last deception will be worse than the first" (Matthew 27:64). They told Pilate that they feared his disciples would perhaps mislead the people in thinking that he was raised from the dead and they did not want his resurrection to cause a greater blow to them than his claim to be Messiah and king.

But were they really afraid of this? They knew that Jesus' disciples were not a threat and that they were terrified at his arrest. In addition, for his disciples to steal his body and prove that he was alive would also prove nothing. The religious leaders knew that his disciples had no power or authority in themselves and that they were among the poor and the lower classes of society. So were they really afraid of this? No! What they really were afraid of was the power of Jesus. They had already witnessed numerous miracles that only God himself could do and they were afraid that what he had previously stated would in deed come true. They were not only afraid of his power but they believed that it would happen and that is why they asked Pilate to help secure the tomb.

Ironically, Jesus' adversaries recalled his prophecy much better than his own disciples, for his disciples were so devastated by all of the events that transpired that they forgot. In addition, even Jesus' enemies knew for a fact that he was dead, for they stated, "we remember that while he was still alive." Soon we will find out that when Jesus was resurrected, the religious leaders did not disagree with this fact but rather tried to find another explanation for his disappearance.

THE SECURING OF THE TOMB

Pilate replied to them saying, "Take a guard. Go, make the tomb as secure as you know how" (Matthew 27:65). He gives Roman soldiers to the Jewish authorities to enable them to make the sepulcher safe proof and there were both Roman soldiers and Jewish soldiers on guard. We have already seen Roman guards act under the authority of the Sanhedrin, but perhaps they needed Pilate's consent for a night watch.

So the religious leaders "went and made the tomb secure by putting a seal on the stone and posting the guard" (Matthew 27:66). Most likely they left the palace of Pilate with the soldiers and they went to the tomb site to plan the security measures. A typical Roman guard consisted of four soldiers. Certainly, some stayed awake while the others were sleeping so that no one would come to the tomb site. They were strapped with weapons if combat was needed. These soldiers were of extreme discipline and were meant to avert anyone who attempted to sabotage or embezzle from the tomb. Anyone trying to get too close was sure to be brutally punished.

A seal was a rope that partly covered the width of the great rock that covered the tomb's entrance. There was wax protecting the rope over the stone and thus, the rock could not be moved unless the rope and wax (seal) was broken. No one person from the inside could move this large stone, especially with a seal. It was just too humanly impossible.

The book of Daniel offers another biblical echo concerning this seal. Daniel 6:17 states that "a stone was brought and placed over the mouth of the den, and the king sealed it with his own signet ring and with the rings of his nobles, so that Daniel's situation might not be changed." But in the morning, the king returned and discovered that Daniel was safe and sound yet there was no mention of taking away the stone. So we see that both Jesus and Daniel went into the grave and they were both faithful to God despite their enemies against them. And like Daniel, his God will soon vindicate his Son as well.

We must also remember that Roman soldiers were not concerned about Jews who were executed, especially since some of them gambled over his clothes. Yet they were responsible for that seal, for if it was broken, their career and maybe their lives were at stake. We understand this fact from Acts 16 when a Roman jailer woke up and saw that the prison doors were open and immediately, "he drew his sword and was about to kill himself because he thought the prisoners had escaped" (16:25-28). In the same way, we see how important it was for these soldiers to make sure that Jesus, the executed criminal, would not escape as well.

The sealing and the setting of the guards describes the measures taken to secure to tomb and this was virtually all humans could do at this time. This security virtually closes the execution and burial of Jesus. Yet little did these Romans and Jewish guards understand was that these obstacles did not matter to God. Man's power, preventative measures, and wisdom did not stand before the One who had decreed that he would rise again on the third day.

CHAPTER 7
THE RESURRECTION AND
THE RISE OF CHRISTIANITY

Friday was hard, Saturday was long, but by Sunday all was resolved.[364] *He was dead and became alive. He is gone but promises to return. The best is yet to come.*[365]

The rise of Christianity begins with the resurrection of Jesus. Up until this point, everything that Jesus had said and did was encompassed within a "movement." And yes it was the religious leaders who wanted to destroy this movement and spiritual cause. If there was no resurrection, Jesus would have only been seen as a religious man who died for a religious cause. But when he rose from the grave, his teachings and actions were no longer wrapped up in a simple movement but in a world religion. And yet, it would not just be a world religion, but a powerful and divine led religion in which none other could compare.

Because of his resurrection, Jesus would have followers who would be converted not out of force and diplomacy but because of the undeniable facts surrounding the resurrection. They would be so convinced that so they would be willing to die for their faith.

The Women Come to the Tomb

As soon as the Sabbath was over, the women wanted to come to the tomb. Matthew 28:1 state that "after the Sabbath, at dawn on the first day of the week" they came and John specifically states that it was still dark (20:1) while Mark states that it was just after sunrise (16:2). We get the picture that the sun had just appeared but yet, it was still mostly dark. The women who came were specifically noted as being "Mary Magdalene, Mary the mother of James, and Salome" (Mark 16:1). In addition to these women, Luke 24:10 states "Joanna" also came.

They came with "the spices they had prepared" (Luke 24:1) and they bought them "so that they might go to anoint Jesus' body" (Mark 16:1). When Jesus was buried, it was recorded that only Joseph, Nicodemus, and these women knew of the exact place where he was buried. So now, they were returning seemingly to give Jesus a more suitable preparation for burial and to make sure that everything was in order as they had left him. It is not recorded that they had to ask anyone where Joseph's tomb was located, for they boldly knew and even more, they had been there just three days earlier. We shall soon see that all of them did not come together, for Mary Magdalene did not hear the good news of the resurrection like the other women did (John 20:1-2).

Why did women come to the tomb three days later and not men? First, it is a fact that women have an intimate involvement with a dead body and in most societies, it is women who tend to the dying, who wash the corpse, and who dress it. They don't need no heightened retelling of the stories of death to comprehend its reality or to quicken their emotional response?[366] Second, although both men and women may both weep for the dead, but it is women who tend to weep longer, louder, and they are the ones who are thought to communicate directly with the dead through their wailing songs. Such a dialogue with the dead places a certain power in their hands.[367] And third, because a woman's identity depends greatly on her relationship to a man, the death of someone deprives her of the crucial component of her identity. It is for this reason that women participate so much more fully than men in the performance of death rituals. They must do so in order to continue to be who they were prior to the death of the men who gave their lives definition and meaning.[368]

As they were on their way to the tomb, "they asked each other, 'Who will roll the stone away from the entrance of the tomb'" (Mark 16:3)? Apparently, they did not think through the process of rolling away the stone, for if they did, good judgment would have told them not to go. Even greater, they probably did not know of the Roman and

Jewish guards at the tomb, and if they came and saw them standing in position, they would have been frightened and would have left. Yet we should soon find out that it was divined orchestrated by God for him to allow them to come at that time in the morning to view the tomb. God had it all planned out in order that the women would be the first witnesses of the empty tomb.

The Angel and the Earthquake

So as they came close to the tomb, "there was a violent earthquake, for an angel of the Lord came down from heaven and, going to the tomb, rolled back the stone and sat on it" (Matthew 28:2). The earthquake must have been centralized, for the women were probably not bothered by it. Although there was a great earthquake just after Jesus died, there is now an earthquake that prepares the way for his resurrection. It was the angel of God that caused the earthquake, for the women saw him come down from heaven. After landing on earth, the angel walked toward the tomb, rolled it back, and sat on it. Most likely, he physically rolled it back with his might and power, and he sat on it demonstrating the power and authority he brought to earth.

The angel's appearance was noted as being "like lightning, and his clothes were white as snow" (Matthew 28:3). His manifestation was certainly visible to those who were at the grave sight and the fact that his appearance was like lightning also shows how quickly he came to earth. Although we shall soon find out that Jesus was taken back to heaven in a more slowly fashion, the angel came to earth with quickness.

After seeing what just happened, "the guards were so afraid of him that they shook and became like dead men (Matthew 28:4). These men must have fainted, for the women's description of them portrays their actions as if someone struck and killed them. Soldiers by nature were not men of fear, especially these soldiers whom Pilate asked to guard Joseph's tomb. Yet when they saw this angel, they quickly understood that the angel was not human like them. When they saw his strength and power as he single-handedly moved the stone, they had no more strength left in them to stand on guard. From their perspective, they were hired to keep a dead man in the grave for just that one day, but not to guard against the power and might of this angel.

After the women found the tomb open, "they entered" but "they did not find the body of the Lord Jesus" (Luke 24:3). Although the actual event of Jesus' resurrection is nowhere described, the discovery is. We do not know exactly what time that Sunday morning he arose and where he went immediately after his resurrection, but what we do know is that women found his tomb to be empty. Undoubtedly, the empty tomb was the first step toward the proof of Jesus' resurrection.

The Angel's Good News

After seeing no person in the tomb, the women were "wondering about this" and were greatly perplexed. They were not planning to see this phenomenon before entering the tomb and surely they did not come looking for the large stone to be rolled away. The fact that there was an empty tomb demonstrated that something extraordinary took place.

While they were greatly perplexed, "suddenly two men in clothes that gleamed like lightning stood beside them" (Luke 24:4). Mark describes them as not just men but "young". They were dressed in white robes and Mark states that one of them was "sitting on the right side" (16:5). Although Mark's gospel does not call him an angel, Matthew's does, and his role is strikingly similar to the role played by angels in apocalyptic visions. When the women saw them, they were "alarmed" (Mark 16:5) and in "fright" (Luke 24:5). Perceiving that these men were probably divine messengers, the "women bowed down with their faces to the ground" symbolizing the dominant act of worship in the Old Testament.

THEIR MESSAGE OF REASSURANCE

Without wasting time, the men first told the women to not be "afraid" and "alarmed". "Why do you look for the living among the dead" (Luke 24:5)? This is certainly a logical question seeing that the women were coming to look for someone in the tomb. But from the angels' point of view, they seemed to be actually surprised that the women were coming to look for Jesus' dead body. They had heard what Jesus said earlier regarding his resurrection and they knew that he had told his followers this news as well. But their concern involved why the women did not remember Jesus' prophetic words.

So the angels had to give them the reassurance of Jesus' whereabouts and they emphatically told them, "He is not here; he has risen, just as he said" (Matthew 28:6). The women had to first be reassured that nothing wrong and dishonest happened to their Lord and this was a means of silencing their fears from not only the angel's disturbing presence but from the empty tomb. The angels knew that the situation at hand would have been to the women's disadvantage if they had told them that he was "not here" without telling them that he was "risen". Both had to go together to reassure them of Jesus' whereabouts as well as his earlier spoken words.

To give them even more reassurance that he was "not hear", the angels told them to "come and see the place where he lay." What great comfort and hope it was for the women to not see Jesus' deceased body in the tomb. By seeing the empty tomb, they knew that the stone was not rolled away to let Jesus out, for he had departed before the stone was rolled away, and we know that Jesus could pass through material barriers such as houses (John 20:19; Luke 24:30-31). Yet God wanted the stone to be rolled away so that potential witnesses could verify that he indeed was "risen".

THEIR MESSAGE OF REMEMBRANCE

After telling the women that Jesus was indeed "risen", the angels desired to specifically refresh their memory of what Jesus had earlier said. They stated, "Remember how he told you, while he was still with you in Galilee: 'The Son of Man must be delivered into the hands of sinful men, be crucified and on the third day be raised again'" (Luke 24:6-7). The angels gently referred the women to Jesus' own words and if they had duly believed and observed the prediction of it, they would easily have believed the thing itself when it came to pass.[369]

We know Jesus stated these exact words in Mark 9 stating "The Son of Man is going to be betrayed into the hands of men. They will kill him, and after three days he will rise." But unfortunately those with him "did not understand what he meant and were afraid to ask him about it." Perhaps the women were around him in the presence of his disciples. Regardless, they were without excuse from hearing and understanding the words of Jesus.

Then, as if a light bulb went off in their brain, they "remembered his words." Yet when Jesus stated this prediction, Luke states that "they did not understand what this meant" and "it was hidden from them, so that they did not grasp it" (9:45). Now, these words of hope are now greater than their message that he had risen, and it was the fact that they remembered Jesus' words that immediately caused their hearts and mind to be completely changed.

This brings another fact of proof in Jesus' resurrection. Understanding the fact that these women did not come to the tomb believing in the resurrection but rather finding the tomb empty shows that they needed a message of reassurance and remembrance. Why, because they came to the tomb and found it empty and were given the message of hope that Jesus has been raised.

THEIR MESSAGE OF REHABILITATION

But the message of remembrance was not the final message from the angels, for they additionally wanted Jesus' disciples to be rehabilitated. Mark 16:7 states that the angels told them to "go, tell his disciples and Peter, 'He is going ahead of you into Galilee. There you will see him, just as he told you to.'" The angels knew that the hope of Jesus' disciples were completely gone and they had no more life within themselves. That is why they told these women to "go quickly and tell his disciples: 'He has risen from the dead' (Matthew 28:7). The angel never told them that they would immediately grasp their message but rather to quickly go and tell them the good news. Thus, the angel's intent was for these men to be rehabilitated.

But why was Peter singled out? Simply because he had denied his Lord just before he was crucified. He was one of the three closest disciples and it was to him specifically that Jesus said, "...on this rock I will build my church, and the gates of Hades will not overcome it. I will give you the keys of the Kingdom of Heaven; whatever you bind on earth will be bound in heaven, and whatever you loose on earth will be loosed in heaven" (Matthew 16:18). The angels knew that if Peter were to hear the good news of Jesus being raised from the dead, he would have been excited and rejuvenated.

The women did not need the rehabilitation but rather the men. So then why did God orchestrate these heavenly beings to appear to women and not the men? Perhaps God knew that they would believe much faster then the men and we will see that this actually took place. Although the women at this time had not seen Jesus but only an empty tomb and divine messengers, some of the men would soon come and see the empty tomb and hear the good news from the women, and yet they would still not grasp the truth of the Scriptures as the women would. Sadly, Jesus had to appear to these men himself in order for them to truly believe. Thus, God knew what he was doing in appearing to the women first.

The Women Report to the Disciples

THEIR STATE OF EMOTIONS

Believing the angel's message, "the women went out and fled from the tomb" (Mark 16:8). It was still very early in the morning for people to have been walking around by the graveyard. These women certainly did not want someone to think that they were tampering with the tomb of a convicted individual and thus, they desired to get as far away from the tomb site as possible, for the large stone rolled away would be quit obvious to those who passed by.

Luke 24:10 gives a list of some of the women who ran and told the report to the disciples. We have already seen Mary Magdalene and Mary the mother of James, but a new woman is mentioned and her name is Joanna. Joanna, which means "Yahweh's gift", was one of the women cured of evil spirits and diseases along with Mary of Magdalene. She was the wife of Cuza, the manager of Herod's household and she was among the women helping to support Jesus out of her own means (Luke 8:2-3).

As they all fled, they were "trembling and bewildered" (Mark 16:8) and although they were "afraid", they were "yet filled with joy" (Matthew 28:8). This word for "bewildered" means displacement and the state of throwing the mind out of its normal state. This word also means amazement. The women left very emotional but as Matthew stated, they were also "filled with joy" for all that had transpired were under good circumstances. It was a joyous occasion for them to see the evidence of the resurrection and more importantly to remember the very words of Jesus. To them, it was joyous to know that Jesus had triumphed over the grave itself, for they knew that he did not just somehow miraculously survived the ordeal of the cross. The fact that he was alive meant more to them then he was simply a survivor.

THEIR SURPRISE VISIT FROM JESUS

Then somewhere on their way, Jesus "suddenly" met them saying, "Greetings." It appeared that he came out of nowhere and met the women right where they were. When the women saw him, they apparently recognized him immediately perhaps by his wounds. So they "came to him, clasped his feet and worshipped him" (Matthew 28:9). The word "clasped" meant to hold and they demonstrated not only heart-felt emotions but expressions of profound reverence.

Jesus did not want them to stay with him and that is why he said to them, "Do not be afraid. Go and tell my brothers to go to Galilee and there they will see me" (Matthew 28:10). He gave them words of comfort but also words of instruction. He appeared seemingly to simply confirm what the angel had already told them. These women were given the privilege to not only hear the first good news of his resurrection, but to be the to see him as well. It must also be noted that Mary Magdalene was not with these women, for she would soon see him by herself.

So the women "said nothing to anyone" (Mark 16:8) as the "ran to tell his disciples" (Matthew 28:8) what had transpired. But why did they not speak to anyone? Why didn't all Jerusalem hear about this empty tomb account that the women and the guards observed? Surely a group of hysterical women rushing about in the early morning would have had the news all over the city within minutes? If nobody proclaimed Jesus as risen for a month or two, as Luke suggest, the question might very well arise as to why did people not hear about this sooner? The answer is that they said nothing because they were afraid. Afraid, of course, because empty tombs and illuminating angels are enough to scare anyone and they were afraid because they had secretly been to the tomb to anoint the body of a condemned would-be Messiah.[370]

THEIR SPEECH TO THE DISCIPLES

When the women finally arrived to where the disciples were, "they told all these things to the Eleven and to all the others" (Luke 24:9). All of Jesus' disciples were not living in the same residence and since there were more than three women who saw the empty tomb, it was possible that they could have split up and have gone to where these men stayed to tell them the news. This makes sense knowing that Mary Magdalene would soon come to Peter and John's residence and tell them the news of what had happened. In addition, there are a couple of incidences where Jesus would soon come during the day and appeared to his disciples at the same time, and we know they were together because of fear of the Jews.

THE SKEPTICISM OF THE DISCIPLES

Regardless of whether the women split up or came to one residence, after telling these men of what had transpired, they "did not believe the women" (Luke 24:11). These women had been faithful followers of Jesus and they continued to believe during his entire earthly ministry. They were obedient to their commission of "evangelism" but sadly the disciples did not believe. Those who had spent so much time with Jesus did not believe that he was alive mainly because they forgot his prophetic words. They had been so often told that he must die and rise again, and then enter into his glory, and they had seen him more than once raised the dead.[371] We can now be shocked that they should be so slow to believe.

The reason why they did not believe was because the women's words "seemed to them like nonsense" (Luke 24:11). This same word for nonsense is "idle talk" which is a medical word used to describe the gibberish of a delirious and insane person. When the women were presenting their chronicle of events, they were testifying to only supernatural events and circumstances. Instead of thinking in the spiritual realm, these men, however, were only thinking in the physical realm knowing for a fact that dead people don't rise. Yet, they completely forgot that Jesus was actually God and was able to do what only God could do. Clearly, they were not expecting their Master to rise from the dead and that is why the women's report was only conceived as "nonsense."

431

Again, these facts only confirm that this account is accurate and verifiable. The writers would not make up an apologetic legend about an empty tomb and having women be the ones who fine it, for women were simply not acceptable as legal witnesses. It was not popular for women, who were considered unclean and below male citizenship, to have been mentioned by men in the First Century to have had a significant role in the resurrection of the Jewish Messiah, even if it was true. By way of example, during the rule of Hitler, it would have been as if Germans wrote in their history books of true and noteworthy acts of the Jews. This type of thing just does not happen. But if it did, it certainly would have been true.

The Guards Report to the Chief Priests

While the women were on their way to tell the disciples what had happened, the guards at the tombs ran to tell the Chief Priests what had happened. Matthew states that "while the women were on their way, some of the guards went into the city and reported to the chief priests everything that had happened" (Matthew 28:11). The soldiers did not waist any time knowing that failing to follow the Pilate's order was punishable by death.

What the guards reported centered in on the supernatural. Everything that occurred that morning would never happen in the ordinary sequence of time. Certainly the chief priests heard about the angel coming down from heaven and rolling the stone away, which only revealed that Jesus himself had already miraculously came out. At the same time, they could not have been terribly surprised understanding that they had seen Jesus perform unbelievable miracles during the past three years.

THE CONSPIRACY AND COVER-UP

After hearing these events, these religious leaders had to come up with a "believable" plan. So they "met with the elders and devised a plan." The terrible sin that the authorities came up with began with a "plan." Interestingly, these men were use to planning and meeting together especially against Jesus ever since the beginning of his earthly ministry. They had wanted to kill him earlier since they saw his miracles and heard his messages condemning their sin and hypocrisy. During Jesus' trial, they sought false testimony against him so that they could condemn him, and lies were used to put him to death and kill his memory from ever existing again. Now that he was unquestionably alive, and yet these same leaders were planning another lie that would go against the plan of God.

The first part of their plan was to give "the soldiers a large sum of money." Bribery is the most widespread form of corruption and its basic act of giving money or gifts would be used to alter these men's behavior. Their plan was not only to pay the soldiers in order to keep them quiet, but to devise another report of how Jesus rose from the dead. So these religious leaders told the soldiers, "You are to say, his disciples came during the night and stole him away while we were asleep. If this report gets to the governor, we will satisfy him and keep you out of trouble" (Matthew 28:13-14). Nowhere do we see that they wanted to tell the Jews throughout Palestine that he miraculous rose from the dead but rather that his disciples came and stole his body to explain why his tomb was empty. In addition, their scheme may have involved them not even choosing soldiers to guard the tomb just before the third day. If the Jews knew that soldiers were there that night and morning, this story would obviously produce numerous questions.

So like most underpaid officers during this era, "the soldiers took the money and did as they were instructed. And this story has been widely circulated among the Jews to this very day." No where do we see that the authorities denied the supernatural events and the appearance of the angels. They actually believed in the resurrection, because their men on guard physically witnessed it. But they decide to commit the terrible sin (which they admit as such) of not announcing that triumph, lest the Jewish people stone their own authorities for leading them astray over Jesus' crucifixion.[372]

The Jewish authorities were not just totally responsible, they were totally guilty. They knew the truth and hid it deliberately from their own people. "All the people," led by their authorities to crucify Jesus, were so repentant after his death that they would have believed the resurrection and stoned their leaders were it not for that cover-up. The Roman authorities were totally guiltless while the Jewish authorities were totally guilty. The Jewish people would all be Christians if only their leaders had not lied.[373] Sadly, the Roman authorities acknowledged Jesus and his deity, but the Jewish leaders scheme with Pilate to mislead their own people and "lie" about Jesus to protect themselves from the Jews. Thus, God makes his Son shine in the conscious of his enemies and there was no way in which these leaders could deny this fact.

THE AMBIGUITY AND LOOPHOLES

However, there are obvious loopholes with the lie that the disciples came and stole the body. First, it was known that there were no third party groups with the backbone and motives for stealing Jesus' body. We have observed that if Pilate thought that Jesus' disciples were capable of any harm or deception, he certainly would not have allowed Joseph to take his body and put him into his tomb.

Second, the lie that the soldiers were bribed is sometimes dismissed as absurd, for it is claimed that to sleep on duty was a capital offense in the Roman army. If this rumor indeed was true, then the soldiers would have known that they were contributing to their own demise despite the promise that the chief priests would persuade the governor, and thus could deliver them from worry.

And third, little did Pilate and the Jewish authorities know that their safekeeping measures would present greater proof to the miracle of Jesus' resurrection. If the burial place were not safeguarded appropriately, there would be room for ambiguity. Without those guards, there would be no eyewitnesses to Jesus' rise from the grave. It even made both Pilate and the Jewish leaders feel dimwitted and senseless for safeguarding the tomb of a condemned poor Jewish criminal. Yet they all knew that there was something about him that was different.

Peter and John Arrive at the Tomb

Mary Magdalene must not have come with the other women, for she had not seen him after he died as the other women did or heard the good news about his resurrection. Yet what she did see when she came to the site was an open tomb and no Jesus. How shocking and terrifying this must have been. Seemingly, she immediately went running to where Jesus' close disciples were located and when she found Simon Peter and John, she said, "They have taken the Lord out of the tomb, and we don't know where they have put him" (John 20:2). Perhaps she was suggesting that the chief priests or even Joseph and Nicodemus must have taken Jesus' body away. Regardless of her suspicion, she was greatly vexed and disturbed that his body was missing and she desired to vent her frustration to the disciples.

After she told Peter and John what she saw at Jesus' gravesite, they unfortunately still did not remember the words of Jesus nor believe that he had the power to overcome death. Rather, the men wanted to see themselves to prove the credibility of the story. So both of them "started for the tomb". John later indirectly states that this same Mary came with them to the tomb. "Both Peter and John were running, but the other disciple outran Peter and reached the tomb first" (John 20:3-4). As a matter of author's humility, John does not refer to himself directly but only as the other disciple. John outran Peter simply because he was much younger, perhaps a teenager or in his early twenties.

THE LINEN

When John came to the tomb, he "bent over and looked in at the strips of linen lying there but did not go in" (John 20:5). This "linen" was most commonly referred to fabric used in the ancient Near East. It was spun from the flax plant and bleached before being woven into clothing, bedding, curtains, and burial shrouds.[374] After John saw this, Simon Peter "arrived and went into the tomb. He saw the strips of linen lying there, as well as the burial cloth that had been around Jesus' head. The cloth was folded up by itself, separate from the linen" (John 20:6-7). Then "finally the other disciple, who had reached the tomb first, also went inside." Peter went in first and made a more exact discovery than John had done. Although John could out run Peter, Peter could out dare John.[375]

But it was what they saw and how they saw it that was unusual and even amazing. They saw grave clothes, but not as if they had been torn off after a brawl or even thrown to the ground. They saw linen lying in perfect order as if someone had passed through them, similarly as Jesus passed through the rock and exited the tomb. The burial cloth that was by his head was not lying with the linen clothes but was folded and lying next to it. They saw that there was no rush for him leaving the tomb but that he took his time to strategically array the cloth and linen inside the tomb. Even amazingly and miraculously, the earthquake that the women clearly saw surrounding the grave site did not alter the linen and the cloth. It was as if the earthquake had no impact on what was inside the tomb.

There were no angels present during Peter and John's visit, yet there were angels present during the women's visit. From this we observe that angels can appear and disappear at pleasure according to the instructions given by God. At the same time, they may become visible to one and not to another as seen in Numbers 22:22-24 and 2 Kings 6:17.

THE FAITH

When John saw this, he "believed" (John 20:8) but Peter "went away wondering to himself what had happened" (Luke 24:12). Peter's boldness encouraged John to enter the tomb after him, which ultimately helped him to believe, and although it seems that John got a head start in believing, neither of them "still did not understand from Scripture that Jesus had to rise from the dead" (John 20:9). Both of these men forgot not only the prophetic words of Jesus but what the prophets of old had been prophetically proclaiming for centuries. John believed in Jesus' "resurrection" at first, not because he remembered Scripture but the facts of the empty tomb and of the linen and the cloth brought about convincing proofs that Jesus was alive. Although these men saw some reliable evidence, nothing still made complete sense because they still did not know the Scriptures.

Jesus Appears to Mary Magdalene

HER CHASE FOR JESUS

Mary probably did not run as fast as Peter and John but I'm sure she came as quickly as she could. After Peter and John went back to their homes", "Mary stood outside the tomb crying. As she wept, she bent over to look into the tomb and saw two angels in white, seated where Jesus' body had been, one at the head and the other at the foot" (John 20-10-12). It is evident that she waited till Peter, John, and anyone else who may have came to look at the tomb had departed to go into the tomb and to see for herself what had happened. Again, we know from John's account that she only "saw that the stone had been removed from the entrance" but she never went inside the tomb herself. She did not encounter the angels as mentioned in Matthew 28 and she never heard their words stating, "Do not be afraid, for I know that you are looking for Jesus, who was crucified. He is not here; he has risen, just as he said. Come and see the place where he lay" (Matthew 28:5-6). If she did, she would not have told Peter and John that "they have taken the Lord out of the tomb, and we don't know where they have put him."

These angels, who are called watchers in Daniel 4:23, are keeping possession of the sepulcher. Their position represents Christ's victory over the powers of darkness. When Mary saw these two "angels", she did not react as others had when they encountered heavenly beings and there is a good explanation as to why. Angels were seen as mere men when they appear, except in the few occasions when they are seen as "glowing". From encounters with Abraham, Jacob, Mary, Zacharias, and others, angels appear as mere men. Yet for Mary and Zacharias, the angel appeared in places in which they knew that no one else was around, and thus, they were startled and greatly afraid. Yet for others, including Abraham and Jacob, there was no fear mentioned. In addition, there are other examples, including some of the ones just mentioned, when individuals encountered angels and they did not know who they were. That is why in many of these occasion, the angel identified himself in the presence of the individual.

Thus, it is easy to conclude that she did not know that these two men in white were angel. It makes sense in understanding the fact of how she would have been able to identify an angelic messenger when she saw one. Although these angels were earlier depicted as having an appearance "like lightning", the fact that their clothes were white did not necessarily show Mary that indeed these two men were angels.

The men asked her, "Woman, why are you crying" (John 20:13). It is even more evident from her response back to them that she did not know that they were angels, for she answered, "They have taken my Lord away and I don't know where they have put him." Once Jacob in the Old Testament saw that he was in the presence of the divine, he wrestled with an angel, for he wanted to receive a blessing. Here, if Mary realized that she was in the presence of the divine, she would not have asked a question like this knowing that angelic beings know much more then humans.

HER COMPREHENSION OF JESUS

Most likely, she heard someone walking which, for her, was perhaps another person who could help her answer the question of Jesus' whereabouts. Then "turned around and saw Jesus standing there, but she did not realize that it was Jesus" (20:14). Probably going toward her, he said to her, "Woman, why are you crying? Who is it you are looking for?" (20:15). He was simply asking her what business she had in the garden so early and why was she so emotional. Jesus had asked questions like this during his entire ministry. To the person he was talking to, it almost sounded absurd that he would ask a question knowing that he knew the answer. But to Jesus, he only wanted to see faith and to him, it was one thing to have faith, but it was another to demonstrate and speak faith.

And Mary did just that. Although she thought he was simply the gardener, she said, "Sir, if you have carried him away, tell me where you have put him, and I will get him" (John 20:15). By stating "sir", we see her respect and she speaks desiring some information concerning someone whom she loved. From her point of view, since this man was in close proximity to Joseph's tomb where Jesus was buried, she purposefully did not state his name as if he knew whom she was talking about. She knew that the stone which was rolled away was obvious enough to anyone in the vicinity, and by seeing this, he should have known what had happened.

Then Jesus said to her, "'Mary'. She turned toward him and cried out in Aramaic, 'Rabboni!' (which means Teacher)." From her view, if someone was to know her name, he must not only know her but must have had a connection with her. And most likely, she comprehended his voice and knew exactly who it was speaking to her. Jesus disclosed himself to her in what has been called the greatest recognition scene in all literature. For her to have called Jesus "teacher" shows that there was no intimacy between the two, for her words actually declared her relationship to him – a pupil. Her most important association with him was at his feet and listening to him, for it was respectable for someone to be a teacher in those days. In addition, we have no reason to suppose that the Gospel writer was making out a case for her primacy.

Then Jesus said, "Do not hold on to me, for I have not yet returned to the Father" (John 20:17). Mary was about to express her joy for her "teacher" but Jesus directs her not to cling on to him. The actual translation of the phrase "do not hold or cling on to me" and "do not grasp me" meant to stop an action already begun rather than to avoid starting it. Basically, Mary was holding on to Jesus and did not want to let him go, and this view makes sense seeing that Jesus said, "Do not hold on to me" right after she recognized who he was. Jesus did not want her to set her affections on him. He knew that he would see her again and was about to instruct her that there were more urgent matters that needed to take place than for her to cling to him.

What this statement from Jesus does not show was that his body was different or supernatural than his body before. Certainly, he was not some see-through spirit or non-graspable human being. He was not a phantom and perhaps his physical appearance was a little different, for Mary did not recognize him at first. Yet after she recognized him, he seemed to look the same from her viewpoint than before. Once she recognized him, she did not say anything concerning why he looked different than he did before he died. In addition, the fact that the "real" Jesus was talking to her provides proof that there was no confusion about having the right tomb where the right body had been buried, as some would like to say otherwise.

HER CHARGE BY JESUS

Instead of wanting Mary to cling on to him, Jesus told her to "go instead to my brothers and tell them, 'I am returning to my Father and your Father, to my God and your God'" (John 20:17). This charge that he said showed a sense of urgency. Who were Jesus' brothers? Matthew 12 states that he asked this question and then pointed to his "disciples" and said, "Here are my mother and my brothers. For whoever does the will of my Father in heaven is my brother and sister and mother" (12:48-50). In addition, Mark states that women also accompanied Jesus' twelve disciples on numerous occasions, so we can not restrict the term "disciples" to just the twelve.

In his mandate, Jesus pointed out a difference between his relationship with God and that with his disciples. Although he had intimate times with his followers, he was telling Mary that he soon would return to his Father. Yet at the same time, he also tells of the relationship that his followers could have with God the Father in heaven. We can even see how he was putting the emphasis of relationship on God and not on himself.

HER OBEDIENCE

As a faithful student, Mary obeys her "teacher" and "went to the disciples with the news: 'I have seen the Lord!' And she told them that he had said these things to her" (John 20:18). Mark 16:10 states that "she went and told those who had been with him and who were mourning and weeping." Peter and John had left her seeking him carefully with tears and would not stay to seek him with her. Now she found it was a living body and a glorified one so that she found what she sought, and what was infinitely better.[376]

We see Mary not just going to one residence but to several, for she went to "those who had been with him." However long it took for her to tell the good news of what she had seen and heard, she was faithful to her task. And Mark gives the emotional state of these men, for although they had seen the empty tomb and heard the good news, they still did not believe. But the women, who had heard the good news, did believed.

HER REJECTION

Now that Mary has shown herself to be a loyal eyewitness to Jesus, the disciples did not trust her words. Mark 16:11 states this truth saying, "when they heard that Jesus was alive and that she had seen him, they did not believe it." They could not give credit to the report she brought them. They heard that he was alive but they fear that she is deceived and that it was but a fancy that she saw him. Had they believed the frequent predictions of it from his own mouth, they would not have been now so incredulous of the report of it.[377]

Yet this narrative again gives historic truth of this account. If someone conjured this account during the First Century, would he state that women, who were regarded as unreliable witnesses, were the first witnesses of the Messiah's resurrection? Would he also say that a woman was the first to see and hear him after he rose from the grave? The answer is undoubtedly no! Although the law during this time did not recognize a women's testimony, Jesus did and trusted women to be the first ones to carry out his commission. In addition, this historic fact builds on to Jesus' character by not being a respecter of persons. He trusted both men and women with his commission and he did not care what culture thought.

<u>Jesus Appears to Two</u>

Mary Magdalene and the women were not the only people that Jesus appeared to that day. Luke tells us that on the "same day" that he rose, which was Sunday morning, "two of them were going to a village called Emmaus, about seven miles from Jerusalem" (Luke 24:13). Emmaus means "hot baths" and its location was 60 furlongs or approximately seven miles from Jerusalem. Josephus, the Jewish historian, mentions "a village called Emmaus" at the same distance. This passage in the Bible is the only clue to this city's identity and location, and today, there are as many as four sites that have been proposed as the location of Emmaus.

By what means of transportation did these two individuals use? The answer is the same transportation that most everyone used during this era – their feet. People mostly walked unless they could pay for transportation like the Pharisees and Sadducees who were of the higher echelons in society. Walking gave people great opportunities to talk, for the seven miles that these men walked would have taken about 2 hours.

Luke states that as they were walking, "they were talking with each other about everything that had happened" (Luke 24:14). We would soon find out that "everything" they were talking about consisted of the unusual circumstances centering on Jesus. These individuals were followers of Jesus and most likely they were among the ones that "did not believe the women because their words seemed to them like nonsense.

441

JESUS' CONCEALED APPEARANCE BEFORE THEM

As they two were talking and discussing "these things with each other, Jesus himself came up and walked along with them" (Luke 24:15). Jesus, seeing them travel down the same path as they, probably asked them that he would be glad to join their company and their conversation. Because of the warm hospitality within the Mediterranean world, the two gladly allowed him to walk with them. Little did they know that in their conversation and reasoning concerning the truth, all their answers were in front of them.

But both Mark and Luke let us know that Jesus was concealed in his appearance before them. Mark states that "Jesus appeared in a different form to two of them while they were walking in the country" (16:12) and Luke states that the two "were kept from recognizing him" (24:16). Jesus intended this to happen so that he could converse with them the truth, to answer all their questions about the unusual events that occurred, and even to rebuke them for their lack of faith and understanding.

THE TWO CONVERSES ABOUT HIM

Now that he had been given the invitation to join their conversation, Jesus asked them, "What are you discussing together as you walk along" (Luke 24:17). He had probably walked silently with them for a while, just paying attention as they carried on their discussion. The Gospel writers show that he was notorious for asking questions that he already knew but he asked with the purpose of inducing faith.

But both of them "stood still" with "their faces downcast" and "one of them, named Cleopas, asked him, 'Are you only a visitor to Jerusalem and do not know the things that have happened there in these days'" (24:17-18). Out of the two followers, one was named and clearly male and one unnamed and probably female, given the protocols of Mediterranean patriarchy. It makes sense later that this person was his wife when they both "asked each other, 'Were not our hearts burning within us.'" The couple was leaving Jerusalem in disappointment and sorrow, and they wondered why this man did not know what was going on. To them, only Jewish strangers were ignorant of the "things that have happened there in these days."

Jesus answered back saying, "What things" as if he did not know what they were talking about, and they answered, "About Jesus of Nazareth." Then the two began to talk about a series of "facts" concerning this Jesus who was from Nazareth so that this "stranger" would be caught up with what everyone else knew about him. They first stated that he was a "prophet" (Luke 24:19). For one to truly have been a prophet, one generally shared several key experiences and characteristics. One had to (1) be called from God; (2) received a word from God through numerous means including declarations, visions, dreams, or divine appearances; (3) speak the word of God; (4) relay God's message by deed and word; (5) performed miracles that would confirm a message; (6) minister to people; (7) have ecstatic experiences.[378] Jesus was distinguished from even a false prophet during his day, for he was consistent in all he said and did.

Second, the two stated that he was "powerful in word and deed before God and all the people" (Luke 24:19). Although this additionally corresponded with him being a prophet, these words carry an additional fact about him. What they were stating was that his teachings were powerful, for they knew that "he taught as one who had authority, and not as their teachers of the law" (Matthew 7:29). In addition, his "deed" or works were powerful and his miracles were astonishing before them all. We even see a religious leader, of whom most were against him, say to Jesus that "we know you are a teacher who has come from God. For no one could perform the miraculous signs you are doing if God were not with him" (John 3:2).

Third, they state that "the chief priests and our rulers handed him over to be sentenced to death, and they crucified him" (Luke 24:20). We see a progression first concentrating on his life and then concentrating on his death. They acknowledged that, although the Romans could only crucify criminal, it was the "chief priests" and their "rulers" who had handed him over. Thus, Jesus' death was a result of their doing and no one else. In addition, they acknowledged that he truly died, for crucifixion was only carried out by the Romans and they certainly left no victims alive.

Their fourth point makes mention of not only their hopes but the hopes of all the Jews and perhaps some Samaritans who were looking for Jesus to be their Messiah. The two stated, "But we had hoped that he was the one who was going to redeem Israel" (Luke 24:21). Their word for "redeem" meant to set free specifically from Roman rule and oppression. From their perspective, their hopes were discontinued when Jesus was executed and now they had no hope. Certainly they were not just speaking about themselves, for all his followers (besides the women who came to the tomb) and all the Jews who had their hope in him. And they mentioned that it was the third day since all this took place" which gives the indication that he is still "missing" or even "dead" and that all hope was still gone.

The last, they stated that "some of our women amazed us. They went to the tomb early this morning but didn't find his body. They came and told us that they had seen a vision of angels, who said he was alive. Then some of our companions went to the tomb and found it just as the women had said, but him they did not see" (Luke 24:22-24). Now we see the progression after mentioning his death in which they talk about him being "missing." We see a time table by the two stating "this morning" which gives the indication that it was late that morning in which they were talking to Jesus. We see them telling of the facts of the empty tomb and that the women had seen angels which told them that Jesus was alive. They also tell of "some" of their companions going to the tomb and finding the women's report to have been accurate. Yet they still did not believe in his resurrection. Although there was proof from the empty tomb, they still saw controversy in the truth.

JESUS CLARIFIES THE SCRIPTURES TO THEM

Jesus stayed quiet to allow them to speak their frustration and confusion pertaining to these events. But now it was time for him to speak and relay the truth, and to clear up the controversy and confusion! He began by saying, "How foolish you are, and how slow of heart to believe all that the prophets have spoken" (Luke 24:25). The two had just spoken that Jesus was a prophet, but sadly, they did not "believe" what the prophets of old had spoken for centuries. Jesus equated their slow belief to the heart and not the head, and he does not call them wicked but rather weak in faith.

Then he told them, "Did not the Christ have to suffer these things and then enter his glory" (Luke 24:26). Although the Jews did not see a Messiah as one who would suffer, Jesus let them know that his suffering was actually proof that he was the Messiah and not proof against it. In other words, the Messiah could not save unless he had to suffer.

He then took them step by step "beginning with Moses and all the Prophets" and "he explained to them what was said in all the Scriptures concerning himself" (Luke 24:27). This word for "explain" meant to expound and to unfold the meaning of what was said. Here, he stayed close to the text and expressed the exact meaning of the passage. Specifically, he probably showed them Scripture pertaining to the fact that the Messiah had to be crushed, bruised, and executed before God would raise him up.

There are numerous passages that he could have stated. He first could have referred them to Isaiah 53:3-5 stating, "He was despised and rejected by men, a man of sorrows, and familiar with suffering. Like one from whom men hide their faces he was despised, and we esteemed him not. Surely he took up our infirmities and carried our sorrows, yet we considered him stricken by God, smitten by him, and afflicted. But he was pierced for our transgressions, he was crushed for our iniquities; the punishment that brought us peace was upon him, and by his wounds we are healed." These passages specifically refer to the fact that the Messiah would be "despised" and "rejected", which actually happened to him during the onset of his ministry. The fact that he would be "pierced", "crushed", and would suffer "wounds" would also be significant in light of the specific punishment that crucifixion would offer.

Second, he could have referred them to Isaiah 50:5-7 which states, "The Sovereign LORD has opened my ears, and I have not been rebellious; I have not drawn back. I offered my back to those who beat me, my cheeks to those who pulled out my beard; I did not hide my face from mocking and spitting. Because the Sovereign LORD helps me, I will not be disgraced." Certainly the "mocking", "spitting" and the fact that they "beat" him played a significant part in his death.

And third, he could have referred them to the fact that the Messiah would actually die. Daniel 9:26 states, "After the sixty-two 'sevens,' the Anointed One will be cut off and will have nothing. The "Anointed One" is the same as the Messiah and "cut off" means to destroy, to be cut down and even to permit to perish.

Thus Jesus was telling them that these facts were destined to take place. Certainly, these two individuals must have been amazed at this man's ability to explain the truth of the Scriptures.

JESUS "CEASES TO EXIST" FROM THEM

"As they approached the village to which they were going, Jesus acted as if he were going farther." This is not the first time that Jesus "acted" as he would continue walking, for Mark 6 states that he did the same thing. Sometime before at "about the fourth watch of the night, he went out to them [his disciples], walking on the lake. He was about to pass by them, but when they saw him walking on the lake, they thought he was a ghost. They cried out, because they all saw him and were terrified" (6:48-50).

But they urged him strongly, 'Stay with us, for it is nearly evening; the day is almost over.'" The fact that they had to "urged" him meant that they had to employ force in order to constrain him. In other words, Jesus initially did not want to stay with them, for he did not want to reveal himself to them or for them to really know who he was. The fact that they asked him to stay shows the hospitality of the Mediterranean society. They thought they were just being kind to a stranger, but little did they know that it was Jesus they were inviting into their home.

So Jesus "went in to stay with them." We don't see in Scripture where someone ever asked him to stay and he refused, and this act of his was consistent to his life before his resurrection. We see that the two showed hospitality to him by giving him food. Whether they asked him to bless the food or whether Jesus initiated it, we will never know. But what we do know is that he "took bread, gave thanks, broke it and began to give it to them" (Luke 24:30). Ironically, this was similar to his actions in Matthew when he fed the five thousand men. There, "he directed the people to sit down on the grass. Taking the five loaves and the two fish and looking up to heaven, he gave thanks and broke the loaves. Then he gave them to the disciples, and the disciples gave them to the people" (14:19). In addition, he used these same actions when he fed the four thousand men (Mark 8).

It was this action of his that allowed their eyes to be "open" and it was at this point that "they recognized him." Now we understand that they were among Jesus' "disciples" who helped to pass out the food to the multitude and it makes sense that they recognized his procedure in distributing the food. To their advantage, it was their invitation which lead to the meal, which lead to their recognition of who was really in their presence. In addition, they probably noticed his nail-scarred wrists but did not put it together until Jesus actually "took", "gave thanks", "broke" and gave it to them.

But as soon as he had given this couple one glimpse of him, he was gone, for he "disappeared from their sight." This word for "disappeared" meant taken out of sight and made invisible. And what actually happened was that he was made invisible before their eyes.

It was at this point that they asked each other, "Were not our hearts burning within us while he talked with us on the road and opened the Scriptures to us" (Luke 24:32). They were simply reflecting over what they were feeling while Jesus "opened" and made plain the Scriptures. They found his presentation as being "powerful in word and deed before God and all the people." Now they knew indeed that it was Jesus before them and no one else.

THE TWO CLAIM JESUS IS ALIVE

With excitement, "they got up and returned at once to Jerusalem." After a seven mile walk one way, they were so overjoyed that they traveled another seven miles back, perhaps even faster, to tell the good news of Jesus' resurrection. Not only did their emotions consist of excitement because of seeing the Lord, but they felt the pain of the others disciples who still did not believe. The two knew that the others were still depressed and emotionally devastated and thus, they had to let them know the good news.

As they returned to Jerusalem, "there they found the Eleven and those with them, assembled together and saying, 'It is true! The Lord has risen and has appeared to Simon'" (Luke 24:13-14). The fact of Jesus appearing to Simon before the rest of the disciples is attested not only here but in 1 Corinthians 15 stating that "Christ died for our sins according to the Scriptures, that he was buried, that he was raised on the third day according to the Scriptures, and that he appeared to Peter." (15:3-5). We don't have a narrative of him appearing to Simon but only the fact that he did. We know that the angels told the women to tell the disciples and Peter mainly for his comfort. Perhaps even though the disciples were mourning because of his death, Peter's morning began way before after he denied him. Thus, he was certainly more emotional than everyone else and it was easy to see why Jesus made a special appearance to him.

As if that was not enough, the two "told what had happened on the way and how Jesus was recognized by them when he broke the bread" (Luke 24:15). Perhaps they saw that the disciples were not taking them seriously and that they needed to continue with their discourse. So they took them step by step of how Jesus appeared to them beginning with their journey to Emmaus and ending with his miraculously disappearance.

But sadly, "they did not believe them either." Perhaps they did not gain credibility with the other disciples of Jesus or perhaps saw a contradiction with the appearances of Jesus with the women. Or better yet, they were just overwhelmed with the news of their Savior being alive that their disbelief worsened.

Jesus' First Appearance to His Disciples

HIS COMING AND SCARE

Perhaps understanding that most of his followers would not believe until they actually saw the risen Lord, Jesus decided to make a personal appearance to them. Little did they know that the empty tomb would serve in some measure to prepare the way for his self-disclosure to them.

Then Luke states that "while they were still talking about this, Jesus himself stood among them" (24:36). "About this" concerns what the two were previously telling the disciples concerning their encounter with Jesus. Perhaps it was towards the onset of the conversation that Jesus appeared or maybe it was sometime after. Regardless, Jesus showed up in their presence among them as they were talking.

Concerning the time of day he came, John states that it was "on the evening of that first day of the week" (20:19) and thus, it was still the same Sunday that he was resurrected. Their meeting was private and certainly not public, and they met in a house. Their reason for gathering was because of their "fear of the Jews." Many of the women and men followers were fearful, unbelieving, and silent concerning what they had heard because perhaps if Jesus were alive, he might have been gathering some new Jewish resistance to overthrow Rome.

Or perhaps they thought that the Jews would think that they stole his body for whatever reason. Regardless of their reasoning, they were fearful not of the Romans but of their own religious leaders.

When Jesus came to them, he "stood among them" with the doors being locked (John 20:19). The fact that the doors were locked and then, all of the sudden, Jesus appears not coming through the doors but standing among them, would certainly be significant enough for John to write about. People only come through doors in order to enter into a house but Jesus came in not by the ordinary way of entrance.

Seeing him just standing among them only "startled and frightened" them, and Luke states that they were thinking they "saw a ghost" (24:37). This was not the first time that his followers thought that he was a ghost. After Jesus fed the 5,000, Mark states that "about the fourth watch of the night he went out to them, walking on the lake. He was about to pass by them, but when they saw him walking on the lake, they thought he was a ghost." And of course, they "were terrified" (48-50). Any person in their right mind would have been scared at his abrupt appearance. But they were about to see that this appearance among them would constitute an infallible proof of his resurrection.

Knowing their fear, Jesus said to them, "Peace be with you" (Luke 24:36). These are similar words he stated to them when they thought they saw a ghost walking on the water. There he stated, "Take courage! It is I. Don't be afraid" (Mark 6:50). During both instances, Jesus did not want any confusion or further emotional fears but rather a calm state of mind by which he would be able to speak to them in an understanding fashion.

HIS CONVINCING PROOFS

Jesus then stated "peace be with you" because he saw that they were troubled. So he continued to say, "Why are you troubled, and why do doubts rise in your minds" (Luke 24:38)? He knew that troublesome thoughts within the mind could bring uncertainty and disbelief concerning his true identity and that is why many, if not all of them, doubted that he was indeed human.

We know that the disciples were not doubtful whether he was Jesus or not but rather if he was truly human. Thus, Jesus had to physically find a way to prove to them that he was truly a human being. So he told them to "'look at my hands and my feet. It is I myself! Touch me and see; a ghost does not have flesh and bones, as you see I have'. When he had said this, he showed them his hands and feet" (Luke 24:39-40). His nail imprints on his hands and feet would show physical proof that he was indeed human. He was showing them the powerful proof that ghosts do not have hands and feet and that ghosts do not have the particular scars of crucifixion.

After this, Luke states that "while they still did not believe it because of joy and amazement, he asked them, 'Do you have anything here to eat'" (24:41). It seems that they were convinced that he was resurrected, but they had a tough time acknowledging it, for it seemed too good to be true. Did they all of a sudden forget the miracles that he himself had performed and the prophecy that he would rise on the third day after being handed over to the Romans?

Upon Jesus' request, his disciples "gave him a piece of broiled fish, and he took it and ate it in their presence (Luke 24:42-43). What Jesus was just trying to do was to convince them that he was the same Jesus and indirectly, he was also letting them know that ghosts do not eat food either. Acts 1:3 states that "after his suffering, he showed himself to these men and gave many convincing proofs that he was alive." To his disciples, these facts were convincing knowing that he was the same Jesus who had died three days earlier. It would be their confirmed belief in the actual resurrection of Jesus that would soon give them boldness to boldly proclaim the truth of their convictions.

HIS COMPLETION OF PROPHECY

For those who still doubted, Jesus would give even more proof from the prophets of old saying, "'This is what I told you while I was still with you: Everything must be fulfilled that is written about me in the Law of Moses, the Prophets and the Psalms.' Then he opened their minds so they could understand the Scriptures" (Luke 24:44-45). These Jews knew the Old Testament Scripture, but they had to be reminded and perhaps educated that whatever they found written concerning the Messiah in the Old Testament must be fulfilled in him.

He told them, "This is what is written: The Christ will suffer and rise from the dead on the third day, and repentance and forgiveness of sins will be preached in his name to all nations, beginning at Jerusalem" (Luke 24:46-47). He most likely repeated the same Old

Testament passages that he told the two who were traveling to Emmaus. He was again letting them know of the necessity for him to have suffered before he could truly save his people from their sins. It was important for his followers to see God's redemptive plan for man's sin, and because of this, he told them that they are "witnesses of these things."

HIS COMMISSION TO THEM

Knowing that he would soon leave them, he would let them know that he would still be among them. He stated, "I am going to send you what my Father has promised; but stay in the city until you have been clothed with power from on high" (Luke 24:49). His "promise" was referring to the Holy Spirit of whom the eleven would personally experience. But they had to stay in Jerusalem until they had experienced his "promise". Certainly, his followers did not know every detail of what Jesus was referring to and how exactly they would be "clothed", but they would find out soon and be assured that this "promise" was what he was referring to.

Possibly Acts 1:4-5 was referring to this first appearance of Jesus with his disciples, for he said virtually the same thing saying, "On one occasion, while he was eating with them, he gave them this command, 'Do not leave Jerusalem, but wait for the gift my Father promised, which you have heard me speak about. For John baptized with water, but in a few days you will be baptized with the Holy Spirit.'" In Luke's writings, he specifically mentions that his disciples would be "clothed" or baptized by the Holy Spirit.

His words of remaining in Jerusalem until the "promise" had come was not his only mandate. He told them, "As the Father has sent me, I am sending you." Although Jesus would soon leave, his followers were instructed to carry on his work and spiritual endeavors. And with that he breathed on them and said, "Receive the Holy Spirit. If you forgive anyone his sins, they are forgiven. If you do not forgive them, they are not forgiven." This was his mark to give certainty to what he said and this action was also a guarantee of him being absolutely alive.

Jesus' Second Appearance to His Disciples

THOMAS ENCOUNTERS THE DISCIPLES AND DISBELIEVES

Although Jesus gave convincing proofs that he was alive, John makes it clear that not all of his disciples were present during his first appearance. He states, "Now Thomas (called Didymus), one of the Twelve, was not with the disciples when Jesus came. So the other disciples told him, 'We have seen the Lord'" (John 20:24-25). Thomas most likely heard the news of Jesus being alive from the women, from the two who were on the road to Emmaus, and now he is hearing the news from all the disciples. How much more proof would he need than for all the disciples to convince him that they really saw Jesus?

"But he said to them, 'Unless I see the nail marks in his hands and put my finger where the nails were, and put my hand into his side, I will not believe it.'" His statement is not that of a doubter but that of an unbeliever. Although both are similar, one who doubts has characteristics of one who is a skeptic. However, one who is a nonbeliever does not have any skepticism but rather believes no part of what is being told. Thomas does not want to accept any part of their valid testimony and from his perspective, he does not even expect to see Jesus although everyone else has told him that he was really alive.

THOMAS ENCOUNTERS JESUS AND BELIEVES

Exactly "a week later, his disciples were in the house again, and Thomas was with them" (John 20:26). Perhaps Jesus' disciples met up daily or they discussed the times that they desired to meet. Again, we see them in a house with "the doors" being "locked" because of fear of the Jews. Although Jesus met up with most of them on one occasion, they were still gripped with fear. Because of this, we will see a pattern of Jesus meeting up with them on several occasions in order to restore their confidence and sanity.

Then suddenly, Jesus "appeared to the Eleven as they were eating" (Mark 16:14) and he "stood among them" (John 20:26). It makes sense that Jesus reserved this second appearance to them on the same day of the week that he arose (resurrection day) and they may have been partaking of the Feast of the Unleavened Bread. Although the Gospels do not state the men's emotions once Jesus appeared, they most likely were scared. Thus, Jesus spoke quickly and said to them "Peace be with you!" most likely to calm their fears.

Then he gets to his main purpose in coming to them. Mark gives the idea that he generally "rebuked them for their lack of faith and their stubborn refusal to believe those who had seen him after he had risen" (Mark 16:14). All we know is that Thomas was "stubborn" and gave a "refusal to believe." Although we don't know of any others, perhaps there were more "disciples" in that house than just the eleven and perhaps some of them gave a "refusal."

But John seems to make it clear that it was only Thomas who did not believe because Jesus began to speak only to him saying, "Put your finger here; see my hands. Reach out your hand and put it into my side. Stop doubting and believe" (20:27). Jesus explicitly showed him his hands and side because Thomas went overboard in telling the other disciples that he would not believe unless he saw "the nail marks in his hands," put his "finger where the nails were," and put his "hand into his side." Jesus was indirectly telling Thomas that he heard exactly what he had said. Certainly Thomas was very embarrassed in front of the other men and perhaps all of them knew what he had said as well.

Then Thomas proclaims the words of belief saying, "My Lord and my God" (John 20:28). The words "Lord" [*Kyrios*] and "God" [*Theos*] are deity titles and Thomas ascribes them specifically to Jesus alone. We don't know if Thomas actually put his finger in Jesus' side and his hands, but we do see him fully content of the certainty of Jesus' resurrection. He quickly recognized that he was the same Jesus who was crucified and that he was no ghost or spirit. This was his giant leap of faith and he demonstrated it by making an open confession. Although a Roman openly proclaimed Jesus' deity by stating him to be the "Son of God" (Mark 15:39), Thomas openly proclaimed that he was both "Lord" and "God." Now Jesus was glorified through both his crucifixion and his resurrection.

JESUS EMPHASIZES THE TRUTH OF BELIEVING

Then Jesus told him, "Because you have seen me, you have believed. Blessed are those who have not seen and yet have believed" (John 20:29). Thomas had been brought to faith in the resurrection by the personal appearance of Christ and blessings would be pronounced on him because he had believed. And soon, multitudes would be brought to faith in Christ by the report of these witnesses.[379] But Jesus was letting him know that everyone will not have the privilege to see the resurrected Christ as he had, and despite that fact, they must also believe. Jesus states that there is a blessing for those who believe without seeing and Thomas has now been commissioned with the others to proclaim this truth.

The faith of Thomas is the climax to this narrative and John emphasizes even more to his listeners concerning the faith that they must have in the risen Jesus. He continues to say that "Jesus did many other miraculous signs in the presence of his disciples, which are not recorded in this book. But these are written that you may believe that Jesus is the Christ, the Son of God, and that by believing you may have life in his name" (20:30-31). The signs given were given to authenticate the person, word, and work of Christ. The resurrection in John's mind was the climactic sign authenticating the person and work of Christ. His purpose in recording the signs was to lead men to personal faith that "Jesus is the Christ, the Son of God" so that "by believing you may have life in his name".[380]

THOMAS' EXAMPLE OF BELIEVING

Although history portrays Thomas simply as one who doubted, a somewhat bad stench has been placed upon him. Outside of his name being listed with the other eleven, the Gospels only mention his name on two other occasions. And sadly, his name is mentioned more in this narrative than anywhere else in the New Testament. So because we don't have much information about him except from this narrative, he is seen in a more negative fashion. Yet this narrative does not show only a deficiency in his character, but something noteworthy.

There are at least two noteworthy qualities from Thomas. First, he refuses to pretend to believe what has been said or done when he does not. That is why he should be classified as an unbeliever and not a doubter. He wanted full proof in order to be persuaded, and he did. Even more, it could have been any disciple who was absent when Jesus appeared the first time, but it happened to be him.

Second, when he finally understood the truth, he believed to the fullest. He was not a half believer but he properly called Jesus both "Lord" and "God". Because of his firm persuasion, he perhaps was the only apostle of Jesus who went outside the Roman Empire to proclaim the gospel. History records that he went to India, and thus, he crossed the largest geographical area including the Persian Empire to preach Jesus. Thus, it was no coincidence that he was absent the first time, because when he was firmly persuaded, he perhaps went where no other apostle journeyed. We see that God can use the strong areas of one's life in order to make the greatest impact for his cause, and he did just that with Thomas.

Jesus' Third Appearance to His Disciples

HIS MIRACLE BEFORE THEM

The Obstacle in Catching Nothing

The apostle John in writing his account had just stated that "Jesus did many other miraculous signs in the presence of his disciples," and now he is about to mention another one of these signs. John 21:1 states, "Afterward Jesus appeared again to his disciples, by the Sea of Tiberias." The Sea of Tiberias, also known as Chinnereth in the Old Testament, the Sea of Galilee, and the Lake of Gennesaret, is located on the western shore of the Sea of Galilee. It was constructed, enlarged, and beautified by Herod Antipas when Jesus was a young man and was named in honor of Tiberias Caesar.

This appearance was about 68 miles north of Jerusalem, which was the place for his first two visits, and we don't know how long it was after Jesus appeared to them the second time. Although Jesus told them all during his first appearance to "stay in the city until you have been clothed with power from on high", they took a temporary trip to Galilee.

John starts from the beginning of the narrative and states, "It happened this way." Then he states, "Simon Peter, Thomas (called Didymus), Nathanael from Cana in Galilee, the sons of Zebedee, and two other disciples were together. 'I'm going out to fish,' Simon Peter told them, and they said, 'We'll go with you'" (21:2). Since we know who Simon Peter was, it is important to know that Thomas, whom we have just seen, was also called Didymus, which means "twin". Nathanael was last mention in the first chapter of John when Philip finds him and tells him "we have found the one Moses wrote about in the Law, and about whom the prophets also wrote - Jesus of Nazareth, the son of Joseph" (1:45). The sons of Zebedee were James and John, and the two who were not named are supposed to be Philip of Bethsaida and Andrew of Capernaum.

These seven disciples follow Peter who tells them that he was going fishing and they proceed out to the sea. History reports a thriving fishing industry around this time with over 200 boats regularly working in the lake. Fishing was not only a leisure activity but a great economic activity along with agriculture. It was not only a way of life but also a means of living. So as they all got into the boat to catch fish, "that night they caught nothing" (John 21:2). It was probably late evening when they began fishing and from that time till late that night, they strangely were not successful. How odd it was for these fishermen who, especially James and John, were good at their trade in the midst of a thriving economy. But little did they know that there was a purpose in the midst of their obstacle.

The Observance of a Miracle

Then "early in the morning, Jesus stood on the shore, but the disciples did not realize that it was him. He called out to them, 'Friends, haven't you any fish?' 'No,' they answered" (John 21:4-5). Seemingly, these seven disciples were still trying to catch fish that morning. Jesus, knowing all along, simply asked them if they had caught any fish.

So he tells them, "Throw your net on the right side of the boat and you will find some" (John 21:6). Jesus is still unrecognized but he is directing operations from the shore. Not knowing who this "fisherman" was, these men obeyed and threw their nets on the other side. It did not take a genius to know that switching directions from the boat would not help to bring in more fish, for there was not much of a directional change in the water.

Yet upon doing so, they caught such a large number of fish that they were unable to haul the net in (John 21:6). There wasn't just a large number of fish but the net "was full of large fish" and amazingly, "the net was not torn" (John 21:11). Because Jesus was present and he initiated the actions of his disciples, we know that this was indeed a miracle. In being consistent with the other miracles, this catch happened instantaneously and not over the process of minutes and hours. Again, it is no miracle to catch a lot of big fish. However, it is a miracle to catch "153" good fishes immediately after throwing one's net over the other side. It was also a miracle for the net to not break when it should have. As a miracle in itself, Christ manifests himself to his people by doing that for them which none else can do.[381] The disciples had the curiosity to count them and perhaps, they were going to split the fishes among the seven.

"Then the disciple whom Jesus loved said to Peter, 'It is the Lord!'" (John 21:7). John seemed to have been the most cerebral and sharp-witted disciple. He had adhered more personally with Jesus in his anguish and affliction than any of them. Thus, it seems that he had a clearer understanding and was more discerning than the rest of the disciples. He knew immediately that it was Jesus because of the instant miraculous catch, for he had seen this happen before. Luke 5 records Jesus telling Simon Peter to put his net out into the deep water for a catch. Although Simon replied that they previously had caught nothing, he obeyed. As a result, they caught such a large amount of fish that they had to ask for help from their partner fisherman. Luke records that Simon "and all his companions were astonished at the catch of fish they had taken, and so were James and John, the sons of Zebedee, Simon's partners" (5:9-10).

The Overwhelming Joy in Seeing Jesus

"As soon as Simon Peter heard him say, 'It is the Lord,' he wrapped his outer garment around him (for he had taken it off) and jumped into the water. The other disciples followed in the boat, towing the net full of fish, for they were not far from shore, about a hundred yards" (John 21:7-8). Although John may have been more intelligent and discerning, Peter had more passion than any of the others. Peter was the most zealous and warmhearted disciple, for as soon as he heard it was the Lord, the boat could not hold him, but into the sea he throws himself that he might come first to Christ. He showed his respect for Christ by wrapping his outer garment around him, that he might appear before his Master in the best clothes he had.[382] His actions showed his overwhelming joy in knowing that Jesus was there. When Jesus performed this similar miracle in Luke 5, Peter fell at Jesus' knees saying, "Go away from me, Lord; I am a sinful man!" (5:8). But now, he shows a different response, for he was no longer feeling the effects of sin but rather the emotions of joy.

These disciples and especially Peter learned that fishing all night without Jesus was to only suffer the embarrassment of catching nothing. But when he showed up to guide and instruct them, they were not only successful but they had a great catch. Both of the miracles regarding Jesus and the large catch of fish were These miracles demonstrate Jesus' assistance to those who were unsuccessful otherwise. Ultimately, he wanted them to be fishers of men just as they were in the business of catching fish, and they were ultimately going to need his assistance in bringing multitudes of people to himself.

HIS MEAL WITH THEM

When the boat had landed, the disciples "saw a fire of burning coals there with fish on it, and some bread. Jesus said to them, 'Bring some of the fish you have just caught'" (John 21:9-10). Jesus was now about to eat with his disciples and we see his desire to maintain his presence with everyone. So Simon, who seemingly was the fishing leader, "climbed aboard and dragged the net ashore. It was full of large fish, 153, but even with so many the net was not torn" (John 21:11). His zeal is seen by him quickly initiating that which Jesus had asked. In addition, the author was simply attesting to the miraculous fact that the net should have also been easily broken, but it was not. Then Jesus said to them, "come and have breakfast." Jesus must have already prepared breakfast for these seven disciples and it must have been ready to eat.

It is important to notice that this greeting with them was much different than his past two "greetings." When he showed up at the house on the two previous occasions where they had gathered, his presence brought fear and doubt. But now his presence was more intimate and there was no fear or doubt present. We even see this fact brought out by the author stating that "none of the disciples dared ask him, 'Who are you?' They knew it was the Lord" (John 21:12). Jesus' first appearance brought skepticism, perhaps even the second as well, but now that he had appeared to them on a third occasion by the sea, they were more comfortable with him and they knew exactly who he was. Fishing was where these men felt "at home" and it was not being locked up into a house because of fear. And Jesus strategically took a third time to establish himself with them in this setting.

So "Jesus came, took the bread and gave it to them, and did the same with the fish" (John 21:13). When it came to eating, Jesus' main actions consisted of him blessing the food, breaking the "food" and giving it to others. We see about nine instances in the gospels when he did just that. For his disciples, they saw the real Jesus, for no one had his unique style in distributing food and thanking God. At the same time, he showed himself fully alive and normal by eating common food, for he had a true body that was capable of eating.

John also makes it clear that "this was now the third time Jesus appeared to his disciples after he was raised from the dead" (John 21:14). Although he had appeared to the women, Mary Magdalene, the two going toward Emmaus, and Peter, this was only the third time that he appeared to the company of his disciples. Each time that he met up with them was only confirming his resurrection and the fact that he was indeed God.

HIS MESSAGE TO PETER

To Feed His Lambs

Now that Jesus had made himself comfortable with these men, he foresaw Peter's future and desired to reinstate his confidence. So "when they had finished eating, Jesus said to Simon Peter, 'Simon son of John, do you truly love me more than these" (John 21:15). Although

Jesus gave him the name Cephas, which when translated is Peter (John 1:42), he calls him Simon, which was his original name. Simon knew that he suffered from embarrassment and reproach because of his three denials, and Jesus knew this and moved to meet his need. From Peter's standpoint, this question carried an undertone that his love for his Savior had weakened because of his disownment. It seemed that his question demonstrated a lack of evidence that seemingly had not been shown. But from another perspective, Peter knew that he had showed his love to him on numerous occasions, but yet he simply made a terrible mistake before his death. He knew that it was evident throughout Jesus' ministry that he demonstrated zeal even when he sometimes went overboard on some occasion.

So he replied back saying, "'Yes, Lord, you know that I love you.' Jesus said, 'Feed my lambs.'" This word for "feed" was strictly intended to give them basic food. Jesus had already told his disciples during the onset of his ministry to be fishers of men and this was his intent for all of his followers. But for Peter, he needed to reinstate him back into the fold, and Jesus wanted to make sure that he understood his desire for them.

Again Jesus said, "'Simon son of John, do you truly love me?' He answered, 'Yes, Lord, you know that I love you.' Jesus said, 'Take care of my sheep'" (John 21:16). Jesus did not say to "feed" this time but rather to "take care" of his sheep. This word meant to not only feed and keep but to tend, to rule and govern, and to nourish.

Strangely, "the third time he said to him, 'Simon son of John, do you love me?' Peter was hurt because Jesus asked him the third time, 'Do you love me?' He said, 'Lord, you know all things; you know that I love you.' Jesus said, 'Feed my sheep'" (John 21:17). Jesus reverts to asking Peter to simply feed his sheep and not the duties of a shepherd. It probably was not hard for Peter to realize that perhaps the three repeated questions of whether he loved Jesus or not corresponded to his three denials.

But Jesus' had a specific purpose he was trying to make to Peter. The particular application here was intended to restore him to his apostleship now that he repented. This commission given was evidence that Jesus was reconciled to him, else he would never have reposed such confidence. Jesus, when he forgave Peter, trusted him with the most valuable treasure he had on earth. It was intended to motivate him to a diligent discharge of his office as an apostle.[383] Again, Jesus gave a basic call to all of his disciples and told them all to be fishers of men. Yet at this moment, Peter needed to be especially reinforced to carry out that call. He was no better than the disciples, yet because he was the only one who boldly denied his Savior, Jesus understood the value to motivate and reconcile him back into the fold.

He Foretell His Death

If Peter truly loved him and if he truly was going to "feed" his "lambs", Jesus wanted to let him know that it would come at a cost. Perhaps Jesus foresaw how Peter's life was going to end and he wanted to make sure that he loved him enough to stay faithful. Jesus then tells him, "I tell you the truth, when you were younger you dressed yourself and went where you wanted, but when you are old you will stretch out your hands, and someone else will dress you and lead you where you do not want to go" (John 21:18). What was Jesus saying when he said this? John states that "Jesus said this to indicate the kind of death by which Peter would glorify God" (John 21:19).

For Jesus to have said "when you are old you will stretch out your hands, someone else will dress you and lead you where you do not want to go," he was giving major hints of the death of crucifixion. Crucifixion was the only death where someone's hands were stretched out by the hands of "someone else", specifically the Romans. Although some people died because of flogging, the actual crucifixion was the main intent of death. The Romans were the ones who "lead" people to the crucifixion cite, just as they did Jesus, so that everyone around would observe their death.

Years after Jesus said these prophetic words, history records that facts of what both Jesus and John had stated. Peter labored in Rome during the last portion of his life and there, his life ended by martyrdom. Christian author and apologist Tertullian who died around 220 A.D. attested to Peter's death, and Christian scholar and theologian Origin who died around 254 A.D. stated, "Peter was crucified at Rome with his head downwards, as he himself had desired to suffer."[384] The Acts of Peter, which was one of the earliest of the apocryphal Acts of the Apostles, attested that Peter was crucified upside down and 64 A.D. has been given as the date of his death.[385] In order to encourage Christians during his era, Clement of Rome who was the first Apostolic Father of the early Christian church, states, "Let us take the noble examples of our own generation. Through jealousy and envy the greatest and most just pillars of the church were persecuted, and came even unto death... Peter, through unjust envy, endured not one or two but many labors, and at last, having delivered his testimony, departed unto the place of glory due to him."[386]

Jesus commissions Peter to be a shepherd, which would unfortunately require him to undergo misery and affliction. Jesus had the motive to first appoint him to do his work, and then he appointed him to suffer the violent death of crucifixion. At the same time, he was letting him know that although it would be an honor to shepherd his people, it would also be an honor to die for his name.

To Follow Him

Then Jesus sums up what he desired to tell Peter and he said to him, "Follow me" (John 21:19). This wasn't the first time he gave him this mandate, for early in his ministry, Jesus saw him casting a net into the lake and he said to him, "come, follow me and I will make you fishers of men" (Matthew 4:19). Although both statements carried the same significance, the second mandate was more personal to Peter. At first, he most likely did not understand the full significance of what Jesus meant, but now he understood his message more clearly.

Jesus' statement was only a further confirmation to his restoration in being a whole-hearted disciple. From Jesus' standpoint, regardless of how his death would end and regardless of his past failures and embarrassments, he simply wanted Peter to follow him. Jesus was looking futuristically which may have been in contrast to Peter only dwelling on his past failures.

While Jesus was saying these words to Peter, "Peter turned and saw that the disciple whom Jesus loved was following them. (This was the one who had leaned back against Jesus at the supper and had said, 'Lord, who is going to betray you?')" (John 21:20). Apparently during most, if not all, of this conversation between Peter and Jesus, they had been walking, perhaps along the shores of the Sea of Galilee. John again does not use his name but rather states that he was "the disciple whom Jesus loved," And it seems that Peter did not know that John was behind him as Jesus and he were talking.

So "when Peter saw him, he asked, 'Lord, what about him?'" (John 20:21). Peter was simply asking Jesus concerning John's task and perhaps what would happen to him when he would get old. He may have wanted to know if John would also suffer the effects of being stretched out and having someone else dress him and lead him where you he does not want to go. At the same time, perhaps Peter was a little uneasy with what Jesus said about his future, which would have been perfectly normal. But Jesus replied to him saying, "If I want him to remain alive until I return, what is that to you? You must follow me" (John 20:22). Jesus simply let Peter know that the business of his conversation centered on him and his future and not John's. Although it was a perfectly normal question, Jesus bluntly stated that he had a different plan for John than he had for Peter.

At the same time, there was an insinuation that John would not die the same type of death as Peter, or maybe not even a violent death at all. Early Christian history even supported the fact that John did not suffer martyrdom as the other disciples or apostles did. John's brother James was the first apostle to die while history supports the fact that John was the last to die. It was during his late years of life that he was exiled to an Island called Patmos, and it was there where he received the apocalypse, the sacred book of Revelation. Yet he did not die on that island, but returned to Ephesus and he helped to establish many churches.

For some reason, what Jesus had said to Peter was misinterpreted by the disciples. John states, "Because of this, the rumor spread among the brothers that this disciple would not die. But Jesus did not say that he would not die. He only said, 'If I want him to remain alive until I return, what is that to you'" (John 21:23). John makes it clear to the other disciples what Jesus said, simply because he was there and was an eyewitness.

Jesus' Forth Appearance to His Disciples

THE ARRIVAL IN GALILEE

John saw the opportunity to mention in detail Jesus' third appearance. But that appearance was not the last time he appeared to his disciples. Matthew simply passed over many of Jesus' intimate times with his disciples to mention his fourth appearance with them. Matthew states the location of this appearance stating, "Then the eleven disciples went to Galilee, to the mountain where Jesus had told them to go" (Matthew 28:16). Galilee is the northern part of Israel and is the region that encompasses the Sea of Galilee, the location of Jesus' third appearance. Perhaps this fourth appearance was not long after the third seeing that they both were around the same region.

Matthew states that "when they saw him, they worshipped him. But some doubted" (Matthew 28:17). Who were the "some" that doubted. Certainly none of the eleven doubted because Jesus had already appeared to them on three occasions, although some were not present for all of them. But we know that all of them believed because they all were trying to tell Thomas the facts of Jesus being alive. So certainly, it is a good case to state that this appearance was not just with the eleven but perhaps with some of his other followers. We know that the angels told the women to tell his disciples that he would go before them into Galilee and perhaps it seemed to the other believers that this was an occasion to see the risen Lord. We know that Paul states that over 500 brethren saw Jesus at one time sometime after he appeared to the eleven in Jerusalem (1 Corinthians 15:6). At the same time, this was Jesus' only recorded appearance in Galilee, outside of being with his disciples by the Sea of Galilee. So the conclusion could be made that although Jesus' disciples met him in Galilee on a mountain, there could have been others there observing him as well.

THE ASSIGNMENT - "GO"

Then Jesus came to them and said, "All authority in heaven and on earth has been given to me" (Matthew 28:18). As if the disciples did not already know, Jesus was letting them know of his power, authority, and dominion over all the earth. The fact that he conquered the grave was proof enough for them to understand that he himself was greater than the laws of nature. The disciples had heard him call upon God as his Father, yet at the same time, they knew that he was God, for only God could do the things that he did.

Because of who he was and the power that was invested in him, he told them to "go and make disciples of all nations, baptizing them in the name of the Father and of the Son and of the Holy Spirit and teaching them to obey everything I have commanded you" (Matthew 28:19-20). His commission summed up what he had told these men from the beginning, for he wanted them to be fishers of men. Now they truly understood that they were to hunt for men even if it took all night just as they had fished all night.

Jesus' first commission consisted of them to "go". This word specifically meant "as you are going" and it gave the connotation that while they were going about in their mission endeavors. These disciples were already familiar with "going", for Luke 10 records Jesus appointing seventy two followers and him sending them ahead of him to towns and cities. During that occasion, he told them, "Go! I am sending you out like lambs among wolves" (10:3). So these disciples had already a familiarity with what Jesus was talking about.

Second, his commission consisted of them going to "all nations" which specifically meant going to all "people-groups". Just to look at large nations without the specific people groups was to miss Jesus' entire commission. We saw that at least Thomas took his charge literally, for history records that he crossed over the Persian Empire and went to the nation of India to preach Jesus.

Third, his commission consisted of them baptizing them, just as Jesus was baptized. Jesus' example in Matthew 3:13-17 was done as an example for his future followers and they were to baptize their soon to be Christian converts in name of the Father, Son, and Holy Spirit. They were not baptizing them in the name of three God's but rather the Father, Son, and Holy Spirit which were three persons making up the same God.

Fourth, as they were going, they were to teach "them to obey everything" that Jesus had said. As we have seen before, Jesus' teachings were entirely strange and countercultural. It was not popular for the Jews to "love" their Roman "enemies" and to "pray for those" Romans "who persecute" them (Matthew 5:44). But they were to do so, for Jesus commanded them to obey everything he said.

But Jesus did not leave them without a promise, for he said, "Surely I am with you always, to the very end of the age" (Matthew 28:20). Although he was about to leave them, Jesus gave the promise that he would actually never leave them. Although his bodily presence would leave, his spiritual presence would stay. These words go back to Jesus telling them that his Father would send "the Counselor, the Holy Spirit" who would "teach you all things and will remind you of everything I have said to you" (John 14:26).

THE ACCOMPANY OF SIGNS

Although it may seem that Mark 16:15-18 occurred during the same time as Mark 16:14, it makes more sense that it occurred during Jesus' fourth appearance. Jesus states to his disciples in Mark 16:15, "Go into all the world and preach the good news to all creation." Matthew specifically records Jesus stating these words when they were on a mountain in Galilee, and what follows in verse 15 gives the notation that Jesus did not say these words in Jerusalem during his first and second appearance to his disciples.

In addition to him telling his disciples to "go", he tells them "whoever believes and is baptized will be saved, but whoever does not believe will be condemned" (Mark 16:16). This condemnation that Jesus was talking about would be when "the Son of Man will send out his angels, and they will weed out of his kingdom everything that causes sin and all who do evil. They will throw them into the fiery furnace, where there will be weeping and gnashing of teeth" (Matthew 13:41-42). But the salvation that he was talking about is stated in Matthew 13:43 which states, "Then the righteous will shine like the sun in the kingdom of their Father." Those who believe will "shine" in the "kingdom" but those who do not believe will be thrown "into the fiery furnace."

Jesus then tells them of the signs that "will accompany those who believe." First he states, "In my name they will drive out demons" (Mark 16:17). When Jesus sent the seventy two into towns ahead of him, they "returned with joy and said, 'Lord, even the demons submit to us in your name'" (Luke 10:17). In other words, the demons came out of man because of the name of Jesus. Although there were not many references to demons being cast out by apostles after Jesus ascended, we know that it took place because it took place before he left.

Second, he states that they would "speak in new tongues" (Mark 16:17). Tongues were actual languages spoken and they were greatly needed during the onset of the church. What Jesus stated actually came true by the hand of the apostles in Acts 2:1-4 stating, "When the day of Pentecost came, they were all together in one place. Suddenly a sound like the blowing of a violent wind came from heaven and filled the whole house where they were sitting. They saw what seemed to be tongues of fire that separated and came to rest on each of them. All of them were filled with the Holy Spirit and began to speak in other tongues as the Spirit enabled them." Because God wanted his church to prosper during its onset, these languages were used to help those who could not hear the good news of Jesus in their language.

Third, Jesus stated that "they will pick up snakes with their hands" (Mark 16:18). Paul the apostle actually fulfilled this prophecy. In Acts 28, when he and others were safely on the shore on the island of Malta, the islanders built a fire because it was raining and cold. As he was gathering dry twigs for the fire, "a viper, driven out by the heat, fastened itself on his hand. When the islanders saw the snake hanging from his hand, they said to each other, 'This man must be a murderer; for though he escaped from the sea, Justice has not allowed him to live.' But Paul shook the snake off into the fire and suffered no ill effects. The people expected him to swell up or suddenly fall dead, but after waiting a long time and seeing nothing unusual happen to him, they changed their minds and said he was a god'" (28:1-6).

Fourth, Jesus prophetically stated that "when they drink deadly poison, it will not hurt them at all" (Mark 16:18). The Gospels and the book of Acts do not record an instance where one of the Saints actually drank poison and it did not hurt them. But Christian history does. During the peak of persecution in Rome, the Roman Emperor Domitian demanded John the apostle to be boiled in a huge basin of boiling oil. But his torturers could not kill him. Then sometime afterwards, he was forced to drink a cup of deadly poison but he was miraculously delivered from death. God was not finished with him because he had to give him a revelation of what was to come. It was after this wave of persecution that he was exiled to the island of Patmos, which was where he wrote the book of Revelation.

And fifth, Jesus told them that "they will place their hands on sick people, and they will get well" (Mark 16:18). More than one instances of this took place in the book of Acts alone. One of these examples was recorded in Acts 3. Here, Peter and John saw a crippled man from birth and Peter took him "by the right hand, he helped him up, and instantly the man's feet and ankles became strong" (3:7).

After looking at these signs in detail from the examples give to us in the New Testament and in Christian history, these were actually signs that took place by the apostles, including Paul who was called an apostle. These were not signs given when a sinner believed in Jesus, but rather were given for the apostles as signs that would "accompany" them because they believed.

Jesus' Fifth Appearance with His Disciples

Jesus' last appearance with his disciples did not occur in the northern vicinity of Israel but in the southern vicinity of Israel. We know that this was his last appearance with his disciples because Luke not only gives the location but states that it was in that specific location where he ascended into heaven. Luke states that he "led them out to the vicinity of Bethany" (Luke 24:50), which is located just outside of Jerusalem and not far from the Dead Sea. John 11:18 specifically states that it was less than two miles from Jerusalem.

HIS ADMONITION

During this fifth appearance, the disciples asked him, "Lord, are you at this time going to restore the Kingdom to Israel" (Acts 1:6). Because Jesus rose from the dead, he was still able to not only be the Jew's Messiah, but was be able to set up his kingdom and deliver his people from foreign control. Because he would be able to complete the duties of Messiahship, his disciples wanted to know if he was going to restore Israel at this moment. From their perspective, they had the right to ask and they were inquisitive to know when his establishment would take place.

Jesus replied to them saying, "It is not for you to know the times or dates the Father has set by his own authority" (Acts 1:7). Sadly, they were only thinking physical, whereas Jesus was thinking both physical and spiritual. Jesus was not only rebuking them but was admonishing them not to set their hopes on dates and times. Perhaps it was at this moment when Peter realized how God's time clock worked, for he stated in his epistle, "But do not forget this one thing, dear friends. With the Lord a day is like a thousand years and a thousand years are like a day. The Lord is not slow in keeping his promise, as some understand slowness. He is patient with you..." (1 Peter 3:8-9). Jesus was letting them know that the knowledge of these things is reserved by God and no one else can reveal these times.

But since Jesus wanted them to keep their minds on his commission, he continued to tell them, "But you will receive power when the Holy Spirit comes on you and you will be my witnesses in Jerusalem, and in all Judea and Samaria, and to the ends of the earth" (Acts 1:8). He told them that they needed to be witnesses of him beginning in the city of Jerusalem and slowly branching out to the ends of the earth.

What Jesus did not say but what actually came true was that they would be martyrs of the faith for him, that is most of them. Yet everyone would know that they were suffering for the cause of Christ. Their deaths would not only be well known but their lives would speak well after their death. Therefore, Jesus wanted to admonish them not to worry about what only God knows but rather to just be witnesses of him.

His Ascension

Then Jesus "lifted up his hands and blessed them" (Luke 24:50) because he was about to leave them. John equated Jesus' blessings to them at this moment to his steadfast and continual love for them. He stated, "Jesus knew that the time had come for him to leave this world and go to the Father. Having loved his own who were in the world, he now showed them the full extent of his love" (John 13:1). Thus, his disciples were able to see this full extend even when he was just about to leave them.

"While he was blessing them, he left them and was taken up into heaven" (Luke 24:51). Luke also states that as he was taken up towards the heavens, "a cloud hid him from their sight" (Acts 1:9). Jesus was not the first in history who had been taken up into heaven. Genesis 5:24 states that Enoch "walked with God and then he was no more, because God took him away." The author actually states that God took him from this earth and that he did not see death. Concerning Elijah, 2 Kings 2:11-12 states that as he and Elisha were "walking along and talking together, suddenly a chariot of fire and horses of fire appeared and separated the two of them, and Elijah went up to heaven in a whirlwind. Elisha saw this and cried out, 'My father! My father! The chariots and horsemen of Israel!' And Elisha saw him no more." These two men never saw death, and, like Jesus, they were taken up to heaven. However, there was one major difference between them. Jesus knew the way to heaven and did not need God to take him, nor a chariot of fire to show him the way. He even said that he was the "truth and the life" and that "no one comes to the Father except through" him.

When he was taken up into heaven, "he sat at the right hand of God" (Mark 16:19). Now Jesus was sitting in the same seat that he had sat before the foundation of the world. He was not better than his Father but rather they both sit in a seat besides each other. Although these men and perhaps some of his followers had seen some amazing miracles during Jesus' ministry, they had never seen something like this. A man seemingly floating up towards the heavens and then all of a sudden, a cloud comes and takes him out of their sight.

THE APPEARANCE OF ANGELS

Understanding what had just occurred, Luke states that all of them "were looking intently up into the sky as he was going" (Acts 1:10). Perhaps they expected to see some change in the visible heavens now at Christ's ascension. Christ had told them that hereafter they should see heaven open (John 1:51), and why should not they expect it now?[387]

Then all of a sudden, "two men dressed in white stood beside them. 'Men of Galilee,' they said, 'why do you stand here looking into the sky? This same Jesus, who has been taken from you into heaven, will come back in the same way you have seen him go into heaven'" (Acts 1:10-11). These men were nothing short of angels and they simply told these men that he was dead and became alive. He is gone but promises to return. The best is yet to come.[388] The prophets of old had even stated that "on that day, his feet will stand on the Mount of Olives, east of Jerusalem" (Zechariah 14:4). Jesus himself told them saying, "I am going there to prepare a place for you. And if I go and prepare a place for you, I will come back and take you to be with me that you also may be where I am" (John 14:2-3). The angels were simply reporting the facts of what the prophets had foretold and what Jesus himself had said that he would do. At the same time, they were telling these men to stop looking for the Messiah to come back at that moment but to continue on with their commission.

THEIR ADORATION OF HIM

Then the disciples stopped looking for Jesus in the clouds but rather "they worshipped him" (Luke 24:52). Their act of worship here was in the form of kneeling down in prostration to show him homage, and this act resembles the respect as one shows men of superior rank. This was their way of showing adoration and gratitude for Jesus blessing them and loving them till the end.

Afterwards, they "returned to Jerusalem with great joy." Their current emotions were totally different than it was weeks before when they were all in a house with the doors locked. They were no longer bound by the chains of depression, disbelief, fear, and skepticism. They were now joyful and in a worshipful state of mind despite what others thought of them.

There in Jerusalem, "they stayed continually at the temple, praising God" (Luke 24:53). When Jesus first told them that he was leaving, their hearts were physically troubled (John 14:1). But now their hearts were spiritually content with their Savior gone and they now had hoped to live the rest of their lives. No longer were they in a small house hiding but they were in a public Jewish building worshipping God.

In addition to their worship, they "went out and preached everywhere" (Mark 16:20). They certainly demonstrated that they were no longer afraid or ashamed of anyone and they boldly obeyed the call of God. Because of their obedience, the "Lord worked with them and confirmed his word by the signs that accompanied it" (Mark 16:20). Again we see the specific application of Jesus' signs that were to be performed, for Mark states that they were specifically carried out by the apostles.

CHAPTER 8
THE GROWTH OF CHRISTIANITY

Does Christianity stand on a strong foundation? Was it just a coincidence that Jesus was resurrected or did God have a purpose? Well looking at Christian history, we see that God indeed had a purpose in allowing his Son to be crucified and resurrected because the years after he left this earth caused growth and transformation for his disciples and followers.

Introduction

The early Christians believed that Jesus was one worth living for. They believed that his life and resurrection carried extreme significance to the point that they were no longer concerned about what people thought of them, nor whether people would fully believe in their message or not. Because of his resurrection, all of his followers who doubted would never doubt again and all those who lived in unbelief would never live in unbelief again. All those who forgot the significance of Scripture applied to Jesus and the kingdom would never forget its significance again. To them, Jesus was truly one worth living for.

The Apostolic Period

The eleven disciples felt that Jesus' resurrection was not only worth living for but was worth dying for as well. They returned to

472

Jerusalem with great joy and they were no longer bound by fear of someone in authority killing them like they did Jesus. In Jerusalem, they stayed continually at the temple, praising God and they "went out and preached everywhere" (Mark 16:20).

It wasn't long, specifically 10 days after his ascension, that Jesus remained true to his promise. He sent the Holy Spirit to his disciples and the church formally started when about 3,000 Jews heard the gospel and responded with faith to Jesus Christ (Acts 2). The Christian movement quickly began to include those who were non-Jews and two of those individuals included an Ethiopian official and a Roman officer and his family (Acts 8:26-39).

Both Jewish and non-Jewish converts increased rapidly after the death of Christ and people were open, receptive, and excited to this new movement of Christianity that was spreading world wide. Some of these areas included the entire Mediterranean world and the entire Roman Empire. Christianity reached even beyond the empire in Ireland, Armenia, and Persia. Now God's Kingdom began to broaden the way God intended and his everlasting covenant would now be able to include one not having to become a Jew by being circumcised and following the Jewish tradition.

THE FELLOWSHIP OF THE CHURCH

Some of the distinctions that signified the early believers as Christians were shown through the reading of Scripture, baptism and communion, fellowship, and daily prayer. Baptism showed the believers union with Jesus Christ and was to be the first act after salvation. Communion gave the believers a preview of the Kingdom of God and of Christ's return.

The fellowship of the church grew because of the believer's common bond and strong convictions, which was mostly shaped by the Jewish synagogue. Daily prayer was apart of the early churches routine and it took place both individually and congregationally. Even if Christians did cease to pray in common with other Jews at an early date, the pattern of their worship was undoubtedly very strongly influenced by the Jewish worship.[389]

THE FALL OF JERUSALEM

Since Jesus himself encouraged Christians to understand that persecution would soon arise, the early church had to undergo hardship and turmoil. Nero, the fifth Roman Emperor who ruled from 54 A.D. to 68 A.D., would be God's instrument to carry out his plan of persecution. During the first 10 years of his reign, he seemed to be benevolent. However, he began to persecute Christians and in 64 A.D., he blamed them for igniting a fire that many believe he started himself.

In 66 A.D., Florus, the last Roman procurator, stole vast quantities of silver from the temple. The outraged Jewish masses rioted and wiped out the small Roman garrison stationed in Jerusalem. This was a heartening victory that had a terrible consequence. Many Jews suddenly became convinced that they could defeat Rome, and the Zealots' ranks grew geometrically. Never again, however, did the Jews achieve so decisive a victory.[390]

But when the Romans returned, they had 60,000 heavily armed and highly professional troops. They launched their first attack against the Jewish state's most radicalized area, the Galilee in the north. The Romans vanquished the Galilee, and an estimate 100,000 Jews were killed or sold into slavery. During the summer of 70, the Romans breached the walls of Jerusalem and initiated an orgy of violence and destruction. Shortly thereafter, they destroyed the second temple. This was the final and most devastating Roman blow against Judea.[391] It is projected that as many as one million Jews died in the revolt against Rome.

The Zealots instigated the "Great Revolt" (66-70) and unfortunately for the Jews, this revolt led to one of the greatest devastations and failures in Jewish history. No one could blame them for wanting to overthrow Rome who continued to oppress them. Yet it was in 63 B.C. that Rome was given the opportunity to rule in Jerusalem, and since that time, their rule had grown more and more onerous. Even the High Priests who represented the Jews before God unfortunately worked with Rome for their benefit.

But it was this fall that caused Christianity to spread even more across the Roman Empire and throughout the world. God had a strategy in allowing his gospel to be brought to even some of the most remote geographical areas around the world. The fall of the Jewish

Temple was just one of the divine purposes in allowing Christianity today to become the largest and extensive religions in the world.

From the Apostolic Period to Constantine

It was not only the early Christians who believe Jesus was worth living for, but Christians throughout the first three centuries carried this same conviction. Church Fathers were instrumental in writing down important historical documents of not only the Christian church and early Christians, but of Jesus himself. These men were not apostles, nor were their works inspired, but their writings can be trust and they do provide a rich source of history of the Christian worship movement. They explain many details that demonstrate their belief in Jesus' heroism and validity.

JUSTIN MARTYR

One of the first recognized great philosophers of early Christianity was a man named Justin Martyr (100 A.D. to 165 A.D.). He not only took a stand for the truth of Scripture but believed that the gospel of Jesus Christ could stand up to the idealistic and rational heritage of the Greek world. His three works include: *First Apology, Second Apology,* and *Dialogue with Trypho.* It is within his work *First Apology* that he wrote to the Emperor Antoninus Pius which gives foundation to the structure and emphasis of early Christian worship. Like many Christians during his time, he died for his faith. Although he was beheaded in 165 A.D., he stayed faithful to Jesus Christ and to his beliefs in worship.

PERSECUTION UNDER DIOCLETANIUS

A Roman soldier named Gaius Aurelius Valerius Diocletanius became Emperor in Rome in 284 A.D. and during a brief period under his reign, Christianity was tolerated as long as it did not endanger or intimidate Diocletanius' Empire. But soon Diocletian became offended when he discovered many officials of the court making the sign of the cross at pagan sacrifices, and he quickly considered their actions to be disrespectful. His presence was soon felt among the Christians when he ordered the destruction of their churches along with their copies of their Bibles. In addition, he ordered everyone to sacrifice to his gods. Yet Christians continued to remain true to their convictions and they stood strong. During his era, approximately 40,000 Christians were martyrs throughout the empire.

It was generally safer for Christians to worship both individually and corporately within the privacy of homes during the start of the Fourth Century because of the great persecution of Diocletian and other leaders. Then in 305 A.D., Diocletian retired and within ten years, Christianity became legal under Emperor Constantine.

THE EMPEROR CONSTANTINE

During an era within history, it was dangerous to call oneself a Christian but with the arrival of Constantine, it became deadly not to become one. Emperor Constantine, who ruled from 306-337 A.D., was the first Roman Emperor to endorse and legalize Christianity. Following the victory of Licinius in 313 A.D. where he defeated Maximinus Daia, the Edict of Milan was signed which set the atmosphere for tranquility for Christians. This allowed Christianity to be both legal and practiced without the fear of persecution.

It was common knowledge among the Christians in the church to understand the physical and divine make-up of Jesus. But after the apostles died, heresies and legalism crept its way into the church. Now Christians were put under pressure to define their beliefs in Jesus the Messiah more clearly. One of the major results of Constantine legalizing Christianity was that the first Council of Nicaea helped established a more defined and distinguished Christian faith amongst believers. The Arian controversy was the main heresy that these bishops gathered together to discuss. Arianism discredited the nature and deity of Jesus Christ by promoting the fact the Jesus Christ was created by God the Father. This belief caused turmoil and confusion amongst Fourth Century Christians.

As a result of the discussion, the bishops organized a profession of faith that gave precision to the true faith of biblical Christianity. Their profession from the First Council of Nicaea included the belief in one God, his Son Jesus who was from the same substance of his

Father, his bringing of salvation, his suffering and his resurrection, and his coming to judge the living and the dead.

As a result of this universal theology of the nature of Jesus, the Christian church grew, formulated its theology and creed, and even developed a more fixed form in its worship. Christians no longer met within the homes but sought fellowship with places of worship. As a result, massive structures of places of worship for Christians came to be and today's worship structures and foundation can be placed back towards the end of the Fourth Century.

Several qualities have defined Jesus throughout his life and ministry that need to be mentioned. He lived a complete life and his qualities have been looked to for centuries as a model of heroism. In no particular order, I will state several characteristics and qualities that, when combined together, consistently set him apart from all others.

CHAPTER 9
JESUS, LIKE NEVER BEFORE

The events surrounding his life and death have been frequently read and spoken more than the stories surrounding any other person in history. Because of this fact, the resurrection established the truthfulness of Jesus and provides hope for millions around the world in several ways.

The Facts of Jesus' Burial

The facts of Jesus' burial set the tone for the facts of his resurrection in numerous ways. First, history proves that victims were to remain on the cross. I have already explained that condemned individuals were allowed to stay on their crosses until their flesh was consumed by the birds, dogs, etc. Sometimes the corpses would be given to family members for proper burial, though this was not done in cases of criminals executed for treason, as Jesus was.[392] Thus, Jesus was to have stayed on the cross like most everyone else until his body was consumed.

This leads us to our second fact which consist of Jewish sensitivity and customs. History itself proves that the Jews had customs and sometimes the Romans would honor them, not because they cared but rather because they were apart of their empire. Thus, it was of no coincidence that Jesus' arrest and crucifixion took place just before the Jewish Passover. As I have already stated, the Jews did not want the bodies of their Jewish victims left on the crosses with this celebration just the next day (Sabbath or Saturday). No historical records show that the Romans would not have honored this Jewish request.

The third fact is that only a wealthy person would have "intimate" access to Pilate and only he could give a condemned criminal executed for treason an honorable burial. Because Arimathea was not a "known" place and had not of yet been discovered, some say that Joseph was only a fabricated figure. Yet there are at least two other aspects that must be understood. First, in looking at cities that have been establish throughout Israel's history, there are many other cities that have not been unearthed. But does that mean that they did not exist? In addition, there have been Old Testament cities excavated such as Ur, Nahor, and Serug that have added validity to the Bible. Second, many scholars fail to understand the fact that Joseph was a member of the same Sanhedrin that condemned Jesus, yet he was not in consent of their decision. Certainly no Jew in their right mind would make up a tale that would incorporate this fact. And adding that he was wealthy and respected shows why he had access to Pilate and why Pilate handed Jesus over to him.

Fourth, the burial story is trustworthy understanding Jewish preservation of the graves of holy men. During Jesus' time, there was an extraordinary interest in the graves of Jewish martyrs and holy men, and these were scrupulously cared for and honored. This suggests that the grave of Jesus would also have been noted so that it too might become such a holy site. The disciples had no inkling of any resurrection prior to the general resurrection at the end of the world, and they would probably have not allowed the burial site of Jesus to go unnoted. This interest makes very plausible the women's lingering to watch the burial and their subsequent intention to anoint Jesus' body with spices and perfumes.[393]

Fifth, Pilate himself noted that Jesus was dead showing the entire world that he "indeed was dead." The biblical account seems to show that Pilate did not check on all the victims who were crucified to see if they were dead, but since Jesus had died so early, he wanted to confirm his dead before releasing him to Joseph. Thus, he served as a double witness from the lead centurion that Jesus was truly dead so that his resurrection was not a resuscitation. Certainly the lead centurion had presided over hundreds of crucifixions, and there was no reason for him to lie to Pilate concerning this one.

Sixth, no other burial tradition exists. No place in history do we have two, three, or even more than one burial story. Outside of the fabricated story that we shall soon see that the Jewish leaders made up, there are no other burial traditions except one. If the burial of

Jesus in the tomb by Joseph is legendary, then it is very strange that conflicting traditions nowhere appear, even in Jewish polemic.[394]

Our seventh fact comes from the Nazareth Inscription that shows that it was a serious violation to disturb tombs. And thus, common knowledge that those who stole a body would be seriously punished by the Romans might cause readers to realize the ridiculousness of the Jewish claim that disciples, who fled when Jesus was arrested, had now gained the courage to steal Jesus' body.[395]

And our eighth and final fact is that our biblical sources are early, which gives more credibility to his actual death. Jesus' burial in the tomb is attest by multiple early sources and this story is found in all four Gospels. Mark suggests that while Matthew and Luke shared the same stream of tradition as Mark, Mark's account was not their only source. In any case, John's narrative is probably literarily independent of the other three Gospels, and thus serves to confirm the main outline of the story.[396] The apostle Paul adds another early fact of Jesus' burial as stated in Romans 6:4, 1 Corinthians 15:4, and Colossians 2:12.

The Facts of Jesus' Resurrection

To reject Jesus' miracles is to disregard accurate inductive procedure where all essentials are investigated before a decision is made. To reject his resurrection is to disregard the same premises. His resurrection, arguably the most important event in the history of Christianity, was not only responsible for the establishment of the Christian Church, but it spawned a movement toward moral perfection from Jesus' followers. Because of this phenomenal event, hundreds of millions of people have found comfort in the Christian Bible and they aspire to live their lives accordingly. Nations have proclaimed to be founded from Jesus' actual resurrection and people everywhere testify to the truth of God and his Son Jesus Christ.

But without investigating, there is no way to claim the occurrence of certain events, such as the resurrection of Jesus Christ. Just to state that there was a resurrection without stating any proof does not stand on solid group. Yet if there were numerous convincing proofs and solid unwavering evidence that he actually rose from the grave, than there is a strong case that he indeed was resurrected. In this section, I desire to state some of this solid unwavering evidence that gives factual proof of Jesus' resurrection.

INTRODUCTION – RESURRECTION AND HOPE

There has only been one single event throughout history which changed the entire world and that event is the resurrection of Jesus of Nazareth. Even the most scientifically minded people remain baffled concerning these events, and what they can't get over is the fact that it is real history. The events surrounding his life and death have been frequently read and spoken more than the stories surrounding any other person in history. Because of this fact, the resurrection established the truthfulness of Jesus and provides hope for millions around the world in several ways.

First, the resurrection provides hope because of Jesus' triumph over death. Emphatically, the triumph of the crucifixion was his resurrection. From the religious leader's perspective, his crucifixion was intended to stop a movement already begun by him, but it failed to do so. Sadly, his execution had aborted their purpose. None of the Gospel accounts ended with Jesus' death, but rather they all included his resurrection account. For these authors, the resurrection reminded them that his crucifixion account was not the end of their record. What made the resurrection a foundation for Christians throughout history was his victory over the grave. Resurrection does not make a covenant with death, it overthrows it, and in the full Jewish and early Christian sense, it is the ultimate affirmation that creation matters.[397]

Second, the resurrection provides hope because Jesus was truly alive after his death and continues to live today. It took five appearances of Jesus after he rose from the grave to ultimately convince his followers of the truth of his resurrection. Not only that, but he presented numerous convincing proofs that he was alive and "normal." He even stayed on earth for forty days to make sure that his followers knew that he still lives (Acts 1:3). Then in their presence, he was taken up alive to his Father in heaven as a proof that he continues to live. Although there have been many different scenarios to explain him being alive after he was crucified, none of even the smarted philosophers can come up with a scenario that makes sense.

Third, the resurrection provides hope because Jesus promised his followers that he would be with them till the end of the age (Matthew 28:20). Followers of Jesus can rest assured that they are guaranteed safe passage throughout this sin infested world. In addition, the Christians who are converted during the tribulation period are given promises that Jesus will continue to be with them till the very end. Although Satan will make huge grounds during this time, Jesus will continue to be there for his people.

Fourth, the resurrection provides hope because of the example given from his disciples and followers. If those who believed in him during his earthly life had not remained steadfast to his teachings and if they had not continued to experience his continuing presence after the ascension, all would have been over. But it was not over because they continued to carry out his commission. They were able to spread the good news all across Jerusalem, Judea, and the Roman Empire, and because of them, Christianity has grown to be the largest religion ever.

Fifth, the resurrection provides hope because it set Jesus apart from everyone else. More than any other miracle he performed, the resurrection put the final stamp that he was not only the Son of God, but was God. Jesus' post death proved to be greater than everything he had done before his death. Even his own disciples were able to see Jesus greater and understand his true work and mission after his death than before.

FROM JESUS' OWN PREDICTIONS

There have been many predictions from people throughout history and some have come true. And yet some have not come true. Yet no one in history has claimed to make so many prophetic predictions, apart from the God of Israel, and all of them have come true. Yet Jesus made numerous predictions and prophecies, and all of them have come true.

Jesus predicted his own death and resurrection on several occasions as he spoke to his disciples. Each of the four Gospels describes his death and resurrection with minor differences in details. In Matthew, Jesus told his disciples he would go to Jerusalem to suffer, die, and rise again (Matthew 16:21). His prophetic references were made more than once in Matthew and instead of referring directly to himself, he refers to the Son of Man being betrayed, killed and resurrected (Matthew 17:22-23, 20:17-19). In the book of Mark, Jesus speaks of his suffering and rejection to come (Mark 8:31, 9:31; 10:33-34) and in the book of Luke, his message was reiterated (Luke 9:21-22, 18:31-32).

One of the true verifications of a prophet was if his prophetic claims came to pass. If one of them did not, he was considered a false prophet. All of Jesus' claims came to pass and not one of them as attested from the Gospel writers came short of Jesus' predictions. He was actually handed over to the Romans and was crucified, but after three days, he rose from the grave. There was no disparity within the writings that Jesus predicted his death on multiple occasions to different people. The slight differences within each account is no different from the slight variations from other narratives, and all of these predictions help support the premise that significant events did actually occur and that the writings were subject to the interpretations of the observer and writer.

FROM HIS DEATH

Supporting Views

The death of Jesus is the most recorded event in ancient, non-Christian history, and perhaps the most important fact that gives credibility to his resurrection comes from the actuality that he literally died and was buried. If there were any loopholes or discrepancies with his actual death, his resurrection would not stand on firm ground. We see key general facts that he actually died. First, the Romans were skilled in executing all criminals who were crucified. Second, there were eyewitnesses present who heard Jesus say his last words and saw him "give up the ghost". Third, eyewitnesses saw a guard pierce his side which caused blood and water to come gushing out. And fourth, the chief guard and Pilate confirmed that he was dead before Joseph buried him in his tomb.

The credibility pertaining to the facts of his burial supports his resurrection. First, Jesus' adversaries and Pilate knew that he was buried, they knew the location of his burial, and they used all of their preventative measures to make sure that his tomb was secure. And second, although his burial in a rich man's tomb would have been rare for any condemned criminal, it is also a fact during this era that crucified victims could receive an honorable burial. And third, the only way Jesus could have been placed in a rich man's tomb was if the rich man had status, money, and influence. And yes, Joseph had all three.

Opposing Views

Yet some people have tried to promote alternate views to do away with the belief that Jesus actually died and was buried. First, some say that after the crucifixion, his corpse was probably laid in a shallow grave, barely covered with dirt and subsequently eaten by wild dogs. They believe that the story of his entombment and resurrection was the result of "wishful thinking."[398] Yet those who believe this theory present no specific evidence for their belief. They just state what they believe without any strong substantiation to support their allegation.

And second, the Swoon Theory has been used to promote his resuscitation and not his resurrection. This theory agrees that Jesus was crucified but claims that he was still alive in a "swoon state". It promotes that because of the "cool restfulness of the sepulcher", Jesus could get up and walk within a few days because he was revived. In addition, his disciples were too ignorant to see that this was no resurrection, but resuscitation

Yet sadly, this theory does not stand up to the thorough investigation that was conducted according to the Gospel writers. It was recorded that after being taken captive in the middle of the night, Jesus was taken on journeys to Herod to Pilate. He was beaten and scourged, and he had to walk his heavy cross most of the way to the crucifixion cite. After he was nailed, he was thirsty and after he showed signs of death, the Roman soldiers had to make sure that he was dead by sticking a spear into his side. The question is, after three days in a tomb in Palestine when it was quite cold at night, could Jesus have survived? Not to mention that he would have had to have unwrapped his body from the grave clothes that covered him. Could he have rolled the stone away and walk around Jerusalem making appearances to his disciples? Certainly not! Thus, this theory cannot possibly be true.

FROM THE EMPTY TOMB

Supporting Views

The empty tomb is a strong fact that supports Jesus' resurrection for several reasons. First, the claim that his tomb was empty and that he had been raised is a good start in proving that his tomb was actually empty. No one could deny, not only the Jewish leaders who condemned him to death, that his tomb, and not someone else's, was indeed empty. Not long after his tomb was found empty, there was a claim by his followers that it was empty and that he had been raised. Although the claim of the empty tomb in itself does not prove his resurrection, it is a good start to proving that he had been raised.

Second, many other Jewish leaders, heroes, and would-be Messiahs died within the same world, but in no way did anyone suggest that they had been raised from the dead. One might imagine other kinds of early faith which could have been generated by events which did not involve an empty tomb. But the specific faith of the earliest Christians could not have been generated by a set of circumstances in which an empty tomb did not play a part. I therefore regard the empty tomb as a necessary condition for the rise of the very specific early Christian belief.[399] The fact is that if the tomb had not been empty from the beginning, there would have been no early Christian belief in the resurrection of Jesus of Nazareth.

Third, the evidence inside the tomb gives not only proof that someone was buried, but that someone had indeed left. The Gospel writers state that there were grave clothes left behind in the tomb. Both Peter and John "saw the strips of linen lying there, as well as the burial cloth that had been around Jesus' head. The cloth was folded up by itself, separate from the linen" (John 20:6-7). The grave clothes showed several facts. First, they seemed to be recognized as a sign of what had transpired with Jesus. The position that they were lying demonstrated that not only was there a person inside the tomb but that the same person had placed the grave clothes in that position. Understanding this, John believed that the tomb was truly empty and that Jesus left. Second, the fact that they were left behind explained the fact that Jesus' body, whether dead or alive, had not been carried off. Because they were lying in perfect order, it seemed that Jesus' body simply passed through the clothes unharmed.

485

Fourth, the empty tomb by itself nor the appearances by themselves, could have generated the early Christian belief. At the same time, an empty tomb without any meetings with Jesus would have been a distressing puzzle.[400] Sightings of an apparently alive Jesus, by themselves, would have been classified as visions or hallucinations, which were well enough known in the ancient world. However, an empty tomb and appearances of a living Jesus, taken together, would have presented a powerful reason for the emergence of the belief. Jesus not only showed himself but repeatedly showed himself over and over again, giving full proof of his resurrection.

And fifth, the fact that Jesus' resurrection was well known when only a small handful of Christians existed gives evidence of the empty tomb. The fact that the tomb was empty would never have arisen unless it was already well known, or at the very least widely supposed. If the empty tomb were itself a late legend, it is unlikely that people would have spread stories about body-stealing.[401] The empty tomb story related a fact that was, so to speak, "common property" of the early Christian fellowship. If this is the case, it seems futile to attempt to construe the empty tomb account as an unhistorical legend.[402]

Opposing Views

In addition, there have been some opposing yet erroneous views that have tried to explain the empty tomb another way. First, the "Wrong Tomb Theory" states that when Mary Magdalene and the other Mary went looking for his grave to anoint the body, it was dim that morning and perhaps they did not know exactly where to look. As a result, they ended up at the wrong grave, assumed it was Jesus' grave, and when they saw it was empty, they announced to everyone that Jesus had been raised. However, it was very unlikely that they went to the wrong tomb, for just three days earlier, they followed Joseph to the right tomb to bury Jesus.

Second, the "Lettuce Theory" states that the gardener for that area around the tomb was planting lettuce seedlings around the grave site and because he was frustrated with people trampling over his seedlings, he moved the Jesus' body to another location. He did so without telling the family and Joseph who owned the tomb what he did. Therefore, when people came to the grave site, they actually came to the right tomb, but they did not receive the information that Jesus was placed in a different tomb. However, this theory is humorous and not possible, for the gardener would not have bypassed the Roman guards who were placed by Pilate to guard Jesus' tomb. In addition, the gardener could not have rolled the stone away by himself.

Third, the "Hallucination Theory" states that the appearances of Jesus were merely wishful thinking on those who saw him. The reason is because when the women first stated to Jesus' followers the "vision" that they saw, then seemingly, everyone else started seeing "visions" as well. They started sighting him at different location. They believe that perhaps Peter had the first vision or hallucination and because of his zeal, all the other disciples believed and professed that they saw Jesus as well. However, this theory contradicts the fact that Jesus made five physical appearances to his disciples and during this time, he talked, ate food, and he showed them his crucifixion scares.

Fourth, the "Twin Brother Theory" states that Jesus had a brother who looked exactly like him. Therefore, after his resurrection, he never really arose but his brother started making appearances to Jesus' followers, but he stayed out of the public most of the time. However, this view does not hold up because his twin brother was not crucified and he could not have showed Jesus' disciples his crucifixion scares. Again, Thomas wanted full proof in seeing Jesus' crucifixion scares, and it was attested in John's gospel that he was fully satisfied with the evidence.

And fifth, the "Rapid Decay Theory" states that because of the hot climate in Palestine, Jesus' body decomposed rather quickly, and that explains why he was never really seen in his tomb. However, this theory is absurd, for no body can ever decay in three days unless it was actually burned into ashes.

In conclusion, all of these theories require unusually strong faith to believe but even if one believes in them, there is strong evidence to refute all of them. There is neither solid base nor historical reconstruction for these theories, and thus, the fact that Jesus' tomb was empty gives substantial evidence to his resurrection.

FROM JESUS' DISCIPLES

Several factors from Jesus' own disciples help prove his resurrection. The first factor comes from their emotional state just before Jesus was resurrected. Matthew states that right after his arrest, "all the disciples deserted him and fled" (26:56). They did not have the courage or physical power to go up against a group of soldiers. The day before his crucifixion, they showed no sign of the kind of bravery it would take to steal the body of Jesus in the middle of the night. On the third day after Jesus was buried, John states that "the disciples were together with the doors locked for fear of the Jews" (20:19). After Mary Magdalene saw Jesus alive on that third day, she "went and told those who had been with him" and they "were mourning and weeping" (Mark 16:9). These men were depressed, distressed, and afraid up until the time Jesus appeared to them the first time in Jerusalem. Even during his second appearance with Thomas present, we still see them all in a house with the doors locked because they were still afraid (John 20:26).

The second factor comes from that fact that they were not expecting his tomb to be empty and ultimately for him to be resurrected. Had the tomb been empty, with no other unusual occurrences, no one would have said that Jesus was the Messiah or the Lord of the world. No one would have imagined that his kingdom had been inaugurated. No one, in particular, would have developed so quickly and consistently a radical and reshaped version of the Jewish hope for the resurrection of the body.[403] His disciples forgot his prophetic words and were too overwhelmed with fear for their very lives after his death. Therefore, if Jesus' very followers were not expecting his tomb to be empty, the case for his tomb actually being empty gains high credibility.

The third factor comes from the transformation of these men after Jesus' resurrection. Throughout the forty days after Jesus was resurrected, he appeared to them, spoke about God's Kingdom, and gave these men proof that he was the same person before he died. Then after his ascension, these men were transformed and as a result, they went preaching the good news of what had occurred.

Knowing this, why would these men, who had shown to be such cowards, risk death in going to the cities where their enemies were present and speak concerning Jesus' resurrection if they did not truly believe what took place? They did not have high status positions, nor were they famous. They had nothing to gain and nothing to loose. Why would they suffer persecution at the hands of the Jews and Romans if the events of Jesus' resurrection did not actually take place? The reason is because they had experiences that were not natural but supernatural and real, and because of this, they were no longer afraid. They were transformed into bold witnesses and the Jewish leaders could not disprove their message. Jesus allowed their messages to be the center of preaching for the Christian church and as a result, the church grew and prospered. At the same time, historical investigation actually proves that the earliest eyewitnesses were convinced that they had seen the risen Jesus.[404]

And the fourth factor comes from the principle of embarrassment. If something reported about Jesus was embarrassing to the early church, the early preachers or the evangelists would not likely to have invented it. That Judas, one of the twelve, gave Jesus over to his enemies, that (most of) the disciples did not remain with Jesus during the passion, and that Peter denied him were all embarrassing to early Christians. Consequently, it is argued that these elements, which are also multiply attested, are likely to have been historical.[405] This factor shows that if Jesus certainly did not rise from the grave, his disciples would not have been transformed, nor would they risk their lives for his cause.

FROM JESUS' OPPONENTS

The fact is, Jesus' own opponents presuppose the empty tomb. They took as a fact that his tomb was empty but tried to cover it up. They remembered his own words in which he predicted his resurrection and they carefully took precautions. They took several soldiers to seal the tomb and to set a watch just for that third day in order to prove him to be a liar. But their plan was dismantled.

In looking at the cover-up, the Jewish leaders did not say that his body was still on the tomb or that he never was placed in Joseph's tomb. But they charged that his disciples were victims of grave robbery. In addition with the religious leaders blaming Jesus' disciples with stealing his body, there was only one other group who could have been involved with his disappearance and they would have been his enemies. But the question is, what would be their motive? If he was dead, why would his enemies want to take his body? Without a motive, there would be no reason for such a thing to happen. Regardless, the enemies of Jesus would have been proved wrong and made a fool in front of all those who put faith in them.

But with the leaders blaming the disciples in taking his body, there are several problems. First, the precautions that were taken by Pilate and the chief priests hurt their proposal. There were extra precautions taken to make sure this disappearance did not occur, including soldiers standing outside of the tomb to make sure his disciples did not steal the body. The fact that these precautions were taken must have shown either they were worried about the disciples making a mockery of them by an empty tomb or there was some divine power that could be involved. Regardless, these precautions proved that the disciples did not take his body.

Second, if it were true that the disciples stole his body while the guards were asleep and they reported this, how would they have actually known the disciples stole the body if they were "asleep"? They would not have been able to see or observe who came and took his body. Therefore, the soldiers would have made up a story to tell the religious leaders and thus, they would have lied.

Third, how could the stone have been rolled away without the guards waking up? They could not have possibly been that ignorant! Certainly, all of them would have awakened if they heard that heavy stone being moved out of its place.

And forth, for many of the Jewish people to have believed the controversy shows that they also had to believe that the tomb was empty. In other words, the rumor that was spreading concerning the empty tomb among the people presupposes that the tomb was empty.

Thus, we know from their own words that the religious leaders believed in Jesus' resurrection. They knew of Jesus' words that he would rise, and indeed he did. Therefore, the actuality that the Jewish leaders never refuted that his tomb was empty, but simply attempted to explain it away, is convincing proof that Jesus was indeed resurrection.

FROM JAMES THE BROTHER OF JESUS

If you only read Paul's letters, you would see both Peter and James as important Christian figures. If you were to read the Gospels, you would see Peter as a future leader and only James as one of Jesus' brothers. However, if you were to read non-Christian sources such as Josephus writing around the First Century, you would only find one other "Christian" person aside from Jesus during the onset of Christianity and that person was James. You would not see Peter or Paul and the great works that they accomplished, but rather only James.

James the brother of Jesus eventually became a follower of Jesus and he helped to validate his resurrection claims. Two major proofs that validate his resurrection were to nonbelievers named Paul and James. During the ministry of Jesus, James was not a believer, and we don't hear anything of him throughout the Gospel narratives. He was not a skeptic as some might say but, like Thomas, he did not believe the truth. Jesus even made a comment concerning those who do the will of God and equated them as being his mother and brothers (Mark 3:35). One of the reasons this might have been said was because some of his own family, including James his brother, did not believe in him.

But after his resurrection, Jesus made special appearances, and one of those appearances was to his own brother James (1 Corinthians 15:7). After his ascension, the brothers of Jesus were said to have been with the disciples and the other believers in Jerusalem (Acts 1:14). James, although not a believer at first, was converted to the faith and he presumptuously believed at that moment when he saw Jesus alive. Paul gives testimony to his conversion by stating in Galatians 1:18-19, "after three years, I went up to Jerusalem to get acquainted with Peter and stayed with him fifteen days. I saw none of the other apostles—only James, the Lord's brother." Here he equates James as one of the "other apostles", which was a testament of not only his faith but of his service to Jesus Christ.

After his conversion, he is portrayed as James the just. He lived a lifelong ascetic piety and was renowned for his asceticism. He was constant in prayer and he was an effective witness. Eusebius states that "control of the church passed to the apostles together with the Lord's brother James whom everyone from the Lord's time till our own has called the "righteous", for there were many James's, but this one was holy from his birth. He used to enter the sanctuary alone, and was often found on his knees beseeching forgiveness for the people so that his knees grew hard like a camels from his continually bending them in worship of God and beseeching forgiveness for the people. Because of unsurpassable righteousness, he was called the "righteous."[406] Josephus confirms that he was highly regarded by loyal and strict Jews, and that he was known as "the brother of Jesus the so-called Messiah."[407]

In time, he assumed the leadership of the Jerusalem church, originally held by Peter. Evidently, such was achieved not through a power struggle but by James' constancy with the church while Peter and the other apostles traveled. In a Jerusalem conference called regarding Paul's Gentile mission, James presided as spokesman for the Jerusalem church.[408] The Jerusalem mother church operated two major missions, one to the Jews and one to the pagans. James was a Christian Jew who believed that Jesus was the Messiah but also followed the full Jewish Law.

His last moments alive were horrifying. Annas the high priest, the same one who presided over Jesus, assembled the judges of the Sanhedrin and brought before them James, the brother of Jesus and others, and accused them of disobeying the Jewish law. As a result, he delivered them to be stoned. Yet many of those who observed the law were offended at this.[409] After he was stoned, he was beaten to death with a fuller's club which only occurred after he was thrown down from the parapet of the temple.[410] He must have had some public standing or he would not have been brought forth by Ananus to be stoned and clubbed to death. He was buried close in proximity to the Jewish Temple and his gravestone still remains there to this day.

Though he was dead, his life was seen as a true witness both to Jews and the Greeks of Jesus' resurrection and Messiahship. Although he was not the only nonbeliever who converted, he helped validate the truth of Jesus' ministry and all that he said and did. His transformation was just one of the results of Paul's early creed in 1 Corinthians 15:9-11 which states, "For I am the least of the apostles and do not even deserve to be called an apostle, because I persecuted the church of God. But by the grace of God I am what I am, and his grace to me was not without effect. No, I worked harder than all of them - yet not I, but the grace of God that was with me. Whether, then, it was I or they, this is what we preach, and this is what you believed."

FROM THE APOSTLE PAUL

Paul was born in a Jewish family and was a Roman citizen. Before his conversion, he was "breathing out murderous threats against the Lord's disciples" (Acts 9:1) and was a persecutor of the Christian Church. He was so adamantly against Christians that on one occasion, he "went to the high priest and asked him for letters to the synagogues in Damascus, so that if he found any there who belonged to the Way, whether men or women, he might take them as prisoners to Jerusalem" (Acts 9:1-2). On the road to Damascus,

Jesus met him and asked why he persecuted him. Paul eventually converted to the Christian faith a few years after James.

Paul was strong willed and believed in what he stood for even before his conversion. His conversion was a valid proof that he would not accept the truth of Christianity if in fact he did not believe in the resurrection. His testimony implied the fact of the empty tomb when he stated that Jesus rose on the third day according to the Scriptures (1 Corinthians 15:4). Although there were false rumors that his disciples came and stole his body, Paul would not have been convinced by such fraud. Understanding that he once persecuted Christians, why would he believe in a phenomenon that never took place? He became a Christian three to five years after the crucifixion of Jesus and he visited Jerusalem three times thereafter - once in the late 30s, again in the late 40s, and finally in the late 50s.[411] Certainly the tomb must have been empty by them. Perhaps he had checked the grave site after Jesus met him on the road to Damascus to make sure indeed that it was indeed empty.

In his testimony, he claims, "Three times I was beaten with rods, once I was stoned, three times I was shipwrecked, I spent a night and a day in the open sea, I have been constantly on the move. I have been in danger from rivers, in danger from bandits, in danger from my own countrymen, in danger from Gentiles; in danger in the city, in danger in the country, in danger at sea; and in danger from false brothers" (2 Corinthians 11:25-26). Would Paul suffer all this if he truly did not believe in the resurrection of Jesus? Certainly not!

Galatians 2:1-10 states that he specifically checked the truth with the apostles. Paul's testimony states that he made a personal and lengthy visit with Peter to cross examine him. He knew at least that the followers of Jesus claimed that his tomb was empty and that this claim had not been falsified. Yet Paul did not have to depend on the statements from others, including the original apostles, for he believed that he was an eyewitness of Jesus himself. Not only was he an eyewitness, but he states that over 500 brethren were eyewitnesses of the resurrected Jesus.

The beauty of Christianity is what Paul found in following Christ. Even though he once lived a life that reflected violence and persecution and was considered unfit to be an apostle, he wrote, "by the grace of God, I am what I am, and his grace to me was not without effect. No, I worked harder than all of them yet not I, but the grace of God that was with me" (1 Corinthians 15:10). Here, he was trying to paint the picture of God's love, not that he deserved it, but simply because God showed him grace.

As a result of his conversion, he undoubtedly became the greatest missionary during the First Century and he helped Christianity to prosper during its early stages. Although he previously worked with the religious leaders who spread false rumors about Jesus' resurrection and who persecuted Jesus' followers, he eventually suffered persecution from those same people. In addition, he was the main person who helped to spread Christianity to non-Jews. Therefore, the facts of him being a follower of Jesus help validate Jesus' resurrection.

FROM WOMEN

The women's low status in Jewish society and them not being qualified to serve as legal witnesses decreased their chances in being mentioned in the writings of important men. Yet, the Gospels state that the resurrection narrative begins with them and that they served as the first believers many hours before the men believed. Therefore from the First Century perspective, to answer the question as to why women and not the male disciples were made discoverers of the empty tomb was that the women were in fact the ones who made this discovery. This conclusion receives confirmation from the fact that there seems to be no reason why the later Christian church should wish to humiliate its leaders by portraying them as cowards hiding in Jerusalem while the women boldly carry out their last devotions to Jesus' body, unless this were in fact the truth.[412]

In addition, the Gospel writers would not have been convinced by the women's testimony if indeed it did not take place. It would have been easy for these writers to highlight Joseph of Arimathea, a respected councilor member, as having been the first one to arrive at the tomb and see the risen Jesus. But they did not highlight him but the women. Were these writers ignorant of the likely reaction they would suffer from the dominant men during their day? Certainly they were aware, but as Luke stated, he had a perfect understanding of all the things that occurred and he received his information from eyewitnesses and ministers of the word (1:2-3). He, under the direction of the Holy Spirit, desired to tell truth rather than a gospel that was socially and culturally acceptable. Therefore, the discovery of the empty tomb by women is highly probable and the fact that the dominant male disciples were not the first to discover Jesus' tomb gives another substantial proof of the resurrection.

FROM EYEWITNESS TESTIMONY

Whether by what we hear on the radio or by what we read in the newspaper, we live everyday by the testimony of others. Our entire court system is based on factual testimony, eyewitness reports, and accurate evidence, and in no way can weaker evidence surpass or destroy a stronger one. There is no species of reasoning more common, more useful, and even necessary to human life, than that which is derived from the testimony of men, and the reports of eyewitnesses and spectators.[413] In addition, there are a number of circumstances to be taken into consideration in all judgments of this kind, and the ultimate standard by which we determine all disputes that may arise concerning them is always derived from experience and observation.[414]

In light of this, a couple distinct groups of eyewitness testimony validates the claims of Jesus' resurrection. First, Jesus had twelve disciples who observed most of his recorded miracles. We have four gospels given in the New Testament. Matthew, Mark, and Luke are very similar, and John was the only disciple to write on an account of the life of Jesus. It must be remembered that, of the four Gospels, John is the only one that claims to be the direct report of an eye witness. The divergences appear very great on first sight, but the fact remains that all of them, without exception, can be made to fall into place in a single orderly and coherent narrative without the smallest contradiction or difficulty, and without any suppression, invention, or manipulation.[415]

Second, the eyewitness testimony of illiterate people helps validate Jesus' resurrection. During this era, people were use to pondering events and circumstances in their heart, just as Mary pondered the events surrounding her son's birth (Luke 2:19). The Jews even had a very good system of law and much of it was memorized. But to a greater degree, perhaps illiterate people have particularly good memories to compensate for being unable to write things down, just as the blind are popularly believed to have especially keen ears or sensitive fingers.[416] Much of those who surrounded Jesus were illiterate and in Acts, both Peter and John were said to be "unschooled, ordinary men" (Acts 4:13). At the same times, most of the people living during the First Century were peasants and although most were unschooled and ordinary, many were illiterate.

So Jesus' resurrection was not proclaimed by people who were educated and astute but rather those who were unlearned. These people at the bottom of their society had no reason to lie or cover up any truth. They had no reason to impress anyone or try to make themselves look important. This fact gives greater testimony that the resurrection of Jesus most likely occurred than it not occurring.

In conclusion, the cohesiveness of the eyewitnesses helps validate Jesus' resurrection. It is one thing to have illiterate people talk about his resurrection, yet, it is another thing to have a lack of cohesiveness. A writer who is known for falsehood does not give good credibility and people entertain a suspicion concerning any matter of fact when the witnesses contradict each other, when they are but few or of a doubtful character, when they have an interest in what they affirm, and when they deliver their testimony with hesitation or with too violent asseverations. There are many others particulars of the same kind, which may diminish or destroy the force of any argument, derived from human testimony.[417] Yet Luke states specifically that he had "carefully investigated everything from the beginning" (1:3). What we have in his Gospel and in all the Gospels are experiences observed by different people who were watching the same event. Although each of the Gospels shares their unique experience, there is cohesiveness. Therefore, the facts of Jesus' resurrection gain more credibility because of this.

FROM THE GOSPEL WRITERS

The Gospel writers give validity to Jesus' resurrection, for it is through their eyes that we see the sequence of events as to what happened that Easter morning. These four authors wrote from their own experiences and from the information that they gathered from eyewitnesses as they were guided by the Holy Spirit. What we have is four versions of the same event, and it is important for the readers to integrate them into a synthetic whole.

There are just a couple important aspects of these stories that I desire to mention in light of their narratives. First, they do not concentrate on themselves at all in their writings, which is unique. John, who had reason to be arrogant because of his close affiliation with Jesus, simply spoke of himself as the "one whom Jesus loved." Certainly his listeners and readers during the First and Second Century understood that he was talking about himself. But they most likely also observed his meekness and humility. In general, there was no one thing of which these writers were more concerned with but to produce extensive confirmation of the resurrection of Jesus. There was something that caused them to want to write a considerable lengthy account of him and they did so without giving themselves credit and praise. This was much different than the accounts of the kings of Assyria, for they never wrote of anything that would cause shame but only of their defeats and victories.

And second, the fact that the Gospel writers wrote very early gives attestation to their validity. The very strong historical probability is that, when Matthew, Luke and John describe the risen Jesus, they are writing down very early oral tradition, representing three different ways in which the original astonished participants told the stories.[418] The accounts were regarded as early, even before Paul wrote, and when placed side by side, they tell a story. As they were giving their accounts, they were not anxious to make everything look right but they were careful with the information that they received. Luke does not prove either that the stories were in fact originally told by eyewitnesses or that everything they say represents a photographic record of what took place.[419]

Because of the facts that show they were written early, some try to point to "inconsistencies" within the Gospels. But the fact that they cannot agree over how man, women, or angels, were at the tomb, or even on the location of the appearances, does not mean that nothing happened. We should not try to domesticate the stories, either by forcing every last detail into harmony, or by forcing them into a hermeneutic of suspicion. The purpose in their writings was not a critical investigation of history, but the reporting of Christian origins.

In addition, the surface of some of the inconsistencies is in fact a strong point in favor of their early character. Perhaps the later they would have been written and edited, the more likely the inconsistencies would be ironed out. Therefore, the inconsistencies between them should not be allowed to stand in the way of taking them seriously as historical sources.[420]

FROM HIS MESSIAHSHIP

The belief in a Messiah and in a Messianic age is so deeply rooted in Jewish tradition that a statement concerning the Messiah became the most famous of Maimonides's Thirteen Principles of Faith stating, "I believe with a full heart in the coming of the Messiah, and even though he may tarry, I will wait for him on any day that he may come."[421] Jewish tradition believes at least five things about the Messiah. 1.) He will be a descendant of King David; 2.) He will gain sovereignty over the land of Israel; 3.) He will gather the Jews in Israel from the four corners of the earth; 4.) He will restore the Jews to full observance of Torah law; 5.) And he will bring peace to the world as a grand finale. Both Jews and Samaritans were awaiting a Messiah figure in the First Century that would come and rescue them from foreign control and restore their land and nation.

When John came baptizing in the desert, he was seen as one who fit the description of a Messiah. The Jews sent priests and Levites from Jerusalem and asked him indirectly if he was the Christ or Messiah and John told them, "no"! When Jesus came on the scene, the question of his Messiahship was the chief concern of the Jews as well, and these claims were surrounded by investigation and argument. Even though many Jews tried to make Jesus their king and many hailed him as their Messiah, all hope was gone when the Romans arrested him, condemned him, and executed him. Unfortunately, this was what the Romans were accustomed to doing with "so-called" prophets and Messiahs within their empires. Just like John's movement crashed and all those who followed him were dismantled, Jesus would be executed and all his followers would dissipate. But three days after his death, his disciples regained their strength and 40 days after his resurrection, his disciples and followers boldly proclaimed his resurrection and his Messiahship.

So then, why would the early Christians acclaim Jesus' Messiahship if he did not rise from the grave and if he obviously wasn't the Messiah? After his death, there were other possible figures that the Jews could have claimed to have been their Messiah. Since Jesus of Nazareth had blood relatives who were known as such two generations after his death, they would have been no problem in finding some reaction on whose shoulders a revived hope might be placed. There was one relative in particular who might have seemed an ideal candidate. James his brother had probably not followed Jesus throughout his public career, but according to the very early tradition, he, like the Eleven, had seen the risen Jesus. He had then quickly become one of the central leaders in the Jerusalem church. He was clearly regarded as the, or at least a, central point of authority in the Jerusalem church, and hence in the worldwide church.[422] But they did not regard him but maintained that Jesus was their Messiah, even though he was not presently with them.

The reason why the early Christians hailed Jesus as their Messiah was because they now understood that he would not fight a military operation but would tackle and defeat evil. They understood that their house of worship would not be of bricks but would consist of the community of Jesus' followers. They reaffirmed the Old Testament's prophecies that pertained to Jesus' Messiahship, and on the basis of the key texts from the Psalm, Isaiah, Daniel and elsewhere, the early Christians declared that Jesus was Lord and Caesar was not. Although Jesus did fulfill much of the Jewish expectations of a Messiah, his resurrection allowed him to still fulfill the rest. In fact, it has already been prophesied that he would fulfill all of the expectations including ushering world peace and protecting his people from their enemies. John the apostle desired his listeners and readers to believe in Jesus' resurrection and in his Messiahship. Matthew wanted his readers to know that Jesus held the role that had been marked out for the Messiah in Psalm 2, 72, and 89.

However, the Jews today as a whole do not believe that Jesus was the Messiah because of at least three reasons. 1.) He did not usher in world peace as a grand finale; 2.) He did not help bring about Jewish political sovereignty for the Jews; 3.) and he did not protect the Jews from their enemies. But as I have stated already, Jesus still has a chance to fulfill all these expectations simply because of his resurrection.

FROM EARLY CHRISTIANITY

Christianity took off after Jesus' ascension beginning with his disciples going into Jerusalem with joy and preaching the good news. Christianity began because the early Christians believed that something phenomenally occurred, something that they were not expecting to happen which caused them to be transformed.

There was a vast spread of the Christian faith across the Roman Empire and even stretching to places like India. Because of this vast spread, those opposing the gospel were trying to contain their "fanatic" beliefs and practices, but they could not disprove their claims. The more persecution arose, the more Christians were converted and the stronger they became. Letters were sent from one Roman authority to another trying to find tactics to control them, but every tactic used became more and more unsuccessful.

Then about three centuries after Christianity was birthed, the Roman Emperor Constantine legalized Christianity within the empire. Twelve years after this, the first Christian archaeological expedition was launched to discover the location of Jesus' tomb site. Led by local Christian authorities, a particular site was stated to be the place and a church was built that sits above the site of Jesus' crucifixion and burial site. All this would not have taken place if Christianity was based on a hoax. Thus, early Christianity and the influence of Constantine gives credibility of Jesus' resurrection and the power of God.

FROM CHRISTIAN AND NON-CHRISTIAN TEXTS

Early Christian texts can be traced historically and they give proof to the resurrection of Jesus. Although through the first three centuries there were groups including the docetists who believed that Jesus was not really human, Ignatius of Antioch affirms that Jesus was truly human. He states, "For I know and believe that after the resurrection, he (Jesus) was in the flesh. And when he came to the people around Peter, he said to them, 'Take, handle me and see, that I am not a bodiless phantom.' And at once they touched him and believed, being mixed together with both his flesh and his spirit. For this reason they scorned even death, and were found to be above death. And after his resurrection he ate with them and drank as a fleshly being, even though he was spiritually united to the father."[423] Ignatius' affirmation even coincides with the biblical account.

The New Testament texts are easily the best attested ancient writings in terms of the number of manuscripts. Ancient classical works have comparatively few manuscripts with twenty entire or partial copies. By comparison, the New Testament has over 5,000 copies. Such a wide difference would provide the New Testament with a much better means of textual criticism, which is crucially important in ascertaining the original readings.[424]

Non-Christian texts also give validity of Jesus' resurrection. Josephus, who was not even a believer in Jesus, stated concerning him, "About this time there lived Jesus, a wise man [if indeed one ought to call him a man.] For he was one who wrought surprising feats and was a teacher of such people as accept the truth gladly. He won over many Jews and many of the Greeks. [He was the Christ.] When Pilate, upon hearing him accused by men of the highest standing amongst us, had condemned him to be crucified, those who had in the first place come to love him did not give up their affection for him. [On the third day he appeared to them restored to life, for the prophets of God had prophesied these and countless other marvelous things about him.] And the tribe of the Christians, so called after him, has still to this day not disappeared."[425] What a power non-Christian affirmation of the resurrection of Jesus from a nonbeliever. Thus, God is not limited in how he works through history to give undeniable evidence for his Son's resurrection.

FROM THE SUPERNATURAL

When Jesus came working miracles and claiming that God was his father, the Pharisees and the other religious leaders were infuriated, for most were not willing to share their supremacy. They did all they could to put him to death by handing him over to the Romans, which showed all the people that he was truly a criminal and outlaw. However, when Jesus baffled their plan by rising from the grave, he brought about a new perspective on where authority came from. Ironically, the very faith that Paul dedicated his life that he once tried to destroy demonstrated that God existed and he had all authority.

To bypass the involvement of God that Sunday morning, some have proposed theories that provide a naturalistic explanation. Some have believed the hallucination theory believing that the women and disciples saw visions and not the actual resurrected Jesus. But the fact is that hallucinations can not explain all the facts pertaining to Jesus' convincing proofs. Again, the disciples were not expecting Jesus to rise from the grave and what they needed was a series of facts that Jesus was indeed alive. If hallucinations were present, they would have been discredited by the second or third public appearance to his disciples. At the same time, hallucinations would not inspire the great outbreak of Jesus' followers nor the fact that Christianity has grown to be the largest religion in the world. In addition, the early Christians would certainly not have been martyred because of alleged visions.

Especially in the First Century when the Jewish elite would not accept the possibilities of anything supernatural, there were arguments that attempted to completely dismiss the possibilities of Jesus' resurrection entirely. Consequently, none of them added up. While the Jewish religious leaders and Pilate were trying to contain Jesus, God only baffles their preventative measures and he simply made use of their precautions in order to show the supernatural.

Thus, the resurrection validates a 'supernatural' view of the world. It means that there really is a 'life after death', that the destiny of Jesus' followers is 'to go to heaven when they die', and that the true realities in this world are 'eternal' or 'spiritual' rather than 'physical'. For others, the meaning of Easter is the invitation to a Jesus centered spirituality in the present.[426] The resurrection proves that God exists and that he is victorious over death. It proves not only the existence in miracles but that God has acted in history. The fact of Jesus being raised shows that he alone was granted the privilege of coming back to life and remain alive, while everybody else had to die and stay dead. His resurrection was not a re-description of death but rather its defeat.

Jesus' Characteristics

First, he was considerate and thoughtful of others. He remained in touch with people by not only living a normal and balanced life, but he treated others as he would have wanted to be treated. Before resurrecting the ruler of the Jews' dead daughter, he told the crowd and those playing musical instruments to go outside (Matthew 9), for they were distractions. He spared the little girl from the trauma that could have been easily brought upon her by the crowd. This was just one example of his consistent consideration of others throughout his ministry.

Second, Jesus lived a life of consistency. He spoke about the consistency of prayer and at the same time, he lived a life of prayer. He often would spend the night praying to God in a secluded area on the mountainside. He consistently demonstrated compassion because of people's physical and spiritual needs. He did not show favoritism to the elite but rather demonstrated love to Jews, Gentiles, and Samaritans, as well as poor and rich.

Third, he lived a life of prudence. He avoided collisions with the religious rulers numerous times. On one occasion, "the Pharisees heard that Jesus was gaining and baptizing more disciples than John, although in fact it was not Jesus who baptized, but his disciples. When the Lord learned of this, he left Judea and went back once more to Galilee" (John 4:1-3). He had accounted confrontation with them and used prudence to get out of the area to most likely avoid possible death. During this same narrative, Jesus used prudence to go through a "hostile" area known as Samaria because he needed to witness to a Samaritan woman.

Fourth, he lived a life of humility. When he was treated unfairly and harsh, he refused to retaliate. On the cross, he never summoned twelve legions of angels to deliver him from his oppressors. He had no desire to be famous and instead of praying in the busy streets surrounding the temple, he went to a lonely mountainside. More than once he tried to tell those whom he healed to keep quiet about what God had miraculously done for them. Yet his fame continued to spread across the surrounding countries. He even performed the despicable practice of washing other men's feet, and he did so to show his humility and service.

And fifth, he lived a life of courage. It took courage to face the rigors of the temptation alone in the wilderness. It took courage to oppose the traditions of men that obscured or even contradicted the word of God. It took courage to tell men that they were evil and to expose their sins so relentlessly that they were left without a cloak for those sins. It took courage to set his face steadfastly to go up to Jerusalem. It took courage to cleanse the temple. It took courage to accept the cup from the Father's and it took courage to face the venom of his accusers and the brutality of his crucifiers.[427] And yet, he maintained courage through them all, and he serves as the model for Christians today.

Jesus' Comparison

TO OTHER MANUSCRIPTS

The stories of Jesus have first been mentioned in the gospels and the New Testament and have proven through history to be trustworthy and even more reliable than many other secular manuscripts in several ways. First, over 5,000 New Testament manuscripts and portions of manuscripts have been produced and this fact can be compared to the majority of classical works that contains less than 20 manuscripts. Second, the dates of the New Testament manuscripts are close to the original writings – 25-150 years, and yet most classical works date from 700-1400 years after the originals. And third, none of the canonical New Testament is lost or missing. By comparison, 107 of Livy's 142 books of history have been lost and about one half of Tacitus' 30 books of Annals and Histories are missing.[428]

TO OTHER MEN IN HISTORY

I must note Jesus' comparisons to other men in history. First, it was specifically stated in the accounts of the Gospels that Jesus was born of the virgin Mary and that the Holy Spirit was his father. Yet it has been noted, whether its true or not, that in the centuries surrounding Jesus' life, that gods and goddesses, spirits and immortals regularly interacted physically and sexually, spiritually and intellectually with human beings, and that the conception of a divine child and the vision of a dead person are neither totally abnormal nor completely unique events.[429] In addition, it was believed that pagans knew of the birth of Aeneas from a divine mother and a human father, and of the claim that Augustus himself was conceived from a divine father and a human mother.[430]

Yet these claims can be dispute in a few ways. First, it must be proven that the "so-called" god was indeed a god with any special powers. Jesus claimed that God his Father sent him and that he was God himself. He even performed miracles that only God could do in the presence of thousands of people and these people could testify of his special powers. So therefore, it must be proven first that the "gods and goddesses, spirits and immortals" had special powers in the first place. Second, it must be proven that these gods "merged" with humanity. From Jesus' standpoint, Joseph, the wife of Mary, could testify that he did not have sexual relations with her before Jesus was born. But who could testify of the divine births of all of these so-called divine births? And third, simple claims alone should not be taken as fact but rather proof and historical evidence must be applied before a conclusion is made. Anyone could claim that other leaders and historical figures had divine birth, but there must be more proof than just someone stating that it happened.

Second, Jesus was not the first Jew of the time to take language about God and apply it to himself. One generation before Jesus, the famous rabbi Hillel made the same kind of claims.[431] Hillel is Judaism's model human being. He is regarded as the greatest scholar of his generation. His greatest legacy was his forceful intellect, which directed Judaism toward the goal of tikkun olam, the ethical bettering of the world.[432] He was attributed with a large number of insightful proverbs as well.

But in what way did he back up his claims? Jesus not only backed up his claims with his miracles but Paul gives him the titles "Son," "Lord" and "Christ." The usage of "Lord," in particular, indicates his view of Jesus' deity. This term indicates that Paul could give Jesus the title of "God," since "Lord" itself "clearly expresses Jesus' deity."[433] Paul writes in Philippians 2:6-11 that Jesus has the form or very nature of God. At the same time, the Jewish tradition has decided that Hillel did not mean what he said.

And third, is Jesus' death any different from other great men in history including John the Baptist, Socrates, and Hillel? What makes Jesus' death stand out as having greater significance to not only the people in his day but to all past and future generations? It is important to understand the connection between the death of Jesus and man's sins. If Jesus was sinful just like the rest of his contemporaries, his death would not be any different from the greatest of Jews. But the fact that he was sinless must be evaluated in light of the undeniable evidence that he was God and that he claimed that he was sent to die for mankind. Then faith is understood as belief in Jesus, a belief which makes what Jesus proclaimed present and real for Christians. No other "important" historical figure gave claims such as Jesus and for him to have risen from the grave demonstrates that he conquers death and sin, and that he is the one who brings hope to past and future generations.

In conclusion, Christianity is a historical religion, meaning that it is not based on myths about gods who never existed but on the story of someone who lived at a particular time in a particular place among real people.[434] Jesus claimed the validity of God's power by his many miracles, signs, and wonders, and he proved his existence and authority over nature, humans, and the physical laws that govern this world.

ENDNOTES

1. Crossan, John Dominic. *God & Empire*. New York: Harper One, 2007. pg. 73

2. Porter, J.R. *Jesus Christ: The Jesus of History, The Christ of Faith*. New York: Oxford University Press, 1999. pg. 12

3. Tenney, Merrill C. *New Testament Survey*. Grand Rapids: Eerdmans Publishing Company and Inter Varsity Press, 1985. pg. 1

4. Mann, Michael. The Sources of Social Power: Volume 1, A History of Power from the Beginning to AD 1760. Cambridge: Cambridge University Press, 1986. pg. 250

5. Tenney, Merrill C. *New Testament Survey*. Grand Rapids: Eerdmans Publishing Company and Inter Varsity Press, 1985. pg. 2

6. Crossan, John Dominic. *God & Empire*. New York: Harper One, 2007. pg. 12

7. Crossan, John Dominic. *God & Empire*. New York: Harper One, 2007. pg. 12

8. Brown, Raymond. *The Death of the Messiah*. 2 Volumes. New York: Doubleday. 1994. pg. 33

9. Buckler, John P., Hill, Bennet D., McKay, John P. *A History of World Societies*. Fourth Edition. Boston: Houghton Mifflin, 1996. pgs. 191-195

10. Buckler, John P., Hill, Bennet D., McKay, John P. *A History of World Societies*. Fourth Edition. Boston: Houghton Mifflin, 1996. pg. 189 and 195

11. Pfeiffer, Charles F. *WyCliffe Bible Dictionary*. Massachusetts. Hendrickson. 1975. pg. 1483

12. Crossan, John Dominic. *God & Empire*. New York: Harper One, 2007. pg. 28-29

13. Perowne, Stewart. *The Life and Times of Herod the* Great. London: Hodder & Stoughton, 1957. pg. 56

14. Perowne, Stewart. *The Life and Times of Herod the* Great. London: Hodder & Stoughton, 1957. pg. 17-23

15. Crossan, John Dominique, Reed, Jonathan. *Excavating Jesus*. New York: Harper Collins, 2001. pg. 89

16. Crossan, John Dominique, Reed, Jonathan. *Excavating Jesus*. New York: Harper Collins, 2001. pg. 93

17. Crossan, John Dominique, Reed, Jonathan. *Excavating Jesus*. New York: Harper Collins, 2001. pg. 93

18. Bailey, Kenneth. *Jesus Through Middle Eastern Eyes*. Downer's Grove: Inter-Varsity Press, 2008. pg. 57

19. Telushkin, Joseph. Jewish Literacy: The Most Important Things to Know about the Jewish Religion, its People, and its History. New York: William Morrow and Company, 1991. pg. 125

20. Josephus, Flavius. *Jewish Antiquities*. Wordsworth Editions, 2006. 17.2.4; #44-45

21. Crossan, John Dominic. *God & Empire*. New York: Harper One, 2007. pg. 109

22. Tenney, Merrill C. *New Testament Survey*. Grand Rapids: Eerdmans Publishing Company and Inter Varsity Press, 1985. pg. 35

23. Crossan, John Dominic. *God & Empire*. New York: Harper One, 2007. pg. 102

24. Klaits, Joseph. *Servants of Satan: The Age of the Witch Hunts*. Indiana University Press, 1987. pg. 67

25. Leacock, Eleanor. "Montagnais Women and the Jesuit Program for Colonization." In *Women and Colonization: Anthropological Perspectives*. Edited by Mona Etienne and Eleanor Leacock, New York: Praeger. 1980. pg. 25-42.

26. Pitt-Rivers, Julian. "Honour," in *Encyclopedia of the Social Sciences*. Second Edition. New York: Macmillan, 1968. pg. 503-511.

27. Scott, Bernard Brandon. *Hear Then the Parable: A Commentary on the Parables of Jesus*. Minneapolis: Fortress Press. 1989. pg. 324

28. Scott, Bernard Brandon. *Hear Then the Parable: A Commentary on the Parables of Jesus*. Minneapolis: Fortress Press. 1989. pg. 326

29. Crossan, John Dominique, Reed, Jonathan. *Excavating Jesus*. New York: Harper Collins, 2001. pg. 195

30. Crossan, John Dominic. *The Birth of* Christianity. New York: Harper One, 1999. pg. 176

31. Hobsbawm, Eric J. *Bandits*. Second Edition. Middlesex: Penguin Books, 1985. pg. 20

32. Crossan, John Dominique, Reed, Jonathan. *Excavating Jesus*. New York: Harper Collins, 2001. pg. 181

33. Crossan, John Dominic. *The Historical Jesus*. New York: Harper One, 1992. pg. 68

34. Crossan, John Dominic. *God & Empire*. New York: Harper One, 2007. pg. 94

35. Buckler, John P., Hill, Bennet D., McKay, John P. *A History of World Societies*. Fourth Edition. Boston: Houghton Mifflin, 1996. pg. 95

36. Clouse, Robert, Pierard, Richard, Yamauchi, Edwin. *Two Kingdoms: The Church and Culture Through the Ages*. Moody Publishers, 1993. pg. 25

37. Crossan, John Dominic. *The Birth of* Christianity. New York: Harper One, 1999. pg. 176

38. Fager, Jeffrey A. *Land Tenure and the Biblical Jubilee*. Sheffield Academic Press, 1993. pg. 27

39. Lenski, Gerhard E. *Power and Privilege: A Theory of Social Stratification*. New York: McGraw-Hill. 1966. pg. 210

40. Crossan, John Dominic. *The Birth of* Christianity. New York: Harper One, 1999. pg. 159

41. Longstaff, Thomas R. W. "Nazareth and Sepphoris: Insights into Christian Origins." *Anglican Theological Review*. 1990. pg. 14

42. Lenski, Gerhard E. *Power and Privilege: A Theory of Social Stratification*. New York: McGraw-Hill. 1966. pg. 172

43. Lenski, Gerhard E. *Power and Privilege: A Theory of Social Stratification*. New York: McGraw-Hill. 1966. pg. 172

44. Lenski, Gerhard E. *Power and Privilege: A Theory of Social Stratification*. New York: McGraw-Hill. 1966. pg. 263

45. Anderson, Leith. *Jesus*. Grand Rapids, MI: Bethany House, 2005. pg. 65

46. Marks, A.J. *The Romans*. London: Usborne Publishing.1990. pg. 10

47. Crossan, John Dominic. *The Birth of* Christianity. New York: Harper One, 1999. pg. 157-158

48. Kautsky, John H. *The Politic of Aristocratic Empire*. Chapel Hill, North Carolina: University of North Carolina Press. 1982. pgs. 280, 281, 288, 289, 91

49. Crossan, John Dominic. *The Birth of* Christianity. New York: Harper One, 1999. pg. 159

50. Zondervan NIV Matthew Henry Commentary. Grand Rapids, Michigan: Zondervan, 1992. pg. 190 New Testament

51. Murphy, Frederick J. *Early Judaism*. Hendrickson, 2002. pg. 286

52. Lenski, Gerhard E. *Power and Privilege: A Theory of Social Stratification*. New York: McGraw-Hill. 1966. pg. 295

53. Kautsky, John H. *The Politic of Aristocratic Empire*. Chapel Hill, North Carolina: University of North Carolina Press. 1982. pgs. 110, 113

54. Crossan, John Dominic. *The Birth of* Christianity. New York: Harper One, 1999. pg. 194

55. Duggan, Alfred. *The Romans*. Cleveland and New York: World Publishing Company, 1964. pg. 76

56. Tenney, Merrill C. *New Testament Survey*. Grand Rapids: Eerdmans Publishing Company and Inter Varsity Press, 1985. pg. 65

57. Tenney, Merrill C. *New Testament Survey*. Grand Rapids: Eerdmans Publishing Company and Inter Varsity Press, 1985. pg. 83

58. Esposito, Fasching, Lewis. *World Religions Today*. Third Edition. New York: Oxford University Press, 2009. pg. 66

59. Alen, Gedaliah. *Jews in their Land in the Talmudic Age*. Harvard University Press. 1989. pg. 42 and 72

60. Tenney, Merrill C. *New Testament Survey*. Grand Rapids: Eerdmans Publishing Company and Inter Varsity Press, 1985. pg. 89

61. Tenney, Merrill C. *New Testament Survey*. Grand Rapids: Eerdmans Publishing Company and Inter Varsity Press, 1985. pg. 84

62. Tenney, Merrill C. *New Testament Survey*. Grand Rapids: Eerdmans Publishing Company and Inter Varsity Press, 1985. pg. 93

63. Levine, L.I., *The Ancient Synagogue: The First Thousand Years*. New Haven, CT: Yale University Press, 1999. pg. 3

64. Levine, L.I., *The Ancient Synagogue: The First Thousand Years*. New Haven, CT: Yale University Press, 1999. pg. 3

65. Tenney, Merrill C. *New Testament Survey*. Grand Rapids: Eerdmans Publishing Company and Inter Varsity Press, 1985. pg. 97

66. Edersheim, Alfred. *The Life and Times of Jesus the Messiah*. Peabody, MA: Hendrickson Publishers, 1993. pg. 632

67. Tenney, Merrill C. *New Testament Survey*. Grand Rapids: Eerdmans Publishing Company and Inter Varsity Press, 1985. pg. 97

68. Esposito, Fasching, Lewis. *World Religions Today*. Third Edition. New York: Oxford University Press, 2009. pg. 80

69. Esposito, Fasching, Lewis. *World Religions Today*. Third Edition. New York: Oxford University Press, 2009. pg. 80

70. Josephus, Flavius. *Jewish Antiquities*. Wordsworth Editions, 2006. 13.16.2; #408-9.

71. Josephus, Flavius. *The War of the Jews: The History of the Destruction of Jerusalem*. IAP; First Edition. 2009. i.110

72. Harrison, Everett. *A Short Life of Christ*. Grand Rapids: Eerdmans Publishing, 1968. pg. 123

73. Meier, John P. *A Marginal Jew*. New York: Doubleday, 2001. pg. 301 and 311

74. Crossan, John Dominique, Reed, Jonathan. *Excavating Jesus*. New York: Harper Collins, 2001. pg. 57

75. Moore, G. F. *Judaism In The First Centuries Of The Christian Area - The Age Of The Tannaim*. Volume I, Bradley Press. 1946. pg. 79

76. Telushkin, Joseph. Jewish Literacy: The Most Important Things to Know about the Jewish Religion, its People, and its History. New York: William Morrow and Company, 1991. pg. 132

77. Josephus, Flavius. *The War of the Jews: The History of the Destruction of Jerusalem*. IAP; First Edition. 2009. 2.124

78. Josephus, Flavius. *The War of the Jews: The History of the Destruction of Jerusalem*. IAP; First Edition. 2009. 5.145

79. Josephus, Flavius. *The War of the Jews: The History of the Destruction of Jerusalem*. IAP; First Edition. 2009. 2.139-142

80. Josephus, Flavius. *The War of the Jews: The History of the Destruction of Jerusalem*. IAP; First Edition. 2009. 2.153-158, Ant. 18.18

81. Josephus, Flavius. *The War of the Jews: The History of the Destruction of Jerusalem*. IAP; First Edition. 2009. 2.122; Ant. 18.20

82. Josephus, Flavius. *The War of the Jews: The History of the Destruction of Jerusalem*. IAP; First Edition. 2009. 2.123, 134

83. Josephus, Flavius. *The War of the Jews: The History of the Destruction of Jerusalem.* IAP; First Edition. 2009. 2.135

84. Philo, *On The Embassy of Gauis.* Book XXXVIII. §75

85. Josephus, Flavius. *The War of the Jews: The History of the Destruction of Jerusalem.* IAP; First Edition. 2009. 2.135

86. Josephus, Flavius. *The War of the Jews: The History of the Destruction of Jerusalem.* IAP; First Edition. 2009. 2.125

87. Josephus, Flavius. *Jewish Antiquities.* Wordsworth Editions, 2006. 18.21

88. Josephus, Flavius. *The War of the Jews: The History of the Destruction of Jerusalem.* IAP; First Edition. 2009. 2.127

89. Josephus, Flavius. *Jewish Antiquities.* Wordsworth Editions, 2006. 18.1.6

90. Esposito, Fasching, Lewis. *World Religions Today.* Third Edition. New York: Oxford University Press, 2009. pg. 81

91. Esposito, Fasching, Lewis. *World Religions Today.* Third Edition. New York: Oxford University Press, 2009. pg. 80

92. Tenney, Merrill C. *New Testament Survey.* Grand Rapids: Eerdmans Publishing Company and Inter Varsity Press, 1985. pg. 117-118

93. Esposito, Fasching, Lewis. *World Religions Today.* Third Edition. New York: Oxford University Press, 2009. pg. 80

94. Schweitzer, Albert. *The Quest of the Historical Jesus.* Translation by J.W. Montgomery. New York: Macmillan, 1968. pg. 487

95. Brown, Raymond. *The Birth of the Messiah.* New York: Doubleday, 1993. pg. 67

96. Rudolf Bultmann, "The Study of the Synoptic Gospels," in Form criticism, transl. by Frederick C. Grant (New York: Harper and Brothers, 1962, p. 60.

97. (Jubilees 41:1).

98. Bailey, Kenneth. *Jesus Through Middle Eastern Eyes.* Downer's Grove: Inter-Varsity Press, 2008. pg. 38

99. Bailey, Kenneth. *Jesus Through Middle Eastern Eyes.* Downer's Grove: Inter-Varsity Press, 2008. pg. 40

100. Bailey, Kenneth. *Jesus Through Middle Eastern Eyes.* Downer's Grove: Inter-Varsity Press, 2008. pg. 41

101. Bailey, Kenneth. *Jesus Through Middle Eastern Eyes.* Downer's Grove: Inter-Varsity Press, 2008. pg. 41

102. Bailey, Kenneth. *Jesus Through Middle Eastern Eyes.* Downer's Grove: Inter-Varsity Press, 2008. pg. 41-42

103. Bailey, Kenneth. *Jesus Through Middle Eastern Eyes.* Downer's Grove: Inter-Varsity Press, 2008. pg. 41

104. Brown, Raymond. *The Birth of the Messiah.* New York: Doubleday, 1993. pg. 73

105. Bailey, Kenneth. *Jesus Through Middle Eastern Eyes.* Downer's Grove: Inter-Varsity Press, 2008. pg. 42

106. Brown, Raymond. *The Birth of the Messiah*. New York: Doubleday, 1993. pg. 259-60

107. Brown, Raymond. *The Birth of the Messiah*. New York: Doubleday, 1993. pg. 280

108. Zondervan NIV Matthew Henry Commentary. Grand Rapids, Michigan: Zondervan, 1992. pg. 213

109. Spence, H. D. M. *The Pulpit Commentary*. Volume 16. Grand Rapids, Michigan: Eerdmans Publishing Company, 1962. pg. 8

110. Ash, Anthony Lee. *The Gospel According to Luke*. Austin, Texas: Sweet Publishing Company, 1972. pg. 39

111. Zondervan NIV Matthew Henry Commentary. Grand Rapids, Michigan: Zondervan, 1992. pg. 214

112. Zondervan NIV Matthew Henry Commentary. Grand Rapids, Michigan: Zondervan, 1992. pg. 215

113. Brown, Raymond. *The Birth of the Messiah*. New York: Doubleday, 1993. pg. 375

114. Borg, Marcus J., Crossan, John Dominic. *The First Christmas* Harper One. New York: Harper One, 2007. pg. 128

115. Liddell, Henry G., Scott, R., *A Greek-English Lexicon*. Oxford: Oxford University Press, 1966. pg. 567

116. Bailey, Kenneth. *Jesus Through Middle Eastern Eyes*. Downer's Grove: Inter-Varsity Press, 2008. pg. 45

117. Crossan, John Dominic. *Jesus, A Revolutionary Biography*. New York: Harper One, 1994. pg. 17

118. Just Martyr places it among the cardinal items of Christian belief. Dialogue 85; Apology 31, 46

119. Bailey, Kenneth. *Jesus Through Middle Eastern Eyes*. Downer's Grove: Inter-Varsity Press, 2008. pg. 46

120. Kierkegaard, Soren, *Fear and Trembling*. Translation by Walter Lowrie. New York: Doubleday Anchor Books, 1954. pg. 66

121. Harrison, Everett. *A Short Life of Christ*. Grand Rapids: Eerdmans Publishing, 1968. pg. 132

122. Brown, Raymond. *The Birth of the Messiah*. New York: Doubleday, 1993. pg. 395

123. Hirschfeld, Yizhar, Vamosh, M.F. "A Country Gentleman's Estate: Unearthing the Splendors of Ramat Hanadiv," *Biblical Archaeology* Review 31, Number 2. 2005. pg. 18-31

124. Bailey, Kenneth. *Jesus Through Middle Eastern Eyes*. Downer's Grove: Inter-Varsity Press, 2008. pg. 28

125. Bailey, Kenneth. *Jesus Through Middle Eastern Eyes*. Downer's Grove: Inter-Varsity Press, 2008. pg. 28-29

126. Bailey, Kenneth. *Jesus Through Middle Eastern Eyes*. Downer's Grove: Inter-Varsity Press, 2008. pg. 32

127. Bailey, Kenneth. *Jesus Through Middle Eastern Eyes*. Downer's Grove: Inter-Varsity Press, 2008. pg. 34

128. Brown, Raymond. *The Birth of the Messiah*. New York: Doubleday, 1993. pg. 401

129. Dalman, G. H. *Sacred Sites and Ways*. Macmillan, 1935. pg. 48-49

130. Brown, Raymond. *The Birth of the Messiah*. New York: Doubleday, 1993. pg. 420

131. TalBab *Sanhedrin* 25b

132. Jeremias, Joachim. *Jerusalem in the Time of Jesus*. Germany: Fortress Press, 1975. pg. 303-304

133. Bailey, Kenneth. *Jesus Through Middle Eastern Eyes*. Downer's Grove: Inter-Varsity Press, 2008. pg. 35

134. Zondervan NIV Matthew Henry Commentary. Grand Rapids, Michigan: Zondervan, 1992. pg. 219

135. Allen, Ronald B. *And I Will Praise Him*. Nashville: Thomas Nelson, 1992. pg. 73

136. Brown, Raymond. *The Birth of the Messiah*. New York: Doubleday, 1993. pg. 169

137. Zondervan NIV Matthew Henry Commentary. Grand Rapids, Michigan: Zondervan, 1992. pg. 4

138. Zondervan NIV Matthew Henry Commentary. Grand Rapids, Michigan: Zondervan, 1992. pg. 5

139. Zondervan NIV Matthew Henry Commentary. Grand Rapids, Michigan: Zondervan, 1992. pg. 5

140. Bailey, Kenneth. *Jesus Through Middle Eastern Eyes*. Downer's Grove: Inter-Varsity Press, 2008. pg. 52

141. Martyr, Justin. *Selections from Justin Martyr's dialogue with Trypho*. Edited by R. P. C. Hanson. London: Lutterworth, 1963. pg. 78

142. Josephus, Flavius. *Jewish Antiquities*. Wordsworth Editions, 2006. XVI v 1; 136-41

143. Brown, Raymond. *The Birth of the Messiah*. New York: Doubleday, 1993. pg. 174

144. Brown, Raymond. *The Birth of the Messiah*. New York: Doubleday, 1993. pg. 204

145. Borg, Marcus J., Crossan, John Dominic. *The First Christmas* Harper One. New York: Harper One, 2007. pg. 145

146. Crossan, John Dominique, Reed, Jonathan. *Excavating Jesus*. New York: Harper Collins, 2001. pg. 66

147. Crossan, John Dominique, Reed, Jonathan. *Excavating Jesus*. New York: Harper Collins, 2001. pg. 55

148. Brown, Raymond. *The Birth of the Messiah*. New York: Doubleday, 1993. pg. 474

149. Brown, Raymond. *The Birth of the Messiah*. New York: Doubleday, 1993. pg. 490

150. Schweitzer, Albert. *The Quest of the Historical Jesus*. Translation by J.W. Montgomery. New York: Macmillan, 1968. pg. 402

151. MacMullen, Ramsay. *Roman Social Relations*: New Haven, CT, and London: Yale University Press, 1974. pg. 17-18, 107-108, 139-140, 198.

152. Bailey, Kenneth. *Jesus Through Middle Eastern Eyes*. Downer's Grove: Inter-Varsity Press, 2008. pg. 147

153. Major, H. D. A., Manson, T. W., Wright, C. J. *The Mission and Message of Jesus*. Sixth Edition. Dutton, 1938. pg. 329

154. Harrison, Everett. *A Short Life of Christ*. Grand Rapids: Eerdmans Publishing, 1968. pg. 102

155. Manson, T.W. *The Teaching of Jesus*. Cambridge: Cambridge University Press 1939. pg. 63-65.

156. Harrison, Everett. *A Short Life of Christ*. Grand Rapids: Eerdmans Publishing, 1968. pg. 98

157. Harrison, Everett. *A Short Life of Christ*. Grand Rapids: Eerdmans Publishing, 1968. pg. 101

158. Montefiore, C. G. *Some Elements of the Religious Teaching of Jesus*. Biblio Bazaar, 2009. pg. 10

159. Bailey, Kenneth. *Jesus Through Middle Eastern Eyes*. Downer's Grove: Inter-Varsity Press, 2008. pg. 155

160. Crossan, John Dominic. *Jesus, A Revolutionary Biography*. New York: Harper One, 1994. pg. 55

161. Harrison, Everett. *A Short Life of Christ*. Grand Rapids: Eerdmans Publishing, 1968. pg. 67

162. Josephus, Flavius. *Jewish Antiquities*. Wordsworth Editions, 2006. pg. 2, 5, and 18

163. Josephus, Flavius. *Jewish Antiquities*. Wordsworth Editions, 2006. pg. 18.116-119

164. Harrison, Everett. *A Short Life of Christ*. Grand Rapids: Eerdmans Publishing, 1968. pg. 139

165. Harrison, Everett. *A Short Life of Christ*. Grand Rapids: Eerdmans Publishing, 1968. pg. 136

166. Eusebius. *The History of the Church*. Translation by G. A. Williamson. Baltimore: Penguin Books, 1965. pg. 353-354

167. Bailey, Kenneth. *Jesus Through Middle Eastern Eyes*. Downer's Grove: Inter-Varsity Press, 2008. pg. 94

168. Davies, W.D., Allison Jr., Dale C. *The Gospel According to Saint Matthew*. New York: T & T Clark, 1988. 2:602

169. Bailey, Kenneth. *Jesus Through Middle Eastern Eyes*. Downer's Grove: Inter-Varsity Press, 2008. pg. 107

170. Bailey, Kenneth. *Jesus Through Middle Eastern Eyes*. Downer's Grove: Inter-Varsity Press, 2008. pg. 68

171. Crossan, John Dominic. *The Birth of* Christianity. New York: Harper One, 1999. pg. 322

172. Crossan, John Dominic. *Jesus, A Revolutionary Biography*. New York: Harper One, 1994. pg. 61

173. Crossan, John Dominic. *The Birth of* Christianity. New York: Harper One, 1999. pg. 321

174. Bailey, Kenneth. *Jesus Through Middle Eastern Eyes*. Downer's Grove: Inter-Varsity Press, 2008. pg. 70

175. Bailey, Kenneth. *Jesus Through Middle Eastern Eyes*. Downer's Grove: Inter-Varsity Press, 2008. pg. 72

176. Bailey, Kenneth. *Jesus Through Middle Eastern Eyes*. Downer's Grove: Inter-Varsity Press, 2008. pg. 77

177. Bultmann, Rudolf. *Theology of the New Testament*. New York: Scribner, 1955. pg. 272-73

178. Bailey, Kenneth. *Jesus Through Middle Eastern Eyes*. Downer's Grove: Inter-Varsity Press, 2008. pg. 82

179. Davies, W.D., Allison Jr., Dale C. *The Gospel According to Saint Matthew*. New York: T & T Clark, 1988. 1:456

180. Rihbany, Abraham. *The Syrian Christ*. Nabu Press, 2010. pg. 214

181. Bailey, Kenneth. *Poet & Peasant and Through Peasant Eyes*. Grand Rapids, Michigan: Eerdmans Publishing Company, 1976. pg. 122

182. Bailey, Kenneth. *Poet & Peasant and Through Peasant Eyes*. Grand Rapids, Michigan: Eerdmans Publishing Company, 1976. pg. 128

183. Bailey, Kenneth. *Poet & Peasant and Through Peasant Eyes*. Grand Rapids, Michigan: Eerdmans Publishing Company, 1976. pg. 119

184. Bailey, Kenneth. *Jesus Through Middle Eastern Eyes*. Downer's Grove: Inter-Varsity Press, 2008. pg. 291

185. Bailey, Kenneth. *Jesus Through Middle Eastern Eyes*. Downer's Grove: Inter-Varsity Press, 2008. pg. 292

186. Bailey, Kenneth. *Jesus Through Middle Eastern Eyes*. Downer's Grove: Inter-Varsity Press, 2008. pg. 293

187. Bailey, Kenneth. *Jesus Through Middle Eastern Eyes*. Downer's Grove: Inter-Varsity Press, 2008. pg. 295

188. Hultgren, Arland J. *The Parables of Jesus*. Grand Rapids: Eerdmans, 2000. pg. 99

189. Bailey, Kenneth. *Jesus Through Middle Eastern Eyes*. Downer's Grove: Inter-Varsity Press, 2008. pg. 294

190. Farb, George, Peter, Armelagos. *Consuming Passions the Anthology of Eating*. Houghton Mifflin, 1980. pg. 4, 211

191. Klosinski, Lee Edward. *The Meals in Mark*. Ann Arbor: University Microfilms, 1988. pg. 56-58

192. Bailey, Kenneth. *Jesus Through Middle Eastern Eyes*. Downer's Grove: Inter-Varsity Press, 2008. pg. 313

193. Lamar, J. S. *The New Testament Commentary*. Volume 2. Cincinnati, Ohio: Chase and Hall, 1877. pg. 191.

194. Crossan, John Dominic. *Jesus, A Revolutionary Biography*. New York: Harper One, 1994. pg. 68

195. Bailey, Kenneth. *Jesus Through Middle Eastern Eyes*. Downer's Grove: Inter-Varsity Press, 2008. pg. 317

196. Zondervan NIV Matthew Henry Commentary. Grand Rapids, Michigan: Zondervan, 1992. pg. 798

197. Barclay, William. *The Gospel of Luke*. Philadelphia: The Westminster Press, 1956. pg. 230

198. Barnes, Albert. *Notes on the New Testament*. Grand Rapids, Michigan: Baker Book House, 1954. pg. 126

199. Bailey, Kenneth. *Poet & Peasant and Through Peasant Eyes*. Grand Rapids, Michigan: Eerdmans Publishing Company, 1976. pg. 137

200. Wesley, John. *Notes on the New Testament*. Naperville, Illinois, 1950. pg. 271

201. Bauer, W. A *Greek-English Lexicon of the New Testament*. Chicago: University of Chicago Press, 1979. pg. 314

202. Bailey, Kenneth. *Poet & Peasant and Through Peasant Eyes*. Grand Rapids, Michigan: Eerdmans Publishing Company, 1976. pg. 157

203. Jeremias, Joachim. *Jerusalem in the Time of Jesus*. Germany: Fortress Press, 1975. pg. 157

204. Jeremias, Joachim. *New Testament Theology: The Proclamation of Jesus*. Charles Scribner's Sons, 1977. pg. 115

205. Bailey, Kenneth. *Poet & Peasant and Through Peasant Eyes*. Grand Rapids, Michigan: Eerdmans Publishing Company, 1976. pg. 143

206. Jarvis, C. S. *Desert and Delta*. London: John Murray, 1938. pg. 217

207. Bailey, Kenneth. *Poet & Peasant and Through Peasant Eyes*. Grand Rapids, Michigan: Eerdmans Publishing Company, 1976. pg. 147

208. Bailey, Kenneth. *Poet & Peasant and Through Peasant Eyes*. Grand Rapids, Michigan: Eerdmans Publishing Company, 1976. pg. 148

209. Bailey, Kenneth. *Poet & Peasant and Through Peasant Eyes*. Grand Rapids, Michigan: Eerdmans Publishing Company, 1976. pg. 149

210. Jeremias, Joachim. *New Testament Theology: The Proclamation of Jesus*. Charles Scribner's Sons, 1977. pg. 115

211. The Roman author Pliny the Elder wrote about the mustard plant in his encyclopedic Natural *History* 19.170-171:

212. Crossan, John Dominic. *Jesus, A Revolutionary Biography*. New York: Harper One, 1994. pg. 65

213. Bailey, Kenneth. *Jesus Through Middle Eastern Eyes*. Downer's Grove: Inter-Varsity Press, 2008. pg. 348

214. Bailey, Kenneth. *Jesus Through Middle Eastern Eyes*. Downer's Grove: Inter-Varsity Press, 2008. pg. 349

215. Marshall. L.H. *The Challenge of New Testament Ethics*. MacMillian, 1947. pg. 60

216. Abrahams. I. *Studies in Pharisaism and the Gospels*. Second Edition. Cambridge: The University Press, 1917. pg. 13-17

217. Bailey, Kenneth. *Jesus Through Middle Eastern Eyes*. Downer's Grove: Inter-Varsity Press, 2008. pg. 300

218. Bailey, Kenneth. *Jesus Through Middle Eastern Eyes*. Downer's Grove: Inter-Varsity Press, 2008. pg. 303

219. Bailey, Kenneth. *Jesus Through Middle Eastern Eyes*. Downer's Grove: Inter-Varsity Press, 2008. pg. 271

220. Hirschfeld, Yizhar, Vamosh, M.F. "A Country Gentleman's Estate: Unearthing the Splendors of Ramat Hanadiv," *Biblical Archaeology* Review 31, Number 2. 2005. pg. 18-31

221. Bailey, Kenneth. *Jesus Through Middle Eastern Eyes*. Downer's Grove: Inter-Varsity Press, 2008. pg. 419

222. Elwell, Walter A. *Evangelical Dictionary of Theology*. Second Edition. Baker Academic, 2001. pg. 778

223. Elwell, Walter A. *Evangelical Dictionary of Theology*. Second Edition. Baker Academic, 2001. pg. 778

224. Geivett, R. Douglas., Habermas, Gary R. *In Defense of Miracles*. Illinois: Inter Varsity Press, 1997. pg. 62-63

225. Geivett, R. Douglas., Habermas, Gary R. *In Defense of Miracles*. Illinois: Inter Varsity Press, 1997. pg. 116

226. Geivett, R. Douglas., Habermas, Gary R. *In Defense of Miracles*. Illinois: Inter Varsity Press, 1997. pg. 33

227. Geivett, R. Douglas., Habermas, Gary R. *In Defense of Miracles*. Illinois: Inter Varsity Press, 1997. pg. 63

228. Geivett, R. Douglas., Habermas, Gary R. *In Defense of Miracles*. Illinois: Inter Varsity Press, 1997. pg. 117

229. Geivett, R. Douglas., Habermas, Gary R. *In Defense of Miracles*. Illinois: Inter Varsity Press, 1997. pg. 163

230. Elwell, Walter A. *Evangelical Dictionary of Theology*. Second Edition. Baker Academic, 2001. pg. 779

231. Elwell, Walter A. *Evangelical Dictionary of Theology*. Second Edition. Baker Academic, 2001. pg. 779

232. Remus, Harold. *Pagan-Christian Conflict over Miracle in the Second Century*. Cambridge, Massachusetts: Philadelphia Patristic Foundation, 1983. pg. 52-72

233. Kee, Howard Clark. *Medicine, Miracle and Magic in New Testament Times*. New York: Cambridge University Press. 1986. SNTSMS 55.

234. Crossan, John Dominic. *The Historical Jesus*. New York: Harper One, 1992. pg. 319

235. Crossan, John Dominic. *The Historical Jesus*. New York: Harper One, 1992. pg. 314

236. Crossan, John Dominic. *The Historical Jesus*. New York: Harper One, 1992. pg. 310

237. Aune, David E. "Magic in Early Christianity." ANRW 2.23.1980. 2.23.1507-1557

238. Schweitzer, Albert. *The Quest of the Historical Jesus*. Translation by J.W. Montgomery. New York: Macmillan, 1968. pg. 44-47

239. Barb, A. A. "The Survival of the Magic Arts." *In The Conflict Between Paganism and Christiantiy in the Fourth Century*. Edited by Arnaldo Momigliano. Oxford: Clarendon Press, 1963. pg. 100-125

240. Smith, Morton. *Clement of Alexandria and a Secret Gospel of Mark*. Cambridge, Massachusetts: Harvard University Press. 1973. pg. 228-229

241. Graham H. Twelftree, Jesus the Exorcist: A Contribution to the Study of the Historical Jesus (Peabody, Mass.: Hendrickson, 1993), p. 173.

242. Josephus, Flavius. *Jewish Antiquities*. Wordsworth Editions, 2006. 8.2.5

243. Harrison, Everett. *A Short Life of Christ*. Grand Rapids: Eerdmans Publishing, 1968. pg. 81

244. Harrison, Everett. *A Short Life of Christ*. Grand Rapids: Eerdmans Publishing, 1968. pg. 85

245. Harrison, Everett. *A Short Life of Christ*. Grand Rapids: Eerdmans Publishing, 1968. pg. 86

246. Harrison, Everett. *A Short Life of Christ*. Grand Rapids: Eerdmans Publishing, 1968. pg. 87

247. Harrison, Everett. *A Short Life of Christ*. Grand Rapids: Eerdmans Publishing, 1968. pg. 122

248. Harrison, Everett. *A Short Life of Christ*. Grand Rapids: Eerdmans Publishing, 1968. pg. 116

249. Harrison, Everett. *A Short Life of Christ*. Grand Rapids: Eerdmans Publishing, 1968. pg. 117

250. Harrison, Everett. *A Short Life of Christ*. Grand Rapids: Eerdmans Publishing, 1968. pg. 121

251. Eisenberg, Leon. "Disease and Illness: Distinctions Between Professional and Popular Ideas of Sickness." *Culture, Medicine, and Psychiatry*, 1977. pg. 11

252. Kleinman, Arthur. *Patients and healers in the Context of Culture*. Berkley: University of California Press, 1980. pg. 72

253. Crossan, John Dominic. *Jesus, A Revolutionary Biography*. New York: Harper One, 1994. pg. 78

254. Harrison, Everett. *A Short Life of Christ*. Grand Rapids: Eerdmans Publishing, 1968. pg. 114

255. Crossan, John Dominic. *Jesus, A Revolutionary Biography*. New York: Harper One, 1994. pg. 80

256. Flew, Anthony. "Theology and Falsification" in *The Existence of God*. Edited by John Hick. New York: Macmillan, 1964. pg. 227

257. Geivett, R. Douglas., Habermas, Gary R. *In Defense of Miracles*. Illinois: Inter Varsity Press, 1997. pg. 222-223

258. Geivett, R. Douglas., Habermas, Gary R. *In Defense of Miracles*. Illinois: Inter Varsity Press, 1997. pg. 223

259. Geivett, R. Douglas., Habermas, Gary R. *In Defense of Miracles*. Illinois: Inter Varsity Press, 1997. pg. 223

260. Blomber, Craig. *The Historical Reliability of the Gospels*. Downers Grove, Ill.: InterVarsity Press, 1987. section 4

261. Geivett, R. Douglas., Habermas, Gary R. *In Defense of Miracles*. Illinois: Inter Varsity Press, 1997. pg. 211

262. Geivett, R. Douglas., Habermas, Gary R. *In Defense of Miracles*. Illinois: Inter Varsity Press, 1997. pg. 207

263. *Ta'anit* 23a.

264. Geivett, R. Douglas., Habermas, Gary R. *In Defense of Miracles*. Illinois: Inter Varsity Press, 1997. pg. 207

265. Vermes, Geza. *Jesus the Magician*. San Francisco: Harper and Row, 1978. pg. 265-76

266. Geivett, R. Douglas., Habermas, Gary R. *In Defense of Miracles*. Illinois: Inter Varsity Press, 1997. pg. 207

267. Bailey, Kenneth. *Jesus Through Middle Eastern Eyes*. Downer's Grove: Inter-Varsity Press, 2008. pg. 141

268. Bishop, E. F. F. "Jesus and the Lake," *Catholic Biblical Quarterly 13*, 1951. pg. 398-414

269. Green, Joel B. *The Gospel of Luke*. Grand Rapids: Eerdmans, 1999. pg. 232

270. Bailey, Kenneth. *Jesus Through Middle Eastern Eyes*. Downer's Grove: Inter-Varsity Press, 2008. pg. 141

271. Zondervan NIV Matthew Henry Commentary. Grand Rapids, Michigan: Zondervan, 1992. pg. 265

272. Brown, Raymond. *The Death of the Messiah*. 2 Volumes. New York: Doubleday. 1994. pg. 149

273. Brown, Raymond. *The Death of the Messiah*. 2 Volumes. New York: Doubleday. 1994. pg. 166

274. Carter, T. T. *The Passion and Temptation of Our Lord*. BiblioLife, 1867. pg. 49

275. Brown, Raymond. *The Death of the Messiah*. 2 Volumes. New York: Doubleday. 1994. pg. 189

276. Brown, Raymond. *The Death of the Messiah*. 2 Volumes. New York: Doubleday. 1994. pg. 196

277. Harrison, Everett. *A Short Life of Christ*. Grand Rapids: Eerdmans Publishing, 1968. pg. 198

278. Brown, Raymond. *The Death of the Messiah*. 2 Volumes. New York: Doubleday. 1994. pg. 215

279. Harrison, Everett. *A Short Life of Christ*. Grand Rapids: Eerdmans Publishing, 1968. pg. 199

280. Josephus, Flavius. *Jewish Antiquities*. Wordsworth Editions, 2006. 14.4.2; #63; 18.9.2; #319-23

281. Josephus, Flavius. *The War of the Jews: The History of the Destruction of Jerusalem*. IAP; First Edition. 2009. 2.8.4; #125

282. Brown, Raymond. *The Death of the Messiah*. 2 Volumes. New York: Doubleday. 1994. pg. 281

283. Brown, Raymond. *The Death of the Messiah*. 2 Volumes. New York: Doubleday. 1994. pg. 303

284. Harrison, Everett. *A Short Life of Christ*. Grand Rapids: Eerdmans Publishing, 1968. pg. 200

285. Brown, Raymond. *The Death of the Messiah*. 2 Volumes. New York: Doubleday. 1994. pg. 594

286. I Macc 12:28-29

287. Brown, Raymond. *The Death of the Messiah*. 2 Volumes. New York: Doubleday. 1994. pg. 402

288. Zondervan NIV Matthew Henry Commentary. Grand Rapids, Michigan: Zondervan, 1992. pg. 421

289. Josephus, Flavius. *Jewish Antiquities*. Wordsworth Editions, 2006. 20.9.1; #198

290. Josephus, Flavius. *Jewish Antiquities*. Wordsworth Editions, 2006. 19.6.4; #316

291. Ensminger, J.J. "The Sadducean Persecution of Christians in Rome and Jerusalem, A.D. 58-65," SWJT 30 #3, 1988. pg. 9-13

292. Brown, Raymond. *The Death of the Messiah*. 2 Volumes. New York: Doubleday. 1994. pg. 421

293. Sanhedrin 4.1

294. Brown, Raymond. *The Death of the Messiah*. 2 Volumes. New York: Doubleday. 1994. pg. 608

295. Josephus, Flavius. *Jewish Antiquities*. Wordsworth Editions, 2006. 18.2.2; #34-35

296. *Holman Illustrated Bible Dictionary*. Nashville: Holman Reference, 1998. pg. 1445

297. Brown, Raymond. *The Death of the Messiah*. 2 Volumes. New York: Doubleday. 1994. pg. 350-351

298. Brown, Raymond. *The Death of the Messiah*. 2 Volumes. New York: Doubleday. 1994. pg. 344

299. Telushkin, Joseph. *Jewish Literacy: The Most Important Things to Know about the Jewish Religion, its People, and its History*. New York: William Morrow and Company, 1991. pg. 69

300. Mishna *Shebu'ot* 4:13

301. Zondervan NIV Matthew Henry Commentary. Grand Rapids, Michigan: Zondervan, 1992. pg. 148

302. Mishna Sanhedrin 4.1

303. Mishna Sanhedrin 4.1

304. Brown, Raymond. *The Death of the Messiah*. 2 Volumes. New York: Doubleday. 1994. pg. 652

305. Dodd, C. H. *Historical Tradition in the Fourth Gospel*. New York: Cambridge University Press, 1963. pg. 108

306. Philo, *On The Embassy of Gauis* Book XXXVIII 299-305

307. Josephus, Flavius. *The War of the Jews: The History of the Destruction of Jerusalem*. IAP; First Edition. 2009. 2.9.2-4; Jewish Encyclopedia article on Pilate, retrieved 5 May 2009

308. Josephus, Flavius. *Jewish Antiquities*. Wordsworth Editions, 2006. 18.3.2

309. Zondervan NIV Matthew Henry Commentary. Grand Rapids, Michigan: Zondervan, 1992. pg. 423

310. Brown, Raymond. *The Death of the Messiah*. 2 Volumes. New York: Doubleday. 1994. pg. 805

311. Blinzler, Joseph. *The Trial of Jesus*. Newman Press, 1959. pg. 222-35

312. Brown, Raymond. *The Death of the Messiah*. 2 Volumes. New York: Doubleday. 1994. pg. 842

313. Brown, Raymond. *The Death of the Messiah*. 2 Volumes. New York: Doubleday. 1994. pg. 847

314. Brown, Raymond. *The Death of the Messiah*. 2 Volumes. New York: Doubleday. 1994. pg. 914-915

315. Brown, Raymond. *The Death of the Messiah*. 2 Volumes. New York: Doubleday. 1994. pg. 923

316. Harrison, Everett. *A Short Life of Christ*. Grand Rapids: Eerdmans Publishing, 1968. pg. 218

317. Brown, Raymond. *The Death of the Messiah*. 2 Volumes. New York: Doubleday. 1994. pg. 938

318. Josephus, Flavius. *The War of the Jews: The History of the Destruction of Jerusalem*. IAP; First Edition. 2009. 1.4.6; #97; Ant. 13.14.2; #380

319. Brown, Raymond. *The Death of the Messiah*. 2 Volumes. New York: Doubleday. 1994. pg. 945

320. Crossan, John Dominic. *Jesus, A Revolutionary Biography*. New York: Harper One, 1994. pg. 124

321. Haas, N. "Anthropological Observations on the Skeletal Remains From Giv' At Ha-Mivtar." *Israel Exploration Journal*. 1970. pg. 20

322. Brown, Raymond. *The Death of the Messiah*. 2 Volumes. New York: Doubleday. 1994. pg. 949

323. Hengel, Martin. *Crucifixion in the Ancient World and the Folly of the Message of the Cross*. Philadelphia: Fortress Press, 1977. pg. 87-88

324. Josephus, Flavius. *The War of the Jews: The History of the Destruction of Jerusalem*. IAP; First Edition 2.75= Jewish Antiquities 17.295

325. Josephus, Flavius. *The War of the Jews: The History of the Destruction of Jerusalem*. IAP; First Edition 2.307

326. Josephus, Flavius. *The War of the Jews: The History of the Destruction of Jerusalem*. IAP; First Edition. 2009. 5.450

327. Crossan, John Dominic. *The Birth of* Christianity. New York: Harper One, 1999. pg. 545

328. Brown, Raymond. *The Death of the Messiah*. 2 Volumes. New York: Doubleday. 1994. pg. 951

329. Habermas, Gary. *The Historical Jesus*. Joplin, Missouri: College Press, 1996. pg. 73-74

330. Brown, Raymond. *The Death of the Messiah*. 2 Volumes. New York: Doubleday. 1994. pg. 951

331. Habermas, Gary. *The Historical Jesus*. Joplin, Missouri: College Press, 1996. pg. 73-74

332. Hengel, Martin. *Crucifixion in the Ancient World and the Folly of the Message of the Cross*. Philadelphia: Fortress Press, 1977. pg. 87-88

333. Crossan, John Dominic. *The Birth of* Christianity. New York: Harper One, 1999. pg. 542

334. Brown, Raymond. *The Death of the Messiah*. 2 Volumes. New York: Doubleday. 1994. pg. 969

335. Brown, Raymond. *The Death of the Messiah*. 2 Volumes. New York: Doubleday. 1994. pg. 963

336. Crossan, John Dominique, Reed, Jonathan. *Excavating Jesus*. New York: Harper Collins, 2001. pg. 214

337. Plummer, Alfred. A Critical and Exegetical Commentary on the Gospel According to St. Luke. BiblioBazaar, 2009. pg. 535

338. Brown, Raymond. *The Death of the Messiah*. 2 Volumes. New York: Doubleday. 1994. pg. 1076-1075

339. Brown, Raymond. *The Death of the Messiah*. 2 Volumes. New York: Doubleday. 1994. pg. 1068

340. Zondervan NIV Matthew Henry Commentary. Grand Rapids, Michigan: Zondervan, 1992. pg. 1132-1133

341. Zondervan NIV Matthew Henry Commentary. Grand Rapids, Michigan: Zondervan, 1992. pg. 429

342. Zondervan NIV Matthew Henry Commentary. Grand Rapids, Michigan: Zondervan, 1992. pg. 430

343. Habermas, Gary. *The Historical Jesus*. Joplin, Missouri: College Press, 1996. pg. 74

344. Brown, Raymond. *The Death of the Messiah*. 2 Volumes. New York: Doubleday. 1994. pg. 1091

345. Josephus, Flavius. *The War of the Jews: The History of the Destruction of Jerusalem*. IAP; First Edition. 2009. 5:5.5; #213-14

346. Zondervan NIV Matthew Henry Commentary. Grand Rapids, Michigan: Zondervan, 1992. pg. 157

347. Brown, Raymond. *The Death of the Messiah*. 2 Volumes. New York: Doubleday. 1994. pg. 1125

348. Brown, Raymond. *The Death of the Messiah*. 2 Volumes. New York: Doubleday. 1994. pg. 1125

349. Brown, Raymond. *The Death of the Messiah*. 2 Volumes. New York: Doubleday. 1994. pg. 1168

350. Brown, Raymond. *The Death of the Messiah*. 2 Volumes. New York: Doubleday. 1994. pg. 1170

351. Josephus, Flavius. *Jewish Antiquities*. Wordsworth Editions, 2006. 17.6.4; #167

352. Eusebius. *The History of the Church*. Translation by G. A. Williamson. Baltimore: Penguin Books, 1965. pg. 60.35.1

353. Josephus, Flavius. *The War of the Jews: The History of the Destruction of Jerusalem*. IAP; First Edition. 2009. 6.5.3; #288-309

354. *Holman Illustrated Bible Dictionary*. Nashville: Holman Reference, 1998. pg. 1326

355. Crossan, John Dominic. *Jesus, A Revolutionary Biography*. New York: Harper One, 1994. pg. 153

356. Crossan, John Dominic. *Jesus, A Revolutionary Biography*. New York: Harper One, 1994. pg. 155

357. Crossan, John Dominic. *Jesus, A Revolutionary Biography*. New York: Harper One, 1994. pg. 153

358. Geivett, R. Douglas., Habermas, Gary R. *In Defense of Miracles*. Illinois: Inter Varsity Press, 1997. pg. 250

359. Brown, Raymond. *The Death of the Messiah*. 2 Volumes. New York: Doubleday. 1994. pg. 1260

360. Brown, Raymond. *The Death of the Messiah*. 2 Volumes. New York: Doubleday. 1994. pg. 1260

361. Josephus, Flavius. The War of the Jews: The History of the Destruction of Jerusalem. IAP; First Edition. 2009. 1.33.9; #673

362. Mishna (*Sabbat* 23.5)

363. Geivett, R. Douglas., Habermas, Gary R. *In Defense of Miracles*. Illinois: Inter Varsity Press, 1997. pg. 250

364. Crossan, John Dominic. *Jesus, A Revolutionary Biography*. New York: Harper One, 1994. 160

365. Anderson, Leith. *Jesus*. Grand Rapids, MI: Bethany House, 2005. pg. 362

366. Holst-Warhaft, Gail. *Dangerous Voices: Women's Laments and Greek Literature*. New York: Routledge, 1992. pg. 22

367. Holst-Warhaft, gail. 1992. *Dangerous Voices: Women's Laments and Greek Literature*. New York: Routledge. 1-2, 3

368. Danforth, Loring M. *The Death Rituals of Rural Greece*. Princeton, NJ: Princeton University Press, 1982. pg. 138

369. Zondervan NIV Matthew Henry Commentary. Grand Rapids, Michigan: Zondervan, 1992. pg. 304

370. Wright, N.T. *The Resurrection of the Son of God*. Fortress Press: Minneapolis, 2003. pg. 630

371. Zondervan NIV Matthew Henry Commentary. Grand Rapids, Michigan: Zondervan, 1992. pg. 304.

372. Crossan, John Dominic. *The Birth of* Christianity. New York: Harper One, 1999. pg. 497

373. Crossan, John Dominic. *The Birth of* Christianity. New York: Harper One, 1999. pg. 506

374. *Holman Illustrated Bible Dictionary*. Nashville: Holman Reference, 1998. pg. 1041

375. Zondervan NIV Matthew Henry Commentary. Grand Rapids, Michigan: Zondervan, 1992. pg. 432

376. Zondervan NIV Matthew Henry Commentary. Grand Rapids, Michigan: Zondervan, 1992. pg. 443

377. Zondervan NIV Matthew Henry Commentary. Grand Rapids, Michigan: Zondervan, 1992. pg. 208-209

378. *Holman Illustrated Bible Dictionary*. Nashville: Holman Reference, 1998. pg. 1334

379. Pentecost, J. Dwight. *The Words and Works of Jesus Christ*. Grand Rapids: Zondervan, 2000. pg. 506

380. Pentecost, J. Dwight. *The Words and Works of Jesus Christ*. Grand Rapids: Zondervan, 2000. pg. 506

381. Zondervan NIV Matthew Henry Commentary. Grand Rapids, Michigan: Zondervan, 1992. pg. 438

382. Zondervan NIV Matthew Henry Commentary. Grand Rapids, Michigan: Zondervan, 1992. pg. 439

383. Zondervan NIV Matthew Henry Commentary. Grand Rapids, Michigan: Zondervan, 1992. pg. 441

384. Eusebius. *The History of the Church*. Translation by G. A. Williamson. Baltimore: Penguin Books, 1965. II.1

385. Stated by the *Annuario Pontificio* which is the lists all the popes to date and all officials of the Holy See's departments

386. Clement of Rome *Letter to the Corinthians* (Chapter 5), 80-98

387. Zondervan NIV Matthew Henry Commentary. Grand Rapids, Michigan: Zondervan, 1992. pg. 446

388. Anderson, Leith. *Jesus*. Grand Rapids, MI: Bethany House, 2005. pg. 362

389. White, James. *A Brief History of Christian Worship*. Nashville, Tennessee: Abingdon Press, 1993. pg. 23

390. Telushkin, Joseph. *Jewish Literacy: The Most Important Things to Know about the Jewish Religion, its People, and its History*. New York: William Morrow and Company, 1991. pg. 134

391. Telushkin, Joseph. *Jewish Literacy: The Most Important Things to Know about the Jewish Religion, its People, and its History*. New York: William Morrow and Company, 1991. 135

392. Geivett, R. Douglas., Habermas, Gary R. *In Defense of Miracles*. Illinois: Inter Varsity Press, 1997. pg. 248

393. Geivett, R. Douglas., Habermas, Gary R. *In Defense of Miracles*. Illinois: Inter Varsity Press, 1997. pg. 251

394. Geivett, R. Douglas., Habermas, Gary R. *In Defense of Miracles*. Illinois: Inter Varsity Press, 1997. pg. 251

395. Brown, Raymond. *The Death of the Messiah*. 2 Volumes. New York: Doubleday. 1994. pg. 1294

396. Geivett, R. Douglas., Habermas, Gary R. *In Defense of Miracles*. Illinois: Inter Varsity Press, 1997. 248

397. Morgan, Robert. "Flesh is Precious: The Significance of Luke 24:36-43." *In Resurrection*. Edited by Stephen Barton and Graham Stanton. London: 1994. pg. 18

398. Ostling, Richard N. "Jesus Christ, Plain and Simple," *Time*, January 10, 1994. pg. 32-33.

399. Wright, N.T. *The Resurrection of the Son of God*. Fortress Press: Minneapolis, 2003. pg. 695

400. Schillebeeckx, Edward. *Jesus: An Experiment in Christology*. New York: Seasbury Press. 1979. pg. 381

401. Wright, N.T. *The Resurrection of the Son of God*. Fortress Press: Minneapolis, 2003. pg. 638

402. Geivett, R. Douglas., Habermas, Gary R. *In Defense of Miracles*. Illinois: Inter Varsity Press, 1997. pg. 254

403. Wedderburn, A. J. M. *Beyond Resurrection*. London: SCM Press, 1999. pg. 65

404. Grant, Michael. *Jesus: An Historian's Review of the Gospels*. Scribner, 1995. pg. 176

405. Brown, Raymond. *The Death of the Messiah*. 2 Volumes. New York: Doubleday. 1994. pg. 18

406. Eusebius. *The History of the Church*. Translation by G. A. Williamson. Baltimore: Penguin Books, 1965. 2,23

407. Josephus, Flavius. *Jewish Antiquities*. Wordsworth Editions, 2006. 20.200.

408. 867 Holmes Illustrated Bi9ble Dictionary

409. Josephus, Flavius. *Jewish Antiquities*. Wordsworth Editions, 2006. 20.197-203

410. History of the Church 1.1, 2.23

411. Crossan, John Dominic. *The Birth of* Christianity. New York: Harper One, 1999. pg. 465

412. Geivett, R. Douglas., Habermas, Gary R. *In Defense of Miracles*. Illinois: Inter Varsity Press, 1997. pg. 257

413. Geivett, R. Douglas., Habermas, Gary R. *In Defense of Miracles*. Illinois: Inter Varsity Press, 1997. pg. 31

414. Geivett, R. Douglas., Habermas, Gary R. *In Defense of Miracles*. Illinois: Inter Varsity Press, 1997. pg. 31

415. Sayer, Dorothy L. *The Man Born to Be King*. Ignatius Press, 1990. pg. 26-29

416. Neisser, Ulric and Hyman, Ira. *Memory Observed*. Second Edition. Worth Publishers, 1999. pg. 241-242

417. Geivett, R. Douglas., Habermas, Gary R. *In Defense of Miracles*. Illinois: Inter Varsity Press, 1997. pg. 32

418. Wright, N.T. *The Resurrection of the Son of God*. Fortress Press: Minneapolis, 2003. pg. 611

419. Wright, N.T. *The Resurrection of the Son of God*. Fortress Press: Minneapolis, 2003. pg. 612-613

420. Wright, N.T. *The Resurrection of the Son of God*. Fortress Press: Minneapolis, 2003. pg. 612-613

421. Telushkin, Joseph. Jewish Literacy: The Most Important Things to Know about the Jewish Religion, its People, and its History. New York: William Morrow and Company, 1991. pg. 545

422. Wright, N.T. *The Resurrection of the Son of God*. Fortress Press: Minneapolis, 2003. pg. 560

423. Letter to the Smyrnaens 3:1-3

424. Bruce, F.F. *The New Testament Documents: Are They Reliable?* Grand Rapids: Eerdmans, 1967. pg. 16 and 36

425. Josephus, Flavius. *Jewish Antiquities*. Wordsworth Editions, 2006. 18:63

426. Lampe, G. W. H. *God as Spirit*. Oxford: Clarendon Press, 1977. pg. 150

427. Harrison, Everett. *A Short Life of Christ*. Grand Rapids: Eerdmans Publishing, 1968. pg. 263-264

428. Habermas, Gary. *The Historical Jesus*. Joplin, Missouri: College Press, 1996. pg. 276

429. Crossan, John Dominic. *The Birth of* Christianity. New York: Harper One, 1999. pg xix

430. Crossan, John Dominic. *The Birth of* Christianity. New York: Harper One, 1999. pg. xviii.

431. Flusser, David "Hillel's Self-Awareness and Jesus," *Judaism and the Origins of Christianity*. Jerusalem: Magnes Press, 1988. pg 509-514

432. Telushkin, Joseph. Jewish Literacy: The Most Important Things to Know about the Jewish Religion, its People, and its History. New York: William Morrow and Company, 1991. pg. 120-121

433. Cullmann, Oscar. *The Christology of the New Testament*, Translation by Shirley Guthrie and Charles Hall. Philadelphia: Westminster, 1963. pg. 311-312

434. Brown, Raymond. *The Death of the Messiah*. 2 Volumes. New York: Doubleday. 1994. pg. 12

BIBLIOGRAPHY

Abrahams. I. *Studies in Pharisaism and the Gospels.* Second Edition. Cambridge: The University Press, 1917.

Alen, Gedaliah. *Jews in their Land in the Talmudic Age.* Harvard University Press. 1989.

Allen, Ronald B. *And I Will Praise Him.* Nashville: Thomas Nelson, 1992.

Anderson, Leith. *Jesus.* Grand Rapids, MI: Bethany House, 2005.

Ash, Anthony Lee. *The Gospel According to Luke.* Austin, Texas: Sweet Publishing Company, 1972.

Aune, David E. "Magic in Early Christianity." ANRW 2.23.1980.

Bailey, Kenneth. *Jesus Through Middle Eastern Eyes.* Downer's Grove: Inter-Varsity Press, 2008.

Bailey, Kenneth. *Poet & Peasant and Through Peasant Eyes.* Grand Rapids, Michigan: Eerdmans Publishing Company, 1976.

Barb, A. A. "The Survival of the Magic Arts." *In The Conflict Between Paganism and Christiantiy in the Fourth Century.* Edited by Arnaldo Momigliano. Oxford: Clarendon Press, 1963.

Barclay, William. *The Gospel of Luke.* Philadelphia: The Westminster Press, 1956.

Barnes, Albert. *Notes on the New Testament.* Grand Rapids, Michigan: Baker Book House, 1954.

Bauer, W. *A Greek-English Lexicon of the New Testament.* Chicago: University of Chicago Press, 1979.

Betz, Hans Dieter. *The Greek Magical Papyri in Translation, Including the Deomotic Spells.* Chicago and London: University of Chicago Press, 1986.

Bishop, E. F. F. "Jesus and the Lake," *Catholic Biblical Quarterly 13,* 1951.

Blinzler, Joseph. *The Trial of Jesus.* Newman Press, 1959.

Blomber, Craig. *The Historical Reliability of the Gospels.* Downers Grove, Ill.: InterVarsity Press, 1987.

Borg, Marcus J., Crossan, John Dominic. *The First Christmas* Harper One. New York: Harper One, 2007.

Brown, Raymond. *The Birth of the Messiah.* New York: Doubleday, 1993.

Brown, Raymond. *The Death of the Messiah*. 2 Volumes. New York: Doubleday. 1994.

Bruce, F.F. *The New Testament Documents: Are They Reliable?* Grand Rapids: Eerdmans, 1967.

Buckler, John P., Hill, Bennet D., McKay, John P. *A History of World Societies*. Fourth Edition. Boston: Houghton Mifflin, 1996.

Bultmann, Rudolf. *Theology of the New Testament*. New York: Scribner, 1955.

Bultmann, Rudolf. "The Study of the Synoptic Gospels," in Form Criticism. Translation by Frederick C. Grant. New York: Harper and Brothers, 1962.

Cahill, Thomas. *The Gifts of the Jews*. New York: Doubleday. 1998.

Carter, T. T. *The Passion and Temptation of Our Lord*. BiblioLife, 1867.

Clouse, Robert, Pierard, Richard, Yamauchi, Edwin. *Two Kingdoms: The Church and Culture Through the Ages*. Moody Publishers, 1993.

Connolly, S. *New Testament Miracles*. New York: Enchanted Lion Books, 2004.

Crossan, John Dominique, Reed, Jonathan. *Excavating Jesus*. New York: Harper Collins, 2001.

Crossan, John Dominic. *God & Empire*. New York: Harper One, 2007.

Crossan, John Dominic. *Jesus, A Revolutionary Biography*. New York: Harper One, 1994.

Crossan, John Dominic. *The Birth of* Christianity. New York: Harper One, 1999.

Crossan, John Dominic. *The Historical Jesus*. New York: Harper One, 1992.

Cullmann, Oscar. *The Christology of the New Testament*, Translation by Shirley Guthrie and Charles Hall. Philadelphia: Westminster, 1963.

Dalman, G. H. *Sacred Sites and Ways*. Macmillan, 1935.

Danforth, Loring M. *The Death Rituals of Rural Greece*. Princeton, NJ: Princeton University Press, 1982.

Davies, W.D., Allison Jr., Dale C. *The Gospel According to Saint Matthew*. New York: T & T Clark, 1988.

Davis, C. Truman. "The Crucifixion of Jesus." Arizona Medicine, 1965.

Dodd, C. H. *Historical Tradition in the Fourth Gospel*. New York: Cambridge University Press, 1963.

Duggan, Alfred. *The Romans*. Cleveland and New York: World Publishing Company, 1964.

Edersheim, Alfred. *The Life and Times of Jesus the Messiah*. Peabody, MA: Hendrickson Publishers, 1993.

Eisenberg, Leon. "Disease and Illness: Distinctions Between Professional and Popular Ideas of Sickness." *Culture, Medicine, and Psychiatry*, 1977.

Elwell, Walter A. *Evangelical Dictionary of Theology*. Second Edition. Baker Academic, 2001.

Ensminger, J.J. "The Sadducean Persecution of Christians in Rome and Jerusalem, A.D. 58-65," SWJT 30 #3, 1988.

Esposito, Fasching, Lewis. *World Religions Today*. Third Edition. New York: Oxford University Press, 2009.

Eusebius. *The History of the Church*. Translation by G. A. Williamson. Baltimore: Penguin Books, 1965.

Fager, Jeffrey A. *Land Tenure and the Biblical Jubilee*. Sheffield Academic Press, 1993.

Farb, George, Peter, Armelagos. *Consuming Passions the Anthology of Eating*. Houghton Mifflin, 1980.

Flew, Anthony. "Theology and Falsification" in *The Existence of God*. Edited by John Hick. New York: Macmillan, 1964.

Flusser, David "Hillel's Self-Awareness and Jesus," *Judaism and the Origins of Christianity*. Jerusalem: Magnes Press, 1988.

Geivett, R. Douglas., Habermas, Gary R. *In Defense of Miracles*. Illinois: Inter Varsity Press, 1997.

Grant, Michael. *Jesus: An Historian's Review of the Gospels*. Scribner, 1995.

Green, Joel B. *The Gospel of Luke*. Grand Rapids: Eerdmans, 1999.

Haas, N. "Anthropological Observations on the Skeletal Remains From Giv' At Ha-Mivtar." *Israel Exploration Journal*. 1970.

Habermas, Gary. *The Historical Jesus*. Joplin, Missouri: College Press, 1996.

Harrison, Everett. *A Short Life of Christ*. Grand Rapids: Eerdmans Publishing, 1968.

Hengel, Martin. *Crucifixion in the Ancient World and the Folly of the Message of the Cross*. Philadelphia: Fortress Press, 1977.

Hirschfeld, Yizhar, Vamosh, M.F. "A Country Gentleman's Estate: Unearthing the Splendors of Ramat Hanadiv," *Biblical Archaeology* Review 31, Number 2. 2005.

Hobsbawm, Eric J. *Bandits*. Second Edition. Middlesex: Penguin Books, 1985.

Holman Illustrated Bible Dictionary. Nashville: Holman Reference, 1998.

Holst-Warhaft, Gail. *Dangerous Voices: Women's Laments and Greek Literature*. New York: Routledge, 1992.

Hultgren, Arland J. *The Parables of Jesus*. Grand Rapids: Eerdmans, 2000.

Jarvis, C. S. *Desert and Delta*. London: John Murray, 1938.

Jeremias, Joachim. "Despised Trades and Jewish Slaves," in *Jerusalem in the Time of Jesus*. Philadelphia: Fortress, 1969.

Jeremias, Joachim. *Jerusalem in the Time of Jesus*. Germany: Fortress Press, 1975.

Jeremias, Joachim. *New Testament Theology: The Proclamation of Jesus*. Charles Scribner's Sons, 1977.

Josephus, Flavius. *Jewish Antiquities*. Wordsworth Editions, 2006.

Josephus, Flavius. *The War of the Jews: The History of the Destruction of Jerusalem*. IAP; First Edition. 2009.

Kautsky, John H. *The Politic of Aristocratic Empire*. Chapel Hill, North Carolina: University of North Carolina Press. 1982.

Kee, Howard Clark. *Medicine, Miracle and Magic in New Testament Times*. New York: Cambridge University Press. 1986.

Kellermann, Bill W. *Seasons of Faith and Conscience*: New York: Orbis Books, 1991.

Kierkegaard, Soren, *Fear and Trembling*. Translation by Walter Lowrie. New York: Doubleday Anchor Books, 1954.

Kirsch, J.P. *St. Peter, Prince of the Apostles*. In The Catholic Encyclopedia. New York: Robert Appleton Company. Retrieved February 20, 2009 from New Advent: 1911.

Klaits, Joseph. *Servants of Satan: The Age of the Witch Hunts*. Indiana University Press, 1987.

Kleinman, Arthur. *Patients and healers in the Context of Culture*. Berkley: University of California Press, 1980.

Klosinski, Lee Edward. *The Meals in Mark*. Ann Arbor: University Microfilms, 1988.

Lamar, J. S. *The New Testament Commentary*. Volume 2. Cincinnati, Ohio: Chase and Hall, 1877.

Lampe, G. W. H. *God as Spirit*. Oxford: Clarendon Press, 1977.

Leacock, Eleanor. "Montagnais Women and the Jesuit Program for Colonization." In *Women and Colonization: Anthropological Perspectives*. Edited by Mona Etienne and Eleanor Leacock, New York: Praeger. 1980.

Lenski, Gerhard E. *Power and Privilege: A Theory of Social Stratification*. New York: McGraw-Hill. 1966.

Levine, L.I., *The Ancient Synagogue: The First Thousand Years*. New Haven, CT: Yale University Press, 1999.

Liddell, Henry G., Scott, R., *A Greek-English Lexicon*. Oxford: Oxford University Press, 1966.

Longstaff, Thomas R. W. "Nazareth and Sepphoris: Insights into Christian Origins." *Anglican Theological Review*. 1990.

MacMullen, Ramsay. *Roman Social Relations*: New Haven, CT, and London: Yale University Press, 1974.

Major, H. D. A., Manson, T. W., Wright, C. J. *The Mission and Message of Jesus*. Sixth Edition. Dutton, 1938.

Manson, T.W. *The Teaching of Jesus*. Cambridge: Cambridge University Press 1939.

Marks, A.J. *The Romans*. London: Usborne Publishing.1990.

Marshall. L.H. *The Challenge of New Testament Ethics*. MacMillian, 1947.

Martyr, Justin. *Selections from Justin Martyr's dialogue with Trypho*. Edited by R. P. C. Hanson. London: Lutterworth, 1963.

Martyr, Justin. *St. Justin Martyr: The First and Second Apologies*. Paulist Press, 1996.

Mann, Michael. *The Sources of Social Power: Volume 1, A History of Power from the Beginning to AD 1760*. Cambridge: Cambridge University Press, 1986.

Meier, John P. *A Marginal Jew*. New York: Doubleday, 2001.

Montefiore, C. G. *Some Elements of the Religious Teaching of Jesus*. Biblio Bazaar, 2009.

Moore, G. F. *Judaism In The First Centuries Of The Christian Area - The Age Of The Tannaim*. Volume I, Bradley Press. 1946.

Morgan, Robert. "Flesh is Precious: The Significance of Luke 24:36-43." *In Resurrection*. Edited by Stephen Barton and Graham Stanton. London: 1994.

Murphy, Frederick J. *Early Judaism*. Hendrickson, 2002.

Neisser, Ulric and Hyman, Ira. *Memory Observed*. Second Edition. Worth Publishers, 1999.

Ostling, Richard N. "Jesus Christ, Plain and Simple," *Time*, January 10, 1994.

Pentecost, J. Dwight. *The Words and Works of Jesus Christ*. Grand Rapids: Zondervan, 2000.

Perowne, Stewart. *The Life and Times of Herod the* Great. London: Hodder & Stoughton, 1957.

Pfeiffer, Charles F. *WyCliffe Bible Dictionary*. Massachusetts. Hendrickson. 1975.

Philo, *On The Embassy of Gauis*. Book XXXVIII.

Pitt-Rivers, Julian. "Honour," in *Encyclopedia of the Social Sciences*. Second Edition. New York: Macmillan, 1968.

Plummer, Alfred. *A Critical and Exegetical Commentary on the Gospel According to St. Luke*. BiblioBazaar, 2009.

Porter, J.R. *Jesus Christ: The Jesus of History, The Christ of Faith*. New York: Oxford University Press, 1999.

Remus, Harold. *Pagan-Christian Conflict over Miracle in the Second Century*. Cambridge, Massachusetts: Philadelphia Patristic Foundation, 1983.

Rihbany, Abraham. *The Syrian Christ*. Nabu Press, 2010.

Sayer, Dorothy L. *The Man Born to Be King*. Ignatius Press, 1990.

Schillebeeckx, Edward. *Jesus: An Experiment in Christology*. New York: Seasbury Press. 1979.

Schweitzer, Albert. *The Quest of the Historical Jesus*. Translation by J.W. Montgomery. New York: Macmillan, 1968.

Scott, Bernard Brandon. *Hear Then the Parable: A Commentary on the Parables of Jesus*. Minneapolis: Fortress Press. 1989.

Smith, Morton. *Clement of Alexandria and a Secret Gospel of Mark.* Cambridge, Massachusetts: Harvard University Press. 1973.

Spence, H. D. M. *The Pulpit Commentary.* Volume 16. Grand Rapids, Michigan: Eerdmans Publishing Company, 1962.

Telushkin, Joseph. *Jewish Literacy: The Most Important Things to Know about the Jewish Religion, its People, and its History.* New York: William Morrow and Company, 1991.

Tenney, Merrill C. *New Testament Survey.* Grand Rapids: Eerdmans Publishing Company and Inter Varsity Press, 1985.

Theissen, Gerd. *The Miracle Stories of the Early Christian Tradition.* Translation by Francis McDonagh. Philadelphia: Fortress, 1983.

Twelftree, Graham H. *Jesus the Exorcist: A Contribution to the Study of the Historical Jesus.* Peabody, Massachusetts: Hendrickson, 1993.

Vermes, Geza. *Jesus the Magician.* San Francisco: Harper and Row, 1978.

Wedderburn, A. J. M. *Beyond Resurrection.* London: SCM Press, 1999.

Wesley, John. *Notes on the New Testament.* Naperville, Illinois, 1950.

White, James. *A Brief History of Christian Worship.* Nashville, Tennessee: Abingdon Press, 1993.

Wright, N.T. *The Resurrection of the Son of God.* Fortress Press: Minneapolis, 2003.

Zondervan NIV Matthew Henry Commentary. Grand Rapids, Michigan: Zondervan, 1992.

INDEX OF CONTENTS